ELEMENTS OF COSTING

ELEMENTS OF COSTING

M.E. Thukaram Rao
Head, Department of Commerce
Sri Sathya Sai University
Brindavan Campus
Bangalore

PUBLISHING FOR ONE WORLD

NEW AGE INTERNATIONAL (P) LIMITED, PUBLISHERS

New Delhi • Bangalore • Chennai • Cochin • Guwahati • Hyderabad
Jalandhar • Kolkata • Lucknow • Mumbai • Ranchi
Visit us at **www.newagepublishers.com**

Published by New Age International (P) Ltd., Publishers
First Edition: 2009

Branches:

- 36, Malikarjuna Temple Street, Opp. ICWA, Basavanagudi, **Bangalore**. ✆ (080) 26677815
- 26, Damodaran Street, T. Nagar, **Chennai**. ✆ (044) 24353401
- Hemsen Complex, Mohd. Shah Road, Paltan Bazar, Near Starline Hotel, **Guwahati**. ✆ (0361) 2543669
- No. 105, 1st Floor, Madhiray Kaveri Tower, 3-2-19, Azam Jahi Road, Nimboliadda, **Hyderabad**. ✆ (040) 24652456
- RDB Chambers (Formerly Lotus Cinema) 106A,1st Floor, S.N. Banerjee Road, **Kolkata**. ✆ (033) 22275247
- 16-A, Jopling Road, **Lucknow**. ✆ (0522) 2209578
- 142C, Victor House, Ground Floor, N.M. Joshi Marg, Lower Parel, **Mumbai**. ✆ (022) 24927869
- 22, Golden House, Daryaganj, **New Delhi**. ✆ (011) 23262370, 23262368

ISBN : 978-81-224-2667-0

Rs. 275 .00

C-09-04-3646

Printed in India at Saras Graphics, Rai.
Typeset at Abro Enterprises, Delhi.

PUBLISHING FOR ONE WORLD
NEW AGE INTERNATIONAL (P) LIMITED, PUBLISHERS
4835/24, Ansari Road, Daryaganj, New Delhi-110002
Visit us at **www.newagepublishers.com**

Preface

I have great pleasure in placing into the hands of esteemed readers this book on Elements of Costing. With the introduction of semester system, the subject of Elements of Costing is prescribed for one of the semester. This book is meant for such students studying under semester system.

This book is written in a simple and lucid style. At the end of each chapter, a large number of standard questions of different varieties are given to test the understanding ability of students. A large number of exercises with answers are also given.

I am thankful to Shri V.R. Damodaran, New Age International (P) Limited Publishers for bringing out this book. I shall appreciate comments and suggestions from readers for the improvement of the book.

M.E. Thukaram Rao

Contents

CHAPTER 1

Nature and Scope of Cost Accounting

In the modern business world, the nature and functioning of business organisations have become very complicated. They have to serve the needs of variety of parties who are interested in the functioning of the business. These parties constitute the owners, creditors, employees, government agencies, tax authorities, prospective investors, and last but not the least the management of the business. The business has to serve the needs of these different category of people by way of supplying various information from time to time. In order to satisfy the needs of all these group of people a sound organisation of accounting system is very essential. In the ancient days the information required by those who were interested with a business organisation was met by practising a system of accounting known as financial accounting system. Financial accounting is mainly concerned with preparation of two important statements, *viz.,* income statement (or profit & loss account) and positional statement (or Balance Sheet). This information served the needs of all those who are not directly associated with management of business. Thus financial accounting is concerned with external reporting as it provides information to external authorities. But management of every business organisation is interested to know much more than the usual information supplied to outsiders. In order to carry out its functions of planning, decision-making and control, it requires additional cost data. The financial accounting to some extent fails to provide required cost data to management and hence a new system of accounting which could provide internal report to mangement was conceived of.

NEED FOR COST ACCOUNTING

The need for cost accounting arises owing to the following:

To Overcome the Limitations of Financial Accounting

Financial accounting records in an overall manner the results of the operations of a business, using conventional double entry book-keeping techniques. It suffers from the following limitations:

(*i*) *It provides only past data*: Financial accounting provide out of date information to management. But management is interested in current data but not past data as it does not serve any purpose to it. Therefore it has been rightly pointed out that financial accounting provide only a post-mortem analysis of past activities.

(ii) *It reveals only over all result of the business*: Financial accounting does not provide data for each and every product, process, department or operation separately. Instead it provides the financial information in a summary form for the entire organization as a whole.

(iii) *It is static in nature:* Modern business is dynamic but not static. Financial accounting does not incorporate the changes that take place within the business.

(iv) *It fails to take into account the impact of price level change:* In the modern inflationary conditions the price level has significant impact over financial statement. Under financial accounting, assets are shown at the actual or historical cost. Consequently depreciation is also charged on actual or historical cost. This under charging of depreciation will distort the profit figure.

(v) *Possibility of manipulation of financial accounting:* Very often financial accounting is manipulated at the whims and fancies of mangement so as to project better image in the minds of prospective investors. The chief forms of manipulating the financial accounting assume the form of over or undervaluation of inventory, excessive or inadequate provision for depreciation, creation of secret reserves, etc.

(vi) *It fails to exercise control over resources:* Financial accounting fail to exercise control over materials, labour and other expenses incurred in a business enterprise. As a results, avoidable wastages and losses go unchecked under this system of accounting.

(vii) *It fails to provide adequate data for price fixation:* Financial accounting fail to provide adequate cost data on the basis of which selling price is fixed. In the absence of fixation of prices in advance, it is not possible to supply quotations to the prospective customers. To that extent the income from such sales diminish.

(viii) *It fails to provide adequate data for management in carrying out its functions:* Management of every organization relies heavily on adequate cost data for formulating policies and in decision-making process. But financial accounting fails to provide such useful cost data to management.

(ix) *It does not provide a basis for cost comparison:* Financial accounting does not help in cost comparison over a period of time or between two jobs or two operations. Thus a basis for judging the efficiency of an year with past year or worthfulness of two different jobs or operations cannot be appraised.

(x) *It does not make use of control techniques:* Financial accounting fail to make use of certain important cost control techniques such as budgetary control and stantard costing. Thus financial accounting does not facilitate measuring the efficiency of the business with the help of control techniques.

(ix) *It fails to ascertain break-even point:* Financial accounting does not help in ascertaining the break-even point, *i.e.,* the sale or output where the revenue equals the cost. Hence, the point of no-profit-no-loss cannot be made out under financial accounts.

To Ensure Optimum Utilisation of Resources

In todays business world, the resources available are very scarce. Hence every business unit must strive hard to obtain maximum output with the available input. In order to ensure the optimum utilization of scarce resources, the value of input is measured against the value of output. This implies matching cost per unit of production against the value of output or selling price. But financial accounting does not provide the information relating to cost per unit of production. Hence the need for cost accounting was felt necessary.

To Achieve Overall Efficiency of Business

Every businessman will make constant effort to improve his business. In order to formulate suitable policy and sound decision, he has to know answers to certain questions such as (*a*) What is the maximum profit which a business can make ? (*b*) Is the profit earned by it is more or less compared to the earlier years ? (*c*) Which product line is making more profit ? (*d*) Has too much capital is blocked in raw materials ? (*e*) Whether the cost of production has gone up compared to earlier years ? (*f*) Should the selling price requires revision ? Cost accounting serves as an useful tool in the hands of management in this direction. By analysing the cost of production of every unit, it helps management to know the answers to the above questions.

GROWTH AND DEVELOPMENT OF COST ACCOUNTING

The history of cost accounting can be traced back to the fourteenth century. In the course of its evolution it passed through following stages:

1. In the first stage of its development, cost accounting was concerned only with the three prime cost elements, *viz.*, direct material cost, direct labour cost and direct expenses. For recording the transactions relating to materials the important documents used were (*a*) stores ledger, (*b*) a material requisition note, and (*c*) materials received note. To account for labour cost, employee time card and labour cost card were devised by Mr. Metcalfe. Later on a distinction between manufacturing and non-manufacturing cost was made by Mr. Norton. Thus material cost, labour cost and manufacturing cost constituted prime cost.
2. Secondly, around the turn of the nineteenth century, the importance of non-manufacturing cost (overheads) was recognized as one of the distinct element of cost. The method of charging non-manufacturing cost to the production cost was devised under this stage.
3. Thirdly, the techniques of estimation and standards are devised. Instead of using actual cost, standard costs are used and by comparing with the actual cost the differences are noted, analysed and disposed off accordingly. This helps in knowing the efficiency of the business undertaking.
4. Fourthly, cost accounting methods were applied to all types of business undertakings. The costing principles and techniques were also extended to important functions of a business.
5. In modern times the development of electronic data processing has occupied significant stage in the growth of cost accounting system.

Cost Accounting in Indian Context

The application of cost accounting methods in Indian industries was felt from the beginning of the twentieth century. The following factors have accelerated the system of cost accounting in our country:

(*a*) Increased awareness of cost consciousness by Indian industrialists with a view to ascertain costs more accurately for each product or job.

(*b*) Growing competition among manufacturers led to fixation of prices at a lower level so as to attract more customers.

(*c*) Economic policy of government which laid emphasis on planned economy with a view to achieve the targets led to cost reduction programmes by Indian industrialists.

(*d*) Increased government control over pricing led the Indian manufacturers to give utmost importance to the installation of cost accounting.

(*e*) The establishment of National Productivity Council in 1958 and the Statutory Recognition of Institute of Cost and Works Accountants of India in 1959 gave further encouragement to install cost accounting system in Indian industries.

DEFINITION AND SCOPE OF COST ACCOUNTANCY

The terminology of cost accountancy published by the Institute of Cost and Management Accountants, London defines cost accountancy as "the application of costing and cost accounting principles, methods and techniques to the science, art and practice of cost control and the ascertainment of profitability. It includes the presentation of information derived therefrom for the managerial decision-making."

On analysis of the above definition, the following features of cost accountancy become evident:

(*a*) "Cost accountancy" is used in the broadest sense when compared to "cost accounting" and "costing". This is so because cost accountancy is concerned with the formulation of principles, methods and techniques to be applied for ascertaining cost and profit.

(*b*) Having ascertained 'cost' and 'profit', cost accountancy is concerned with presentation of information to management. To enable management to carry out its functions, reports must be promptly made available at the right time, to the right person and in a proper form.

(*c*) The information so provided is to serve the purpose of managerial decision-making such as introducting a new line of product, replacement of manual labour by machnies, make or buy, decisions, etc.

SCOPE OF COST ACCOUNTANCY

The scope of any subject refers to the various areas of study included in that subject. As regards the scope of cost accountancy is concerned, it has vast scope. The following topics fall under the purview of cost accountancy: (1) Costing, (2) Cost Accounting, (3) Cost Control Techniques, (4) Budgeting and (5) Cost Audit.

1. Costing

The terminology of ICMA, London, defines costing as "the technique and process of ascertaining the cost." According to the revised terminology of ICMA, London, *"Costing is the process of determining the costs of products, services or activities."*

The above definiton is very significant in as much as it carries the main theme of cost accountancy. This definition emphasizes two important aspects, *viz*.

(*a*) **The technique and process of costing:** The technique of costing involves two distinct steps, namely, (*i*) collection and classification of costs according to various elements and (*ii*) allocation and apportionment of the expenses which cannot be directly charged to production. As a process, costing is concerned with the routine ascertainment of cost with a formal procedure.

(*b*) **Ascertainment of cost:** It involves three steps, *viz.* (*i*) collection and analysis of expenses, (*ii*) measurement of production at different stages and (*iii*) linking up of production with the expenses. To achieve the first step, costing has developed different systems such as Historical, Estimated and Standard Cost. For achieving the second step, costing has developed different methods such as single or output costing. Job costing, contract costing, etc. Finally, for achieving the last step costing has developed important techniques such as *Absorption Costing, Marginal Costing and Standard Costing.*

The three terms indicated as 'systems', 'methods', 'techniques' are independent factors but co-exist together. Ascertainment of cost of production is based on all these terms. For example, continuous type of industries may use process costing as a method, using actual cost as a system, under Standard Costing Technique.

2. Cost Accounting

Kohler in his dictionary for Accountants defines cost accounting as "that branch of accounting dealing with the classification, recording, allocation, summarization and reporting of current and prospective costs."

Mr. Wheldon defines cost accounting as "the classifying, recording and appropriate allocation of expenditure for the determination of the costs of products or services, the relation of these costs to sales values, and the ascertainment of profitability."

The above definitions reveal the following aspects of cost accounting:

(*a*) *Cost classification:* This refers to grouping of like items of cost into a common group.

(*b*) *Cost recording:* This refers to posting of cost transactions into the various ledger maintained under cost accounting system.

(*c*) *Cost allocation*: This refers to allotment of costs to various products or department.

(*d*) *Cost determination or cost finding:* This refers to the determination of the cost of goods or services by informal procedure, *i.e.,* procedures that do not carry on the regular process of cost accounting on a continuous basis.

(*e*) *Cost reporting:* This refers to furnishing of cost data on a regular basis so as to meet the requirements of management.

Differences between Cost Accountancy, Costing and Cost Accounting

Points of Differences	*Cost Accountancy*	*Costing*	*Cost Accounting*
1. Scope	Cost accountancy is broadest in its scope.	It is broader in its scope.	It is narrow in its scope.
2. Function	It is concerned with formulation of costing principles, methods, techniques to be adopted by a business.	It is concerned with ascertainment of cost.	It is concerned with recording of cost.

3. Periodicity of functioning	It is a starting point.	It begins where cost accountancy ends.	It begins where costing ends.
4. Persons involved	The persons involved are experts in the field of cost accountancy such as management accountant.	The person involved is cost accountant.	The persons involved are cost clerks.

3. Cost Control

According to Kohler, cost control represents the employment of management devices in the performance of any necessary operation so that pre-established objectives of quality, quantity and time may be attained at the lowest possible outlay for goods and services. The terminology published by ICMA, London, defines cost control as "The guidance and regulation by executive action of the cost of operating an undertaking." According to this definition, cost control aims at guiding the actuals towards the lines of target and regulates the actuals if they deviate from the targets. This guidance and regulation is done by the executive who is responsible for causing the deviation. This process will become clear by enumerating the steps involved in any cost control technique.

(*a*) Fixation of targets in terms of cost and production performance.

(*b*) Ascertaining the actual cost and production performance.

(*c*) Comparison of actuals with the targets.

(*d*) Analysing the variance by causes and the person responsible for it.

(*e*) Taking remedial steps to set right unfavourable variations.

Cost control is exercised through a variety of techniques such as inventory control, quality control, budgetary control, standard costing, etc. The advantages of cost control are as follows:

(*a*) It helps in utilizing the resources to the full extent.

(*b*) It helps in reduction of prices which are benefited by customers.

(*c*) It helps in competing successfully in the market.

(*d*) It increases the profit earning capacity of the business.

(*e*) It increases the goodwill of the business.

4. Budgeting

Mr. Heiser in his book *Budgeting-Principles and Practice,* defines budget as "an overall blue print of a comprehensive plan of operations and actions expressed in financial terms. According to him budgeting process involves the preparation of a budget and its fullest use not only as a devise for planning and co-ordinating but also for control."

5. Cost Audit

The terminology of ICMA, London, defines cost audit, as "the verification of the correctness of cost accounts and the adherence to the cost accounting plan."

NATURE OF COST ACCOUNTING

The nature of cost accounting can be brought out under the following headings:

1. **Cost accounting is a branch of knowledge:** Though considered as a branch of financial accounting, cost accounting is one of the important branch of knowledge, *i.e.,* a discipline by itself. It is an organised body of knowledge consisting of its own principles, concepts and conventions. These principles and rules vary from industry to industry.
2. **Cost accounting is a science:** Cost accounting is a science as it is a body of systematic knowledge relating to not only cost accounting but relating to a wide variety of subjects such as law, office practice and procedure, data processing, production and material control, etc. It is necessary for a cost accountant to have intimate knowledge of all these field of study in order to carry on his day-to-day activities. But it is to be admitted that it is not a perfect science as in the case of natural science.
3. **Cost accounting is an art:** Cost accounting is an art in the sense it requires the ability and skill on the part of cost accountant in applying the principles, methods and techniques of cost accountancy to various management problems. These problems include the ascertainment of cost, control of costs, ascertainment of profitability, etc.
4. **Cost accounting is a profession:** In recent years cost accounting has become one of the important professions which has become more challenging. This view is evident from two facts. First, the setting up of various professional bodies such as National Association of Accountants (NAA) in USA. The Institute of Cost and Management Accountants in UK, the Institute of Cost and Works Accountants in India and such other professional bodies both in developed and developing countries have increased the growing awareness of costing profession among the people. Secondly, a large number of students have enrolled in these institutes to obtain costing certificates and memberships for earning their livelihood.

RELATIONSHIP BETWEEN FINANCIAL ACCOUNTING AND COST ACCOUNTING

Cost accounting is very closely-related to financial accounting. Some authorities on the subject consider cost accounting to be the branch of financial accounting. But it may he said that cost accounting is complementary to financial accounting, *i.e.,*a subject which is necessary to make financial accounting whole or complete. Financial accounting and cost accounting are similar in certain respects. But in some other respects they differ from one another. These points of similarities and dissimilarities are enumerated below:

Points of Similarities

(*a*) The fundamental principles of double entry is applicable to both the systems of accounting.

(*b*) The invoices and vouchers constitute the common basis for recording transactions under both the systems of accounting.

(*c*) The results of business are revealed by both the systems of accounting.

(*d*) The causes for losses and wastages of a business are provided by both these systems of accounting.

(*e*) The determination of future business policy is guided by both these systems of accounting.

(*f*) A basis for comparison of expenses is being provided by both the accounting systems.

(g) Accuracy of accounts is maintained under both the systems by means of exercising check over errors and commissions which might creep in either of accounting.

Points of Dissimilarities

Points of Differences	*Financial Accounting*	*Cost Accounting*
1. Purpose	The purpose of financial accounting is external reporting mainly to owners, creditors, tax authorities, government, and prospective investors.	The purpose of cost accounting is internal reporting, *i.e.,* to the mangement of every business.
2. Obligation to maintain accounts	This is to be maintained compulsorily by higher forms of business organizations. The preparation of accounts must be in accordance with the statutory provisions.	Cost accounting are maintained voluntarily. In some cases government has directed some companies to maintain cost accounts to improve efficiency.
3. Recording	(*a*) Financial accounting records transactions in a subjective manner, *i.e.,* according to the nature of expenditure.	(*a*) Cost accounting records transactions in an objective manner, *i.e.,* according to purpose for which costs are incurred.
	(*b*) In financial accounting expenses are recorded in totals.	(*b*) In cost accounting costs are expressed by proper analysis and classification in order to find out cost per unit.
	(*c*) Financial accounting records all transactions which takes place in the business.	(*c*) Cost accounting records only those costs which affect production and sales.
	(*d*) Financial accounting records only historical costs.	(*d*) Cost accounting records both historical and estimated costs.
4. Analysis of profit	Financial accounting discloses profit for the entire business as a whole.	Cost accounting shows the profitability or otherwise of each product, process or operation so as to reveal the areas of profitability.
5. Control	(*a*) It does not make use of any control techniques.	(*a*) It makes use of some important control techniques such as Marginal Costing, Budgetary Control, Standard Costing, etc., in order to control cost.

	(*b*) It does not control materials by using any technique. (*c*) Control over labour is not exercised.	(*b*) It exercises control over materials using some techniques such as ABC analysis, level setting, economic order quantity, etc. (*c*) Control over labour is exercised and efforts are taken to minimise idle time, over time etc.
6. Duration of reproting	Generally, financial accounting provides financial information once a year.	Cost accounting furnishes cost data at frequent intervals. Some reports are daily. Some are weekly and some monthly.
7. Evalution of efficiency	The information provided by financial accounting is not sufficient to evaluate the efficiency of the business.	The cost data helps in evaluating the efficiency of the businesses.
8. Pricing	It fails to guide the formulation of pricing policy.	It provides adequate data for formulating pricing policy.
9. Valuation of stock	Stock is valued at cost or market price whichever is less.	Stock is always valued of cost price.

DIFFERENCES BETWEEN COST AND MANAGEMENT ACCOUNTING

The American Accounting Association 1958, committee on management accounting defines management accounting as "the application of appropriate techniques and concepts in processing the historical and projected economic data of an entity to assist management in establishing a plan for reasonable economic objectives and in the making of rational decisions with a view towards achieving these objectives." It includes the methods and concepts necessary for effective planning for choosing among alternative business actions, and for control through the evaluation and interpretation of performance. Its study involves consideration of ways in which accounting information may be accumulated, synthesised, analysed and presented in relation to specific problems, decisions and day-to-day tasks of business management.

The terminology published by ICMA, London, defines management accounting as "the application of professional knowledge and skill in the preparation and presentation of accounting information in such a way as to assist management in the formulation of policies and in the planning and control of the operation of the undertaking."

If we examine the above two definitions of management accounting, it appears that both the systems of accounting serve the same purpose. However, they differ from one another in respect of the following:

Points of Differences	***Cost Accounting***	***Management Accounting***
1. Growth of Accounting	The history of cost accounting dates back to fourteenth century.	This system of accounting evolved in the middle of 20th century. Hence it is of recent origin when is compared to cost accounting.

2. Object	The main objects of cost accounting is to ascertain and control cost.	The main objective of management accounting is to provide useful information to management for decision-making.
3. Basis of recording	It is based on both present and future transactions for cost ascertainment.	It is concerned purely with the transactions relating to future.
4. Scope	Cost accounting has narrow scope as it covers matters relating to ascertainment and control of cost.	It has a wide scope in as much as it covers the areas of financial accounting, cost accounting, taxation, etc.
5. Utility	Cost accounting serves the needs of both internal management and external parties.	Management accounting serves the needs of only internal management.
6. Types of transactions dealt with	It deals only with monetary transactions. *i.e.,* it covers only quantitative aspect.	It deals with both monetary and non-monetary transaction, *i.e.,* both quantitative and qualitative aspects.
7. Observation of principles and format	Cost accounting follows a definite principle for ascertaining cost and a format for recording.	It does not follow a definite principle and format. Instead, the data to be presented depends upon the need of the management.

RELATIONSHIP BETWEEN COST, ESTIMATE AND PRICE

The terms 'estimates', 'costs' and 'prices' are closely related to each other in costing. An estimate is a forecast of the probable cost of a product, job, or process for a future date. Estimation is purely based on past experience. Cost accounting provide reliable data on the basis of which future cost is estimated. However, an estimate is only an opinion because there is every chance of committing mistake while estimating. Estimation is also based on the future conditions and much depends on guesswork. But such guesswork must be as far as possible closer to the facts.

Cost represents actual total cost incurred in manufacturing a product or in completing a job. The total cost of manufacturing a product broadly consists of material, labour and other expenses. The true cost is ascertained either at the various stages of completing the production or at the end of completion of the job. The current cost serves as the basis for future estimates. Thus cost is considered as a fact as it represents the actual or true cost of manufacturing a product or completing the job.

Price in costing refers to selling price of product. Selling price is arrived at after adding a certain margin of profit to the actual cost. Of course, certain other factors also determine the price fixation policy such as demand for the product, tastes and preferences of customers, price of competitive products, future trends of prices and so on. So price fixing is regarded as a matter of policy. Hence it has been popularly said that an "estimate is an opinion, cost is a fact and price is a policy."

PURPOSES OR OBJECTS OF COST ACCOUNTS

Costing serves number of purposes among which the following are considered to be most important:

1. **Ascertainment of cost:** This was considered to be the primary objective of cost accounting in the initial stages of its development. However, in modern times this has assumed the secondary objective of cost accounting. Cost ascertainment involves the collection and classification of expenses at the first instance. Those items of expenses which are capable of charging directly to the products manufactured are allocated. Then the other expenses which are not capable of direct allocation are apportioned on some suitable basis. Thus the cost of production of goods manufactured is ascertained. In this process, cost accounting involves maintenance of different books to record various elements of cost. Cost of production is ascertained by using any of the costing technique such as historical costing, marginal costing, etc.
2. **Cost control:** At one time cost control was considered as secondary objective of cost accounts. But in modern times it constitutes the primary purpose because of its utmost importance in all business undertakings. Cost control is exercised at different stages in a factory, *viz.,* acquisition of materials, recruiting and deployment of labour force, during the production process and so on. As such we have material cost control, labour cost control, production control, quality control and so on. However, control over cost is exercised through the techniques of budgetary control and standard costing. The control techniques enable the management in knowing the operating efficiency of a business.
3. **Determination of selling price:** Every business organisation aims at maximising profit. Total cost of production constitutes the basis on which selling price is fixed by adding a margin of profit. Cost accounting furnishes both the total cost of production as well as cost incurred at each and every stage of production. No doubt other factors are taken into consideration before fixing price such as market conditions, the area of distribution, volume of sales, etc. But cost plays the dominating role in price fixation.
4. **Frequent preparation of accounts and other reports:** The management of every business constantly rely upon the reports on cost data in order to know the level of efficiency relating to purchase, production, sales and operating results. Financial accounting provides information only at the end of the year because closing stock value is available only at the end of the year. But cost accounts provide the value of closing stock at frequent intervals by adopting a "continuous stock verification" system. Using the value of closing stock it is possible to prepare final accounts and know the operating results of the business.
5. **To provide a basis for operating policy:** Cost data to a great extent helps in formulating the policies of a business and in decision-making. As every alternative decisions involve investment of capital outlay, costs play an important role in decision making. Therefore availability of cost data is a must for all levels of management. Some of the decisions which are based on cost are (a) make or buy decision, (b) manufacturing by mechanisation or automation, (c) whether to close or continue operation in spite of losses.

FUNCTIONS OF COST ACCOUNTANT

The functions of cost accountant may be enumerated under the following:

Traditional Functions

The traditional functions comprise of the routine functions of cost accountant. Such functions are as follows:

(*a*) To establish various cost centres in the organisation.

(*b*) To ascertain the cost of every product, job or process both in terms of total and per unit of product.

(*c*) To design suitable system for defining responsibilities and controlling cost.

(*d*) To provide necessary data to enable management in fixing the price.

(*e*) To prepare reports on wastages of material, loss of labour time, idle capacity of machines so as to improve profitability of business.

(*f*) To implement cost control techniques such as budgetary control and standard costing.

(*g*) To prepare cost schedules to assist management in making decisions and in formulating policies.

(*h*) To design suitable forms for organising an effective system of reporting which ensures provision of adequate cost data to all levels of management.

(*i*) To assist management in the valuation of closing stock of raw materials and work-in-progress so that too much of capital is not locked up in unnecessary inventories.

(*j*) To prepare periodical cost statements and profit and loss account.

Modern Functions

In recent times the functions of a cost accountant are not only confined to ascertain and control cost but extend far beyond these functions. This is on account of the additional responsibilities arising from the various branches of accounting, works organisation, office management and administration, methods of statistical analysis, system analysis O and M studies, modern principles of management, use of computers, etc. These modern functions are as follows:

(*i*) Supervising the functions of mechanised accounting.

(*ii*) Organisation of internal audit in the field of accounting.

(*iii*) To work in close co-ordination with various departmental managers so as to implement cost reduction programmes and methods of improvement.

(*iv*) To undertake cost audit programmes as per the directives issued by the government and the provision of the Indian Companies Act of 1956.

As regards the role of cost accountant in an industry, it has been beautifully summarised by Mr. Wilmot in his article on "the cost accountant's place in management". According to him, the role of cost accountant, is "that of a historian, news agent, and prophet". As historian he must be meticulously accurate, *i.e.*, while supplying cost information to management he has to furnish in greater detail with carefulness and exactness. As news agent, he must be up-do-date, selective and provide full cost information to the needy person. As a prophet he must combine knowledge and experience with foresight and courage.

INSTALLATION OF COST ACCOUNTS

At the outset it is to be understood that a common cost accounting system cannot be installed for all types of business undertakings. The cost accounting system depends upon the nature of business and the product manufactured. Before a suitable system of cost accounting is installed it is necessary to undertake a preliminary investigation so as to know the feasibility of installing cost accounting system to such business. While introducing a system of cost accounts it should be borne in mind that cost accounting system must suit the business. There should not be any attempt to make the business suit the system. One more consideration that is of practical importance is that the benefits derived from cost accounting system must be more than the investment made on it. This means the system must be simple and it must lead to savings through the control of materials, labour and overheads when compared to expenses incurred in maintaining it. For the successful functioning of the costing system, the following conditions are essential:

(*a*) There must be an efficient system of material control.

(*b*) A sound and well-designed method of wage payment must be set up.

(*c*) The existence of sound basis for collection of all indirect expenses and a basis for its apportionment to various production departments.

(*d*) The integration of cost and financial accounts to facilitate reconciliation of profit as shown by these two system of accounting.

(*e*) The use of printed forms so as to facilitate quick compilation of cost reports.

(*f*) The duties and responsibilities of cost accountant must be made clear.

Factors to be Considered before Installing a Cost Accounting System

The following factors are to be considered before installing a cost accounting system:

1. **History of business unit:** The history of a business unit implies the duration of its existence, position in the industry, the rate of growth, policy and philosophy of management and the like. The history of business unit serves as the basis for designing the cost accounting in respect of necessity, simplicity, and investment involved in installing cost accounting.
2. **Nature of the industry:** The nature of business such as manufacturing, mining, trading, etc., determines the costing techniques to be applied. Similarly, the type of product manufactured also determine the method of costing that is to be employed. In other words, there is no all purpose technique and method of costing that can be applied universally.
3. **Product range:** The range of products manufactured and sold also determine the method of costing to be selected. Accordingly range of products must be analysed in terms of size, models, fashions, area of market, competitors and whether the products are made to customers specification or for stocking and selling.
4. **Technical considerations:** Technical considerations that influence the installation of cost accounting are as follows:

   (*a*) Size and layout of the factory

   (*b*) The existence of production and service departments

   (*c*) Flow of production

(*d*) Capacity of machines and degree of mechanisation

(*e*) Existence of laboratories

(*f*) Internal transport and material handling equipments

(*g*) Production control techniques

(*h*) Inspection and testing of materials and finished goods.

5. **Organisational factors:** The problem of installing cost accounting is somewhat difficult in case of an existing business when compared to new business. However, the existing set up of the organisation should be least disturbed should the need arise. In order to fix up responsibility to the executives it may be necessary to group the departments. The organisational factors to be considered are: (*a*) size and the type of organisation such as line, line and staff, functional and committee organisation, (*b*) the levels of management, *viz.*, top level, middle level and bottom level management, (*c*) extent of delegation and responsibility, (*d*) extent of centralization and decentralization, (*e*) extent of of departmentation, (*f*) availability of modern office equipments, and (*g*) number of managerial and supervisory staff.

6. **Selling and distribution method:** The chief factors to be considered with regard to distribution process are the warehousing facilities, external transport, market research and other promotional measures, terms of sale and procurement of orders from customers.

7. **Accounting aspects:** The factors to be considered in respect of accounting are: (*a*) number of financial records, (*b*) existing forms, (*c*) registers used, and (*d*) number of copies required.

8. **Area of control to be exercised:** The areas where cost control is to be exercised is to be identified so that each manager may take action relevant to his activities. If material control occupies significant area of control, it must be given topmost priority for exercising control over materials.

9. **Reporting:** The cost accounting system to be installed must ensure frequency and promptitude in reporting cost data to all levels of management. It must also to be pointed out that duplication of reporting is to be avoided. Further, only those information which are relevant for the management in a particular context alone should be reported.

10. **Uniformity:** The practice of adopting uniform costing facilitates inter-firm comparison among various firms belonging to the same industry. Further it also has the benefit of adopting common costing practice if a holding company has number of subsidiaries.

11. **Use of electronic data processing:** In modern days, it has become a common practice to use electronic data processing equipments and computers. In this situation, it is essential to ensure that the equipment meets the needs of the system but not the other way round.

12. **Practical consideration:** The cost accounting system to be installed must be flexible in operation and must be capable of adaptation to changing conditions. The system must be periodically scrutinised so as to make necessary changes owing to development in business.

STEPS INVOLVED IN THE INSTALLATION OF COST ACCOUNTING

The steps involved in the installation of a cost accounting system are as follows:

1. **Determination of objectives:** The costing system will be simple if the objective is only to determine cost. It will have to be elaborate if the objective is to have information which will help the management in exercising control and taking decisions.
2. **Studying the existing organisations and routine practice:** The various matters to be considered in this regard are the nature of the business, the various operations carried on, extent of responsibility and authority attached to the various functionaries, the lay-out of the factory with particular reference to the manufacturing department, the methods of dealing with wastage of materials, the system of time recording and the methods of computing and paying wages, the system of issuing orders for production to the factory and the method of treating fixed, semi-variable and variable overheads.
3. **Deciding the structure of cost accounts:** This refers to deciding the system of costing based on a thorough study of the manufacturing process and their anciliary services. The structure of cost accounting should follow the natural production line. The sequence can be simple, analytical or synthetic. The designing of the system should be such that there is gradual build up of the cost at each significiant stage of production as the product proceeds to completion.
4. **Determining the cost rates:** This entails a thorough study of factory conditions, classification of cost into direct and indirect, grouping of indirect costs into production, selling, administration etc., treatment of wastes of all kinds, methods of pricing issues, methods of recovering overheads and calculation of overheads rates. A complete cost accounting code should be drawn up so that expenditure may be quickly classified in the office as to both source and cause.
5. **Introducing the system:** No costing system can be expected to function effectively unless cooperation of all the officials could be obtained. Before the system is put into effect, the implications of the system should be explained to all indicating to them the benefits that will accrue to each and to the business as a whole. However, instead of introducing the complete system, it should be introduced only by stages and the existing routines and practices should be utilised unless, there are good grounds to supersede them.
6. **Organising the cost office:** It is always better that the cost office is situated adjacent to the factory so that delay in routing out documents or in clearing up discrepancies and doubts is avoided. The costing staff must be allowed to perform their duties properly. The size of staff would depend on the volume of work involved. The duties of cost office fall into the following spheres.
   (a) *Stores accounts.* Posting of materials, receipts and stores issues in stores ledgers, preparing material abstracts.
   (b) *Labour accounting.* Evaluation of time sheets, jobs cards etc., preparing labour abstracts. In some cases preparation of actual pay rolls.
   (c) *Cost accounts.* Posting of all cost accounts, whether job or process or service accounts.

(*d*) *Cost control.* Posting cost control accounts from data supplied from sections (*a*) and (*b*) above. Preparation of special statistical and other information for management for carrying out special investigation and preparation of periodical trading statements.

7. **Relationship of cost office to other department:** The cost department should function independently. The cost accountant being made directly responsible to the General Manager or Managing Director. The costing system should be designed to serve management at all levels. The cost accountant, therefore, should design his whole system of records and reports; with this end in view. He must know and understand the problems faced in the process of production and try to translate them into financial implications so that correct decisions may be taken.

Practical Difficulties in Installing Cost Accounting

In addition to the above problems, a cost accountant will encounter the following practical difficulties at the time of installation of cost accounting system:

1. **Lack of support from management:** Wherever costing system is installed, it is essential to seek the support of various departmental managers. Very often the managers show hostile attitude towards the costing system. They feel that this system will interfere in their routine work and probably as a means of checking their efficiency. Under such circumstances it is better to convince them about the utility of costing system for the business as a whole.
2. **Resistance by existing accounting staff:** Very often the existing accounting staff resist the installation of the cost accounting system on two grounds. Firstly, they feel that the new system of accounting might lead to excess work. Secondly, they are afraid of their job security. But this difficulty may be overcome by encouraging them about the usefulness of cost accounting as a supplement to financial accounts and the generation of more employment opportunities from the installation of cost accounting system.
3. **Non-cooperation from middle and bottom level management:** At times the middle and bottom level managers such as foremen, supervisors and inspectors also fail to extend their wholehearted cooperation fearing additional work which may be entrusted to them. This problem may be overcome by suggesting them about the simplicity of the system and the existence of a separate cost accounting department to look after costing matters. However, they may be required to provide necessary reports concerning their area of activity so as to enable functioning of cost accounting department efficiently.
4. **Lack of trained staff:** This was no doubt a problem in olden days. Today this problem is overcome, thanks to the establishment of The Institute of Cost and Works Accountant of India in our country which offers professional course in costing and also offers training facilities through various companies to the candidates undergoing the course. In spite of this facility, it is somewhat difficult to get the competent and experienced staff at the time of installation. This problem can be overcome by paying attractive salaries to the cost accountants.
5. **Heavy expenses in installing and maintaining the system:** The setting up of a separate costing department with staff often poses a problem. In addition to installation, the operating expenses in the form of printing and stationery, heating and lighting, depreciation and insurance, rent and rates are to be incurred. However,

as was mentioned earlier, the system of cost accounting must be a useful investment, *i.e.,* benefits derived from it must be more than the investment made on it. If this is not possible, for the time being the system must be discarded.

REQUISITES OR ESSENTIALS OF COST ACCOUNTING SYSTEM

The following are the essentials of an ideal cost accounting system:

1. **Accuracy:** The system of cost accounting must provide for accuracy in terms of both cost ascertainment and presentation. Otherwise it will prove to be misleading.
2. **Simplicity:** Cost accounting system involves detailed analysis of cost. To avoid complications in the procedure of cost ascertainment an elaborate system of costing should be avoided and every care must be taken to keep it as simple as possible.
3. **Elasticity:** The costs accounting system should be capable of adapting itself to the changing situations of business. It must be capable of expansion or contraction depending upon the needs of the business.
4. **Economy:** The cost of operating costing system must be less. It must result in increased benefit when compared to the expenditure incurred in installing it.
5. **Comparability:** The records to be maintained must facilitate comparison over a period of time. The past records must serve as a basis to guide the future.
6. **Promptness:** An ideal costing system is one which provides cost data in an analytical form to the management. So all the departments of a factory must analyse and record the relevant items of cost promptly in order to furnish cost information on a regular basis to various levels of management. This helps in checking up the progress of the business on a regular basis.
7. **Periodical preparation of accounts:** With a view to facilitate the comparison of results frequently, it is desirable to prepare accounts periodically. Constant comparison of actual result with standard result enables to spot out areas of inefficiency. This can be set right by taking remedial measures.
8. **Reconciliation with financial accounts:** The system of cost accounts must be capable of reconciling with financial accounts so as to check accuracy of both the system of accounts.
9. **Uniformity:** The various forms and documents used under costing system must be uniform in size and quality of paper. Printed forms must be used to avoid delay in the preparation of reports. This also reduces the burden of clerical staff. Forms of different colours can be used to distinguish different documents.
10. **Equity:** The basis of apportioning indirect expenses to products, departments or jobs must be fair and equitable.

ORGANISATION OF COST ACCOUNTING DEPARTMENT

The organisation of cost accounting department depends upon the size of the concern. Whatever may be the structure of cost accounting department in a factory, it is established to serve the following purposes: (*i*) To compile cost data in order to meet the statutory requirement wherever applicable, (*ii*) To provide necessary cost data to management to carry out its functions efficiently, and (*iii*) To ensure efficiency and economy in the functioning of cost accounting department. To achieve the above purposes cost accounting department usually performs the following functions:

1. Designing and installation of appropriate method of costing.
2. Accumulation of cost data by process, department and product.
3. Analysis of such cost by elements of cost.
4. Estimation of cost of production.
5. Reporting of cost information to all levels of management.
6. Advising management in relation to investment based on cost information.

In a small and medium-sized concern, the cost accounting department may be set up as a section of financial accounting system. The cost accountant who is incharge of cost accounting department may be authorised to report to the chief accountant. In large-sized concern, a separate cost accounting department is established under the supervision of a full-fledged cost accountant. The cost accounting department is equipped with sufficient staff each to look after different facets of cost accounting function. While important functions such as budgeting, cost analysis, etc., are performed by cost accountant, cost recording, cost reporting and such other functions are performed by cost clerks.

The cost accounting department may be organised either on the principle of centralisation or decentralisation. Under centralised system, the functions of cost accounting departments relating to all firms belonging to same industry is performed at a common central place. The extent of centralisation of cost accounting department depends upon the following factors:

(*a*) The philosophy of management regarding divisional responsibility.

(*b*) The ready availability of cost data from each firm.

(*c*) Size of the firm.

(*d*) The area of operations of every firm.

(*e*) The economy involved in centralisation process.

Advantages of Centralised Cost Accounting Department

1. It facilitates full utilisation of services of costing staff.
2. It permits mechanisation of accounting which is not possible under decentralisation system.
3. It reduces paper work and economise stationery costs.
4. It facilitates prompt reporting.

Under decentralisation system a separate cost accounting department is set up for each and every firm under the supervision of a competent cost accountant. This system has certain advantages.

(*a*) It tends to increase the initiative of the cost accountants of every firm as the responsibility to control lies in their hands.

(*b*) It eliminates duplication of recording and reporting.

(*c*) It increases the speed of functioning of cost accounting department.

Relationship of Cost Department to Other Departments

1. **Cost accounting department and production department:** It can well be said that production department and cost department are interwoven together as the former cannot function efficiently without the existence of the latter. The production process is concerned with the utilisation of materials, money and human resources. The cost department helps in estimating the material cost, labour cost and other expenses for manufacturing a product. It also helps in controlling these costs so as to minimise the cost of production. In fact, the main objective of cost accounting system is to reduce the cost of production of goods or services manufactured and rendered by business units.

   The other areas where cost accounting department is helpful in manufacturing process are:

   (*a*) Engineering department which is concerned with designing a prodouct,

   (*b*) Research and development department which is concerned with development of a new product,

   (*c*) Production planning and control department which ensures completion of production within the time schedule, and

   (*d*) Quality control section, which ensures quality of products. All these departments heavily rely on cost accounting department because costs to be incurred in these departments have a direct impact over the functioning of these departments.

2. **Cost accounting department and personnel department:** The personnel department which is concerned with proper recruitment, selection, training, time-keeping, fixation of wage rate and preparation of payroll, will work with close coordination of cost department. Each and every function performed by personnel department is again influenced by additional cost to be incurred on such function as for example promotion of employees leads to incurrence of additional wages.

3. **Cost accounting department and finance department:** The finance department is concerned with receiving and disbursement of cash. The allocation of investments on fixed and working capital entirely depends upon the cost reports submitted to it by the cost department. Judicious utilisation of available capital is possible only when priority is given for more important areas of investment. This is facilitated by furnishing prompt report by cost department.

4. **Cost accounting department and purchase department:** In majority of firms purchase of raw materials at right quantity, of right quality, from right supplier, at a right time not only ensures ready supply but also at a reasonably low price. Any purchase of substandard quality of materials will lead to dissatisfaction among customers and consequently it leads to loss of orders. Further, purchase of materials at high rate will increase the cost of production tremendously. Delay in getting supplies of materials lead to delay in executing customers orders. In these respects cost accounting department can assist purchase department to ensure efficient purchasing. Cost department also helps in reducing (*a*) waste of materials, (*b*) the risk from theft, and (*c*) excessive investment in inventories.

5. **Cost accounting department and marketing department:** Marketing department relies on cost information in order to (*a*) Estimate future product cost for fixing the selling price, (*b*) In knowing the expenses incurred in marketing the products so that if the amount exceeds the target, control measures can be taken to reduce such

expenses, (*c*) To consider alternative selling methods and promotional measures, and (*d*) To make further investment in warehousing and distribution process. Cost department provides all such information as is required by the marketing department for its efficient functioning.

6. **Cost accounting department and financial accounting department:** The existence of cost accounting department makes the financial accounting department a complete organisation by furnishing additional cost data to the chief accountant. Cost department enables financial accounts department in carrying out the latter's function furnishing necessary data in respect of the following:
   (*a*) Supply of material cost, labour cost and expenses to facilitate preparation of manufacturing account.
   (*b*) Provision of the value of closing stock frequently to facilitate the preparation of interim final accounts.
   (*c*) Assist financial accounting department in matters relating to taxation, insurance and in solving legal matters.
   (*d*) Enables financial accounting department to settle the bills by duly approving them.
   (*e*) Helps financial accounting department in budgeting.

ADVANTAGES OF COST ACCOUNTING

A good costing system serves the needs of a large sections of people. The advantages of cost accounting are discussed below:

Advantages of Cost Accounting to Management

1. **Fixation of responsibility:** Whenever a cost centre is established, it implies establishing a kind of relationship between superior and subordinates. Thus, responsibilities are fixed on every individual who is concerned with incurrence of cost.
2. **Measures economic performance:** By applying cost control techniques such as budgetary control and standard costing it helps in knowing the performance of business.
3. **Fixation of price:** By providing cost data it helps management to fix the selling price in advance. Hence, quotations can be supplied to prospective customers to secure orders.
4. **Aids in decision-making:** It helps management in making suitable decisions such as make or buy, replace manual labour by machines, shut down or continue operations based on cost reports.
5. **Helps in the preparation of interim final accounts:** By the process of continuous stock taking it enables to know the value of closing stock of materials at any time. This facilitates preparation of final accounts wherever desired.
6. **Helps in minimising wastages and losses:** Cost accounting system enables to locate the losses relating to materials, idle time and under utilisation of plant and machinery.

7. **Facilitates comparison:** It facilitates cost comparison in respect of jobs, process, departments and also between two periods. This reveals the efficiency or otherwise of each job, process or department.
8. **Assists in increasing profitability:** Costing reports provide information about profitable or unprofitable areas of operation. The management can discontinue that product line or that department which are responsible for incurring losses and only profitable line of activities alone are retained.
9. **Reconciliation with financial accounts:** A well maintained cost accounting system facilitates reconciliation with financial accounts to check the arithmetical accuracy of both the systems.
10. **It guides future production policy:** Cost data help management in determining future production policy. Any expansion or contraction of production for the future is based on past cost data.

Advantages to Employees

1. Cost accounting system enables employees to earn better wages through overtime wages and incentive systems of wage payment.
2. By providing better facilities it ensures job security to employees.
3. Employees benefit by merit rating techniques which is conducted by scientific process.

Advantages to Creditors

1. It increases the confidence of creditors in the capital employed in the business.
2. The frequent preparation of reports and statements help in knowing solvency position of the business.

Advantages to Government

1. It helps government in formulating policies regarding export, import, taxation, price control measures, wage fixation, etc.
2. It helps in assessing excise duty, sales tax and income tax of the business.
3. Costing information helps in preparing national plans.

Advantages to Society

1. Cost reduction and cost control programmes go to minimise cost of production of goods and services. A portion of the reduced cost of production is shared by customers by paying less price for goods and services.
2. It offers employment opportunities in the cost accounting department in the capacity of cost accountants and cost clerks.

LIMITATIONS OF COST ACCOUNTING

1. **It is expensive:** The system of cost accounting involves additional expenditure to be incurred in installing and maintaining it. However, before installing it, care must be taken to ensure that the benefits derived is more than the investment made on this system of accounting.

2. **The system is more complex:** As the cost accounting system involve number of steps in ascertaining cost such as collection and classification of expenses, allocation and apportionment of expenses, it is considered to be complicated system of accounts. Moreover the system makes use of several documents and forms in preparing the reports. This will tend to delay in the preparation of accounts.
3. **Inapplicability of same costing method and technique:** All business enterprises cannot make use of a single method and technique of costing. It all depends upon the nature of business and type of product manufactured by it. If a wrong technique and method is used, it misleads the results of business.
4. **Not suitable for small-scale units:** A cost accounting system is applicable only to a large-sized business but not to small-sized one. Hence, there is limitation to its application to all types of business.
5. **Lack of accuracy:** The accuracy of cost accounts get distorted owing to the use of notional cost such as standard cost, estimated cost, etc.
6. **It lacks social accounting:** Cost accounting fails to take into account the social obligation of the business. In other words, social accounting is outside the purview of cost accounts.

CRITICISMS OR OBJECTIONS LEVELLED AGAINST COST ACCOUNTS

Despite several benefits offered by cost accounts, critics have levelled the following criticisms against it:

1. **Cost accounting is merely a system of estimates and probabilities:** Though the main purpose of cost accounting is to ascertain the cost of production with a reasonable degree of accuracy, yet absolute accuracy is not possible owing to the two reasons. (*a*) Indirect expenditures are absorbed on the basis of predetermined rates instead of actual rates, and (*b*) The material cost and labour cost is inflated so as to cover the normal loss and wastage of materials and normal idle time of workers.
2. **Cost accounting is unnecessary in such business enterprises which make large profit:** It is argued that industries which earn large amount of profit need not have a system of cost accounting. This statement is absolutely wrong. Earning of more profit by industry does not necessarily mean that its cost of production is lowest and there is no scope for further reduction in the cost. Profit represents the difference between the selling price and the cost of a product. Profit earned by a business may be high because of increased price prevailing in the market. Two or more than two products manufactured by business may earn profit for one line of product and loss by other. The profit earned by one product may outweight the loss suffered by other product thus resulting in overall profit. So it is wrong to judge the efficiency of the business on the basis of overall profitability of the business. If necessary steps are taken to reduce or eliminate losses suffered by a second line product, the industry would earn more amount of profit. It is in this context that a system of costing is felt.
3. **It is unnecessary:** This criticism is levelled owing to lack of understanding of the objectives and advantages of costing. In the present-day competitive world, every manufacturer must know the cost of production for each article so that he can fix

selling price on a reliable and reasonable basis. Further he can also compare his selling price thus fixed with the price prevailing in the market. Cost ascertainment involves application of certain principles and techniques. Having ascertained the cost, control techniques are used to keep the costs under check and thereby increase the profit. Thus it can be said that cost accounting is necessary in most of the concerns.

4. **It is expensive:** This criticism is true as long as the benefits derived from this system is not commensurate with the investment made on it. But by carefully designing the system so as to suit the business, the criticism can be nullified.
5. **Competition governs price and hence there is no need for costing system:** Some critics contend that in these days of competition prices are determined by the forces of demand and supply as against fixation of selling price by adding a desired margin of profit on the cost price. This argument is incorrect. Even in this situation cost accounts disclose the margin of profit that is earned by comparing the market price and cost of production. It impresses upon management the need to reduce cost by increasing the volume of production or by elimination of losses and wastages if any. If the cost price tend to be higher than the market price, it is desirable to abandon such product line and pay attention to profitable line of products.
6. **There is no need for costing where production efficiency is high:** The statement is misleading as without a yardstick to measure the efficiency it is not possible to appraise the efficiency of a business. Cost accounting system offers number of techniques such as standard costing, budgetary control, inter-firm comparison and so on. The cost of production can also be compared between two periods of time to know whether business is currently running efficiently when compared to previous year. In case of inefficient operation remedial measures can be taken to improve the business.
7. **Other objections:** Some other objections that are raised against the installation of cost accounting system are as follows:

   (*a*) *It is a mere matter of forms and rulings:* Often it is argued that the cost accounting system degenerates into a matter of mere forms and rulings. This is not the defect of cost accounting system but the way in which the system is maintained. No doubt different forms are necessary under costing system but they must be simplified and altered to meet the changing condition.

   (*b*) *Failure in many cases:* The system of cost accounting is often condemned as defective in as much as it has failed to produce the desired result. The defect does not lie in the costing system but for some other reasons such as indifferent attitude of the management, lack of adequate facilities, non-cooperations or opposition from employees. These defects can be overcome by reversing the above trend.

   (*c*) *For want of necessity:* It is contended by some that costing is of recent origin and that its application was not felt in the past. Though it was not used earlier, still many industries prospered. So it is felt by some critics that the installation of costing involves unnecessary expenditure. However, it is to be remembered that todays business functions in a competitive conditions and every manufacturer must know the actual cost of production in order to reduce the selling price. Many industrial failures in the past may be attributed to the lack of knowledge on the part of management relating to the actual cost of production thereby selling product below cost.

Questions

I. A. Indicate whether the following statements are True or False

1. Cost accounting is not needed for a non-profit organisation such as a club. *T/F*
2. If management is not interested in costing information, there should be no costing department. *T/F*
3. The cost accounting system is designed in such a way the flow of costs parallel the physical movement of products. *T/F*
4. Effective control of cost can be secured only if the responsibility for cost incurrence is clearly defined. *T/F*
5. Installation of a suitable system of cost accounting is restricted to manufacturing concerns only. *T/F*
6. Cost Audit is a part of cost accounting. *T/F*
7. Both financial accounting and cost accounting are written up with the same basic documents. *T/F*
8. Since pricing is a matter of management policy cost information is useless for price fixation. *T/F*
9. A concern that has been quite prosperous needs no costing system. *T/F*
10. Cost accounting is a branch of financial accounting. *T/F*

[***Answers:*** *True*–2, 3, 4, 6, 7
False–1, 5, 8, 9, 10]

B. Choose the correct answer from the following:

1. Which one of the following is most important tool in cost planning
   (*a*) cost unit (*b*) direct cost
   (*c*) cost statement (*d*) budgeting
2. Cost accounting concepts include all the following except:
   (*a*) planning (*b*) profit sharing
   (*c*) controlling (*d*) product costing
3. The principal factor to be considered in designing a cost system include:
   (*a*) company organisation structure (*b*) nature of business
   (*c*) manufacturing process (*d*) all of the above
4. The chief objective of cost accounting is to
   (*a*) earn more profit (*b*) increase production
   (*c*) provide information for management for planning and control
   (*d*) fix the prices
5. Cost accounting is
   (*a*) nothing more than a detailed analysis of expenditure
   (*b*) an instrument of management control
   (*c*) useful only in such organisation as have profit as the aim
   (*d*) not needed if prices are beyond the control of the firm
6. The need for cost accounting arises as it helps in
   (*a*) ascertaining and control of cost (*b*) increasing the sales
   (*c*) increasing the production (*d*) solving labour problem

7. The primary objective of cost accounting in modern time is

(*a*) cost ascertainment (*b*) cost control

(*c*) ascertainment of profit (*d*) preparation of reports

8. The purpose of financial accounting is to provide information for

(*a*) fixing prices (*b*) recording expenses

(*c*) locating factors leading to wastage and losses

(*d*) assessing the profitability and financial position of the firm

9. Which one of the following is not a factor to be considered in designing a cost system

(*a*) price factor (*b*) organisational factor

(*c*) economy factor (*d*) reporting factor

10. Cost accounting differs from financial accounting in respect of

(*a*) recording cost (*b*) ascertaining cost

(*c*) control of cost (*d*) reporting of cost

[***Answers:*** 1. (*d*), 2. (*b*), 3. (*d*), 4. (*c*), 5. (*b*), 6. (*a*), 7. (*b*), 8. (*d*), 9. (*a*), 10. (*c*)]

C. Match the following:

List A	*List B*
1. Financial accounting provides	(*a*) management needs
2. One of the objections against costing	(*b*) ascertainment of profit of business
3. Cost accounting was evolved	(*c*) is expensive
4. Financial accounting is concerned with	(*d*) find the actual cost of product
5. Cost accounting is concerned with	(*e*) factual financial information

[***Answers:*** 1. (*e*), 2. (*c*), 3. (*d*), 4. (*b*), 5. (*a*)]

SECTION–A

Simple questions

1. Define Cost Accounting. *(Bangalore University, B.Com., April 2000)*

2. Distinguish between costing and cost accounting. *(Bangalore University, M.Com., 1998)*

3. Mention any two uses of cost accounting system to management.
(Bangalore University, B.Com., November 1999)

4. Mention two limitations of costing. *(Bangalore University, B.Com., November 1997)*

5. Distinguish between cost, estimate and price.
(Sri Krishnadevaraya University, B.Com., March 1997)

6. State any four items which are not included in cost accounts.
(Bangalore University, B.Com., April 1995)

7. Mention steps that you should take to instal cost accouning.
(Bharathidasan University, B.Com., November 1995)

8. Mention two objects of cost accounting. *(M.G. University, B.Com., April 1994)*

9. What are the limitations of financial accounting ? *(Osmania University, B.Com., October 1996)*

SECTION–B

Short answer questions

1. "Cost accounting is becoming more and more relevant in the emerging economic scenario in India." Comment. *(C.S. Intermediate, June 2000)*

2. "Cost accounting system that simply records for the purpose of fixing sale price has accomplished only a small part of its mission." Explain. *(C.S. Intermediate, June 1999)*
3. "Selling price is always based on total cost." Comment. *(C.S. Intermediate, June 1999)*
4. "Cost accounts are key to economy in manufacture and one indispensable to the intelligent and economical management of a factory." Discuss. *(C.S. Intermediate, June 1998)*
5. State the steps involved in the installation of a costing system in a large manufacturing company. *(C.S. Intermediate, June 1997) (S.V. University, B. Com., Sept. 94)*
6. Cost accounting is a system of foresight and not a postmortem examination, it turns losses into profits, speeds up activities and eliminates wastes. Comment. *(C.S. Inter, December 1997)*
7. State two differences between financial accounts and cost accounts. *(Bharathidasan University, B.Com., April 1998)*
8. What are the main characteristics of an ideal cost accounting system ? *(M.G. University, B.Com., September 1994)*
9. What is costing ? What are its objectives ? *(Calcutta University, B.Com., October 1994)*
10. Describe the pre-requisites for the installation of cost accounting system. *(Karnataka University, M.Com., April 1997)*
11. Write a note on cost control. *(Mangalore University, B.Com., April 1997)*
12. What is cost accounting ? What are its objectives ? In what respects does cost accounting differ from financial accounting ? *(Mangalore University, B.Com., October 1996)*
13. Distinguish between cost, estimation and cost ascertainment. *(University of Kerala, B.Com., April 1996)*
14. State the advantages of cost accounting. *(Bangalore University, B.Com., November 1992)*

SECTION–C

Long answer questions

1. State the objectives of cost accounting. Briefly explain the advantages of cost accounting. *(University of Mysore, B.Com., April 1998)*
2. Define "Costing", "Cost" and "Cost Accountancy." Distinguish between cost accounting and financial accounting. *(University of Mysore, B.Com., April 2000)*
3. "A Good system of costing must place the same emphasise on cost control as on cost ascertainment." Comment on this statement. *(University of Mysore, B.Com., October 1999)*
4. "Cost accounting is better understood as a cost control and cost reduction exercise and not a mere cost ascertainment process." Discuss. *(University of Mysore, B.Com., April 1997)*
5. "Cost accounting is a system of foresight like pre-natal care, but financial accounting is just a post-mortem examination." Critically examine this statement. *(University of Mysore, B.Com., October 1996)*
6. What are the limitations of financial accounting ? How do you overcome them in cost accounting ? *(University of Mysore, B.Com., November 1995)*
7. Define costing. How does it differ from financial accounting ? Explain its importance under present circumstances. *(University of Mysore, B.Com., November 1998)*
8. State the advantages of costing. How it aids the management and what objections are raised against cost accounts ? *(University of Mysore, B.Com., November 1991)*
9. Define costing. Discuss briefly the objectives and advantages of costing. *(S.V. University, B.Com., April 1998)*
10. Define cost accounting and bring out the differences between Cost accounting and Financial accounting. *(Madurai Kamaraj University, B.Com., April 1998)*

11. Define costing. Critically evaluate the arguments for the installation of costing system in an industry. *(Mangalore University, B.Com., April 1998)*

12. What are the objectives of cost accounting ? What are its advantages and limitations ? *(Nagarjuna University, B.Com., March 1998)*

13. Cost accounting has become an essential tool of management. Mention the steps to be taken while installing cost accounting system in a manufacturing concern. *(Sri Krishnadevaraya University, M.Com., April 1998)*

14. What are the objectives of cost accounting and what is the relation with Management accounting department ? *(S.V. University, B.Com., September 1995)*

15. "Cost accounting has become an essential tool of modern management." Comment. *(Mangalore University, B.Com., April 1994)*

16. Explain briefly the objects, advantages and limitations of costing. *(Sri Krishnadevaraya University, B.Com., April 1994)*

17. Define cost accounting. How does a good system of cost accounting serve the management? *(Bharathidasan University, B.Com., April 1994)*

18. Discuss the limitations of financial accounting and explain the importance of cost accounting. *(M.G. University, B.Com., April 1996)*

19. "An efficient system of costing is essential factor for industrial control under modern conditions of business and as such may be regarded as an important part in the efforts of any management to secure business stability." – Elaborate. *(Mangalore University, B.Com., September 1997)*

20. What is meant by cost accounting ? Discuss in detail the advantages of the cost accounting. *(Madurai Kamaraj University, B.Com., April 1997)*

21. What do you mean by installation of costing system ? Explain the practical difficulties involved in installing such a system in a manufacturing concern. *(Osmania University, B.Com., October 1996)*

22. Explain the advantages of cost accounting. What are the differences between cost accounting and Financial accounting? *(Sri Krishnadevaraya University, B.Com., October 1996)*

23. "A good costing system is an invaluable aid to management." Discuss. *(Osmania University, B.Com., March 1996)*

24. How cost accounting is superior over financial accounting ? Explain the technique of costing and their application and suitability. *(Karnataka University, M.Com., May 1996)*

25. What is cost accounting ? What are its objectives ? Discuss. *(Mangalore University, B.Com., October 1995)*

26. "Cost accounting has become an essential tool of management." Comment and state the steps to be taken while installing a costing system in a manufacturing concern. *(Bangalore University, M.Com., May 1995)*

27. Explain the advantages of cost accounting. *(University of Kerala, M.Com., May 1995)*

28. Explain the significance of cost accounting in a manufacturing company. *(Sri Krishnadevaraya University, M.Com., April 1995)*

29. Enumerate the main objectives of introduction of a cost accounting system in a manufacturing organisation. *(C.A. PE-II November 2002)*

30. Distinguish between costing and cost accounting. *(C.S. June 2004)*

31. Explain the advantages and limitations of cost accounting system for a modern manufacturing organisation. *(Osmania University, M.Com., (Final) June 2003)*

32. State the objectives of cost accounting and list out the characteristics of an ideal costing system. *(Osmania University, M.Com., (Final) June 2002)*

33. Enumerate the matters which you will investigate and the problems which you expect to face before installing a costing system in a manufacturing company. *(Osmania University, M.Com., April 2000)*

34. Explain the need for the development of cost accounting and state its objectives.
(Osmania University, B.Com., March 2004)

35. Explain the significance of cost accounting. *(Osmania University, B.Com., October 2003)*

36. Explain the differences between cost accounting and financial accounting.
(Osmania University, B.Com., March 2003)

37. Define costing and explain the advantages and limitations of costing.
(Kakatiya University, B.Com., July 2003)

38. (*a*) State any five differences between financial accounting and cost accounting.
(Sri Sathya Sai University, B.Com., (Hons) March 2005)

(*b*) Explain any five essential features of an ideal cost accounting system.
(Sri Sathya Sai University, B.Com., (Hons) March 2005)

39. "Cost accounting is considered to be an invaluable aid to management." Bring out the advantages of cost accounting to management of an organisation.
(Sri Sathya Sai University, B.Com., (Hons) March 2001)

❑❑❑

CHAPTER 2

Cost Analysis and Classification

DEFINITION OF COST

The term 'cost' connotes different meanings to different people. But in cost accounting it is used in a special sense. The terminology published by ICMA, defines cost as "the amount of expenditure (actual or notional) incurred on or attributable to a specified thing or activity."

According to Crowningshield cost represents, "an expenditure made to secure an economic benefit, generally resources that promise to produce revenue. The resources may have tangible substance (material or machinery) or they may take the form of services (wages, rent, power)."

In the words of Shillinglaw (Cost Accounting, Analysis and Control) cost represents the resources that must be sacrificed to attain a particular objective.

The AICPA Committee on terminology defines cost as "the amount measured in money, of cash expended or other property transferred, capital stock issued, services performed or a liability incurred in consideration of goods or services received or to be received."

The committee on cost concepts and standards of the American Accounting Association defines cost as "cost is a foregoing, measured in monetary terms incurred or potentially to be incurred to achieve a specific objective."

The term cost is denoted by "expenses" when the cost is incurred after deriving the benefit. The AICPA Committee on terminology defined expenses as "all expired cost which are deductible from revenue." In a narrow sense, expense refers to such items as operating, selling or administrative expenses. Examples of 'expired cost' or 'expense' are rent paid for using the building, wages and salaries paid for deriving the services.

When the cost is incurred before deriving the benefit it is termed as "deferred cost". Examples of deferred costs are insurance premium paid, advertisement expenses incurred and cost of research and development.

When no benefit is derived by the incurrence of cost, it is termed as "loss". Examples of loss are materials destroyed by fire, salary paid for a period of strike, materials spoiled through bad workmanship, high prices paid for materials because of faulty purchases, wages paid to workers for idle time arising from breakdown of machines.

ROLE OF COST IN COST ACCOUNTING

1. It helps in choosing from among various alternative courses of action.
2. It helps in pricing decisions.
3. It helps in determining the optimum level of operation depending upon the behaviour of cost in relation to scale of operation.
4. It helps to make or buy decisons in respect of a component.
5. It helps in matters relating to replacement of capital equipments by a new one.
6. It helps in deciding whether to sell a product at a particular stage of production or to further process and sell at the stage of its completion.
7. It is useful in deciding the acquisition of fixed assets.
8. It helps in deciding to shut down or continue the operation of a certain department owing to losses and wastages arising from such department.
9. It helps in deciding whether an asset is to be bought or hired.
10. It helps in evaluating the incurrence of different elements of cost on different projects.

COST UNIT AND COST CENTRE

Cost Unit

Cost unit is defined by the terminology of ICMA as "a quantitative unit of product or service in relation to which costs are ascertained." A cost unit is a device used for the purpose of splitting total cost into smaller subdivisions attributable to products or service. A cost unit simply stated is a unit of finished product, service or time or combination of these in relation to which cost is ascertained and expressed. The following are some of the examples of cost units selected by different industries.

Names of the Industry	***Products***	***Cost Units***
1. Brick kilns	Bricks	1,000 bricks
2. Cement industry	Cement	Ton
3. Pharmaceutical industry	Tablets	1,000 tablets
4. Cosmetics industry	Talcum powder	1 tin
5. Furniture industry	Table	1 table
6. Hardware industry	Bolts and nuts	100 pieces
7. Cotton textile	Yarn	1 Kg
8. Breweries	Beer	1 barrel
9. Quarry	Granite stone	Ton
10. Construction company	House	Contract
11. Transport companies	Service	Passenger-mile
12. Hospital	Service	Bed-day

Cost Centre

A cost centre refers to a section of a factory for which costs are accumulated separately. In order to facilitate charging of costs to cost units, it is necessary to divide the factory into various sections which can be used to accumulate costs for subsequent distribution. Each section of a such factory is known as cost centre. This also facilitates fixation of responsibility for every officer-in-charge of that section. Hence, cost centre is also known as responsibility centre.

Cost centre has been defined by ICMA terminology as "a location, person or item of equipment (or group of these) in respect of which costs may be ascertained and related to cost units."

Types of Cost Centre

1. **Personal and impersonal cost centre:** Personal cost centre consists of a person or group of persons. Personal cost centre follows the organisational structure of a factory. Under this type of cost centre, costs are analysed and accumulated according to, say, works manager, sales manager, store-keeper, etc.

   Impersonal cost centre consists of a location or item of equipment. A cost centre relating to location may represent a region of sales, a warehouse or storeroom. Cost centre relating to an item of equipment could be a machine or group of machines.

2. **Operation and process cost centre:** Operation cost centre consist of those machines which carry out the same operation.

   A process cost centre is a cost centre in which a specific process or a continuous sequence of operation is carried out.

3. **Production and service cost centre:** A production cost centre is one where actual production process is carried out. The manufacturing and non-manufacturing costs are charged to production cost centre.

   A service cost centre is one which provides services to other cost centre. Only non-manufacturing costs are charged to service cost centre

4. **Other cost centres**

   (*a*) **Profit centre:** A part of a business accountable for both cost and revenues.

   (*b*) **Responsibility centre:** A department or organisational function whose performance is the direct responsibility of a specific manager.

   (*c*) **Revenue centre:** A centre devoted to raising revenue with no responsibility for costs, *e.g.*, a sales centre often used in a non-profit organisation.

Whatever may be the type of cost centre, it is determined by taking into consideration the following factors:

(*a*) The volume of work to be performed.

(*b*) The extent of cost control that can be exercised.

(*c*) Responsibilities to be identified.

(*d*) The uses of cost centres to the cost accounting department.

COSTING TECHNIQUES

Some of the important techniques of costing are as follows:

(a) **Absorption costing:** Under this technique both fixed and variable costs are charged to costs of production.

(b) **Marginal costing:** Under this technique, a distinction is made between variable cost and fixed cost. Only variable costs are charged to cost of production. Fixed costs are written off to the costing profit and loss account.

(c) **Historical costing:** Under this technique, the actual cost incurred is taken into the cost of production.

(d) **Standard costing:** Under this technique, standard costs are established for each item of expense based on past experience. The actual cost is compared with standard cost to know the variance. This reflects the efficiency or otherwise of the performance of the organisation.

(e) **Differential costing:** A technique used in the preparation of *ad hoc* information in which only cost and income difference between alternative courses of action are taken into consideration.

(f) **Uniform costing:** The use by several undertakings of the same costing systems, *i.e.*, the costing principles and method.

COSTING SYSTEMS

Neuner in his *Accounting System* has defined an accounting system as "an organisation of forms, records and reports, closely coordinated to facilitate business management through determining certain basic and required information." A cost system is an aspect of the accounting system designed specifically to provide information concerning costs and efficiency. The following are some of the costing systems:

1. **Historical cost system:** A historical system is one which accumulates actual costs after the operations have taken place. So, under this system cost of a product is ascertained after they have been actually incurred. This system is not so popular because it suffers from the following limitations.
   (*i*) As historical costs are recorded after the event takes place, it is not possible to rectify the defect until the inefficiency is discovered.
   (*ii*) It does not provide any basis against which efficiency can be measured.
   (*iii*) It does not facilitate preparation of tender statements and quotations.
   (*iv*) It is expensive system as a large number of records and forms are to be maintained under this system.
2. **Estimated cost system:** It is a system under which the various elements of costs are estimated or predetermined for recording the cost in the books of accounts. Estimated cost system helps in comparing such cost with actual cost to know variations between estimated and actual costs. Estimated cost serve as a basis for fixation of selling price. A serious limitation of estimated cost system is that estimated costs are seldom accurate.

3. **Standard cost system:** It is a system of cost accounting which makes use of predetermined standards relating to various elements of cost. Having fixed the standard costs, they are compared with actual costs to develop variances to know the efficiency of business. Standard cost system is applicable where the production process is standardised.

Although estimated costs and standard costs are predetermined cost they differ from each other in respect of the following:

(*i*) Estimated costs are established on an average basis taking into account the past performance. While standard costs are established on a scientific basis.

(*ii*) Estimated costs only constitute a statistical information and are not recorded in the books. Standard costs are recorded in the accounting books.

(*iii*) Estimated cost does not serve the purpose of cost control. They are useful in fixing the prices. Whereas standard cost serves the purpose of cost control.

COSTING METHODS

Costing methods help in finding out cost per unit of a product or service. Cost finding is defined as the determination of the cost of goods or services by informal procedure, *i.e.*, procedure that do not carry on regular process of cost accounting on a continuous basis. There are number of methods of cost finding which are used in practice depending upon the nature of the business and the type of its products. The most popular methods of cost finding is shown in the following chart.

Methods of Cost Finding

- Specific order costing
  - Job costing
  - Batch costing
  - Contract costing
  - Cost plus costing
- Operation costing
  - Single or output costing
  - Process costing
  - Service or operating costing
  - Departmental costing
  - Composite costing

Specific Order Costing

The terminology of ICMA defines specific order costing as "the category of basic costing methods applicable where the work consists of separate contracts, jobs or batches each of which is authorised by a special order or contract." This method is adopted in made-to-order type of products which depends entirely on the specification of customers. As such there is no standardisation in the production process for want of uniformity. This method may take any of the following:

1. **Job costing:** The terminology of ICMA defines job costing as "that form of specific order costing which applies where work is undertaken to customers' special requirements." The work is usually carried out within a factory or workshop where each job moves, through the processes or operations as a continuously identifiable

unit although the term may also be applied to such work as building repairs carried out in the customer's premises.

A job costing is also known as terminal costing' as the recording of costs ends after the completion of job. Under this method of costing each job is dissimilar in nature and is therefore identified separately by a job order number. Costs are ascertained job wise and profit or loss is known for each job separately.

This methods is used in repair workshops, printing press, foundries, film studios, interior decoration, etc.

2. **Contract costing:** The terminology of ICMA defines contract costings as "that form of specific order costing which applies where work is undertaken to customers' special requirements and each order is of long duration." The work is usually of a constructional nature. In general, the method is similar to job costing although it has certain distinctive features. These features of contract costing are as follows:
   (*a*) Most of the contracts take several months (even years) for completion.
   (*b*) The work is performed in all cases without exception in the premises of contractee.
   (*c*) Most of the expenses chargeable to contracts are direct in nature.

   This method is adopted in constructional companies engaged in building houses, road repairs, construction of dams and bridges.
3. **Cost plus contract:** This is a variation of contract costing which was very popular during the First World War. At present, it is used in USA and India to a large extent by constructional contractors. Under this method, the contract price is fixed by adding a percentage of profit to the prime cost, *i.e.,* aggregate of direct material cost, direct labour cost and direct expenses. This method is followed only when there is need for quick execution of contracts without waiting for the fixing of definite contract price. This method is disapproved because of the following limitations:
   (*a*) The contractor may unduly fix a higher margin of profit on a high notional cost.
   (*b*) There may be fraudulent agreement between contractor and sub-contractor in arriving at a high total cost, on which profit margin is to be fixed.
   (*c*) It may lead to inefficiency and thus, resulting in overtime work to complete the work within the time schedule.
4. **Batch costing:** The terminology of ICMA defines batch costing as "that form of specific order costing which applies where similar articles are manufactured in batches either for sale or for use within the undertaking." In most cases the costing is similar to job costing. Under this method a convenient batch of production is treated as a job. Cost is ascertained for each batch separately. This method is used in biscuit factories, bakeries, ready-made garments, hardwares like bolts, nuts, screws, drugs and pharmaceuticals.

Operation Costing

The terminology of ICMA defines operation costing as "the category of basic costing methods applicable where standardised goods or services results from a sequence of repetitive and more or less continuous operations or process to which costs are charged before being averaged over the units produced during the period." The following are the distinctive methods of costing which fall under this category.

1. **Single or output or unit costing:** It is a method of costing by the unit of production, where manufacturing is continuous and the units are identical. In some cases, the units may differ in terms of size, shape, quality, etc. This method is called single costing as only single type of product alone is manufactured. Examples of industries which make use of this method of costing are collieries, quarries, flour-mills, paper mills, textile mills, brick-making.
2. **Process or continuous or average costing:** The terminology of ICMA defines process costing as "that form of operation costing which applies where standardised goods are produced." It is a method of costing where cost is ascertained at the stage of every process and also after completing the finished production. The industries which make use of this method of costing have the following distinct features:
   (*a*) The output of one process is passed on as input of subsequent process until production is complete.
   (*b*) The cost of every process is transferred to subsequent process as is done in the above feature.
   (*c*) The process industries incur normal and abnormal losses usually.
   (*d*) In majority of process costing industries by-products are obtained in addition to main product.
   (*e*) The cost of semi-finished goods are expressed in terms of fully finished goods and this process is known as equivalent production.

   The examples of industries which make use of process costing are breweries, chemicals, paints, soap, sugar, etc.
3. **Service or operating costing:** The terminology of ICMA defines service costing as "that form of operation costing which applies where standardised services are provided either by an undertaking or by a service cost centre within an undertaking". This method of costing is used by those undertakings which render service as against manufacturing and supply of tangible products. The important features of industries where this method of costing is applied are as follows:
   (*a*) They render uniform service for those who apply for it or who depend on it.
   (*b*) It involves heavy capital expenditure in manufacturing and in the supply of services.
   (*c*) The cost of production is classified into fixed and variable as economy of operation affects unit cost of service rendered.
   (*d*) They make use of composite unit to express the cost per unit.

   Examples of industries which make use of this method of costing are (*i*) Transport undertakings, which may take the form of Roadways, Railways and Airways, (*ii*) Supply services which may take the form of supply of gas, electricity, water, (*iii*) Welfare services such as Canteen, Hospital and Library.
4. **Departmental costing:** Under this method of costing the cost incurred in maintaining a particular department is ascertained. There are two reasons for using this method of costing, *viz.*, (*a*) to control the cost of a department as for example the cost of running a research department or a dispensary belonging to the factory, (*b*) to charge the costs of a department to the finished product, as for example, charging the costs of maintenance department to production department.

5. **Multiple or hybrid or composite costing:** This method of costing is used in those industries which assemble the various component parts. Such industries make use of more than one method of costing. For example, in bicycle manufacturing industries batch costing may be used to ascertain the costs of various component parts. Upon assemblage of these parts output costing may be used in ascertaining the cost of a single bicycle. Other examples of industries which make use of this method of costing are radio manufacturing concerns, refrigeration industries, aeroplane, TV industries, automobiles and so on.

COST CLASSIFICATION

According to Robert I. Dickey, classification is the process of grouping like facts under a common designation on the basis of similarities of nature, attributes or relations. The Committee on National Association of Accountants define classification as "the identification of each item and the systematic placement of like items together according to their common features. Items grouped together under common heads are further defined according to their fundamental differences."

Need for Cost Classification

The need for classification arises owing to use of cost data for a variety of purposes. The same cost data cannot serve all purposes equally well. For different purposes, different kinds of cost information are required. Hence, costs must be arranged and classified in such a way that they can be combined in different ways to serve different purposes. The cost classification is directed towards the attainment of the following purposes:

(*a*) ascertainment of profits periodically

(*b*) in budgeting and planning process

(*c*) controlling cost

(*d*) pricing policy, and

(*e*) current application of plans and policies.

METHODS OF COST CLASSIFICATION

Costs are classified on the basis of large number of methods. This is shown in the following chart. *(see next page)*

On the Basis of Element of Cost

Under this basis costs can be classified into the following:

(*a*) **Material cost:** The terminology of ICMA defines material cost as "the cost of commodities, other than fixed assets, introduced into products or consumed in the operation of an organisation." Materials cost may be either direct material cost or indirect material cost. The terminology defines direct material cost as "the cost of materials entering into and becoming constituent element of a product or saleable service." Examples of direct materials are cotton in Cotton Textiles, timber in furniture

CHART SHOWING CLASSIFICATION OF COST

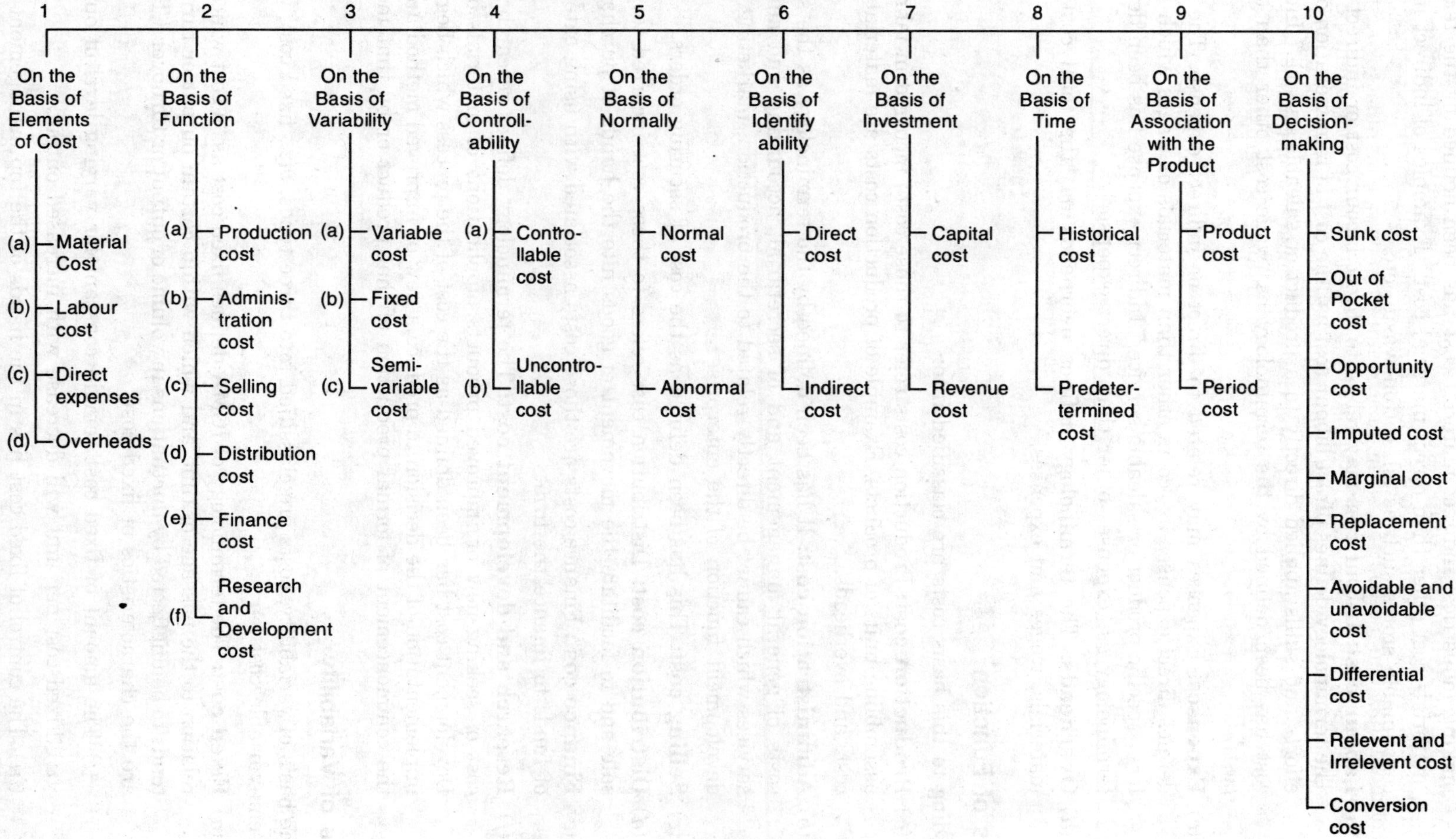

making industries. Indirect material cost has been defined by the terminology as "materials cost other than direct material cost." Examples of indirect materials are consumable stores such as oil, cotton waste, etc.

(*b*) **Labour cost:** Labour cost may relate to direct labour cost or indirect labour cost. The terminology defines direct labour cost as "the cost of remuneration of employees' efforts and skills applied directly to a product or saleable service." Indirect wages cost has been defined by the terminology as "wage cost other than direct wages cost."

(*c*) **Expenses:** Expenses may related to direct or indirect expense. The terminology defines direct expenses as "costs other than materials or wages which are incurred for a specific product or saleable service." Indirect expense has been defined by the terminology as "expenses other than direct expense."

(*d*) **Overheads:** The terminology defines overheads as "the total cost of indirect materials, wages and expenses."

Basis of Function

According to this basis costs are classified into:

(*a*) **Production cost:** Production costs refer to those costs incurred in fabricating, and assembling units of products. Example of production costs are material cost, labour cost, and overheads.

(*b*) **Administration cost:** It has been defined by the terminology as the sum of those costs of general management and of secretarial, accounting and administrative services which cannot be directly related to the production, marketing, research or development function of the enterprise.

(*c*) **Selling cost:** This has been defined as the cost of securing orders.

(*d*) **Distribution cost:** Distribution cost refers to those cost incurred to promote the sale and to facilitate the movement of goods into the hands of purchasers.

(*e*) **Finance cost:** Finance costs are those costs associated with using external sources of funds to finance the firm.

(*f*) **Research and development cost:** The terminology defines research cost as "the cost of seeking new or improved products, applications of materials or methods." Development cost has been defined as the cost of the process which begins with the implementation of the decision to produce a new or improved method and ends with the commencement of formal production of that product or by that method.

Basis of Variability

On the basis of variability, costs are classified into three types, *viz.,* fixed cost, variable cost and semi-variable cost.

(*a*) **Fixed cost:** The terminology of ICMA defines fixed cost as "a cost which accrues in relation to the passage of time and which within certain output or turnover limits, tends to be unaffected by fluctuations in volume of output or turnover." The following are the characteristics of fixed cost:

(*i*) The amount of fixed cost remain constant for varying level of output.

(*ii*) Fixed cost per unit will decrease with increased output.

(*iii*) The control of fixed cost lies in the hands of the top management rather than departmental heads.

Examples of fixed costs are rent and rates, insurance, salaries and such their items.

(*b*) **Variable cost:** The terminology of ICMA defines variable cost as "a cost which in aggregate tends to vary in direct proportion to changes in the volume of output or turnover." The characteristics of variable costs are as follows:

(*i*) They vary in in direct proportion to volume of output or sales.

(*ii*) The variable cost per unit of product remains constant.

(*iii*) It is easy to assign variable cost to products or departments.

(*iv*) Control over variable cost lies in the hands of departmental heads.

Examples of variable costs are direct material cost, and direct labour cost.

(*c*) **Semi-variable cost:** The terminology defines semi-variable cost as "a cost containing both fixed and variable elements, which is, therefore, partly affected by fluctuations in the volume of output or turnover." Examples of semi-variable costs are telephone charges (as telephone bill for local calls are fixed and for outstation calls it varies depending upon number of calls made) depreciation (for efflux of time is fixed, for wear and tear it is variable).

Basis of Controllability

On this basis, cost is classified into two types, *viz.*, (*i*) controllable cost, and (*ii*) non-controllable cost.

(*a*) **Controllable cost:** The ICMA terminology defines controllable cost as "cost chargeable to a cost centre, which can be influenced by the actions of the person in whom control of the centre is vested." Practically all variable costs are controllable cost.

(*b*) **Non-controllable cost:** The ICMA terminology defines non-controllable cost as a "cost chargeable to a cost centre which cannot be influenced by the actions of the person in whom control of the centre is vested." Practically, all fixed costs are non-controllable cost.

Basis of Normality

According to this basis, costs are classified into two types, *viz.*, (*a*) normal cost and (*b*) abnormal cost.

(*a*) **Normal cost:** Normal cost is defined as a "cost" which is normally incurred at a given level of output in the condition in which that level of output is normally attained.

(*b*) **Abnormal cost:** It is defined as a "cost which is not normally incurred at a given level of output in the conditons in which that level of output is normally attained." Only normal cost is charged to cost of production. Abnormal cost is charged to costing Profit & Loss Account.

Basis of Identifiability

On this basis, costs are clsssified into two types, *viz.*, (*i*) direct cost, and (*ii*) indirect cost.

(*i*) **Direct cost:** All costs which can be conveniently allocated to cost unit or cost centre is known as direct cost.

(*ii*) **Indirect cost:** Those costs which cannot be allocated to, but which can be apportioned to cost unit or cost centre are known as indirect cost.

This classification is important because of the following:

(i) It facilitates accurate ascertainment of cost by means of identifying direct cost to cost unit and by appropriate apportionment and absorption of indirect cost by cost unit.

(ii) It facilitates controlling of costs because most of the direct costs are controllable whereas indirect costs are not amenable for control.

(iii) It enables in fixing the responsibility to the executives.

Basis of Investment

On this basis, costs are classified into (a) capital cost, and (b) revenue cost.

(a) **Capital cost:** A captial cost is intended to benefit future periods.

(b) **Revenue cost:** A cost which is incurred to benefit the current period is treated as revenue cost.

Capital cost is treated as an asset while revenue cost is treated as an expense.

Basis of Time

On this basis, costs are classified into two types: (a) Historical cost, and (b) Predetermined cost.

(a) **Historical cost:** This refers to costs which are incurred after the event takes place.

(b) **Predetermined cost:** This refers to a cost which is computed in advance of production on the basis of a specification of all the factors affecting cost. Predetermined costs are costs which are set up from analysis and forecast made before the event and represent not what has happened but what is expected to happen. Predetermined costs take a number of forms such as budgeted cost, estimated cost, standard cost and so on.

Basis of Association with the Production

On this basis, costs are classified into two types, *viz.*, (a) product cost, and (b) period cost.

(a) **Product cost:** These are the costs which are directly associated with the product. These costs provide no benefit until the product is sold. When the products are sold, the total product costs are recovered as an expense. This expense is called the cost of goods sold. Examples of product costs are direct material, direct labour and factory overheads.

(b) **Period cost:** Period costs are those costs that can be associated with a particular accounting period rather than with the products delivered to the customers.

Basis of Decision-making

The following costs are classified on the basis of managerial decision-making:

(a) **Sunk cost:** The National Association of Accountants defines a sunk cost as "an expenditure for equipment of productive resources which has no economic relevance to the present decision-making process." Sunk cost as its name implies is an historical cost that are irrevocable in a given situation. It is a cost which has been created by a decision that was made in the past which cannot be changed by any decision that will be made in the future. For example, an equipment which is to be discarded at its book value having no scrap value is not affected by a decision to continue or shutdown the operation of a department where such equipment is used.

(*b*) **Out-of-pocket cost or explicit cost:** It signifies the cash outlay required for undertaking a project. Here the management is interested in knowing whether the income from a particular project will at least cover the expenditure incurred on that project.

(*c*) **Opportunity cost:** The terminology of ICMA defines opportunity cost as "the value of benefit sacrificed in favour of an alternative course of action." Edwards Hermanson and Salmonson define it as "the benefit lost by rejecting the best competing alternatives to the one chosen." The benefit lost is usually the net earnings or profit that might have earned from the rejected alternative. Opportunity costs are not recorded in the books. It is important in decision-making and in comparing various alternatives to decide the best alternative. An example of opportunity cost would be investment on plant and machinery, cannot be invested on shares of a company. The loss of dividend that would have been earned had the investment is made on shares is the opportunity cost.

(*d*) **Imputed cost or notional cost or implicit cost:** The terminology of ICMA defines notional cost as "a hypothetical cost taken into account to represent a benefit enjoyed by the undertaking in respect of which no actual expense is incurred." Examples of imputed costs are rent of owned land, salary of owner and interest on owned capital.

(*e*) **Marginal cost:** The terminology of ICMA defines marginal cost as "the variable cost of one unit of product or a service, *i.e.*, a cost which would be avoided if the unit was not produced or provided."

(*f*) **Replacement cost:** It refers to the cost of replacing an asset at current market value. For example, when the cost of replacing a machinery is considered, it means the cost of purchasing the machinery at the current market price and not at which it was purchased.

(*g*) **Avoidable cost and unavoidable cost:** Avoidable cost can be eliminated, in case the product or department is discontinued.

Unavoidable costs are the indirect costs which cannot be eliminated with the discontinuation or a product or department. Such costs are merely allocated if the product or department is discontinued. Example of unavoidable cost is rent of factory and salary of factory manager which cannot be eliminated if a particular product line or a department is discontinued.

(*h*) **Differential cost:** Differential cost has been defined as the increase or decrease in total cost resulting out of (*i*) producing and distributing a few more or few less of products, (*ii*) a change in the method of production or distribution, (*iii*) an addition or deletion of product or a territory, and (*iv*) the selection of an additional sales channels.

(*i*) **Relevant and irrelevant cost:** Relevant costs are those costs that would change by the decision. Irrelevant costs are those costs that would not be affected by the decision. For example, when a manufacturer decided to close a warehouse, the wages associated with the maintenance of such warehouse is relevant cost as wage payment cease if the warehouse is closed. But rent which was already paid under lease agreement which cannot be recovered is irrelevant cost.

(*j*) **Conversion cost:** This is the aggregate of direct labour cost and overheads. Such costs assume more importance where material value is negligible as in the case of brick manufacturing industries.

COST CONVENTIONS

The cost accounting conventions may be summarised as under:

1. **Classification of expenses according to nature of cost:** In order to facilitate control over costs, the total cost incurred in manufacturing a product is divided into (*a*) direct material cost, (*b*) direct labout cost, (*c*) direct expenses, and (*d*) overheads.
2. **Classification of costs into fixed and variable:** In order to know the behaviour of costs, total cost is classified into fixed and variable.
3. **Classification of costs into normal and abnormal:** To facilitate comparison of cost of one period with other period, costs are classified into normal cost and abnormal cost. Normal cost is charged to cost of production and abnormal cost is taken into costing profit and loss account.
4. **Principle of exception:** Principle of exception which is a technique of management science is used in reporting cost data to management. Under this convention, only such report which are useful in management decision-making is reported and all irrelevant matters are not disclosed to management.
5. **Establishment of standards:** The standards to be set for each and every task should be practical one which is attainable under a given condition and for attaining a given level of output. In other words, standards to be set must be a realistic approach.
6. **Classification of costs as controllable and uncontrollable:** In order to fix the responsibility on the executives, it is necessary to classify the costs into controllable and uncontrollable cost.
7. **Consistency:** Whenever any method or system or technique is used for ascertaining cost, it should be continued for a reasonably long period of time unless the situation demand for its change. For example, the method of wage payment should not be changed very often. Frequent changes in the methods and techniques will vitiate comparison of cost data. In other words, consistency must be maintained for a relatively longer period of time.
8. **Cost control to be exercised through close contact with those who incur the costs:** The control of cost should not only be the job of cost accountant alone. Everyone such as foreman, supervisors, and departmental managers should be consulted and involved in cost control process.
9. **Cost should represent sacrifice involved when a business is operating at an efficient level of operation:** Certain items of expenses will not affect cost of production and as such they are not recorded. For example, interest on capital is not recorded in cost accounts being a matter of pure finance.
10. The system of cost accounting should be designed so as to meet the specific requirements of a business.

COMPONENTS OF TOTAL COST

The various components of total cost are as follows:

(*a*) Prime cost (*b*) Factory cost or works cost

(*c*) Office cost or cost of production (*d*) Cost of sales or total cost.

These components of total cost are explained below.

1. **Prime cost:** Prime cost is also called by other names such as first cost, basic cost, and foundation cost as it is incurred first in the sequence when compared to other components of total cost. Prime cost consists of three important elements of costs, namely, direct material cost, direct labour cost and direct expenses. Prime cost is important for three reasons. *Firstly*, this is the most important component of total cost because in terms of elements of cost they constitute highest percentage of total cost. It is the foundation upon which stands the whole structure of total cost. *Secondly*, some of the overheads are absorbed on the basis of prime cost elements. *Thirdly*, by analysing and comparing every element of prime cost of one period with the corresponding element of the previous year, management can know to what extent the prime cost element has varied and take appropriate steps to control such element of prime cost. Expressed in the form of an equation:

   Prime cost = Direct material cost + Direct labour + Direct expenses

2. **Factory cost or works cost:** It comprises of prime cost and factory overheads which includes indirect material cost, indirect labour cost and indirect expenses. Works cost denotes the actual expenses that are incurred in converting raw materials into finished products. Works cost is important for two reasons. *Firstly,* by comparing works cost of current year with the previous year, it shows the variation of the work cost. Management can take suitable steps to control if the variation is adverse. *Secondly,* works cost constitute the basis for absorption of office overheads in certain cases. Expressed in the form of an equation:

   Factory cost or work cost = Prime cost + Factory or works overhead

3. **Office cost or cost of production:** Office cost is the aggregate of works cost and office and administration overheads. Office cost is important as it serves the purposes of (*a*) knowing the cost of production, (*b*) knowing the percentage of office overheads to office cost. This in turn reflects the relative importance of office department and its efficient functioning, (*c*) selling price is fixed on the basis of cost of production in case of made-to-order type of industries. Expressed in the form of an equation:

   Office cost or cost of production = Works cost or factory cost + Office and administration overhead

4. **Total cost or cost of sales:** When selling and distribution expenses are added to office cost or cost of production, it is known as total cost or cost of sales. Total cost serves the purposes of (*a*) fixing the selling price by adding a margin of profit to the total cost, (*b*) knowing the relation between selling and distribution expenses with office overheads on the one hand and works overheads on the other hand, (*c*) by comparing the total cost of present year with past year it is possible to know increase

or decrease in the total cost and thereby to control the total cost if it has gone up. Expressed in the form of an equation:

Total cost or cost of sales = Office cost or cost of production + Selling and distribution overhead

The Fig. 2.1 summarises the various components of total cost.

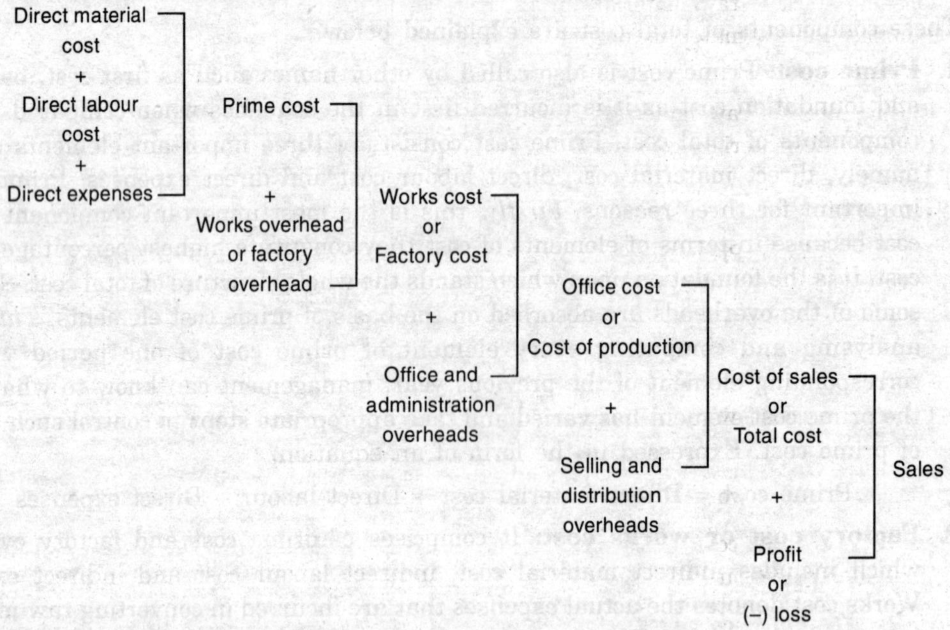

Fig. 2.1. *Chart showing components of total cost.*

COST SHEET

A cost sheet is a statement which shows the details regarding the total cost of the job or a product. A cost sheet may include as many columns as is desired to show in detail (*a*) Cost per unit of the product, (*b*) Total cost of all the units produced, (*c*) Particulars of cost relating to the previous year, (*d*) Estimated cost for the succeeding year, and (*e*) A column showing the variation of each and every elements of cost. A cost sheet not only shows the total cost but also the various components of total cost. It serves the following purposes:

1. It discloses the cost per unit as well as total cost of output.
2. It discloses the various elements of cost which go to make up total cost.
3. By fixing selling price in advance it facilitates preparation of tender price.
4. It facilitates comparison of total cost with previous year's cost and standard cost and thereby help management in locating inefficiency in production.

The following is the pro forma of a cost sheet:

PRO FORMA COST SHEET (*For the period ending........*)

		Total	*Cost per unit*
Direct material cost:			
Opening stock of raw material during the year	xx		
Add : Purchase of raw materials during the year	xx		
Add : Carriage inwards	xx		
Less : Closing stock of raw materials	xx		
Cost of raw materials consumed	xx	xx	xx
Direct labour cost		xx	xx
Direct expenses		xx	xx
Prime cost		xx	xx
Factory overhead		xx	xx
		xx	xx
Add : Opening stock of work-in-progress		xx	xx
		xx	xx
Less : Closing stock of work-in-progress		xx	xx
Works cost		xx	xx
Office and Administration Overheads		xx	xx
Office cost or cost of production		xx	xx
Add : Opening stock of finished goods		xx	xx
Cost of goods available for sale		xx	xx
Less : Closing stock of finished goods		xx	xx
Cost of goods sold		xx	xx
Selling and Distribution overheads		xx	xx
Total cost or cost of sales		xx	xx
Profit		xx	xx
Sales		xx	xx

Problem-1

Indicate giving reasons, whether the following items are to be dealt within cost accounts mentioning whether and how any of these items are to be included in the total cost.

(1) Surplus realised on sale of factory plant and machinery.

(2) Royalties paid on patents of other party used in own manufacturing process.

(3) Royalties received for allowing other to use own patents.

(4) Carriage and freight inwards in respect of raw materials purchased.

(5) Carriage and freight outwards in respect of finished products sold.

(6) Advertising expenses for selling goods.

(7) Cash discount received from suppliers of raw materials.

(8) Packing materials required for making a product saleable.

(Calcutta University, B.Com (Hons) 1994)

Solution:

(1) Surplus realised on sale of factory plant and machinery is not an item of cost. It is purely a financial matter. Therefore, it is to be kept outside the purview of total cost.

(2) Royalties paid on patents is an item of Direct expenses. Therefore, it is to be charged to prime cost.

(3) Royalties received from others is a financial matter. Therefore, it is to be excluded from cost.

(4) Such expenses are to be added to cost of materials *i.e.*, charged to prime cost.

(5) Such expenses are the items of distribution overhead and charged to costs accordingly.

(6) This is an item of selling overhead.

(7) This is a financial matter. Therefore, it is to be excluded from costs.

(8) This is an item of distribution overhead and charged to costs accordingly.

Problem-2 (Calculation of Material Cost Purchased)

Calculate the cost of raw materials purchased from the following data:	*Rs.*
Opening stock of raw materials	*20,000*
Closing stock of raw materials	*30,000*
Expenses on purchases	*10,000*
Direct wages	*50,000*
Prime cost	*1,50,000*

(University of Madras, B.Com., May 2005)

Solution:

Calculation of Cost of Raw Materials Purchased

Prime cost = Opening Stock of Raw Materials + Purchases + Expenses on Purchases − Closing Stock of Raw Materials + Direct Wages

$$1{,}50{,}000 = 20{,}000 + P + 10{,}000 - 30{,}000 + 50{,}000$$

$$1{,}50{,}000 = 50{,}000 + P$$

$$1{,}50{,}000 - 50{,}000 = P$$

$$\text{Purchases} = 1{,}00{,}000$$

Problem-3

From the following information, compute the raw material purchased	*Rs.*
Opening stock of raw materials	*20,000*
Closing stock of raw materials	*30,000*
Direct wages	*2,10,000*

Factory overheads	*60% of Direct wages*
General overheads	*10% of Works cost*
Cost of production	*6,88,600*

(Calcutta University, B.Com (Hons.) 2000)

Solution:

Statement Showing Raw Materials Purchased

Cost of production	6,88,600
Less : General overhead (10% of works cost *i.e.*, $\frac{1}{11}$ of cost of production)	62,600
Works cost	6,26,000
Less : Factory overhead $2{,}10{,}000 \times \frac{60}{100}$	1,26,000
Prime cost	5,00,000
Less : Direct wages	2,10,000
Raw materials consumed	2,90,000
Add : Closing stock of raw materials	30,000
	3,20,000
Less : Opening stock of raw materials	20,000
Purchase of raw materials	3,00,000

Problem-4 (Cost Sheet)

The following data have been extracted from the books of M/s Moon Shine Industries Ltd. for the Calender year 2004.

	Rs.
Opening stock of raw materials	25,000
Purchases of raw materials	85,000
Closing stock of raw materials	40,000
Carriage inwards	5,000
Wages : Direct	75,000
Indirect	10,000
Other direct expenses	15,000
Rent and Rates : Factory	5,000
Office	500
Indirect consumption of materials	500
Depreciation : Plant	1,500
Office furniture	400
Salary : Office	2,500
Salesman	2,000

Other factory expenses	*5,700*
Other office expenses	*900*
Managing Director's remuneration	*12,000*
Other selling expenses	*1,000*
Travelling expenses of salesman	*1,100*
Carriage outwards	*1,400*
Advance income tax paid	*15,000*
Advertisement	*2,000*
Sales	*2,50,000*

Managing Director's remuneration is to be allocated in the ratio of 2 : 1 : 3 for Factory, Office, and Sales departments respectively.

From the above information prepare a Cost Sheet.

(Sri Sathya Sai University B.Com. (Hons), March 2005)

Solution:

Cost Sheet of M/s Moon Shine Industries Ltd for the year 2004

Opening stock of raw materials	25,000	
Add: Purchases	85,000	
Add: Carriage inward	5,000	
	1,15,000	
Less : Closing stock	40,000	
Materials consumed		75,000
Direct wages		75,000
Direct expenses		15,000
	Prime cost	1,65,000
Indirect wages	10,000	
Factory rent and rates	5,000	
Indirect materials	500	
Depreciation on plant	1,500	
Other factory expenses	5,700	
Managing director's expenses $12{,}000 \times \frac{2}{6}$	4,000	26,700
	Works cost	1,91,700
Office and Administration oh:		
Office rent and rates	500	
Dep. on office furniture	400	
Salary to office staff	2,500	
Other office expenses	900	
M.D's remuneration $12{,}000 \times \frac{1}{6}$	2,000	6,300
	Office cost	1,98,000

Selling and Distribution overheads:		
Salary to Salesmen	2,000	
Managing Directors remuneration $12{,}000 \times \frac{3}{6}$	6,000	
Other selling expenses	1,000	
Travelling expenses of salesman	1,100	
Carriage outward	1,400	
Advertisement	2,000	13,500
	Cost of sales	2,11,500
	Profit	38,500
	Sales	2,50,000

Problem-5

Prepare cost sheet showing the different elements of cost from the following information:

	Rs.
Opening Balances:	
Raw materials	*25,000*
Work-in-progress	*1,000*
Finished goods	*2,000*
Purchase of materials	*85,000*
Direct wages	*75,000*
Direct charges	*15,000*
Indirect materials	*500*
Other factory expenses	*5,700*
Prepaid income tax	*15,000*
Salaries:	
Office	*2,500*
Godown	*2,000*
Other office expenses	*900*
Bad debts	*1,000*
Travelling expenses	*1,100*
Sales	*2,50,000*
Closing balances:	
Raw materials	*40,000*
Work-in-progress	*500*
Finished goods	*1,000*
Carriage inwards	*5,000*
Indirect wages	*10,000*

Rent & Rates:	
Factory	*5,000*
Office	*500*
Depreciation:	
Plant & machinery	*1,500*
Furniture	*100*
Manager's remuneration	*12,000*
Advertisement	*2,000*
Carriage outwards	*1,000*

Manager's remuneration is to be allocated Rs. 4,000 to factory, Rs. 2,000 to office and Rs. 6,000 to sales departments. *(Kakatiya University, B.Com., March 2004)*

Solution:

Cost Sheet

Opening stock of raw material	25,000	
Add : Purchases	85,000	
Carriage inwards	5,000	
	1,15,000	
Less : Closing stock of raw materials	40,000	
Cost of materials consumed		75,000
Direct wages		75,000
Direct charges		15,000
	Prime cost	1,65,000
Factory overheads:		
Indirect materials	500	
Indirect wages	10,000	
Factory rent and rates	5,000	
Depreciation on plant and machinery	1,500	
Managers remuneration	4,000	
Other factory expenses	5,700	26,700
		1,91,700
Add : Opening stock of work-in-progress		1,000
		1,92,700
Less : Closing stock of work-in-progress		500
	Works cost	1,92,200
Office and administration overhead:		
Office salaries	2,500	
Office rent and rates	500	
Depreciation on furniture	100	

Other office expenses	900	
Managers remuneration	2,000	6,000
	Office cost	1,98,200
Add : Opening stock of finished goods		2,000
		2,00,200
Less : Closing stock of finished goods		1,000
	Cost of goods sold	1,99,200
Selling and distribution expenses:		
Godown salaries	2,000	
Bad debts	1,000	
Travelling expenses	1,100	
Advertisement	2,000	
Carriage outwards	1,000	
Managers remuneration	6,000	13,100
	Cost of sales	2,12,300
	Profit	37,700
	Sales	2,50,000

Problem-6

The following data of costing information related to 'A' Handicraft Association for the month of 31-3-2002.

	Rs.
Stock (1-3-2002):	
Raw materials	*2,50,000*
Finished goods	*1,70,000*
Purchase of raw materials	*3,00,000*
Direct wages	*1,70,000*
Works expenses	*88,000*
Office expenses	*30,000*
Selling and distribution expenses	*40,000*
Work-in-progress (1-3-2002)	*80,000*
Work-in-progress (31-3-2002)	*90,000*
Stock (31-3-2002):	
Raw materials	*2,60,000*
Finished goods	*1,60,000*
Sale of finished goods	*6,70,000*
Income tax	*2,00,000*
Dividend	*10,000*

Prepare a statement of cost showing

(1) Materials consumed

(2) Prime cost

(3) Factory cost

(4) Cost of production

(5) Cost of sales

(6) Net profit

(Bangalore University, B.Com., April 2003)

Solution:

Cost Sheet of 'A' Handicraft for the Month 31-3-2002

Opening stock of raw materials	2,50,000	
Add : Purchases of raw materials	3,00,000	
	5,50,000	
Less : Closing stock of raw materials	2,60,000	
Cost of materials consumed		2,90,000
Direct wages		1,70,000
Prime cost		4,60,000
Works expenses		88,000
		5,48,000
Add : Opening stock of work-in-progress		80,000
		6,28,000
Less : Closing stock of work-in-progress		90,000
Works cost		5,38,000
Office expenses		30,000
Office cost		5,68,000
Add : Opening stock of finished goods		1,70,000
		7,38,000
Less : Closing stock of finished goods		1,60,000
Cost of goods sold		5,78,000
Selling and distribution expenses		40,000
Cost of sales		6,18,000
Profit		52,000
Sales		6,70,000

Note: Income tax and dividend are items of pure finance. They don't affect cost of production directly. Therefore, they are excluded from cost accounts.

Problem-7

The following are the particulars of a product for the half year ending 30-6-2000.

Materials purchased	*1,32,000*
Wages	*1,10,000*
Rent and rates (office)	*44,000*
Carriage inwards	*1,584*
Stock on 1-1-2000:	
Raw materials	*22,000*
Work-in-progress	*5,280*
Finished goods (1600 tonnes)	*17,600*
Stock on 30-6-2000:	
Raw materials	*24,464*
Work-in-progress	*17,600*
Finished goods (3200 tonnes)	*35,200*
Factory supervision	*8,800*
Sales	*3,30,000*

Advertisement and selling expenses are 0.80 paise per tonne sold. Total units produced during the above period 25,600 tonnes. Prepare cost sheet showing the elements of cost.

(Kakatiya University, B.Com., July 2003)

Solution:

Cost Sheet for the Half Year Ending 30-6-2000

Opening stock of raw materials	22,000	
Add : Materials purchased	1,32,000	
Carriage inwards	1,584	
	1,55,584	
Less : Closing stock of raw materials	22,464	
Cost of raw materials consumed		1,31,120
Wages		1,10,000
	Prime cost	2,41,120
Factory supervision		8,800
		2,49,920
Add : Opening stock of work-in-progress		5,280
		2,55,200
Less : Closing stock of work-in-progress		17,600
	Works cost	2,37,600
Office rent and rates		44,000
	Office cost	2,81,600
Add : Opening stock of finished goods		17,600

		2,99,200
Less : Closing stock of finished goods		35,200
	Cost of goods sold	2,64,000
Selling and advertisement expenses 24,000 × 0.80		19,200
	Cost of sales	2,83,200
	Profit	46,800
	Sales	3,30,000

Working Note:

Calculation of tonnes sold

Opening stock of finished goods		1,600
Add : Tonnes produced during the year		25,600
		27,200
Less : Closing stock of finished goods		3,200
	Tonnes sold	24,000

Problem-8

Calculate cost per unit by preparing a Cost Sheet

Opening stock:	
Materials	*2,00,000*
Work-in-progress	*60,000*
Finished goods	*5,000*
Closing stock:	
Materials	*1,80,000*
Work in progress	*50,000*
Finished goods	*15,000*
Materials purchased	*5,00,000*
Direct wages	*1,50,000*
Manufacturing expenses	*1,00,000*
Sales	*8,00,000*
Selling and distribution expenses	*20,000*
No. of units produced : 10000	

(University of Madras, B.Com., April 2001)

Solution:

Cost Sheet

Particulars		***Total***	***Cost per unit***
Opening stock of raw materials	2,00,000		
Add : Purchases of materials	5,00,000		
	7,00,000		
Less : Closing stock of materials	1,80,000	5,20,000	52.00
Direct wages		1,50,000	15.00
	Prime cost	6,70,000	67.00
Manufacturing expenses		1,00,000	10.00
		7,70,000	77.00
Add : Opening stock of work-in-progress		60,000	6.00
		8,30,000	83.00
Less : Closing stock of work-in-progress		50,000	5.00
	Works cost	7,80,000	78.00
Add : Opening stock of finished goods		5,000	
		7,85,000	
Less : Closing stock of finished goods		15,000	
	Cost of goods sold	7,70,000	
Add : Selling and distribution expenses		20,000	
	Cost of sales	7,90,000	
	Profit	10,000	
	Sales	8,00,000	

Problem-9

A manufacturing company provides you with a summary of its production costs at three production levels

Cost Items	*1,000 Units Rs.*	*2,000 Units Rs.*	*3,000 Units Rs.*
A	5,000	5,000	5,000
B	1,400	1,800	2,200
C	3,000	6,000	9,000

(i) Indicate cost behaviour for the cost items

(ii) What would be total cost if the company produce 2500 units ?

(Calcutta University, B.Com. (Hons.) 2001)

Solution:

(1) Cost item 'A' is fixed for all levels of production. Therefore it is a fixed cost.

(2) Cost item 'B' is jumping by Rs. 400 for every 1000 units increase in output *i.e.*, it

is a semi-variable cost having a variable cost of $\frac{400}{1000}$ = Rs. 0.40 per unit and having a fixed cost of (1,400 – 1,000 × 0.40) = Rs. 1,000

(3) Cost item 'C' is increasing directly by Rs. 3 for each unit of increase in production. So it is a variable cost.

Cost Sheet Showing Total Cost of 2500 Units

Cost item A :	(Fixed)		5,000
Cost item B :	–Fixed	1,000	
	–Variable	1,000	
	2,500 × 0.40		2,000
Cost item C :	(Variable) 2,500 × 3		7,500
		Total cost	14,500

Problem-10

Following information has been obtained from the records of a manufacturing concern for the year ended December 2002.

	1-1-2002 *Rs.*	*31-12-2002* *Rs.*
Stock of finished goods	15,000	15,000
Stock of raw materials	40,000	50,000
Stock of work-in-progress	20,000	10,000
Purchase of raw materials		5,00,000
Carriage inwards		12,000
Wages		2,00,000
Works managers salary		30,000
Factory workers salary		60,000
Power expenses		10,000
Factory rent		8,000
Drawing office salaries		15,000
Unproductive wages		50,000
General expenses		?
Sales for the year		16,00,000
Income tax		20,000
Debenture interest		5,000
Dividend received		1,000
Transfer to sinking fund		10,000
Goodwill written off		10,000
Advertising and publicity		40,000
Sale of soap		1,000
Packing and forwarding on sales		10,000
Purchase of computer for sales department		1,00,000
Commission paid on sales		10,000

There was a stock of finished goods on 1-1-2002 worth 10000 units. During the year, the ompany manufactured 1,00,000 units out of which 10,000 units remained in hand on 1-12-2002. Using the above information, prepare a Cost Sheet and find out the missing gure. It is the policy of the company to sell goods uniformly at a profit of 25% on its cost.

(Sri Sathya Sai University, B.Com (Hons.), March 2004)

olution:

Cost Sheet

Opening stock of raw materials	40,000	
Add : Purchases	5,00,000	
Carriage inwards	12,000	
	5,52,000	
Less : Closing stock of raw materials	50,000	
Cost of materials consumed		5,02,000
Wages		2,00,000
Prime cost		7,02,000
Factory overheads:		
Works manager's salary	30,000	
Factory workers salary	60,000	
Power expenses	10,000	
Factory rent	8,000	
Drawing office salary	15,000	
Unproductive wages	50,000	1,73,000
		8,75,000
Less : Sale of scrap		1,000
		8,74,000
Add : Opening stock of work-in-progress		20,000
		8,94,000
Less : Closing stock of work-in-progress		10,000
Works cost		8,84,000
General expenses (see working note)		3,36,000
Office cost		12,20,000
Add : Opening stock of finished goods		15,000
		12,35,000
Less : Closing stock of finished goods		15,000
Cost of goods sold		12,20,000
S & D. overhead		
Advertising and publicity	40,000	
Packing and forwarding on sales	10,000	
Commission paid on sales	10,000	60,000
Cost of sales		12,80,000
Profit		3,20,000
Sales		16,00,000

Working notes:

Works Cost	+	General Expenses	+	Opening Stock of FG	–	Closing Stock of FG	+	S&D overhead	+	Profit	=	Sales
8,84,000	+	GE	+	15,000	–	15,000	+	60,000	+	3,20,000	=	16,00,000

$$12{,}64{,}000 + GE = 16{,}00{,}000$$
$$GE = 16{,}00{,}000 - 12{,}64{,}000$$
$$GE = 3{,}36{,}000$$

Calculation of profit on sales:

Let cost price = 100

Add profit % = 25

Selling price = 125

$$\frac{25}{125} \times 16{,}00{,}000 = 3{,}20{,}000$$

Items excluded from cost sheet:

Income tax, debenture interest, dividend received, transfer to sinking fund, goodwill written off are matters of pure finance. Hence, they are excluded from cost sheet. Purchase of computers for sales department is an asset. Hence, it is excluded from cost sheet.

Problem-11

A fire occurred in the factory premises on October 31, 2003. The accounting records hav been destroyed. Certain accounting records were kept in another building. They reveal th following, for the period September 1, 2003 to October 31, 2003.

(i) Direct materials purchased	*Rs. 2,50,000*
(ii) Work-in-process inventory 1 - 9 - 2003	*Rs. 40,000*
(iii) Direct materials inventory 1 - 9 - 2003	*Rs. 20,000*
(iv) Finished goods inventory 1 - 9 - 2003	*Rs. 37,750*
(v) Indirect manufacturing costs	*40% of conversion cos*
(vi) Sales revenue	*Rs. 7,50,000*
(vii) Direct manufacturing labour	*Rs. 2,22,250*
(viii) Prime cost	*Rs. 3,97,750*
(ix) Gross margin percentage based on revenues	*30%*
(x) Cost of goods available for sale	*Rs. 5,55,775*

The loss is fully covered by insurance company. The insurance company wants to knou the historical cost of the inventories as a basis for negotiating a settlement, although th settlement is actually to be based on replacement cost, not historical cost. Required.

(i) Finished goods inventory, 31-10-2003

(ii) Work-in-process inventory, 31-10-2003

(iii) Direct materials inventory, 31-10-2003

(CA, PE-II November, 2003

Solution:

Calculation of Direct materials cost consumed during the month

= Prime cost – Direct labour cost

= 3,97,750 – 2,22,250 = Rs 1,75,500

Calculation of conversion cost and indirect manufacturing cost:

Conversion Cost = Direct labour cost + Indirect manufacturing cost

Conversion Cost = 2,22,250 + 40% of conversion cost

r, 0.60 Conversion cost = 2,22,250

r, $\text{Conversion cost} = \dfrac{2,22,250}{0.60} = \text{Rs. } 3,70,417$

Indirect manufacturing cost = 40% of conversion cost

$= \dfrac{40}{100} \times 3,70,417$

= 1,48,167

(*b*) **Calculation of cost of goods manufactured**

Cost of goods available for sale	5,55,775
Less : Finished goods on 1-9-2003	37,750
Cost of goods manufactured	5,18,025

(*i*) Finished goods inventory 31-10-2003

Sales revenue	7,50,000
Less Profit $\frac{30}{100} \times 7,50,000$	2,25,000
Cost of goods sold (*a*)	5,25,000
Cost of goods available for sale (*b*)	5,55,775
Finished goods inventory 31-10-2003 (*b–a*)	30,775

(*ii*) Work-in-process inventory 31-10-2003

Prime cost	3,97,750
Add : Indirect manufacturing cost	1,48,167
Add : Opening stock of work-in-progress	40,000
Manufacturing cost to account for	5,85,917
Less : Cost of goods manufactured	5,18,025
Work-in-progress on 31-10-2003	67,892

(*iii*) Direct material inventory 31-10-2003

Direct material inventory 1-9-2003	20,000
Add : Direct materials purchased	2,50,000
	2,70,000
Less : Direct materials consumed	1,75,500
Direct materials inventory 31-10-2003	94,500

Problem-12

On June 30, 1996, a flash flood damaged the warehouse and factory of ABC Corporatio completely destroying the work-in-progress inventory. There was no damage to either the ra materials or finished goods inventories. A physical verification taken after the flood reveale the following valuation

Raw materials	*Rs. 62,600*
Work-in-progress	*0*
Finished goods	*Rs. 1,19,000*

The inventory on 1-1-1996 consisted of the following

Raw materials	*Rs. 30,000*
Work-in-progress	*1,00,000*
Finished goods	*1,40,000*
	2,70,000

A review of the books and records disclosed that the gross profit margin historicall approximated 25% of sales. The sales for the first 6 months of 1996 were Rs. 3,40,000. Ra materials purchases were Rs. 1,15,000. Direct labour cost for this period were Rs. 80,000 an manufacturing overhead has historically been 50% of direct labour.

Compute the cost of work-in-progress inventory lost at June 30, 1996 by preparing statement of cost and profit. *(University of Delhi, B.Com (Hons.), April 199*

Solution:

Cost Sheet of ABC Corporation

Opening stock of raw materials	30,000	
Add: Purchases	1,15,000	
	1,45,000	
Less: Closing stock of raw materials	62,000	
Cost of materials consumed		83,000
Direct Labour		80,000
Prime cost		1,63,000
Factory overhead $\frac{50}{100} \times 80{,}000$		40,000
		2,03,000
Add : Opening stock of work-in-progress		1,00,000
		3,03,000
Less : Closing stock of work-in-progress (see note below)		69,000
Factory cost		2,34,000
Add : Opening stock of finished stock		1,40,000
		3,74,000
Less : Closing stock of finished stock		1,19,000
Cost of goods sold		2,55,000
Profit		85,000
Sales		3,40,000

Working Notes:

(1) Calculation of profit:

$$\frac{25}{100} \times 3{,}40{,}000 = 85{,}000$$

(2) Calculation of closing stock of work-in-progress

Sales		3,40,000
Less : Profit		85,000
		2,55,000
Add : Closing stock of finished stock		1,19,000
		3,74,000
Less : Opening stock of finished stock		1,40,000
	Factory cost	2,34,000
Less : Cost before closing work-in-progress		3,03,000
Closing work-in-progress		69,000

Problem-13

For each of the following cases, find the unknown designated by letters

	Case I *Rs.*	*Case II* *Rs.*
Direct materials used	*8,000*	*6,000*
Direct labour	*13,000*	*11,000*
Purchase of direct materials	*9,000*	*7,000*
Factory overhead	*7,000*	*D*
Finished goods inventory 1-1-88	*5,000*	*4,000*
Finished goods inventory 31-12-88	*B*	*5,300*
Sales	*42,000*	*31,800*
Cost of goods sold	*A*	*22,000*
Profit	*11,300*	*C*
Work-in-progress on 1-1-88	*Nil*	*800*
Work-in-progress on 31-12-88	*Nil*	*3,000*

(Sri Sathya Sai University, B.Com., October 1989)

Solution:

Cost Sheet

	Case I	*Case II*
Raw materials	8,000	6,000
Direct materials purchased	9,000	7,000
Direct labour	13,000	11,000
Prime cost	30,000	24,000
Factory overheads	7,000	(*D*) 1,500

		37,000	25,500
Add : Opening stock of WIP		Nil	800
		37,000	26,300
Less : Closing stock of WIP		Nil	3,000
	Factory cost	37,000	23,300
Add : Opening stock of finished goods		5,000	4,000
		42,000	27,300
Less : Closing stock of finished goods	(B)	11,300	5,300
Cost of goods sold	(A)	30,700	22,000
	Profit	11,300	(C) 9,800
	Sales	42,000	31,800

Problem-14

For each of the following cases find out the unknown balances for a given year

	Case A	*Case B*
Stock of raw materials (1-1-2008)	(*a*)	3,500
Stock of raw materials (31-12-2008)	3,600	2,900
Work-in-progress (1-1-2008)	2,700	6,720
Work-in-progress (31-12-2008)	3,800	3,100
Finished stock of goods (1-1-2008)	1,900	(*d*)
Purchase of raw materials	16,100	12,000
Cost of production	(*b*)	27,220
Cost of goods sold	56,050	27,200
Gross profit	(*c*)	16,400
Direct labour	26,450	3,800
Direct materials consumed	15,300	(*e*)
Factory overhead	13,800	7,200
Sales	1,03,300	(*f*)

Solution:

Cost Sheet

	Case 'A'	*Case 'B'*
Opening stock of raw materials	(*a*) 2,800	3,500
Add : Purchases of raw materials	16,100	12,000
	18,900	15,500
Less : Closing stock of raw materials	3,600	2,900
Cost of materials consumed	15,300	(*e*) 12,600

Direct labour		26,450	3,800
	Prime cost	41,750	16,400
Factory overheads		13,800	7,200
		55,550	23,600
Add : Opening stock of work-in-progress		2,700	6,720
		58,250	30,320
Less : Closing stock of work-in-progress		3,800	31,00
	Cost of production	(*b*) 54,450	27,220
Add : Opening stock of finished goods		(*d*) 1,900	4,380
		56,350	31,600
Less : Closing stock of finished goods		300	4,400
	Cost of goods sold	56,050	27,200
	Profit	(*c*) 47,250	16,400
	Sales	1,03,300	(*f*) 43,600

Problem-15

Prepare a cost sheet showing cost and profit for 1000 bricks.

Fuel (Coal)	*2,500 kgs @ Rs. 15 per kg*
Wages	*10 labourers for 150 days @ Rs. 50 per day*
Royalties	*0.75 per 1000 bricks*
Depreciation on equipment	*@ 10% on Rs. 1,50,000*
Handling charges	*0.50 per 1000 bricks*
Works expenses	*10% of wages and coal*
Administrative expenses	*5% of wages and coal*
Production data:	
Bricks made	*52,00,000*
Stock on 1-1-2008	*1,00,000 @ Rs. 40 per 1000*
Stock on 30-6-2008	*11,00,000*
Actual breakage	*2,00,000*
Bricks sold	*40,00,000 @ Rs. 50 per 1000*

Solution:

Cost Sheet

		Cost per 1,000 bricks	***Total cost for 50,00,000***
Coal : 2500 kgs @ m 15 per kg		7.50	37,500
Wages : 10 × 150 × 50		15.00	75,000
Royalty		0.75	3,750
	Prime cost	23.25	1,16,250

Works expenses –10% of wages and coal	2.25	11,250
Handling charges	0.50	2,500
Depreciation –10% on Rs. 1,50,000	3.00	15,000
Works cost	29.00	1,45,000
Administration expenses –5% of wages and coal	1.125	5,625
Cost of production	30.125	1,50,625
Add : Opening stock of bricks 1,00,000 × $\frac{40}{100}$		4,000
		1,54,625
Less: Closing stock of bricks 11,00,000 × $\frac{30.125}{1000}$		33,138
Cost of brick sold		1,21,487
Profit		78,513
Sales		2,00,000

Problem-16

From the books of accounts of M/S Raja Rajeswari Enterprises the following details have been extracted for the quarter ending December 31, 2006.

	Rs.
Stock of materials – Opening	*2,70,000*
Stock of materials – Closing	*3,00,000*
Purchases of materials	*12,48,000*
Direct wages	*3,57,600*
Direct expenses	*1,20,000*
Indirect wages	*24,000*
Salaries to administrative staff	*60,000*
Carriage inwards	*48,000*
Carriage outwards	*37,500*
Manager's salary	*72,000*
General charges	*37,200*
Legal charges for criminal suit	*20,000*
Commission on sales	*28,000*
Fuel	*96,000*
Electricity charges (Factory)	*72,000*
Director's fees	*36,000*
Repairs to plant and machinery	*63,000*
Rent, rates and taxes—Factory	*18,000*
Rent, rates and taxes—Office	*9,600*
Depreciation on plant and machinery	*45,000*
Depreciation on office furniture	*3,600*
Salesmen's salary	*50,000*
Audit fees	*18,000*

(1) *The manager's time is shared between the factory and office in the ratio of 20 : 80*
(2) *Carriage outwards include Rs. 7500 being carriage inwards on plant and machinery*
(3) *Selling price is 120% of the cost price. From the above details, prepare a cost sheet for the quarter ending 31-12-2006 and ascertain sales.*

(Sri Sathya Sai University, B.Com. (Hons.), March 2007)

Solution:

Cost Sheet of Raja Rajeshwari Enterprises for the Quarter Ending 31-12-2006

Opening stock of materials	2,70,000	
Add : Purchases of materials	12,48,000	
Add : Carriage inwards	48,000	
	15,66,000	
Less : Closing stock of materials	3,00,000	
Cost of materials used		12,66,000
Direct wages		3,57,600
Direct expenses		1,20,000
Prime cost		17,43,600
Works overhead:		
Indirect wages	24,000	
Manager's salary (20%)	14,400	
Fuel	96,000	
Electricity	72,000	
Repairs—plant	63,000	
Factory rent	18,000	
Depreciation—plant	45,000	3,32,400
Works cost		20,76,000
Office and administration overheads:		
Salaries to staff	60,000	
Manager's salary (80%)	57,600	
General charges	37,200	
Director's fees	36,000	
Office rent	9,600	
Depreciation - furniture	3,600	
Audit fees	18,000	2,22,000
Office cost		22,98,000
Selling & distribution overheads:		
Carriage outwards (37500–7500)	30,000	
Commission on sales	28,000	
Salesmen's salary	50,000	1,08,000
Cost of Sales		24,06,000
Profit		4,81,200
Sales		28,87,200

Note: Legal charges for criminal suit is a financial charge and hence ignored in preparing the cost sheet.

Problem-17

From the following particulars' prepare cost sheet showing various elements of cost

	Rs.
Opening stock of raw materials	*1,10,000*
Purchases of raw materials	*8,25,000*
Carriage outwards	*28,500*
Direct wages	*4,21,400*
Direct power	*25,840*
Technical directors salary	*40,590*
Factory rent, rates and insurance	*10,140*
Sale of factory scraps	*1,460*
Depreciation on factory buildings	*75,200*
Closing work-in-progress	*1,20,260*
Factory stationery	*12,340*
Opening stock of finished goods	*45,280*
Closing stock of raw materials	*36,920*
Fees to brand ambassador	*2,00,000*
Stationery and printing	*12,200*
Staff salaries	*6,30,000*
Trade discount	*1,20,000*
Office rent	*60,000*
Free sample expenses	*20,320*
Closing stock of finished goods	*50,240*

Sales are made to earn profit @ 10% on cost price.

(University of Bombay, B.Com., October 2006)

Solution:

Cost Sheet

Opening stock of raw materials	1,10,000	
Add : Purchases of raw materials	8,25,000	
	9,35,000	
Less : Closing stock of raw materials	36,920	
Cost of materials consumed		8,98,080
Direct wages		4,21,400
Direct power (expenses)		25,840
Prime cost		13,45,320

Works overheads:		
Technical directors salary	40,590	
Factory rent rates and insurance	10,140	
Depreciation on factory building	75,200	
Factory stationery	12,340	
	1,38,270	
Less : Sale of scrap	1,460	
		1,36,810
Less : Closing stock of work-in-progress		1,20,260
Works cost		13,61,870
Office and administration overheads:		
Printing and stationery	12,200	
Office rent	60,000	
Staff salaries	6,30,000	7,02,200
Cost of production		20,64,070
Add : Opening stock of finished goods		45,280
		21,09,350
Less : Closing stock of finished goods		50,240
Cost of goods sold		20,59,110
Selling and distribution overheads:		
Carriage outwards	28,500	
Fees paid to brand ambassador	2,00,000	
Free samples	20,320	2,48,820
Cost of sales		23,07,930
Profit 10% on 23,07,930		2,30,793
Sales		25,38,723

Problem-18

The following details are available for the year ending 2004

	Rs.
Direct wages	*60,000*
Purchase of materials	*72,000*
Indirect materials	*3,600*
Indirect wages	*5,400*
Office salaries	*7,200*
Employees' contribution to employees state insurance	*600*
Printing and stationery	*1,200*
Power and fuel	*5,400*
Legal charges	*864*

Office rent	*1,200*
Sales (9000 units)	*1,80,000*
Opening stock:	
Raw materials	*12,000*
Work-in-progress	*2,880*
Finished goods (600 units at the rate of Rs. 16.25 per unit)	—
Closing stock:	
Raw materials	*13,344*
Work-in-progress	*9,600*
Finished goods (1200 units)	*?*

Value the finished stock at cost of production

Prepare a cost sheet showing different elements of cost.

(University of Mumbai, B.Com., April 2005)

Solution:

Cost Sheet for the Year Ended 31-3-2005

Opening stock of raw materials	12,000	
Add : Purchases	72,000	
	84,000	
Less : Closing stock of raw materials	13,344	
Cost of materials consumed		70,656
Direct wages		60,000
Prime cost		1,30,656
Works overheads:		
Indirect materials	3,600	
Indirect wages	5,400	
Employees contribution to employees state insurance	600	
Power and fuel	5,400	
	15,000	
Add : Opening stock of work-in-progress	2,880	
	17,880	
Less : Closing stock of work-in-progress	9,600	8,280
Works cost		1,38,936
Office and administration overhead:		
Office salaries	7,200	
Legal charges	864	
Office rent	1,200	
Printing and stationery	1,200	10,464
Cost of production		1,49,400

Add : Opening stock of finished stock 600 units × 16.25		9,750
		1,59,150
Less : Closing stock of finished stock		18,675
Cost of goods sold		1,40,475
Profit		39,525
Sales		1,80,000

Working Notes:

1. **Calculation of units produced:**

Units produced = Units sold + Closing stock of finished goods – Opening stock of finished goods

= 9,000 + 1,200 – 600

= 9,600

2. **Value of closing stock of finished goods:**

$$\frac{1,49,400}{9,600} \times 1,200 = \text{Rs. } 18,675$$

3. Employees State Insurance contribution is normally in respect of low-paid employees (*i.e.*, workers) and hence is treated as works overhead.

Problem-20

A and B are manufacturers of bangles. Their factory has three departments viz., foundry, carpentry and finishing. From the following information, you are required to show the week's result of each department, total factory cost and cost per bangle.

	Rs. Per week
Fuel consumed in foundry	*600*
Pig iron used	*2,750*
Lime used	*660*
Foundry wages	*1,200*
Timber and fitting used	*850*
Carpenter's wages	*480*
Paint and polish used	*330*
Finisher's wages	*320*

The number of bangles produced per week was 317 of which 17 were found defective and may be assumed to be worth Rs. 10 each as scrap iron. The departments required equal supervision by a manager and his assistant, who received salaries of Rs. 100 and Rs. 50 per week respectively. The expenditure on factory overhead amount to Rs. 500 per week and the basis of apportionment may be taken to be the departmental wages.

(Osmania University, M.Com (Final), May 2000)

Solution:

Cost Sheet

Foundry Dept. cost:		
Pig iron used	2,750	
Lime used	660	
Fuel consumed in foundry	600	
Foundry wages	1,200	
Factory overhead $\frac{15}{25} \times 500$	300	
Supervisor's salary	50	
		5,560
Carpentary Dept. cost:		
Timber and fittings used	850	
Carpenter's wages	480	
Factory overhead $\frac{6}{25} \times 500$	120	
Supervisor's salary	50	
		1,500
Finishing Dept. cost:		
Paints and polish used	330	
Finisher's wages	320	
Factory overhead $\frac{4}{25} \times 500$	80	
Supervisor's salary	50	
		780
Total cost		7,840
Less : Sale of defective items		170
Net factory cost		7,670

$$\text{Net output} = \text{Total output} - \text{wastage}$$
$$= 317 - 17 = 300$$

$$\text{Cost per unit} = \frac{\text{Net factory cost}}{\text{Net output}}$$
$$= \frac{7670}{300} = 25.57.$$

Problem-20

The state Government granted licence to Sweet Sugar Ltd. to manufacture and sell sugar with a stipulation that 40% of the output should be sold to the state Government at a controlled price of Rs. 3000 per ton and the balance output can be sold in the open market ct any price. Following are the details of Sweet Sugar Ltd. for the year ended 31st March, 2004.

During the year 3600 tons sugarcane was consumed @ Rs. 1000 per ton. Direct labour amounted to Rs. 825 per ton of sugar produced. The details of other expenses are as follows:

	Rs.
Direct expenses	*4,20,000*
Telephone charges	*3,52,695*
Office computer purchased	*2,75,350*
Factory rent and insurance	*3,54,760*
Machinery purchased	*4,25,560*
Machinery repairs	*98,847*
Commission on sales	*3,37,650*
Factory salaries	*2,19,588*
Carriage outward	*1,54,090*
Packing expenses	*1,94,450*
Bank interest	*1,65,895*
Factory electricity	*2,61,880*
Delivery van expenses	*1,06,850*
Coal consumed	*3,80,125*
Depreciation on machinery	*2,49,600*
Depreciation on computer	*204,180*
Depreciation on delivery van	*1,57,360*
Office salaries	*1,89,325*
Printing and stationery	*1,13,000*

During the year 2400 tons of sugar was produced.

The Company's profit target for the year for fixing the open market selling price on the basis of cost sheet is 10% of its average paid-up capital of Rs. 1,42,56,000.

Prepare Cost Sheet and find various components to total cost and per unit cost and suggest the selling price for open market. *(University of Mumbai, B.Com., April 2005)*

Solution:

Cost Sheet in the Books of Sweet Sugar Limited
for the year ended 31st March 2004

		Total Cost	***Cost per Ton***
Direct materials—sugarcane		36,00,000	1,500
Direct labour		19,80,000	825
		4,20,000	175
Prime cost		60,00,000	2,500
Factory overheads:			
Factory rent	3,54,760		
Coal consumed	3,80,125		
Factory salary	2,19,588		
Machinery repairs	98,847		
Factory electricity	2,61,880		

Machinery depreciation	2,49,600	15,64,800	652
	Works cost	75,64,800	3,152
Office overheads:			
Salary	1,89,325		
Printing and stationery	1,13,000		
Telephone	3,52,695		
Depreciation on computers	2,04,180	8,59,200	358
	Cost of production	84,24,000	3,510
Selling and distribution o/h:			
Commission		3,37,650	
Carriage outward		1,54,090	
Packing expenses		1,94,450	
Delivery van expenses		1,06,850	
Depreciation on vans		1,57,360	
	Cost of sales	93,74,400	3,906
Less : Sold to Government (960 Tons × 3,000)		28,80,000	—
		64,94,400	—
Profit $\frac{10}{100} \times 1,42,56,000$		14,25,600	—
Sales (Open Market)		79,20,000	

Problem-21

Prepare a Cost Sheet showing the total and per tonne cost of paper manufactured by Times Paper Mills Ltd for the month of March 1996. There were 26 working days in the month. Also find the profit earned by the company. The details are as under:

Direct raw materials:	
Paper pulp	*6000 tons @ Rs. 900 tonne*
Direct labour:	
280 skilled workmen	*Rs. 250 per day*
300 semi-skilled workmen	*Rs. 150 per day*
470 unskilled workmen	*Rs. 100 per day*
Direct expenses:	
Special equipment hire charges	*Rs. 12,000 per day*
Special dyes	*Rs. 250 per tonne of total raw materials input*
Works overheads:	
Variable	*@ 50% of direct wages*
Fixed	*Rs. 2,70,000 p.m.*
Administration overheads	*@12% of works cost*
Selling and distribution overheads	*Rs. 80 per tonne sold*

Opening stock of paper *500 tonnes valued @ Rs. 2501.60 per ton*
Closing stock of paper *300 tonnes valued at cost of production*
The paper is sold @ Rs. 3000 per tonne

(University of Mumbai, B.Com., April 1997)

Solution:

Cost Sheet of Times Paper Mills Ltd.
for the month ending 31-3-1996

		Total Cost	Unit Cost
Direct materials:			
Raw materials 6000 × 900		54,00,000	900
Direct wages:			
Skilled workmen (280 × 250 × 26)	18,20,000		
Semi-skilled workmen (300 × 150 × 26)	11,70,000		
Unskilled workmen (470 × 100 × 26)	12,22,000		
		42,12,000	702
Direct expenses:			
Equipment hire charges (12000 × 26)	3,12,000		
Special dyes (250 × 6000)	15,00,000		
		18,12,000	302
	Prime cost	1,14,24,000	1,904
Works overheads:			
Variable (50% of Direct wages)	21,06,000		
Fixed	2,70,000	23,76,000	396
	Works cost	1,38,00,000	2,300
Administrative overheads (12% of works cost)		16,56,000	276
	Office cost	1,54,56,000	2,576
Add : Opening stock of finished goods (500 × 2501.06)		1,25,0800	
		1,67,06,800	
Less : Closing stock of finished goods (300 × 2576)		7,72,800	
	Cost of goods sold	1,59,34,000	2,570
Selling and Distribution o/h (80 × 6200)		4,96,000	80
	Cost of sales	1,64,30,000	2,650
	Profit	21,70,000	350
	Sales	1,86,00,000	3,000

Working Notes:

(1) Calculation of cost of goods sold per unit $\frac{1,59,34,000}{6,200} = 2,570$

(2) The rate for equipment hire charges has been given on per day basis. Hence, they have been computed only for 26 working days.

Problem-22

From the following particulars relating to the production and sales for the year ended 31st December, 2004. Prepare a cost statement showing therein (i) Prime cost (ii) Works cost (iii) Cost of production (iv) Total cost, and (v) Profit per unit.

	Rs.
Raw materials as on 1-1-2004	*12,500*
Work-in-progress as on 1-1-2004	*18,000*
Finished goods at cost as on 1-1-2004 (8,000 units)	*60,000*
Raw materials purchased	*1,10,000*
Freight on raw materials purchased	*5,000*
Factory expenses	*65,000*
Chargeable expenses	*25,000*
Direct labour	*1,35,000*
Administrative expenses	*60,000*
Selling and distribution expenses	*45,000*
Sales of finished goods (28,000 units)	*4,00,000*
Raw materials as on 31-12-2004	*20,000*
Work-in-progress as on 31-12-2004	*19,000*
Stock of finished goods as on 31-12-2004 (10,000 units)	*?*

(Calcutta University, B.Com (Pass) 2005)

Solution:

Cost Sheet for the Year Ended 31-12-2004

Opening stock of raw materials		12,500	
Add : Purchases of raw materials		1,10,000	
Freight on raw materials purchased		5,000	
		1,27,500	
Less : Closing stock of raw materials		20,000	
Raw materials consumed			1,07,500
Direct labour			1,35,000
Chargeable expenses			25,000
	Prime cost		2,67,500
Factory expenses			65,000
			3,32,500
Add : Opening stock of work-in-progress			18,000
	Work cost		3,50,500
Less : Closing stock of work-in-progress			19,000
	Office cost		3,31,500
Administration overhead			
	Office cost		60,000
			3,91,500

		Rs.
Add : Opening stock of finished goods		60,000
		4,51,500
Less : Closing stock of finished goods		1,30,500
	Cost of goods sold	3,21,000
Selling and distribution overheads		45,000
	Cost of sales	3,66,000
	Profit	34,000
	Sales	4,00,000

Working Notes:

(1) Calculation of no. of units produced:

= Sales + Closing stock – Opening stock

= 28,000 + 10,000 – 8,000 = 30,000 units

(2) Calculation of value of closing finished goods:

$$= \frac{\text{Cost of production}}{\text{No. of units produced}} \times \text{Closing stock of finished goods}$$

$$= \frac{3{,}91{,}500}{30{,}000} \times 10{,}000 = 1{,}30{,}500$$

(3) Calculation of profit per unit:

$$\frac{\text{Profit}}{\text{Units sold}} = \frac{34{,}000}{28{,}000} = 1.2143.$$

Problem-23

From the following particulars, you are required to prepare a monthly Cost Sheet of Soap Manufacturers Ltd showing therein:

(i) Prime cost (ii) Works cost (iii) Cost of production (iv) Cost of sales and profit per unit.

	Rs.
Opening Inventory (1-1-2004):	
Raw materials	6,000
Work-in-progress	9,620
Finished goods (1000 units)	13,680
Closing Inventory (31-1-2004):	
Raw materials	7,000
Work-in-progress	8,020
Finished goods	?
Donations to home for destitutes	2,100
Raw materials purchased	72,000
Import duty on raw materials purchased	14,400

Productive wages	*18,000*
Machine hours worked	*21,600 hours*
Machine hour rate	*Re. 1.50*
Chargeable expenses	*Rs. 2,000*
Office and administration expenses	*Rs. 1 per unit*
Selling expenses	*Rs. 0.90 per unit*
Units sold	*8,000 units*
Units produced	*8,200 units*
Profit on sale	*10%*

(University of Delhi, B.Com (Pass) 2005)

Solution:

Cost Sheet

		Total Cost	***Cost per unit***
Opening stock of raw materials	6,000		
Add : Purchases of materials	72,000		
Import duty on purchases	14,400		
	92,400		
Less : Closing stock of raw materials	7,000		
Cost of materials consumed		85,400	10.414
Productive wages		18,000	2.195
Chargeable expenses		2,000	0.243
Prime cost		1,05,400	12.852
Works overhead 21,600 Machine hours @ Rs.1.50		32,400	3.951
		1,37,800	16.803
Add : Opening stock of work-in-progress		9,620	1.173
		1,47,420	17.976
Less : Closing stock of work-in-progress		8,020	0.976
Works cost		1,39,400	17.000
Office and administration overhead @ Re 1 per unit		8,200	1.000
Cost of production		1,47,600	18.000
Add : Opening stock of finished goods		13,680	
		1,61,280	
Less : Closing stock of finished goods 1200 units @ Rs. 18		21,600	
Cost of goods sold (8000 units)		1,39,680	17.46
Selling overhead @ Rs. 0.90 per unit sold 8000 × 0.90		7,200	0.90
Cost of sales		1,46,880	18.36
Profit $\frac{1}{9} \times 1,46,880$		16,320	2.40
Sales		1,63,200	20.40

Working Note:

Calculation of quantity of closing stock of finished goods

Closing stock of finished = Opening stock of finished goods + Qty. produced – Qty. sold

= 1000 + 8200 – 8000

= 1200 units

Problem-24

Popeye Company is a metal and woodcutting manufacturer, selling products to the home construction market. Consider the following data for the month of October, 2004.

	Rs.
Sand paper	*5,000*
Material handling costs	*1,75,000*
Lubricants and coolants	*12,500*
Miscellaneous indirect manufacturing labour	*1,00,000*
Direct manufacturing labour	*7,50,000*
Direct materials October 1, 2004	*1,00,000*
Direct materials October 31, 2004	*1,25,000*
Finished goods, October 1, 2004	*2,50,000*
Finished goods, October 31, 2004	*3,75,000*
Work-in-process, October 1, 2004	*25,000*
Work-in-process, October 31, 2004	*35,000*
Plant-leasing costs	*1,35,000*
Depreciation-plant equipment	*90,000*
Property taxes on plant equipment	*10,000*
Fire insurance on plant equipment	*7,500*
Direct materials purchased	*11,50,000*
Sales revenues	*34,00,000*
Marketing promotions	*1,50,000*
Marketing salaries	*2,50,000*
Distribution costs	*1,75,000*
Customer-service costs	*2,50,000*

Required:

(1) *Prepare an income statement with a separate supporting schedule of cost of goods manufactured* *(CA, PE-II, Nov. 2004)*

Solution:

Schedule for Cost of Goods Manufactured
for the month ending Oct. 2004

Opening stock of materials	1,00,000	
Add : Purchase of materials	11,50,000	
	12,50,000	
Less : Closing stock of materials	1,25,000	
Direct materials used		11,25,000

Direct manufacturing labour			7,50,000
	Prime cost		18,75,000
Factory overheads:			
Sand paper		5,000	
Material handling cost		1,75,000	
Lubricants and coolants		12,500	
Misc. Indirect manufacturing labour		1,00,000	
Plant leasing cost		1,35,000	
Depreciation on plant & equipment		90,000	
Property tax on plant and equipment		10,000	
Fire insurance on plant & equipment		7,500	5,35,000
			24,10,000
Add : Opening stock of work-in-progress			25,000
			24,35,000
Less : Closing stock of work-in-progress			35,000
	Factory cost		24,00,000
Add : Opening stock of finished goods			2,50,000
			26,50,000
Less : Closing stock of finished goods			3,75,000
	Cost of goods sold		22,75,000
Selling and distribution overheads:			
Marketing promotions		1,50,000	
Marketing salaries		2,50,000	
Distributions cost		1,75,000	
Customer service cost		2,50,000	8,25,000
	Cost of sales		31,00,000
	Profit		3,00,000
	Sales		34,00,000

Questions

I. A. Indicate whether the following elements of cost is (1) Direct Material (2) Direct Labour or, (3) Factory Overheads

(*i*) Machine repairs
(*ii*) Bottles for packing medicines
(*iii*) Salary of supervisor
(*iv*) Wages of carpenter
(*v*) Plant depreciation
(*vi*) Carriage on materials purchased
(*vii*) Wages of shoemaker
(*viii*) Thread used in stitching
(*ix*) Salary of works manager
(*x*) Bags used in cement mill

[**Answer:** Direct Materials. (*ii*), (*vi*), (*x*)
Direct Labour. (*iv*), (*vii*)
Factory overheads. (*i*), (*iii*), (*v*), (*viii*), (*ix*)]

B. State the method of costing to be used in the following industries:

(*a*) Petroleum refiner (*b*) Meat packing (*c*) Automobile repair shop (*d*) Chocolate manufacturer (*e*) T.V. sets (*f*) Soft drink (*g*) Furniture making (*h*) Coal (*i*) Textile (*j*) Interior decoration (*k*) Hospital (*l*) Scooter (*m*) Toys-making (*n*) Nuts and Bolts (*o*) Drugs.

[**Answer:** Single or output costing – (*h*)
Job costing – (*c*), (*g*), (*j*)
Process costing – (*a*), (*b*), (*f*), (*i*)
Batch costing – (*d*), (*m*), (*n*), (*o*)
Multiple costing – (*e*), (*l*)
Operating costing – (*k*)]

C. State whether the following costs are (1) Fixed (2) Variable (3) Semivariable:

(*a*) Sundry supplies used in a factory, (*b*) Supervisor's salary, (*c*) Cost of electric power for the factory, (*d*) Life insurance premium of employee, (*e*) Rent payable on leased land, (*f*) Maintenance on the physical facilities, (*g*) Telephone expenses, (*h*) Cost accountants salary, (*i*) Rent of factory godown (*j*) Raw materials cost, (*k*) Depreciation, (*l*) Heating, lighting and power, (*m*) Repairs.

[**Answer:** Fixed cost – (*b*), (*d*), (*e*), (*h*), (*i*)
Variable cost – (*a*), (*c*), (*j*), (*l*)
Semi-variable cost – (*f*), (*g*), (*k*), (*m*)]

D. Classify the following industries with respect to the method of costing:

(*a*) Steel, (*b*) Paper box, (*c*) Cooking utensils, (*d*) Pianos, (*e*) Nylon, (*f*) Baby food, (*g*) Office machines, (*h*) Paint, (*i*) Tyres and tubes.

[**Answer:** Single or output – (*a*), (*b*), (*c*), (*d*)
Process costing – (*e*), (*h*)
Batch costing – (*h*), (*i*)
Multiple costing – (*g*)]

E. Classify each of the following costs using the following classes:

(*a*) Direct materials, (*b*) Direct labour, (*c*) Manufacturing overheads, (*d*) Non-manufacturing overheads, (*i*) Managing director's salary, (*ii*) Oil for machine, (*iii*) Wages of machine operator, (*iv*) Salary of supervisor of assembly department for product A, B and C, (*v*) Depreciation on the factory building, (*vi*) Depreciation in the administrative office building, (*vii*) Rent on the sales office, (*viii*) Insurance on the truck used for delivery of finished goods sold.

[**Answer:** Direct labour cost – (*iii*)
Manufacturing overhead – (*ii*), (*iv*), (*v*)
Non-manufacturing overhead – (*i*), (*vi*), (*vii*), (*viii*)]

F. Classify the following manufacturing costs as direct or indirect product cost:

(*a*) Rent on the factory building, (*b*) Salary of the supervisor of costing department, (*c*) Fire insurance on the factory equipment, (*d*) Labour cost for material handling, (*e*) Power cost for operating machinery, (*f*) Storage for raw materials, (*i*) Wages for tool and die-maker.

[**Answer:** Direct cost – (*b*), (*c*), (*g*), (*i*)
Indirect cost – (*a*), (*d*), (*e*), (*f*), (*h*)]

II. Indicate whether the following statements are True or False:

1. All costs are fixed in long run. *T/F*

2. Fixed cost per unit vary with changes in volume. *T/F*

3. Total variable costs remain constant with changes in volume. *T/F*

4. Fixed cost per unit increases with increase in production volume. *T/F*

5. Notional costs and inputed costs mean the same. *T/F*

6. Conversion cost and overheads are interchangeable terms. *T/F*

7. Abnormal cost is uncontrollable. *T/F*

8. The term 'Cost' means price. *T/F*

9. The process of converting raw materials to finished product is known as conversion cost. *T/F*

10. An item of cost that is direct for one business may be indirect for another. *T/F*

11. The salary paid to salesman is an example of a period cost. *T/F*

12. Product costs are inventoriable; period costs are not. *T/F*

13. The job order costing is most suitable for a large steel mill. *T/F*

14. Factory overhead cost applied to job is usually based on a predetermined rate. *T/F*

15. Cost unit in a college may be a student. *T/F*

[**Answer:** (1) *T*, (2) *F*, (3) *F*, (4) *F*, (5) *T*, (6) *F*, (7) *T*, (8) *F*, (9) *F*, (10) *T*, (11) *T*, (12) *T*, (13) *F*, (14) *T*, (15) *T*]

III. Select the correct answer from the following:

1. Which one of the following constitute conversion cost

(*a*) Material cost and direct wages
(*b*) Material cost and factory overheads
(*c*) Direct wages and factory overheads
(*d*) Direct expenses and factory overheads

2. Which one of the following is a best example of a variable cost

(*a*) Interest on capital
(*b*) Depreciation on machinery
(*c*) Cost of materials
(*d*) Rent and taxes

3. Which one of the following constitute the cost of production

(*a*) Prime cost + factory overhead
(*b*) Works cost + office and administration overhead
(*c*) Works cost + prime cost
(*d*) Works cost + selling and distribution overhead

4. Fixed cost per unit increases when

(*a*) Variable cost per unit increases
(*b*) Variable cost per unit decreases
(*c*) Production value increases
(*d*) Production value decreases

5. Increases in total variable cost is due to

(*a*) Increase in fixed cost
(*b*) Increase in sales
(*c*) Increase in production
(*d*) Increase in semi-variable cost

6. Which one of the following industry adopts batch costing in determining the total cost

(*a*) Biscuit making
(*b*) Oil refinery
(*c*) Cycle manufacturing
(*d*) Cement industry

7. Multiple costing is following in

(*a*) Garment making
(*b*) Steel industry
(*c*) Brick making
(*d*) Cycle manufacturing

8. Which one of the following method of costing is adopted by quarries

(*a*) Single costing
(*b*) Multiple costing
(*c*) Contract costing
(*d*) Batch costing

9. If the total cost of production is Rs. 40,000 and 20% of the sale price is the profit to be added to cost, what is the profit ?

(*a*) Rs. 6,000
(*b*) Rs. 8,000
(*c*) Rs. 10,000
(*d*) Rs. 12,000

10. The total cost of a product is Rs. 32,000 and if 20% of the sale price is the profit to be added, what is the sale price ?

(*a*) Rs. 34,000
(*b*) Rs. 36,000
(*c*) Rs. 38,400
(*d*) Rs. 40,000

11. Welfare expenses will be shown in the cost sheet under

(*a*) Selling overhead
(*b*) Administrative overhead
(*c*) Office overhead
(*d*) Works overhead

12. When a change is made in the level of production the resulting change in the total cost in known as

(*a*) Imputed cost
(*b*) Opportunity cost
(*c*) Out of pocket cost
(*d*) Differential cost

13. An example of a variable cost is

(*a*) Insurance on machinery
(*b*) Manager's salary
(*c*) Labour cost
(*d*) Depreciation

14. An example of fixed cost is

(*a*) Direct material cost
(*b*) Direct labour cost
(*c*) Taxes
(*d*) Lubricants

[**Answer:** 1. (*c*), 2. (*c*), 3. (*b*), 4. (*d*), 5. (*c*), 6. (*c*), 7. (*d*), 8. (*a*), 9. (*c*), 10. (*d*), 11. (*d*), 12. (*d*), 13. (*c*), 14. (*c*)]

IV. Fill in the blanks:

1. In cement industries cost unit is ....

2. .... costing is based on the classification of costs into fixed and variable.

3. .... costing is used in cinemas.

4. In .... costing the cost of group of products is ascertained.

5. .... is a location, person, or item of equipment in relation to which cost is ascertained.

6. The use by several undertaking of the same technique of costing is known as .... costing.

7. .... is desirable as a common denominator for comparing costs from period to period.

8. .... costs are those chargeable as expenses in the current period, while .... costs are those carried forward to future periods.

9. .... costs remain constant with changes in volume, while .... costs fluctuate with volume.

10. .... cost are those which follow the item into inventory, and .... costs are those chargeable against current income.

11. .... departments work directly with the product, while .... department render a benefit for other departments.

12. .... costs benefit the current period only, while .... cost benefit more than one period.

13. .... costs are determined in advance of production, while .... costs are accumulated as they occur.

[**Answer:** 1. tonne 2. marginal 3. operating 4. batch 5. cost centre 6. uniform 7. cost unit 8. expired and unexpired 9. fixed and variable 10. product and period 11. production and service 12. revenue and capital 13. standard and actual]

V. Match the following:

Industry	*Methods of costing*
1. Nursing home	(*a*) Process
2. Coal	(*b*) Job
3. Bicycle	(*c*) Multiple
4. Bridge construction	(*d*) Single
5. Interior decoration	(*e*) Operating
6. Sugar industry	(*f*) Contract
	(*g*) Batch

[Answer: 1. (*e*), 2. (*d*), 3. (*c*), 4. (*f*), 5. (*b*), 6. (*a*)]

A	B
1. Sunk cost	(*a*) Increases in production to output
2. Opportunity cost	(*b*) Remains constant
3. Incremental cost	(*c*) Not suitable for decision
4. Fixed cost	(*d*) Added cost of a new product
5. Variable cost	(*e*) Cost of displaced alternative

[Answer: 1. (*c*), 2. (*e*), 3. (*d*), 4. (*b*), 5. (*a*)]

A	B
(*a*) Pencil	1. One gross
(*b*) Bricks	2. One litre
(*c*) Cement	3. One bottle
(*d*) Chemical	4. Cubic metre
(*e*) Medicines	5. One thousand
	6. One bag
	7. One batch

[Answer: (*a*) –1, (*b*) –5, (*c*) –6, (*d*) –2, (*e*) –7]

A	B
1. Batch costing	(*a*) Railways
2. Multiple costing	(*b*) Buildings
3. Contract costing	(*c*) Garments
4. Unit costing	(*d*) Cycle manufacturing
5. Operating costing	(*e*) Mines
	(*f*) Toys
	(*g*) Painters

[Answer: 1. (*c*), 2. (*d*), 3. (*b*), 4. (*e*), 5. (*a*)]

A	B
(*a*) Process costing	1. Ship building
(*b*) Contract costing	2. Hospital
(*c*) Operating costing	3. Chemicals
(*d*) Unit costing	4. Printing Press
(*e*) Batch costing	5. Breweries
	6. Pharmaceuticals

[Answer: (*a*) –3, (*b*) –1, (*c*) –2, (*d*) –5, (*e*) –6]

VI. Simple questions

1. What do you mean by cost sheet ? *(Bangalore University, B.Com., April 2000)*
2. What is a cost centre ? *(Bangalore University, B.Com., April 2000)*
3. What is a cost units ? *(Bangalore University, B.Com., April 1997)*
4. Distinguish between Fixed and Variable cost. *(Sri Krishnadevaraya University, B.Com., March 1998)*
5. State the difference between cost of goods sold and cost of sales. *(Bangalore University, B.Com., April 1999)*
6. What are the techniques of costing ? *(Bangalore University, B.Com., April 1999)*
7. What are the different methods of costing ? *(Bangalore University, B.Com., Nov. 1997)*
8. What is prime cost ?
9. Define cost. *(Bangalore University, B.Com., Nov. 1997)*
10. Define the following :

    (*a*) cost unit (*b*) cost centre (*c*) conversion cost (*d*) controllable cost.

    (Osmania University, B.Com., April 1994)
11. What is meant by Semi-variable expenses ? *(Bharathidasan University, B.Com., April 1994)*
12. Name any four industries in which unit costing would be suitable. *(Bangalore University, B.Com., April 1995)*
13. Mention two purposes served by a cost sheet. *(M.G. University, B.Com., April 1997)*
14. Define service costing. *(M.G. University, B.Com., April 1997)*
15. What is batch costing ? *(M.G. University, B.Com., April 1996)*
16. Mention four essentials of job costing. *(M.G. University, B.Com., April 1995)*
17. What is indirect labour ? *(M.G. University, B.Com., September 1994)*
18. What is sunk cost ? *(M.G. University, B.Com., September 1994)*
19. What is direct labour ? *(M.G. University, B.Com., April 1994)*
20. What is total cost ? *(M.G. University, B.Com., April 1994)*
21. What are indirect materials ? *(M.G. University, B.Com., April 1994)*
22. Explain the term direct expense. *(M.G. University, B.Com., October 1993)*
23. Explain the term indirect expense. Give two examples. *(Bangalore University, M.Com., May 1996)*
24. What is variable cost ? *(Karnataka University, B.Com., April 1997)*
25. What is prime cost ? *(M.G. University, B.Com., April 1997)*
26. State the elements of cost. *(Sri University, B.Com., Oct. 1997)*
27. Distinguish between

    (*a*) Cost centre and cost unit (*b*) Fixed cost and variable cost.

    (Kolkata University, B.Com., October 1997)
28. Write short notes on

    (*a*) Concept of cost (*b*) Oncost (*c*) Semi-variable cost.

    (Karnataka University, M.Com., 1997)
29. What is historical costing ? *(Bangalore University, B.Com., April 1996)*
30. What is uniform costing ? *(Bangalore University, B.Com., April 1996)*
31. Give examples of industries which adopt Batch costing. *(Bangalore University, B.Com., April 1996)*

32. What is cost classification ? *(Bangalore University, B.Com., April 1996)*

33. What do you mean by imputed cost ? *(University of Kerala, B.Com., April 1996)*

34. How and why do you distinguish between fixed and variable cost ?
(University of Kerala, B.Com., April 1996)

35. What is opportunity cost ? *(University of Kerala, M.Com., April 1996)*

36. Classify the following into fixed variable and semi-variable cost
(*a*) Office rent (*b*) Direct materials
(*c*) Telephone expenses (*d*) Insurance of factory building
(Kuvempu University, B.Com., October 1995)

37. State the methods of costing suitable to the following establishments
(*a*) Printing press (*b*) Transport company
(*c*) Mining company (*d*) Construction company
(*e*) Breweries *(University of Mysore, B.Com., Nov. 1999)*

38. Distinguish between Direct and Indirect cost. *(University of Mysore, B.Com., April 1996)*

SHORT AND LONG ANSWER QUESTIONS

1. Explain the terms "product cost" and "period cost" with at least two examples of each.
(C.S. Inter., December 1998)

2. "While variable costs are controllable fixed costs are not"? Comment.
(C.S. Inter., December 1997)

3. "The term "cost" must be qualified according to its context". Comment
(C.S. Inter., June 1996)

4. Draw a pro forma cost sheet. *(C.S. Inter., December 1994)*

5. Describe briefly the different methods of costing together with industries to which they can be applied ? *(University of Mysore, B.Com., May 1999)*

6. Distinguish between
(*a*) Cost centre and profit centre (*b*) Direct and indirect cost
(Madurai Kamaraj University, B.Com., April 1998)

7. What are period cost and product cost ? Give a few examples of such cost. Explain the significance of such classification. *(Sri Venkateshwara University, B.Com., April 1998)*

8. Define costing and explain the different classification of costing.
(University of Madras, B.Com., March 1994)

9. What are the components of total cost ? *(Bharathidasan University, B.Com., April 1994)*

10. State the important ways of classification of cost and discuss each of item in detail.
(Bharathidasan University, B.Com., April 1994)

11. Fundamentally, it is said that there are only two methods of costing. Explain them.
(M.G. University, B.Com., April 1993)

12. What is the proper method and unit of cost for the following:
(*a*) Shipping company (*b*) Cold storage plant (*c*) Advertising company
(*d*) Pottery (*e*) Oil refinery (*f*) Architect
(*g*) Aircraft factory (*h*) Hospital (*i*) Toy company
(*j*) Vegitable Ghee Co. *(M.G. University, B.Com., April 1993)*

13. What are the elements of cost ? Explain the terms with appropriate examples.

(Sri Krishnadevaraya University, B.Com., April 1996)

14. Distinguish between cost control and cost reduction. *(CA, PE-II, May 2003)*

15. Write short notes on:

(*a*) Conversion cost (*b*) Sunk cost (*c*) Opportunity cost *(CA, PE-II, May 2003)*

16. What do you understand by the term cost centre ? *(CA, PE-II, November 2002)*

17. Distinguish between controllable cost and uncontrollable cost.

(CA, Inter, November, 2001)

18. Define explict costs. How is it different from implicit costs. *(CA, Inter, May, 2001)*

19. Define and explain the terms (*a*) cost centre (*b*) profit centre. *(CS, Inter, December, 2002)*

20. Explain the different elements of the total cost of a product.

(Bangalore University, B.Com., April 2005)

21. Discuss the various methods of cost classification.

(Osmania University, B.Com., October 2004)

22. Discuss briefly the methods and techniques of costing.

(Osmania University, B.Com., March 2004)

23. Explain different types of costing. *(University of Madras, B.Com., April 2002)*

PRACTICAL EXERCISE

1. From the following information, prepare a cost sheet for the month of April 2002.

Stock of raw materials (April 1st)	2,50,000
Stock of finished goods (April 1st)	1,73,000
Stock of raw materials (April 30th)	2,62,000
Stock of finished goods (April 30th)	1,57,000
Purchase of raw materials	2,19,000
Carriage on purchases	11,000
Work-in-progress : on April 1	82,000
Work-in-progress : on April 30	91,000
Sale of finished goods	7,23,000
Direct wages	1,72,000
Non-productive wages	8,000
Direct expenses	12,000
Factory overheads	83,000
Administrative overheads	32,000
Selling and distribution overheads	42,000

(Sri Sathya Sai University, B.Com (Hons), March 2003)

[**Answer:** Profit Rs. 1,49,000]

2. The following extracts of costing information related to 'X' Handicraft Association for the year ended 31st March 1999.

Stock on 1-3-1999 :

Raw materials	2,50,000
Finished goods	1,70,000

Purchase of raw materials	3,00,000
Direct wages	1,70,000
Works expenses	88,000
Office expenses	30,000
Selling and distribution expenses	40,000
Work-in-progress in the beginning (1-3-1999)	80,000
Work-in-progress (31-3-1999)	90,000
Stock on 31-3-1999:	
Raw materials	2,60,000
Finished products	1,60,000
Sale of finished goods	6,70,000
Income tax	2,00,000
Dividend	10,000

Prepare a statement of cost showing:

(*a*) Materials consumed (*b*) Prime cost

(*c*) Factory cost (*d*) Cost of production

(*e*) Cost of sales (*f*) Net profit

(*Bangalore University, B.Com., October 2000*)

[**Answer:** (*a*) Cost of materials consumed Rs. 2,90,000
(*b*) Prime cost Rs. 4,60,000
(*c*) Factory cost Rs. 5,38,000
(*d*) Cost of production Rs. 5,68,000
(*e*) Cost of sales Rs. 6,18,000
(*f*) Net profit Rs. 52,000]

3. From the following particulars of the AB Ltd., prepare a statement showing:

(*a*) The cost of materials used

(*b*) The works cost

(*c*) Total cost

(*d*) The percentage of works expenses to productive wages:

Stock of materials on 1-1-1998	20,000
Stock of finished goods on 1-1-1998	51,000
Purchases of raw materials	5,80,000
Productive wages	3,90,000
Sale of finished goods	12,10,000
Stock of raw materials on 31-12-98	25,000
Works overhead charges	86,000
Office and general expenses	70,000
Stock of finished goods on 31-12-98	50,000

(*University of Madras, B.Com., April 2000*)

[**Answer:** Cost of materials used 5,75,000
Works cost 10,51,000
Cost of goods sold 11,22,000
Percentage of works expenses to productive wages 22.05%]

4. From the following particulars, prepare cost sheet showing the different elements of cost for the year ending 31-12-1999.

	Rs.
Materials purchased	1,25,000
Works overhead	45,000
Direct wages	1,00,000
Opening stock of materials	23,400
Carriage inwards	1,600
Opening stock of work-in-progress	15,000
Closing stock of materials	20,000
Opening stock of finished goods (2000 tons)	30,000
Closing stock of work-in-progress	4,800
Closing stock of finished goods (3000 tons)	46,000

Selling and distribution expenses Rs. 1.50 per ton sold. During the above period 16,000 tons were produced. *(Kakatiya University, B.Com., July 2004)*

[**Answer:** Cost of sales Rs. 2,91,700]

5. The following extract of costing information relates to commodity 'A' for the half year ending 31st December, 2000.

Purchase of raw materials	1,20,000
Rent, rates and works oncost	40,000
Direct wages	1,00,000
Carriage inwards	1,440
Stock (on 1st July 2000) :	
Raw materials	20,000
Finished products (1000 tons)	16,000
Stock (on 31st December 2000):	
Raw materials	22,240
Finished products (2000 tons)	32,000
Work-in-progress on 1st July 2000	4,800
Work-in-progress on 31st December 2000	16,000
Sale of finished products (16,000 tons)	3,00,000
Cost of factory supervision	8,000

Advertising and selling cost Re 1 per ton sold. You are required to ascertain : (*a*) The value of raw materials used (*b*) Cost of production (c) The cost of goods sold (*d*) The cost of sale (*e*) The net profit *(Sri Sathya Sai University, B.Com (Hons) March 2001)*

[**Answer:** (*a*) The value of materials used Rs. 1,19,200
(*b*) Cost of production 2,56,000
(*c*) Cost of goods sold 2,40,000
(*d*) Cost of sale 2,56,000
(*e*) Net profit 44,000]

6. From the following information prepare a monthly cost sheet of the Selhagiri Bricks Works showing cost per 1000 bricks. Also find out the profit per 1000 bricks.

Materials used:

Lime	895 kgs @ Rs. 30 per kg
Coal	829 kgs @ Rs. 25 per kg
Sand	Rs. 10 per 1000 bricks made
Others	Rs. 700

Labour:

Sand digging	Rs. 1,800
Brick making	Rs. 8,000
Factory overhead	25% of Direct charges
Office overhead	10% of factory overhead
Bricks sold	35,00,000 @ Rs. 20 per 1000 bricks
Stock of bricks at the beginning of the month	1,00,000
Stock of bricks at the end of the month	6,00,000

[**Answer:** Loss Rs. 38,189]

7. Andhra Auto Limited supplies you the following information and requires you to prepare cost sheet.

	Rs.
Stock of raw materials on 1-9-2005	75,000
Stock of raw materials on 30-9-2005	91,500
Direct wages	52,500
Indirect wages	2,750
Sales	2,00,000
Work-in-progress on 1-9-2005	28,000
Work-in-progres on 30-9-2005	35,000
Purchase of raw materials	66,000
Factory rent, rates and power	15,000
Depreciation on plant and machinery	3,500
Expenses on purchases	1,500
Carriage outwards	2,500
Advertising	3,500
Office rent and taxes	2,500
Salesman's wages and commission	6,500
Stock of finished goods on 1-9-2005	54,000
Stock of finished goods on 30-9-2005	31,000

(*Sri Sathya Sai University, B.Com (Hons). March 2006*)

[**Answer:** Prime cost Rs. 1,03,500 Works cost Rs. 1,17,750, Cost of sales 1,55,750, Profit Rs. 44,250]

8. The following extract of costing information related to X' Handicraft Association for the year ended 31st March 1999.

	Rs.
Stock on 1-3-1999:	
Raw materials	2,50,000
Finished goods	1,70,000

Purchase of raw materials	3,00,000
Direct wages	1,70,000
Work expenses	88,000
Office expenses	30,000
Selling and Disrtibution expenses	40,000
Work-in-progress on 1-3-1999	80,000
Work-in-progress on 31-3-1999	90,000
Stock on 31-3-1999:	
Raw materials	2,60,000
Finished products	1,60,000
Sale of finished goods	6,70,000
Income tax	2,00,000
Dividend	10,000

Prepare a statement of cost showing:

(1) Materials consumed (2) Prime cost

(3) Factory cost (4) Cost of production

(5) Cost of sales (6) Net profit

(*Bangalore University, B.Com., October 2000*)

[**Answer:** (1) Matetrials consumed 2,90,000
(2) Prime cost 4,60,000
(3) Factory cost 5,38,000
(4) Cost of production 5,68,000
(5) Cost of sales 6,18,000
(6) Sales 6,70,000]

9. The following data have been extracted from the books of Surya Industries Ltd. for the calender year 1998.

		Rs.
Opening stock of raw materials		25,000
Purchases of raw materials		85,000
Closing stock of raw materials		40,000
Carriage inward		5,000
Wages :	Direct	75,000
	Indirect	10,000
Other direct charges		15,000
Rent and rates :	Factory	5,000
	Office	500
Indirect material consumption		500
Depreciation :	Plant	1,500
	Office furniture	100
Salary :	Office	2,500
	Salesman	2,000
Other factory expenses		5,700
Other office expenses		900

Managing Director's remuneration	12,000
Other selling expenses	1,000
Travelling expenses of salesman	1,100
Carriage outwards	1,000
Sales	2,50,000
Advertisement	2,000

Managing Director's remuneration is to be allocated Rs. 4,000 to factory, Rs. 2,000 to office and Rs. 6,000 to selling department. From the above information calculate : (*a*) Prime cost (*b*) Works cost (*c*) Cost of production (*d*) Cost of sales (*e*) Net profit

(*Bangalore University, B.Com., April 2002*)

[**Answer:** (*a*) Prime cost Rs. 1,65,000; (*b*) Works cost Rs. 26,700; (*c*) Cost of production Rs. 1,97,700; (*d*) Cost of sales Rs. 2,10,800; (*e*) Net profit Rs. 39,200]

10. The following data of costing information related to 'A' handicraft association for the month ending 31-3-2002.

	Rs.
Stock on 1-3-2002:	
Raw materials	2,50,000
Finished goods	1,70,000
Purchase of raw materials	3,00,000
Direct wages	1,70,000
Works expenses	88,000
Office expenses	30,000
Selling and distribution expenses	40,000
Work-in-progress (1-3-2002)	80,000
Work-in-progress (31-3-2002)	90,000
Stock (31-3-2002):	
Raw materials	2,60,000
Finished goods	1,60,000
Sales of finished goods	6,70,000
Income tax	2,00,000
Dividend	10,000

(*Calcutta University, B.Com (Pass) 1999*)

[**Answer:** Prime cost Rs. 27,600
Works cost Rs. 35,280
Office cost Rs. 37,080
Cost of goods sold Rs. 37,680
Cost of sales Rs. 40,080
Sales Rs. 50,100]

11. From the following information, prepare a statement of cost for the year 1996, showing therein (*a*) Prime cost (*b*) Works cost (*c*) Cost of production (*d*) Profit or loss.

	Rs.
Raw materials consumed	60,000
Direct wages	40,000
Direct expenses	8,000
Indirect wages	10,000

Depreciation on machinery	12,000
Office overhead	20% of works cost
Selling overhead	Rs. 2 per unit
Units produced	15,000
Units sold	12,000 @ Rs. 15 each

(Calcutta University, B.Com., (Pass) 1997)

[**Answer:** (*a*) Prime cost Rs. 1,08,000
(*b*) Works cost Rs. 1,30,000
(*c*) Cost of production Rs. 1,56,000
(*d*) Profit Rs. 31,200]

12. From the following particulars, prepare a cost sheet showing major elements of cost and profit.

	Opening Stock (Rs.)	*Closing Stock (Rs.)*
Raw materials	15,000	15,000
Finished goods	10,200	9,600
Work-in-progress	4,800	5,400

	Rs.
Purchase of raw materials	18,000
Direct wages	10,200
Works expenses	5,280
Office expenses	1,800
Selling expenses	2,400
Depreciation on plant and machinery	4,800
Sales of scrap	1,800
Rate of profit	20% on sales

(Calcutta University, B.Com (Pass), 1999)

[**Answer:** Prime cost Rs. 27,600
Works cost Rs. 35,280
Office cost Rs. 37,080
Cost of goods sold Rs. 37,680
Cost of sales Rs. 40,080
Sales Rs. 50,100]

13. The Vardhaman Ltd. manufactures one product. A summary of its activities for the year 1998 is given below.

	Units	*Rs.*
Sales	80,000	8,00,000
Material inventory 1-1-98		40,000
Material inventory 31-12-98		32,000
Work-in-progress 1-1-98		55,000
Work-in-progress 31-12-98		72,000
Finished goods 1-1-98	16,000	
Finished goods 31-12-98	34,000	

Material purchases	1,52,000
Direct labour	1,45,000
Manufacturing overhead	1,08,000
Selling expenses	50,000
General expenses	40,000

Prepare a cost sheet

(University of Delhi, B.Com., (Hons) 2003)

[**Answer:** Prime cost Rs. 3,05,000
Factory cost Rs. 3,96,000
Office cost Rs. 4,36,000
Cost of goods sold Rs. 3,48,735
Profit Rs. 4,01,265]

14. From the following particulars prepare cost sheet, percentage of works overhead to productive wages, percentage of general overhead to works cost and the percentage of net profit on sales.

	Rs.
Sales	12,00,000
Works overhead	75,000
Stock of materials on 1-7-2005	30,000
Purchases	5,50,000
Office expenses	50,000
Stock of finished goods on 31-7-2005	25,000
Productive wages	2,50,000
Stock of materials on 31-7-2005	70,000
Work-in-progress on 1-7-2005	10,000
Work-in-progress on 31-7-2005	25,000

(Sri Krishnadevaraya University, B.Com., March 2006)

[**Answer:** (1) Profit Rs. 3,45,000
(2) % of works overhead to production wages 30%
(3) % of general overheads to works cost 6% (Approximately)
(4) % of profit to sales 28.75%]

15. From the following data relating to a company during the month of September 2003, prepare a statement showing cost and profit per unit.

	Rs.
Raw materials	40,000
Wages	24,000
Machine hours worked	9500 hours
Machine hour rate	Rs. 4 per hour
Office overheads	20% on works cost
Selling overheads	Re 1 per unit
Units produced	20,000
Units sold 18,000 at Rs. per unit	

(Sri Krishnadevaraya University, B.Com., March 2005)

[**Answer:** Profit Rs. 49,840]

❑❑❑

CHAPTER 3

Materials Cost—Purchase Control

INTRODUCTION

Purchase control is concerned with controlling the kind, amount, location, movement and timing of the various commodities used and produced by industrial enterprise. Materials cost constitute a substantial portion of the capital invested in factories and thus demand a continuing and considerable attention from its management. Many factory failures are the direct outgrowth of excessive inventories. Too much materials cause idle funds, storage and obsolescence problems and marketing difficulties. On the other hand, if the materials are not adequate to meet the needs of the operating and distribution segments of the enterprise, efficiency suffers, costs skyrocket, manufacturing delays are frequent and broken delivery promises will be inevitable.

The term "materials" denote the commodities or substances supplied to factories for the sake of converting them into finished goods. The term "stores" is often interchangeably used to denote the materials. However, it is used in a broader sense to include sundry supplies, maintenance, stores, tools and jigs in addition to raw materials used in the production process. Sometimes materials are also denoted by the term "inventory" which is used in the broadest sense. Inventory includes raw materials, semi-finished goods and finished goods. The Institute of Chartered Accountants of India define inventory as "tangible property held *(i)* for sale in the ordinary course of business or *(ii)* in the process of production for sale or *(iii)* for consumption in the production of goods or service for sale, including maintenance supplies and consumables other than machinery spares."

TYPES OF MATERIALS

The following are some of the important types of materials used in a factory:

1. **Raw materials:** These are the basic materials which undergo change during the manufacturing process so as to become finished goods. Examples of raw materials are coal, steel, lead, copper, rubber, cotton, wool, timber, limestone, etc.
2. **Component parts:** These are the piece parts manufactured from raw materials so as to assemble them to get a finished product. Usually, component parts are the

finished products of one industry which become the raw materials of another industry. Some examples of component parts are collar in dress-making, tyres and tubes in cycle industries, battery cells in transistors.

3. **Equipments and spares:** This type of stock is usually more important in extractive industries, public utility undertakings and such other organisations. They include machines installations, vehicles and other spare parts associated with such equipments.
4. **Tools:** These may relate to hand tools such as hammers, screwdrivers, etc. used on machines or machine tools such as drills, milling cutters, portable electric and pneumatic tools.
5. **Gauges:** Gauges are the materials which are used to measure the dimensions of shapes of materials or components. Examples of gauges used are calliper, screw gauge, common balance, etc.
6. **Jigs and fixtures:** These are the equipments used for handling the materials when they are in the process of manufacturing, fitting, assembly or other processes. They are used mainly in mass-production factories.
7. **Wrok-in-progress:** Work-in-progress refers to partly finished goods and which require further processing so as to convert them into finished products.
8. **Primary packing materials:** Primary packing materials which are used for easy handling of finished goods such as bottles, tins, polythene bags, etc. Constitute one of the important types of materials in some factories.
9. **Scraps and residues:** These are the waste, used or surplus materials arising out of the manufacturing processes which are reused for further manufacturing processes. Examples of materials falling under this category are iron filing and other scrap metals, rejected components, saw dust, etc.
10. **Sundry materials or supplies:** All other materials which do not fall under any of the above category are classified as sundry materials. Examples of sundry materials are cleaning materials such as cotton waste, jute waste, sand paper, oil, grease, etc.

DIRECT AND INDIRECT MATERIALS

From the cost accounting point of view materials used in a manufacturing organisation may be classified into two types: (*i*) Direct materials (*ii*) Indirect materials. Materials are called as direct materials when they satisfy the following characteristics:

(*a*) They are capable of being identified with the finished product.

(*b*) They vary directly with the volume of output.

(*c*) They become part and parcel of finished goods.

(*d*) They are measurable in terms of related production units.

(*e*) They are significant in amount and determination of the cost of the same is of practical use for control.

The following are some of the specific examples of direct materials:

- Jute in manufacturing gunny bags
- Steel in manufacturing cars

- Fruits in manufacturing jams
- Timber in manufacturing furniture
- Turpentine oil in manufacturing paint
- Polythene grannules in manufacturing plastic products.

Materials are said to be indirect when a direct relationship cannot be established between materials used with the specific production units. Indirect materials are ancillary to production although some such materials are also used in repairs department, canteen, department office and administration department and selling and distribution department as no specific production unit consumes them. Whereas direct materials cost forms part of prime cost, indirect materials cost is treated as part of overheads. Some of the examples of indirect materials are sewing thread used in dress-making, nails used in furniture making, glue used in book binding, polishing compound used in vessels manufacturing and so on.

DEFINITION AND IMPORTANCE OF PURCHASING

Alford and Beatty in their book *Industrial Organisation and Management* define purchasing as "the procuring of materials, supplies, machine tools and services required for the equipment, maintenance and operation of a manufacturing plant. Dr. Walters defines scientific purchasing as the procurement by purchase of the proper materials, machinery, equipment and supplies of stores used in the manufacture of a product adapted to marketing in the proper quantity and quality at the proper time and the lowest price consistent with the quality desired." The objective of scientific purchasing is to procure materials at:

(*a*) Right price
(*b*) Right quality
(*c*) Right contractual terms
(*d*) Right time
(*e*) Right source
(*f*) Right materials
(*g*) Right place
(*h*) Right mode of transportation
(*i*) Right quantity
(*j*) Right attitude.

The importance of purchasing may be summarised under the following:

(*i*) Purchasing is a primary function and as such it directly influences the total cost of production. The increased or decreased amount of profit earned in a factory is determined by the efficient purchasing.

(*ii*) The purchase department ensures receipt of proper materials, in sufficient quantities, when needed to maintain production process on a continuous basis. It checks unnecessary or excessive investment of capital on purchase of materials.

(*iii*) It is possible to discover new materials which may be used as a substitute for existing material. This is ensured by the purchase department by coming into close contact with other factories.

(*iv*) By discovering new substitute of materials, it enables to introduce new lines of products.

(*v*) It helps in framing plans and policies relating to scheduling of production and marketing.

ORGANISATION OF PURCHASE DEPARTMENT

The organisation of purchase department depends upon the size, the relative importance of procurement, the availability of personnel and the management policy. The purchase function is common for all factories irrespective of the size. But in a large-sized factory, it is under the control of a chief purchase manager who is assisted by assistant purchase officers. In small factories all the purchase functions are performed by a single individual. The organisation of purchase department may be based on any of the following three systems:

1. Centralisation of Purchases

Centralisation of purchases refers to purchase of materials under one purchase department, headed by a competent purchase manager. If the firm has one plant, then it has to invariably follow centralisation of purchases. When a firm has many plants certain factors are to be considered before centralising the purchases. These factors are geographical location of plants, similarity of products manufactured, type of materials, the quantity of materials, the location of suppliers and other conditions peculiar to industry. According to National Association of Purchasing Management, a firm having several plants in the same country manufacturing similar products requiring the same general types of materials should have centralised purchasing.

Advantages of Centralised Purchasing

(*a*) The purchase manager can be solely held responsible for inefficient purchasing.

(*b*) It helps in maintaining a consistent buying policies such as terms of payment, (payment on delivery, cash with order, cash before delivery) packing, marking, etc.

(*c*) It results in economy of purchase records.

(*d*) It tends to reduce the inventories that must be carried and thus helps in low capital investment on materials.

(*e*) Bulk purchasing results in reduced price of materials on account of trade discount, cash discount facilities.

(*f*) Free home delivery facility is available under centralised system owing to bulk purchases.

(*g*) It relieves the departmental heads, the responsibility of procuring variety of materials.

(*h*) Specialised and expert knowledge on the purchasing problems connected with specific items of materials can be made available to all the units.

Disadvantages of Centralised Purchasing

(*a*) The benefits arising out of local purchase cannot be availed of.

(*b*) This system of purchases leads to communication difficulties between centralised purchasing office and the plants.

(*c*) Emergency purchases cannot be made under this system.

(*d*) Delay in receiving, checking and approving the invoices as central purchasing office has to receive all the reports and invoices from all the plants.

2. Decentralised Purchasing

Under decentralised purchasing system a separate purchase department is established to make purchases independently. Decentralised purchasing is applicable to those manufacturing concerns which operates several plants in different localities manufacturing different products and each plant requiring different types of materials. Each purchase department will have a purchase authority who enjoys the freedom of making purchases of materials required for his department. The purchasing authority in each department reports to the chief purchase officer who establishes the general purchase policies and coordinates the purchasing functions in all plants.

Advantages of Decentralised Purchasing

(*a*) *Greater flexibility:* If a centralised buyer is purchasing for a number of plants he will find it difficult to react rapidly to changes in the requirements of individual plant. But under decentralisation system, the buyer can buy the required quantity and quality and at the time when materials are required.

(*b*) *Close liaison:* A local buyer will be in close contact with his own manufacturing unit. Therefore, he is in a position to make scientific purchase of all kinds of materials.

(*c*) *Quick procurement of materials:* The delay involved in centralised purchasing system where in pooling all the purchase requisition and placing the order and then supply of materials to each and every plant is avoided under this system.

3. Centralised-Decentralised System

Firms which have more than one plant located in and around, adopt this system of purchasing. Though such plants produce different products, there are some materials which are common to all plants. Under such circumstance, it is desirable to partially centralise and partially decentralise the purchase function. Under this system, it is necessary to make clear that which type of materials are to be bought by the centralised buying officer and which type of materials by departmental buying officer. For the successful operation of this system of buying, the following requirements are essential:

(*a*) The centralised purchase manager has to establish policies, procedures, record keeping methods and exercise central control and restrict the authority and range of buying by each decentralised purchase officer.

(*b*) All decentralised purchases must be reported immediately to the central office.

(*c*) The decentralised buying officer must buy materials for his plant only within the budgeted amount.

(*d*) Approval of the central office must be obtained by the decentralised buying officer for special and excess quantity purchases.

(*e*) The plan should be kept flexible so that specific buying authorities can be reassigned as conditions change.

QUALIFICATIONS OF PURCHASE MANAGER

- He must have considerable experience in buying and must be conversant with the purchasing techniques.

- He must possess technical ability to decide upon the most suitable source and the required quality of material.
- He must know as to how to negotiate with the suppliers.
- He must acquaint himself closely with current quotations and sources of supply.
- He must have practical knowledge of the finance and business methods.
- He must have knowledge of the materials which he is required to purchase and their specification, quality and quantity.
- He must be honest and reliable.
- He must be aware of the policy of management and financial resource of the factory and its impact on purchases.
- He must have an up-to-date knowledge of government policies regarding import and export restrictions and various duties and taxes on materials.
- He must be well-conversant with economic principles of demand and supply, price, etc.
- He must have a working knowledge of laws relating to Contracts, Sale of Goods Act, Negotiable Instruments Act, etc., which have a bearing on purchase of materials.
- He must be aware of the market conditions, and should have a complete knowledge of the market, source of supply, price and purchase formalities.
- He must be able to maintain records and documents like catalogues, price lists, trade magazines, journals, etc., to assist him in locating the best market.

Duties and Responsibilities of Purchase Manager

The duties of Purchase Manager can be summarised as under:

1. To establish purchase policies for his department to execute.
2. To locate and select the best source of supply for materials and services required.
3. To receive purchase requisitions from all the departments and know the exact quantity of material requirements of the factory.
4. To purchase the required quantity of materials at the lowest price and at the best possible terms.
5. To place purchase orders with the supplier.
6. To follow-up suppliers so that delivery of materials can be obtained at the proper time.
7. To make sure that materials received from suppliers conform to the orders placed.
8. To verify and check the invoices and approve them for payment.
9. To secure adjustment on claims for materials received which are not in accordance with quality or quantity or which have been damaged.
10. To manitain proper records for efficient operation of the purchase department.
11. To keep constant touch with market conditions and try to secure new goods which are better than existing materials.
12. To analyse the effects of changes in general business trends upon purchase plants.
13. To advise on prices for materials to be used in new or modified designs.
14. To prepare and present all reports regarding the purchase of materials to the General Manager.
15. To take part in departmental conferences for planning, formulation of policies or other purposes.

The responsibilities of the Purchase Manager can be summarised as under:

(*a*) He is responsible for organising and directing the purchase department.

(*b*) He is responsible for timely purchase of materials so that production process is not interrupted.

(*c*) He is responsible for judicious utilisation of funds while purchasing various types of materials.

(*d*) He is responsible for maintaining the factory's regulation for integrity and fair dealings.

(*e*) He is responsible for preparing purchase budget.

(*f*) He is responsible for conducting research on mateials, tools, etc.

(*g*) He is responsible for final check on all goods requisitioned, questioning the need, quantity, quality and specification of materials.

PURCHASE PROCEDURE

The main steps involved in the purchase procedure are as follows:

1. Receiving purchase requisitions.
2. Decision regarding what, when and how much to buy.
3. Determining the source of supply.
4. Selecting the supplier by issuing tenders.
5. Preparing and placing purchase orders.
6. Follow-up of purchase orders.
7. Receiving of materials.
8. Inspection of materials.
9. Checking the invoices and settling the accounts.

The above steps are discussed below.

1. Receiving Purchase Requisitions

The purchase requisition is a formal request made to the Purchase Manager to arrange for the purchase of materials described in the purchase requisition. It is a statement which contains a list of materials and a request to purchase them. It serves as a basis for purchasing the materials when it is signed and approved by authorised person. The requisition should give clearly and completely all the information that is required for initiation of the purchase procedure. This particulars ensure that the purchases can be made with speed and accuracy. It must contain the following essential information:

(*a*) Name and exact description of materials wanted.

(*b*) Quantity required.

(*c*) Date on which materials are needed.

(*d*) Statement of need or record of the use that justifies requisition.

(*e*) The place of delivery within the factory after passing through receiving and inspection or directly in case of machinery which should be unloaded as close to the point of use as possible.

(*f*) Vendor's name, in certain special cases as in repair parts for equipment.

(*g*) Signature of the authority initiating the purchase requisition.

(*h*) A space for use of the purchase department to add supplier's name, price, terms.

The above particulars are presented to depict a typical purchase requisition hereunder:

WELLMAN (INDIA) PRIVATE LIMITED

Purchase Requisition

Department ....
Requisition No. ....

To,
Purchase Manager

Date of Initiating
Purchase Requisition
Required on ....

Dear Sir,

Please purchase the following items in accordance with the following specfications:

S. No	*Quantity*	*Description*	*Material in hand*	*Average consumption*	*Remark*

Required by........... Approved by............
Special Instructions...............

Fig. 3.1. *Purchase requisition form.*

The purchase requisition form may originate from (*a*) Storekeeper for the purchase of raw materials which have reached reorder level. (*b*) Production control department for special type of materials. (*c*) Head of the concerned department for buying equipment such as almirah, filing cabinet, etc. (*d*) Plant engineer for the purchase of plant and machinery and other tools and equipments. (*e*) Office manager for purchase of office stationery.

Whenever a purchase requisition is received it is reviewed to see whether the items are available in the storeroom or whether the request for some materials could be replaced by a standard item which is readily obtained at lesser price.

The purchase requisition is generally prepared in triplicate so that the original is sent to the purchase department, the duplicate is sent to the production control department and triplicate is retained in the department which initiates the purchase requisition.

2. Decision Regarding What, When and How Much to Buy

The Purchase Manager before proceeding further in purchasing the materials has to decide the quality, quantity, price and time at which materials are to be purchased.

(*a*) ***Buying the proper quality of purchase specification:*** A specification is an accurate description of material to be purchased. Buying proper quality of materials depends upon (*i*) the accurate specification of materials required ; (*ii*) placing the order with a reliable supplier ; and (*iii*) checking materials against specification. Definiteness in the specification of materials always tend to minimise cost of materials. The form of specification may be indicated by (*a*) trade name or brand name, (*b*) blue print, (*c*) physical characteristics or chemical analysis, (*d*) detail of materials, (*e*) description of purpose or use, (*f*) suppliers sample, (*g*) buyer's sample.

(*b*) ***Buying the proper quantity:*** As a rule, the quantity of a material to be purchased is specified in the purchase requisition. The quantity is often changed to take advantage to market or speculative purchasing. Quantity of materials required are determined by taking the following factors into consideration: (*i*) sales forecast, (*ii*) customer's orders, (*iii*) production authorisation, (*iv*) transfers from other departments, and (*v*) time taken to supply the materials by the suppliers.

(*c*) ***Buying at proper price:*** In order to purchase materials at reasonable price, the purchase manager must obtain and record the price. Material prices may be classified into: (*i*) Prices obtained from market reports and newspapers, (*ii*) prices listed in catalogues, (*iii*) price quoted by the suppliers when tenders are issued.

3. Determining the Source of Supply

After determining the quality and quantity of materials to be bought, the sources of supply are to be tapped. The following are the important sources of supply of materials:

(*i*) Trade directories
(*ii*) Telephone directories
(*iii*) Purchasing periodicals
(*iv*) Newspapers and commerce magazines
(*v*) Catalogues
(*vi*) Supplier's index files
(*vii*) Exhibitions and trade shows
(*viii*) Market survey
(*ix*) Quotations
(*x*) Experience of purchase manager.

While considering suitable source of supply, the following factors should be given due consideration.

(A) Whether to purchase from a single supplier or a multiple of them.

Advantages of a Single Source

(*a*) The Purchase Manager will place an order for all items of materials with a single supplier and thereby get the largest possible discount.

(*b*) There is less administration work in the purchase department.

(*c*) A good relation will prevail between buyers and suppliers, wherein the supplier offers all facilities to the buyer such as credit facilities, after sale services, exchange facilities, free transport facility, etc.

Advantages of Multiple Source

Many factories avoid relying on a single source for all items. Then try to have at least two suppliers for each item of materials. The main advantages of multiple source are:

(*a*) With several sources, there is less risk of interruption of supply. If one supplier fails, the other supplier can take up the supply of materials.

(*b*) With two or more suppliers for one item a healthy competitive spirit can develop in which each vie to improve methods and reduce costs in order to get greater share of the business.

(*c*) Whether to purchase from the local sources or from some distant place.

(*d*) Whether to purchase directly from the manufacturer or through wholesaler.

Problem-1 (Selecting the source of supply)

A company has the option to procure a particular material from two sources:

Source I, assures that defectives will not be more than 2% of supplied quantity.

Source II, does not give any assurance but on the basis of past experience of supplies received from it, it is observed that defective percentage is 2.8%.

The material is supplied in lots of 1000 units. Source II supplies the lot at a price, which is lower by Rs. 100 as compared to source I. The defective units of materials can be rectified for use at a cost of Rs. 5 per unit.

You are required to find out which of the two sources is more economical.

(C.A. Inter, May 2001)

Solution:

	Materials Source I	*Material Source II*
Defectives (in %)	2	2.8
	(Future estimate)	(Past experience)
Total defective units in a lot	$\frac{2}{100} \times 1000 = 20$	$\frac{2.8}{100} \times 1000 = 28$
	Rs.	*Rs.*
Additional price paid per lot	100	—
Rectification cost of defective		
Source I–20 units × Rs. 5	100	—
Source II–28 units × Rs. 5	—	140
Total additional cost per lot	200	140

Decision:

On comparing the total additional cost incurred per lot of 1000 units. We observe that it is more economical if the required material units are procured from material source II.

4. Selecting the Supplier by Issuing of Tenders

When there are more than one supplier dealing with materials, the Purchase Manager has to select the best supplier with whom the Purchase Manager has confidence as to quality of materials, ability to deliver the materials promptly, at the cheapest price and with better terms of sale. The selection of such a supplier is decided by issuing tenders. A tender is a written letter or an advertisement given in newspaper inviting the prospective suppliers to quote their lowest price and other terms and conditions of sale. The request for quotation should give the following information:

(*i*) Quantity to be ordered.

(*ii*) Name and full specification of materials.

(*iii*) Place where materials are to be delivered.

(*iv*) Other terms and conditions of sale which the supplier wishes to make.

Types of Tender

(*i*) ***Single tender:*** Such a tender is issued where an item is of a proprietary nature or where the material is dealt with by a single supplier.

(*ii*) ***Limited tender:*** When the value of the tender is moderate, limited tenders are issued. Here, tenders are invited only from those suppliers who are on the approved list of suppliers. The merits of this method are: (*a*) Being regular suppliers they submit realistic quotations, (*b*) They are fully conversant with the materials, (*c*) The chances of selecting the supplier is better.

(*iii*) ***Open tender:*** This type of tender is issued when the sources are many and the value is large. Anybody who deals with such material and who is willing to supply the materials can quote his prices in response to this tender.

(*iv*) ***Global tender:*** This type of tender is issued for the suppliers even beyond the boundaries of the country. This tender is mostly used when the factory is under the collaboration of foreign government.

Earnest Money

Earnest money is demanded from the supplier to discourage unreliable suppliers. This is also insisted upon so that the prospective supplier subsequently does not back out from the rate he has quoted for supplying the materials. A specimen of tender form is given below:

ABC CO. LTD.

Request for Quotation

Date............

To, Quotation No. ....

.... (Name of Supplier)

.... Address

....

Dear Sir,

Please submit your quotation for the materials listed below so as to reach the office of the undersigned on or before......... at .... Please send full details, specifications and other literature, if any, along with the quotation. Please note the terms and conditions mentioned below:

(*a*) Please mention on the top of the envelop enquiry number .... date on which due.

(*b*) Submit quotations in duplicate.

(*c*) Preferably quote in the same order as in the enquiry letter.

(*d*) Price each item separately and the prices quoted should be for destination............

(*e*) If you are unable to furnish materials as per our descriptions and wish to offer a substitute, please give details.

(*f*) Quotations should be valid for at least one month from the date of opening.

(*g*) Quotations should be sent in sealed covers.

(*h*) Taxes should be mentioned for each item.

(*i*) The right is reserved to accept or reject quotations on each item separately or as a whole.

The quotations will be opened on ....at........... in the office of the undersigned.

S. No	*Description*	*Quantity*	*Unit*	*Price*	*Discount*	*Total price*

Yours faithfully

Sd/-

Fig. 3.2. *Tender form.*

The sealed quotations are opened on the last date on which it is to be submitted by all competitive suppliers. The Purchase Manager will then prepare a comparative tender statement to know the lowest quotation price and best terms and conditions of sale offered.

Thus, the supplier is choosen with whom the purchase order is to be placed. A specimen form of comparative tender statement is given below.

Comparative Tender Statement

Section ....

Tender Number ....

Date of Opening Quotations ....

Comparative Tender Statement prepared by ....

Checked by ....

S. No	*Description of materials*	*Quantity*	*Rates*		
			Supplier 1	*Supplier 2*	*Supplier 3*
			Terms and Conditions		
	Delivery Date Places of Delivery Terms of Payment Taxes Packing and Forward Charges				

Fig. 3.3. *Comparative tender statement.*

Problem-2

The stock position and requirements of a certain material used in a factory are as follows:

Present stock	*7,000 units*
Average weekly requirement	*2,000 units*
Maximum level	*16,000 units*
Minimum level	*6,000 units*

The manager invited tenders for the supply of materials and received the undernoted quotations:

(a) Any quantity up to 20,000 units @ Rs. 2.40 per unit, immediate delivery.

(b) Any quantity @ Rs. 2.20 per unit plus Rs. 1,000 fixed charges irrespective of quantity ordered ; immediate delivery.

Give your decision as regards the choice of tender and quantity to be ordered.

Solution:

Comparative Statement

Quantity ordered (units)	*Quotation price as per tender (a) @ Rs. 2.40 per unit*	*Quotation price as per tender (b)*		*Total*
		Variable cost @ Rs. 2.20 per unit	*Fixed cost*	
	Rs.	*Rs.*	*Rs.*	*Rs.*
2,000	4,800	4,400	1,000	5,400
3,000	7,200	6,600	1,000	7,600
4,000	9,600	8,800	1,000	9,800
5,000	12,000	11,000	1,000	12,000
6,000	14,400	13,200	1,000	14,200
7,000	16,800	15,400	1,000	16,400
8,000	19,200	17,600	1,000	18,600
9,000	21,600	19,800	1,000	20,800
10,000	24,000	22,000	1,000	23,000
20,000	48,000	44,000	1,000	45,000

From the above comparative tender statements, it is clear that at 5,000 units the amount quoted by both tenderer is same, *viz.*, Rs. 12,000. The present stock is 7,000 units Whereas the maximum level is 16,000 units. So, the Purchase Manager can purchase 9,000 units. (16,000—7,000). As the quotation price for the purchase of 9,000 units are quoted by tenderer (*b*) is less, *i.e.*, Rs. 20,800, he is to be preferred over tender (*a*).

Problem-3

After inviting tenders, two quotations are received as under.

Supplier A — *Rs. 2.20 per unit*

Supplier B — *Rs. 2.10 per unit plus Rs. 2,000 fixed charges irrespective of units ordered*

(i) Calculate the order quantity for which the purchase price per unit will be the same.

(ii) Select the supplier, if the purchase officer wants to place an order for 15,000 units.

(C.S. Dec. 1990; Sri Sathya Sai University, B.Com., Oct., 1991)

Solution:

(*i*) Calculation of the order quantity for which the purchase price per unit will be the same.

Difference in tender price:

Quotation per unit by supplier 'A'	=	Rs. 2.20
Quotation per unit by supplier 'B'	=	Rs. 2.10
Difference per unit		0.10

In order to cover the fixed charges of Rs. 2,000 of supplier *B*, the order quantity should be 20,000 units *i.e.*, Rs. 2,000 ÷ Re. 0.10. At the quantity of 20,000 units, the purchase price will be the same in both cases as shown below:

Supplier *A* 20,000 × Rs. 2.20 = Rs. 44,000

$$\text{Per unit} = \frac{44{,}000}{20{,}000} = \text{Rs. } 2.20$$

Supplier *B* 20,000 × Rs. 2.10 + 2,000 fixed cost

= 42,000 + 2,000 = Rs. 44,000

$$\text{Per unit} = \frac{44{,}000}{20{,}000} = 2.20$$

(*ii*) Selection of the best supplier for the purchase of 15,000 units.

Quotation price of supplier *A* = 15,000 × Rs. 2.20 = Rs. 33,000

Quotation price of supplier *B* = 15,000 × Rs. 2.10 + Rs. 2,000

= 31,500 + 2,000 = Rs. 33,500

As the quotation price of supplier *A* is less compared to supplier *B*, it is suggested to select supplier *A* by the purchase officer.

Problem-4

When two tenders were invited for a stores, two quotations were received as under:

Supplier (A) (*a*) *Rate Rs. 2 each,* (*b*) *Trade discount 10%* (*c*) *Cash discount 5%, if bills are paid within a fortnight after receipt,* (*d*) *Transport charge Re. 1 per 100 units.*

Supplier (B) (*a*) *Rate Rs. 1.80 each (up to 1,000 units)*

Rs. 1.60 each (for order above 1,000 units)

(*b*) *6% interest per annum will be added, if bills are not paid within a fortnight after receipt of the material.*

(*c*) *Transport charges Rs. 3 per 100 units.*

Assuming that above 5,000 units are required every month and that quality and other conditions of supply are the same offer your comments as to on whom purchase orders can be issued. The factory pays 50% of its monthly bills every fortnight.

Solution:

	Supplier A	Supplier B	
		up to 1,000 units	above 1,000 units
Basic rate	2.00	1.80	1.60
Less: Trade discount	0.20		
Net price per unit	1.80	1.80	1.60
Add: Total transport charges	0.01	0.03	0.03
Purchase price per unit	1.81	1.83	1.63
Purchase bill	5,000 × 1.81 = 9,150.00	5,000 × 1.83 = 9,150.00	5,000 ×1.63 = 8,150.00
Less: Cash discount – 5% on Rs. 9,050 for fortnight	= 226.25	—	—
	8,823.75	9,150.00	8,150.00
Add: Interest at 6% on Rs. 9,150 and Rs. 8,150 for fortnight	—	11.28	10.04
Final cost	8,823.75	9,161.28	8,160.04

Comments: As the price quoted by supplier *B* is less when more than 1,000 units are bought he must be selected for placing order of 5,000 units.

Working Note:

(1) Calculation of cash discount:

$$9,050 \times \frac{1}{2} \times \frac{5}{100} = 226.25$$

(2) Calculation of interest:

$$9,150 \times \frac{6}{100} \times \frac{15}{365} \times \frac{1}{2} = 11.28$$

$$8,150 \times \frac{6}{100} \times \frac{15}{365} \times \frac{1}{2} = 10.04$$

(3) In the above calculations $\frac{1}{2}$ is equal to 50% of bill paid.

5. Preparing and Placing Purchase Order

A purchased order is a contractual document which authorises the supplier to supply the materials. Once the purchase order is issued to a supplier, it is obligatory on the part of Purchase Manager to take delivery of materials and arrange for the payment of invoice. The purchase order must be carefully drafted by precisely including all essential elements of purchases to be made. It must be prepared in such a manner so as to avoid future misunderstanding and minimise the necessity of correspondence. The purchase order should include the following particulars:

(*a*) ***Purchase order number:*** Purchase order number helps in identifying the transaction in future correspondence. It also helps the supplier in preparing the invoice and in despatching the materials.

(*b*) ***Quantity ordered:*** The quantity ordered is expressed in different units depending upon the type of materials.

(*c*) ***Description:*** The full description of materials enable the supplier to supply the right quality of materials. It also helps the receiver to inspect the materials on its receipt.

(*d*) ***Delivery instructions:*** This relate to the data on which the materials are to be delivered. It also includes the place of delivery, packing, marking, insurance and mode of transportation.

(*e*) ***Terms of payment:*** The terms of payment, *i.e.,* cash basis, credit basis, FOB, FOR, CWO, CBO, COD can be made clear under this point.

(*f*) **Price:** The unit rate and the total amount of materials purchased are to be included.

(*g*) Name and address of the purchasing company.

(*h*) Name and address of supplier.

(*i*) Date of placing purchase order.

(*j*) Signature of purchase manager.

A specimen form of purchase order is given below:

WELLMAN (INDIA) PRIVATE LIMITED

Regd. Office: Neville House, Currimnbhoy Road, Mumbai.

Factory & Adm. Office: Kolshet Road, Thana, Maharashtra

Purchase Order

Phone.............. Purchase Order No. ....

Cable .... Date ....

Telex .... CST Reg. No. ....

To,

....

....

....

Your reference.........dated.........

[Please deliver the undermentioned materials subject to conditions printed on the reverse, quoting the order number on all delivery challans.]

S. No	*Quantity*	*Description*	*Unit rate*		*Price*	
			Rs.	*P.*	*Rs.*	*P.*

Delivery: Deliveries at our stores should be made before 4.00 p.m. on working days.

Insurance: On despatch of the consignment please Telegraph following information to the attention of purchase department.

(*a*) Our order reference, (*b*) Invoice value, (*c*) Freight charges payable.

For Wellman (India) Pvt. Ltd.

Purchase Manager

Fig. 3.4. *Purchase order.*

Conditions

(*a*) **Acceptance:** The acceptance of this order will constitute the contract. The buyer reserves the right to cancel or amend this order or any part thereof without assigning any reason.

(*b*) **Quality:** All materials must conform to samples, specification, description and drawings and will be subject to our inspection and approval at any time within a reasonable time from the date of delivery. If not up to specification, they will be held for deposition or returned at your risk and expenses. If required, free replacement for rejected materials/equipment should be made.

(*c*) **Quantity:** The buyer assumes no obligation in relation to any goods delivered in excess of those specifically ordered. In any case, the quantity of the material must not exceed without permission in writing being first obtained.

(*d*) **Delivery:** Delivery is to be undertaken within the stipulation of the order and the buyer reserves the right to rescind or cancel the order without prior notice or intimation if the delivery is not affected within the time stated on this purchase order.

(*e*) **Partial delivery:** The buyer may accept partial delivery on condition that the balance will be delivered within a stipulated time from thereon.

(*f*) All the materials must be forwarded by the particular route named. Otherwise difference in freight and extra cost of cartage, etc., will be charged to the account.

(*g*) **Payment:** Ninety days after receipt and inspection of goods at our factory at Thana, unless otherwise specified.

(*h*) **Advice notes:** Advice notes are to be sent to the purchase department at the time after goods are despatched.

(*i*) **Bill or invoices:** All bills or invoices must be sent to us in TRIPLICATE mentioning our order number and our Sales Tax Registration number thereon. The RR number or L.R. number and data under which the materials are despatched must appear on Bills/Invoices.

Itemised bills or invoices should be sent to the purchase department immediately along with a copy of delivery note and a copy of rail/lorry receipt.

A copy of the invoice should be sent along with consignment despatched by lorry or motor to avoid seizure at sales tax check posts.

(*j*) **Cartage and freight:** No charges will be allowed for cartage, freight and/or packing, etc., unless accepted by previous agreement.

(*k*) The statement of account must be sent at stated intervals mutually agreed upon.

The purchase order is prepared in five copies: (*i*) two copies are sent to supplier and the supplier will return back the duplicate as acknowledgement, (*ii*) third copy is sent to production department or department which initiated purchase requisition, (*iii*) fourth copy is sent to costing department, and (*iv*) fifth copy is retained by purchase manager.

6. Follow-up of Purchase Order

The continuation of production process to a large extent depends upon the regular and ready delivery of materials. While placing purchase order the date on which materials are to be delivered must be clearly mentioned. It is the duty of follow-up section to see that this date is kept. Where it is not possible to get delivery of material on the promised date, the follow-up section can take necessary steps to prevent crippling the production process due to lack of materials. To avoid late delivery of materials the following points must be remembered:

(*a*) Use clear and complete specifications.

(*b*) Keep demands for "rush" delivery to minimum.

(*c*) Keep records of the delivery performance of suppliers.

(*d*) Try to find good alternative suppliers to those whose delivery performances are consistently bad.

(*e*) Keep abreast of suppliers current range of delivery times.

(*f*) Know supplier's policy regarding stock of raw materials.

(*g*) Visit suppliers regularly.

(*h*) Pay suppliers promptly.

7. Receiving of Materials

Before materials are taken delivery of, it is very essential to receive and inspect materials so as to ensure that the supplier has supplied the exact quantity and quality of materials. In large factories, a separate receiving and inspection department is set up and receiving clerks are incharge of receiving the materials. To facilitate the receiving clerk to receive and inspect the materials, a copy of purchase order without filling up the quantity of materials can be supplied. This serves as the basis for recording the entries by the receiving clerks. The duties of receiving department are as follows:

(*a*) To check the incoming materials to know whether all items of materials in terms of quantities conform to the purchase order.

(*b*) To record the receipt of the materials.

(*c*) To inform the storekeeper about the receipt of materials.

(*d*) To inform the purchase manager the fact which require an adjustment to be made with supplier in respect of shortage or defective materials.

(*e*) To deliver the materials either to the department where it is required or to the storeroom.

Having received and checked the materials, the receiving clerk will prepare a material received report. A material received report is useful for checking the supplier's invoice. It contains the following particulars:

(*a*) Date of receipt.

(*b*) Supplier's name and address.

(*c*) Types of materials received.

(*d*) Quantity of materials received.

(*e*) Condition in which materials are received.

(*f*) Type of container.

(g) Mode of transportation.

A specimen of materials received note is given below.

USHA MARTIN BLACK LTD.

58, Main Road, Whitefield, Bangalore - 560 066

Material Received Note

MRN No. ....

Name of the supplier .... Date ....

RR no. .... Order no. & date ....

S. No.	*Particulars*	*Unit*	*Qty as per order no.*	*Shortage*	*Excess*	*Rejected*	*Accepted*

Signature of receiving clerk ....

Fig. 3.5. *Materials received note.*

8. Inspection of Materials

The next step involved in the purchase procedure is inspection of materials received. Inspection refers to comparison or checking of quality, size and quantity of materials. The quality of material is ensured if the properties such as shape, colour, dimension, weight, composition, strength, etc., of the required standard are present in the materials. Some times materials such as chemicals are taken to laboratory and tested to know their quality.

Importance of Inspection of Materials

Inspection of materials is necessary to ensure that:

(*a*) Materials received are in strict specification of purchase order. In other words, only those materials that were ordered have been received.

(*b*) The quantity of materials conform to the quantity of materials ordered.

(*c*) The quality of materials are those specified in purchase order.

(*d*) No damage is caused to materials during transit.

Inspection of materials in a large factory is usually undertaken by Inspection Officer. In small factories, inspection function is performed by the receiving clerk or by the storekeeper himself. The duties and responsibilities of Inspection Officer are as follows:

(*a*) To sort out defective raw materials received.

(*b*) To report the management about the quality of materials received.

(*c*) To suggest action regarding rejected materials, *i.e.*, whether they are to be returned to the supplier or deducted from the supplier's invoice.

(*d*) To prepare and sign the material inspection certificate.

(*e*) To maintain and use various inspection devices such as steel rules, callipers, micrometer, electric insturments, etc., for the purpose of inspection.

9. Checking the Invoice and Settling the Account

This is the last step in the purchase procedure. The invoice is checked with the purchase order and the materials received report. The rates and the terms of invoice is compared with those of purchase order. Similarly, the quantity received, must tally with the quantity ordered. If there is any discrepancy or defective materials is received, the same is brought to the notice of supplier and accordingly a debit note or credit note is prepared. Finally, if everything is in order, the invoice is approved by purchase manager and forwarded to the costing section for payment.

ASCERTAINING PURCHASE COST OR VALUATION OF MATERIALS RECEIVED

As a matter of rule, the invoice price quoted by the supplier is used for accounting purposes. However, the following items are to be considered while valuing the materials:

(*a*) **Invoice price or supplier's price:** Invoice quoted by suppliers are of different types such as net price or list price subject to discounts, inclusive or exclusive of freight, customs, insurance or packages. However, for costing purposes we must arrive at a figure which will represent the cost actually incurred up to the point of delivery of the goods. For this reason, 'purchase price' is calculated by taking the invoice price as the basis, deducting any trade or quantity discounts and adding other expenses not already included.

(*b*) **Trade discount:** It is a discount allowed by manufacturers to distributors. This is to enable the distributors to cover the cost of storage, repacking goods if any, and such other expenses.

(*c*) **Quantity discount:** It is a discount allowed by the manufacturers to customers who buy goods on large-scale basis. This discount takes the form of special rebates with a view to encourage them to purchase in bulk quantities.

(*d*) **Cash discount:** This is a deduction allowed by manufacturer if payment is made promptly within a specified period. But the treatment of this item depends upon the decision taken by the purchaser to pay the bill promptly to avail the benefit. In some cases, this item is kept outside the purview of costing considering this as an item of pure financial matter.

(*e*) **Transport charges:** Sometimes the manufacturer undertakes to supply the materials meeting the transport charges. But when the supplier fails to meet the transport cost, it is the purchaser who has to bear the transport cost and hence included in the cost of materials.

(*f*) **Storage cost:** The expenses incurred by the purchaser to store the purchased materials is to be taken into account while determining the purchase price.

(*g*) **Insurance:** Any insurance taken to cover the materials in transit is again added to materials cost to calculated its purchase price.

(*h*) **Customs duties:** When raw materials are imported from other countries, it involves payment of custom duties. This is to be added while calculating purchase price of materials.

(*i*) **Excise, duty, sales tax, octroi:** These items of expenses are to be paid when materials are bought from a local manufacturer or goods manufactured indegenously are bought. This is added to the cost of materials while calculating purchase price of materials.

(*j*) **Cost of containers:** Sometime the manufacturer will not charge any amount to the containers or packing materials. In such circumstances, the cost of containers are not included in the materials cost. Where the manufacturer charges for the containers it will be treated as follows:

(*i*) *Non-returnable containers:* In this situation, the cost of container will be added to the purchase price of materials.

(*ii*) *Crediting returnable containers at its full value:* Where the purchaser returns all the containers safely, it will no be included in the purchase price.

(*iii*) *Crediting returnable containers at reduced value:* Under this situation, the difference between the cost of container and the amount credited by the supplier will be added to purchase price of materials.

(*k*) **Apportionment of joint purchase cost:** Where materials are purchased in different grades in one lot, by incurring common cost, it becomes necessary to apportion the common cost or joint cost to all the grades of materials on an average basis. This may result in undercharging or overcharging of cost to all the grades of materials. To eliminate such differences the existing rates of material can be taken into consideration and the receipt of materials priced accordingly. If any difference is still found, it can be distributed proportionately to the various grades on the basis of market price.

(*l*) **Extra quantity or free supply of excess spare parts:** Sometimes the manufacturer may supply extra quantities of certain types of spare parts at a free of cost. This will reduce the unit price of the consignment.

Problem-5

Ramprakash & Co. purchases certain quantities of mixed grades of materials for Rs. 9,00,000. On sorting out into the following grades they revealed the following market rates:

Grades	*Units*	*Selling rate per unit*
Grade X	*50,000*	*Rs. 12.00*
Grade Y	*30,000*	*Rs. 10.00*
Grade Z	*20,000*	*Rs. 5.00*

Find out the purchase rate per unit of each grade of materials assuming all grades yield the same rate of profit.

Solution:

This problem is worked out based on equation

Selling Price = Cost price or purchase price + Profit

Statement showing profit

Grade X	50,000 units @ Rs. 12 each	Rs. 6,00,000
Grade Y	30,000 units @ Rs. 10 each	Rs. 3,00,000
Grade Z	20,000 units @ Rs. 5 each	Rs. 1,00,000
	Total sale price	10,00,000
	Less: Purchase price	9,00,000
	Profit	1,00,000

Calculation of percentage of profit on sale price

For Rs. 10,00,000 sales, Profit is Rs. 1,00,000

For 100 – ?

$$\frac{1,00,000 \times 100}{10,00,000} = 10\%$$

Ascertainment of purchase rate

Grades	*Selling price per unit (A)*	*Profit 10% per unit of sales (B)*	*Purchase rate per unit (A) – (B)*
X	Rs. 12	Rs. 1.20	Rs. 10.80
Y	Rs. 10	Re. 1.00	Rs. 9.00
Z	Rs. 5	Re. 0.50	Rs. 4.50

Verification

Purchase price of grade X materials	50,000 × Rs. 10.80	= Rs. 5,40,000
Purchase price of grade Y materials	30,000 × Rs. 9.00	= Rs. 2,70,000
Purchase price of grade Z materials	20,000 × Rs. 4.50	= Rs. 90,000
	Total purchase price	Rs. 9,00,000

Problem-6

A factory received a consignment of four grades of a material for Rs. 1,20,000. These were sorted in stores and recorded as below:

Grade-I	*4,000 units,*	*Grade-III*	*10,000 units*
Grade-II	*8,000 units,*	*Grade-IV*	*12,000 units*

Grade—I total sales was Rs. 16,000 at a profit of $33\frac{1}{3}\%$ *on cost.*

Grade—II was totally sold at a price one and a half time that of Grade-I fetching $33\frac{1}{3}\%$ *profit on sales.*

Grade—III Sales of Rs. 50,000 brought at a profit of 20% on sales.

Find out the purchase price of each grade of materials from the above information.

(Madurai University, B.Com., April 1986)

Solution:

This problem is worked out based on the formula

Selling price = Cost price + Profit

Calculation of profit on Grade-I material

Percentage of profit is given on selling price but not on cost price.

Let cost price be = Rs. 100

Add: Percentage of profit on cost price = $33\frac{1}{3}\%$

$\therefore$ Selling price = $133\frac{1}{3}\%$

$$\text{Profit on sales} = \frac{33\frac{1}{3}\%}{133\frac{1}{3}\%} \times 16{,}000$$

$$= \frac{100}{3} \times \frac{3}{400} \times 16{,}000 = 4{,}000$$

Purchase price of Grade-I materials = Sales – Profit

= 16,000 – 4,000 = Rs. 12,000

Calculation of profit on Grade-II materials

Selling price of Grade-II materials is $1\frac{1}{2}$ times that of Grade-I materials

i.e., $= \frac{3}{2} \times$ Rs. 4 = Rs. 6

Total sales of Grade-II materials

= 8,000 units × Rs. 6 = Rs. 48,000

Percentage profit on sales is $33\frac{1}{3}\%$

i.e., $= \frac{33\frac{1}{3}}{100} \times 48{,}000$

or, $\frac{100}{3} \times \frac{1}{100} \times 48{,}000$ = Rs. 16,000

Purchase price of Grade-II materials

= Sales – Profit

= 48,000 – 16,000 = Rs. 32,000

Calculation of profit on Grade-III materials

Percentage of profit on sales is 20%

i.e., $\frac{20}{100} \times 50{,}000$ = Rs. 10,000

Purchase price of Grade-III materials = Sales – Profit

= 50,000 – 10,000 = Rs. 40,000

Calculation of purchase price of Grade-IV materials

Total purchase price – (Purchase price of Grade I, II, III materials)

Rs. 1,20,000 – (12,000 + 32,000 + 40,000)

Rs. 1,20,000 – 84,000 = Rs. 36,000

Problem-7

The following details are available in respect of a consignment 1,250 kgs of materials x.

(a) Invoice price – Rs. 20 per kg

(b) Excise duty – 25% on invoice price

(c) Sales tax – 8% on invoice price including excise duty

(d) Trade discount – 10% on the invoice price

(e) Insurance – 1% on aggregate net price

(f) Delivery charges – Rs. 250

(g) Cost of containers @ Rs. 60 per container of 50 kgs of materials, Rebate is allowed @ Rs. 40 per container, if returned within six weeks, which is a normal feature.

(h) One container load of materials was rejected on inspection and not accepted.

(i) Cost of unloading and handing @ 0.25% of the cost of materials ultimately accepted. On the basis of above you are required to find out the landed cost of per kg of material X. *(ICWA Inter., Dec. 1991)*

Solution:

Statement showing cost per kg of material 'X'

		Amount (Rs.)	Cost per kg (1,200 kgs)
Invoice price:			
Total Qty. ordered	1,250 kgs		
Less: Qty. rejected	50 kgs		
Qty. accepted	1.200		
1,200 kgs. @ Rs. 20		24,000	20.00
Less: Trade discount – 10% on invoice price	2,400	2.00	
		21,600	18.00
Excise duty – 25% on invoice price $\left(\frac{25}{100} \times 24{,}000\right)$		6,000	5.00
		27,600	23.00
Sales tax – 8% on invoice price and excise duty $\frac{8}{100} \times 30{,}000$ (24,000 + 6,000)		2,400	2.00
Delivery charges		250	0.21
Cost of containers = $\frac{1250}{20}$	= 25		
Less: Return of 1 container full of materials	$\frac{1}{24}$		

24 Containers @ Rs. 60	= 1,440		
Less: Credited at Rs. 40 when returned (24 × 40)	= 960	480.00	0.40
	Net Purchase Price	30,730.00	25.61
Insurance : 10% on Rs. 30,730		307.30	0.25
Cost of materials ultimately accepted		31037.30	25.86
Cost of unloading and handling			
@ Rs. 0.25% of the cost of Material accepted		75.60	0.60
Landed Cost of Materials		311114.90	25.92

Problem-8 (Ascertaining Purchase Cost of Materials)

Modern Manufacturing Company Kolkata, purchased a material of 20 tonnes from a mining company. The following data is available for the lot of material purchased.

(i) *Invoice price of material @ Rs. 2,000 per tonne*
(ii) *Trade discount @ 20% on Invoice price*
(iii) *Excise duty @ 10% on Invoice price*
(iv) *Sales tax @ 10%*
(v) *Freight and Insurance @ 2%*
(vi) *Other charges for delivery @ Rs. 100 per tonne*
(vii) *Cost of containers @ Rs. 20 per box of one quintal*
(vii) *Cost of loading and unloading @ 1% of total cost*

Compute total material purchase cost and cost per tonne to Modern Manufacturing Company. *(Calcutta University, B.Com (Hons) 2001)*

Solution:

Statement Showing Total Material Purchase Cost of 20 Tonnes

Invoice price of materials (20 tonnes × Rs. 2,000)	40,000
Less: Trade discount @ 20% on Invoice price	8,000
	32,000
Add: Excise duty @ 10% on Invioce price	4,000
	36,000
Add: Sales tax @ 10%	3,600
	39,600
Add: Freight and Insurance @ 2%	792
	40,392
Add: Other charges for delivery (Rs. 100 × 20 tonnes)	2,000
	42,392
Add: Cost of containers (20 × 10 quintal × 20 tonnes)	4,000
	46,392
Add: Cost of loading and unloading 1% of 46,392	464
Total cost of materials (20 tonnes)	46,856

$$\text{Cost per tonne} = \frac{46{,}856}{20} = \text{Rs } 2342.80$$

Note:

100 kgs	= 1 Quintal
1000 kgs	= 1 Tonne
10 Quintals	= 1 Tonne

Problem-9 (Purchase Cost of Materials)

The following quotation is received from a supplier in respect of materials

		Rate per kg
		Rs.
Let price	*1,000 kg*	*5.00*
	5,000 kg	*4.50*
	10,000 kg	*4.00*

Trade discount 20% and cash discount 5%, if payment is made within 15 days. One container is required for every 1,000 kg of the material and containers are charged at Rs. 100 each but credited Rs. 90, if returned within 3 months. Transport charges for one order is Rs. 500. Storage charges Rs. 150. Calculate material cost for 5,000 kg of the material when the purchaser decides to purchase 5,000 kg of the material assuming containers are returned in time. *(Sri Sathya Sai University, B.Com (Hons.), March 2002)*

Solution:

Calculation of material cost

Purchase of 5,000 kg	*Amount*	*Cost per kg*
Invoice price – 5,000 kgs × 4.50	22,500	4.50
Less: Trade Discount @ 20%	4,500	0.90
	18,000	3.60
Add: Cost of containers 5 × 100 = 500		
Less: Credited on return 5 × 0.90 = 450	50	0.01
Transport charges	500	0.10
Storage charges	150	0.03
Total cost of material	18,700	3.74

Problem-10

The following details are available in respect of a consignment of 1200 kg of material 'x'

(i) Lot price quoted by the supplier and accepted by the company:

Lot upto 1,000 kg @ Rs. 22 per kg

1000 – 1,500 kg @ Rs. 20 per kg

1,500 – 2000 kg @ Rs. 18 per kg

(ii) Trade discount 20%

(iii) Additional charge for containers @ Rs. 10 per drum of 25 kg

(iv) Credit allowed on return of containers @ Rs. 8 per drum

(v) Sales tax at 10% on raw materials and 5% on drums

(vi) Total freight paid by the purchaser Rs. 240

(vii) Insurance at 2.5% (on net invoice value) paid by the purchaser

(viii) Stores overhead applied at 5% on total purchase cost of material

The entire quantity was received and issued to production. The containers are returned in due course. Draw up a suitable statement to show:

(a) Total cost of materials purchased

(b) Unit cost of materials issued to production

Solution:

Statement of total and per unit cost of materials

	Total	*Per unit*
Invoice price 1200 kg × 20 per kg	24,000	20.00
Less: Trade Discount 20%	4,800	4.00
	19,200	16.00
Cost of containers $\frac{1200}{25}$ = 48 @ Rs. 10 per container	480	0.40
	19,680	16.40
Sales Tax.:		
10% on 19,200 = 1920		
5% on 480 = 24	1,944	1.62
Net Invoice Value	21,624	18.02
Freight paid	240	0.20
Insurance $\frac{2.5}{100} \times 21{,}624$	540	0.45
	22,404	18.67
Less: Credit for containers 48 × 8	384	0.32
	22,020	18.35
Stores overhead @ 5% on Rs. 22,020	1,101	0.92
	23,121	19.27

Questions

I. Mark True or False

1. Purchase requisition note is prepared by the purchase department. *T/F*
2. The Purchase Manager is himself the controller of materials. *T/F*
3. Routing the purchase requisition through the purchase department entails an unnecessary delay in receiving the required materials. *T/F*

4. The direct materials as a type of materials usually includes materials that are in their raw or natural state. *T/F*
5. Some materials used in the manufacture of a product may not be classified as direct materials. *T/F*
6. The primary criterion for classifying a material as direct is whether it can be clearly traced to and associated with a product. *T/F*
7. The duties and responsibilities of the purchase department differ from factory to factory. *T/F*
8. Centralised purchasing should not be used for any concern operating a single plant. *T/F*
9. Specification of materials means the material standards which are established by the factory to define its major materials requirement. *T/F*
10. Tenders are invited when time permits and money involved is in large amount. *T/F*
11. Once a tender has been received, no alteration or modification is allowed. *T/F*

[**Answer:** (1) *F*, (2) *F*, (3) *F*, (4) *F*, (5) *T*, (6) *T*, (7) *T*, (8) *F*, (9) *T*, (10) *T*, (11) *T*]

II. Indicate whether each of the following items represent direct or indirect material

(*a*) Clay in bricks (*b*) Lubricants (*c*) Jars for cosmetics (*d*) Nails in wooden furniture (*e*) Sand paper used in polishing (*f*) Ink used in printing (*g*) Shop pattern (*h*) Thread used in stitching shirts (*i*) Fruits in canning industry (*j*) Pig iron in foundry.

[**Answer:** Direct Materials: (*a*), (*c*), (*f*), (*e*), (*i*), (*j*), rest are Indirect Materials]

III. Choose the correct answer from the following:

(*a*) Which one of the following would not be treated as direct material in the manufacture of furniture:

(1) Lumber for frames (3) Adhesive paste
(2) Foam rubber padding (4) Steel wire spring

(*b*) Purchase requisition is generally prepared in:

(1) Single (3) Triplicate
(2) Duplicate (4) Quadruplicate

(*c*) Which of the following items of cost should not be treated as direct material:

(1) Electricity representing 90% of the total cost
(2) Sand paper used in production
(3) Thread use in stitching garments (4) All of the above

(*d*) A purchase requisition is prepared by:

(1) Purchase manager (3) Supplier
(2) Foreman (4) Storekeeper

[**Answer:** (*a*) –3, (*b*) –3, (*c*) –4, (*d*) –4]

IV. Match the following

A	*B*
1. Raw materials	(*a*) Materials that are used in production but do not become part of the product.
2. In-process materials	(*b*) Materials used directly in the production but have not undergone a major change.
3. Finished products	(*c*) Products ready to be packaged and sold.
4. Supplies	(*d*) Machine parts that are used in manufacturing.

5. Equipment items — (e) Materials used in the product whose form has changed as a result of the production process.

[**Answer:** 1 –*e*, 2 –*b*, 3 –*c*, 4 –*a*, 5 –*d*]

V. Simple questions

1. State two advantages of centralised purchasing. (*M.G. University, B.Com., April 1996*)
2. Mention two disadvantages of centralised purchasing. (*M.G. University, B.Com., April 1995*)
3. What are direct materials ? (*M.G. University, B.Com., September 1994*)
4. What is materials received note ? (*Bangalore University, B.Com., April 1995*)
5. What are the stages in materials purchase cycle ? (*Bangalore University, M.Com., May 1995*)
6. Classify the following into direct materials and indirect materials:
   (1) Oil & grease used in machine
   (2) Leather used in shoe
   (3) Cotton in textile industry
   (4) Nails used in furniture
   (*Kuvempu University, B.Com., April 1995*)
7. What is meant by Direct materials cost ? (*Bangalore University, B.Com., Nov. 1997*)
   (*Karnataka University, B.Com., Nov. 1994*)
8. What is meant by centralised buying ? (*Bangalore University, B.Com., November 1999*)

VI. Short answer questions

1. Explain the different stages involved in purchase procedure.
   (*University of Mysore, B.Com., Nov. 1997*)
2. Explain in brief the functions of:
   (1) Purchasing Department
   (2) Receiving Department
   (3) Inspection Department
   (4) Stores Department
   (*University of Mysore, B.Com., April 1997*)
3. Describe the procedure to be followed for purchase of stores till the payment of the bill.
   (*Sri Krishnadevaraya University, B.Com., Nov. 1998*)
4. What buying process followed in an industrial organisation ?
   (*Nagarjuna University, B.Com., March 1998*)
5. Describe the procedure for purchasing materials from outside.
   (*Nagarjuna University, B.Com., April 1994*)
6. What do you understand by Double-bin system ?
   (*Sri Krishnadevaraya University, B.Com., March 1997*)
7. Describe the material purchase procedure. (*Osmania University, B.Com., October, 1996*)
8. Explain the functions of the Purchase Department.
   (*Kuvempu University, B.Com., October 1995*)

EXERCISES

Exercise on tender

1. After inviting tenders, two quotations are received as follows:
   (*a*) Rs. 1.20 per unit
   (*b*) Rs. 1.10 per plus unit Rs. 3,000 fixed charges to be added irrespective of units ordered.
   Advise with your arguments on whom orders should be placed and what quantity to be ordered. The following additional information may be of interest:

	Units
Present stock	35,000
Average monthly requirements	10,000
Maximum level	80,000
Minimum level	30,000

Sales tax may be ignored.

[**Answer:** Materials can be bought up to 45,000 units considering the maximum level of 80,000 units and the present stock of 35,000 units. In this case the tender price of supplier I for 45000 units comes to Rs. 54000 and Rs. 52500 by supplier II. Hence supplier II is to be selected.]

Exercises on ascertaining purchase price

2. A small factory purchases different types of materials for Rs. 80,000. After sorting them out the selling price is recorded against each as shown below:

Category *A* 6,000 kgs selling price per unit is Rs. 8.

Category *B* 4,000 kgs selling price per unit is Rs. 6.

Category *C* 7,000 kgs selling price per unit is Rs. 4

Find out the purchase rate per unit of each category of the materials presuming that all categories yield the same rate of profit.

[**Answer:** Purchase Rates of A = Rs. 6.40, B = Rs. 4.80, C = Rs. 3.20]

3. The following quotation is received from a supplier in respect of Material A.

		Rate per kg.
Lot Price –	100 units	5.00
–	500 units	4.50
–	1,000 units	4.00

Trade discount 20% and cash discount 5% if payment is made within 15 days. One container is required for every 100 units of the materials and containers are charged at Rs. 10 each but credited Rs. 9, if returned within 3 months.

Transport charges for order	Rs. 50
Storage charges	Rs. 15

Calculate the material cost for 500 units and per unit cost of materials when the purchaser decides to by 500 units of the materials.

[**Answer:** Assuming that containers are returned within 3 months and cash discount not availed the purchase price amounts to Rs. 1,870 for 500 units and Rs. 3.74 per units of material.]

4. A consignment was received by a small business containing four types of materials. The invoice reveals the following.

		Rs.
Material *A* –	2,000 litres @ Rs. 2 per litre	4,000.00
Material *B* –	1,000 litres @ Rs. 3 per litre	3,000.00
Material *C* –	1,500 litres @ Rs. 4 per litre	6,000.00
Material *D* –	500 litres @ Rs. 4.50 per litre	2,250.00

Insurance	152.50
Freight paid by buyer	1,000
Expenses incurred by the buyer	1,600
Tax paid by the supplier	610

Loss due to breakage was recorded as follows:

Material *A*	– 120 litres,	Material *B*	– 20 litres
Material *C*	– 45 litres,	Material *D*	– 10 litres

It has been a policy of the materials management to keep a further provision of 10% for evaporation. Calculate the rate at which these should be priced when issued to various departments.

[Answer: Apportioning insurance and taxes on the basis of value of materials and freight and other expenses' on the basis of number of unit, the issue prices are A–3.05. B–4.11, C–5.36, D–5.88]

❑❑❑

CHAPTER 4

Materials Cost—Storekeeping

OBJECTIVES OF STOREKEEPING

Storekeeping is that aspect of materials management which is concerned with the physical storage of materials. Storekeeping is essentially a service function and as such it should aim at providing this service efficiently and effectively at a minimum cost. The main objectives of storekeeping are as follows:

1. Easy identification of materials: Identification of materials become very difficult especially when varieties of materials are bought in bulk quantities. Unless they are sorted out and stored properly identifying the materials will pose a problem. Production will be delayed to the extent of identification and its issue.

2. To prepare purchase requisitions: By seeing the quantity of materials reaching the reorder level, it is possible to replenish the exhausting materials by requesting the purchase manager to arrange for the purchase of materials. So the danger in the stoppage of production can be overcome by timely purchase of materials.

3. Safe keeping of materials: To ensure the safety of all types of materials it is essential to store the materials. Proper storage of materials also facilitates quick issue of materials to various production departments.

4. To maintain store records: The object of maintaining store records is to know the quantity of materials on hand, slow moving and fast moving, dormant and obsolete materials so that prompt action can be taken in respect of each of these materials.

5. Co-ordination with other departments: Co-ordination of storage department with other departments is necessary to know the exact requirements of material and their specifications, so that only required quantity and quality of materials can be procured.

6. Store verification: To exercise control over materials stock verification is necessary.

IMPORTANCE OF STOREKEEPING

(*a*) Proper maintenance of stores will help the storekeeper to know the actual quantity of materials available in storeroom. On the other hand, if the materials are not properly stored it does not help in assessing the exact requirements of materials.

Whereas those materials which are already available are initiated for purchasing again and again the one which must be bought may go unnoticed by the storekeeper.

(*b*) Systematic arrangement of stores help in easy location of materials. Delay in the process of issue of materials can be avoided once materials are easily located. In fact, a store item 'misplaced' is a store item 'lost' for all practical purposes.

(*c*) By submitting frequent reports regarding the stock position of materials it facilitates the top level management to formulate purchase policies.

(*d*) Losses arising from theft, can be avoided by proper storage of materials.

ESSENTIALS OF GOOD STOREKEEPING

Storekeeping is both an art and a science. It is an art as it involves the day-to-day receipt, storage and issue of materials. It is a science, as it involves recording the stores transactions as per the prescribed principles and rules. Good storekeeping results from experienced and enthusiastic storekeeper and his assistants. The essentials of good storekeeping are outlined below:

(*a*) Allot a proper place for every item of store.

(*b*) Keep every item of store in the allotted place.

(*c*) Maintain proper records of stores and keep them up-to-date.

(*d*) To issue the materials promptly to various departments.

(*e*) Storing the materials in an orderly fashion.

(*f*) Protecting materials against damage and pilferage.

(*g*) Issue oldest materials first.

(*h*) Classify and codify the materials for easy identification.

(*i*) Adequate space must be provided in between rack and almirah for easy movement of store's assistants.

(*j*) Undertake continuous verification of materials.

LOCATION AND LAYOUT OF STORES DEPARTMENT

The selection of appropriate site for establishing a storeroom is known as location of stores. The ideal location of storeroom must be such that the movement of the materials from the receiving department to the storeroom and from the storeroom to the production departments is minimum. Further the ideal location of store is that where the most efficient transportation and material handling equipment could be utilised. The following storage location factors should be taken into account in order to select the best locality:

(*a*) **Materials classification:** Materials of the same classification may be stored at a place irrespective of differences in size, weight and place of consumption. For example, one area may be designated for raw materials, sundry supplies and component parts: another area may be designated for semi-finished products and another for finished stock.

(*b*) **Similarity of materials:** Items of similar size, shape and weight may be stored together although they may be classified differently or required at different production departments. For example, all small items may be kept in one place and bulk items in another place.

(*c*) **Materials handling consideration:** Materials requiring similar handling equipment may be grouped together. For example, those materials which are to be moved by trucks alone may be stored separately. Similarly liquids which are to be specially measured and moved by trolleys may be placed together.

(*d*) **Character of materials to be stored:** The character of the materials to be stored affects the location of storage areas. Materials that are not damaged by weather can be stored in a shed. Materials subject to corrosion must be stored in dry place. Materials whose character is altered by high temperature must be stored in cold storage room. Finished goods which are damaged by dust must be stored in dust proof bins.

(*e*) **The quantity, weight and bulk of materials:** The quantity of each of the materials to be stored must be carefully considered in determining the location of storeroom. When the quantities of materials are known, the weight and bulk of materials can be determined and required space can be allotted.

(*f*) **Miscellaneous factors**

(*i*) Security aspect to prevent theft and explosion of certain types of materials.

(*ii*) The storeroom may be located near the main road, railway stations or wharf to facilitate easy handling of materials.

(*iii*) Heavy and bulky items should be stored near the departments using them.

(*iv*) Location of doors, size of platforms, etc., should suit the storeroom.

(*v*) Fast moving items should be stored near the point of issue.

Layout of Stores

Stores layout refers to physical arrangement of storage space facilities so as to provide for most efficient receipt, storage and issue of materials. The arrangement of storeroom includes arrangement of space for storing materials, records and files and materials handling equipments. The basic principles of good stores layout are:

1. The layout of stores must reduce (*a*) the distance of moving the stores item, (*b*) storage equipment, (*c*) storage spaced and (*d*) handling cost.
2. The stores layout must be flexible enough to allow for changed condition and future expansion.
3. Free flow of materials into and outside the storeroom, *i.e.*, the principle of minimum distance is to be followed.
4. Provision of different storage facility for different types of materials.
5. Facilitate better supervision of stores.

A well planned layout offers the following advantages:

(*a*) Full utilisation of storage space.

(*b*) Easy accessibility to all the materials.

(*c*) More security of all materials and stores records.

(*d*) Lesser time to receive, issue and store the materials.

(*e*) Minimum spoilage, damage and other kinds of losses.

ORGANISATION OF STORES DEPARTMENT

The organisation of storekeeping department depends upon (*a*) design and layout of the factory, (*b*) the degree of centralisation required, (c) need for departmental storeroom, and (*d*) frequency of issues of materials. Generally, speaking storekeeping department can be organised under (1) Centralised System, (2) Decentralised System and (3) Imprest System.

1. Centralised System: In centralised system all the materials are received and issued from one stores department. The advantages of this system according to *Wheldon* is outlined below:

(a) Economy in staff and concentration of experts in one department.
(*b*) Reduced clerical costs and economy in records and stationery.
(*c*) Better supervision is possible.
(*d*) Staff become acquainted with different types of stores, which is very useful, if any one is absent from work.
(*e*) Better layout of stores.
(*f*) Inventory check facilitated.
(*g*) Stocks are kept to a minimum, thus reducing storage space.
(*h*) Fewer obsolete articles.
(*i*) The amount of capital invested in stock is minimised.
(*j*) Better security arrangements can be made.

The disadvantages of this system are as follows:

(*a*) When centralised storeroom is located far away from other departments it involves high transportation cost.
(*b*) The supply of materials to distant production department may cause delay and inconvenience.
(*c*) Breakdown of transport or hold-ups in storeroom will hamper production.
(*d*) The chance of risk of loss on account of natural calamities such as occurrence of fire, flood, etc., are high.

2. Decentralised System: Under this system, a separate storeroom is located adjacent to the production department from where materials can be drawn. This system is particularly suitable where the plants are dispersed over wider geographical areas. The disadvantages of centralised store system can be overcome by adopting this method.

3. Imprest System: This system is followed in order to minimise materials handling expenses. Under this system, a sub-store is located near production department. The exact requirements of stores for each production department is decided in advance and so much of materials are kept on hand in the beginning. At the end of the month, the sub-storekeeper will obtain the quantity of materials required so as to replenish the exhausted stock of materials. The advantages of this system are as follows:

(*a*) It facilitates personal supervision of materials by the sub-storekeeper.
(*b*) It reduces transport cost involved during frequent issue of materials.
(*c*) It facilitates prompt issue of materials.
(*d*) Space in the main storeroom can be saved.
(*e*) Risk due to fire is spread over a number of departments.

The disadvantages of this system are:

(a) It lacks centralised control over materials.

(b) The cost of storage is more with the involvement of more sub-storekeepers and other storekeeping expenses.

(c) Additional space is to be provided for every sub-store.

DUTIES AND RESPONSIBILITIES OF STOREKEEPER

The stores department is headed by a competent authority known as storekeeper. He takes care of the stores and keeps a watchful eye on the movement of both men and materials with a view to keep the whole organisation moving. The extent of functions to be performed by him varies depending upon the nature, size and composition of the stores department. However, a good storekeeper must possess the following requisities:

(a) He must be hard working.

(b) He must be honest.

(c) He must have knowledge of accounts.

(d) He must possess leadership abilities so as to command his subordinates to carry out storekeeping functions efficiently.

(e) He must possess an academic qualification which depend upon the type of industry. For example, the storekeeper of an engineering storeroom should be a science graduate.

Duties of Storekeeper

(a) To prepare and issue purchase requisition note for such types of materials which have reached reorder level.

(b) To receive the purchased materials from receiving department.

(c) To enter the particulars of materials in the bin card.

(d) To store materials in their appropriate place for easy identification.

(e) To issue the materials to production departments on the basis of, "materials requisition note".

(f) To take back the surplus materials returned by production departments.

(g) To undertake stock verification of materials.

(h) To report on scrap, waste, surplus, obsolete materials to management for taking necessary action.

(i) To equip the storeroom with material handling equipments for easy and economical handling.

(j) To prevent unauthorised persons from entering into the storeroom.

Responsibilities of Storekeeper

(a) The storekeeper is responsible for the materials which he receives. Therefore, at the time of receiving the materials into the storeroom he must verify the quantity, quality and the specification of materials.

(b) He is responsible for the timely issue of materials. So the storekeeper has to classify and codify the materials and store them at appropriate place.

(*c*) He is responsible for shortage of materials on account of theft, damage and spoilage.

(*d*) It is the responsibility of the storekeeper to work in close coordination with purchase, production and accounts departments for the smooth functioning of the factory.

(*e*) He is responsible for the negligence of his as well as his subordinates duties.

STOREKEEPING RECORDS

The need for keeping stock records are as follows:

(*a*) To know the amount of materials without depending on physical stock taking.

(*b*) To know the reasons for the discrepancies in the balance of materials as shown by different stock records and the actual balance of materials.

(*c*) To know the quantity and time at which such materials are to be bought.

(*d*) To facilitate valuation of materials.

The following documents are used in recording the sotres items:

(*a*) **Material receipt book:** This book records the receipt of materials by the storekeeper in a chronological order. This book forms the basis of stores accounting. Before the materials are stored in bins, they are verified in respect of quantity and quality. If there is any shortage or damage of materials, the storekeeper prepares accordingly a shortage or damage report.

(*b*) **Bin card:** A bin card is made out of a thick paper and is meant for recording the receipt, issue and balance of materials in stores. The bin card is attached to the bin or rack in which materials are stocked. It enables to know the quantity of materials on hand, whenever materials are issued or when received from suppliers or returned by the departments as surplus stock. A bin card helps storekeeper to prepare purchase requisition to replenish the exhausted materials. It also helps in locating the discrepancy when physical stock verification is undertaken and the balance compared with bin card. It contains particulars such as bin number, description of materials, code number of materials, maximum, minimum, reorder and danger levels and the columns for the quantity of materials received, issued and in balance. The specimen of a Bin Card is given below.

KMA–BANGALORE

Bin Card

Description ....

Group .... Units .... Bin card No. ....

Materials Code ....

Location ....

Max. Level ....

Min. Level ....

Order Level ....

Date	*Ref. No.*	*Receipts (qty.)*	*Issues (qty.)*	*Balance (qty.)*	*Remarks*

Fig. 4.1 *Bin card*

Problem-1

The Kamani Metal and Alloys Co. furnishes the following information to you. Draw up the Bin Card (Number 32)

2008 Jan,	1,	Opening balance	200	Tons
	2,	Issued on requisition no. 10	57	Tons
	4,	Issued on requisition no. 11	83	Tons
	5,	Received from supplier by Challan no. 74	120	Tons
	8,	Issued on requisition no. 12	92	Tons
	12,	Issued on requisition no. 13	30	Tons
	17,	Received from supplier by Challan no. 76	100	Tons
	24,	Issued on requisition no. 14	69	Tons
	28,	Issued on requisition no. 15	29	Tons
	30,	Received from supplier by Challan no. 80	125	Tons
	31,	Issued on requisition no. 16	85	Tons

Examination by stock verifier on Jan. 27, 2008 revealed a shortage of 5 tons. The maximum quantity of stock permissible at any time is 200 tons and the minimum 50 tons. The ordering level is 100 tons.

Solution:

Bin Card

Name of Materials. **Steel** **Bin Card No. : 32**
Unit **Tons** **Max. Qty. : 200 Tons**
Min. Qty. : 50 Tons
Ordering Level : 100 Tons

Date	*Receipts*		*Issues*		*Balance*	*Remarks*
	Ch. No	*Qty.*	*Requisition No.*	*Qty.*		
2008 Jan.1	–	–	–	–	200	
2	–	–	10	57	143	
4	–	–	11	83	60	
5	74	120	–	–	180	
8	–	–	12	92	88	
12	–	–	13	30	58	
17	76	100	–	–	158	
24	–	–	14	69	89	
27	–	–	–	5	84	Shortage
28	–	–	15	29	55	
30	80	125	–	–	180	
31	–	–	16	85	105	

(*c*) **Stores ledger card:** A stores ledger card is a record of materials showing receipts, issues and balance of materials both in quantities and values. It is maintained in stores accounting section and is outside the control of storekeeper. A specimen of stores ledger card is given below.

STORES LEDGER CARD

Name of the Materials ....
Code No. of Material ....

Maximum Level ....
Minimum Level ....
Reorder Level ....
Danger Level ....

	Receipts				Issues				Balance		
Date	PRN	Qty.	Rate	Amount	MRN	Qty	Rate	Amount	Qty.	Rate	Amount

Fig. 4.2. *Stores ledger card.*

A stores ledger card differs from a bin card in the following respects:

Bin Card	*Stores Ledger Card*
1. It is maintained in the storeroom.	1. It is maintained in the cost accounting department.
2. It contains particulars of materials only in terms of quantities.	2. It contains particulars of materials both in terms of quantity and value.
3. Entries in the bin card is made by storekeeper or his assistants.	3. Entries in the stores ledger card is made by the stores clerks or stores accountant.
4. Entries are made on the basis of actual quantity received or issued.	4. Entries are supported by materials received note, materials requisition note, etc.
5. Inter-departmental transactions do not appear in a bin card.	5. Inter-departmental transfer of materials are recorded in the stores ledger card.
6. Entries are posted before the transactions takes place.	6. Entries are posted after the transactions takes place.
7. Entries are posted individually.	7. Entries are posted periodically.

(*d*) **Stock verification sheet:** This record is prepared at the time of stock taking in the storeroom. After physical verification is over, they may be valued to incorporate the value of materials to record in the Balance Sheet.

Two-Bin System

Under this system, a certain quantity of materials termed as reserve stock is set apart which is not used for daily use. Under this system, two bins are used. The first bin is termed as "running bin" which serves the purpose of day-to-day issues. The second bin which is termed as "reserve bin" is set aside with a certain quantity of materials. The reserve stock is set apart by taking into account the time taken by the supplier to deliver the materials. When the materials in the running bin exhaust, the materials of reserve bin is used for issuing them. This serves as a caution for the storekeeper to make immediate arrangement to prepare and place a purchase requisition for procuring the required materials. However, the reserve bin should be kept rotated, *i.e.*, old materials must be issued and reserve should be created out of fresh stock.

MATERIALS HANDLING

Material handling refers to the study of the movement of materials from one place to another place within the factory. The importance of materials handling cannot be underestimated in spite of the fact that mechanical equipments are largely being used. It has been estimated that one out of ten in labour force is involved in handling materials and in a typical factory, fifty tons of product must be handled to produce one ton of finished product. In some factories at least one-quarter of the cost is attributable to the handling of the materials.

Objectives of Material Handling

(*a*) **Reduce the cost for each part handled:** The main objective of material handling is to reduce the overall costs of materials handling by reducing the number of handling involved. But the overall material handling costs can be reduced only if the unit cost, *i.e.,* cost for each part handled are reduced. This approach requires that costs of handling be allocated to its component parts that are moved.

(*b*) **Reduce the manufacturing-cycle time:** Effective handling of materials from the stage of receipt to the stage of completion involves reduction in production time. By means of speedling up or handling over short distance it results in the reduction of inventory cost.

(*c*) **Contribute towards a better control of the flow of goods:** In continuous manufacturing factories, where all the process of production are predetermined and where production of one process depends upon another process, material handling plan can effect considerable amount of savings in flow of materials. Thus, the production control can be exercised more efficiently.

(*d*) **Provide for improved working conditions and greater safety:** The Factories Act requires adherence to safe handling practices. Safe handling of materials also reduces industrial accidents. This reduces the tangible saving in the form of reduced insurance rates and an intangible saving in the form of improved employee movable.

(*e*) **Lesser rejection of goods:** Handling of materials carefully to a large extent reduces breakages and damages of the finished product. This is more so in case of fragile goods, such as glass and ceramics. Excess damages and breakages add to the increased cost of production and so a careful material handling plan is necessary.

(*f*) **Increases storage capacity:** A well-designed material handling plan saves to a considerable extent storage space in factories.

(*g*) **Increased productivity at lower manufacturing cost:** A material handling system improves productivity by moving materials in the fastest, most efficient and economical way possible.

Factors Affecting the Selection of Material Handling Equipment

The following factors are to be considered when choosing material handling equipment:

(*a*) **Types of materials to be handled:** This include size, weight and strength of the material to be handled.

(*b*) **Type of production:** For the sake of material handling purpose, the type of production can be considered as continuous production or batch production. If continuous production is envisaged, conveyor belts and overhead conveyor might be suitable. In case of batch production, powered truck and portable conveyors are useful.

(*c*) **Factory building:** The determining factors are number of floors, provision of lifts, heights of ceiling, etc.

(*d*) **Handling costs:** It is difficult to assess material handling costs. However, a full study of cost should be made not only of labour but also of handling equipments and containers.

(*e*) **Adaptability:** The carrying capacity of the equipment should fit the material handling problem. Whenever possible the equipment should have flexibility to handle more than one material.

(*f*) **Speed:** Rapidity of movement of material within the limits of production process should be considered.

(*g*) **Space requirements:** The space required to install or operate materials handling equipment is an important factor in selecting the material handling equipment.

(*h*) **Supervision required:** This refers to the degree of automaticity designed into the equipment.

(*i*) **Ease of maintenance:** Equipment selected should be easily maintained at reasonable cost.

(*j*) **Environment:** Equipment selected must conform to any environmental regulation.

Advantages of Mechanised Handling

1. The manufacturing-cycle time can be reduced by the elimination of non-productive time in the manufacturing process. Research has indicated that at least 30 per cent of the total time required in manufacturing is consumed by material handling.
2. Human fatigue in lifting and handling manually can be reduced and in some cases eliminated.
3. Idle time can be brought to a minimum. Most of the waiting for work that occurs where intermittent and non-mechanical delivery of material is involved can be eliminated by equipment that ensures a steady constant flow of materials.
4. The productivity of employees working on the product is increased by a reduction of time they would otherwise spend in handling materials.
5. Increased safety of handling results where materials are not 'man-handled'.
6. Storage space is conserved, particularly where mechanical equipment is used to stock materials vertically.
7. Non-productive indirect labour can be released for more productive, direct-labour activities.
8. Certain types of mechanised handling equipment tied in with automatic machine controls open up vast vistas in the field of automation.

Materials Handling Cost

The cost of material handling arises from two sources *viz.*, (1) the cost of acquiring and maintaining equipment, and (2) the cost of operating the system. The material handling cost can be classified on the basis of variability and character of costs. This is shown under the following chart:

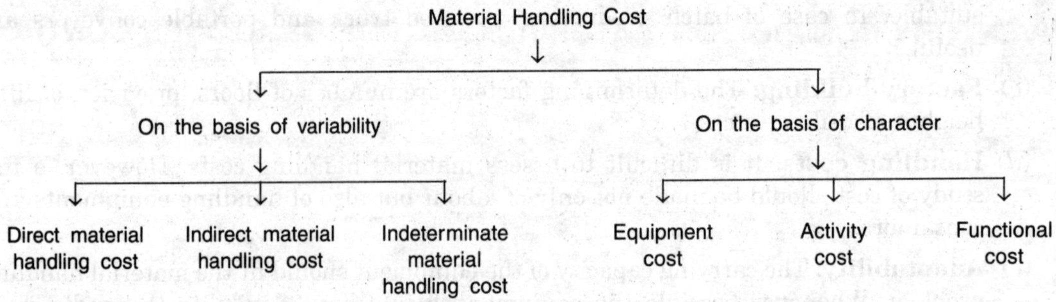

Fig. 4.3 *Chart showing material handling cost*

On the basis of variability material handling cost can be classified into the following types:

(*a*) **Direct material handling cost:** Direct costs are those commonly associated with the operation of material handling equipment. Both equipment and manpower costs are included in this category. Some examples of direct material handling costs are depreciation, interest on investment, wages of operating personal, fuel and power, etc.

(*b*) **Indirect material handling cost:** Indirect material handling costs are those associated with the investment. Sometimes this cost also include operation cost of an equipment but not in direct proportion. Examples of indirect materials handling costs are rent for space occupied, repair parts, etc.

(*c*) **Indeterminate material handling cost:** Indeterminate material handling costs are those which cannot be precisely determined or which are not known in advance or which do not lend themselves to the determination of a definite cost figure. This category might include some of the following costs, safety, clerical costs, plants for expansion.

On the basis of character of costs, material handling cost can be classified into the following types of costs:

(*a*) **Equipment cost:** Equipment costs are those related to the actual capital investment.

(*b*) **Activity cost:** Activity costs are those expenditures required by a specified handling activity.

(*c*) **Functional cost:** Functional costs are concerned with such organisational units as receiving, warehousing and the like.

Suggestions to Reduce Material Handling Costs

In order to reduce the material handling cost the following suggestions are made.

(*a*) Keep all handling at a minimum.

(*b*) Handle as many pieces in one unit as is practical.

(*c*) Provide large, heavy or bulky objects with handling aids such as hooks.

(*d*) Always consider handling problems in analysing and designing the overall production system.

(*e*) Modify existing building facilities to permit full use of available capacity.

(*f*) Wherever possible manufacturing processing should take place while the product is being moved.

(*g*) Move the greatest weight or bulk material to the least possible distance.

INVENTORY CONTROL OR MATERIAL CONTROL OR STORES CONTROL

Material control can be defined as the systematic control concerned with procuring, storing and using of materials so as to minimise wastage and losses and at the same time avoiding excess investment in materials.

Objectives of Material Control

1. **To ensure continuity in production:** The success of an undertaking depends upon the continuity in production. Stoppage of production has adverse impact not only in terms of restarting of production as in the case of furnaces but also in the cancellation of orders by the customers. Therefore, care must be taken to ensure that production is not stopped for want of raw materials and other sundry supplies.
2. **To purchase requisite quality of materials:** The quality of finished goods depend upon the quality of raw materials used. Any purchase of inferior quality of materials lead to sub-standard production of goods which are likely to be rejected by customers. At the same time, a very superior quality of materials should also be avoided as it may entail payment of high prices. This may lead to the increased cost of production and consequently increased selling price, which is also likely to be rejected by the customers.
3. **To eliminate losses and wastages:** Materials are subjected to rust, dust, dirt, moisture. Sometimes they are also lost due to theft and careless handling of materials. Hence, it must be the endeavour of material management to investigate the causes for the losses and wastages of materials and take prompt action to eliminate such losses.
4. **To avoid overstocking of materials:** Overstocking of materials lead to incurring of the following expenses:
   (*a*) *Capital cost.* Any excess purchase of materials result in the sinking of capital in the purchase of materials which could otherwise yield a higher rate of return, if invested in profitable investment.
   (*b*) *Storage cost.* Storage or excess quantity of materials require incurrence of additional amount of rent, heating, lighting, etc.
   (*c*) *Equipment cost.* Additional equipments such as bins, racks, etc., are required to store overstocked materials.
   (*d*) *Personal cost.* Personal costs such as salaries and wages are to be paid for additional staff recruited for storing, stock verification security, etc.
   (*e*) *Obsolescence.* The higher the stock of materials, higher is the chances of obsolescence because they are kept in storeroom for longer duration.
   (*f*) Loss on account of deterioration and evaporation in case of certain types of liquid materials.
5. **To avoid understocking of materials:** The understocking of materials results in the following consequences:
   (*a*) There is a danger in the stoppage of production for want of materials.
   (*b*) Stoppage in production results in delayed deliveries thereby leading to cancellation of orders.
   (*c*) While there may not be any revenue earned during the period of stoppage in production, it involves incurring of fixed expenses such as wages, rent etc.

6. **Purchase at reasonable price:** Purchase of materials must be always at a reasonably low price. Otherwise a large amount of money is lost in purchasing the materials. However, quality should not be sacrificed at the cost of lower price.
7. **Knowledge about the sources of materials:** A good system of material control must facilitate ready availability of information about various sources of suppliers, so that the best terms of purchase can be resorted to.

ESSENTIALS OF MATERIAL CONTROL

Buyers and Holmes in their book *Principles of Cost Accountancy* have summarised the essential requirements of material control as listed below:

(*a*) Co-ordination between the departments involved in the buying, receiving, inspection and storage of materials and in accounting for them.

(*b*) Centralisation of purchasing under the authority of a competitive buyer.

(*c*) The planning and programming of materials requirements.

(*d*) Standardisation and simplification of materials.

(*e*) The proper classification and codification of materials.

(*f*) The use of standard forms for orders, requisition, etc., upon which written and signed instructions are given.

(*g*) Control by budget of material and equipment purchases.

(*h*) The operation of internal check to ensure that all transactions involving materials and equipment are checked by reliable and independent officials.

(*i*) The storage of all materials is well-planned and porperly designated subject to adequate safeguards and supervision.

(*j*) The operations of efficient stock control procedures and records.

(*k*) Adequate records to control materials during production and the quantities manufactured for stock.

(*l*) Regular reports to management upon purchases of materials, issues, stocks and in particular obsolete stocks, returns to suppliers, spoilage and waste, etc.

TECHNIQUES OF MATERIAL CONTROL

The important techniques used to exercise control over materials are as follows:

1. ABC analysis.
2. Level setting.
3. Economic order quantity.
4. Inventory turnover.
5. Stock checking and stock taking—Perpetual inventory system.
6. Input-output ratio analysis.
7. Classification and codification of materials.
8. Miscellaneous techniques.
9. New techniques of material control.

1. ABC Analysis or Selective Inventory Control: The concept of ABC analysis was coined by Pareto, an Italian philosopher in the nineteenth century, who illustrated graphically the fact that most of the wealth in Italy was owned by a small proportion of the population. This analysis is based on the principle "Vital few—Trivial many". On an analysis of materials consumption in all factories it is revealed that about 80 per cent of total value of issues accounts for 20 per cent of the items. So this technique is sometimes expressed 80 : 20 rule. When this techniques is used as a tool of material control, the materials are classified into three categories, designated as 'A' category materials, 'B' category materials and 'C' category materials. The features of such materials can be stated as under:

Category 'A' items—Small in number, high in usage value—the 'vital few' from a financial point of view.

Category 'B' items—Medium number, medium usage value—'normal items'.

Category 'C' items—High number, low usage value—the 'trivial many'.

This is illustrated in the following graph.

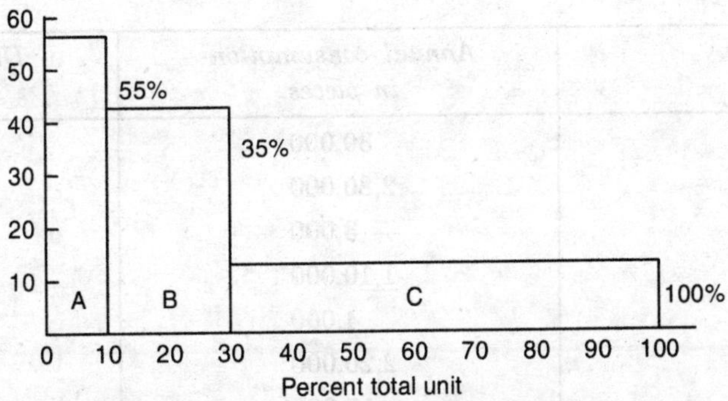

Fig. 4.4 *Graph showing ABC analysis.*

According to this technique, a strict control is exercised over 'A' category material, perhaps under the supervision of an experienced person, a moderate control is exercised over 'B' category materials and relatively lesser degree of control over 'C' category materials. The object of carrying out ABC analysis is to develop policy guidelines for selective controls. Normally once ABC analysis has been done, the following broad policy guidelines can be established in respect of each category.

From the point of view	*'A' Items*	*'B' Items*	*'C' Items*
1. Degree of control	Very strict control	Moderate control	Low control
2. Safety stock	No safety stock	Low-safety stock	High-safety stock
3. Ordering	Frequent ordering	Once in 3 weeks	Bulk ordering once in 6 months
4. Periodicity of control	Weekly control statements	Monthly control reports	Quarterly control reports
5. Value analysis	Rigorous value analysis	Moderate value analysis	Minimum value analysis
6. Forecasting	Accurate forecasting and planning	Estimate based on past data and present plans	Rough estimates
7. Lead time	Maximum efforts to reduce lead time	Moderate efforts	Minimum efforts

Advantages of ABC Analysis

(*a*) A strict control is exercised on costlier items of materials while exercising moderate control over less costlier materials.

(*b*) Investment on materials are judiciously utilised.

(*c*) Storage cost also will be less as only the required quantity of materials alone are bought.

(*d*) Quick purchase of materials can be ensured by concentrating on fewer items that are required at one time.

(*e*) It is based on the principle of control by exception which gives best results especially when resources and staff are less.

Problem-2

The following information is known about a group of items. Classify the materials, as A, B and C classification.

Model no.	*Annual consumption in pieces*	*Unit price in paise*
501	30,000	10
502	2,80,000	15
503	3,000	10
504	1,10,000	5
505	4,000	5
506	2,20,000	10
507	15,000	5
508	80,000	5
509	60,000	15
510	8,000	10

Solution:

Statement showing value of materials consumed and its relative ranks

Model no.	*Annual consumption*	*Unit price*	*Value of annual consumption*	*Ranks based on value*
501	30,000	0.10	3,000	6
502	2,80,000	0.15	42,000	1
503	3,000	0.10	300	9
504	1,10,000	0.05	5,500	4
505	4,000	0.05	200	10
506	2,20,000	0.10	22,000	2
507	15,000	0.05	750	8
508	80,000	0.05	4,000	5
509	60,000	0.15	9,000	3
510	8,000	0.10	800	7
Total	8,10,000		87,550	

STATEMENT OF ABC CLASSIFICATION

Category		Model no.	Percentage items	Annual consumption value	Percentage to total value	Rank
A		502	10%	42,000	48%	1
		506	10%	22,000	25%	2
	Total		20%	64,000	73%	
B		509	10%	9,000	10%	3
		504	10%	5,500	6%	4
		508	10%	4,000	5%	5
	Total		30%	18,500	21%	
C		501	10%	3,000	3.4%	6
		510	10%	800	1.0%	7
		507	10%	750	1.0%	8
		503	10%	300	1.4%	9
		505	10%	200	0.2%	10
	Total		50%	5,050	6.00%	
	Grand Total		100%	87,550	100%	

Problem-3

A factory uses 4,000 varieties of inventory. In terms of inventory holding and inventory usage, the following information is compiled.

No of varieties of inventory	*%*	*% value of inventory holding (average)*	*% of inventory usage (in end product)*
3875	96.875	20	5
110	2.750	30	10
15	0.375	50	85
4000	100.00	100	100

Classify the items of inventory as per ABC analysis with reasons.

(C.A. Inter November, 1998)

Solution:

Classification of the items of inventory as per ABC analysis:

1. **15 number of varieties of inventory items should be classified as 'A' category items because of the following reasons:**
   - (*a*) **They constitute 0.375% of total number of varieties of inventory items handled by stores of the factory, which is minimum as per given classification in the table.**
   - (*b*) **50% of total use value of inventory holding (average) which is maximum according to the given table.**

(c) Highest consumption of about 85% of inventory usage (in end-product).

2. 110 number of varieties of inventory items, should be classified as 'B' category item because of the following reasons:
   (a) They constitute 2.75% of total number of varieties of inventory items handled by stores of factory.
   (b) They require moderate investment of about 30% of total use value of inventory holding (average).
   (c) Moderate consumption of about 10% of inventory usage (in end-product).
3. 3,875 number of varieties of inventory items, should be classified as 'C'category items because of the following reasons:
   (a) They constitute 96.875% of total varieties of inventory items handled by stores of the factory.
   (b) They require investment of 20% of total use value of inventory holding.
   (c) Minimum consumption, *i.e.,* about 5% of inventory usage (in end-product).

2. Level Setting: This technique of material control is helpful in avoiding overstocking and understocking of materials in storeroom. The stock levels are fixed by the management and it is the duty of storekeeper to observe them. The various stock levels commonly fixed are as follows.

(a) ***Maximum level:*** It is the level beyond which storage of raw materials are not allowed to go. The main purpose of this level is to avoid blocking up of capital unnecessarily on materials. The following factors guide in fixing up this level:
   (i) Rate of consumption of materials.
   (ii) Time necessary to obtain new supplies.
   (iii) Finance—if stocks are unnecessarily high, capital is locked up which could probably be otherwise employed.
   (iv) Storage cost.
   (v) Possibility of loss by evaporation, deterioration, etc.
   (vi) Extent to which price fluctuates.
   (vii) Risk of changing specification and obsolescence.
   (viii) Seasonal considerations as to both price and availability of supplies.
   (ix) Economic order quantity.
   (x) Rules framed by the government for importing raw materials.

(b) ***Minimum level:*** It is the level below which materials should not be allowed to fall. This level serves as safety stock and is not generally used for issue purposes. As soon as this level is reached, it indicates the possibility of stoppage in production unless quick arrangement is made for further purchases of materials. Hence, the storekeeper and purchase manager have to give the topmost priority for the acquisition of new supplies. The following factors are to be considered while fixing up this level:
   (i) Rate of consumption of the materials.
   (ii) Time necessary to obtain delivery of materials.
   (iii) Nature of materials, for example, for purchase of special materials against customer's specific order, no minimum level is necessary.

(*c*) ***Danger level:*** This level is fixed in between minimum level and nil stock or zero stock. This level is fixed for such types of materials which are used against more than one order or product. As and when this level is reached, the storekeeper normally does not issue materials unless authorised by the production control department as to which job or product is to get the priority for the use of these items. This level is particularly fixed to control materials during the period of emergency so that urgent and priority orders are not held up.

(*d*) ***Reorder level:*** This is the level on reaching of which a fresh order is prepared and placed with a supplier. This level is fixed in between maximum level and minimum level. This level is fixed after considering the following factors:

(*i*) Maximum usage
(*ii*) Delivery time
(*iii*) Rate of consumption
(*iv*) Economic order quantity.

Lead Time and Delivery Time

In connection with fixation of various levels for materials, the term 'lead time' refers to the time required for the whole procurement procedure and delivery time refers to the period which is required for execution of orders by the suppliers, *i.e.*, from the time the order reaches the supplier till the commodities are despatched to the purchaser.

Problem-4

Compute various stock levels from the following data.

Normal consumption	300 units per day
Maximum consumption	420 units per day
Minimum consumption	240 units per day
Reorder quantity	3,600 units
Reorder period	10 to 15 days
Normal reorder period	12 days

(*Nagarjuna University, M. Com., March 1992*)

Solution:

Reorder level = Maximum usage × Maximum reorder period
= 420 × 15 = 6,300 units

Minimum level = Reorder level – (Normal usage × Normal reorder period)
= 6,300 – (300 × 12)
= 6,300 – 3,600 = 2,700 units

Maximum level = (Reorder level + Reorder quantity) – (Minimum usage × Minimum reorder period)
= (6,300 + 3,600) – (240 × 10)
= 9,900 – 2,400 = 7,500 units

$$\text{Average stock level} = \frac{\text{Minimum level} + \text{Maximum Level}}{2}$$

$$= \frac{2{,}700 + 7{,}500}{2}$$

$$= \frac{10,200}{2} = 5,100 \text{ units}$$

Problem-5

Calculate Reorder level, minimum stock level, maximum stock level and average stock level from the following information.

Normal usage	—	300 Units per week
Maximum usage	—	450 Units per week
Minimum usage	—	150 Units per week
Reorder period	—	4 to 6 weeks
Reorder quantity	—	2,400 units (*University of Madras, B.Com., March 1997*)

Solution:

1. Reorder level = Maximum usage × Maximum reorder period
   = 450 × 6 = 2,700 units per week
2. Minimum stock level = Reorder level – (Normal usage × Normal reorder period)
   = 2,700 – (300 × 5)
   = 2,700 – 1,500 = 1,200 units per week
3. Maximum stock level = (Reorder level + Reorder quantity) – (Minimum usage × Minimum reorder period)
   = (2,700 + 2,400) – (150 × 4)
   = 5,100 – 600 = 4,500 units per week
4. Average stock level = Minimum level + $\frac{1}{2}$ (Reorder quantity)
   = 1,200 + $\frac{1}{2}$ × 2,400
   = 1,200 + 1,200 = 2,400 units per week

Problem-6

Two components A and B are used as follows:

(*a*) Reorder qunatity.

A	:	3,000 units
B	:	4,000 units

(*b*) Reorder period

A	:	4 to 6 weeks
B	:	2 to 4 weeks

(*c*) Normal usage	:	3,000 units per week each
(*d*) Minimum usage	:	1,500 units per week each
(*e*) Maximum usage	:	4,500 units per week each

You are required to calculate for each of the component (1) Reorder level, (2) Minimum level, (3) Maximum level, (4) Average stock level.

(*Sri Venkateshwara University, B. Com., April 1998*)

Solution:

1. Reorder level = Maximum usage × Maximum reorder period

A = 4,500 × 6 = 27,000 units per week

B = 4,500 × 4 = 18,000 units per week

2. Minimum level = Reorder level – (Normal usage × Average reorder period)

A = 27,000 – (3,000 × 5)

B = 27,000 – 15,000 = 12,000 units per week

= 18,000 – (3,000 × 3) = 9,000 units

3. Maximum level = (Reorder level + Reorder quantity) – (Minimum usage × Maximum reorder period

A = (27,000 + 3,000) – (1,500 × 4)

= 30,000 – 6,000 = 24,000 units per week

B = (18,000 + 4,000) – (1,500 × 2)

= 22,000 – 3,000 + 19,000 units per week

4. Average stock level $= \frac{\text{Minimum level} + \text{Maximum level}}{2}$

$$A = \frac{12,000+24,000}{2} = \frac{36,000}{2} = 18,000 \text{ units per week}$$

$$B = \frac{9,000+19,000}{2} = \frac{28,000}{2} = 14,000 \text{ units per week.}$$

Problem-7

Kerala producers furnish the following information regarding the requirements of material *x*, *y* and *z* in their production activity.

Raw materials	*Usage per unit of production (kgs.)*	*Reorder quantity (kgs.)*	*Price per kg. (Rs.)*	*Delivery period (weeks)*	*Order level (kg.)*	*Minimum level (kg.)*
X	20	20,000	1.00	1 to 3	16,000	—
Y	8	10,000	3.00	3 to 5	9,500	—
Z	12	20,000	1.50	2 to 4	—	4,000

Weekly production vary from 350 to 450 units averaging to 400 units. What would you expect the quantities of the following to be.

(*a*) Minimum stock level of *x*

(*b*) Maximum stock level of *y*

(*c*) Reorder stock level of *z*

(*d*) Average stock level of *x* (*Calicut University, M.Com., April 1992*)

Solution:

(*a*) Minimum level of *x* = Reorder level – (Average usage × Average delivery period)

= 16,000 – (400 × 20 × 2)

= 16,000 – 16,000 = 0

(*b*) Maximum level of y = (Reorder level + Reorder quantity) – (Minimum usage × Minimum reorder period)
= (9,500 + 10,000) – (350 × 8 × 3)
= 19,500 – 8,400 = 11,100 units

(*c*) Reorder level of z = Maximum usage × Maximum reorder period
= 450 × 12 × 4 = 21,600 units

(*d*) Average stock level of x = Minimum level + $\frac{1}{2}$ Reorder quantity

= 0 + $\frac{1}{2}$ × 20,000 = 10,000 units.

Problem-8

The following particulars are furnished by Kiran Stamping Ltd.

Month	*Budget consumption (in units)*	*Month*	*Budget consumption (in units)*
2000 Jan.	300	July	1,000
2000 Feb.	300	Aug.	1,000
2000 Mar.	500	Sept.	1,000
2000 Apr.	600	Oct.	900
2000 May	800	Nov.	600
2000 June	1,000	Dec.	400

Delivery period : 2 to 4 months
Reorder quantity : 1,000 units
Calculate : (1) Maximum level, (2) Minimum level, (3) Reorder level, (4) Average stock level using reorder quantity.

Solution:

1. Reorder level = Maximum consumption × Maximum delivery period
= 1,000 × 4 = 4,000 units

2. Minimum level = Reorder level – (Normal usage × Average reorder period)
= 4,000 – (700 × 3)
= 4,000 – 2,100 = 1,900 units

3. Maximum level = (Reorder level + Reorder quantity) – (Minimum usage × Minimum reorder period)
= (4,000 + 1,000) – (300 × 2)
= 5,000 – 600 = 4,400 units

4. Average stock level = Minimum level + $\frac{1}{2}$ reorder quantity

= 1,900 + $\frac{1}{2}$ × 1,000

= 1,900 + 500 = 2,400 units

Working Note:

Normal usage is calculated by the following formula:

$$\frac{\text{Total consumption per year}}{\text{Number of months in the year}} = \frac{8{,}400}{12} = 700 \text{ units.}$$

Problem-9

From the following information calculate the four important levels of stocks:

(*a*)	Average delivery time	= 20 days
(*b*)	Maximum delivery time	= 30 days
(*c*)	Minimum delivery period	= 15 days
(*d*)	Maximum delivery period for emergency purchase	= 5 days
(*e*)	Agerage rate of consumption per day	= 25 units
(*f*)	Maximum rate of consumption	= 35 units per day
(*g*)	Minimum rate of consumption	= 14 units per day
(*h*)	Standard ordering quantity	= 600 units

Solution:

1. Reorder level = Maximum usage × Maximum reorder period
   = 35 × 30 = 1,050 units
2. Minimum level = Reorder level – (Normal usage × Average reorder period)
   = 1,050 – (25 × 20)
   = 1,050 – 500 = 550 units
3. Maximum level = (Reorder level + Reorder quantity) – (Minimum usage × Minimum reorder period)
   = (1,050 + 600 – (14 × 15)
   = 1,650 – 210 = 1,440 units
4. Danger level = Average usage × Maximum reorder period for emergency purchase
   = 25 × 5 = 125 units.

Problem-10

If the minimum stock level and average stock level of raw-material A are 4,000 and 9,000 units respectively, find out its 'Reorder quantity'.

Solution:

Minimum stock level of material A = 4,000 units

Average stock level of material A = 9,000 units

Average stock level = Minimum level + $\frac{1}{2}$ reorder quantity

9000 = 4,000 + $\frac{1}{2}$ reorder quantity

or $-\frac{1}{2}$ reorder quantity = – 9,000 – 4,000 units

or Reorder quantity = 5,000 × 2 = 10,000 units

Problem-11

From the following information calculate:

1. Reorder level
2. Maximum level
3. Minimum level
4. Average stock level

Lead time	:	2 to 4 weeks
Usage of materials	:	3000 units to 9000 units per month
Reorder quantity	:	36000 units

(Mangalore University, B. Com, April 2006)

Solution:

1. Reorder = Maximum usage × Maximum delivery period
   = 9000 × 4 = 36000 units
2. Minimum level = Reorder level – (Normal usage × Normal delivery period)
   = 36,000 – (6,000 × 3)
   = 36,000 – 18,000 = 18,000 units

Working Note:

$$\text{Normal usage} = \frac{\text{Min. usage} + \text{Max. usage}}{2}$$

$$= \frac{3{,}000 + 9{,}000}{2} = 6{,}000 \text{ units}$$

$$\text{Normal delivery period} = \frac{2+4}{2} = 3 \text{ Weeks}$$

3. Maximum level = (Reorder level + Reorder qty.) – (Min usage × Min delivery period)
   = (18,000 + 36,000) – (3,000 × 2)
   = 54,000 – 6,000 = 48,000 units
4. Average stock level

$$= \frac{\text{Min. level} + \text{Max. level}}{2}$$

$$= \frac{18{,}000 + 48{,}000}{2}$$

$$= \frac{66{,}000}{2} = 33{,}000 \text{ units.}$$

3. Economic Order Quantity (EOQ): This technique of material control helps in deciding the purchase of most favourable quantity of materials when fresh supplies are required. One of the problems encountered by the purchase manager at the time of preparing a purchase order is deciding about the quantity of materials to be ordered. The quantity of materials to be ordered at a time is affected by two conflicting cost, termed as "Ordering cost" and "Cost of carrying the inventory". The important components of these are outlined below:

Ordering cost. Ordering cost can be again classified into: (*i*) Fixed ordering cost and (*ii*) Variable ordering cost. Examples of fixed ordering costs are salaries of staff, establishment cost, rent and unalterable services in running the department. However, fixed ordering cost does not affect the quantity of materials to be ordered. It is the variable ordering cost that affect the quantity of materials that is to be ordered. The examples of variable ordering costs are : cost of documents, postage and stationery, cost of follow-up, telephone and telegram expenses, etc. The fact to be underlined at this stage is that smaller the quantities ordered more frequently, larger is the ordering cost and *vice versa*. Again, if a small order is placed at a time, the benefits arising out of large-scale purchases such as trade discount, cash discount, free home delivery services, exchange facilities, credit facilities, after sales services cannot be derived.

Cost of carrying the inventory. The important components of carrying cost can be enumerated as under:

(*a*) *Investment cost.* This include the cost of foregone liquidity, interest on borrowed capital and the opportunity cost of investment.

(*b*) *Storage cost.* This include rent, salary of watch and ward staff, electricity charges, maintenance expenses of store room and handling and equipment costs.

(*c*) *Wastage cost.* This include deterioration and damages, obsolescence and handling losses.

(*d*) *Miscellaneous cost.* This include insurance, pilferage, etc.

In addition to the above costs, the following costs also affect the determination of EOQ.

(*a*) **Stock-out cost or outage cost.** Such costs are incurred to make product continue without interruptions. Whenever the usual type of materials are not readily available, often a suitable material which may be quite expensive or an inferior quality of materials are bought. Stock-out cost includes the additional cost of an expensive substitute, delayed production cost and customer's dissatisfaction owing to the use of inferior item. If customers reject such goods the cost of waste product is also treated as stock-out cost.

(*b*) **Systemic cost.** This type of cost arises from stock-out cost. They include additional cost of emergency purchases such as higher rates, increased transportation costs, cost of job rescheduling, set-up cost, etc.

The cost of carrying inventory will be less when the quantity of materials bought is also less and *vice versa*. Therefore, EOQ is a problem of balancing the two conflicting kinds of cost, *i.e.*, the cost of ordering and cost of carrying the inventory. The EOQ is taken at that level where the total cost of purchases must be the lowest which is possible when the cost of ordering is equal to cost of carrying the inventory. There are three different methods of presenting EOQ. They are: (1) Graphic method (2) Algebraic method, and (3) Tabular method. The graphic method of presenting EOQ is shown below. In the graph, the ordering cost shows a downward slope to indicate that it will be less when the quantity ordered is more. The cost of carrying inventory shows a rising trend to indicate that it will be more when the quantity ordered is more. The point of intersection between the ordering cost and carrying cost indicates EOQ. The total cost is minimum at EOQ point which is A. The total cost curve is the lowest at the point of EOQ. This is represented by AB. At C the ordering cost and inventory carrying cost are equal.

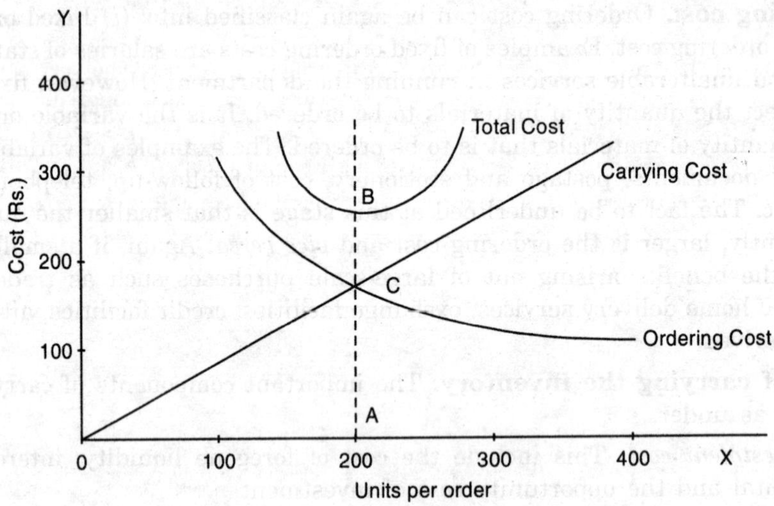

Fig. 4.5. *Graph showing EOQ.*

The following formula is used to calculate economic order quantity.

$$EOQ = \sqrt{\frac{2AB}{CS}}$$

where, A = Annual usage

B = Buying cost per order or ordering cost per order

C = Cost per unit

S = Storage cost or the cost of carrying the inventory.

2. Algebraic Method

Problem-12

The annual demand for a product is 6,400 units. The unit cost is Rs. 6 and inventory carrying cost per unit per annum is 25% of the average inventory cost. If the cost of procurement is Rs. 75. Determine:

(*i*) economic order quantity (EOQ)

(*ii*) number of orders per annum, and

(*iii*) time between two consecutive orders (*C.S. Inter, December 1998*)

Solution:

(*i*) $EOQ = \sqrt{\frac{2AB}{CS}} = \sqrt{\frac{2\times 6{,}400\times 75}{6\times\frac{25}{100}}} = \sqrt{\frac{2\times 6{,}400\times 75\times 100}{6\times 25}}$

$= 800$ units

(*ii*) Number of orders per annum. $= \frac{\text{Annual usage}}{\text{EOQ}} = \frac{6{,}400}{800} = 8$ orders

(*iii*) Time between two orders $= \frac{\text{Number of months in a year}}{\text{Number of orders}}$

$= \frac{12 \text{ months}}{8 \text{ orders}} = 1.5$ months

Problem-13

ABC company buy in lots of 125 boxes which is a three months supply. The cost per box is Rs. 125 and the ordering cost is Rs. 250 per order. The inventory carrying cost is estimated at 20% of unit value per annum. You are required to ascertain.

(*i*) What is the total annual cost of the existing inventory policy?

(*ii*) How much money would be saved by employing the economic order quantity (EOQ)?

(*C.S. Inter, Dec 1999*)

Solution:

$$\text{EOQ} = \sqrt{\frac{2AB}{CS}} = \sqrt{\frac{2\times(125\times4)\times250}{125\times\frac{20}{100}}}$$

$$= \sqrt{\frac{2\times500\times250\times100}{125\times20}} = \sqrt{10{,}000} = 100 \text{ units}$$

Statement showing annual cost of existing policy

Cost of purchase		
125 × 4 × 125=		62,500
Ordering cost 4 orders		
each costing Rs. 250	=	1,000
Average inventory cost	=	1562.50
$125 \times 125 \times \frac{20}{100} \times \frac{1}{2}$		
	=	65062.50

Statement showing annual cost with EOQ

Cost of purchase	=	62,500
Ordering cost 5 orders		
each costing Rs. 250	=	1,250
Average inventory cost	=	1,250
	$100 \times 125 \times \frac{20}{100}\times\frac{1}{2}$	
	=	65,000

Hence, savings = 65,062.50 – 65,000 = Rs. 62.50

Problem-14

The complete Gardener is deciding on the economic order quantity for two brands of lawn fertilizer; Super Grow and Native's own. The following information is collected:

	Fertilizer	
	Super grow	*Natives own*
Annual demand	2,000 bags	1,280 bags
Relevant ordering cost per purchase order	Rs. 1,200	Rs. 1,400
Annual relevant carrying cost per bag	Rs. 480	Rs. 560

Required:

(*i*) Compute EOQ for super grow and native's own.

(*ii*) For the EOQ what is the sum of the total annual relevant ordering costs and total annual relevant carrying costs for super grow and native's own?

(*iii*) For the EOQ compute the number of deliveries per year of super grow and native's own.

(*C.A. Inter, November 1999*)

Solution:

(*i*) $EOQ = \sqrt{\frac{2AB}{CS}}$

Super grow fertilizer $= \sqrt{\frac{2 \times 2{,}000 \times 1{,}200}{480}}$

$= \sqrt{10{,}000}$

= 100 bags

Native's own fertilizer $= \sqrt{\frac{2 \times 1{,}280 \times 1{,}400}{560}}$

= 80 bags

(*ii*) **Total annual relevant costs for super grow fertilizer**

= Total annual ordering cost + Total annual carrying cost

$= \frac{\text{Annual demand}}{\text{EOQ}} \times \text{Ordering cost} + \frac{1}{2}\text{EOQ} \times \text{Cost of carrying}$

$= \frac{2{,}000}{100} \times 1{,}200 + \frac{1}{2} \times 100 \times 480$

= 24,000 + 24,000

= Rs. 48,000

Total annual relevant costs for native's own fertilizer.

$= \frac{1{,}280}{80} \times 1{,}400 + \frac{1}{2} \times 80 \times 560$

= 22,400 + 22,400

= Rs. 44,800

(*iii*) **Number of deliveries (*i.e.*, orders)**

$= \frac{\text{Annual usage}}{\text{EOQ}}$

Super grow $= \frac{2{,}000}{100} = 20$ orders

Native's own $= \frac{1280}{80} = 16$ orders

Problem-15

G. Ltd. produces a product which has a monthly demand of 4,000 units. The product requires a component *x* which is purchased at Rs. 20. For every finished product, one unit of component is required. The ordering cost is Rs. 120 per order and the holding cost is 10% per annum.

You are required to calculate.

(*i*) Economic order quantity.

(*ii*) If the minimum lot size to be supplied is 4,000 units. What is the extra cost, the company has to incur?

(*iii*) What is the minimum carrying cost the company has to incur? (*C.A. Inter, May 1999*)

Solution:

(*i*)
$$\text{EOQ} = \sqrt{\frac{2AB}{CS}}$$
$$= \sqrt{\frac{2\times 48{,}000\times 120}{20\times\frac{10}{100}}}$$
$$= 2{,}400 \text{ units}$$

(*ii*) **Extra cost incurred by the company**

Total cost (where order size is 4,000 units) = Total ordering cost + Average carrying cost

$$= \frac{\text{Annual demand}}{\text{Order size}} \times \text{Ordering cost} + \frac{1}{2}\ \text{Order size} \times \text{Cost of carrying}$$
$$= \frac{48{,}000}{4{,}000}\times 120 + \frac{1}{2}\times 4{,}000\times 20\times\frac{10}{100}$$
$$= 1{,}440 + 4{,}000$$
$$= \text{Rs. } 5{,}440 \qquad ...(a)$$

$$\text{Total cost (when order size is 2400)} = \frac{48{,}000}{2{,}400}\times 120 + \frac{1}{2}\times 2{,}400\times 20\times\frac{10}{100}$$
$$= 2{,}400 + 2{,}400$$
$$= \text{Rs. } 4{,}800 \qquad ...(b)$$

Extra cost $= (a - b)$

$= 5{,}440 - 4{,}800 = \text{Rs. } 640.$

(*iii*) **Minimum Carrying Cost:** Carrying Cost depends upon the size of the order. It will be minimum on the least order size. In this problem, the two orders are 2,400 units and 4,000 units. Here, 2,400 units is the least of the two order sizes. At this order size, carrying cost will be minimum.

The minimum carrying cost in this case can be computed as under:

$$= \frac{1}{2}\times 2{,}400\times 20\times\frac{10}{100}$$
$$= \text{Rs. } 2400$$

Problem-16

A publishing house purchase 2,000 units of a particular item per year at unit cost of Rs. 20, the ordering cost per order is Rs. 50 and the inventory carrying cost is 25%. Find the optimal order quantity and the minimum total cost including purchase cost.

If a 3% discount is offered by the supplier for purchase in lots of 1,000 or more, should the publishing house accept the order?

(*C.S. Inter, December 1996, Sri Sathya Sai University, B.Com (Hons), March 2003*)

Solution:

EOQ without discount.

$$EOQ = \sqrt{\frac{2AB}{CS}}$$

$$= \sqrt{\frac{2\times 2{,}000\times 50}{20\times \frac{25}{100}}}$$

$$= \sqrt{\frac{2\times 2{,}000\times 50\times 100}{20\times 25}}$$

= 200 units

Number of orders to be placed $= \frac{\text{Annual purchase}}{\text{EOQ}}$

$= \frac{2{,}000}{200} = 10$ orders

Total cost of purchase without discount

Purchase cost	– 2,000 units @ Rs. 20	40,000
Ordering cost	– 10 orders @ Rs. 50	500
Carrying cost of average inventory		
Average inventory	$= \frac{200}{2} = 100$ units	
Cost of carrying per unit		
	$\frac{25}{100}\times 20$ = Rs. 5	
for 100 units @ Rs. 5 per unit		500
		Rs. 41,000

Total cost of purchase with discount

Purchase cost – 2000 units @ Rs. 19.40 = (20 – 3% of 20)	38,800
Ordering cost – Number of order is 2	
$\left(i.e., \frac{2{,}000}{1{,}000}\right)$ @ Rs. 50	= 100
Carrying cost of average inventory	
Average inventory = 500 units $\left(i.e., \frac{1{,}000}{2}\right)$	
Carrying cost $\frac{25}{100}\times 19.4$ = 4.85	
for 500 units @ Rs. 4.85	= 2,425
	= 41,325

Problem-17 (EOQ)

Harsha Ltd. produces a product which has a monthly demand of 4,000 units. The product requires a component x which is purchased at Rs. 20. For every finished product, one unit of component x is required. The ordering cost is Rs. 120 per order and the holding cost is 10% per annum.

You are required to calculate.

(*i*) Economic order quantity

(*ii*) If the minimum lot size to be supplied is 4,000 units, what is the extra cost the company has to incur. (*C.S. Inter, June 2003*)

Solution:

(*i*) $\text{EOQ} = \sqrt{\dfrac{2AB}{CS}}$

$$= \sqrt{\frac{2\times(4{,}000\times12)\times120)}{20\times\dfrac{10}{100}}}$$

= 2,400 units

(*ii*) **Calculation of extra cost if the minimum lot size is 4,000 units.**

(*a*) **Number of orders where order size is 4,000 units = 12**

		Rs.
Ordering cost = Rs. 120 × 12 orders	=	1,440
Carrying cost = $\frac{1}{2}$ × 4,000 × Rs. 2	=	4,000
Total ordering cost and carrying cost	=	5,440

(*b*) **Number of orders with EBQ**

$$\frac{\text{Annual usage}}{\text{EBQ}} = \frac{48{,}000}{2{,}400} = 20 \text{ orders}$$

		Rs.
Ordering cost = Rs. 120 × 20 orders	=	2,400
Carrying cost = $\frac{1}{2}$ × 2,400 × Rs. 2	=	2,400
Total ordering cost and carrying cost		4,800
Extra cost = (5440 – 4800)	=	Rs. 640

Problem-18

A factory requires 1,500 units of an item per month. The cost of each unit is Rs. 27. The cost per order is Rs. 150 and inventory carrying charges works out to 20% of the average inventory. Find out the economic order quantity (EOQ) and ascertain the number of orders to be placed per year. Would you accept a 2% price discount on a minimum supply of 1,200 units? (*C.S. Inter, June 2007*)

Solution:

$$EOQ = \sqrt{\frac{2AB}{CS}}$$

$$= \sqrt{\frac{2\times(1{,}500 \text{ units}\times 12)\times 150}{27\times\frac{20}{100}}}$$

$$= \sqrt{\frac{2\times 18{,}000\times 150}{5.40}}$$

$$= \sqrt{10{,}00{,}000} = 1{,}000 \text{ units}$$

If 2% discount is given (original price – 2% discount)

Cost price = Rs. 27 – 0.54 = Rs. 26.46

No of orders to be placed when 1,200 units are to be bought.

$$\frac{18{,}000}{1{,}200} = 15 \text{ orders}$$

No of orders to be placed when 1,000 units (EOQ are bought)

$$\frac{18{,}000}{1{,}000} = 18 \text{ orders}$$

Total cost without discount.

Purchase price – 18,000 × 27	=	4,86,000
Ordering cost – 18 × Rs. 150	=	2,700
Carrying cost – $\frac{1}{2}\times 1{,}000\times 5.40$	=	2,700
		Rs. 4,91,400

Total cost with 2% discount

Purchase price – 18,000 × 26.46	=	4,76,280
Ordering cost – 15 × Rs. 150	=	2,250
Carrying cost – $\frac{1}{2}\times 1{,}200\times 5.40$	=	3,175
		Rs. 4,81,705

Since the total cost is less with 2% discount, the proposal may be accepted

Problem-19

Your factory buys and uses a component for production at Rs. 10 per unit. Annual requirement is 20,000 units. The carrying cost of inventory is 10% per annum and ordering cost is Rs. 40 per order. The purchase manager argues that as the ordering cost is very high, it is advantageous to place a single order for the entire annual requirement. He also says that if we order 20,000 units at a time, we can get a 3% discount from the supplier. You are required to evaluate this proposal and make your recommendations. *(C.S. Inter, December 2006)*

Solution:

$$EOQ = \sqrt{\frac{2AB}{CS}}$$

$$= \sqrt{\frac{2\times 20{,}000\times 40}{10\times\frac{10}{100}}}$$

$$= \sqrt{16{,}00{,}000}$$

= 1265 units

No of orders to be placed

$$= \frac{\text{Annual usage}}{\text{EOQ}}$$

$$= \frac{20{,}000}{1{,}265} = 15.8 \text{ or } 16 \text{ orders}$$

Total cost in case of EOQ.

Buying cost	– 20,000 × Rs. 10	=	2,00,000
Ordering cost	– 16 orders × Rs. 40	=	640
Carrying cost	– $\frac{1}{2}\times 1265\times 10\times\frac{10}{100}$	=	632
			2,01,272

Total cost of acquiring 20,000 units in one lot.

Buying cost	– 20,000 × Rs. 9.70	=	1,94,000
Ordering cost	– 1 order × Rs. 40	=	40
Carrying cost	– $\frac{1}{2}\times 20{,}000\times\frac{10}{100}\times 9.70$	=	9,700
			2,03,740

By the economic order quantity, the total cost is less by Rs. 2467 (Rs. 2,03,740 – 2,01,272) as compared to buying in one lot of 20,000 units. Hence, the view of the purchase manager is incorrect.

Problem-20 (EOQ)

Given below is the information pertaining to a material in a manufacturing organisation

Annual consumption of the material	: 25,000 unit for 360 days
Cost per unit of the material	: Rs. 20
Ordering cost	: Rs. 50 per order
Inventory carrying cost	: 25 %
Normal lead time	: 20 days
Safety stock	: 20 days consumption

You are required to find out:

1. How much should be ordered each time?
2. When should the order be placed?
3. What should be the inventory level immediately before the material ordered is received?

(Sri Sathya Sai University, B.Com (Hons) March, 2004)

Solution:

$$EOQ = \sqrt{\frac{2AB}{CS}}$$

$$= \sqrt{\frac{2\times 25{,}000\times 50}{20\times \frac{25}{100}}}$$

$$= \sqrt{\frac{2\times 25{,}000\times 50\times 100}{20\times 25}}$$

$$= \sqrt{5{,}00{,}000} = 707 \text{ units.}$$

2. Time of placing order.

For 25,000 units, the period is 360 days

For 707 units ⟶?

$$\frac{707\times 360}{25{,}000} = 10 \text{ days}$$

3. Inventory level before the order is received

(Delivery period × Normal usage) + Safety stock

$$= \left(20\times \frac{25{,}000}{360}\right) + 1389$$

$$= 20 \times 69.45 + 1389$$

$$= 1388 + 1389 = 2777 \text{ units}$$

Working Note:

Calculation of safety stock

For 360 days, safety stock is 25,000 units.

For 20 days ⟶?

$$\frac{25{,}000}{360} \times 20 = 1389.$$

Problem-21 (EOQ)

The following data are available in respect of a material 'MMI' used in the production of goods of M/s Bright Ltd. for the year 2001:

Cost of the materials per unit	Rs. 50
Weekly consumption	300 units
Ordering cost per order	Rs. 650
Stock holding cost	2% per month on cost

Compute: (*a*) Economic order quantity (*b*) optimum number of orders per year, and (*c*) Time lag between two consecutive orders.

(Calcutta University, B.Com (Hons), 2002)

Solution:

$$EOQ = \sqrt{\frac{2AB}{CS}}$$

$$= \sqrt{\frac{2 \times 15{,}600 \times 650}{50 \times \frac{2}{100} \times 12}}$$

$$= \sqrt{\frac{2 \times 15{,}600 \times 650}{12}} = 1300 \text{ units.}$$

> **Note.**
> Annual consumption 300 × 52 = 15,600 units

(*b*) **Optimum number of orders per year**

$$\frac{\text{Annual usage}}{\text{EOQ}} = \frac{15{,}600}{1300} = 12 \text{ orders.}$$

(*c*) **Time lag between two consecutive orders**

$$\frac{\text{No. of months}}{\text{No. of orders}} = \frac{12 \text{ months}}{12 \text{ orders}} = 1 \text{ month}$$

Problem-22 (EOQ)

A company purchases a spare part from its suppliers @ Rs. 60 per unit. Annual requirements are 1,600 units. The following further information are available:

Cost of one procurement	Rs. 100
Tax, insurance, rent etc. per unit per annum	Rs. 2
Annual return on investment	10%

Find out (*a*) Economic order quantity, (*b*) Time gap between two consecutive orders.

(Calcutta University, B. Com. (Hons), 2004)

Solution:

$$(a)\ EOQ = \sqrt{\frac{2AB}{CS}}$$

$$= \sqrt{\frac{2 \times 1{,}600 \times 100}{\left(60 \times \frac{10}{100}\right) + 2}}$$

$$= \sqrt{\frac{2 \times 1{,}600 \times 100}{8}} = 209 \text{ units.}$$

(*b*) **Time gap between two orders.**

Calculation of number of orders per annum

$$\frac{\text{Annual usage}}{\text{EOQ}} = \frac{1{,}600}{209} = 7.6 \text{ or } 8 \text{ orders.}$$

$$\text{Time gap between two orders} = \frac{\text{Number of months in a year}}{\text{No. of orders}}$$

$$= \frac{12}{8} = 1.5 \text{ months or 45 days.}$$

Problem-23 (Level setting with EOQ)

Annual consumption of a material of a company is 1,00,000 units at Rs. 2.40 per unit. Each order costs Rs. 90 and carrying cost is 15% of the annual average inventory value. Company operates 250 days per year. The procurement time is 10 days and safety stock is 1000 units. Calculate Maximum stock level. *(Calcutta University, B.Com (Hons.) 2003)*

Solution:

$$\text{EOQ} = \sqrt{\frac{2AB}{CS}}$$

$$= \sqrt{\frac{2 \times 1,00,000 \times 90}{2.40 \times \frac{15}{100}}}$$

$$= \sqrt{\frac{2 \times 1,00,000 \times 90}{0.36}} = 7071 \text{ units}$$

Consumption (maximum) per day.

$$\frac{1,00,000}{250} = 400 \text{ units.}$$

Reorder level = Maximum consumption × Maximum delivery period

= 400 × 10 = 4,000 units

Maximum level = (Reorder level + Reorder Qty) – (Minimum consumption × Min. delivery period)

= 7071 + 4,000 – (Nil)

= 11,071 units (assuming minimum consumption = 0)

If safety stock is added then maximum stock level will be 11,071 + 1,000 = 12,071 units.

Problem-24

P. Ltd. furnished the following regarding the details of its manufacturing operation during 2004:

Average monthly market demand	4,600 units
Ordering cost	Rs. 52 per order
Inventory carrying cost	20% per annum
Cost of material	Rs. 630 per unit
Normal usage	245 units per week
Minimum usage	70 units per week
Maximum usage	380 units per week
Lead time to supply	4-6 weeks

Compute Maximum level and Minimum level of stock. *(Calcutta University, B.Com. (Hons), 2005)*

Solution:

$$\text{EOQ} = \sqrt{\frac{2AB}{CS}}$$

$$= \sqrt{\frac{2 \times 4,600 \times 12 \times 52}{630 \times \frac{20}{100}}}$$

= 235 units

Reorder level = Maximum consumption × Maximum delivery period

= 380 × 6 = 2280 units

Minimum level = Reorder level – (Normal consumption × Normal delivery period)

= 2280 – (245 × 5)

= 2280 – 1125 = 1155 units

Maximum level = (Reorder level + Reorder Qty.) – (Min. consumption × Min. delivery period)

= (2280 + 235) – (70 × 4)

= 2515 – 280 = 2235 units.

Problem-25 (EOQ)

P. Ltd. is engaged in the manufacture of industrial pumps of a standard description. The company uses about 75,000 valves per year for its production and the uasge is fairly constant at 6250 valves per month. The valves cost Rs. 1.50 per unit when bought in quantities and the carrying cost is estimated to be 20% of average inventory investment on the annual basis. The cost to place an order and process the delviery is Rs. 18. It takes 45 days to receive delivery from the date of an order and a safety stock of 3200 valves is desired. You are required to determine

(*i*) the most economical order quantity

(*ii*) the reorder point *(University of Delhi, B.Com. (Hons.), 2002)*

Solution:

(*i*) $$\text{EOQ} = \sqrt{\frac{2AB}{CS}}$$

$$= \sqrt{\frac{2 \times 75,000 \times 18}{1.50 \times \frac{20}{100}}}$$

$$= \sqrt{\frac{27,00,000}{0.3}}$$

$$= \sqrt{90,00,000} = 3,000 \text{ units}$$

Reorder level = Minimum stock + (Normal usage × Normal reorder period)

= 3200 + (6250 × 1.5 months)

= 3,200 + 9,375 = 12,575 units.

Problem-26 (EOQ)

A company manufactures a product having a monthly demand of 2,000 units. For one unit of finished product, 2 kgs of a particular raw material item is needed. The purchase price of the material is Rs. 20 per kg. The ordering cost is Rs. 120 per order and the holding cost is 10% per annum.

Calculate: (*a*) Economic order quantity

(*b*) Annual cost of purchasing and storage of the raw material at that quantity

(*University of Delhi, B.Com. (Hons), 2004*)

Solution:

$$\text{EOQ} = \sqrt{\frac{2AB}{CS}}$$

$$= \sqrt{\frac{2 \times 48{,}000 \times 120}{20 \times \frac{10}{100}}}$$

$$= \sqrt{57{,}60{,}000} = 2{,}400 \text{ kgs}$$

$$\text{Annual cost} = \text{Cost of purchasing} + \text{Cost of storage}$$

$$= \left(\frac{48{,}000}{2{,}400} \times 120\right) + \frac{2400 \times 20 \times 10}{2 \times 100}$$

$$= 2{,}400 + 2{,}400 = \text{Rs. } 4{,}800$$

Problem-27 (EOQ Tabular presentation)

RST Limited has received an offer of quantity discount on its order of materials as under:

Price per ton	Tonnes number
Rs. 9,600	Less than 50
Rs. 9,360	50 and less than 100
Rs. 9,120	100 and less than 200
Rs. 8,880	200 and less than 300
Rs. 8,640	300 and above

The annual requirement for the material is 500 tonnes. The ordering cost per order is Rs. 12,500 and the stock holding cost is estimated at 25% of the material cost per annum

Required:

(*i*) Compute the most economical purchase level.

(*ii*) Compute EOQ, if there are no quantity discounts and the price per tonne is Rs. 10,500.

(*CA PE-II, November, 2004*)

Solution:

Order size Q (1)	No. of orders $\frac{A}{Q}$ (2)	Cost of purchase A × cost per unit (3)	Ordering cost $\frac{A}{Q} \times$ Rs.12,500 (4)	Carrying cost $\frac{Q}{2} \times C \times 25\%$ (5)	Total cost (3+4+5) (6)
40	12.5	48,00,000 (500 × 9,600)	1,56,250	48,000 $\left(\frac{40}{2}\times 9{,}600\times 0.25\right)$	50,04,250
50	10	46,80,000 (500 × 9,360)	1,25,000	58,500 $\left(\frac{50}{2}\times 9360\times 0.25\right)$	48,63,500
100	5	45,60,000 (500 × 9,120)	62,500	1,14,000 $\left(\frac{100}{2}\times 9120\times 0.25\right)$	47,36,500
200	2.5	44,40,000 (500 × 8,880)	31,250	$\left(\frac{200}{2}\times 8{,}880\times 0.25\right)$	46,93,250
300	1.67	43,20,000	20,875	3,24,000 $\left(\frac{300}{2}\times 8{,}640\times 0.25\right)$	46,64,875

The above table shows that the total cost of 500 units including ordering and carrying cost is minimum (Rs. 46,64,875), where the order size is 300 units. Hence, the most economical purchase is 300 units

$$\text{EOQ} = \sqrt{\frac{2AB}{CS}}$$

$$= \sqrt{\frac{2\times 500\times 12{,}500}{10{,}500\times \frac{25}{100}}} = 69 \text{ units.}$$

Problem-28

A company manufactures a product from a raw material, which is purchased at Rs. 60 per kg. The company incurs a handling cost of Rs. 360 plus freight of Rs. 390 per order. The incremental carrying cost of inventory of raw material is Re 0.50 per kg per month. In addition, the cost of working capital finance on the investment in inventory of raw material is Rs. 9 per kg per annum. The annual production of the product is 1,00,000 units and 2.5 units are obtained from one kg of raw material.

Required:

(*i*) Calculate the economic order quantity of raw materials.

(*ii*) Advise how frequently should orders for procurement be placed.

(*iii*) If the company proposes to rationalise placement of orders on quarterly basis, what percentage of discount in the price of raw materials should be negotiated?

(*CA Inter, November, 2001*)

Solution:

1. **Annual usage of raw materials in kgs:**

For 2.5 units : 1 kg

For 1,00,000 units ⟶?

$$\frac{1,00,000 \times 1}{2.5} = 40,000 \text{ kgs.}$$

2. **Handling and freight cost per order.**

Rs. 360 + Rs 390 = Rs. 750

3. Carrying cost per kg per annum + Investment cost per kg per annum

= 0.50 × 12 months + Rs. 9

= 6 + 9 = Rs. 15 per kg

(*i*) EOQ $= \sqrt{\frac{2AB}{CS}}$

$$= \sqrt{\frac{2 \times 40,000 \times 750}{15}}$$

= 2,000 kgs

(*ii*) Frequency of orders: per annum

$$\frac{\text{Annual usage}}{\text{EOQ}} = \frac{40,000}{2,000} = 20 \text{ orders}$$

$$\text{Frequency of placing orders} = \frac{\text{No. of months in a year}}{\text{No. of orders}}$$

$$= \frac{12}{20} = 0.6 \text{ month or 18 days (App)}$$

(*iii*) Percentage of discount in the price of raw materials to be negotiated

No. of quarters in a year = 4

$$\text{Quarterly orders} = \frac{\text{Annual usage}}{\text{No. of quarters in a year}}$$

$$= \frac{40,000}{4} = 10,000 \text{ kgs per orders}$$

Total cost (When order size is 10,0000 units)

Order placing cost (4 orders × Rs. 750)	3,000

	Rs.
Carrying cost $\left(\frac{10,000}{2} \times Rs.15\right)$	75,000
	78,000
Total cost (When order size is equal to EOQ)	
Order placing cost (20 orders × Rs. 750)	15,000
Carrying cost $\left(\frac{2,000}{2} \times Rs.15\right)$	15,000
	30,000

Increase in cost to be compensated by discount = Rs. 48,000 (78,000 – 30,000)

Reduction per kg in the purchase price of raw materials

$$\frac{Rs.48,000}{40,000\,kg} = 1.20 \text{ per kg}$$

percentage of discount in the price of raw material to be negotiated = 2%

For Rs. 60 : The reduction is Rs. 1.20

For Rs. 100 →?

$$\frac{1.20}{60} \times 100 = 2\%.$$

Problem-29 (EOQ—Tabular presentation)

A manufacturer requires 9,600 units of a certain component annually. This is currently purchased from a regular supplier at Rs. 50 per unit. The cost of placing an order is Rs. 60 per order and the annual carrying cost is Rs. 5 per piece. What is the economic order quantity (EOQ) for placing order?

Recently, the supplier has expressed his willingness to reduce the price to Rs. 48, if the total requirements are obtained from him in two equal orders and to Rs. 47, if the entire quantity required is purchased in one lot. Analyse the cost of the three options and recommend the best course.

(I.C.W.A. Inter December, 2003)

Solution:

$$EOQ = \sqrt{\frac{2AB}{CS}}$$

$$= \sqrt{\frac{2 \times 9,600 \times 60}{5}}$$

$$= \sqrt{2,30,400} = 480 \text{ units.}$$

Analysis of costs of three options

No of orders (options)	20	2	1
Size of orders (units)	480	4,800	9,600
Average stock (units)	240	2,400	4,800
	Rs.	Rs.	Rs.
Total ordering cost @ Rs. 60	1,200	120	60
Total carrying cost @ Rs. 5	1,200	12,000	24,000
Total cost of components	4,80,000	4,60,800	4,51,200
Total cost	4,82,400	4,72,920	4,75,260

Recommendation

From the above analysis it reveals that the most economical order quantity is 4,800 units of components. Therefore, placing 2 orders is bolt.

Working Note:

1. Calculation of no. of orders with EOQ.

$$\frac{\text{Annual}}{\text{EOQ}} = \frac{9,600}{480} = 20 \text{ orders}$$

2. Size of order units:

For 1 order = 9,600 units

$$\text{For 2 orders} = \frac{9,600}{2} = 4,800 \text{ units}$$

$$\text{For 20 orders} = \frac{9,600}{20} = 480 \text{ units}$$

3. Average stock:

$$= \frac{480}{2} = 240 \text{ units}$$

$$= \frac{4,800}{2} = 2,400 \text{ units}$$

$$= \frac{9,600}{2} = 4,800 \text{ units}$$

4. Total ordering cost:

No. of orders × Cost per order

= 20 × Rs. 60 = Rs. 1,200

= 2 × Rs. 60 = Rs. 120

= 1 × Rs. 60 = Rs. 60

5. Total carrying cost:

240 × Rs. 5 = Rs. 1,200

2,400 × Rs. 5 = Rs. 12,000

4,800 × Rs. 5 = Rs. 24,000

6. Purchase cost:

9,600 × Rs. 50 = Rs. 4,80,000

9,600 × Rs. 48 = Rs. 4,60,800

9,600 × Rs. 47 = 4,51,200

Problem-30 (Tabular presentation)

A manufacturing company purchases 24,000 pieces of a component from a sub-contractor at Rs. 500 per piece and uses them in its assembly department, at a steady rate. The cost of placing an order and following it up is Rs. 2,500. The estimated stock holding cost is approximately 1% of the value of average stock hold. The company is at present placing orders which at present vary between an order placed every two months (*i.e.*, 6 orders p.a) to one order per annum. Which policy would you recommend?

(*ICWA Inter, December, 2001*)

Solution:

Statement showing costs for optimum number of orders placed

1. No of orders per year	1	2	3	4	5	6
2. Order sizes (pieces)	24,000	12,000	8,000	6,000	4,800	4,000
3. Average stock (pieces)	12,000	6,000	4,000	3,000	2,400	2,000
4. Value of average stock @ Rs. 500 (Rs in thousand)	6,000	3,000	2,000	1,500	1,200	1,000
5 Stock holding cost @ 1% (Rs.)	60,000	30,000	20,000	15,000	12,000	10,000
6. Ordering cost @ Rs. 2500 per order	2,500	5,000	7,500	10,000	12,500	15,000
Total cost (5 + 6)	62,500	35,000	27,500	25,000	24,500	25,000

Working Note:

Calculation of order size pieces

$$= \frac{\text{No of pieces}}{\text{No of orders}}$$

$$2 \text{ orders} = \frac{24,000}{2} = 12,000$$

$$3 \text{ orders} = \frac{24,000}{3} = 8,000 \text{ and so on}$$

$$\text{EOQ} = \sqrt{\frac{2AB}{CS}}$$

$$= \sqrt{\frac{2 \times 24,000 \times 2,500}{500 \times 0.01}}$$

$$= 4899 \text{ (Appr).}$$

$$\text{No. of orders} = \frac{24,000}{4899} = 4.90 \text{ or } 5 \text{ orders}$$

Total inventory carrying cost and ordering cost:

Ordering cost 5 orders	12,500
Carrying cost (Average inventory *i.e.,* 2449.50 × 5)	12,247.50
	24,747.50

Recommendation:

From the above table as the total cost is least *i.e.,* 24,500, when 5 orders are placed; it is recommended to management to place 5 orders.

Problem-31 (Level setting)

In a manufacturing company a material is used as follows:

Maximum usage	12,000 units per week
Minimum usage	4,000 units per week
Normal usage	8,000 units per week
Reorder quantity	48,000 units

Time required for delivery is 4 to 6 weeks. You are required to calculate:

(*a*) Reorder level (*b*) Minimum level

(*c*) Maximum level (*d*) Average stock level

(*Sri Sathya Sai University, B.Com. (Hons.) August, 2007*)

Solution:

Reorder level = Maximum usage × Maximum delivery period

= 12,000 × 6

= 72,000 units

Minimum level = Reorder level – (Normal usage × Normal delivery period)

= 72,000 – (8,000 × 5)

= 72,000 – 40,000 = 32,000 units

Maximum level = (Reorder level + Reorder qty) – (Minimum usage × Minimum delivery period)

= (72,000 + 48,000) – (4,000 × 4)

= 1,20,000 – 16,000

= 1,04,000 units

$$\text{Average stock level} = \text{Minimum level} + \frac{1}{2}\text{ (Reorder quantity)}$$

$$= 32{,}000 + \frac{1}{2} \times 48{,}000$$

= 56,000.

Problem-32 (Level setting with economic order quantity)

ABC Ltd., manufactures a special product "RUBY". The following particulars were collected for the year 2006.

(*a*) Cost of placing an order Rs. 100

(*b*) Annual carrying cost per unit Rs. 15

(*c*) Usage rate for input; 25 units to 75 units per week

(*d*) Reorder period : 4 to 6 weeks

(*e*) Normal usage : 50 units per week

Compute for the input for Ruby:

1. Economic order quantity
2. Minimum level
3. Reorder level
4. Maximum level
5. Average stock level

(*Sri Sathya Sai University, B. Com. (Hons.) March, 2007*)

Solution:

$$\text{EOQ} = \sqrt{\frac{2AB}{CS}}$$

$$= \sqrt{\frac{2 \times 2{,}600 \times 100}{15}}$$

= 186 units

Working Note:

Annual usage = Normal usage × Number of weeks in a year
= 50 × 52 = 2600

(*b*) Reorder level = Maximum usage × Maximum reorder period
= 75 × 6 = 450 units

(*c*) Minimum level = Reorder level – (Normal usage × Normal reorder period)
= 450 – (50 × 5)
= 450 – 250 = 200 units

(*d*) Maximum level = (Reorder level + Reorder qty) – (Minimum usage × Minimum reorder period)
= (450 + 186) – (25 × 4)
= 636 – 100
= 536 units

(*e*) Average stock level $= \frac{\text{Minimum level} + \text{Maximum level}}{2}$

$= \frac{200+536}{2} = 368$ units.

Problem-33

Shagoon India Limited provides the following information in respect of material 'A':

Supply period:	5 to 15 days
Rate of consumption:	
Average	15 units per day
Maximum	20 units per day
Yearly	5,000 units

Ordering costs are Rs. 20 per order. Purchase price per unit is Rs. 50. Storage costs are 10% of unit value. Compute (*a*) Economic order quantity (*b*) Reorder level (*c*) Minimum level (*d*) Maximum level (*e*) Average stock level. (*Sri Sathya Sai University, B. Com (Hons.) March, 2006*)

Solution:

(*a*) Economic order qty $= \sqrt{\frac{2AB}{CS}}$

$= \sqrt{\frac{2 \times 5{,}000 \times 20}{50 \times \frac{10}{100}}}$

$= \sqrt{\frac{2 \times 5000 \times 20 \times 100}{50 \times 10}}$

$= \sqrt{40{,}000} = 200$ units

Working Note:

Calculation of minimum consumption:

Average consumption $= \frac{\text{Minimum consumption} + \text{Maximum consumption}}{2}$

$15 = \frac{x+20}{2}$

$$15 \times 2 = x + 20$$
$$30 = x + 20$$
$$-x = -30 + 20$$
$$x = 10$$

(*b*) Reorder level = Maximum usage × Maximum delivery period
= 20 × 15 = 300 units

(*c*) Minimum level = Reorder level – (Normal usage × Normal delivery period)
= 300 – (15 × 10)
= 300 – 150 = 150 units

(*d*) Maximum level = (Reorder level + Reorder qty) – (Minimum usage × Minimum delivery period)
= (300 + 200) – (10 × 5)
= 500 – 150 = 450 units

(*e*) Average stock level $= \dfrac{\text{Minimum level} + \text{Maximum level}}{2}$

$= \dfrac{150+450}{2} = \dfrac{600}{2} = 300$ units.

Problem-34

'Zee' is the product manufactured out of three raw materials 'M', 'N', and 'O'. Each unit of "Zee" requires 10 kg, 8 kg, and 6 kg of M, N, and O respectively. The reorder levels of M and N are 15,000 kg and 10,000 kg respectively, while the minimum level of O is 2500 kg. The weekly production of "Zee" varies from 300 to 500 units while the weekly average production is 400 units. You are required to compute:

1. The minimum stock level of M
2. The maximum stock level of N
3. The reorder level of O

The following additional data is given

	M	N	O
Reorder Qty (in kg)	20,000	15,000	20,000
	Delivery (in weeks)		
Minimum	2	4	3
Average	3	5	4
Maximum	4	6	5

Solution:

1. Minimum level of M = Reorder level – Average usage × Average delivery time
= 15,000 – 400 × 10 × 3
= 15,000 – 12,000 = 3,000 kg

Working Note:

Average delivery time $= \dfrac{2+3+4}{3} = \dfrac{9}{3} = 3$

2. Maximum level of N = Reorder level + Reorder qty. – Minimum usage × Minimum reorder period
   = 10,000 + 15,000 – 300 × 8 × 4
   = 25,000 – 9,600 = 15,400 units
3. Reorder level of O = Maximum usage × Maximum reorder period
   = 500 × 6 kgs × 5 weeks
   = 15,000 kg.

Problem-35

In respect of material M-04, the following data are available.

Budgeted consumption.

Maximum — 300 units per month
Minimum — 50 units per month
Average — 150 units per month
Annual — 1,800 units
Lead time — 2 – 4 months

Storage costs are 25% p.a. of average stock value

Ordering costs are Rs. 2 per order, price per unit of material is 0.32 paise

Calculate: 1. EOQ
2. Reorder level
3. Minimum level
4. Maximum level
5. Average stock level

(Bangalore University, B.Com., April 2004)

Solution:

(1) EOQ $= \sqrt{\dfrac{2AB}{CS}}$

$= \sqrt{\dfrac{2 \times 1800 \times 2}{0.32 \times \dfrac{25}{100}}}$

$= \sqrt{\dfrac{2 \times 1800 \times 2 \times 100}{0.32 \times 25}}$

$= \sqrt{90{,}000}$ = 300 units

(2) Reorder level = Max. usage × Max delivery period
= 300 × 4 = 1200 units

(3) Minimum level = Reorder level – (Normal usage × Normal delivery period)
= 1200 – (150 × 3)
= 1200 – 450 = 750 units

(4) Maximum level = (Reorder level + Reorder qty) – (Minimum usage × Minimum delivery period)
= (1200 + 300) – (50 × 2)
= 1500 – 100 = 1,400 units

(5) Average stock level = $\dfrac{\text{Minimum level} + \text{Maximum level}}{2}$

$= \dfrac{750+1400}{2} = 1075$ units

Problem-36

The following information is available in respect of a component. Calculate reorder level and reorder quantity.

Maximum stock level	:	8,400 units
Budgeted consumption	:	Maximum 1,500 units per month
		Minimum 800 units per month
Estimated delivery period	:	Maximum 4 months
		Minimum 2 months (*Osmania University, B. Com, October 2004*)

Solution:

Reorder level = Maximum consumption × Maximum delivery period

= 1,500 × 4 = 6,000 units

Maximum level = (Reorder level + Reorder qty) – (Minimum consumption × Minimum delivery period)

8,400 = (6,000 + Reorder qty) – (800 × 2)

(–) Reorder qty. = – 8,400 + 6,000 – (1,600)

(–) Reorder qty. = – 2,400 – 1,600

Reorder qty. = 4,000 units.

Problem-37 (Level setting)

Two components A and B are used as follows:

Normal usage	—	50 units per week
Minimum usage	—	25 units per week
Maximum usage	—	75 units per week
Reorder quantity	—	A—300 units
		B—500 units
Reorder period	—	A—4 to 6 weeks
		B—2 to 4 weeks

Calculate for each component:

(*a*) Reorder level (*b*) Minimum level

(*c*) Maximum level (*d*) Average stock level

(*Sri Krishnadevaraya University, B.Com., March 2006*)

Solution:

(*a*) Reorder level = Maximum consumption × Maximum reorder period

A = 75 × 6 = 450 units

B = 75 × 4 = 300 units

(*b*) Minimum level = Reorder level – (Normal usage × Normal reorder period)

A = 450 – (50 × 5)

= 450 – 250 = 200 units

Working Note:

Normal reorder period $= \frac{4+6}{2} = 5$ weeks

B $= 300 - (50 \times 3)$

$= 300 - 150 = 150$ units

Working Note:

Normal reorder period $= \frac{2+4}{2} = 3$ weeks

(*c*) Maximum level = (Reorder level + Reorder qty) – (Minimum usage × Minimum reorder period)

A $= (450 + 300) - (25 \times 4)$

$= 750 - 100 = 650$ units

B $= (300 + 500) - (25 \times 2)$

$= 800 - 50 = 750$ units

(*d*) Average stock level $= \frac{\text{Minimum level} + \text{Maximum level}}{2}$

A $= \frac{200+650}{2} = 425$ units

B $= \frac{150+750}{2} = 450$ units.

Problem-38 (Level setting)

Two materials *x* and *y* are used as follows:

Minimum usage — 50 units per week each

Maximum usage — 150 units per week each

Normal usage — 100 units per week each

Ordering quantity — $x = 600$ units

— $y = 1{,}000$ units

Delivery period — $x = 4$ to 6 weeks

— $y = 2$ to 4 weeks

Calculate for each material:

(*a*) Minimum level

(*b*) Maximum level

(*c*) Ordering level

(*Sri Krishnadevaraya University, B. Com., October 2006*)

Solution:

(*a*) Reorder level = Maximum consumption × Maximum reorder period

x $= 150 \times 6 = 900$ units

y $= 150 \times 4 = 600$ units

(*b*) Minimum level = Reorder level – (Normal consumption × Normal reorder period)

x $= 900 - (100 \times 5)$

$= 900 - 500 = 400$ units

y = 600 – (100 × 3)
= 600 – 300 = 300 units

(c) Maximum level = (Reorder level + Reorder qty.) – (Minimum consumption × Minimum reorder period)

x = (900 + 600) – (50 × 4)
= 1500 – 200 = 1300 units

y = (600 + 1000) – (50 × 2)
= 1600 – 100 = 1500 units.

Problem-39

A company manufactures 5,000 units of a product per month. The cost of placing an order is Rs. 100. The purchase price of the raw material is Rs. 10 per kg. The reorder period is 4 to 8 weeks. The consumption of raw materials varies from 100 to 450 kg per week, the average consumption being 275 kg. The carrying cost of inventory is 20% per annum.

You are required to calculate:

(i) Reorder quantity
(ii) Reorder level
(iii) Maximum level
(iv) Minimum level
(v) Average stock level *(CA PE-II, November 2002)*

Solution:

(i) EOQ $= \sqrt{\frac{2AB}{CS}}$

$$= \sqrt{\frac{2 \times 14,300 \times 100}{10 \times \frac{20}{100}}}$$

= 1196 kgs

Note:

Annual usage = 275 kg × 52 weeks = 14,300 kg

(ii) Reorder level = Maximum usage × Maximum reorder period
= 450 × 8 = 3600 kg

(iii) Maximum level = (Reorder level + Reorder qty) – (Min usage × Min reorder period)
= (3600 + 1196) – (100 ×4)
= 4396 kg

(iv) Minimum level = Reorder level – (Normal usage × Normal reorder period)
= 3600 – (275 kg × 6)
= 1950 kg

(v) Average stock level $= \frac{\text{Max level} + \text{Min level}}{2}$

$$= \frac{4396 + 1950}{2} = 3173 \text{ kg}$$

OR

$$= \text{Minimum level} + \frac{1}{2}\ \text{Reorder quantity}$$

$$= 1950 + \frac{1}{2} \times 1196$$

$$= 2548 \text{ kg.}$$

Problem-40

A firm requires 50 items every day for a machine. A fixed cost of Rs. 50 per order is incurred for placing an order. The inventory carrying cost per item amounts of Re. 0.02 per day. The lead period is 32 days. You are required to compute : (*i*) Economic order quantity, and (*ii*) Reorder level.

(*CS Inter, December 2002*)

Solution:

(*i*) EOQ $= \sqrt{\frac{2AB}{CS}}$

$$= \sqrt{\frac{2 \times (50 \times 365) \times 50}{0.02 \times 365}}$$

$$= \sqrt{\frac{2 \times 18250 \times 50}{7.30}}$$

$= 500$ units

(*ii*) Reorder level = Maximum usage per day × Maximum lead time

= 50 units per day × 32 days

= 1600 items (units).

Problem-41

The following details are available from the books of Ruby Engineering Works Ltd. for the year ended 31st March 2005.

Monthly demand (units)	2,000
Cost of placing an order (Rs)	200
Annual carrying cost (Rs. per unit)	30
Normal usage (units per month)	100
Maximum usage (units per month)	150
Minimum usage (units per month)	50
Reorder period (weeks)	4–6

Based on the above details, calculate:

1. Reorder quantity
2. Reorder level
3. Minimum level
4. Maximum level

Assume 52 weeks in a year

(*C.S. Inter, June 2006*)

Solution:

In the question normal usage, maximum usage and minimum usage have been given in units per month instead of in weeks as the reorder period is given in weeks. It is further given that 52 weeks in a year. Therefore, in order to make the uniformity in usage of materials and reorder period, the reorder period given in weeks has been converted into months.

Therefore, maximum reorder period = $\frac{12}{52} \times 6 = 1.38$ months

Minimum reorder period = $\frac{12}{52} \times 4 = 0.92$ months

1. EOQ $= \sqrt{\frac{2AB}{CS}}$

$= \sqrt{\frac{2 \times 1200 \times 200}{30}} = 128$ units (Approx)

2. Reorder level = Maximum usage × Maximum reorder period

= 150 × 1.38 months = 207 units

3. Minimum level = Reorder level – (Normal usage × Average delivery period)

= 207 – (100 × 1.15)

= 207 – 115 = 92 units

Note:

Average delivery period or normal delivery period

$$\frac{1.38 + 0.92}{2} = 1.15 \text{ months}$$

4. Maximum level = (Reorder level + Reorder qty) – (Minimum usage × Minimum delivery period)

= (207 + 126) – (50 × 0.92)

= 333 – 46 = 287 units.

Problem-42

From the following particulars find out

(*a*) how much should be ordered each time

(*b*) when should the order be placed, and

(*c*) what should be the inventory level immediately before the material order is received?

Annual Consumption	= 12,000 units (360 days)
Cost per unit	= Re. 1
Ordering cost	= 12 per order
Inventory carrying charge	= 24%
Normal lead time	= 15 days
Safety stock	= 30 days consumption

(*Bangalore University, M.Com., May 1989, CA PE-II May 2005*)

Solution:

(*i*) EOQ $= \sqrt{\frac{2AB}{CS}} = \sqrt{\frac{2\times12{,}000\times12}{1\times\frac{24}{100}}} = \sqrt{\frac{2\times12{,}000\times12\times100}{1\times24}}$

$= \sqrt{12{,}00{,}000} =$ 1,095 units

(*ii*) **Time of placing the order.**

For 12,000 units, the period is 12 months (360 days)

For 1,095 units ⟶? $\frac{1{,}095}{12{,}000}\times12$

= 1.095 months

or 33 days

(*iii*) **Inventory level before the order is received.**

(Delivery period × normal usage) + safety stock

$\left(15\,\text{days}\times\frac{12{,}000}{360}\right)$ + 1,000 (see note)

= 15 × 33.34 + 1,000

= 500 + 1,000 = 1,500

Working Note:

For 360 days safety stock is 12,000

For 30 days → $= \frac{12{,}000\times30}{360}$ = 1,000 units.

Problem-43

Following information relating to a type of raw material is available

Annual demand	2,400 units
Unit price	Rs. 2.40
Ordering cost per order	Rs. 4.00
Storage cost	2% per annum
Interest rate	10% annum
Lead time	half month

Calculate EOQ and total annual inventory cost in respect of the particular material.

(*Sri Sathya Sai University, B.Com, (Hons.) August 2000*)

(*University of Madras, B.Com, May 2003*)

Solution:

(*i*) EOQ $= \sqrt{\frac{2AB}{CS}} = \sqrt{\frac{2\times2{,}400\times4}{2.40\times\frac{(10+2)}{100}}} = \sqrt{\frac{2\times2{,}400\times4}{2.40\times\frac{(12)}{100}}} = \sqrt{\frac{19.200}{0.288}}$ = 258 units

Calculation of total annual inventory cost:

Cost of 2,400 units @ Rs. 2.40 5,760.00

Ordering cost $= \frac{2,400}{258} = 9.3$ orders

or say 10 orders

@ Rs. 4 40.00

Carrying cost of average inventory

$258 \times 2.40 \times \frac{1}{2} \times \frac{12}{100}$ 37.15

5,837.15

Problem-44

Exe Ltd. has received an offer of quantity discount in its order of materials as under.

Price per ton	*Tonnes*
(Rs.)	
1,200	less than 500
1,180	500 and less than 1,000
1,160	1,000 and less than 2,000
1,140	2,000 and less than 3,000
1,120	3,000 and above

The annual requirements for materials is 5,000 tonnes. The ordering cost per order is Rs. 1,200 and the stock holding cost is estimated at 20% of materials cost per annum. You are required to compute the most economical purchase level.

What will be your answer to the above question, if there are no discounts offered and the price per tonnes is Rs. 1,500? (*CA. Inter, November 1990*)

Solution:

EOQ with Discount

Ordering qty. (tonnes)	*Price per ton (Rs.)*	*Cost of purchasing 5,000 tonnes*	*Cost of ordering (Rs.)*	*Cost of carrying average inventory*	*Total cost (Rs.)*
Q	*P*	*(Rs.) 5,000 × P*	$\frac{5,000}{Q} \times 1,200$	$\frac{Q}{2} \times P \times 20\%$	
400	1,200	60,00,000	15,000	48,000	60,63,000
500	1,180	59,00,000	12,000	59,000	59,71,000
1,000	1,160	58,00,000	6,000	1,16,000	59,22,000
2,000	1,140	57,00,000	3,000	2,28,000	59,31,000
3,000	1,120	56,00,000	2,000	3,36,000	59,38,000

From the above table it is clear that the most economical purchase level is at 1,000 ordering quantity in tonnes. Because it is at this level that total cost. *i.e.,* cost of ordering and cost of carrying inventory is minimum.

EOQ without discount and when the price is Rs. 1,500 per tonne.

EOQ $= \sqrt{\frac{2AB}{CS}}$

$$= \sqrt{\frac{2 \times 5{,}000 \times 1{,}200}{1{,}500 \times \frac{20}{100}}}$$

$$= \sqrt{\frac{2 \times 5{,}000 \times 1{,}200 \times 100}{1{,}500 \times 20}}$$

$$= \sqrt{40{,}000}$$

$$= 200 \text{ units.}$$

Problem-45

Anil company buys its annual requirement of 36,000 units in 6 instalments. Each unit cost Re. 1, and the ordering cost is Rs. 25. The inventory carrying cost is estimated of 20% of unit value. Find the total annual cost of the existing inventory policy. How much money can be saved by economic order quantity? *(C.A. Final, May 1986)*

$$\text{EOQ} = \sqrt{\frac{2AB}{CS}}$$

$$= \sqrt{\frac{2 \times 36{,}000 \times 25}{1 \times \frac{20}{100}}}$$

$$= \sqrt{\frac{2 \times 36{,}000 \times 25 \times 100}{1 \times 20}}$$

$$= \sqrt{90{,}00{,}000} = 3000 \text{ units.}$$

Solution:

Statement showing annual cost of the existing policy:

Cost of purchase	=	36,000
Ordering cost — $\frac{36{,}000}{6{,}000}$ = 6 orders @ Rs. 25 per order	=	150
Carrying cost — 6,000 × 1 × $\frac{1}{2} \times \frac{20}{100}$	=	600
Total cost		36,750

Statement showing annual cost with EOQ

Cost of purchase	=	36,000
Ordering cost — $\frac{36{,}000}{3{,}000}$ = 12 orders @ Rs. 25	=	300
Carrying cost – 3,000 × 1 × $\frac{1}{2} \times \frac{20}{100}$	=	300
Total cost		36,600

Problem-46 (Problem on level setting and EOQ)

The following data pertain to material x.

Supply period	4 to 8 months
Consumption rate:	
Maximum	600 units per month
Minimum	100 units per month
Normal	300 units per month
Yearly	3,600 units

Storage cost are 50% of stock value. Ordering costs are Rs. 400 per order. Price per unit of material Rs. 64.

Compute:

(*i*) Reorder level
(*ii*) Minimum stock level
(*iii*) Maximum stock level
(*iv*) Average stock level

(University of Delhi, B.Com. (Pass), April 1999)

Solution:

1. Reorder level = Maximum usage × Maximum reorder period
= 600 × 8 = 4,800 units

2. Minimum stock level = Reorder level – (Normal usage – Normal reorder period)
= 4,800 – (300 × 6)
= 4,800 – 1,800 = 3,000 units

Note: Normal reorder period is the average reorder period *i.e.,* $\frac{4+8}{2}$ = 6 months

3. Maximum stock level = (Reorder level + Reorder quantity) – (Minimum consumption × Minimum reorder period)
= (4,800 + 300) – (100 × 4)
= 5,100 – 400 = 4,700 units

Note:

$$\text{Reorder quantity or EOQ} = \sqrt{\frac{2AB}{CS}}$$

$$= \sqrt{\frac{2\times 3{,}600\times 400}{64\times\frac{50}{100}}}$$

$$= \sqrt{\frac{2\times 3{,}600\times 400}{32}}$$

$$= 300 \text{ units}$$

4. Average stock level $= \frac{\text{Minimum stock level} + \text{Maximum stock level}}{2}$

$$= \frac{3{,}000+4{,}700}{2}$$

$$= \frac{7{,}700}{2} = 3{,}850 \text{ units.}$$

Problem-47

ACE Ltd. manufactures a product and the following particulars are collected for the year ended March 2000.

Monthly demand (units)	1,000
Cost of placing on order (Rs.)	100
Annual carrying cost (Rs. per unit)	15
Normal usage (units per week)	50
Minimum usage (units per week)	25
Maximum usage (units per week)	75
Reorder period (weeks)	4–6

You are required to calculate:

1. Reorder quantity
2. Reorder level
3. Minimum level
5. Average stock level

(*C.S. Inter, June 2000*)

Solution:

(*i*) Reorder quantity $= \sqrt{\dfrac{2AB}{CS}}$

$= \sqrt{\dfrac{2 \times 2{,}600 \times 100}{15}}$

$=$ 186 units

Since normal usage is 50 units per week the annual consumption for the year is — 52 weeks × 50 = 2,600 units.

(*ii*) Reorder level = Maximum usage × Maximum delivery period

= 75 × 6 = 450 units per week

(*iii*) Minimum level = Reorder level – (Normal usage × Average delivery period)

= 450 – (50 × 5)

= 450 – 250 = 200 units per week

(*iv*) Maximum level = (Reorder level + Reorder qty.) – (Minimum usage × Minimum delivery period)

= (450 + 186) – (25 × 4) = 536 units per week

(*v*) Average stock $= \dfrac{\text{Minimum level} + \text{Maximum level}}{2}$

$= \dfrac{200 + 536}{2}$ = 368 units per week.

Note:

Alternatively, since the monthly demand given in the Problem is 1,000 units, it can be presumed that the annual consumption would be 12,000 units. Then, the answers would be changed accordingly as regards (*i*) Reorder quantity, (*ii*) Maximum level, and (*iii*) Average stock level.

Problem-48

Shagoon India Ltd., provides the following information in respect of material '*x*'.

Supply period	:	5 to 15 days
Rate of consumption		
Average	:	15 units per day
Maximum	:	20 units per day
Yearly	:	5,000 units

ordering costs are Rs. 20 per order. Purchase price per unit is Rs. 50. Storage costs are 10% of unit value.

Compute:

(*i*) Reorder quantity

(*ii*) Reorder level

(*iii*) Minimum level

(*iv*) Maximum level (*University of Delhi, B.Com., (Hons), April 1998*)

Solution:

(*i*) Reorder quantity $= \sqrt{\frac{2AB}{CS}}$

$$= \sqrt{\frac{2 \times 5{,}000 \times 20}{50 \times \frac{10}{100}}}$$

$$= \sqrt{\frac{2 \times 5{,}000 \times 20 \times 100}{50 \times 10}}$$

= 200 units

(*ii*) Reorder level = Maximum consumption × Maximum delivery period

= 20 × 15 = 300 units

(*iii*) Minimum level = Reorder level – (Normal consumption × Normal delivery period)

= 300 – (15 × 10)

= 300 – 150 = 150 units

(*iv*) Maximum level = (Reorder level + Reorder qty.) – (Minimum consumption × Minimum delivery period)

= (300 + 200) – (10 × 5)

= 500 – 50 = 450 units.

Problem-49

M/s Tubes Ltd., are the manufactures of picture tubes for T.V. The following are the details of their operation during 1997.

Average monthly market demand	2,000 tubes
Ordering cost	Rs. 100 per order
Inventory carrying cost	20% per annum
Cost of tubes	Rs. 500 per tube
Normal usage	100 tubes per week

Minimum usage	50 tubes per week
Maximum usage	200 tubes per week
Lead time to supply	6–8 weeks

Compute from the above:

1. Economic order quantity. If the supplier is willing to supply quarterly 1,500 units at a discount of 5% is it worth accepting.
2. Maximum level of stock
3. Minimum level of stock
4. Reorder level

(*C.A. Inter, May 2000*)

Solution:

1. EOQ $= \sqrt{\frac{2AB}{CS}}$

$$= \sqrt{\frac{2 \times 5{,}200 \times 100}{500 \times \frac{20}{100}}}$$

$= 102$ tubes

Note. Annual usage = 100 × 52 weeks = 5200.

If the supplier is willing to supply 1,500 units at a discount of 5%, is it worth accepting.

Total cost (When order size is 1,500 units)

= cost of 5,200 units + ordering cost + carrying cost

$$= 5{,}200 \times 475 + \frac{5{,}200}{1{,}500} \times 100 + 1{,}500 \times \frac{1}{2} \times 475 \times \frac{20}{100}$$

= 24,70,000 + 346.67 + 71.250

= 25,41,596.67

Total cost (when order size is 102 units)

$$= 5200 \times 500 + \frac{5{,}200}{102} \times 100 + 102 \times \frac{1}{2} \times 500 \times \frac{20}{100}$$

= 26,00,000 + 5,098.03 + 5,100

= 26,10,198.03

Since, the total cost under quarterly supply of 1,500 units with 5% discount is lower than that when order size is 102 units, therefore, the offer should be accepted. While accepting this offer consideration of capital blocked on order size of 1,500 units per quarter has been ignored.

2. Maximum level of stock = (Reorder level + Reorder quantity) – (Minimum usage × Minimum reorder period)

   = (1,600 + 102) – (50 × 6)

   = 1,402 units

3. Minimum level = Reorder level – (Normal usage × Average reorder period)

   = 1,600 – (100 × 7)

   = 900 units

4. Reorder level = Maximum usage × Maximum reorder period

   = 200 × 8.

   = 1,600 units

4. Inventory Turnover Ratio or Material Turnover Ratio. Inventory turnover ratio as a technique of material control is useful to avoid unnecessary investment on those materials whose consumption is much less. In addition to this, it also helps to avoid obsolescence of stock and incurring of unnecessary storage costs. It may be defined as the ratio of cost of materials consumed to the average stock held during the period. Expressed in the form of formula,

$$\text{Inventory turnover ratio} = \frac{\text{Cost of materials consumed during the period}}{\text{Average stock of materials during the period}}$$

Inventory turnover may be denoted in terms of number of days in which the average inventory is consumed. This is obtained by using the following formula.

$$\text{Inventory turnover ratio in terms of days} = \frac{\text{365 days}}{\text{Inventory turnover ratio}}$$

In this case, if the duration of the inventory turnover period is short (than the anticipated period), material is said to be fast moving.

Whenever the consumption of different types of materials are analysed, it will be observed that not all materials are consumed in the same quantities. Some materials move fast while others are slow in their movement for consumption purposes. On the basis of rate of consumption of materials, the following categories of materials become evident.

(*a*) ***Slow-moving materials.*** Such materials have a low turnover ratio and hence they must not be stocked in excess quantities.

(*b*) ***Dormant materials.*** Materials which are currently not in demand for consumption purpose are regarded as dormant materials. Such materials should not be bought until the entire stock is made use of.

(*c*) ***Obsolete materials.*** Obsolete materials represent a kind of materials for which there is no longer a demand. This may be on account of the fact that the production of goods using this kind of materials must have been discontinued or a better substitute must have been found. The obsolete stock may be treated as scrap.

Problem-50

The following information is available from the books of a company for the year ended 31st December, 1990.

	Material A	*Material B*
	(Rs.)	(Rs.)
Opening stock	14,000	20,000
Purchases	2,30,000	36,000
Closing stock	10,000	24,000

Calculate the material turnover ratio of the above type of materials and determine which of the two materials is more fast moving.

(*University of Kerala, M.Com., May 1992*)

Solution:

Calculation of materials consumed

	Material A	Material B
Opening stock	14,000	20,000
Add : Purchases	2,30,000	36,000
	2,44,000	56,000
Less : Closing stock	10,000	24,000
Cost of material consumped	2,34,000	32,000

Calculation of average inventory

$$\frac{\text{Opening stock + closing stock}}{2}$$

$$\text{Material A} \quad \frac{14{,}000+10{,}000}{2} = 12{,}000$$

$$\text{Material B} \quad \frac{20{,}000+24{,}000}{2} = 22{,}000$$

Calculation of inventory turnover ratio

$$\text{Inventory turnover ratio} = \frac{\text{Cost of materials consumed}}{\text{Average inventory}}$$

$$\text{Material A} = \frac{2{,}34{,}000}{12{,}000} = 19.5$$

$$\text{Material B} = \frac{32{,}000}{22{,}000} = 1.4$$

Material A is fast moving.

Problem-51

From the following data for the year ended 31st December 1986. Calculate the inventory ratio of the two items and put forward your comments on them.

	Material A (Rs.)	Material B (Rs.)
Opening stock on 1.1. 1986	10,000	9,000
Purchase during the year	52,000	27,000
Closing stock on 31.12.1986	6,000	11.000

(ICWA, Inter, Dec. 1987)

Solution:

Calculation of materials consumed

	Material A (Rs.)	Material B (Rs.)
Opening stock	10,000	9,000
Add : Purchases	52,000	27,000
	62,000	36,000
Less : Closing stock	6,000	11,000
Cost of materials consumption	56,000	25,000

Calculation of average inventory

$$\frac{\text{Opening stock + Closing stock}}{2}$$

Material A $= \dfrac{10{,}000 + 6{,}000}{2} = \text{Rs. } 8{,}000$

Material B $= \dfrac{9{,}000+11{,}000}{2} = \text{Rs. } 10{,}000$

Inventory turnover ratio $= \dfrac{\text{Cost of materials consumed}}{\text{Average inventory}}$

Material A $= \dfrac{56{,}000}{8{,}000} = 7 \text{ times}$

Material B $= \dfrac{25{,}000}{10{,}000} = 2.5 \text{ units}$

Inventory turnover ratio in terms of number of days $= \dfrac{\text{Number of days in a year}}{\text{Inventory turnover ratio}}$

Material A $= \dfrac{365}{7} = 52 \text{ days}$

Material B $= \dfrac{365}{2.5} = 146 \text{ days.}$

Problem-52

(Calculation of inventory turnover ratio when stock levels are given): From the following particular calculate the inventory turnover ratio:

Minimum stock level	Rs. 1,000
Maximum stock level	Rs. 3,000
Issues during the period	Rs. 10,000

Solution:

Inventory turnover ratio $= \dfrac{\text{Cost of materials consumed during period}}{\frac{1}{2}(\text{Maximum level} + \text{Maximum stock level})}$

$$= \frac{10{,}000}{\frac{1}{2}(3{,}000+1{,}000)} = 5 \text{ items}$$

Problem-53

(Calculation of inventory turnover ratio when reorder quantity is given) : From the following particulars, calculate the inventory turnover ratio:

Maximum stock level	1,500 units
Minimum stock level	600 units
Reorder quantity	800 units
Issues during the year	4,000 units

Solution:

$$\text{Inventory turnover ratio} = \frac{\text{Units of materials consumed during period}}{\text{Minimum level} + \frac{1}{2}\text{ Reorder quantity}}$$

$$= \frac{4{,}000}{600 + \frac{1}{2} \times 800} = 4 \text{ times.}$$

Problem-54

(*a*) From the following information available from the Bin Cards of a concern for the period of one year, calculate inventory ratios of materials A, B and C.

(*b*) If the prices of A, B, and C be respectively Rs. 10 per unit, Rs. 8 per kg and Rs. 5 per litre, then what is the total turnover of materials A, B and C?

(*c*) Find the period for which the average inventory in respect of each of A, B and C is held?

	Material A	*Material B*	*Material C*
Opening stock	7,000 units	2,000 kg.	10,000 litres
Purchases	1,15,000 units	1,10,000 kg.	12,000 litres
Closing stock	2,000 units	12,000 kg.	18,000 litres

Solution:

$$(a)\ \text{Inventory turnover ratio} = \frac{\text{Annual consumption of materials in units}}{\text{Average inventory}}$$

$$\text{Material A} = \frac{1{,}20{,}000}{4{,}500} = 26.67$$

$$\text{Material B} = \frac{1{,}00{,}000}{7{,}000} = 14.29$$

$$\text{Material C} = \frac{4{,}000}{14{,}000} = 0.29$$

Note: 1. Annual consumption of material = Opening stock + Purchases – Closing stock.

Material A	= 7,000 + 1,15,000 – 2,000	= 1,20,000 units
Material B	= 2,000 + 1,10,000 – 12,000	= 1,00,000 kg.
Material C	= 10,000 + 12,000 – 18,000	= 4,000 litres

Note 2. Average inventory $= \dfrac{\text{Opening stock} + \text{Closing stock}}{2}$

Material A $= \dfrac{7{,}000 + 2{,}000}{2} = 4{,}500$ units

Material B $= \dfrac{2{,}000 + 12{,}000}{2} = 7{,}000$ kg.

Material C $= \dfrac{10{,}000 + 18{,}000}{2} = 14{,}000$ litres

(*b*) Total turnover of materials A, B & C

$= \dfrac{\text{Value of materials consumed during the year}}{\text{Value of average inventory}}$

$= \dfrac{20{,}20{,}000}{1{,}71{,}000} = 11.81$

Note 3. Value of materials consumed:

Material A	1,20,000 units	@ Rs. 10	=	12,00,000
Material B	1,00,000 kg.	@ Rs. 8	=	8,00,000
Material C	4,000 litres	@ Rs. 5	=	20,000
				20,20,000

Note 4. Value of average inventory:

Material A	4,500 units	@ Rs. 10	=	45,000
Material B	7,000 kg.	@ Rs. 8	=	56,000
Material C	14,000 litres	@ Rs. 5	=	70,000
				1,71,000

(*c*) Inventory turnover expressed in days $= \dfrac{\text{No. of days in the year}}{\text{Inventory turnover ratio}}$

Material A $= \dfrac{365}{26.67} = 14$ days

Material B $= \dfrac{365}{14.29} = 26$ days

Material C $= \dfrac{365}{0.29} = 1{,}259$ days.

Problem-55

The following data are available in respect of material '*x*' for the year ended 31st March, 1997.

	(Rs.)
Opening stock	90,000
Purchases during the year	2,70,000
Closing stock	1,10,000

Calculate: (*i*) Inventory turnover ratio and, (*ii*) Number of days for which the average inventory is held. (*C.A. Inter, November 1997*)

Solution:

Cost of materials consumed

Opening stock of raw materials	90,000
Add : Material purchased during the year	2,70,000
	3,60,000
Less : Closing stock of raw materials	1,10,000
Cost of raw materials consumed	2,50,000

Average stock of raw materials

$$= \frac{\text{Opening stock of raw materials + Closing stock of raw materials}}{2}$$

$$= \frac{90,000 + 1,10,000}{2}$$

$$= 1,00,000$$

(*i*) Inventory turnover ratio $= \dfrac{\text{Cost of raw materials consumed}}{\text{Average stock of raw materials}}$

$$= \frac{2,50,000}{1,00,000} = 2.5$$

(*ii*) Average number of days for which the average inventory is held

$$= \frac{365}{\text{Inventory turnover ratio}}$$

$$= \frac{365}{2.5} = 146 \text{ days.}$$

5. Stock Checking or Stock Taking. The term stock taking refers to the process of verifiying the quantity balances of the entire range of materials held in the storeroom. The term stock checking is used to denote verification of materials in terms of quantities which may be undertaken either regularly or intermittently. It is process of counting, weighing or measuring all items of materials and recording the results. Stock checking serves the following purposes.

(*a*) To verify the accuracy of stores records.

(*b*) To furnish value of closing stock to prepare final accounts of the enterprise.

(*c*) To disclose frauds, thefts and losses of materials.

(*d*) To reveal any weakness in the system of storage and control over materials.

Methods of stock taking. There are two methods of stock taking, *viz.,* periodic or annual and continuous or perpetual.

1. ***Periodic or annual stock taking.*** Under this method, the entire stock of materials are covered at the same time at the end of given period, which is usually the end of the financial year. However, in a large factory it may be impossible to do all the verification work in one day and hence it is extended over several days. Annual stock taking involves a great deal of preparation. Firstly, a programme should be drawn up and it is agreed upon by all concerned. Secondly, stock verification sheets are to be prepared in advance. Thirdly, all personnel concerned must be instructed as to their duties. The following points are to be considered while conducting annual stock verification.

(*a*) Appoint one person to control the whole operation.

(*b*) While stock taking is in progress, do not open storeroom for issues and receipts.

(*c*) Consider for verification all normal stock of materials such as packages, scraps, residues and materials under inspection.

(*d*) The stock taking sheets must be under the control of one individual, consecutively numbered and issued to staff on duty as required.

(*e*) All damaged, deteriorated or used items must be recorded separately.

(*f*) Make each person taking stock responsible for a particular section or clearly defined area of the storeroom and record everything that is found in that area. Stock takers should proceed in an orderly manner and mark each bin or rack as it is dealt with to avoid the chance of checking any items twice and to ensure that nothing is missed.

(*g*) List separately materials received, but still under inspection.

(*h*) Show the method of checking, *i.e.,* count weight, measurement on the stock sheet for each item.

(*i*) The method of pricing should be known and if possible, it is desirable to enter all prices in terms of units of issue on the stock sheets in advance.

(*j*) In case of decentralised store systems, the materials in transit at the date of stock taking must be taken into account.

Having verified the stock of materials, a stock verification report is to be prepared. A specimen form of such a report is given below.

ABC CO. LTD

Stock Verification Report

Store room no. .... Section .... Date of verification ....

Date of completion.............

Number of items checked .... Number of items found incorrect ....

Code	*Description of materials*	*Physical balance*	*Book balance*	*Physical balance over or under book balance*	*Unit code*	*Remarks*

Physical count by .... Unit cost entered by ....

Checked by ....

Fig. 4.6 *Stock verification report.*

Disadvantages of Annual Stock Taking System

(*a*) Under this system the factory has to be closed during the period of stock verification which results in the loss of production time.

(*b*) Sometimes a complete check on materials may not be exercised. Often those materials which are not used go unnoticed.

(*c*) It takes more time to verify the stock.

2. *Continuous or perpetual inventory control.* In its broad sense, it means a method of recording stores balance after every receipt and issue, to facilitate regular checking and to obviate closing down of factory for stock taking. Under this method the balance of materials as shown by the bin card and stores ledger card for the same item of materials is compared along with the actual quantity of materials in stock. The book balance and the physically verified balance must agree with each other. The discrepancy if any go to indicate the deficit in the materials for which prompt action is taken to avoid such defects.

Under this system, to verify the materials on a regular basis, a team may be constituted which verifies the stock continuously throughout the year in accordance with a predetermined programme so that each item is physically verified at least once in the course of year or more frequently. The programme is so designated that a certain number of materials are taken on every working day and compared with the bin cards and the store ledger. Having verified the materials, a stores audit note is prepared. A specimen form of it is given below:

XYZ CO. LTD.
Store Audit Note

Note. no. .... Bin no. ....
Items .... Location code...........
Code no. .... Date ....

Date of verification	*Actual stock*	*Bin card stock*	*Shortage*	*Surplus*	*Reasons*	*Adjustment*	*Remarks*

Stock .... Storekeeper .... Stores accountant ....

Fig. 4.7. *Stores audit note.*

When the stock is incorrect, an enquiry is made and the discrepancies are adjusted in the records to make them correspond with the physical balance. A surplus or deficiency should be prevented. Deficiency in materials may arise out of malpractice in stores whereas a surplus may tend to introduce and encourage malpractice.

Causes for the discrepancies in the materials. The causes for the discrepancies in the materials may be analysed as shown in the following chart:

Discrepancy in the materials

- Apparent
- Real
  - Abnormal
  - Normal
    - Avoidable
    - Unavoidable

Fig. 4.8. *Chart showing causes for discrepancies.*

Apparent cause of discrepancy is owing to wrong entry in the bin card or because of wrong verification of materials. These discrepancies can be set right by correcting the bin card entries or by re-verifying the stock.

If the discrepancy is not because of the above reasons, it is termed as 'real' discrepancy which requires further investigation.

The causes for abnormal discrepancies are due to occurrence of fire, riot, burglary, etc. They are not within the reach of management. Hence, they are written off as losses. Normal discrepancies are within the control of management and hence effective steps are to be taken to prevent them.

Avoidable discrepancies arise on account of (*i*) incorrect measurement of issues, (*ii*) carelessness in material handling, (*iii*) improper storage of materials, and (*iv*) Pilferage. It is the duty of storekeeper to be vigilant on all these causes and is personally responsible for all surpluses and deficiencies arising out of avoidable causes.

Unavoidable deficiencies are caused by (*i*) handling losses arising out of issuing in small units, (*ii*) loss or gain arising out of atmospheric conditions. For example, evaporation in case of liquids and gain in weight of exposure to air in case of certain chemicals like caustic soda, (*iii*) gains arising out of seasoning of materials. Though it is unavoidable, the control lies in foreseeing the nature of unavoidable causes, the extent of the differences that could arise out of these and to decide a proper method of treating them.

Advantages of Perpetual Inventory Control

The advantages of perpetual inventory system are as follows:

(*a*) The long and costly work of stock taking is avoided. The stock of materials as shown by the stores ledger can be obtained quickly for the preparation of final accounts at interim periods.

(*b*) A detailed and reliable check on the stores is obtained.

(*c*) It is not necessary to stop production during the period of stock verification.

(*d*) Discrepancies are readily located and appropriate measures can be taken to avoid their recurrence.

(*e*) It boosts the moral effect on the storekeeper and the practice of dishonesty can be curbed.

(*f*) It helps in avoiding the understocking and overstocking of materials and the dangers associated with them.

(*g*) It helps storekeeper in replenishment of stocks on item as he is always in touch with reorder level because of continuous stock taking.

(*h*) The investment in stock can be kept to the minimum in view of the operational requirements.

(i) It reveals the existence of surplus, dormant, obsolete and slow moving materials and hence remedial action can be taken.

Limitations

(a) The system is expensive and a small concern cannot afford to implement this system.

(b) The information about actual stock of a particular item on a particular day may not be available. Instead only book figures are available.

Differences between Periodic Stock Taking and Perpetual Inventory System

Periodic stock taking	*Perpetual inventory system*
1. Stock verification is done once in the year.	1. Stock verification is spread all over the year.
2. It is undertaken by Technical staff.	2. It is undertaken by staff of accounts or the audit department.
3. Discrepancies are adjusted in one consolidated figure.	3. Dicrepancies are adjusted all over the year.
4. There is no secrecy about the items of materials to be verified.	4. Secrecy can be maintained as to the items and dates on which they are verified.
5. It involves closure of the factory during the period of stock verification.	5. It is carried out without affecting the stores and production departments.
6. Discrepancies are brought to the notice of management at the end of the year and hence it becomes too late to take corrective measures.	6. Discrepancies are brought to the notice of management as and when it is detected and hence immediate action can be taken.
7. It is suitable only for small sized concerns as it will be very expensive to have a continuous stock taking system.	7. It is suitable for large sized concern which can easily afford to incur expenses on this system.

Accounting of Surpluses and Shortages

1. Apparent discrepancies need no adjustment. The only thing to be done is to correct the bin card or to reverify the stock depending upon the circumstance.
2. Abnormal discrepancies are to be written off to costing profit and loss account.
3. Avoidable discrepancies should be valued and adjusted through the stores consumption account. The difference in the amount is recovered as an item of stores overhead.
4. Unavoidable discrepancies should be estimated in terms of percentages. When materials are issued, the issue quantities should be adjusted by this percentage.

Reconciliation between the Bin Card Balance, Stores Ledger Balance and the Physical Balance

Reconciliation is a three-tier process. They are:

(a) ***Reconciliation between physical balance of stores and bin card balances.*** If the physical balance of stores is less than the bin card balance, the shortage is to be entered in the issue column and the excess, should be entered in the receipt column in red ink.

(b) ***Reconciliation between bin card and stores ledger with respect to quantities.*** The differences can be avoided by writing the serial number of documents used in connection with recording the material transactions. Another method is by indicating the balance of stock in each and every material document after posting in the bin card. This facilitates automatic reconciliation at the time of posting in stores ledger card.

(*c*) ***Reconciliation between stores ledger and cost ledger in regard to value.*** Various transactions relating to materials such as receipts, issues, returns, shortages, excesses are valued, posted and journalised. The entries are posted in the cost ledger. The value of closing stock of all the stores ledger card should be equal to the value of closing stock in the cost ledger. Any differences should be corrected at regular intervals.

Problem-56

After the annual stock taking you come to know of some significant discrepancies between book stock and physical stock. You gather the following information.

Item	*Stock card (units)*	*Stores ledger (units)*	*Physical (units)*	*Cost per unit*
A	600	600	560	60
B	380	380	385	40
C	750	780	720	10

(*a*) What action should be taken to record the information shown above?

(*b*) Suggest reasons for the shortage and discrepancies above and recommend a possible course of action by management to prevent losses. (*C.A., Inter, May 1991*)

Solution:

The following action is to be taken to record the information given in the question.

(*i*) Check the stock card and stores ledger and to record the correct physical quantities.

(*ii*) Investigate the causes for the losses or gains in the stock.

(*iii*) Once the causes are known, the following treatment is to be given.

(*a*) Factory Overhead A/c *Dr.*
To Stores Ledger Control A/c
(When the shortage is normal)

(*b*) Costing Profit and Loss A/c *Dr.*
To Stores Ledger Control A/c
(When the shortage is abnormal

(*c*) Work-in-progress A/c Dr.
To Stores Ledger Control A/c
(When the shortage is due to non-recording or short-recording)

(*iv*) If there are any clerical errors rectification entries are to be passed.

(*v*) If there is any gain, the following entries are required to be passed.

(*a*) Stores Ledger A/c *Dr.*
To Factory Overhead A/c
(When the excess of stock is due to normal course)

(*b*) Stores Ledger Control A/c *Dr.*
To Costing P & L A/c
(When the excess of stock is due to abnormal circumstances)

(c) Stores Ledger Control A/c Dr.
To work-in-progress A/c
(When the excess of stock is due to wrong recording)

(vi) In the given problem, the losses are with reference to items A (Rs. 60 × 40 units = 2,400) and C (Rs. 10 × 60 = 600). As the reasons for these losses are not given, they may be debited to Profit & Loss A/c and Stores Ledger Control A/c is credited accordingly.

(vii) The gains are in respect of stock item B (Rs. 40 × 5 = 200). This gain is debited to stores Ledger Control Account and Profit & Loss Account is credited.

Reasons for shortage and discrepancies

(i) Wastage of materials due to spoilage, evaporation, etc., which may be normal or abnormal.
(ii) Units issued for production without entering in stock card and stores ledger.
(iii) Theft.
(iv) Clerical errors.

Recommendations for Preventing Future Losses

(i) Only authorised persons should make entries.
(ii) Materials should be issued only against material requisition notes.
(iii) A system of internal check should be undertaken for all types of materials.
(iv) Materials are to be issued in the order of their receipts to avoid deterioration or obsolescence.
(v) Entries must be carefully made in both stores ledger card and stock card.

Problem-57

In the course of physical verification of stores as on 31st March 1991, following differences are revealed in case of AB Ltd.

Material	*Unit*	*Rate per unit (Rs.)*	*Balance*		*Remarks*
			Physical	*Ledger*	
A	Nos.	700	600	680	Wrong entry
B	Litres	1,200	1,100	1,155	Normal evaporation loss
C	Nos.	600	350	400	Material losses not accounted for
D	Kgs.	2,200	900	930	Shortage due to pilferage and theft
E	Nos.	1,500	1,475	1,325	150 Nos. received but not entered in ledger.
F	Meters	1,000	291	291	Obsolete materials realised sale value Rs. 1,650 awaiting despatch.

Prepare journal entries in the cost ledger to give effects to the above adjustments as called for.
(ICWA, Inter, June 1991)

Solution:

Material A. No journal entry is required. The stock verification record should be altered to 680 numbers to match with the book balance which is the correct balance.

Material B.

Stores Adjustment A/c	Dr.	660	
To Stores Ledger Control A/c			660

(Being the adjustment of normal evaporation loss of material B, charged off to production overheads)

Material C.

Work-in-progress Control A/c	Dr.	300	
To Stores Ledger Control A/c			300
(Being adjustment of issue of materials)			

Material D.

Costing Profit & Loss A/c	Dr.	660	
To Stores Ledger Control A/c			660
(Being the abnormal loss of materials caused by theft charged P & L A/c			

Material E.

Stores Ledger Control A/c	Dr	2,250	
To General Ledger Control A/c			2,250
(Being entry for materials received not taken into stock)			

Material F.

General Ledger Adjustment A/c	Dr.	1,650	
Stores Adjustment A/c	Dr.	1,260	
To Stores Ledger Control A/c			2,910
(Being obsolete materials written off sale value transferred to general ledger)			

6. Input-output Ratio Analysis: This technique of material control is helpful in knowing the utility or usage of materials in manufacturing a finished product. It refers to the ratio of quantity of a material put in the manufacturing process to the quantity of the material in the finished product. Expressed in the form of a formula.

$$\text{Input-output ratio} = \frac{\text{Input quantity of materials}}{\text{Quantity of materials in the output}}$$

Very often this ratio is expressed in percentages. To know whether the input-output ratio is favourable or adverse a standard input-output ratio is determined. The actual ratio is compared with the standard ratio. If the actual ratio is higher than the standard ratio, it denotes an inferior quality of materials or inefficiency in the manufacturing process. Accordingly, the reasons may be traced and appropriate action is taken. This ratio helps in exercising control over scrap and wastages in the production.

Advantages

(*a*) It helps in knowing whether the usage of material is favourable or adverse.

(*b*) It helps in evaluating the efficiency of production department.

(*c*) It helps in knowing the cost of raw material in the finished product. This is calculated by multiplying cost per unit of the raw material by the input-output ratio.

Problem-58

The pure chemical industry is using chemical *A* as its raw materials. This chemical costs Rs. 10 per kg. and its input-output ratio is 125 per cent. On account of scarcity of this material, the industry is forced to use one of the following alternative keeping in view, of course the quality of materials.

Material	*Rate per kg.*	*Input-output ratio*
Chemical B	Rs. 12	110%
Chemical C	Rs. 9	150%

Recommend which material is to be used.

Solution:

In order to select the right type of substitute, it is necessary to calculate the cost of raw material in the finished product. The following formula is to be adopted.

$$\frac{\text{Input}}{\text{Output}} \times \text{rate per unit}$$

$$\text{Chemical B} = \frac{110}{100} \times 12 = \text{Rs. } 13.20 \text{ per kg.}$$

$$\text{Chemical C} = \frac{150}{100} \times 9 = \text{Rs. } 13.50 \text{ per kg.}$$

As the cost per kg. of chemical B is less it has to be preferred to chemical 'C'.

7. Classification and Codification of Materials: This technique of material control helps in easy identification of materials and in issuing them quickly to various production departments. Large factories involve purchase of varieties of materials in bulk quantities and they tend to mix up with other materials. Classification of materials prevents from mixing up of materials and in issuing them easily to various departments.

Classification of materials may be defined as a standardised arrangement of materials under a common designation according to its similarities, attributes or relations. Classification of materials are made on the basis of its nature or usage. The following principles of classification helps in quick identification of materials.

(*a*) Every item of material and all related components thereof, should be grouped into logical divisions or classes.

(*b*) Divisions should be specific enough to exclude all duplicate listing of items or ambiguity.

(*c*) Arrangement should be broad enough so that divisions will not become numerous as to be cumbersome.

Having classified the materials the next step is to codify the materials. A code may be defined as mark, character or group of characters which may consist of figures, letters or signs chosen to typify or represent material. The following principles are to be followed while coding the materials:

(*a*) A code should be exclusive and should completely differentiate the item, it represents from every other item in the system.

(*b*) A code should indicate, by its form, the class and principal sub-classes in which the item represented by it belongs.

Methods of Codifying the Materials

(*a*) ***Alphabetic method:*** Under this method, each item of material is indicated by a letter or combination of letters. This method is conveniently used when the materials used are few in number.

(*b*) ***Numerical method:*** Under this method, each item of material is indicated by a number or combination of numbers.

(*c*) ***Mnemonic method :*** When the codes chosen for classification is meant for memory assisting, it is known as mnemonic codification. This includes the use of both alphabetic letters and numbers. The first letter or number of the code denotes the general class to which the material belong and successive letters or numbers indicate sub-class for which the materials belong.

Advantages of Codification of Materials

(*a*) It helps in easy identification of materials which facilitates quick and prompt issue of materials. Codification is more useful where the same material is known by more than one name.

(*b*) It dispenses with writing full names and other particulars of materials. This also economises space in forms.

(*c*) Codification is a must for mechanised accounting.

(*d*) Codification ensures secrecy as code numbers are known to all.

8. Miscellaneous Techniques: The following are some of the techniques used to exercise control over materials:

(*a*) ***Automatic order system:*** Under this technique purchase orders are automatically placed as soon as the materials reach the reorder level. This technique is used where materials accounting is mechanised. The punched cards are used to record the receipts and issues of materials. When the reorder level is reached, computer automatically sorts the material card. It is then processed by a clerk who places an order for the necessary quantity. This technique enables the purchase department to review material items, forecast the requirements and the lead time, establishes safety stock and in determining economic order quantity.

(*b*) ***Order cycling:*** Under this technique a review of materials in storeroom is made on a regular basis. For example, a review can be made once in a month. Those materials which are more essential can be reviewed more frequently compared to other materials. On review, an order is placed to bring the materials to a desired level, say fortnightly supply. One of the review that is made frequently covering small items of materials (indirect materials) is termed as 90 ÷ 60 – 30 day method. When the materials fall to a 60-day supply, an order is placed for 30-day supply. Similarly adjustments can be made for procuring the materials at the time desired.

(*c*) ***Minimum-maximum method:*** This is based on the technique of level setting. Under this technique, the minimum level represents reordering level. It means as and when the minimum level is reached an order is placed with a view to increase the materials to the maximum level.

9. New Techniques of Materials Control: The following are some of new techniques of material control:

(*a*) ***FSN analysis (Fast-slow and non-moving materials) :*** Fast moving materials are consumed very frequently in the production process and hence they are to be replenished at very frequent intervals. Slow moving materials on the other hand are consumed less frequently. Non-moving materials may be termed as dormant stock. These are the materials whose demand for the current production requirements are not felt but are needed in the near future. A careful watch is to be kept on all these three category of materials so as to keep further stock of slow moving and dormant stock to a minimum while increasing the stock of fast moving materials.

(*b*) ***HML analysis (High, Medium and Low valued items):*** As compared to ABC analysis which takes into account the consumption value of materials under this technique the unit value of stores item is considered. Those materials with a high unit value will be given utmost importance and a tight control is exercised. The medium items of materials with a moderate unit value will be given lesser degree of control whereas low valued items will receive least degree of control.

(*c*) ***VED analysis (Vital, Essential, Desirable materials):*** The technique of material control is applicable to spare parts. Spares are classified into vital, essential and desirable. Whereas vital category of spares are to be stocked adequately, essential and desirable categories can be stocked as and when required if the lead time of such materials is low.

A modified form of this technique is termed as **VEIN** (Vital, Essential, Important and Normal) which is used to control plant and machineries. When this technique is used in conjunctions with VED analysis it becomes one of the effective technique of material control. Under this technique, vital spares are arranged for all plants, *viz.,* vital, essential, important and normal. Similarly, essential spares are arranged for all the four categories of machines.

(*d*) ***SDE analysis:*** This technique is used to exercise control over materials depending upon their ready availability. Accordingly, materials are classified into scarce, difficult and easy to obtain the materials. Any item of materials which is scarce in supply is to be stocked in excess quantities irrespective of its value, volume and frequency of its movement in order to avoid stoppage in the production process. So also constant efforts are to be made to procure difficult-to-obtain type of materials. However, no extra efforts are required/to be taken in the case of 'easy-to-obtain' type of materials.

(*e*) ***SOS analysis:*** Under this technique of material control, materials are classified into two types, *viz.,* seasonal and off-seasonal materials. It is seasonal materials which are given more importance in terms of its procurements.

(*f*) ***GOLF analysis:*** Under this technique of material control, materials are classified on the bases of nature of supply. Accordingly, materials are classified into (*i*) government supplies *i.e.,* through government department like STC, MMTC, etc., (*ii*) open supplies, (*iii*) local supplies, and (*iv*) foreign supplies. No problem is posed in case of open and local supplies. Whereas certain formalities are to be observed in case of government and foreign supplies.

(*g*) ***Just-in-time system (JIT):*** Just-in-time (JIT) purchase means the purchase of goods or materials such that delivery immediately preceeds their use. It is one of the latest management practice that has originated from Japan. JIT is at the core of Japanese production management, inventory management as well as improvement strategies.

JIT is a system whose objective is to procure or produce products or components as they are required by a customer or for use rather than stock. A just-in-time system is a pull system which responds to demand, in contrast act to a "push" system in which stocks net as buffer between the different elements of the system, such as purchasing, production and sales.

The JIT approach involves a continuous commitment to the pursuit of excellence in all phases of manufacturing system, design and operation. The aims of JIT are to produce required items, at required quality, in required quantities, at the precise time they are required.

Just-in-time philosophy is used in manufacturing and purchasing. "JIT manufacturing" is a system of manufacturing that aims to eliminate waste and reduce scrap and down time and thereby improve the production system. JIT purchasing is defined as a purchasing system in which material purchases are contracted so that the receipt and usage of material to the maximum extent match or coincide.

Features of a JIT system

(1) Low or zero inventories
(2) Emphasis on customer service and timing
(3) Short lead time
(4) Flexibility of operations
(5) Efficient flow

Advantages of JIT

(1) The suppliers of goods or materials cooperate with the company and supply requisite quantity of goods or materials for which order is placed before the start of production.
(2) JIT purchases results in cost savings as for example, the cost of stock out, inventory carrying, material handling and breakage are reduced.
(3) Due to frequent purchases of raw materials its issue price is likely to be very close to the replacement price. Consequently, the method of pricing to be followed for valuing material issues becomes less important for companies using JIT purchasing.
(4) JIT purchasing are now attempting to extend daily deliveries to as many areas as possible so that the goods spend less time in warehouses or on store shelves before they are exhausted.

Pre-requisities of JIT

(1) Low variety
(2) Demand stability
(3) Vendor reliability
(4) Defect free material
(5) Good communication
(6) Elimination of non-value added activities
(7) Total quality control.

Questions

I. A. Mark *T* or *F* in the space provided.

(*a*) Storeroom does not store finished products manufactured in the factory. *T*/*F*
(*b*) "Providing a place for everything and everything in its place" is the key to success in a stores organisation. *T*/*F*
(*c*) Centralised stores system is more suitable for a large-sized factory. *T*/*F*
(*d*) A good layout of stores need not give a good appearance. *T*/*F*
(*e*) A bin card is not filled by the storekeeper. *T*/*F*
(*f*) A stores ledger card contains the quantity and value of materials received, issued and in balance. *T*/*F*
(*g*) The returned material is received by the stores accountant. *T*/*F*
(*h*) Under a decentralised 'storekeeping' system several employees working out of one storeroom are responsible for the issue and control of all items. *T*/*F*
(*i*) Stores ledger is maintained in the stores room. *T*/*F*

(*j*) A high inventory turnover rate indicates that material in question is a fast moving one. *T/F*

(*k*) Bin cards are not a part of accounting records. *T/F*

(*l*) An efficient and experienced storekeeper need not bother himself about classification and codification of materials. *T/F*

(*m*) The two extremes of overstocking and understoking of materials may be avoided by the fixation of inventory level. *T/F*

(*n*) The stores ledger is written by the storekeeper. *T/F*

(*o*) Maintenance of the stores ledger involves additional clerical labour since it contains the same particulars as those in bin card. *T/F*

[***Answers:*** (*a*) *F*, (*b*) *T*, (*c*) *T*, (*d*) *F*, (*e*) *F*, (*f*) *T*, (*g*) *F*, (*h*) *F*, (*i*) *F*, (*j*) *T*, (*k*) *T*, (*l*) *F*, (*m*) *T*, (*n*) *F*, (*o*) *F*]

II. Fill in the blanks:

(*a*) The process of physical verification of stores throughout the year is known as ....

(*b*) .... level is that level of materials at which a new order for material is placed.

(*c*) Allotting symbols to the different items of stores is known as ....

(*d*) The quantity of materials that is to be ordered with a supplier is known as ....

(*e*) Bin card is maintained by ....

[***Answers:*** (*a*) Perpetual inventory system, (*b*) reorder, (*c*) codification, (*d*) economic order quantity, (*e*) storekeeper]

III. Select the correct answers from the following:

(*a*) Which of the following method of stock control aims at concentrating efforts on selected items of materials

(*i*) Perpetual inventory system (*ii*) Material turnover

(*iii*) Level setting (*iv*) ABC analysis

(*b*) The formula to be used to calculate minimum level is

(*i*) Reorder level × Minimum reorder period

(*ii*) Reorder level + Reorder quantity × Minimum reorder period

(*iii*) (Reorder level + Reorder quantity) – (Minimum usage × Minimum reorder period)

(*iv*) Reorder level – Normal usage × Average reorder period

(*c*) The storekeeper should initiate a purchase requisition when stock reaches

(*i*) Minimum level (*ii*) Maximum level

(*iii*) Reorder level (*iv*) Average level

(*d*) Lead time refers to

(*i*) The time interval between the date of production and the date of sale

(*ii*) The time interval between the date of purchase and the date of sale

(*iii*) The time required to order and receive the materials

(*iv*) The time required to process the order

(*e*) Economic order quantity is computed so that

(*i*) The ordering and carrying costs are least

(*ii*) The ordering and stock out costs are least

(*iii*) The ordering and back ordering costs are least

(*iv*) The cost of materials are least

[***Answers:*** (*a*) *iv*, (*b*) *iv*, (*c*) *iii*, (*d*) *iii*, (*e*) *i*]

IV. Simple questions

1. Give two advantages of codification of materials. *(Bangalore University, B.Com., April 2000)*
2. What is perpetual inventory system? *(Bangalore University, B.Com., April 2000)*
3. State two differences between Bin Card and Stores Ledger Card. *(Bangalore University, B.Com., April 2000)*
4. What do you mean by ABC analysis? *(Bangalore University, B.Com., April 2000)*
5. What is Bill of materials? *(Bangalore University, B.Com., November 1999)*
6. What do you mean by stores discrepancies? State its causes. *(Bangalore University, B.Com., April 1997)*
7. Mention the methods of codification. *(Bangalore University, B.Com., November 1997)*
8. What is EOQ? Give its utility? *(Bharathisadan University, B.Com., April 1994)*
9. What is Bin card? *(Bangalore University, B.Com., November 1997)*
10. What do you mean by maximum level? *(Bangalore University, B.Com., April 1994)*
11. What is danger level of materials? *(Bangalore University, B.Com., April 1994)*
12. Write a specimen of Bin card. *(Bangalore University, B.Com., April 1994)*
13. Give the formula to calculate reorder level? *(Karnataka University, B.Com., April 1994)*
14. What do you mean by material control? *(Bangalore University, B.Com., April 1995)*
15. On what bases is the reorder quantity determined? *(Bharathisadan University, B.Com., November 1995)*
16. What is minimum level? *(M.G. University, B.Com., April 1994)*
17. What is material turnover ratio? *(Karnataka University, B.Com., April 1997)*
18. What is stores ledger card? *(Karnataka University, B.Com., April 1997)*
19. What is danger level? *(Bangalore University, B.Com., April 1996)*
20. What is economic order quantity? *(University of Kerala, M. Com., May 1995)*

V. Short answer questions

1. What is 'economic order quantity'? How is it determined? Is it different from reorder quantity? *(C.S. Inter, June 2000)*
2. Differentiate between 'bin card' and stores ledger card. *(C.S. Inter, December 1999, C.A., Inter, May 1999)*
3. State briefly the various techniques used for inventory control. *(C.S. Inter, June 1999)*
4. Explain perpetual inventory system. *(C.S. Inter, June 1998)*
5. Outline a system of stores control. *(C.S. Inter, June 1997)*
6. "Perpetual inventory system is an integral part of material control." Explain. *(C.S. Inter, December 1997)*
7. Explain ABC analysis of inventory control. *(C.S. Inter, December 1996)*
8. How do you determine economic order quantity? *(C.S. Inter, December 1996)*
9. What is material handling cost? How will you deal it in cost accounts? *(C.S. Inter, May 1999)*
10. At the time of physical stock taking it was found that actual stock level was different from the clerical or compute records? What can be possible reason for such differences? How will you deal with such differences? *(C.S. Inter, May 1998)*
11. What is perpetual inventory system? Explain its merits over periodic system. *(University of Mysore, B.Com., April 1998)*
12. Explain the meaning and importance of material control and the main requisites of an adequate system of material control. *(University of Mysore, B.Com., October 1999)*

13. Describe the factors which influence different stock levels of a manufacturing unit.
(University of Mysore, B.Com., April 1995)

14. Explain the tools and techniques of material control. *(S.V. University, B.Com., April 1995)*

15. What do you mean by ABC analysis? What are its advantages?
(S.V. University, B.Com., September 1994)

16. What is codification of materials? Describe the methods of codification of materials.
(University of Mysore, B.Com., April 1994)

17. What is meant by 'maximum level', 'minimum level' and 'reorder level' with regard to maintenance of stocks? What are the factors that govern the fixing of levels?
(Bharathisadan University, B.Com., April 1994)

18. What is a bin card? Give a specimen form of it and discuss its utility.
(Bharathisadan University, B.Com., April 1994)

19. What are the duties of a storekeeper? *(M.G. University, B.Com., September 1994)*

20. What is two-bin system? What are the advantages? *(M.G. University, B.Com., September 1994)*

21. What is meant by inventory turnover? Explain it with the help of an example.
(M.G. University, B.Com., September 1994)

22. Explain the objectives of inventory control. *(M.G. University, B.Com., October 1993)*
(Mangalore University, B.Com., April 1997)

23. Give the advantages resulting from classification of materials.
(Mangalore University, B. Com., April 1996)

EXERCISES

Exercise on bin card

Exercise 1: Sirdhar and Co. furnish the following information regarding receipts and issues of materials:

			kg.
1992, April	1	Opening stock	25,000
	2	Issued against requisition no. 1	13,000
	3	Issued against requisition no. 2	2,000
	4	Received from a supplier by challan no. 13	30,000
	10	Issued on requisition no. 3	10,000
	15	Issued on requisition no. 4	5,000
	25	Received from supplier by challan no. 14	10,000
	30	Issued on requisition no. 5 examination by the stock verifier on 26th morning revealed a shortage of 500 kg.	50,000
Maximum limit			50,000
Minimum limit			50,000
Ordering level			8,000
You are required to prepare bin card no.			25,000

[*Answer:* Balance 30,000 kg.]

Exercise on ABC analysis

Exercise 2: Analyse the following items into A, B and C categories on the basis of information given below. Show the percentage of material in quantity and value under A, B, and C categories.

Category A – Rs. 4,000 and above (total value)

Category B – Rs. 1,000 to Rs. 3,999 of (total value)
Category C – Rs. Below Rs. 1,000 (total value)

S.No.	*Code No.*	*Quantity*	*Unit rate*
1	*A*	147	3.00
2	*B*	986	2.00
3	*C*	353	4.00
4	*D*	8,931	0.10
5	*E*	1,239	0.15
6	*F*	100	0.25
7	*G*	18	513.00
8	*H*	3,770	2.50
9	*I*	683	2.00
10	*J*	134	0.70
11	*K*	190	0.40
12	*L*	1	43.00
13	*M*	52	0.70
14	*N*	426	0.10
15	*O*	4,725	0.06
16	*P*	10	30.27
17	*Q*	20	0.40
18	*R*	6,542	0.02
19.	*S*	329	0.40
20	*T*	10	134.00

[***Answer:***

Category	*Quantity in percentage*	*Value of percentage*	*Value of materials*
A	10%	68%	Rs. 18,659
B	20%	22%	Rs. 6,090
C	70%	10%	Rs. 2,715]

Exercise on level setting

Exercise 3: Calculate the minimum stock level, maximum stock level, average stock level reorder level from the following information:

Minimum consumption	– 240 units per day
Normal consumption	– 300 units per day
Maximum consumption	– 420 units per day
Reorder period	– 10 – 15 days
Reorder quantity	– 3600 units
Normal recorder period	– 12 days

(University of Madras, B. Com., April 2005)

[***Answer:*** (1) Reorder level = 6,300 units
(2) Minimum Level = 2,700 units
(3) Maximum level = 7,500 units
(4) Average stock level = 4,500 units (using reorder quantity formula)]

Exercise 4 : Calculate reorder level, minimum stock level and maximum stock level from the following information:

Minimum consumption	=	100 units per day
Maximum consumption	=	150 units per day
Normal consumption	=	120 units per day
Reorder period	=	10 to 15 days
Normal reorder period	=	12 days

(University of Madras, B.Com., May 2004)

[***Answer:*** (1) Reorder level = 2250 units
(2) Minimum level = 810 units
(3) Maximum level = 2750 units]

Exercise 5 : From the following information for the last 12 months, compute

(*a*) Reorder level

(*b*) Minimum level

(*c*) Average stock level, and

(*d*) Maximum stock level of a component

Maximum usage in a month 300 nos

Minimum usage in a month 200 nos

Average usage in a month 225 nos

Time lag for procurement of material

Maximum	–	6 months
Minimum	–	2 months
Reorder quantity	=	750 nos

(University of Madras B. Com., April 2003)

[***Answer:*** (*a*) Reorder level = 1,800 nos (*b*) Minimum level = 900 nos (*c*) Maximum level 2150 nos (*d*) Average stock level 1275 nos.]

Exercise 6 : Two components A and B are used as follows:

Normal usage	:	300 units per week each
Maximum usage	:	450 units per week each
Minimum usage	:	150 units per week each
Reorder quantity	:	A – 2400 units
		B – 3600 units
Reorder period	:	A – 4 to 6 weeks
		B – 2 to 4 weeks

Calculate for each component:

(*a*) Reorder level (*b*) Minimum level

(*c*) Maximum level (*d*) Average stock level

(University of Madras. B.Com., October 2002)

[***Answer:***

(1) Reorder level	'A'	– 2,700 units
	'B'	– 1,800 units
(2) Minimum level	'A'	– 1,200 units
	'B'	– 900 units
(3) Maximum level	'A'	– 4,500 units
	'B'	– 5,100 units

(4) Average stock level 'A' – 2,400 units
(Using oeorder 'B' – 2,700 units
qty. formula)]

Exercise 7 : Calculate : (*a*) Minimum stock level (*b*) Maximum stock level (*c*) Reordering level from the following:

Minimum consumption	–	100 units per day
Maximum consumption	–	150 units per day
Normal consumption	–	120 units per day
Reorder period	–	10 to 15 days
Reorder quantity	–	1500 units
Normal reorder period	–	12 days

(University of Madras, B. Com., May 2002)

[***Answer:*** (1) Reorder level = 2,250 units
(2) Minimum level = 810 units
(3) Maximum level = 2,750 units]

Exercise 8 : Two items X and Y are used as follows :

Normal usage	–	50 units per week each		
Minimum usage	–	25 units per week each		
Maximum usage	–	75 units per week each		
Economic order qty.	–	X	–	300 units
		Y	–	500 units
Reorder period	:	X	–	4 to 6 weeks
		Y	–	2 to 4 weeks

Calculate for each item:
(*a*) Reorder level (*b*) Minimum level
(*c*) Maximum level (*d*) Average stock level

(University of Madras, B.Com., April 2001)

[***Answer:*** (1) Reorder level = X — 450 units
Y — 300 units
(2) Minimum level = X — 200 units
Y — 150 units
(3) Maximum level = X — 650 units
Y — 750 units
(4) Average stock level = X — 350 units
Y — 400 units]

Exercise 9 : Calculate the minimum stock level, maximum stock level, reordering level and average stock level

(*a*) Minimum consumption	=	100 units per day
(*b*) Maximum consumption	=	150 units per day
(*c*) Normal consumption	=	120 units per day
(*d*) Reorder period	=	10–15 days
(*e*) Reorder quantity	=	1,500 units
(*f*) Normal reorder period	=	12 days

(Sri Krishnadevaraya University, B. Com., March 2005)

[*Answer:* (1) Reorder level = 2,250 units
(2) Minimum level = 810 units
(3) Maximum level = 2,750 units
(4) Average stock level = 1,780 units]

Exercise 10 (EOQ): Calculate Economic Order quantity from the following information and number of orders per annum.

Annual consumption	–	12,000 units
Cost per unit	–	Rs. 320
Ordering cost per order	–	Rs. 400

Carrying cost 20% of the inventory value.

(Calcutta University, B.Com., (Pass) 2001)

[*Answer:* EOQ = 1225 units
Number of orders per annum = 10 orders]

Exercise 11: Calculate EOQ from the following:

(*i*) Quantity	:	600 units
(*ii*) Ordering cost	:	Rs. 12 per order
(*iii*) Carrying cost	:	20%
(*iv*) Price per unit	:	Rs. 20

(Calcutta University, B.Com., (Pass) 2003)

[*Answer:* EOQ = 60 units]

Exercise on level setting

Exercise 12: From the following particulars, compute : (1) Maximum stock level (2) Minimum stock level, and (3) Reorder level

Normal consumption per month	–	1,000 litres
Maximum consumption per month	–	8,000 litres
Minimum consumption	–	4,000 litres
Lead time	–	2 to 4 months
Reorder quantity	–	10,000 units

(Calcutta University, B.Com., (Pass) 2003)

[*Answer:* Reorder level = 32,000 units
Minimum level = 29,000 units
Maximum level = 34,000 units]

Exercise 13: Two materials X and Y are used as follows:

Minimum usage – 50 units per week in both cases

Maximum usage – 150 units per week in both cases

Ordering quantity	X	–	600 units
	Y	–	1000 units
Delivery period	X	–	4 to 6 weeks
	Y	–	2 to 4 weeks

Calculate for X and Y:

(*i*) Reorder level (*ii*) Minimum level
(*iii*) Maximum level (*iv*) Average stock level

(Calcutta University, B. Com., (Pass) 2005)

[*Answer:* (1) Reorder level = X – 900 units
Y – 600 units
(2) Minimum level = X – 400 units
Y – 300 units
(3) Maximum level = X – 1,300 units
Y – 1,500 units
(4) Average stock level = X – 850 units
Y – 900 units]

Exercise on economic order quantity

Exercise 14: Find out the Economic order quantity from the following:

Annual usage	–	Rs. 1,20,000
Cost of placing and receiving one order	–	Rs. 15
Annual carrying cost	–	10% of inventory value

(University of Madras, B.Com., April 2005)

[*Answer:* Rs. 6000 (in value)]

Exercise 15: From the following particulars calculate EOQ

Annual requirements	–	1600 units
Cost of material per unit	–	Rs. 40
Cost of placing and receiving One order	–	Rs. 50
Annual carrying cost of inventory	–	10 % of inventory value

(University of Madras, B.Com., May 2005)

[*Answer:* EOQ = 200 units]

Exercise 16: From the following information determine EOQ

Annual usage	–	90000 units
Cost per unit	–	Rs. 50
Buying cost per order	–	Rs. 10
Cost of carrying inventory	–	10 % of cost

(University of Madras, B.Com., April 2004)

[*Answer:* EOQ = 600 units]

Exercise 17: Inventory turnover ratio

From the following data, calculate the Inventory Turnover Ratio

	Material X (Rs.)	Material Y (Rs.)
Opening stock	25,000	87,500
Closing stock	15,000	62,500
Purchases	1,90,000	1,25,000

Determine the fast moving materials

(University of Madras, B.Com., October 2003)

[*Answer:* Inventory Turnover
Ratio of material X – 10 times
Y – 2 times
Material X is fast moving]

Exercise on EOQ

Exercise 18: From the following figure, calculate Economic Order Quantity and number of orders to be placed in each year

Annual consumption of materials	=	4,000 units
Cost of buying per order	=	Rs. 5
Cost per unit	=	Rs. 2 per unit
Storage and carrying cost	=	8 % on average inventory

(University of Madras, B.Com., October 2002)

[***Answer:*** EOQ = 500 units]

Exercise 19: In a company, the weekly minimum and maximum consumption of material A are 25 and 75 units respectively. The reorder quantity as fixed by the company is 300 units. Material A is received within 4 to 6 weeks from the date of issue of supply order. Calculate minimum level and maximum levels of material A

(C.S. Inter, June 2005)

[***Answer:*** Reorder level – 450 units.
Minimum level – 200 units
Maximum level – 650 units]

Exercise on inventory turnover ratio

Exercise 20: From the following date for the year ended 31st December 2,000, calculate (*i*) Inventory turnover ratio of the two items and (*ii*) Their average stock holding in terms of number of days

	Material A Rs.	Material B Rs.
Opening stock (1-1-2,000)	20,000	18,000
Purchases during the year	1,04,000	54,000
Closing stock (31-12-2000)	12,000	22,000

(ICWA. Inter June, 2001)

[***Answer:*** ITR of material 'A' 7 material 'B' 2.5 ITR in terms of days material 'A' 14 days material 'B' 14.6 days.]

❑❑❑

CHAPTER 5

Materials Cost—Issue Control

INTRODUCTION

Issue control is that phase of material control which is exercised in the course of usage of materials. Materials for consumption and issue purposes can be classified into three types *viz* (*i*) raw materials which are to be issued to production department. (*ii*) spare parts and components, which are to be issued to maintenance department and (*iii*) indirect materials and sundry supplies which are to be issued to both production and service departments. It is desirable to estimate in advance the requirement of materials for every product, job or process both item-wise and quantity-wise so that the exact requirements can be issued to ensure continuity in production. When standard costing is in operation, a standard material schedule is prepared for each job or product. Otherwise for bulk issue of materials, a document known as bill of materials is used.

OBJECTS OF MATERIALS ISSUE CONTROL

The following are the objects of materials issue control:

1. Every Issue must be Authentically Authorised: A person is said to be authentically authorised if he derives the power to draw the required quantity of materials from a specified lot. Usually the foreman or a supervisor is authorised to draw materials from the storeroom. The storekeeper keeps a specimen signature of the authority to draw the materials. The document which is used to draw materials is termed as a material requisition note or a stores requisition note. This document is prepared in triplicate. The original and duplicate copies are sent to storekeeper which serves as the basis for issuing the materials. The storekeeper sends the original copy to the stores accountant to facilitate him for pricing the issues. The triplicate copy is retained by the department which initiated the material requisition note. The contents of material requisition note are as follows:

(*a*) Number and date of requisition. The materials requisition note is centrally numbered in the storeroom by a serial number to ensure that all the notes are accounted for.

(*b*) Name of the department needing the materials.

(*c*) Particulars and code number of materials to facilitate the correct issue of materials.

(*d*) The quantity of materials demanded and its unit of measurement.

(*e*) The rate at which the issue is to be priced. This is obtained from stores ledger which is worked out under FIFO, LIFO or other methods of issuing price.

(*f*) The total value of materials which is obtained by multiplying the unit cost with the quantity issued on the requisition.

(*g*) The signature of the person initiating the materials requisition note.

A specimen form of material requisition note is given below.

W.S. INSULATORS OF INDIA LIMITED
Factory, Porur, Madras

Material requisiton note

Please issue the following materials. No. ....

Date ....

S. no.	*Description of materials*	*Material code*	*Quantity required*	*Quantity issued*	*Unit*	*Rate*	*Value*

Cost centre ☐

Authorised by........... *Issued by* .... *Received by* ....

Fig. 5.1 *Material requisition note.*

When all the types of materials required to execute a job is to be drawn at a time, a document known as a 'Bill of materials' is made use of. It is a list of all materials required for a specific job, process or work order. Usually this document is prepared by the production planning department and presented to the storekeeper in lieu of one or more material requisition slips. It serves the following purposes:

(*a*) It serves as an advance intimation to all the persons concerned about the execution of the job.

(*b*) It facilitates the storekeeper to prepare a purchase requisition note and thus ensures ready availability of materials for issue purpose.

(*c*) It facilitates quick accounting of materials consumed as entries can be posted in totals to the concerned jobs.

(*d*) It serves as a substitute to material requisition note especially when all the materials for executing a job is to be drawn.

A specimen form of bill of materials is given below.

ABC CO. LTD.

Bill of materials

Department authorised .... Number ....

Job or work order no. .... Date of issue ....

Item no.	*Code no.*	*Description of materials*	*Quantity*	*For department use*		
				MRN no.	*Date*	*Qty*

Fig. 5.2. *Bill of materials.*

The authority to draw materials from storeroom must be extended to return the surplus materials from the production departments to storeroom. Otherwise it may involve misappropriation of materials and may go unaccounted. The document used to accompany the return of surplus materials is known as materials return note. This note is used to record not only the return of excess materials but also the rejected materials, scraps, etc. arising out of the materials received in the department. On the basis of this document the returned materials are priced. A specimen form of materials return note is given below:

W.S. INSULATORS OF INDIA LIMITED

Porur, Madras - 602 104

MATERIALS RETURN NOTE No. ....

Date ....

S.no.	*Description of materials*	*Material code*	*Quantity*	*Rate*	*Amount*	*Remarks*

Returned by .... Cost centre .... Received by ....

Fig. 5.3. *Material return note.*

Sometimes the excess quantity of materials of one department may be needed by other departments. In such situations it may not be prudent to return back the surplus materials to the storeroom. Instead it can be directly transferred to the department where it is needed. Though inter-departmental transfer of materials is not generally allowed, under the following two circumstances it is to be encouraged (*a*) where the excess materials are very heavy in weight involving more material handling expenses, (*b*) where the production is not to be delayed for want of materials. A specimen form of material transfer note is given below.

ABC CO. LTD.

From .... (cost centre) No. ....

To .... (cost centre) Date ....

Material Transfer Note

Transfer from job no. .... To job no. ....

S. no.	*Description of materials*	*Material code*	*Quantity*	*Rate*	*Amount*	*Remarks*

Sent by .... *Received by* .... *Stores clerk*............

Fig. 5.4. *Material transfer note.*

2. Proper Accounting of Every Authorised Issue: The materials issued to various departments from storeroom must be properly accounted both in storeroom as well as in stores accounting section. This ensures proper usage of materials and helps in knowing the correct requirements of materials for every department.

3. Proper Pricing of Materials: Pricing of material issues to a large extent influences the cost of product and the value of closing stock. The method to be followed depends upon number of factors. However, the following basic factors must be satisfied by a good method of pricing material issue:

(*a*) The issue price must cover the cost of purchases of materials.

(*b*) It must reflect current market price.

(*c*) It should not destabilise cost from time to time.

(*d*) It should not lead to adjustment of stock at the end of accounting year.

4. Proper Charging of Material Cost to Product, Process or Job: This objective enables the proper charge of materials cost to various jobs executed. The basis of charging material cost is material requisition notes, which are analysed first on the basis of cost centres and then by job number. Charging of materials cost to every job as and when materials are issued leads to cumbersome process. Sometimes this may also lead to omission of entries thereby underestimating materials cost. So, to facilitate charging of materials cost for all the jobs without omission, a document known as materials abstract or material analysis sheet is prepared. This document contains the analysis of materials by jobs and cost centres. This document is prepared once in a week or fortnight on the basis of various materials requisition notes used during that week or fortnight. From this document entries are posted into stores ledger card at one time and the cost of materials issued to every job or work order ascertained. This document is prepared both for direct and indirect materials. But the cost of indirect materials are charged to factory overheads.

A specimen form of materials abstract or material analysis sheet is given below.

ABC CO. LTD.

Material Analysis Sheet

Period............

Job no.	*Material requisition no.*	*Stores ledger folio no.*	*Quantity*	*Rate*	*Amount*	*Progressive total for each order no.*

Fig. 5.5 *Material analysis sheet.*

PRINCIPLES REGARDING MATERIALS ISSUE

While issuing that materials to various departments, the following principles should be followed:

(*a*) The exact requirement of materials is to be planned. This ensures the correct issue of materials (neither less nor more) to all the departments.

(*b*) All the materials (direct and indirect) must be issued, only on the basis of written requisition forms signed by competent authority.

(*c*) There should be a system of material audit of issues of materials. This helps in checking over-issue of materials.

(*d*) A proper control must be exercised on wastages, scraps and defective materials so that they can be kept to a minimum.

METHODS OF PRICING MATERIALS ISSUE

Before issues of materials are recorded in the stores ledger, the cost accounting department must decide upon the method of pricing the materials issue. However, materials issues could have been recorded at its actual cost, if prices of materials reamin uniform. But this phenomenon is rarely observed in practice. The adoption of particular method of pricing material issues serves two purposes, *viz,* (*a*) To charge cost of materials to the jobs on a consistent basis and (*b*) To value the closing stock properly for the preparation of final accounts. Different methods of pricing materials have been devised and the choice of a method is left to the discretion of the enterprise. These methods of pricing materials issues is shown in the following chart.

Methods of Pricing Materials Issues

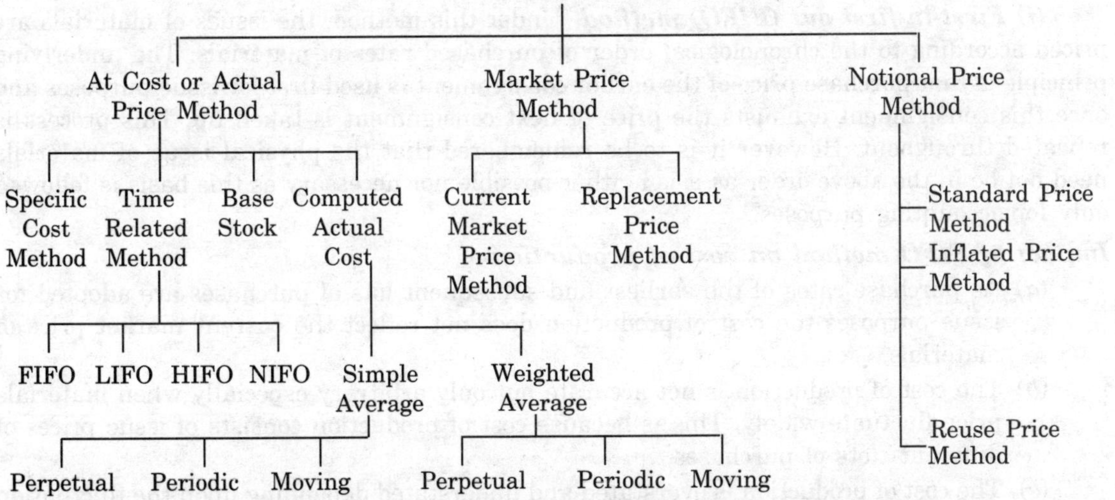

Fig. 5.6 *Chart showing various methods of pricing materials.*

I. At Cost or Actual Price Method

This method takes into account the price of materials at which they are bought for the purpose of valuing them at the time of issues. The following methods fall under this classification.

1. Specific cost method. This method of pricing material issues is adopted where special types of materials are bought for the execution of a job or a contract. The materials to be issued to jobs are identified with the invoice prices and if any handling and inspection costs are incurred such expenses are also included to constitute issue prices. The materials which are thus priced is commonly known as special materials as they are specifically purchased at the instance of customers Thus under this method, the production is charged with the actual cost of materials. The inventory is also similarly valued at the actual cost.

Advantages

(*a*) No calculation is involved for calculating issue prices when compared to other methods.

(*b*) The production is charged with the acutal cost. Therefore, production is neither undercharged nor overcharged.

(*c*) The closing stock of materials are also valued at actual cost and therefore we do not come across any unrealised profit or loss.

Limitations

(*a*) This method is not suitable in case of continuous manufacturing industries involving repetitive and frequent purchase of materials.

(*b*) As each job differs from other jobs a separate register is to be maintained for the issue of materials which involves more of clerical work.

(*c*) If materials purchased are too frequent it becomes difficult to maintain their identity. Similarly if issues are too frequent it becomes difficult to relate the materials to each and every job.

(*d*) As this method depends on invoices non-receipt of an invoice will obstruct the issue procedure.

2. Time related method.

(i) First-in-first out (FIFO) method. Under this method, the issues of materials are priced according to the chronological order of purchased rates of materials. The underlying principle is that purchase price of the earlier consignment is used first for issue purposes and once this consignment exhausts the price of next consignment is taken up. This process is repeated throughout. However it is to be remembered that the physical issue of materials need not be in the above order as it is neither possible nor necessary as this basis is followed only for accounting purposes.

Impact of FIFO method on cost of production

(*a*) As purchase rates of the earliest and subsequent lots of purchases are adopted for issue purposes the cost of production does not reflect the current market price of materials.

(*b*) The cost of production is not accurate but only arbitrary especially when materials price fluctuate widely. This is because cost of production consists of issue prices of different lots of purchases.

(*c*) The cost of production is overstated and understated depending upon the fluctuation in the prices of materials in the market.

Impact of FIFO method on inventory valuation

(*a*) When the materials price increase, the value of stock is understated and when the material price decreases, the value of closing stock is overstated.

(*b*) The total value of stock fluctuates with the rise and fall in the cost of materials. This distorts the valuation of the stock accurately.

(*c*) The value of closing stock reflects current market price.

Impact of FIFO method on the profit

(*a*) The total profit is unaffected by the overstatement in cost as this is compensated by a corresponding understatement in closing stock value and *vice versa*. However as production cost of a particular product or job is distorted by a rise or fall in the material cost, consequently profit on such product or job will also fall or rise.

Advantages

(*a*) As materials are issued at actual cost but not on estimates and approximation, unrealised profit or loss will not arise.

(*b*) Where FIFO principle is adopted even for the physical issue of materials, this method gives correct cost of materials consumed. Further oldest materials are exhausted first to avoid deterioration and obsolescence.

(*c*) The value of closing stock will reflect current market price.

(*d*) If purchases are few and if the prices of materials remain stable the method will be simple to operate.

Disadvantages

(*a*) Issue prices do not reflect current market price and so does cost of production.

(*b*) Two similar jobs cannot be compared as different rates of materials are used to execute the jobs.

(*c*) During the period of falling prices cost of production tend to be high. This may lead to cancellation of prospective sales because of high quotations.

Pricing of materials returned to storeroom under FIFO. Materials returned to storeroom is recorded at the price at which they were issued originally. These units are to be issued at the old price on the next material requisitions received.

Pricing of materials returned to vendor. Materials returned to the vendor is recorded at the price of the oldest materials in stock on the date on which the materials are returned.

Problems on FIFO method

Problem-1

From the following information prepare a stores ledger account under FIFO method.

1.1.96	Opening stock	1,000 units at Rs. 5 each
5.1.96	Purchased	900 units at Rs. 6 each
10.1.96	Issued	1,200 units
12.1.96	Purchased	800 units at Rs. 6.20 each
15.1.96	Purchased	300 units at Rs. 6.40 each
19.1.96	Issued	400 units
22.1.96	Issued	600 units
27.1.96	Purchased	200 units at Rs. 6.50 each
31.1.96	Issued	600 units

(University of Madras, B.Com., September 1997)

Solution:

Stores ledger card-FIFO method

Date	Receipts			Issues			Balance		
	Qty.	*Rate*	*Amount*	*Qty.*	*Rate*	*Amount*	*Qty.*	*Rate*	*Amount*
1.1.96	—	—	—	—	—	—	1,000	5	5,000
5.1.96	900	6	5,400	—	—	—	1,000	5	5,000
							900	6	5,400
10.1.96	—	—	—	1000	5	5,000	700	6	4,200
				200	6	1,200			
12.1.96	800	6.20	4,960	—	—	—	700	6	4,200
							800	6.20	4,960
15.1.96	300	6.40	1,920	—	—	—	700	6	4,200
							800	6.20	4,960
							300	6.40	1,920
19.1.96	—	—	—	400	6	2,400	300	6	1,800
							800	6.20	4,960
							300	6.40	1,920
22.1.96	—	—	—	300	6	1,800	500	6.20	3,100
				300	6.20	1,860	300	6.40	1,920
27.1.96	200	6.50	1,300	—	—	—	500	6.20	3,100
							300	6.40	1,920
							200	6.50	1,300
31.1.96	—	—	—	500	6.20	3,100	200	6.40	1,280
				100	6.40	640	200	6.50	1,300

(ii) Last-in-first-out (LIFO) Method. This method is exactly the opposite of FIFO method. For pricing the materials issues the price of the latest batch or lot of materials is adopted. If this lot exhausts then the price of earlier lot is made use of. However, before the current lot of materials are used fully, if any further purchases are made, any issue of materials are priced at the rate of recently purchased lot of materials. This process is continued throughout.

Impact of LIFO method on cost of production

(*a*) As the prices of the latest purchased materials are used for issue purpose, the issue price conforms to the current market prices. Consequently, the cost of production also reflects to the current market price.

(*b*) In a rising market, cost of production is overstated and in a falling market the cost of production is understated.

Impact of LIFO method on inventory valuation

(*a*) The value of closing stock does not reflect the current market price as all the rates of latest purchased materials are used for issue purposes. Thus closing stock is valued at old rates but not at the current rates of materials.

Impact of LIFO method on profit

(*a*) The total profit will not get affected under this method because a rise in price may be compensated by a fall in prices over a period of time. However, profits of every product or job differs because of charging of different rates of materials to different products or jobs.

(*b*) In period of rising prices, the higher rates of materials are charged to production, thereby inflating the cost of production. This results in a reduced margin of profit resulting in tax deduction.

Advantages

(*a*) As all issues are priced at the actual cost no unrealised profit or loss is derived.

(*b*) Issue prices reflect current market rates and hence cost of production also conforms to the current market rates which is more realistic.

(*c*) Because of the above reason, it will be possible to fix the selling price easily.

(*d*) The method is easy to operate where purchases are made less frequently.

(*e*) As mentioned earlier, because of inflation in the cost of production, the reduced profit margin result in savings in tax.

Disadvantages

(*a*) Two similar jobs cannot be compared because of charging of different rates of materials to different jobs.

(*b*) The closing stock does not reflect current market price. This may not be accepted by income tax authorities.

(*c*) This method cannot be operated when the invoice price does not reach before issues are to be priced.

(*d*) Calculation will be more if transactions are many with frequent price fluctuations.

Pricing of materials returned to storeroom under LIFO method. Materials returned should be recorded at the price at which they were originally issued, and these units should be issued at the old price on the next requisition received.

Pricing of materials returned to vendor under LIFO method. The materials returned to the vendor should be valued at the price of the latest units received and still in stock.

Problem-2 (Problems on LIFO method)

From the following receipts and issues of material during the month of January 1997, prepare store ledger account according to LIFO method.

1997 Jan. 1, Received	500 units @ Rs. 10 per unit
1997 Jan. 5, Received	250 units @ Rs. 11 per unit
1997 Jan. 8, Issued	300 units
1997 Jan. 10, Received	400 units@ Rs. 12 per unit
1997 Jan. 13, Issued	250 units
1997 Jan. 20, Received	100 units @ Rs. 11 per unit
1997 Jan. 28 Issued	400 units

On 1st Januray 1997, stock-on-hand was 200 units valued at Rs. 9 per unit.

(University of Delhi, B.Com., (Pass), April 1998)

Stores ledger card-LIFO method

Solution:

Date	*Receipts*			*Issues*			*Balance*		
	Qty.	*Rate*	*Amount*	*Qty.*	*Rate*	*Amount*	*Qty.*	*Rate*	*Amount*
1997									
Jan. 1.	—	—	—	—	—	—	200	9	1,800
1.	500	10	5,000	—	—	—	200	9	1,800
							500	10	5,000
5	250	11	2,750	—	—	—	200	9	1,800
							500	10	5,000
							250	11	2,750
8	—	—	—	250	11	2,750	200	9	1,800
				50	10	500	450	10	4,500
10	400	12	4,800	—	—	—	200	9	1,800
							450	10	4,500
							400	12	4,800
13	—	—	—	250	12	300	200	9	1,800
							450	10	4,500
							150	12	1,800
20	100	11	1,100	—	—	—	200	9	1,800
							450	10	4,500
							150	12	1,800
							100	11	1,100
28	—	—	—	100	11	1,100			
				150	12	1,800			
				150	10	1,500			
							200	9	1,800
							300	10	3,000

Problem-3 (Problems on FIFO and LIFO methods)

In pricing the diesel sold, service station of *A* follows FIFO method, while station *B* follows LIFO methods. On 1 January 1992 both had 6,000 litres each @ Rs. 2.60 per litre. During the month, each station received additional supply of 6,000 litres at Rs. 2.75 per litre. Sales for each of these two stations during the month were 8,000 litres @ Rs. 2.90 per litre. Calculate for each station the profit earned during the month and value of diesel in stock at the close of the period.

Solution:

Stores ledger card–FIFO method

Particulars	*Receipts*			*Issues*			*Balance*		
	Qty.	*Rate*	*Amount*	*Qty.*	*Rate*	*Amount*	*Qty.*	*Rate*	*Amount*
Opening stock	—	—	—	—	—	—	6,000	2.60	15,600
Receipts	6,000	2.75	16,500	—	—	—	6,000 6,000	2.60 2.75	15,600 16,500
Issues	—	—	—	6,000 2,000	2.60 2.75	15,600 5,500	4,000	2.75	11,000

Profit = Sale price – Issue price
= 8,000 × Rs. 2.90 – 21,100 (15,600 + 5,500)
= 23,200 – 21,100 = Rs. 2,100

Stores ledger card–LIFO method

Particulars	*Receipts*			*Issues*			*Balance*		
	Qty.	*Rate*	*Amount*	*Qty.*	*Rate*	*Amount*	*Qty.*	*Rate*	*Amount*
Opening stock	—	—	—	—	—	—	6,000	2.60	15,600
Receipts	6,000	2.75	16,500	—	—	—	6,000 6,000	2.60 2.75	15,600 16,500
Issues	—	—	—	6,000 2,000	2.75 2.60	16,500 5,200	4,000	2.60	10,400

Profit = Sale price – Issue price
= 23,200–21,700 (16,500 + 5,200)
= 1,500

Problem-4

The following transactions occur in the purchase and issue of a material during the first quarter of 1999.

Jan. 2, Purchased 4,000 units @ Rs. 4.00 per unit

Jan. 20, Purchased 500 units @ Rs. 5.00 per unit

Feb. 5,	Issued	2,000 units
Feb. 10,	Purchased	6,000 units @ Rs. 6.00 per unit
Feb. 12,	Issued	4,000 units
Mar. 2,	Issued	1,000 units
Mar. 5,	Issued	2,000 units
Mar. 15,	Purchased	4,500 units @ Rs. 5.50 per unit
Mar. 20,	Issued	3,000 units

From the above, prepare the stores ledger card by using (*a*) FIFO method, (*b*) LIFO method of issuing materials. What would be the value of stock-on-hand at the end of the period according to each of the two methods. *(Sri Sathya Sai University B.Com. (Hons.) March 1999)*

Solution:

Stores ledger card–FIFO method

Date	*Receipts*			*Issues*			*Balance*		
	Qty.	*Rate*	*Amount*	*Qty.*	*Rate*	*Amount*	*Qty.*	*Rate*	*Amount*
Jan. 2,	4,000	4	16,000	—	—	—	4,000	4	16,000
Jan. 20,	500	5	2,500	—	—	—	4,000	4	16,000
							500	5	2,500
							2,000	4	8,000
Feb. 5,	—	—	—	2,000	4	8,000	500	5	2,500
							2000	4	8,000
10	6,000	6	36,000	—	—	—	500	5	2,500
							6,000	6	36,000
12	—	—	—	2000	4	8,000			
				500	5	2,500			
				1,500	6	9,000	4,500	6	27,000
Mar. 2,	—	—	—	1,000	6	6,000	3,500	6	21,000
5	—	—	—	2,000	6	12,000	1,500	6	9,000
15	4,500	5.50	24,750	—	—	—	1,500	6	9,000
							4,500	5.50	24,750
20,	—	—	—	1,500	6	9,000			
				1,500	5.50	8,250	3,000	5.50	16,500

Closing Stock 3,000 units @ Rs. 5.50 = Rs. 16,500

Stores ledger card–LIFO method

Date	*Receipts*			*Issues*			*Balance*		
	Qty.	*Rate*	*Amount*	*Qty.*	*Rate*	*Amount*	*Qty.*	*Rate*	*Amount*
Jan. 2,	4,000	4	16,000	—	—	—	4,000	4	16,000
Jan. 20,	500	5	2,500	—	—	—	4,000 500	4 5	16,000 2,500
Feb. 5,	—	—	—	500 1,500	5 4	2,500 6,000	2,500	4	10,000
Feb. 10,	6,000	6	36,000	—	—	—	2,500 6,000	4 6	10,000 36,000
Feb. 12,	—	—	—	4,000	6	2,400	2,500 2,000	4 6	10,000 12,000
Mar. 2,	—	—	—	1,000	6	6,000	2,500 1,000	4 6	10,000 6,000
Mar. 5,	—	—	—	1,000 1,000	6 4	6,000 4,000	1,500	4	6,000
Mar. 15,	4,500	5,50	24,750	—	—	—	1,500 4,500	4 5.50	6,000 24,750
Mar. 20,	—	—	—	3,000	5.50	16,500	1,500 1,500	4 5.50	6,000 8,250

Closing stock = 1,500 units @ Rs. 4 = 6,000
1,500 units @ Rs. 5.50 = 8,250
Rs. 14,250

(iii) Highest-in-first-out (HIFO) method. This is a variation of LIFO method and gives similar result as in case of LIFO during the period of continuous rising prices. Under this method issues are priced at the highest rates of materials in stock irrespective of the dates of purchases. The purpose of this method is to charge with the highest rate of materials to the current cost of production.

The impact of the method over cost of production is that cost is overstated. On profit, its impact is understatement of profit. On valuation of closing stock its impact is understatement of the value of stock and a hidden reserve is created in the valuation of stock.

Problem-5 (Problem on HIFO method)

The South India Chemical Works had a opening stock of materials of 500 units at Re. 1 per unit on 1.4.2003. The following purchases and issues were made thereafter.

Purchases			Issues	
Date	*Units*	*Rate*	*Date*	*Units*
6.4.03	100	1.10	9.4.03	500
20.4.03	700	1.20	22.4.03	500
27.4.03	400	1.30	30.4.03	500
13.5.03	1,000	1.40	15.5.03	500
20.5.03	500	1.50	22.5.03	500
17.6.03	400	1.60	18.6.03	500
28.6.03	600	1.70	29.6.03	500

Prepare a store ledger card and determine the value of closing stock as on 30.6.03 under HIFO method.

Solution:

Stores ledger card HIFO method

Material ———— Bin no. ———— Max. level ————
Description ———— Location code no. ———— Reorder level ————
Code no. ———— Unit of quantity ———— Danger level ————

Date	*Receipts*			*Issues*			*Balance*		
	Qty.	*Rate*	*Amount*	*Qty.*	*Rate*	*Amount*	*Qty.*	*Rate*	*Amount*
1.4.03							560	1	500
6.4.03	100	1.10	110				500	1	500
							100	1.10	110
				100	1.10	110			
9.4.03									
				400	1	400	100	1	100
20.4.03	700	1.20	840				100	1	100
							700	1.20	840
22.4.03				500	1.20	600	100	1	100
							200	1.20	240
27.4.03	400	1.30	520				100	1	100
							200	1.20	240
							400	1.30	520
30.4.03				400	1.30	520			
				100	1.20	120	100	1	100
							100	1.20	120
13.5.03	1,000	1.40	1,400				100	1	100
							100	1.20	120
							1,000	1.40	1,400
15.5.03				500	1.40	700	100	1	100
							100	1.20	120
							500	1.40	700
20.5.03	500	1.50	750				100	1	100
							100	1.20	120
							500	1.40	700
							500	1.50	750

22.5.03				500	1.50	750	100	1.00	100
							100	1.20	120
17.6.03	400	1.60	640				500	1.40	700
							100	1.00	100
							100	1.20	120
							500	1.40	700
							400	1.60	640
18.6.03				400	1.60	640	100	1.00	100
				100	1.40	140	100	1.20	120
							400	1.40	560
28.6.03	600	1.70	1,020				100	1.00	100
							100	1.20	120
							400	1.40	560
							600	1.70	1,020
29.6.03				500	1.70	850	100	1.00	100
							100	1.20	120
							400	1.40	560
							100	1.70	170

(iv) Next-in-first-out (NIFO) method. Under this method, the issues are priced at the purchased rates of materials which are yet to arrive, in simple words, the materials rates which have been agreed upon by the supplier is used for issue purpose, though materials are not physically received. In this method, materials are issued at the price at which a new order has been placed and this price will hold good for all future issues until a next order is placed. As this method is somewhat complicated it is not normally adopted.

3. Base stock method. Strictly speaking this is not a distinct method of pricing materials issue. However, this method is used by some concerns as a safety device to ensure continuity in production. This method works out under the assumption that a certain minimum quantity of materials are set aside which is to be used during the period of emergency. This minimum stock is treated as a fixed asset and is known as 'Base Stock'. Materials which are in excess of base stock are issued by adopting either FIFO or LIFO principle. The base stock is deemed to have been created out of the first consignment and therefore valued at this price. The advantages and disadvantages of this method depends upon FIFO or LIFO principle used.

Problem-6 (Problems on Base stock method)

From the following particulars, write up the priced stores ledger card:

2003 Jan	1	Purchased 500 kg. @ Rs. 2 per kg.
	10	Purchased 300 kg. @ Rs. 2.10 per kg.
	15	Issued 600 kg.
	20	Purchased 400 kg. @ Rs. 2.20 per kg.
	25	Issued 300 kg.
	27	Purchased 500 kg. @ Rs. 2.10 per kg.
	31	Issued 200 kg.

Adopt base stock method of issues using LIFO principle and ascertain the value of closing stock. Base stock being 200 kg. (*University of Madras, B.Com, April 2003*)

Solution:

Stores ledger card (Base stock method—LIFO)

Materials ________ Bin no. ________ Max. level ________

Description ________ Location code no. ________ Min level ________

Code no. ________ Unit of quantity ________ Reorder level ________

Danger level ________

Date	*Receipts*			*Issues*			*Balance*		
	Qty.	*Rate*	*Amount*	*Qty.*	*Rate*	*Amount*	*Qty.*	*Rate*	*Amount*
1.1.03	500	2	1,000				500	2	1,000
10.1.03	300	2.10	630				500	2	1,000
							300	2.10	630
15.1.03				300	2.10	630	200	2	400
				300	2	600			
20-1-03	400	2.20	880				200	2	400
							400	2.20	880
25-1-03				300	2.20	660	200	2	400
							100	2.20	220
27-1-03	500	2.10	1.050				200	2	400
							100	2.20	220
							500	2.10	1,050
31-1-03				200	2.10	420	200	2	400
							100	2.20	220
							300	2.10	630

4. Computed actual cost. This method is based on the assumption that when materials are frequently bought and put in storeroom, they loose their identity. This is more common in industries like chemicals, paints, varnishes, oil refineries, etc. As materials cannot be identified for issue purpose, its actual cost cannot be used for pricing the materials issue. Therefore instead of using actual cost computed actual costs are used. The following are the various methods which fall under this category of pricing materials issues.

A. Simple average price methods

1. *Perpetual simple average price.* Under this method issue price is calculated by dividing the total of unit purchase price of different lots of materials from which the materials to be priced could be drawn by the number of prices constituting the total. Expressed in the form of a formula.

$$\text{Simple average price} = \frac{\text{Total unit prices of materials in stock}}{\text{Number of purchases}}$$

The new simple average price is to be calculated when a fresh purchase is made. Similarly the issue rates also changes when the materials from a consignment the price of which was taken into consideration for calculating issue price is exhausted.

Advantages

(*a*) The method smoothens out the variations in the material price.

(b) Issue rate remains same until a fresh purchase is made or the consignment which gets exhausted before the current issue is made. This reduces clerical work.

Disadvantages

(a) The issue prices do not confirm the current market price. So we come across an element of unrealised profit or loss in every job.

(b) Closing stock value also does not conform to current market price. This distorts the balance sheet of the concern.

(c) It takes into account only the purchase prices but not the quantities.

Pricing of materials returned to storeroom under average price method. Materials returned to storeroom is recorded at the price originally issued but a new average cost is to be computed at the time of such issue as if the goods returned is a new purchase.

Pricing of materials returned to vendor. Materials returned to vendor is valued at the latest average price.

Problem-7

Record the following transactions in a stores ledger card under simple average price method.

Date	*Receipts*		*Issues*
	Qty	*Rate*	
1-1-03	1,000	1.00	
10-1-03	260	1.05	
20-1-03			700
4-2-03	400	1.15	
21-2-03	300	1.25	
16-3-03			620
12-4-03			240
10-5-03	500	1.10	
25-5-03			380

Solution:

Stores ledger card (Simple average price method)

Materials ____________ Bin no. ____________ Max. level ____________

Description ____________ Location code no. ____________ Min level ____________

Code no. ____________ Unit of quantity ____________ Reorder level ____________

Danger level ____________

Date	*Receipts*				*Issues*				*Balance*	
	Qty.	*Cumulative qty.*	*Rate*	*Amt.*	*Qty.*	*Cumulative qty.*	*Rate*	*Amt.*	*Qty.*	*Rate*
1.1.03	1,000	1,000	1	1,000					1,000	1,000
10.1.03	260	1,260	1.05	273					1,260	1,273
20-1-03					700	700	1.025	718	560	555
4-2-03	400	1,660	1.15	460					960	1,015

21-2-03	300	1,960	1.25	375					1,260	1,390
16-3-03					620	1,320	1.11	682	640	708
12-4-03					240	1,560	1.20	288	400	420
10-5-03	500	2,460	1.10	550					900	970
25-5-03					380	1,940	1,165	443	520	527

Calculation of 1st issue price:

Cumulative receipts 1,260: Cumulative issue *Nil.* So the price is

$$\frac{1.00+1.05}{2} = 1.025$$

Calculation of IInd issue price:

Cumulative receipt 1,960: Cumulative issue 700. So issue price is

$$\frac{1.00+1.05+1.15+1.25}{4} = 1.11$$

Calculation of IIIrd issue price:

Cumulative receipt is 1,960: Cumulative issues 1,320 which exceeds the cumulative receipts to January 10 (1,260). So the price is

$$\frac{1.15+1.25}{2} = 1.20$$

Calculation of IVth issue price:

Cumulative receipt is 2,460. Cumulative issues 1,560 which exceeds the cumulative receipts to January 10 (1,260) but is still less than cumulative receipts to February 4 (1,660). So price is

$$\frac{1.15+1.25+1.10}{3} = 1.165$$

2. *Periodic simple average price method.* Unlike simple average price method, where issue are calculated depending upon purchases and issues of materials, under this method issue prices are calculated for a particular period. Hence the name periodic simple average price method. The issue rate is computed by dividing the total of purchase rates of all materials for a period by the number of rates used in that period. However, rate of opening stock is not included, as it is included in the previous year's calculation. The issue rate thus obtained is used for pricing the material issues.

Problem-8 (Problem on Periodic simple average method)

For the problem number 7 prepare a stores ledger card using periodic simple average price method.

Solution:

Stores ledger card (Periodic simple average price method)

Materials ________	Bin no. ________	Max. level ________
Description ________	Location code no. ________	Min. level ________
Code no. ________	Unit of quantity ________	Reorder level ________
		Danger level ________

Date	Receipts			Issues			Balance	
	Qty.	*Rate*	*Amount*	*Qty.*	*Rate*	*Amount*	*Rate*	*Amount*
1-1-03	1,000	1	1,000				1,000	1,000
10-1-03	260	1.05	273				1,260	1,273
20-1-03				700			560	
9-2-03	400	1.15	460				960	
21-2-03	300	1.25	375				1,260	
16-3-03				620			640	
12-4-03				240			400	
10-5-03	500	1.10	550				900	
25-5-03				380			520	505
	2,460	5.55	2,658	1,940	1.11	2,153		

Note. The issue rate is calculated at the end of the given period. The issue rate of Rs.1.11 is calculated as under:

$$\text{Periodic simple average price} = \frac{\text{Total rates of materials}}{\text{Number of rates}}$$

$$= \frac{5.55}{5} = 1.11$$

Value of closing stock = Value of receipts – Value of issues

= 2.658 – 2.153 (1,940 × 1.11)

= Rs. 505

3. *Moving simple average price method.* This method is particularly used when, there is drastic changes in the price level and where it is desired to spread total cost over all the jobs executed. The issue rate is calculated by dividing the total of periodic simple average prices relating to a given period by the number of period. This method therefore involves the fixation of period which can be a month, two months and so on. For example, if the monthly period is fixed, the simple moving average rate is to be calculated for the month of April. The number of prices of purchases for the month of January to March is added and then it is divided by three. Similarly, for calculating issue rate of April, the purchase rate of January is ignored and that of April month is included. The total rates of February to April is then divided by 3 to get the issue rate for April.

Problem-9 (Problem on Simple moving average price method)

Voltas Ltd. follows simple moving average price method of pricing materials issue. The periodic average prices are given in order to calculate 3 monthly simple moving average price for use for the period from May to September 1992

Month:	Jan.	Feb.	Mar.	April	May	June	July	Aug	Sept.
Periodic Simple Average price:	2.00	2.10	2.20	2.30	2.40	2.50	2.60	2.70	2.80

Solution:

Calculation of 3 monthly simple moving average price

Month	*Periodic average price*	*3 Monthly moving total*	*Simple moving average price*
Jan.	2.00		
Feb.	2.10	6.30	2.10
Mar.	2.20	6.60	2.20
Apr.	2.30	6.90	2.30
May	2.40	7.20	2.40
June	2.50	7.50	2.50
Jul.	2.60	7.80	2.60
Aug.	2.70	8.10	2.70
Sept.	2.80		

B. Weighted average price methods

1. *Perpetual weighted average price method.* Under this method the weighted average price is calculated by taking into account both the quantity and amount of materials. Issue rates are calculated by dividing the amount of materials in balance column of stores ledger by the quantity of materials in stock. Issue rates are to be calculated only when a fresh purchase is made, till then all are priced at the same issue rate. In other words, the issue rate remains same until a fresh purchase is made. However, the issue rate is calculated up to four decimal places to get more accurate results.

Advantages

(*a*) The method smoothens out a drastic fluctuation in the prices of materials.

(*b*) Issue rates need be calculated only when materials are purchased. Hence clerical work is reduced.

(*c*) This method gives satisfactory result compared to simple average price method becuase it takes into account both the quantity and value of materials.

Disadvantages

(*a*) Calculation will be more when transactions are many.

(*b*) Issue rate does not correspond to current market price. Hence we come across an element of unrealised profit or loss.

(*c*) Closing stock value also does not correspond to current market price. Hence balance sheet does not reflect the true position of the business.

(*d*) Issue rates are to be calculated up to four decimal places to ensure more accuracy.

Problem-10 (Problem on Weighted average cost method)

The following purchases have been extracted in respect of material 'Exe'. Prepare stores ledger account under 'weighted average method' of pricing material issues.

Receipts:

3rd Oct. 90	Purchased	500 units @ Rs. 4.00 per unit.
4th Oct. 90	Purchased	100 units @ Rs. 4.20 per unit.

10th Oct. 90	Purchased	50 units @ Rs. 4.25 per unit.
13th Oct. 90	Purchased	800 units @ Rs. 4.30 per unit.
23rd Oct. 90	Purchased	850 units @ Rs. 3.80 per unit.

Issues.

5th Oct. 90	Issued	400 units.
10th Oct. 90	Issued	50 units.
15th Oct. 90	Issued	900 units.
25th Oct. 90	Issued	450 units.

(*Bangalore University, B.Com., May 1992*)

Solution:

Stores ledger card

Date	*Receipts*			*Issues*			*Balance*	
	Qty.	*Rate*	*Amount*	*Qty.*	*Rate*	*Amount*	*Qty.*	*Amount*
3rd Oct.	500	4	2,000	—	—	—	500	2,000
4th Oct.	100	4.20	420	—	—	—	600	2,420
5th Oct.				400	4.0333	1613	200	807
10th Oct.	50	4.25	213				250	1,020
10th Oct.				50	4.08	204	200	1,780
13th Oct.	800	4.30	3,440				1,000	5,220
15th Oct.				900	5.22	4,698	100	522
23rd Oct.	850	3.80	3,230				950	3,752
25th Oct.				450	3.95	1,777	500	1,975

Problem-11

The stores ledger account of a manufacturing company reveals the following entries of a particular material.

Date	*Receipts*			*Issues*		
	Qty.	*Rate*	*Amount*	*Qty.*	*Rate*	*Amount*
2-1-03	4,000	1.80	7,200			
5-1-03	2,000	1.75	3,500			
18-1-03				10,000		19,500
3-2-03				5,000		9,750
14-2-03	3,000	1.85	5.550			
18-2-03	3,000	1.90	5,700			
20-2-03				10,000		19,200

Opening stock as on 1-1-03 was 20,000 units valued at Rs. 40,000. Closing stock as per physical verification on 28-2-03 was 6,950 units.

Work out the method of pricing the issue which you consider to have been adopted for the issue of the material and show the working of the issue rates (correct to 2 places of decimal). Complete the account of the material and work out the value of the closing stock as on 28-2-03 on the basis of valuation adopted.

Solution:

Stores ledger card (Weighted average price method)

Materials X ———— Bin no. ———— Max. level ————
Description ———— Location code no. ———— Min. level ————
Code no. ———— Unit of quantity ———— Reorder level ————
Danger level ————

Date	*Receipts*			*Issues*			*Balance*	
	Qty.	*Rate*	*Amount*	*Qty.*	*Rate*	*Amount*	*Qty.*	*Amount*
1-1-03							20,000	40,000
2-1-03	4,000	1.80	7,200				24,000	47,200
5-1-03	2,000	1.75	3,500				26,000	50,200
18-1-03				10,000	1.95	1,9500	16,000	31,200
3-2-03				5,000	1.95	9,750	11,000	21,450
14-2-03	3,000	1.85	5,550				14,000	27,000
18-2-03	3,000	1.90	5,700				17,000	32,700
20-2-03				10,000	1.92	19,200	7,000	13,500
28-2-03				50 (Loss being difference of balance of stock)	1.92	96	6,950	13,404

Working Note: In the above problem, weighted average method of pricing issues has been followed as is evident from the working of issue price as given below:

(1)On 18-1-03, the issue price units is

$$\frac{19{,}500}{10{,}000} = \text{Rs. } 1.95$$

This corresponds to weighted average rate which is calculated from the following receipts prior to 18-1-92

		Qty (Units)	Value (Rs.)
Opening stock	1-1-03	20,000	40,000
Purchases on	2-1-03	4,000	7,200
Purchases on	5-1-03	2,000	3,500
		26,000	50,700

$$\therefore \text{Weighted average rate per unit} = \frac{50{,}700}{26{,}000} = \text{Rs. } 1.95$$

(2) On 3 February 2003, the issue price per unit is

$$= \frac{9{,}750}{5{,}000} = \text{Rs. } 1.95$$

(3) On 20 February, the issue price is

$$= \frac{19,200}{10,000} = \text{Rs. } 1.92$$

This corresponds to weighted average rate which is calculated from the following receipts in the stores prior to 20-2-03

	Qty. (Units)	Value (Rs.)
Balance of materials in stores on 30-2-03, i.e., balance left after issue on 3.2.03	11,000	21,450
Purchases on 14-2-03	3,000	5,550
Purchases on 18-2-03	3,000	5,700
	17,000	32,700

$$\text{Weighted average rate} = \frac{32,700}{17,000} = \text{Rs. } 1.92$$

Problem-12 (Problem on FIFO, LIFO and weighted average method)

Oil India is a bulk distributor of high octane petrol. A periodic inventory of petrol on hand is taken when the books are closed at the end of each month. The following summary of information is available for the month of June 1985.

	Rs.
Sales	9,45,000
General administrative cost	25,000
Opening stock : 1,00,000 litres @ Rs. 3 per litre	3,00,000

Purchases :

June 1, 2,00,000 litres @ Rs. 2.85 per litre

June 30, 1,00,000 litres @ Rs. 3.03 per litre

Closing stock June 30—1,30,000 litres

Compute the following data by the first-in-first-out weighted average and last-in-first-out method of inventory costing:

(*a*) Value of inventory on June 30

(*b*) Amount of the cost of goods sold for June

(*c*) Profit or Loss for June. (*Sri Sathya Sai University, B.Com., Oct., 1988*)

Solution:

Stores ledger card (FIFO method)

Materials X ————	Bin no. ————	Max. level ————
Description ————	Location code no. ————	Min level ————
Code no. ————	Unit of quantity ————	Reorder level ————
		Danger level ————

Date	Receipts Qty.	Receipts Rate	Receipts Amount	Issues Qty.	Issues Rate	Issues Amount	Balance Qty.	Balance Rate	Balance Amount
June 1							1,00,000	3	3,00,000
June 1	2,00,000	2.85	5,70,000				1,00,000	3	3,00,000
							2,00,000	2.85	5,70,000
June 1 to				1,00,000	3	3,00,000			
June 30				1,70,000	2.85	4,84,500			
June 30	1,00,000	3.03	3,03,000				30,000	2.85	85,500
							1,00,00	3.03	3,03,000

Stores Ledger Card (Weighted average method)

Date	Receipts Qty.	Receipts Rate	Receipts Amount	Issues Qty.	Issues Rate	Issues Amount	Balance Qty.	Balance Amount
June 1							1,00,000	3,00,000
June 1	2,00,000	2.85	5,70,000				3,00,000	8,70,000
June 1 to June 30				2,70,000	2.90	7,83,000	30,000	87,000
June 30	1,00,000	3.03	3,03,000				1,30,000	3,90,000

Stores ledger card (LIFO method)

Date	Receipts Qty.	Receipts Rate	Receipts Amount	Issues Qty.	Issues Rate	Issues Amount	Balance Qty.	Balance Rate	Balance Amount
June 1							1,00,000	3	3,00,000
June 1	2,00,000	2.85	5,70,000				1,00,000	3	3,00,000
							2,00,000	2.85	5,70,000
June 1 to June 30				2,00,000	2.85	5,70,000			
				70,000	3	2,10,000			
June 30	1,00,000	3.03	3,03,000				30,000	3	90,000
							1,00,000	3.03	3,03,000

(b) Statement showing cost of goods sold for June

	FIFO	Weighted average	LIFO
Opening stock of materials	3,00,000	3,00,000	3,00,000
Add : Purchases :			
June 1, 2,00,000 litres @ Rs. 2.85 per litre	5,70,000	5,70,000	5,70,000
June 30, 1,00,000 litres @ Rs. 3.03 per litre	3,03,000	3,03,000	3,03,000

	11,73,000	11,73,000	11,73,000
Less : Closing stock of materials	3,88,500	3,90,000	3,93,000
Cost of goods sold	7,84,500	7,83,000	7,80,000

(c) Statement showing profit:

	FIFO	*Weighted average*	*LIFO*
Sales	9,45,000	9,45,000	9,45,000
Less : Cost of goods sold	7,84,500	7,83,000	7,80,000
Gross Profit	1,60,500	1,62,000	1,65,000
Less : General adm. cost	25,000	25,000	25,000
Profit	1,35,500	1,37,000	1,40,000

2. *Periodic weighted average price method.* This method is also known as month-end weighted average method. Under this method the issue rate is calculated by dividing the total cost of materials purchased for a month (or quarter) by the total quantity of materials purchased during the period. The opening stock of materials (both quantity and value) is not considered while calculating the issue rate as this is included in calculating the previous year's issue rate. The issue of materials and closing stock is valued at the rate so obtained.

Advantages

(*a*) Issue rate is calculated once in a month. Hence it reduces clerical work.

(*b*) This method is more accurate when compared to periodic simple average method since it takes into account both the quantity and cost.

(*c*) This method is particularly useful in continuous manufacturing industries where accounting entries are made periodically.

(*d*) It even's out wide fluctuation in the prices of materials in a given period.

Disadvantages

(*a*) This method is not based on actual cost. Hence it gives rise to unrealised profit or loss.

(*b*) The value of closing stock neither reflects current market price nor actual cost.

Problem-13

Prepare stores ledger card for problem no. 7 adopting periodic weighted average method considering 5 month duration.

Solution:

Stores ledger card (Periodic weighted average method)

Materials ————	Bin no. ————	Max. level ————
Description ————	Location code no. ————	Min level ————
Code no. ————	Unit of quantity ————	Reorder level ————
		Danger level ————

Date	Receipts			Issues			Balance	
	Qty.	Rate	Amount	Qty.	Rate	Amount	Qty.	Amount
1-1-03.	1,000	1	1,000				1,000	1,000
10-1-03	260	1.05	273				1,260	1,273
20-1-03				700				
4-2-03	400	1.15	460					
21-2-03	300	1.25	375					
16-3-03				620			640	
12-4-03				240			400	
10-5-03	500	1.10	550				900	
25-5-03				380			520	563
	2,460		2,658	1,940	1.08	2,095		

Note : Calculation of issue rate $= \dfrac{\text{Total cost of purhases of materials}}{\text{Total quantity of materials purchased}}$

$= \dfrac{\text{Rs. } 2{,}658}{2{,}460} = \text{Rs. } 1.08$

Closing stock = Receipts – Issues

= 2,658 – 2,095 = Rs. 563

or closing stock = 520 units @ Rs. 1.08 = 563 (App.)

3. *Moving weighted average price method.* Under this method the issue price is calculated by dividing the total of the weighted price of the current period and weighted average price of a given number of preceding period by the total number of current and preceding periods. The issues of current month or period are valued at this rate.

Problem-14 (Problem on Moving weighted and periodic weighted average price method)

From the following transactions extracted from the books of accounts of a manufacturing concern as on 31-12-2002, work out.

(*a*) The consumption value of raw materials in the month and (*b*) value of closing stock as on 31-1-2002 under the following methods of pricing issues.

(*i*) Moving weighted average price method

(*ii*) Periodic weighted average price method

Show the results in a tabuler form.

			Quantity in unit	*Rate per unit*
2002 Dec.	1	Opening stock	300	9.70
	3	Purchases	250	9.80
	11	Issues	400	
	15	Purchases	300	10.05
	20	Issues	210	

25	Purchases	150	10.30
29	Issues	100	

(*I.C.W.A., Inter; 1981*)

Solution:

Stores ledger card (Moving weighted average price)

Material ———	Bin no. ———	Max. level ———
Description ———	Location code no. ———	Min. level ———
Code no. ———	Unit of quantity ———	Reorder level ———
		Danger level ———

Date	*Receipts*			*Issues*			*Balance*	
	Qty.	*Rate*	*Amount*	*Qty.*	*Rate*	*Amount*	*Qty.*	*Amount*
1-1-02							300	2,910
3-12-02	250	9.80	2,450				250	2,450
							550	5,360
11-12-02				400	9.75	3,900	150	1,460
15-12-02	300	10.05	3,015				300	1,015
							450	4,475
20-12-02				210	9.94	2087.40	240	2,387.60
25-12-02	150	10.30	1,545				150	1,545.00
							390	3,932.60
29-12-02				100	10.08	1008	290	2,924.60

Note: Calculation of 1st issue rate $= \dfrac{5,360}{550} = 9.75$

Calculation of 2nd issue rate $= \dfrac{4,475}{450} = 9.94$

Calculation of 3rd issue rate $= \dfrac{3,932.60}{390} = 10.08$

Value of consumption of 710 units is as follows:

(*i*) 400 units @ 9.75 per unit	3,900.00
(*ii*) 210 units @ 9.94 per unit	2,087.40
(*iii*) 100 units @ Rs. 10.08 unit	1,008.00
	6,995.40

Stores ledger card (Periodic weighted average price method)

Material ______	Bin no. ______	Max. level ______
Description ______	Location code no. ______	Min. level ______
Code no. ______	Unit of quantity ______	Reorder level ______
		Danger level ______

Date	*Receipts*			*Issues*			*Balance*		
	Qty.	*Rate*	*Amount*	*Qty.*	*Rate*	*Amount*	*Qty.*	*Rate*	*Amount*
1-1-02	300	9.70	2,910				300	9.70	2,910
3-12-02	250	9.80	2,450				250	9.50	2,450
15-12-02	300	10.05	3,015				300	10.05	3,015
25-12-02	150	10.30	1,545				150	10.30	1,545
							1,000		9,920
11-12-02				400	9.92	3,968.00			
20-12-02				210	9.92	2,083.20			
20-12-02				100	9.92	992.00	290		2,876.80
	1,000		9,920	710	992	7,043.30			

Note : Calculation of issue rate $= \dfrac{9,920}{1,000} = 9.92$

Value of consumption = Rs. 7,043.20

Value of closing stock = Rs. 2,876.80

II. Market Price Method

This method is based on market price as against actual cost of material under the earlier discussed methods. The following two methods fall under this clssification of pricing materials issue.

1. Current market price method. As the name itself suggests, under this method, the materials are issued at the current prices prevailing in the market. This method is based on the principle that the cost of production must reflect the current market price. Thus this method is an improvement over the earlier methods discussed as all these methods are historical in nature and hence the cost of production does not reflect the current market price. This limitation is overcome by market price method. As the cost of production is charged with the current market price, the value of closing stock will reflect the historical cost.

Advantage

Cost of production reflects current market price.

Disadvantages

(*a*) Issues are not based on actual cost of materials at which they were bought. This results in notional profits.

(*b*) It is diffcult to ascertain market price.

(*c*) The cost of production varies depending upon fluctuation in market prices.

(*d*) The closing stock value does not conform to current market price.

2. Replacement price method. This method is based on the principle that at every issue of material, it is possible to determine the replacement cost of materials. However, determination of replacement price is not so easy and hence involves more work. Under this method, the issues are valued at the replacement price prevailing in the market on the date of issue.

Advantages

(*a*) No calculations are involved for pricing the material issues. The determined rates of issues are used instead.

(*b*) The cost of production reflects current market price.

Disadvantages

(*a*) It is difficult to determine replacement prices of materials.

(*b*) Issues are not made at the actual cost at which they were bought. Hence we come across notional profit or loss.

(*c*) Closing stock value does not conform to current market price.

Problem-15 (Problem on Replacement price method)

Prepare stores ledger card showing pricing of material issues in replacement price basis from the following particulars.

10-3-03	Opening balance 400 units @ Rs. 4 each
10-3-03	Received 100 units @ Rs. 4.10 each
15-3-03	Issued 300 units to job X vide MRN 1
17-3-03	Received 200 units @ Rs. 4.30 each
20-3-03	Issued 250 units to job Y vide MRN 2
25-3-03	Received 400 units @ Rs. 4.50 each
26-3-03	Issued 200 units to job Z vide MRN 3
27-3-03	Received 100 units @ Rs. 4.60 each
30-3-03	Issued 300 units to job A vide MRN 4
	Replacement price on various dates
	15-3-03—Rs. 4.20, 20-3-03—Rs. 4.40, 26-3-03—Rs. 4.60 and 30-3-03—Rs. 4.80

Solution: **Stores ledger card (Replacement price method)**

Material ————	Bin no. ————	Max. level ————
Description ————	Location code no. ————	Min. level ————
Code no. ————	Unit of quantity ————	Reorder level ————
		Danger level ————

Date	*Receipts*			*Issues*			*Balance*	
	Qty.	*Rate*	*Amount*	*Qty.*	*Rate*	*Amount*	*Qty.*	*Amount*
1-3-03							400	1,600
10-3-03	100	4.10	410				500	2,010
15-3-03				300	4.20	1,260	200	750
17-3-03	200	4.30	860				400	1,610
20-3-03				250	4.40	1,100	150	510
25-3-03	400	4.50	1,800				550	2,310
26-3-03				200	4.60	920	350	1,390
27-3-03	100	4.60	460					
30-3-03				300	4.80	1,440	150	410

III. Notional Price Method of Pricing Material Issues

1. Standard price method. The terminology of ICMA London defines standard price as "a predetermined price fixed on the basis of a specifications of all the factors affecting price." These factors are as follows:

(*a*) The quantity of materials to be purchased which will affect quantity discount.

(*b*) The possibility of a rise in price due to expected wage increase.

(*c*) The likelihood of a rise or fall in prices due to market condition.

(*d*) The charging of freight and warehousing expenses to the material.

(*e*) The charging of containers to the materials.

Although this method works out in those industries which make use of standard costing techniques, yet it can be adopted in other industires as well. This method is used both as a control technique for ensuring efficient purchases as well as to price the materials issues. The actual price of materials purchased is compared with the standard price. If the actual price paid exceeds standard it results in loss. On the other hand if the actual price is less than standard price, it results in profit.

Under this method receipts of materials are recorded in the stores ledger card at the actual prices and all issues at the standard price. The difference between actual and standard price is disposed off through price variance account.

Advantages

(*a*) The method enables to know the efficiency of purchases made. As was mentioned earlier if actual price paid is more than standard price it amounts to inefficient purchase.

(*b*) Comparing of two similar jobs is possible as all materials are priced at the same standard price.

(*c*) The method is simple to operate as all materials are issued at the same standard price.

(*d*) It facilitates fixation of selling price in advance.

Disadvantages

(*a*) The issue prices do not correspond to the current market price. So an unrealised profit or loss will arise.

(*b*) The closing stock value also does not correspond to the current market price. Hence balance sheet will not show the realistic position.

(c) It is difficult to fix up standard price in practice.

(d) It involves adjustment of profit or loss arising under this method.

Problem-16 (Problems on Standard price method)

The purchases and issues of materials in the month of December 2002 of Shriram & Co. are as follows:

1-12-02	Purchases 400 units @ Rs. 20.00 per unit
5-12-02	Purchases 350 units @ Rs. 18.00 per unit
10-12-02	Issues 300 units
15-12-02	Issues 400 units
20-12-02	Purchases 400 units @ Rs. 20.00 per unit
25-12-02	Purchases 250 units @ Rs. 25.00 per unit
30-12-02	Issues 500 units

The standard price per unit of materials is fixed at Rs. 20 for the year. Prepare the store ledger and determine the price variance for the month of December 02.

Solution: **Stores ledger card (Standard price method)**

Date	Receipts			Issues			Balance	
	Qty.	Rate	Amount	Qty.	Rate	Amount	Qty.	Amount
1-12-02	400	20	8,000				400	8,000
5-12-02	350	18	6,300				750	14,300
10-12-02				300	20	6,000	420	8,300
15-12-02				400	20	8,000	50	300
20-12-02	400	20	8,000				450	8,300
25-12-02	250	25	6,250				700	14,550
30-12-02				500	20	10,000	200	4,550
	1,400		28,550	1,200		24,000		

Standard cost of purchases 1,400 units @ Rs. 20	=	28,000
Actual cost of purchases	=	28,550
Adverse material price variance		550

Alternatively value of closing stock of 200 units @ Rs. 20 is 4,000. But the actual value shown in the stores ledger is 4,550. Hence, 550 is transferred to material price variance. The following entry is passed to dispose off the variance.

Material Control A/c	Dr	24,000	
Material Price Variance A/c	Dr	550	
To Cost Ledger Control A/c			24,550

(Being the adverse variance transferred to cost ledger control a/c)

Problem-17

Stock are issued at standard price and the following transactions have occurred with respect to high speed steel, a basic raw materials of a small tool factory.

Opening stock on 1-1-03 1,000 kg. @ Rs. 9.00 per kg.

Purchased on 5-1-03 5,000 kg. @ Rs. 8.50 per kg.

Issued on 10-1-03 600 kg.

Issued on 15-1-03 3,750 kg.

Issued on 20-1-03 650 kg.

Purchased on 25-1-03 2,500 kg. @ Rs. 8.00 per kg.

The credit balance of price variance account before transfer to costing profit & loss a/c was Rs. 500. Find out the standard rate at which the above issues should be made and determine the closing stock.

Solution: Stores ledger card (Standard price method)

Material ————	Bin no. ————	Max. level ————
Description ————	Location code no. ————	Min. level ————
Code no. ————	Unit of quantity ————	Reorder level ————
		Danger level ————

Date	*Receipts*			*Issues*			*Balance*	
	Qty.	*Rate*	*Amount*	*Qty.*	*Rate*	*Amount*	*Qty.*	*Amount*
1-1-03							1,000	9,000
5-1-03	5,000	8.50	42,500				6,000	51,500
10-1-03				600	8.50	5,100	5,400	46,400
15-1-03				3,750	8.50	31,875	1,650	14,525
20-1-03				650	8.50	5,525	1,000	9,000
25-1-03	2,500	8	20,000				3,500	29,000
	7,500		62,500	5,000		42,500		

Note: Calculation of issue price or standard price: In the previous year the standard price was Rs. 9 per kg. Therefore the total value was 9,000 (1,000 × 9). As there is a credit balance in the material price variance a/c, the standard rate of current year should be less than Rs. 9.00 (*i.e.,* to be debited). Hence the issue rate is calculated as follows.

Opening balance	Rs. 9,000
Less : Credit variance	500
	8,500

$$\frac{8{,}500}{1{,}000} = 8.50$$

Calculation of material price variance

Material price variance = Std. value of closing stock – Actual value of closing stock

= 3,500 × 8.50 – 29,000

	= 29,750 – 29,000	
	= 750 (*F*)	
Cost ledger control a/c	Dr. 43,250	
To material control a/c		42,500
To material price variance a/c		750
(Being material price variance transferred to cost ledger a/c.)		

2. Inflated price method. This is not a distinct method of pricing material issues. Instead it is a method of materials taking into account the losses, wastages deterioration, evaporation of materials. It was discussed earlier in the previous chapter that all costs related to losses and wastages, materials receiving and handling expenses, etc, are absorbed by the cost of production through a overhead recovery rate. But where it is desired that the actual cost of materials are to be known in the cost of production of a job, this method treats all such losses and wastages as also receiving, storages and handling cost as a charge to material consumed. In other words the cost of good materials is inflated to the extent of loss, scrap and waste materials together with other expenses incurred in procuring, storing and issuing them.

Problem-18

A manufacturer of Surat purchased three chemicals *A, B* and *C* from Bombay. The invoice gave the following information.

		Rs.
Chemical *A*	3,000 kg. @ Rs. 4.20 per kg.	12,600
Chemical *B*	5,000 kg. @ Rs. 3.80 per kg.	19,000
Chemical *C*	2,000 kg. @ Rs. 4.75 per kg.	9,500
Sales tax		2,055
Railway freight		1,000
	Total cost	44,155

A shortage of 200 kg. in chemical *A*, of 280 kg. in chemical *B* and 100 kg. in chemical *C* was noticed due to breakages. At Surat, manufacturer paid octroi duty @ Re. 0.10 per kg. He also paid cartage, Rs. 22 for chemical *A*, Rs. 63.12 for chemical B, Rs. 31.80 for chemical *C*. Calculate the stock rate that you would suggest for pricing issue of chemicals assuming a provision of 5 per cent towards further deterioration. (*C.A., Inter., Nov. 1991*)

Solution:

Statement showing the total price

		Chemicals		
		A (*Rs.*)	B (*Rs.*)	C (*Rs.*)
	Purchase price	12,600	19,000	9,500
Add :	Sales tax @ 5% of purchase price (*See Note 1*)	630	950	475

		A	B	C
Add :	Railway freight in the ratio of 3:5:2 (*See Note 2*)	300	500	200
Add :	Octroi @ Re. 0.10 per kg on the quantity of material received	280	472	190
Add :	Cartage	22	63.12	31.80
	Total price	13,832	20,985.12	10,396.80

Statement showing the net quantity of chemcial available for issue

		A (*kg.*)	B (*kg.*)	C (*kg.*)
	Quantity purchased	3,000	5,000	2,000
Less :	Shortage (assumed to be normal)	200	280	100
	Qty. Received at the stores	2,800	4,720	1,900
Less :	Provision for further deterioration 5%	140	236	95
	Quantity available for issue	2,660	4,484	1,805
	Rate of issue per kg.	$\frac{13,832}{2,660}$	$\frac{20,985.12}{4,484}$	$\frac{10,396.80}{1.805}$
		= 5.20	4.68	5.76

Working Notes:

(1) Rate of sales tax = $\frac{\text{Sales tax}}{\text{Total purchase price of chemcial}} \times 100 = \frac{2,055}{11,100} \times 100 = 5\%$

(2) Railway freight : The quantity purchased is taken as the basis. *i.e.,* 3,000 : 5,000 : 2,000

3. Re-use price method. Sometimes materials issued to production departments are returned back to stores being considered unfit or in excess. Such returned materials are again re-issued to other department not at its original price but at a different price. The price at which they are valued is known as the re-use price.

ADDITIONAL PROBLEMS

Problem-19 (FIFO method)

The following are the receipts and issues of materials during January 2002.

1, Opening balance 1000 units @ Rs. 50 each.

3, Issue 500 units.

13, Received from vendor 400 units @ Rs. 48 each.

15, Refund of surplus from a work order 34 units @ Rs. 48 per unit.

16, Issue 360 units.

20, Received from vendor 640 units @ Rs. 50 per unit.

26, Issue 800 units.

28, Refund of surplus from a work order 24 units (issued on 3rd January).

From the above write the stores ledger using FIFO method of pricing material issues.

(*Osmania University, B.Com., March 2004*)

Solution:

Stores ledger card—FIFO method

Date	Receipts			Issues			Balance		
	Qty.	Rate	Amount	Qty.	Rate	Amount	Qty.	Rate	Amount
2002									
Jan. 1	—	—	—	—	—	—	1,000	50	50,000
3	—	—	—	500	50	25,000	500	50	25,000
13	400	48	19,200	—	—	—	500	50	25,000
							434	48	20,832
15	34 (Refund)	48	1,632	—	—	—	500	50	25,000
							434	48	20,832
16	—	—	—	360	50	18,000	140	50	7,000
							434	48	20,832
							640	50	32,000
20	640	50	32,000	—	—	—	140	50	7,000
							434	48	20,832
							640	50	32,000
26	—	—	—	140	50	7,000			
				434	48	20,832			
				226	50	11,300	414	50	20,700
28	24 (Refund)	50	1,200	—	—	—	414	50	20,700
							24	50	1200

Problem-20 (FIFO and LIFO method)

The following are the particulars of the receipt and issue of materials in a factory during January 1998

Jan. 2	Opening balance	1,000 kg. at Rs. 30
3	Issued	140 kg.
4	Issued	200 kg.
8	Issued	160 kg.
13	Received from vendor	400 kg. at Rs. 35
15	Returned surplus from a work order	30 kg. at Rs. 28
16	Issued	300 kg.
18	Received from vendor	600 kg. at Rs. 32
20	Issued	550 kg.
22	Received from vendor	400 kg. at Rs. 34
24	Issued	250 kg.
29	Return of surplus from a work order	40 kg. at Rs. 32
30	Received from vendor	200 kg. at Rs. 36

Prepare stores ledger showing the above transactions under FIFO and LIFO method.

(Sri Krishnadevaraya University, B. Com., October 2005)

Solution: **Stores ledger card-FIFO method**

Date	*Receipts*			*Issues*			*Balance*		
	Qty.	*Rate*	*Amount*	*Qty.*	*Rate*	*Amount*	*Qty.*	*Rate*	*Amount*
1998									
June 2	—	—	—	—	—	—	1,000	30	30,000
3	—	—	—	140	30	4,200	860	30	25,800
4	—	—	—	200	30	6,000	660	30	19,800
8	—	—	—	160	30	4,800	500	30	15,000
13	400	35	14,000	—	—	—	500	30	15,000
							400	35	14,000
15	30	28	840	—	—	—	500	30	15,000
	(Refund)						400	35	14,000
							30	28	840
16	—	—	—	300	30	9,000	200	30	6,000
							400	35	14,000
							30	28	840
18	600	32	19,200	—	—	—	200	30	6,000
							400	35	14,000
							30	28	840
							600	32	19,200
20	—	—	—	200	30	6,000	50	35	1750
				350	35	12,250	30	28	840
							600	32	19,200
22	400	34	13,600	—	—	—	50	35	1750
							30	28	840
							600	32	19,200
							400	34	13,600
24	—	—	—	50	35	1,750	430	32	13,760
				30	28	840	400	34	13,600
				170	32	5,440			
29	40	32	1,280	—	—	—	430	32	13,760
	(Refund)						400	34	13,600
							40	32	1,280
30	200	36	7,200	—	—	—	430	32	13,760
							400	34	13,600
							40	32	1,280
							200	36	7,200

Stores ledger card—LIFO method

Date	Receipts			Issues			Balance		
	Qty.	*Rate*	*Amount*	*Qty.*	*Rate*	*Amount*	*Qty.*	*Rate*	*Amount*
1998									
June 2	—	—	—	—	—	—	1,000	30	30,000
3	—	—	—	140	30	4,200	860	30	25,800
4	—	—	—	200	30	6,000	660	30	19,800
8	—	—	—	160	30	4,800	500	30	15,000
13	400	35	14,000	—	—	—	500	30	15,000
							400	35	14,000
15	30 (Refund)	28	840	—	—	—	500	30	15,000
							400	35	14,000
							30	28	840
16	—	—	—	30	28	840	500	30	15,000
				270	35	9,450	130	35	4550
18	600	32	19,200	—	—	—	500	30	15,000
							130	35	4550
							600	32	19,200
20	—	—	—	550	32	17,600	500	30	15,000
							130	35	4,550
							50	32	1,600
22	400	34	13,600	—	—	—	500	30	15,000
							130	35	4,550
							50	32	1,600
							400	34	13,600
24	—	—	—	250	34	8,500	500	30	15,000
							130	35	4,550
							50	32	1,600
							150	34	5,100
29	40 (Refund)	32	1280	—	—	—	500	30	15,000
							130	35	4,550
							50	32	1,600
							150	34	5,100
							40	32	1,280
30	200	36	7,200	—	—	—	500	30	15,000
							130	35	4550
							50	32	1,600
							150	34	5,100
							40	32	1,280
							200	36	7,200

Problem-21 (FIFO and LIFO method)

From the records of a company distributing petrol, the following information is available for the month of March 2002

Sales for the month	: Rs. 79,10,000
Opening stock as on 1-3-2002	: 1,25,000 litres @ Rs. 30 per litre
Purchases	
March 5	: 1,50 000 litres @ Rs. 31.10 per litre
March 27	: 1,00,000 litres @ Rs. 31.20 per litre

Closing stock as on 31 March 2002 : 1,30,000 litres

General Administration expenses for the month of March 2002 : Rs. 1,72,000

From the information given above, work out the following using FIFO and LIFO method of inventory valuation, assuming pricing of issues being done at the end of month after all receipts during the month.

(*a*) value of closing stock as on 31-3-2002

(*b*) cost of sales for March 2002

(*c*) profit or loss for March 2002 (*I.C.W.A., Inter., December 2002*)

Solution: **(*a*) Valuation of Closing Stock as on 31-3-2002**

Particulars	*FIFO*			*LIFO*		
	Qty.	*Rate*	*Amount*	*Qty.*	*Rate*	*Amount*
Opening stock	1,25,000	30	37,50,000	1,25,000	30	37,50,000
Add : Purchases						
March 5	1,50,000	31.10	46,65,000	1,50,000	31.10	46,65,000
March 27	1,00,000	31.20	31,20,000	1,00,000	31.20	31,20,000
	2,50,000	—	77,85,000	2,50,000	—	77,85,000
Total (*A*)	3,75,000	—	1,15,35,000	3,75,000	—	11,53,5000
Less : Issues						
March 31	1,25,000	30	37,50,000	1,00,000	31.20	31,20,000
	1,20,000	31.10	37,32,000	1,45,000	31.10	45,09,500
Total (*B*)	2,45,000	—	74,82,000	2,45,000	—	76,29,500
Closing stock	30,000	31.10	9,33,000	5,000	31.10	1,55,500
as on 31-3-2002	1,00,000	31.20	31,20,000	1,25,000	30	37,50,000
(A – B)	1,30,000	—	40,53,000	1,30,000	—	39,05,500

(*b*) Statement showing cost of sales for March, 2002

	FIFO	**LIFO**
	(*Rs.*)	**(*Rs.*)**
Opening stock	37,50,000	37,50,000
Add : Purchases	77,85,000	77,85,000
	1,15,35,000	1,15,35,000
Less : Closing stock	40,53,000	39,05,500
Cost of petrol sold	74,82,000	76,29,500
Add : General Administration expenses	1,72,000	1,72,000
Cost of sales	76,54,000	78,01,500

(c) Statement showing profit or loss for March 2002

	FIFO	LIFO
Sales for the month	79,10,000	79,10,000
Less : Cost of sales	76,54,000	78,01,500
	2,56,000	1,08,500

Problem-22 (LIFO method)

The following is an extract of the record of receipts and issues of a material 'x' during March 2006. On March 1, 2006 opening balance was 300 units @ Rs. 20 per unit

2006

March 3, Issues 150 units
4, Issues 100 units
10, Received from supplier 200 units @ Rs. 19 per unit
16, Issued 65 units
20, Received from supplier 240 units @ Rs. 22 per unit
24, Returned to supplier 20 units out of purchases of 20 March 2006
25, Purchases 100 units @ Rs. 24 per unit
26, Issues 180 units

On March 14 received back from production department to stores 15 units. Stock verification on 18th March revealed a shortage of 10 units and on 31st March showed an excess of 5 units. Write up Stores Ledger Account under LIFO method.

(Mangalore University, B.Com., April 2006)

Solution: **Stores ledger card-LIFO method**

Date	*Receipts*			*Issues*			*Balance*		
	Qty.	*Rate*	*Amount*	*Qty.*	*Rate*	*Amount*	*Qty.*	*Rate*	*Amount*
2006									
Mar. 1	—	—	—	—	—	—	300	20	6,000
3	—	—	—	150	20	3,000	150	20	3,000
4	—	—	—	100	20	2,000	50	20	1,000
10	200	19	3,800	—	—	—	50	20	1,000
14	15	20	300	—	—	—	50	20	1,000
	Ret to Stores						190	19	3,610
16	—	—	—	65	19	1235	50	20	1,000
							125	19	2,375
18	—	—	—	10	19	190	50	20	1,000
				Shortage			115	19	2,185
20	240	22	5,280	—	—	—	50	20	1,000
							115	19	2,185
							240	22	5,280

24	—	—	—	20	22	440	50	20	1,000
				Ret to			115	19	2,185
				Supp			220	22	5,280
26	—	—	—	180	22	3,960	50	20	1,000
							115	19	2,185
							40	22	880
31	5	22	110	—	—	—	50	20	1,000
	(Surplus)						115	19	2,185
							40	22	880
							5	22	110

Problem-23 (Base stock method)

The stock of materials in hand on 1st April 2003 was 800 units at Rs. 50 per unit. The following receipts and issues were recorded. You are required to prepare stores ledger account, showing how the values of issues would be calculated under base stock method through "FIFO" method, base stock being 200 units.

April

2 Purchased 200 units @ Rs. 55 per unit

6 Issued 800 units

10 Purchased 1200 units @ Rs. 60 per unit

13 Issued 1,000 units

20 Purchased 1,000 units @ Rs. 65 per unit

25 Issued 1,200 units

May

10 Purchased 1,600 units @ Rs. 70 per unit

12 Issued 1,000 units

13 Issued 400 units

15 Purchased 1,000 units @ Rs. 75 per unit

June

6 Issued 800 units

15 Purchased 600 units @ Rs. 80 per units

(*Osmania University, B.Com., October 2004*)

Solution: Stores ledger card-base stock method with FIFO principle

Date	Receipts			Issues			Balance		
	Qty.	*Rate*	*Amount*	*Qty.*	*Rate*	*Amount*	*Qty.*	*Rate*	*Amount*
2003									
Apr. 1	—	—	—	—	—	—	800	50	40,000
2	200	55	11,000	—	—	—	800	50	40,000
							200	55	11,000
6	—	—	—	600	50	30,000			
				200	55	11,000	200	50	10,000
10	1,200	60	72,000	—	—	—	200	50	10,000
							1,200	60	12,000
13	—	—	—	1,000	60	60,000	200	50	10,000
							200	60	12,000
20	1,000	65	65,000	—	—	—	200	50	10,000
							200	60	12,000
							1,000	65	65,000
25	—	—	—	200	60	12,000			
				1,000	65	65,000	200	50	10,000
May 10	1,600	70	1,12,000	—	—	—	200	50	10,000
							1,600	70	1,12,000
12	—	—	—	1,000	70	70,000	200	50	10,000
							600	70	42,000
13	—	—	—	400	70	28,000	200	50	10,000
							200	70	14,000
15	1,000	75	75,000	—	—	—	200	50	10,000
							200	70	14,000
							1,000	75	75,000
June 6	—	—	—	200	70	14,000	200	50	10,000
				600	75	45,000	400	75	30,000
15	600	80	48,000	—	—	—	200	50	10,000
							400	75	30,000
							600	80	48,000

Problem-24 (Simple average cost method)

The following transaction took place in respect of a raw material during the month of January 1993

Date	Particulars	kg.	Rate per kg. (Rs.)
Jan. 1	Balance	1,000	9
2	Purchased	1,500	10
5	Issued	390	—
8	Shortage	10	—
15	Surplus returned by a production department	200	12
20	Issued	1,000	—
25	Recevied from vendor	300	14
28	Issued	1,200	—
31	Issued	100	—

You are required to write up the stores ledger account applying the simple average method of pricing of issues

(Calcutta University, B.Com. (Hons) 1993)

Solution: **Stores ledger card-simple average cost method**

Material ....
Max. level ....

Code no. ....
Min. level ....

Bin no. ....
Reorder level ....

Location ....

Date	Receipts			Issues			Balance	
	Qty.	Rate	Amount	Qty.	Rate	Amount	Qty.	Amount
1-1-93	—	—	—	—	—	—	1,000	9,000
2-1-93	1,500	10	15,000	—	—	—	2,500	24,000
5-1-93	—	—	—	390	9.50	3,750	2,110	20,295
8-1-93	—	—	—	10	9.50	95	2,100	20,200
15-1-93	200	12	2,400	—	—	—	2,300	22,600
20-1-93	—	—	—	1,000	10.33	10,330	1,300	12,270
25-1-93	300	14	4,200	—	—	—	1,600	16,470
28-1-93	—	—	—	1,200	12	14,400	400	2,070
31-1-93	—	—	—	100	13	1,300	300	770

Working Notes:

1. Issue price on 5-1-93 will be the average price of the stocks held on that date

$$\frac{9+10}{2} = \text{Rs. } 9.50 \text{ per unit}$$

2. Shortage are treated exactly as an issue on 8-1-93 *i.e.,* at simple average cost , *i.e.,*

$$\frac{9+10}{2} = \text{Rs. } 9.50$$

3. Issue price on 20-1-93 will be the average price of the stocks held on that date

$$\frac{9+10+12}{3} = \text{Rs. } 10.33 \text{ per unit}$$

4. On 28-1-93 entire stock of opening balance of 1,000 kg. was exhausted. Hence the lot remains @ Rs. 10 + 12 + 14 respectively. So the issue price will be

$$\frac{10+12+14}{3} = \text{Rs. } 12.00$$

5. On 31-3-93 upto the second lot of 15 kg. @ Rs. 10 is exhausted. Hence the lot remains is of 200 kg @ Rs. 12 per kg and the lot of 300 kg @ Rs. 14 per kg remains. So issue price will be

$$\frac{14+12}{2} = \text{Rs. } 13$$

Problem-25 LIFO

From the following information select the most suitable method of pricing material issues and write up a stores ledger card based on that method.

1996

Jan 1 Opening balance 24,400 kg. @ Rs. 7,500 per tonne
1 Purchased 44,000 kg. @ Rs. 7600 per tonne
3 Issued 10,000 kg.
5 Issued 16,000 kg.
12 Purchased 10,000 kg. @ Rs. 7,800 per tonne
13 Issued 24,000 kg.
18 Issued 25,000 kg.
22 Purchased 50,000 kg. @ Rs. 8,000 per tonne
28 Issued 20,000 kg.

On 24th January 1996, a shortage of 200 kg. was noticed in stock taking.

(*Calcutta University, B.Com. (Hons) 1996*)

Solution:

Note:

1. The quantity purchased is expessed in kg. whereas the purchase rate is expressed as rate per tonne. 1,000 kg. = 1 Tonne. So the purchase rate is to be converted from tonne to kg. by dividing the amount by 1,000 kg. The purchase rate of opening balance is $\frac{7,500}{1,000}$ = Rs. 7.50 per kg. and so on.
2. Since the price of materials is going up with time last in first out (LIFO) method of pricing of issues will be appropriate. Under LIFO method production will be charged with materials at close to market price to show true cost of production.

Stores ledger Card-LIFO method

Date	Receipts			Issues			Balance		
	Qty.	Rate	Amount	Qty.	Rate	Amount	Qty.	Rate	Amount
1996									
Jan. 1	—	—	—	—	—	—	24,000	7.50	1,80,000
1	44,000	7.60	3,34,400	—	—	—	24,000	7.50	1,80,000
							44,000	7.60	3,34,400
3	—	—	—	10,000	7.60	76,000	24,000	7.50	1,80,000
							34,000	7.60	2,58,400
5	—	—	—	16,000	7.60	1,21,600	24,000	7.50	1,80,000
							18,000	7.60	1,36,800
12	10,000	7.80	78,000	—	—	—	24,000	7.50	1,80,000
							18,000	7.60	1,36,800
							10,000	7.80	78,000
13	—	—	—	10,000	7.80	78,000	24,000	7.50	1,80,000
				14,000	7.60	1,06,000	4,000	7.60	30,400
18	—	—	—	4,000	7.60	30,400			
				21,000	7.50	1,57,500	3,000	7.50	22,500
22	50,000	8	4,00,000	—	—	—	3,000	7.50	22,500
							50,000	8	4,00,000
24	—	—	—	2000 (Shortage)	8	1,600	3,000	7.50	22,500
							49,800	8	3,98,400
28	—	—	—	20,000	8	1,60,000	3,000	7.50	22,500
							29,800	8	2,38,400
31	—	—	—	22,000	8	1,76,000	3,000	7.50	22,500
							7,800	8	62,400

Problem-26 (LIFO and weighted average cost method)

Record the following transations in a specimen stores ledger using: (*a*) weighted average method and (*b*) LIFO method of pricing issues

Date	Particulars	Units	Price (Rs.)
Mar. 1	Balance in hand	3,000	2
2	Purchased	2,000	2.20
3	Issued	1,500	?
5	Purchased	2,000	2.30
10	Issued	1,500	?
15	Issued	2,000	?
20	Purchased	2,000	2.40
31	Issued	1,500	?

In the above situation what are the effects of each method ?

(Calcutta Univesity, B.Com. (Hons) 2003)

Solution: **Stores ledger card-weighted average cost method**

Date	Receipts			Issues			Balance	
	Qty.	Rate	Amount	Qty.	Rate	Amount	Qty.	Amount
Mar. 1	—	—	—	—	—	—	3,000	6,000
2	2,000	2.20	4,400	—	—	—	5,000	10,400
3	—	—	—	1,500	2.08	3,120	3,500	7,280
5	2,000	2.30	4,600	—	—	—	5,500	11,880
10	—	—	—	1,500	2.16	3,240	4,000	8,640
15	—	—	—	2,000	2.16	4,320	2,000	4,320
20	2,000	2.40	4,800	—	—	—	4,000	9,120
31	—	—	—	1,500	2.28	3,420	2,500	5,700

Stores ledger card-LIFO method

Date	Receipts			Issues			Balance		
	Qty.	Rate	Amount	Qty.	Rate	Amount	Qty.	Rate	Amount
Mar. 1	—	—	—	—	—	—	3,000	2	6,000
2	2,000	2.20	4,400	—	—	—	3,000	2	6,000
							2,000	2.20	4,400
3	—	—	—	1,500	2.20	3,300	3,000	2	6,000
							500	2.20	1,100
5	2,000	2.30	4,600	—	—	—	3,000	2	6,000
							500	2.20	1,100
							2,000	2.30	4,600
10	—	—	—	1,500	2.30	3,450	3,000	2	6,000
							500	2.20	1,100
							500	2.30	1,150
15	—	—	—	500	2.30	1,150			
				500	2.20	1,100			
				1,000	2	2,000	2,000	2	4,000
20	2,000	2.40	4,800	—	—	—	2,000	2	4,000
							2,000	2.40	4,800
31	—	—	—	1,500	2.40	3,600	2,000	2	4,000
							500	2.40	1,200

Problem-27 (LIFO and weighted average cost method)

From the following information, prepare stores ledger for the month of February 2005 under (*i*) LIFO and (*ii*) weighted average method.

Date	Particulars	Units	Rate per unit
Feb. 3	Purchased	450	Rs. 16.20
7	Purchased	780	17.50
13	Purchased	340	16.80

18	Returned from workshop (issued on Feb 7)	65	
24	Purchased	670	16.50

Date	Issues (units)
Feb. 4	350
6	220
9	670
16	325
21	270
26	430

Further Information:

Opening balance on 1-2-2005 - 620 units @ Rs. 15.40 per unit. A shortage of 24 units was noticed and recorded on 15th February. *(Calcutta University, B.Com. (Hons) 2005)*

Solution: **Stores ledger card—LIFO method**

Date	*Receipts*			*Issues*			*Balance*		
	Qty.	*Rate*	*Amount*	*Qty.*	*Rate*	*Amount*	*Qty.*	*Rate*	*Amount*
2005									
Feb. 1	—	—	—	—	—	—	620	15.40	9,548
3	450	16.20	7,290	—	—	—	620	15.40	9,548
							450	16.20	7,290
4	—	—	—	350	16.20	5,670	620	15.40	9,548
							100	16.20	1620
6	—	—	—	100	16.20	1,620	500	15.40	7,700
				120	15.40	1,848			
7	780	17.50	13,650	—	—	—	500	15.40	7,700
							780	17.50	13,650
9	—	—	—	670	17.50	11,725	500	15.40	7,700
							110	17.50	1,925
13	340	16.80	5,712	—	—	—	500	15.40	7,700
							110	17.50	1,925
							340	16.80	5,712
15	—	—	—	24	16.80	403	500	15.40	7,700
							110	17.50	1,925
							316	16.80	5,309
16	—	—	—	316	16.80	5,309	500	15.40	7,700
				9	17.50	158	101	17.50	1,767

Date	Receipts Qty.	Rate	Amount	Issues Qty.	Rate	Amount	Balance Qty.	Rate	Amount
18	65	17.50	1,138	—	—	—	500	15.40	7,700
	(Reurns from Workshop)						166	17.50	2,905
21	—	—	—	166	17.50	2,905			
				104	15.40	1,602	396	15.40	6,098
24	670	16.50	11,055	—	—	—	396	15.40	6,098
							670	16.50	11,055
26	—	—	—	430	16.50	7,095	396	15.40	6,098
							240	16.50	3,960

Store ledger card-weighted average cost method

Date	*Receipts*			*Issues*			*Balance*	
	Qty.	*Rate*	*Amount*	*Qty.*	*Rate*	*Amount*	*Qty.*	*Amount*
2005								
Feb. 1	—	—	—	—	—	—	620	9,548
3	450	16.20	7,290	—	—	—	1,070	16,838
4	—	—	—	350	15.736	5,508	720	11,330
6	—	—	—	220	15.736	3462	500	7,868
7	780	17.50	13,650	—	—	—	1,280	21,518
9	—	—	—	670	16.811	11,263	610	10,255
13	340	16.80	5,712	—	—	—	950	5,967
15	—	—	—	24 (Shortage)	16.807	403	926	15,564
16	—	—	—	325	16.807	5,462	601	10,102
18	65 Return	16.811	1,093	—	—	—	666	11,195
21	—	—	—	270	16.809	4,539	396	6,656
24	670	16.50	11,055	—	—	—	1,066	17,711
26	—	—	—	430	16.614	7,144	636	10,567

Problem-28 (FIFO and LIFO)

X Ltd has purchased and issued the materials '*N*' in the following order.

		Units	Unit cost Rs.
2007 March 01	Purchases	300	3
04	Purchases	600	4
06	Issue	400	—
10	Purchases	600	4
15	Issue	1,000	—
20	Purchases	400	5
31	Issue	200	—

Prepare stores ledger card under FIFO and LIFO methods. Which of the method of pricing issue of materials would you recommend in ths case?

(Sri Sathya Sai University, B. Com., August 2007)

Solution: **Stores ledger card-FIFO method**

Date	Receipts			Issues			Balance		
	Qty.	*Rate*	*Amount*	*Qty.*	*Rate*	*Amount*	*Qty.*	*Rate*	*Amount*
2007									
Mar. 1	300	3	900	—	—	—	300	3	900
4	600	4	2,400	—	—	—	300	3	900
							600	4	2,400
6	—	—	—	300	3	900			
				100	4	400	500	4	2,000
10	600	4	2,400	—	—	—	500	4	2,000
							600	4	2,400
15	—	—	—	500	4	2,000			
				500	4	2,000	100	4	400
20	400	5	2,000	—	—	—	100	4	400
							400	5	2,000
31	—	—	—	100	4	400			
				100	5	500	300	5	1,500

Stores ledger card-LIFO method

Date	Receipts			Issues			Balance		
	Qty.	*Rate*	*Amount*	*Qty.*	*Rate*	*Amount*	*Qty.*	*Rate*	*Amount*
2007									
Mar. 1	300	3	900	—	—	—	300	3	900
4	600	4	2,400	—	—	—	300	3	900
							600	4	2,400
6	—	—	—	400	4	1,600	300	3	900
							200	4	800
10	600	4	2,400	—	—	—	300	3	900
							200	4	800
							600	4	2,400
15	—	—	—	600	4	2,400			
				200	4	800			
				200	3	600	100	3	300
20	400	5	2,000	—	—	—	100	3	300
							400	5	2,000
31	—	—	—	200	5	1,000	100	3	300
							200	5	1,000

Recommendation

Since the prices are showing increasing trend LIFO method of pricing issues may be recommended as in this case cost of production reflects current market trends and the balance of stock is not shown at the high rate.

Problem-29 (Weight average method and LIFO method)

Prepare the stores ledger card by using (*a*) weighted average method and (*b*) LIFO method of pricing issues in connection with the following transactions

Date	*Particulars*	*Units*	*Value* Rs.
2006			
March 1	Balance b/d	300	600
2	Purchased	200	440
4	Issued	150	—
6	Purchased	200	460
11	Issued	150	—
19	Issued	200	—
22	Purchased	200	480
27	Issued	250	—

In a period of rising prices such as above what are the effects of each method.

(Sri Sathya Sai University, B.Com. (Hons), March 2006)

Solution: **Stores ledger card-weighted average method**

Date	*Receipts*			*Issues*			*Balance*		
	Qty.	*Rate*	*Amount*	*Qty.*	*Rate*	*Amount*	*Qty.*	*Rate*	*Amount*
2006									
Mar. 1	—	—	—	—	—	—	300		600
2	200	2.20	440	—	—	—	500		1,040
4	—	—	—	150	2.08	312	350		728
6	200	2.30	460	—	—	—	550		1,188
11	—	—	—	150	2.16	324	400		864
19	—	—	—	200	2.16	432	200		432
22	200	2.40	480	—	—	—	400		912
27	—	—	—	250	2.28	570	150		342

Stores ledger card-LIFO method

Date	*Receipts*			*Issues*			*Balance*		
	Qty.	*Rate*	*Amount*	*Qty.*	*Rate*	*Amount*	*Qty.*	*Rate*	*Amount*
2006									
Mar. 1	—	—	—	—	—	—	300	2	600
2	200	2.20	440	—	—	—	300	2	600
							200	2.20	440
4	—	—	—	150	2.20	330	300	2	600
							50	2.20	110
6	200	2.30	460	—	—		300	2	600
							50	2.20	110
							200	2.30	460
11	—	—	—	150	2.30	345	300	2	600
							50	2.20	110
							50	2.30	115
19	—	—	—	50	2.30	115			
				50	2.20	110			
				100	2.00	200	200	2	400
22	200	2.40	480	—	—	—	200	2	400
							200	2.40	480
27	—	—	—	200	2.40	480			
				50	2.00	100	150	2	300

Pricing methods and rising prices.

1. Weighted average method. This method evens out the effect of widely varying prices. Thus when the prices are showing a rising trend the effect of rise in prices is reduced. This is because the rise in prices is spread over a large number of units.

2. LIFO method. This method charges production with the latest prices paid. Thus higher prices of the most recent purchases are charged to operations. This keeps the profit figure low and may result in tax saving. However, the value of closing stock is at the older prices and is thus undervalued.

Problem-30 (FIFO and LIFO method)

Morewell limited is a distributor on 30th June, stock on hand was 200 units which had a value of Rs. 8,400. Transactions for the six months to 31st December were as follows.

Date	*Purchases qty.* *(Units)*	*Cost per unit* *Rs.*
July	200	46.00
August	500	49.40
September	1,000	52.50 (net)

The purchase manager obtained a bulk purchase discount of Rs. 7.50 per unit on the September purchase.

Date	*Sales qty. (Units)*	*Unit sale price (Rs.)*
October	500	66
November	700	70
December	500	75

There were no sale during the first three months of the period. You are required to

(*a*) Prepare a stores ledger card applying the method.

(*i*) Where closing stock should correspond to the current market price.

(*ii*) Where issue price should correspond to the current market price.

(*b*) Show the profit earned under the above methods by preparing a statement of cost

(*Sri Sathya Sai University, B.Com. (Hons), March 2005*)

Solution:

Note. 1. FIFO method is suitable when closing stock should correspond to the current market price. This is because, under FIFO method all issues are made at old prices and therefore the closing stock is valued at the current market pric.

2. LIFO method is to adopted when issue prices should correspond to the current market price.

Stores ledger card-FIFO method

Date	*Receipts*			*Issues*			*Balance*		
	Qty.	*Rate*	*Amount*	*Qty.*	*Rate*	*Amount*	*Qty.*	*Rate*	*Amount*
July	—	—	—	—	—	—	200	42	8,400
July	200	46	9,200	—	—	—	200	42	8,400
							200	46	9,200
Aug.	500	49.40	24,700	—	—	—	200	42	8,400
							200	46	9,200
							500	49.40	24,700
Sept.	1000	52.50	52,500	—	—	—	200	42	8,400
							200	46	9,200
							500	49.40	24,700
							1,000	52.50	52,500
Oct.	—	—	—	200	42	8,400			
				200	46	9,200	400	49.40	19,760
				100	49.40	4,940	1,000	52.50	52,500
Nov.	—	—	—	400	49.40	19,760			
				300	52.50	15,750	700	52.50	36,750
Dec.	—	—	—	500	52.50	26,250	200	52.50	10,500

Stores ledger card-LIFO method

Date	Receipts			Issues			Balance		
	Qty.	*Rate*	*Amount*	*Qty.*	*Rate*	*Amount*	*Qty.*	*Rate*	*Amount*
July	—	—	—	—	—	—	200	42	8,400
July	200	46	9,200	—	—	—	200	42	8,400
							200	46	9,200
Aug.	500	49.40	24,700	—	—	—	200	42	8,400
							200	46	9,200
							500	49.40	24,700
Sept.	1,000	52.50	52,500	—	—	—	200	42	8,400
							200	46	9,200
							500	49.40	24,700
							1,000	52.50	52,500
Oct.	—	—	—	500	52.50	26,250	200	42	8,400
							200	46	9,200
							500	49.40	24,700
							500	52.50	52,500
Nov.	—	—	—	500	52.50	26,250	200	42	8,400
				200	49.40	9,880	200	46	9,200
							300	49.40	14,820
Dec.	—	—	—	300	49.40	14,820			
				200	46	9,200	200	42	8,400

Statement of Cost

		FIFO	LIFO
Sales —	500 units × 66 = 33,000		
	700 units × 70 = 49,000		
	500 units × 75 = 37,500		
		1,19,500	1,19,500
Add :	Closing stock	10,500	8,400
		1,30,000	1,27,900
Less :	Purchases		
	200 units × 46 = 9,200		
	500 units × 49.40 = 24,700		
	1,000 units × 52,50 = 52,500		
		86,400	86,400
		43,600	41,500
Less :	Opening stock	8,400	8,400
	Profit	35,200	33,100

Alternate method to calculate profit

Profit = Sales – Total issue price

FIFO = 1,19,500 – 84,300 = 35,200

LIFO = 1,19,500 – 8,640 = 33,100

Problem-31 (Simple average, weighted average and standard cost method)

With the help of the following information prepare a stores ledger card. To even out the fluctuations in the prices of materials, company decided to follow simple average method for the first two issues, followed by weighted average method for the next two issues. For the last two issues, the company decided that if the per unit value standing as the balance after purchasing on Nov. 22 is greater than 0.15 paise, it will follow a standard price of 0.15 paise per unit. If not, it will continue its weighted average method.

Nov. 1	Opening balance	24,000 kg.	for Rs. 7,500
1	Purchases	44,000 kg.	for Rs. 7,600
1	Issue	10,000 kg.	
5	Issue	16,000 kg.	
12	Issue	24,000 kg.	
13	Purchase	10,000 kg.	for Rs. 7,800
18	Issue	24,000 kg.	
22	Purchase	50,000 kg.	for Rs. 8,000
28	Issue	30,000 kg.	
30	Issue	22,000 kg.	

Find out the value of closing stock from the stores ledger card.

(Sri Sathya Sai University, B.Com. (Hons), March 2004)

Solution:

Stores ledger card

Date	*Receipts*			*Issues*			*Balance*	
	Qty.	*Rate*	*Amount*	*Qty.*	*Rate*	*Amount*	*Qty.*	*Amount*
Nov. 1	—	—	—	—	—	—	24,000	7,500
1	44,000	0.172	7,600	—	—	—	68,000	15,100
1	—	—	—	10,000	0.242	2,420	58,000	12,680
5	—	—	—	16,000	0.242	3,872	42,000	8,808
12	—	—	—	24,000	0.20	5,028	18,000	3,708
13	10,000	0.78	7,800	—	—	—	28,000	11,580
18	—	—	—	24,000	0.41	9,840	4,000	1,740
22	50,000	0.16	8,000	—	—	—	54,000	9,740
28	—	—	—	30,000	0.15	4,500	24,000	5,240
30	—	—	—	22,000	0.15	3,300	2,000	1,940

Working Notes:

1. Calculation of issue rate on Nov. 1

Rate of opening stock = $\dfrac{7,500}{24,000}$ = 0.312

$= \dfrac{0.312 + 0.172}{2} = 0.242$

2. Calculation of issue rate on Nov. 5

$= \dfrac{0.312 + 0.172}{2} = 0.242$

3. Calculation of weighted average issue rate on Nov. 12

$= \dfrac{8,800}{42,000} = 0.20$

4. Calculation of weighted average issue rate on Nov. 18

$= \dfrac{11,580}{28,000} = 0.41$

5. Calculation of issue rate on Nov. 22

$= \dfrac{9,740}{54,000} = 0.18$

As the issue rate after purchasing on Nov. 22 is greater, *i.e.,* 0.18 is greater than 0.15, the company will follow standard cost method, *i.e.,* 0.15 for the last two issues.

Problem-32 (Weighted average cost method)

The stores ledger account for material '*x*' in a manufacturing concern reveals the following data for the quarter ended September 30

Date	*Receipts Qty*	*Rate Rs.*	*Issues Qty*	*Value*
July 1 Balance b/d	1,600	2	—	—
9	3,000	2.20	—	—
13	—	—	1,200	2,556
Aug. 5	—	—	900	1,917
17	3,600	2.40	—	—
24	—	—	1,800	4,122
Sept. 11	2,500	2.50	—	—
27	—	—	2,100	4,971
29	—	—	700	1,656

Physical verification on september 30 revealed on actual stock of 3,800 units. You are required to:

(*a*) Indicate the method of pricing employed in the above.

(*b*) Complete the above account by making entries you would consider necessary including adjustments if any, and giving explanation for such adjustments.

(Sri Sathya Sai University, B.Com. (Hons), March 2002)

(Stores ledger card–weighted average cost method)

Solution:

Date	Receipts			Issues			Balance	
	Qty.	*Rate*	*Amount*	*Qty.*	*Rate*	*Amount*	*Qty.*	*Amount*
July 1	—	—	—	—	—	—	1,600	3,200
9	3,000	2.20	6,600	—	—	—	4,600	9,800
13	—	—	—	1,200	2.1304	2,556	3,400	7,244
Aug. 5	—	—	—	900	2.1305	1,917	2,500	5,327
17	3,600	2.40	8,640	—	—	—	6,100	13,967
24	—	—	—	1,800	2.2896	4,122	4,300	9,845
Sept 11	2,500	2.50	6,250	—	—	—	6,800	16,095
27	—	—	—	2,100	2.3669	4,971	4,700	11,124
29	—	—	—	700	2.3669	1,656	4,000	9,468
30	—	—	—	200	2.367	474	3,800	8,994

Note:

1. Weighted average cost method is adopted in this problem as the value of issues confirm to the weighted average rates as shown below:

Issue rate on 13th July

$$= \frac{9,800}{4,600} = 2.1304$$

Issue value will be 1200 × 2.1304 = Rs. 2556 as given in the problem

Issue rate on 5th Aug.

$$= \frac{7,244}{3,400} = 2.1305$$

Issue value will be 900 × 2.1305 = Rs. 1,917 which is same as given in the problem

Issue rate on 24th Aug.

$$= \frac{9,845}{4,300} = 2.2896$$

Issue value will be 1,800 × 2.2896 = Rs. 4,121 which is same as given in the problem.

Issue rate on 27th Sept.

$$= \frac{11,124}{4,700} = 2.3669$$

Issue value will be 2,100 × 2.3669 = Rs. 4970 which is the same as given in the problem.

Issue rate on 29th Sept.

$$= \frac{9,468}{4,000} = 2.3669$$

Issue value will be 700 × 2.3669 = Rs. 1,656 which is the same as given in the problem.

2. The closing stock on 30th September as given in the problem is 3,800 units whereas the stores ledger shows the closing stock quantity to be 4,000 as on 29th September. The difference between the two *viz.*, 200 units (4,000 units – 3,800 units) are treated as normal loss units and valued at weighted average price.

Problem-33 (Simple average and weighted average cost method)

Prepare a stores ledger card showing the prcing of issues on the basis of : (*i*) Simple average and (*ii*) weighted average cost methods from the information pertaining to meterial -'*x*'.

Date		*Particulars*
2007		
Jan. 1,	Purchased	100 units @ Rs. 10 each
2,	Purchased	200 units @ Rs. 10.20 each
5,	Issued	250 units to Job A, vide MRN 1
7,	Purchased	300 units @ Rs. 10.50 each
10,	Purchased	200 units @ Rs. 10.80 each
13,	Issued	200 units to Job B vide MRN 2
18,	Issued	200 units to Job C vide MRN 3
20,	Purchased	100 units @ Rs. 11.00 each
25,	Issued	150 units to Job D vide MRN 4

(*Sri Sathya Sai University, B.Com. (Hons), March 2007*)

Solution:

Stores ledger card-simple average cost method

Date	*Receipts*			*Issues*			*Balance*	
	Qty.	*Rate*	*Amount*	*Qty.*	*Rate*	*Amount*	*Qty.*	*Amount*
2007								
Jan 1	100	10	1,000	—	—	—	100	1,000
2	200	10.20	2,040	—	—	—	300	3,040
5	—	—	—	250	10.10	2,525	50	515
7	300	10.50	3,150	—	—	—	350	3,665
10	200	10.80	2,160	—	—	—	550	5,825
13	—	—	—	200	10.50	2,100	350	3,725
18	—	—	—	200	10.65	2,130	150	1,595
20	100	11	1,100	—	—	—	250	2,695
25	—	—	—	150	10.90	1,635	100	1,060

Working Notes:

Calculation of simple average cost.

1. Issue rate on 5th Jan.

$$\frac{10.20 + 10}{2} = 10.10$$

2. Issue rate on 13th Jan.

$$\frac{10.80+10.50+10.20}{3} = 10.50$$

3. Issue rate on 18th Jan.

$$\frac{10.50+10.80}{2} = 10.65$$

4. Issue rate on 25th Jan.

$$\frac{10.80+11}{2} = 10.90$$

Stores ledger card-weighted average cost method

Date	*Receipts*			*Issues*			*Balance*	
	Qty.	*Rate*	*Amount*	*Qty.*	*Rate*	*Amount*	*Qty.*	*Amount*
2007								
Jan. 1	100	10	1,000	—	—	—	100	1,000
2	200	10.20	2,040	—	—	—	300	3,040
5	—	—	—	250	10.13	2,533	50	507
7	300	10.50	3150	—	—	—	350	3,657
10	200	10.80	2,160	—	—	—	550	5,817
13	—	—	—	200	10.58	2,116	350	3,701
18	—	—	—	200	10.58	2,116	150	1,585
20	100	11	1,100	—	—	—	250	2,685
25	—	—	—	150	10.74	1,611	100	1,074

COMPARISON OF DIFFERENT METHODS OF PRICING

Points of differences	*FIFO*	*LIFO*	*Average cost*	*Market price*	*Standard price*
1. Recovery of cost	It recovers cost	It recovers cost	It recovers cost	It does not recover the cost	It does not recover the cost
2. Reflection of market price	Does not reflect market Price	It reflects market price	It does not reflect market price. But if the rise and fall in prices is uniform then it reflects market price	It reflects market price	It does not reflect market price
3. Elimination of variation	It does not eliminate price variation	It does not eliminate price variation	It eliminates price variation	It does not eliminate price variation	It eliminates price variation
4. Stock adjustment	Avoids stock adjustment	It does not avoid stock adjustment	It avoids stock adjust-ment	It does not avoid stock adjustment	It avoids stock adjustment

FACTORS INFLUENCING PRICING OF MATERIAL ISSUES

From the foregoing discussion of various method of pricing the material issues it is possible to decide which particular method is best suited for adoption. There are no rigid rule which can be applied for selecting a particular method of pricing the material issues. The choice depends upon the following factors:

(*a*) The nature of materials used: If materials are kept for ripening as in the case of fruits or seasoning as in the case of timber, then inflated price is useful.

(*b*) The policy of management wherein if the cost of production is to reflect market price, then market price method is used.

(*c*) The ability to meet clerical expenses in calculating the issue price. Small sized concerns will not have more amount to invest. So they choose a method which does not involve much clerical labour.

(*d*) The frequency of purchases made, receipts obtained and issues to be made.

(*e*) Fluctuations in the price of material in which case weighted average cost method can be used.

(*f*) The application of standard costing technique in which case standard price method is applicable.

(*g*) The nature of business: If it is job order industries it requires use of special type of materials in which case specific price method is to be adopted.

(*h*) The accuracy desired in which case weighted average price method is to be selected.

(*i*) The length of material turnover period. If the material turnover ratio is less FIFO method is to be used.

(*j*) The method of stock valuation.

(*k*) The effect of pricing method on tax payable.

(*l*) Identification of materials in the purchase lot. Where materials lose their identity average price method is to be adopted.

ACCOUNTING OF MATERIAL SUPPLIED BY CUSTOMERS

Sometimes the material required for processing the goods might be supplied by customers themselves. The examples are supply of dress materials in case of readymade garment factory, gold and silver in case of jewellery, leather in case of footwear industry and other controlled commodities. In accounting of such materials, the following problems arise.

Valuing the Stock of Materials on Hand Supplied by Customers

The quantity of materials supplied by customers must be recorded in the stores ledgers pricing them either at nil value or at a notional value. The clerical work related to receipts and issues will be reduced if materials are valued at nil value. However, this method will not help in claiming the insurance as the value of stock is under-insured. So a prudent manufacturer will always value the materials supplied by the customer at a notional price. The following entries are passed for the receipt and issue of such material.

1. For receiving the stock of materials from customers store
   Stock A/c Dr.
   To stores suspense A/c
2. For issuing the materials to production
   Work-in-progress A/c Dr.
   To stores stock A/c
3. For writing back at the year end the notional value of customer's material taken into stock A/c
   Stores suspense A/c Dr.
   To stores stock A/c
   To work-in-progress A/c

Charging of Handling Charges to Materials Supplied by Customers. Whenever the manufacturer arranges to obtain the material from the premises of customer, the cost of receiving, handling and storage of such materials is to be charged to customer's account. A separate rate is calculated for such materials on a percentage basis and on this basis it is levied.

Treatment of Wastage of Materials Supplied by Customers

An agreement is entered into between manufacturer and customer in respect of a percentage of wastage of material which is common in production process. The output to be delivered must be in accordance with the given quantity of input subject to the provision for waste percentage. Any excess of wastage than the agreed percentage is to be borne by the manufacturer. Thus an excess waste constitutes a loss to manufacturer.

Questions

I. A. Indicate whether the following statements are True or False

1. Stores ledger is maintained in the stores room. *T/F*
2. Bill of materials is a cash bill sent by the supplier along with the materials. *T/F*
3. The standard pricing method is a tool of material cost control. *T/F*
4. A bill of material is a special form of material requisition. *T/F*
5. The adoption of FIFO method results in a profit inflation during period of rising prices. *T/F*

[***Answer:*** *1-F, 2-F, 3-T, 4-T, 5-T*]

II. Fill in the blanks

1. In...........method of pricing the materials evens out the fluctuations in purchase prices.
2. Under the ....method of pricing the material issues, a new issue price is determined after each purchase.
3. Under............method of pricing material issues, materials are issued to production at a predetermined price.
4. The stores ledger card contains information relating to ....as well as..........
5. The document used to draw material from stores room for production departments is known as.............

6. When excess materials are returned to stores..........note is prepared in the department where the materials are in excess.

[***Answer***: (1) average cost method, (2) weighted average price, (3) standard price, (4) quantity and value, (5) material requisition note (6) materials returned note or stores debit note]

III. Choose the correct answer

1. Materials from the storeroom are issued to production departments on presentment of
   (*a*) Purchase requisition note
   (*b*) Stores requisition note
   (*c*) Stores credit note
   (*d*) Materials received note
2. Pricing of material issues closely resembles the current market value under
   (*a*) Last-in-first-out
   (*b*) First-in-first-out
   (*c*) Simple average
   (*d*) Weighted average
3. In base stock method of pricing the material issues, the term base stock represents
   (*a*) Quantity of stock being issued
   (*b*) Stock balance
   (*c*) Minimum stock
   (*d*) Maximum stock
4. In which of the following methods of pricing costs lag behind the current economic value
   (*a*) LIFO
   (*b*) FIFO
   (*c*) Simple average
   (*d*) Weighted average
5. Under which method issue of material is priced at the latest purchase price
   (*a*) FIFO
   (*b*) LIFO
   (*c*) NIFO
   (*d*) HIFO
6. Material requisition note is prepared by
   (*a*) Purchase department
   (*b*) Accounts department
   (*c*) Production department
   (*d*) Production control department
7. Materials analysis sheet is also known as
   (*a*) Material requistion note
   (*b*) Purchase requisition note
   (*c*) Materials abstract
   (*d*) Bill of materials
8. When prices fluctuate widely the method of pricing that smooth out the effect of fluctuation is
   (*a*) Simple average
   (*b*) Weighted average
   (*c*) FIFO
   (*d*) LIFO
9. A material transfer note is prepared to
   (*a*) Transfer materials from one job to another
   (*b*) Transfer materials from main stores to sub-sotre
   (*c*) Return materials to stores from production department
   (*d*) Return defective materials to suppliers
10. FIFO method of pricing the issues is suitable
    (*a*) During period of rising prices
    (*b*) During a period of falling prices
    (*c*) During a period of constant prices
    (*d*) During a period when prices move erratically

11. The value of closing stock approximates to the market value under
    (a) LIFO
    (b) FIFO
    (c) Base stock method
    (d) Standard price method
12. Given: Opening stock on 1-1-2008 200 kg. @ Rs. 4 per kg.
    Purchased on 4-1-2008, 300 kg. @ Rs. 5 per kg.
    Issued on 8-1-2008, 350 kg.
    Market price on 8-1-2008 was Rs. 5 per kg.
    (a) The value of materials issued on 8th under FIFO is
        (i) Rs. 1,100
        (ii) Rs. 1,450
        (iii) Rs. 1,700
        (iv) Rs. 1,750
    (b) The amount at which issues are charged under LIFO method is
        (i) Rs. 1,550
        (ii) Rs. 1,575
        (iii) Rs. 1,700
        (iv) Rs. 1,750
    (c) Under simple average method it will be
        (i) Rs. 1,550
        (ii) Rs. 1,575
        (iii) Rs. 1,610
        (iv) Rs. 1,700
    (d) Under weighted average the amount at which issues are charged will be
        (i) Rs. 1,575
        (ii) Rs. 1,610
        (iii) Rs. 1,625
        (iv) Rs. 1,700

[***Answers:*** 1. (b), 2. (a), 3. (c), 4. (a), 5. (b), 6. (c), 7. (c), 8. (b), 9. (a), 10. (b), 11. (a), 12. (a) (ii), (b) (iv), (c) (ii), (d) (ii)]

IV. Match the following.

A	B
(1) Puchase requisition note	(a) Person nominated by the management
(2) Purchased order	(b) Stores attendant
(3) Materials received note	(c) Head of the department
(4) Bill of materials	(d) Laboratory technician
(5) Materials requisition note	(e) Cost clerk
(6) Stores ledger card	(f) Foreman
(7) Material stock verification note	(g) Purchase manager
(8) Materials transfer note	(h) Production control department
(9) Material inspection note	(i) Storekeeper
(10) Bin card	(j) Material inspection clerk
	(k) Cost accountant
	(f) General manager

[***Answer:*** (1)-(i), (2)-(g), (3)-(j), (4)-(h), (5)-(f), (6)-(e), (7)-(a), (8)-(c), (9)-(d), (10)-(b)]

V. Simple questions

1. What do you mean by material requisition note? Give its specimen form.
2. What do you mean by a bill of material ? Give its specimen from.
3. Distinguish between a material requsition note and bill of materials.

6. What do you mean by material transfer note ? Give its specimen form.
7. What do you mean by FIFO method of pricing material issues ?
8. What do you mean by LIFO method of pricing material issues ?
9. What do you mean by base stock of pricing material issues ?
10. State any two merits and two demerits of FIFO method.
11. State any two merits and two demerits of LIFO method.
12. What do you mean by HIFO method ?
13. What do you mean by NIFO method ?
14. What do you mean by simple average price method.
15. What do you mean by weighted average price method.
16. State the advantages and disadvantages of simple average price method.
17. State the advantages and disadvantages of weighted average.
18. Distinguish between simple average and weighted average price method of pricing the material issues.
19. What do you mean by periodic simple average price ?
20. What do you mean by periodic weighted average price ?
21. What do you mean by inflation price method ?
22. What do you mean by replacement price method ?
23. What do you mean by standard price method ?
24. State the advantages of standard price method.
25. State the disadvantages of standard price method.

VI. Short and long answer questions

1. Explain the standard cost method of pricing the material issues.
   (Bangalore University, B.Com., April 1987)
2. Explain the FIFO and LIFO methods of valuation of materials issues State under what cirumstances these methods are used.
   (Sri Sathya Sai University, B.Com., Feb. 1991)
3. Make a comparative study of the following methods pricing materials issues and state in what situations each method would be appropriate (*a*) LIFO, (*b*) FIFO, (*c*) Weighted average and (*d*) Standard price method. *(Sri Sathya Sai University, B.Com., Oct. 1989)*
4. Explain how LIFO and FIFO method affect (*i*) Valuation of inventories and (*ii*) Profit during a period of rising prices and falling prices. *(Sri Sathya Sai University, B.Com., Oct. 1987)*
5. Discuss the methods of pricing the issues of materials.
   (Bangalore University, M.Com., May 1991)

Exercise-1 (FIFO method)

From the following details prepare stores ledger account by adopting FIFO method.

Dec. 1 Opening stock 1,000 units at Rs. 2 each
3 Purchased 800 units at Rs. 2.10 each
5 Issued 1,200 units
12 Purchased 1,600 units at Rs. 2.10 each *(University of Madras, B. Com., May 2005)*

[***Answer:*** Closing stock 2,200 units at Rs. 2.10 Rs. 4,620)

Exercise-2 (LIFO method)

Prepare a stores ledger from the following transactions under LIFO method.

Jan.	1	Received 1,000 units at Rs. 1.00 per unit
	10	Received 260 units at Rs. 1.05 per unit
	20	Issued 700 units
Feb.	4	Received 400 units at Rs. 1.15 per unit
	21	Received 300 unit at Rs. 1.25 per unit
Mar.	16	Issued 620 units·
Apr.	12	Issued 240 units
	20	Received 500 units at Rs. 1.10 per unit
	25	Issued 380 units

(University of Madras, B. Com., May 2003)

[***Answer:*** Closing stock 400 units amounting to Rs. 400, 120 units Rs. 132]

Exercise-3 (Simple average and weighted average cost method)

The following transactions took place in respect of a material item.

Date	*Receipts (in units)*	*Rate*	*Issues (in units)*
2-1-03	200	2	—
10-1-03	300	2.40	—
15-1-03	—	—	250
18-1-03	250	2.60	—
20-1-03	—	—	200

Prepare the stores ledger accounts using the issues at (*a*) simple average price method and (*b*) weighted average price method. *(University of Madras, B.Com., May 2004)*

[***Answer:*** Closing stock under simple average method 300 units amounting to Rs. 720 and under weighted average method 300 units amounting to Rs. 726]

Exercise-4 (Standard price method)

The standard price of a material is fixed at Rs. 10 per unit. Prepare the stores ledger account showing how the cost of materials issued and value of balance in stock will be recorded under the standard price method from the following purchases and issues made during January 1995.

Date	*Particulars*	*Quantity Units*	*Rate Rs.*
January 2	Received	2,000	11
5	Received	1,000	10
10	Issued	1,200	—
18	Received	800	9
25	Issued	900	—
29	Received	500	12
30	Issued	1,100	

Also find out the efficiency of purchasing materials

(University of Madras, B.Com., October 2003)

[***Answer:*** Closing stock 1,100 units accounting to Rs. 13,200]

Exercise-5 (Weighted average cost method)

The following transactions took place in respect of material 'x' during the month of January 2002.

Date	*Particulars*	*Quantity (kg.) Units*	*Rate per kg. Rs.*
January 2	Received	3,000	10
6	Received	500	12
9	Issued	2,000	—
10	Received	400	14
15	Issued	1,000	—
25	Received	300	11
31	Issued	200	—

Prepare stores ledger card under weighted average price system.

(*Osmania University, B.Com., October 2003*)

[***Answer:*** Closing stock 1,000 units amounting to Rs.10,974]

Exercise-6 (Simple average cost method)

The following information is provided by Swetha Industries for the month of May 2002. Stock on 1.5.2002 100 units @ Rs. 5 per unit.

Purchases

5-5-2002	300 units @ Rs. 6 each
8-5-2002	500 units @ Rs. 7 each
12-5-2002	600 units @ Rs. 8 each

Issues

6-5-2002	250 units
10-5-2002	400 units
14-5-2002	500 units

Calculate using "simple average" method of pricing issues.

1. The value of materials consumed during the period and
2. The value of stock of materials on 15-5-02

(*Osmania University, B.Com., March 2003*)

[***Answer:*** (*a*) Value of material consumed Rs. 7725, (*b*) Closing stock 350 units accounting to Rs. 2,875]

Exercise-7 (FIFO method)

Draw up a "stores ledger" for the following transactions adopting "FIFO" method of pricing of issues.

01-8-98	Opening balance 50 units @ Rs. 3 per unit
05-8-98	Issued out to production 2 units
07-8-98	Purchased 48 units @ Rs. 4 per unit
09-8-98	Issued out 20 units to production
19-8-98	Purchased 76 units @ Rs. 3 per unit
24-8-98	Received back into stores 19 units out of 9th August issue
27-8-98	Issued to production 10 units

31-8-98 Stock verifier found shortage of 5 units of stock

(Andhra University, B. Com., April 2004)

[***Answer:*** Value of closing stock Rs. 516]

Exercise-8 (FIFO method)

From the following transactions, prepare stores ledger account using FIFO method.

Oct. 1	Opening balance 100 units at Rs. 5 each
2	Received 500 units at Rs. 5 each
20	Issued 300 units
Nov. 5	Issued 200 units
6,	Received 500 units at Rs. 5 each
Dec. 10	Issued 300 units
12	Issued 250 units

(University of Madras, B.Com., April 2002)

[***Answer:*** Closing stock 50 units amounting to Rs. 250]

Exercise-9 (FIFO and weighted average cost method)

Prepare a stores ledger statement from the following particulars adopting "weighted average method" and first in first out method of pricing of issues.

1999	
Jan. 1	Opening balance 500 units at Rs. 25 per units
3	Issue 250 units
4	Purchases 200 units at Rs. 26 per unit
12	Return from a work order 15 units at Rs. 24 per unit
15	Issue 180 units
16	Stock verification reveals loss of 5 units
20	Purchases 320 units at Rs. 30 per unit
28	Stock verification reveals a loss of 8 units
30	Issue 112 units

(Andhra University, B.Com., April 2003)

[***Answer:*** Closing stock under weighted average method is 480 units amounting to Rs. 13,369 and under FIFO method accounting to Rs. 13,730]

Exercise-10 (LIFO and weighted average cost method)

Date	Particulars	Units	Rate
01-1-90	Purchases	300	3.00
04-1-90	Purchases	600	4.00
10-1-90	Purchases	700	5.00
20-1-90	Purchases	300	6.00
06-1-90	Issues	500	
15-1-90	Issues	800	
23-1-90	Issues	100	

(Kakatiya University, B.Com., July 2004)

[***Answer:*** Closing stock under LIFO method is 500 units, amounting to Rs. 2,100 and under weighted average cost method 500 units amounting to Rs. 2,631]

Exercise-11 (LIFO and weighted average cost method)

From the following receipts and issues of materials, prepare stores ledger under the following methods. (*i*) LIFO (*ii*) Weighted Average

Date	*Particulars*	*Units*	*Rate*
1-12-97	Purchases	300	3
4-12-90	Purchases	600	4
10-12-97	Purchases	600	4
20-12-97	Purchases	400	5
6-12-97	Issues	400	
15-12-97	Issues	1,000	
23-12-97	Issues	200	

(*Kakatiya University, B.Com., March 2003*)

[***Answer :*** Closing stock under LIFO method amounts to Rs. 1,300 and under weighted average cost method is 300 units amounting to Rs. 1,436]

Exercise-12 (FIFO method)

The following transactions occur in January 2005. From the given particulars, prepare stores ledger A/c by FIFO method

2005 Jan.		
1st	Balance	2,000 units @ Rs. 2.00 per unit
4th	Purchases	250 units @ Rs. 2.50 per unit
7th	Issues	1,000 units
15th	Purchases	300 units @ Rs. 3.00 per unit
20th	Issues	1,000 units
25th	Issues	1,000 units
30th	Purchases	500 units @ Rs. 3.50 per unit

(*Sri Krishnadevaraya University, B.Com., October 2006*)

[***Answer:*** Closing stock 2,750 units amounting to Rs. 8,500]

❑❑❑

CHAPTER 6

Accounting of Material Losses

INTRODUCTION

It is a normal tendency in most of the industries to lose a part of materials at all the three stages of dealing with materials, *viz.,* receiving, storing and issuing. Materials like cement, sand, coal and such other materials are lost at least in part at the time of its receipt. During the stage of storage some materials are lost owing to evaporation, shrinkage, breaking the bulk and so on. Similarly during the stage of issue and usage of materials, the quantity of output will be less compared to the quantity of input, which represents the loss of materials. Such losses assume the form of waste, scrap, spoilage and defectives. These losses often pose special problem in dealing with them in cost accounts. Unless the causes and circumstances which give rise to such losses are carefully analysed, it becomes difficult not only in accounting but also in exercising control over them.

CLASSIFICATION OF MATERIAL LOSSES

For proper accounting and control of material losses, material losses can be classified into the following types. This is shown in the following chart:

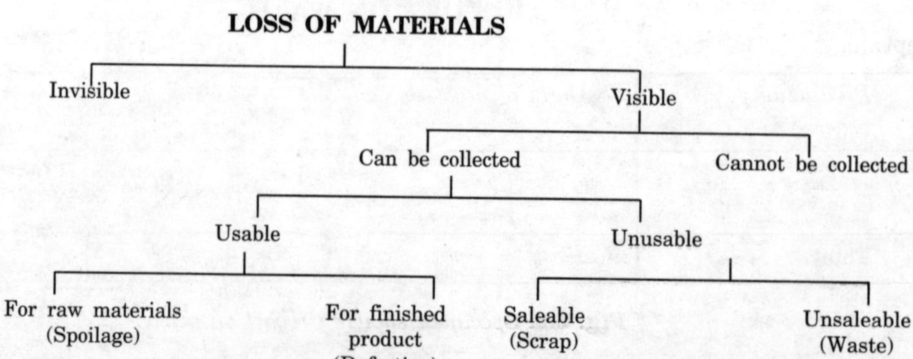

Fig. 6.1. *Chart showing types of material losses.*

Invisible Loss

This represents loss in weight on account of shrinkage, evaporation, absorption by moisture, flow of materials in the form of dust, etc.

Visible Loss

Visible loss can be visualised and its presence can be identified.

Collectable and non-collectable loss. The portion of visible loss which is usefully collected and measured is known as collectable loss. The remaining portion of visible loss which is not worthwhile to collect is known as waste.

Usable and unusable loss. Usable loss is that portion of collected loss which can be used internally for further processing. This is used either as raw material or rectified to constitute a finished product. In the former case it is termed as a spoilage and in the latter case it is termed as a defective material. Whereas unusable material cannot be used for further processing, they can at best be sold as a scarp or thrown away as a waste.

ACCOUNTING TREATMENT OF WASTE

The residue which is left behind by a production process is known as a waste. Wastage is inevitable and is inherent in the technological process. It has comparatively insignificant value. It cannot be reused nor reworked so as to convert into good units. Waste comprises of (*a*) Invisible loss as for example, shrinkage, in a tanning industry, evaporation in an oil refinery, loss in energy transmission, etc., (*b*) Visible loss that cannot be collected as for example, sand in construction industry and (*c*) Unsaleable portion of collected loss as for example, saw dust in furniture making industry, churnings in a machining operation, cuttings in a garment industry, ash in coke industry and so on. In certain cases waste involves further costs of disposing it, as for example, cost incurred for the disposal of effluent, obnoxious gases, etc.

Whenever a waste occurs it is necessary to prepare a report to facilitate accounting and controlling such waste. A specimen form of report on waste materials is given below:

REPORT ON WASTE

Dept.................. Period..................

Production order No.	*Units of product*	*Waste qty.*	*Percentage of waste to production*
Total			

Fig. 6.2. *Specimen showing report on waste.*

Accounting Treatment of Wastage

For the sake of treatment of wastages in cost accounting, it is classified into two types, *viz.*, (*a*) Normal wastage and (*b*) Abnormal wastage.

Normal wastage is unavoidable and uncontrollable and is treated as part of the product cost. The wastage cost is borne by the good units.

Abnormal wastage is unanticipated and is valued as if the output is good. This cost is transferred to the costing profit & loss account.

Sometimes a demand may arise for the wastage, as for example, it may be used as a substitute raw material. In such a case, the selling price has to be suitably fixed on the basis of the market value of the raw material substituted.

ACCOUNTING OF SCRAP

A scrap refers to the incidental residue derived from certain types of manufacture recoverable without further processing. The main feature of scrap is it has some disposable value and it arises from normal production process. Scrap arises from faulty operation, bad supervision, wrong tool setting, defective process and use of defective raw material.

Types of Scrap

(*a*) *Normal scrap.* This is considered to be inevitable in the manufacturing process and hence it is predetermined or anticipated much in advance of production and provided for in the books of accounts.

(*b*) *Administrative scrap.* This arises owing to the decision taken by management such as use of a different method of production or a different design of product.

(*c*) *Defective scrap.* This arises mainly due to the use of substandard quality of materials and/or for bad workmanship.

Differences between a Waste and a Scrap

(*i*) The degree of inherence of waste is more when compared to the inherence or the element of inevitability in scrap.

(*ii*) The chance of re-using scrap in the same production process is high when compared to waste.

(*iii*) Scrap has a higher saleable value when compared to waste.

Examples of scraps in engineering industry takes the form of turnings, borings, filings, etc., from the metal. In leather industry, it takes the form of pieces of leather. In timber industry, it takes the form of saw dust.

To facilitate accounting of scrap a daily or weekly scrap report is to be prepared. This reveals the unexpected items and abnormal variations in scraps. A specimen form of such a report is given below:

SCRAP REPORT

Name of the production dept........... Scrap report for the week ending ....

No.	*Description*	*Units issued*	*Units scrapped*	*Percentage of scrap*	*Cost*	*Reasons*
Total for the week						

Fig. 6.3. *Specimen showing scrap report.*

Accounting Treatment of Scrap

Depending upon the quantity of scrap and its sale value, it is treated according to the following methods:

(*a*) If the scrap has negligible value, the income earned by such sale is treated as other income.

(*b*) The sale value can be used to mitigate or to reduce the cost of materials by deducting it from materials cost.

(*c*) It can be credited to the cost of production, so as to minimise cost of production and thereby minimising selling price.

(*d*) If the scrap, arising from one job is transferred to another job to be used a raw material, the latter job is debited and the former job is credited with the cost of scrap.

ACCOUNTING OF SPOILAGES

Spoilage is man-made scrap. It results when materials are so damaged in manufacturing operations that they are taken out of process and disposed of in some manner without further processing. They cannot be repaired or reconditioned into a product of acceptable quality. It is either sold as second hand product or reused for further manufacturing as a basic raw material. Spoilages occur due to faults in operation, bad workmanship, use of defective raw materials, defective machines and faulty tool setting.

Spoilage differs from scrap in the following two respects:

(*a*) Spoilage occurs more towards the finishing stage with higher loss of added value whereas scraps occur in the beginning and intermediary stage of production with less added value.

(*b*) Spoilage arises because of some defects in production process or materials which may or may not be inherent in the production process. Whereas scrap arises as a result of inherent production process. Thus, it can be said that scrap is inevitable whereas spoilage is not so in all cases.

To facilitate accounting and control of spoilages, a spoilage report is to be prepared. A specimen form of spoilage report is given below:

SPOILAGE REPORT

Dept. no. .... Date ....

Production order no. ....

Units produced	*Units spoilt*	*Normal spoilage*	*Abnormal spoilage*	*Cost of abnormal spoilage*	*Reason*	*Action taken*

Fig. 6.4. *Specimen showing spoilage report.*

Accounging Treatment of Spoilages

(*a*) Loss arising due to normal spoilage can be debited to the job, product or process in which it occurs.

(*b*) Abnormal loss arising out of spoilage which is unexpected and uncontrollable is transferred to costing profit & loss a/c.

(*c*) Where it becomes difficult to identify the normal loss arising out of spoilage to any of the product or job or process, it is charged to factory overhead so that the loss is borne by all products.

ACCOUNTING OF DEFECTIVES

Defectives refer to imperfect products which are transformed into the standard specifications by the application of additional material, labour or both. Defectives differes from spoilage in one important respect, *viz.*, defectives can be reworked and restored to original condition but spoilages cannot be rectified. Defectives occur on account of the following reasons:

(*i*) Substandard raw materials,
(*ii*) Bad maintenance of machines,
(*iii*) Wrong setting-up of tools,
(*iv*) Bad workmanship,
(*v*) Machines used for unscheduled operations,
(*vi*) Lack of control such as temperature, humidity, etc.
(*vii*) Bad design of the product,
(*viii*) Bad working conditions.

Defective goods should be separated from spoilages to facilitate reconditioning of work. However, reconditioning work is justifiable only when the revenue earned by the sale of rectified defective goods is more than the cost incurred in rectification of defectives. The rework to be done on defectives should be authorised by a senior official. For this a defective work report is to be prepared and attached to production order representing the defective work. A specimen form of defective work report is given below:

DEFECTIVE WORK REPORT

Production order no. .... No. ....
No. of units. .... Date ....
Dept. responsible ....
Nature of defective ....

Job no.	*Description of additional work required*	*Rework cost*			*Total cost*
		Material cost	*Labour cost*	*Overhead*	

Fig. 6.4. *Specimen showing defective work report.*

Accounting Treatment of Defectives

1. The estimated quantity or number of defectives are considered to be normal and are treated in the following manner:
   (*a*) Charging of loss to good units manufactured.
   (*b*) The additional cost of rectifying defectives is charged to factory overhead and apportioned to various units as part of the factory overhead.
   (*c*) If a particular department is responsible for the additional cost of rectification, it can be charged to that department.
2. Where the defective units are traceable to a specific job or work-order, the additional costs can be charged to that job or work-order.
3. Where the defectives are considered abnormal and beyond control, the cost of such defectives is to be charged to costing P & L a/c.

CONTROL OF WASTE, SCRAP, SPOILAGE AND DEFECTIVES

The first step in designing a control system is to classify the losses into controllable and uncontrollable losses. Secondly, standards must be set in respect of all types of losses and actual losses are to be compared with standard losses to know whether they are normal or abnormal. Standard levels should be frequently reviewed because some losses may be uncontrollable in the short run but controllable in the long run. A good control system should calculate and report data relating to losses, wastages, defectives and spoilage to management. This facilitates management to evaluate performance and take remedial action. Control over material losses is exercised at the stage of (*a*) Occurrence, (*b*) Recovery, handling and storage and (*c*) Disposal.

Control over Occurrence

Before control is exercised it is necessary to identify the causes for the occurrence of losses of materials. Material losses occur on account of several reasons. The main causes can be summarised under the following:

(*i*) **Causes related to production method.** The various causes which fall under this category are use of defective equipment, bad design, overloading, excessive utilisation of resources, problems associated with new products.

(*ii*) **Material related causes.** These causes are mainly due to use of sub-standard quality of materials, obsolete materials and deteriorated quality of materials. Other causes which fall under this category are shrinkage, evaporation, breaking the bulk, etc.

(*iii*) **Labour related causes.** The causes which fall under this category are inadequate training to the operator, inadequate supervision, lack of skill, damage caused by mishandling, fatigue, etc.

At each and every stage of occurrence of losses, it is necessary to keep a strict vigilance so that they can be minimised, if not eliminated.

Control over Handling and Storage

As soon as materials are received they must be properly stored. The corks of containers should be tightly closed. Material handling equipments must be used to handle heavy and bulk quantity of materials. Proper care must be taken to avoid theft and misappropriation of materials.

Control over Disposal

To increase the revenue of waste, spoilages and defectives it is necessary to consider the following points:

(*i*) To make available such scrapped, spoilt or defective material ready for sale,

(*ii*) To select the best buyer. Quotations can be obtained and the revenue receivable should be compared with market price,

(*iii*) Control the quantity of losses. Physical control is to be exercised over such materials before they leave the factory and there must be frequent review of the quantities produced, repaired and sold.

Problem-1

The normal handling waste is 10 per cent of material *A*. The average price is Rs. 18 per kg. Total material drawn from stores were 170 kg. Job-wise analysis of consumption of this material was as follows:

Job	1	30 kg.
	2	40 kg.
	3	24 kg.
	4	50 kg.

Find out: (1) the effective rate of material per kg. to be charged to jobs so that cost of normal wastage is covered, (2) quantity and value of abnormal loss.

Solution:

Calculation of effective rate of materials

Normal handling waste is	10%
∴ Good units must be	90%
Average price of materials is Rs. 18	
For 90% of units, materials cost is Rs. 18	
For 100% – ?	$\frac{18 \times 100}{90}$ = Rs. 20

Total materials drawn form stores	=	170 kg.
Less: Normal of 10%	=	17 kg.
Net units used	=	153 kg.

Total units of materials used on Jobs

Job	1	30
Job	2	40
Job	3	24
Job	4	50
	Total	144 kg.

Calculation of abnormal wastage

Units of materials used subject to normal loss	=	153 kg.
Less: Actual units used on various job	=	144 kg.
Abnormal wastage	=	9 kg.
Value of abnormal loss : 9 kg. @ Rs. 20	=	Rs. 180

Problem-2

2,000 kg. of Art board valued at Rs. 8,000 were issued for the manufacture of medium-sized cartons. The following details were collected.

(*a*) 2,400 nos. medium-sized cartons weighted 0.50 kg. each were manufactured.

(*b*) 480 kg. of off cuts were used for the manufacture of small-sized cartons. This would have amounted to Rs. 1,000.

(*c*) 320 medium-sized cartons were damaged and rectification costs came up to Rs. 160.

(*d*) 120 kg. of off cuts were sold as scrap for Rs. 20.

You are required to calculate the cost of one medium sized carton assuming that there are no opening and closing stock.

Solution:

Calculation of cost of one medium-sized carton

	Qty (*kg.*)	*Value* (*Rs.*)
Input	2,000	8,000
Less: Offcuts transferred to small-sized cartons	480	1,000
	1,520	7,000
Less: Value of scrap sold	120	20
	1,400	6,980
Add: Cost of rectification	–	160
	1,400	7,140
Less: Waste in process (Balancing figure)	40	
Output	1,360	7,140

$$\text{Cost per carton} = \frac{7,140}{2,720} = \text{Rs. } 2.62$$

Note 1: Calculation of quantity of output.

2,400 + 320 = 2,720 cartons and expressed in terms of kg. it is (Cartons) (Cartons)

$$\frac{2,720}{2} = 1,360 \text{ kg.} \left(\text{each carton weighing } \frac{1}{2}\right)$$

Note 2: Calculation of number of cartons.

Total output is 1,360 kg. and expressed in terms of cartons it will be 2,700 cartons.

Problem-3

XYZ Co. draws up the standard cost of a product as follows:

	Rs.	*Rs.*
Direct material		12
Direct wages:		
Dept. A–3 hrs.	15	
Dept. B–2 hrs.	12	
Dept. C–5 hrs.	20	47

Factory overheads			
Dept. A		18	
Dept. B		18	
Dept. C		40	76
	Factory cost		135
Administration cost			12
Selling cost			15
Distribution cost			18
	Total cost		180
	Net profit		20
	Selling price		200

Factory overhead is absorbed by means of departmental hour rates. Analysis of these overhead reveal that in each department a rate of Rs. 2 per hour is required to absorb the variable portion, the balance being of a fixed nature. As a general rule, all production is of first class quality.

After a batch of 1,000 units has been processed through all three departments, inspection reveals that half are faulty. The faulty products can be rectified by completely reprocessing through departments B and C. Alternatively, they can be sold for Rs. 120 each.

Present figures which indicate to management the most economic method of dealing with the faulty product.

Solution:

Calculation of time taken for original processing and rectification

Dept.	A—1,000 units @ 3 hrs.	=	3,000 hrs.
	B—1,000 units @ 2 hrs. plus 500 units @ 2 hrs.	=	3,000 hrs.
	C—1,000 units @ 5 hrs. plus 500 units @ 5 hrs.	=	7,500 hrs.

Calculation of fixed cost per unit

Dept. A—Rs. 18 – (Rs. 2 × 3 hrs.) = Rs. 12 per unit

B—Rs. 18 – (Rs. 2 × 2 hrs.) = Rs. 14 per unit

C—Rs. 40 – (Rs. 2 × 5 hrs.) = Rs. 30 unit

***Alternative* I**

Statement showing cost of production (including reprocessing cost)

Direct Materials— 1,000 units @ Rs. 12				12,000
Wages:	Dept.	A	3,000 × Rs. 7 (5 + 2)	21,000
		B	3,000 × Rs. 8 (6 + 2)	24,000
		C	7,500 × Rs. 6 (4 + 2)	45,000
			Prime cost	1,02,000
Overheads:	Dept.	A	1,000 × 12	12,000
		B	1,500 × 14	25,000
		C	1,500 × 30	45,000
			Factory cost	1,84,000

Administration, selling and distribution overhead for 1,000 units [@ Rs. 45 per unit]	45,000	
Loss on non-recovery of 500 units reprocessed	22,500	67,500
Total cost		2,47,500
Loss		(–) 47,500
Sales		2,00,000

***Alternative* II**

Cost of production of 1,000 units of which 500 units are disposed off

Sales 500 × 200 + 500 × 120	=	1,60,000
Less: Total cost 1,000 × 180	=	1,80,000
Loss	=	(–) 20,000

The second alternative is better as the loss involved is less.

Questions

I. Fill in the blanks:

(*a*) Abnormal loss of materials are charged to .... a/c.

(*b*) Normal loss is charged to .... a/c.

[***Answers:*** (*a*) costing profit & loss all. (*b*) cost of production]

II. Mark 'T' or 'F' in the space provided

(*a*) The cost of abnormal wastage is added to the cost of product. *T/F*

(*b*) Defectives can be sold as finished goods without being processed. *T/F*

[***Answers:*** (*a*) *F*, (*b*) *F*]

III. Choose the correct answer:

1. Which one of the following is considered to be the normal loss of materials.
   (*a*) Loss due to accident
   (*b*) Loss due to breaking the bulk
   (*c*) Pilferage
   (*d*) Loss due to careless handling of materials

2. Defectives are those items
   (*a*) Which are rectifiable, made into good units ?
   (*b*) Which are useless and beyond rectification ?
   (*c*) Which has scrap value and thus be sold ?
   (*d*) Which is waste having no recoverable value ?

[***Answers:*** 1 (*b*). 2 (*a*)]

IV. Simple questions

1. What do you mean by 'invisible loss' ?

2. What do you mean by 'visible loss' ?

3. Distinguish between usable and unusable loss.

4. What do you mean by 'waste' ?

5. What do you mean by 'scrap' ?

6. Distinguish between a 'waste' and 'scrap'.

7. What do you mean by spoilage ?

8. Distinguish between a 'scrap' and 'spoilage'.

9. What do you mean by defective ?

V. Short and long answer questions

1. Distinguish between scrap, spoilage and defectives in an engineering industry with specific reference to accounting treatment and control for each.

(Madras University, B.Com., March 1991)

2. Explain how would you differentiate between normal and abnormal wastage of materials and their treatment in cost accounts. *(ICWA, Inter., December 1990)*

3. Distinguish amongst waste, spoilage, salvage, rectification scrap. How are they treated in cost accounts? *(C.A., Inter., May 1986)*

4. Distinguish between waste, scrap, spoilage and defective and indicate the accounting treatment of each. *(Kerala University, B.Com., April 1989)*

5. Explain the terms waste, scrap, spoilage and defectives. Enumerate the steps for control and the principles of accounting of such losses to be followed in a manufacturing concern.

(ICWA, Inter., December 1991)

6. What is scrap ? How is treated in cost accounts ?

(Madurai Kamaraj University, B.Com., April 1992)

7. What do you understand by normal and abnormal waste of materials during the process of manufacture ? State briefly how each should be treated in cost accounts.

(Madras University, B.Com., April 1992)

8. Explain the accounting treatment and control of the following in cost accounts.

(*a*) Waste (*b*) Scrap (*c*) Defective and (*d*) Spoilages *(Madras University, B.Com., April 1992)*

9. State briefly the problems connected with waste, scrap, spoilage and defectives and indicate the principle to be followed in control and accounting of such losses.

(Kakatiya University, M.Com., August 1991)

10. Illustrate normal wastage and abnormal wastage in cost accounts. Also explain how does it affect the cost of the production and the necessity to minimise the same.

(Sri Krishnadevaraya University, B.Com., April 1992)

CHAPTER 7

Tools, Patterns, Designs, Blue Prints and Packing Materials

TOOLS

These are small equipments which are used in machine operations. Though they cost relatively less when compared to plant and machines yet they play an important role and has significant financial implications. Where tools constitute an important means of production, a separate tool room is established and it will be under the supervision of a tool room-keeper. His duties among other things include maintenance of tool, its issue to various departments, receive them back after their use and undertake verification of tools from time to time.

Types of Tools

The following are the different types of tools used in manufacturing concerns:

(*a*) **Tool.** A tool is a device used for working or cutting a material into a desired shape, for holding workpieces or for measuring parts after work has been completed.

(*b*) **Fixture.** A fixture is a device that holds one or more pieces while work is being done.

(*c*) **Jig.** A Jig is a device that keeps the work in position while cutting operations are being performed.

In addition to above tools many other tools such as locating devices, centralisers, clamping devices, dies, gages, etc., are used depending upon the nature of work involved.

Treatment of Tools Cost in Cost Accounting

For the sake of treating tools in cost accounting it is classified into following types:

(*a*) **Loose tools, jigs, etc.** The value of these tools are charged to departmental overheads by means of revaluing them.

(*b*) **Tools, jigs of standard types.** The depreciated value of such tools are charged to departmental overhead.

(*c*) **Special tools.** The cost of such tools are directly charged to the order on which special tools are used. The cost to be charged is not only the cost but also the cost of upkeep during the processing of the product.

(*d*) **Maintenance of old tools.** Such costs are charged to various departments in proportion to number of tools used.

Controlling Tool Cost

The tools required for production purpose may be manufactured or purchased. When it is to be manufactured, it involves the following steps:

(*a*) Prepare an estimate of tools required.

(*b*) Determine the unit cost and total cost of production.

(*c*) Add to the above cost of tools.

Instructions are then issued to manufacture such tools. Standard cost is established and used as yardstick for control of actual cost of tool manufacture.

When they are procured they are stored in the tool room. They are subjected to perpetual inventory control.

For costly tool a separate tool ticket is maintained. This shows the number of times the tools are used, the extent of wastage and extent of recovery of tool cost.

Whenever any tools are to be drawn, it is to be authorised by a competent authority and the tools are issued only against presentment of a tool ticket. Alternatively, metal tokens can be used for drawing the tools. Such tokens are kept in the relevant vacant bin and handed back when tools are returned at the end of day's work. This eliminates the paper work connected with issue of tools. Tools are examined when they are returned.

Damaged tools are sent for repairs. Every employee is made responsible for careful handling, using and return of tools.

The following steps should be taken while controlling the tool cost:

(*a*) The design of tool must be according to the design of the product for which the tools are required. In other words while manufacturing or procuring the tools care must be taken to see that they suit the design of the product to be manufactured.

(*b*) Tools are to be classified according to its requirements for various jobs.

(*c*) Conducting periodic inventory of tools.

(*d*) Recording of receipts, issues and wastages in stock ledger of tools.

(*e*) Inspection of tools when they are returned back after use in various departments.

(*f*) The life span of every tool must be indicated on the tools. If they wear out before its life span, the causes for the same is to be investigated.

PATTERNS

A pattern is a model according to which the finished product is to be developed or manufactured. Patterns are mostly used by ready-made garment industry, plastic industry, iron and steel industry, etc.

Patterns can be obtained in two different ways, *viz.*,

(*i*) They can be manufactured and

(*ii*) They may be supplied by customers themselves.

Treatment of Pattern Cost in Cost Accounts

(*i*) Where the patterns are manufactured by the manufacture, its cost is charged to the job. Thus, the cost of production of job will be higher to the extent of the pattern cost.

(*ii*) Where the pattern is supplied by customers, the cost of pattern is charged to the job.

A separate register is maintained for various types of patterns used so as to enable return of patterns to customers. Records are also necessary for revaluing the patterns and for its depreciation. In big industries, a pattern shop and pattern stores is set up as in the case of a tool room.

DESIGNS

The dictionary meaning of design is "a drawing or sketch, a plan in outline". However, the term design is much more than a drawing as it gives the three-dimensional view of the various parts and the whole assembly of a product. It is a sketch which preceeds the drawing and takes into consideration the shape, constructional materials, method of manufacture, handling and the ultimate function of the various parts and the complete product. Though a design represents a paper sketch, it is supported by notes as to the kind of materials to be used, method of manufacture and so on. Design should be developed by the coordinated efforts of designers and cost accountant. This is because the cost of design exerts a powerful influence over the total cost of production. The design so developed must meet the functional efficiency, widest in its use, good in appearance and cheap in its development.

Treatment of Cost of Designs in Cost Accounts

(*a*) When the design is drawn for a specific job, the cost of design should be charged to that job wholly.

(*b*) When the design is meant for production of goods on a repetitive basis, an estimated design cost per unit is predetermined and charged to products manufactured in course of time as research and development cost.

DRAWINGS AND BLUEPRINTS

The term 'drawings' refers to the representation of the products by lines drawn, shades, etc. They are prepared according to a choosen scale. The term 'blueprint' refers to the original or altered (diminished or enlarged) copies of the drawings.

Drawings are prepared as per the list of specification for various parts and the final assembly of the parts into a finished product illustrating the dimensions of raw materials, parts made from such raw materials and finished dimension of the assembled product.

A separate department known as drawing office is established to prepare drawings and blueprints. This is essential in order to prepare the selling price in advance of production for quoting to prospective customers. The draughtsmen will maintain a record of drawings made by him.

Treatment of Cost of Drawings and Blueprints

The cost of drawings and blueprints are charged directly to the customer's orders. Where drawings and blueprints are prepared for manufacturing standard products, its cost are charged over the period of life of drawings.

PACKING MATERIALS

Packing materials are those materials which are used to pack the finished products before they are distributed to customers. Examples of packing materials are wrapping papers, bags, cartons, boxes, bottles, tins, etc. For the sake of accounting of packing materials, it can be classified into two types, *viz.*,

(*a*) Primary packing materials,

(*b*) Secondary packing materials.

Primary packing materials are required to pack finished goods before they are ready for sale. Whereas secondary packing materials are those which are required for safe and convenient distribution of the finished product.

Treatment of Primary Packing Materials in Cost Accounts

(*a*) The cost of primary packing materials are charged as part of the direct materials cost to the finished product. In other words, it forms part of prime cost.

(*b*) The cost of secondary packing materials is treated as distribution overhead.

Control over Packing Materials

(*a*) Select the best packing materials among various available ones. This can be done by a comparative study of the relative merits and demerits of various packing materials in relation to damage, deterioration and pilferage.

(*b*) Select the most durable and economical type of packing materials.

(*c*) By studying the turnover of packing material the slow moving type is to be eliminated.

(*d*) When packing materials such as drums, etc., are used the empty containers returned by customers can be revised for further packing of goods.

(*e*) The cost of packing materials can be reduced by bulk buying or manufacturing on mass scale basis.

(*f*) Manual method of packing is to be replaced by mechanical method.

Questions

Short and long answer questions

1. How would you treat the following in cost accounts?
   (*a*) Tools
   (*b*) Designs
   (*c*) Drawings and blueprints
   (*d*) Packing materials
2. Suggest what control measures would you recommend for (a) Tools and (b) Packing materials.

❑❑❑

CHAPTER 8

Labour Cost Control

INTRODUCTION

Labour cost constitutes the second important element of cost next only to material cost. Research has shown that in majority of the cases labour cost constitutes about 40 per cent to 50 per cent of total cost of production. Though in modern days machines are used on a large scale basis, the importance of manual labour cannot be under estimated. This is so because efficient utilisation of labour reduces the labour cost, increases the productivity and quality and reduces the wastage and spoilage of goods. For the successful utilisation of labour force, it is necessary to account and control the labour. However, payment of low labour cost need not result in decreased cost of production as it may result in delayed production, involving more wages and increased overhead. Similarly payment of higher wages need not result in higher cost of production because it may boost the morale of employee, thereby increasing their efficiency, speedier production and reduced overhead cost.

DIRECT AND INDIRECT LABOUR

Labour engaged in a factory may be classified into two types, *viz.*, (1) Direct labour and (2) Indirect labour.

Direct Labour

It refers to labour engaged in altering the construction, composition, conformation or condition of the product. In other words, it is the labour which can be conveniently identified with a particular cost centre or cost unit. The remuneration payable to direct labour is known as direct wages. As such labour cost can be allocated to the cost unit or cost centre. It is the wages which is paid for those employees who actually convert raw materials into finished goods. The examples of direct labour are wages payable to furniture-maker, shoemaker, baker, tailor, masons, drivers, etc. The following are the important features of direct labour:

(*a*) Direct labour is a part of prime cost.

(*b*) It can be attributed to finished goods.

(*c*) Its cost can be identified with total cost of production.

(*d*) It varies with change in output.

(*e*) It can be controlled.

The ICMA terminology defines direct labour cost as "the cost of remuneration for employees' efforts and skills applied directly to a product or saleable service".

Indirect Labour

Labour that does not alter the construction, conformation, composition or condition of the product, but which contributes to the completion of the product is known as indirect labour. It is the labour which serves as ancillary to the direct labour used in completing the production. The remuneration paid to indirect labour is termed as indirect wages. It is defined by the ICMA terminology as "wage cost other than direct wage cost". Examples of indirect labour are services of watch and ward, supervisor, inspector, foreman, cleaners, time keeping officers, storekeeper, general manager, etc. The following are the important features of indirect labour:

1. It is secondary in importance as compared to direct labour.
2. Its cost cannot be allocated but can only be apportioned.
3. It does not vary with the change in production.
4. It cannot be controlled.
5. Its cost is treated as overheads.
6. It cannot be identified with the finished product.

The nature of work performed need not be necessarily taken as a basis for classifying labour into direct and indirect. It is instead based on practicability and expediency. A worker who is engaged on a particular job is treated as direct if the above two conditions are satisfied. Thus, wages or salary payable to an inspector or supervisor who can devote all his time for a single job is a direct labour. Whereas if he devotes his time on different jobs, his wages or salary is treated as indirect labour. Nevertheless, the following are the important points of differences between direct and indirect labour.

Direct labour	*Indirect labour*
1. It can be identified with finished product.	1. It cannot be identified with finished product.
2. The direct labour cost can be allocated to cost centre or cost unit.	2. The indirect labour cost cannot be allocated but can only be apportioned.
3. It is a part of prime cost.	3. It is a part of overheads.
4. It is primary in the production process.	4. It is secondary or subsidiary to the production.
5. Direct labour cost can be easily ascertained.	5. It is somewhat difficult to ascertain indirect labour cost.
6. It varies according to change in output.	6. It remains fixed.
7. It can be controlled.	7. It cannot be easily controlled.

Need for Classifying Labour into Direct and Indirect

1. To ascertain the cost accurately in order to provide a basis for control.
2. To maintain efficiency.
3. To allocate overheads.
4. To introduce incentives.

5. To facilitate inter-firm comparison.
6. To estimate the total labour cost.

LABOUR CONTROL

It may be defined as a control exercised over labour cost by proper employment and there afterwards efficient utilisation of labour force. The important aspects over which labour control is exercised are as follows:

(*a*) Recruitment and selection of employees.
(*b*) Provision of good working conditions.
(*c*) Calculation and payment of correct amount of wages.
(*d*) Proper recording of attendance time.
(*e*) Accounting of wages.

By far the most important aspect over which control is exercised is labour cost. For better control, labour cost is classified into the following types.

Monetary Reward

The following are some of the examples of monetary reward:

(*i*) Basis wages.
(*ii*) Dearness allowance.
(*iii*) Production bonus.

Deferred Monetary Reward

These include the following:

(*i*) Employer's contribution to provident fund.
(*ii*) Employer's contribution to state insurance.
(*iii*) Gratuity.
(*iv*) Pension fund.
(*v*) Bonus based on profit.

Fringe Benefits or Non-monetary Benefits

These include the following:

(*i*) Canteen.
(*ii*) Housing.
(*iii*) Dispensary.
(*iv*) Education.

Labour-related Costs

These include the following:

(*i*) Holiday pay.
(*ii*) Leave pay.
(*iii*) Premium pay.
(*iv*) Idle time pay
(*v*) Overtime pay.

In big industries five separate departments are established to control labour cost. They are as follows:

1. Personnel department. This department is concerned with recruitment and selection of employees. Having selected, the employees are inducted and trained on the jobs. On appointment of an employee, this department intimates to the timekeeping and payroll department. This department maintains two important documents, *viz.*, (*a*) labour placement requisition and (*b*) employee history card.

A labour placement requisition is prepared by various departments which are in need of employees. The personnel manager verifies from his records in order to know whether the required number of employees are available within the factory. Otherwise he will arrange for the recruitment of said number of employees by advertising in newspaper or by consulting the employment exchange. The necessary action is then taken to receive applications, to conduct interviews, tests, etc.

An employee history card is maintained to keep the record of every employee. It contains the details such as name, address, department where he works, name of the former employers, date of appointment, rate of pay, etc. Whenever any employee leaves the factory on his own or when his services are terminated the cause for such leaving or termination is recorded. This helps to control excessive labour turnover.

2. Time recording department. Time recording serves two purposes, *viz.*, (*i*) Time keeping and time booking. Time keeping refers to recording of incoming and outgoing time of employees in a factory. Time booking refers to recording the time of employees spent on various jobs.

3. Payroll department. This department is concerned with calculation and disbursement of wages to employees. It performs the following functions:

(*a*) Maintenance of job classification record and wage rate of employees.

(*b*) To collect the hours of time spent in factory as well as on jobs by various employees.

(*c*) To calculate the wages of employees.

(*d*) To prepare payroll for every department separately.

(*e*) To calculate various deductions to be made from gross wages.

(*f*) To pay the net wages to the employees.

(*g*) To maintain payroll record of every employee.

4. Engineering department. This department carries out the following functions:

(*a*) To determine and provide for good working conditions.

(*b*) To determine production method for each job.

(*c*) To prepare designs for each job.

(*d*) To conduct time and motion study.

(*e*) To determine the rate of pay.

5. Cost accounting department. Cost accounting department is concerned with proper recording and control of labour cost. It will classify the labour cost into direct and indirect labour cost. The former is recorded under prime cost and the latter under overheads. Proper reports are prepared by the cost accountant and submitted to management for controlling excess idle time, overtime, labour turn over, etc. It will also compare actual labour cost with estimated labour cost to know variance between the two.

TIME KEEPING AND TIME BOOKING

Time Keeping

Time keeping refers to the process of recording the arrival and departure time of employees in a factory. In other words, it records the incoming and outgoing time of employees in a factory. Every factory will establish a separate time keeping department which is situated near the entrance of factory gate. The time keeping officer will be incharge of the department. His duty is to arrange for accurate time recording of all employees of the factory. Usually time recording is done twice in a day, *i.e.,* at the starting time and at the closing time of the factory. However, where employees are allowed to go out of the factory during lunch interval it will be recorded on four occasions. Time keeping serves the following objects:

(*a*) To calculate the wages payable to the employees.

(*b*) To calculate the normal working hours and overtime working hours of the employees.

(*c*) To meet statutory requirements.

(*d*) To calculate labour cost of an operation or job.

(*e*) To apportion overheads if they are based on number of workers or wages.

(*f*) To provide a basis for preparing statistical record which help in controlling labour cost.

(*g*) To introduce incentive system of wage payment.

(*h*) To ensure discipline among workers, *i.e.,* regularity and punctuality. This information is also useful for the management in deciding matters relating to promotion, sanction of increments, termination, etc.

Methods of Time Keeping

Broadly speaking there are two methods for time keeping. These are (*i*) Manual method and (*ii*) Mechanical method.

1. Manual method. Under this method the attendance time of employees are recorded either by the time keeping officer or by employees themselves. The manual method of time keeping are as follows:

(*a*) ***Muster roll method or attendance register method.*** Under this method, an attendance register is maintained for recording the attendance time. This method is followed in small-sized concerns. This method is more suitable for recording the attendance time of clerical staff and other staff officers. Two separate columns are maintained corresponding the names of every employee. One column is to record the arrival time and second column for recording departure time. The attendance time can be marked by the time keeping officer by calling out the name of every employee or alternatively the attendance register may be signed by every employee.

Merits

1. It is simple to maintain attendance register.
2. It is economical when compared to other methods.

Demerits

1. The method is not suitable for medium and large sized business.

2. Where the attendance is marked by calling out the names of employees, there will be hold-ups near the factory gate.

3. Dishonest employees may mark the attendance of their absentee employee.

4. Time keeping officer may show step-motherly treatment to his friends and this will defeat the purpose of time keeping.

5. It involves additional work for posting the entries into the individual working record.

(*b*) ***Token or disc method.*** A disc or token is a small metallic plate which bears the identification number of an employee. The disc of all employees may be arranged in a spike file or in a box. Whenever a worker enters into the factory gate, he is supposed to pick up his token and place it on another file or box meant for this purpose. The box can be replaced at frequent intervals to know the extent of late arrival of employees. Alternatively, instead of replacing the box, the employees may be asked to report to time keeping officer who in turn will record the late attendance time of employees. The time keeping officer will then prepare an attendance record with the help of disc and the absentees are denoted by the missing discs.

Merits

1. It is simple to operate.
2. It does not involve heavy investment.
3. It suits to a factory which employs more number of employees.

Demerits

1. The dishonest practice of inserting a disc of an absentee worker by another employee may take place.
2. It involves more clerical work to prepare an attendance record with the help of disc. Where any mistake is committed in recording attendance time on the basis of disc and in case of any disputes between an employee and time keeping officer, disc cannot offer any proof.

2. Mechanical method. In modern days mechanical methods of time keeping is used to save time and ensure greater accuracy. The machines record the exact time of the arrival and departure of employees. Thus, they avoid possible disputes and difference of opinions between employees and time keeping officers. Mechanical methods are used in medium and large sized industries as small sized concerns cannot afford to invest more capital on such equipments. The following are the important mechanical methods of time recording.

(*a*) ***Dial time recorder.*** The features and functioning of this equipment can be summarised as under:

(*i*) It consists of a large dial on which there are about 150 holes corresponding to the number of workers.

(*ii*) A clock is fitted within the circles of the dial together with a dial arm which operates from the centre of the circle.

(*iii*) The worker while entering into the gate turns the dial arm. He then presses the button corresponding to his clock number. The time of his arrival is recorded on a sheet of paper kept inside the machine.

(*iv*) The same procedure is followed before the employee leaves the factory gate.

Merits

(*i*) Time is recorded strictly according to payroll order.

(*ii*) Provision can also be made out not only to record time but also to calculate wages.

Demerits

(*i*) A worker can record the time of absentee worker.

(*ii*) Time of arrival and departure are separated out in two different sheets of paper which require additional clerical work.

(*iii*) A worker cannot see the time he has booked and disputes may arise afterwards.

(*b*) ***Card time recorder.*** This is a machine which is fitted with a clock on each side of which there is an 'in' and 'out' rack which contains the cards of the employees. The worker who enters the gate takes his card from the 'in' rack, inserts it in the machine. On pressing a lever the time of arrival is recorded on the card. Then, the card is placed in the 'out' rack. At the time of departure from the factory the worker removes his card, inserts it in the machine to record the time of departure and finally places it in the 'in' rack.

Merits

(*i*) For each and every worker time is recorded individually.

(*ii*) The absence of worker can be checked by a mere look at the 'out' rack.

(*iii*) This can be taken as a basis for wage calculation.

Demerits

(*i*) An employee can record the time of absentee worker.

(*ii*) Controlling and checking cards becomes difficult.

(*c*) ***Autograph or signature type time recorder.*** This type of machine is most commonly used in small sized business enterprise where supervision for time recording does not arise. Its features can be summarised as follows:

(*i*) It is a machine which is fitted with a clock and is connected to a printing mechanism on a roll of paper.

(*ii*) To operate the machine, the employee opens the shutter by pressing a lever which is at the side of the machine. This enables to uncover a small signature window.

(*iii*) The employee signs in this signature window and as he signs, the day and time is automatically recorded.

(*iv*) When the lever is released, the paper roll inside the machine (which now bears worker's signature, day and time) is advanced, the shutter slides back over the signature window, and the machine is ready for the signature of the next worker.

Merits

(*i*) Recording of time is automatic and accurate.

(*ii*) Employees can see the recorded time.

Demerits

(*i*) The worker's name does not appear as per the payroll order.

(*ii*) The signature may not be legible.

(*iii*) Breakdown in the machine leads to stoppage in the recording of attendance time.

Time Booking

Time booking refers to the process of recording the time spent by workers on various jobs in a factory. In other words, it is the recording of the starting time and finishing time of employees on a job. Time booking comes next in the sequence after the time keeping in respect of recording time.

Distinction between Time Keeping and Time Booking

Time keeping	*Time booking*
1. It records attendance time of employees.	1. It records the total time worked by employees on jobs.
2. It is the first step involved in time recording.	2. It is the second step involved in time recording.
3. It records the time spent by the employees in the factory.	3. It records the time spent by the employees on various jobs.
4. Time keeping is done at the time keeping office.	4. It is done at various production departments.
5. It is recorded by time keeping officer.	5. It is recorded by a foreman or by employees.
6. Its purpose is to enable preparation of payroll.	6. Its aim is to ascertain the labour cost of job.

Methods of Time Booking

Time booking can be entrusted to the foreman or to time booking clerks. Sometime it is done even by employees. It can be recorded either manually or mechanically. The following are the various methods of time booking:

1. Daily time sheet system. Under this method the time spent by workers on different jobs for a certain day is recorded. For each worker a sheet of paper is issued wherein his time spent on various jobs are recorded. This method is suitable under two situations, *viz.*, (*a*) Size of the factory is small, (*b*) Where the worker has to attend to more jobs instead of few jobs on the same day. Daily time sheet consists of the following particulars:

(*a*) Worker's name
(*b*) Worker's identification number
(*c*) Name of the department
(*d*) Date of work
(*e*) Job number
(*f*) Nature of work done
(*g*) Starting time on the job
(*h*) Finishing time on the job
(*i*) Actual or normal hours and overtime hours of work done
(*j*) Signature of time booking authority.

A proforma of daily time sheet is shown below:

DAILY TIME SHEET

Name of the worker .... Department ....

No. ....

Machine no. ....

Worker order no.	*Work done*	*Time*		*Total hrs.*	*Rate*	*Total wages*
		Start	*Finish*			

Signature of time booking authority ....

Fig. 8.1. *Specimen showing daily time sheet.*

Merits

(*a*) It is simple to operate.

(*b*) It enables the foreman to know how much of work is done by employee each day.

(*c*) The record shows accurate information as it is checked by the foreman everyday.

(*d*) This method is particularly useful where more number of jobs are to be performed on the same day.

Demerits

(*a*) It involves more of clerical work by way of consolidation of all the daily time sheets for one full month.

(*b*) It is not suitable for large business concerns.

2. Weekly time sheet. This method resembles to daily time booking. But instead of booking the time daily, it is recorded for the week. It provides the data relating to the time spent on various jobs for a period of one week. The proforma of such document is shown below:

WEEKLY TIME SHEET

Name of the employee .... Week ending ....

No. ....

Name of the job	*No. of the job*	*Nature of work*	*M*	*T*	*W*	*T*	*F*	*S*	*Total*	
									Ordinary	*OT*

Signature of supervisor/foreman ....

Fig. 8.2. *Weekly time sheet.*

3. Job cards or job tickets. Under this method a card is made use of for recording the time spent by workers on various jobs instead of sheets of paper. Each employee will be given a card which contains the particulars of work to be performed by him. This card is to be filled in by employees by noting down the starting time and finishing time of the job which he attends to. When a worker completes a job he will be given a separate job card to book the time on such job. A specimen form of job card is given below:

JOB CARD

Department .... Job no. ....
Work order no. .... Date ....
Machine no. .... Starting time. ....
Finishing time. ....

Description of job	*Hours*	*Rate*	*Amount*

Signature of foreman ....

Fig. 8.3. *Specimen showing daily time sheet.*

Merits

(*a*) It provides information relating to the job to be performed by workers. Thus it serves as an authority to start the work, besides recording the total time spent by workers on jobs.

(*b*) It provides correct and clear information for costing department.

Demerits

(*a*) It involves more paper work when workers perform several jobs everyday.

(*b*) Reconciliation of attendance time and time booked on job becomes difficult when idle time is not properly recorded.

4. Combined time and job card. This document contains two parts. The first part is to be filled in as attendance time and the second part, the total time spent on jobs. This facilitates reconciliation of gate time with the work time and the extent of idle time can be easily detected. This method fulfils the objectives of both time keeping and time booking. A proforma of this document is shown below:

COMBINED TIME AND JOB CARD

Name of worker .... Week ending ....
No. .... Department ....

Days in the week	*Job no.*	*Attendance time*		*Job time*		*Total hrs.*		*Rate*	*Amount*
		Arrival	*Departure*	*From*	*To*	*Ordinary*	*OT*		
Monday Tuesday Wednesday Thursday Friday Saturday									

Idle hours

Signature of time keeping officer Signature of time booking officer

Fig. 8.4. *Speciman showing combined time and job card.*

Merits

(*a*) It combines the merits of both attendance time and time booking.

(*b*) Compared to maintaining time keeping and time booking separately, it is more economical.

(*c*) The idle time is properly accounted for.

Demerit It is not suitable for large sized undertakings.

5. Labour cost card. A labour cost card is used to record the time spent by all the workers on various operations of the job. In other words, the time spent by a group of workers attending on a job is recorded in labour cost card. This card is meant for a job instead of workers. As and when a worker records time spent on the job, it shall be passed on to other workers. This record thus shows the total time spent on a job and the wages to be charged to that job. As this card shows the total labour cost of a particular job it is termed as labour cost card.

6. Piece work card. This card shows the number of units produced by the worker and the time spent in manufacturing the units. This method is adopted where piece rate system of wage payment is adopted. A separate card is prepared and used by every worker to record the number of units produced and the total time spent by him. A proforma of piece work card is shown below:

PIECE WORK CARD

Name of worker ....

No. ....

Department ....

Job no.	*Description of the job*	*Units*		*Hours*		*Piece rate*	*Amount*
		Produced	*Rejected*	*Starting*	*Finishing*		

Signature of worker/foreman — Signature of inspector

Fig. 8.5. *Specimen of piece work card.*

MOTION STUDY, TIME STUDY AND WORK STUDY

In order to fix wage rates it is necessary to classify the jobs in relation to their importance, the skill and time required to complete the jobs and such other factors. Motion study, time study and work assume more importance in fixing wage rates.

Motion Study

Motion study has been defined by F.B. Gilberth as "The science of eliminating, wastefulness resulting from using unnecessary, ill directed and inefficient motions." Motion study consists of dividing work into the most fundamental elements possible, studying these elements separately and in relation to one another and from these elements, the unnecessary movement of workers' organ's are eliminated.

A micro-motion study is the subdivision of an operation into motion and their analysis for the improvement of the work cycle. Detailed bodily movements, especially highly skilled motions are recorded and the time is measured by taking motion pictures at a constant speed with a micrometer from the background.

Advantages of Motion Study

(*a*) By simplifying the movements and reducing the sequence, it enables the worker to produce more units per hour and earn more wages. The employer is also benefitted by the increased production.

(*b*) It helps in carefully planning material handling equipments which not only increases speed of production but also reduces material handling cost.

(*c*) It helps the foreman to know the causes for the slow progress of work and enables him to train the workers the best method of performing the task.

(*d*) It helps the personnel department to induct the right type of workers into the jobs for which they are best suited.

(*e*) It leads to better safety measures.

Time Study

The concept of time study was introduced by F.W. Taylor. It refers to the analysis and determination of the time necessary to perform a given task. It replaces the old practice of using past performance, judgement of trial as a method of establishing the time allowed for the performance of a task. Time study has been defined by Alford and Beatty (in their *Industrial Management*) as a scientific analysis of methods and equipments used or planned in doing a piece of work, development in practical detail the best way of doing it and determination of the time required.

Time Study Procedure

The following steps are involved in a time study procedure:

1. The objective of the study is to be clear. This includes a definition of the use of the results, the precision required and the desired confidence in the estimation of the time parameter.
2. The purpose of the study and necessary preparations are reviewed by the supervisor of the operating department.
3. A preliminary analysis of the operation is made to determine whether standard methods and conditions prevail and whether the operator is properly trained.
4. When there is more than one operator, the operator to be chosen is studied.
5. A detailed record is made for the standard methods and conditions, either in writing or by a motion picture.
6. The operation is divided into time study elements.
7. A number of time study observations are taken.
8. The actual measurement is made with the requisite number of observations over a specified time period.
9. The operator is rated during the study by a comparison of his performance level with that of the normal operator.
10. Allowances for various job interruptions and delays are determined by policy.
11. The standard time is derived from the observed time, the rating factor and allowance.

Utility of Time Study

The management makes use of time study for the following purposes:

(*a*) To determine the standard time for the performance of an operation and use the data for establishing a fair incentive system of wage payment.

(*b*) To estimate the time and cost involved in new production orders.

(*c*) To achieve a uniform flow of work in developing or improving the layout of a plant.

(*d*) To aid the analysis of work methods conducted during motion studies.

Work Study

Keith Lockyer (in his *Production Management*) has defined work study as "a management service based on those techniques, particularly method study and work measurement, which are used in the examination of human work in all its contexts and which lead to systematic investigation of all the resources and factors which affect the efficiency and economy of the situation being reviewed, in order to effect improvement." Work study is one of the important tools of management which indicates the areas requiring investigation, so as to set right the defects in manufacturing. Work study includes two closely related techniques *viz.*, (1) Method study and (2) Work measurement.

1. Method study. Method study is the systematic recording and critical examination of the existing and proposed ways of doing work, as a means of developing and applying easier and more effective methods and reducing costs. The following are some of the reasons for which method study is conducted:

(*a*) Bottlenecks generating high work-in-progress, link delivery times or unbalanced work-flow.

(*b*) Idle plants giving rise to under utilisation of resources.

(*c*) Poor morale on account of trivial complaints, high absenteeism.

(*d*) Inconsistent earnings.

(*e*) Poor quality, which may arise from poor working methods or conditions.

2. Work measurement. The procedure involved in measuring or forecasting the rate of output of an existing or newly designed operation, as well as in determining how much time is consumed for various productive and non-productive activities of a process, operation or job is known as 'work measurement'. The management of a factory makes use of work measurement as a technique for evaluation of work methods and in determining the standard time for each job.

JOB EVALUATION

Kimball and Kimball (in their *Industrial Organisation*) have defined job evaluation as "an effort to determine the relative value of every job in a plant and to determine what the fair basic wage for such a job should be."

Objectives of Job Evaluation

The main objectives of job evaluation are as follows:

(*a*) To eliminate wage inequalities.

(*b*) To establish sound wage differentials among the jobs.

(*c*) To provide a sound wage for incentive and bonus plan.

(*d*) To establish a sound wage structure.

(*e*) To facilitate maintenance of a consistent wage policy.

Advantages of Job Evaluation

(*a*) Wage rates can be fixed accurately in an organisation by deciding the proper worth of the different jobs.

(*b*) Job evaluation technique is useful for proper selection, training, promotion, transfers of employees within the organisation. These activities can be performed objectively and impartially through job evaluation.

(*c*) It facilitates objective control on the entire organisation and eliminates nepotism and wastage.

(*d*) It eliminates or at least minimises the grievances of the workers about the absolute and relative wage rate. It avoids confusion in the minds of employees as regards the wage rates fixed by the management.

(*e*) Job evaluation technique raises the morale of the employees and also efficiency of labour force in factories.

Methods of Job Evaluation

There are four methods of job evaluation. They are as follows:

1. Ranking method. This method is also known as the grading method as it involves assigning grades to various jobs in the order of their relative importance. Under this method, three steps are involved, *viz.*, (*a*) making a thorough job analysis, (*b*) expressing the findings of this analysis in job description and (*c*) ranking each job by arranging them in an ascending order, starting with the job of minimum requirements of various characteristics and ending with maximum requirements of various characteristics of the job. Ranking can be based on: (*i*) difficulty of work, (*ii*) volume of work, (*iii*) responsibility involved, (*iv*) supervision required, (*v*) Knowledge, (*vi*) Conditions under which work is done.

After ranking is completed, the jobs are generally grouped into ten or twelve groups, according to their position. The jobs are then evaluated by determining the wage rates prevailing in similar factories. Accordingly, wage rates are increased either by a fixed percentage or by a fixed amount.

2. Job classification method. Under this method, standard grade descriptions are used in classifying the various jobs. As and when each job is reviewed, it is placed in the category having the most appropriate description. This is opposite of what happens in the job ranking system, since in that system, jobs are first ranked and then divided into grades.

3. Points method. This method is by far the most widely used method in factories. It consists of a yardstick containing various factors such as skill, education, responsibility and so on that are inherent in the jobs. The degree of importance of each factor is determined by an arbitrary decision, and a suitable point value is specified for each factor. The total points for all the factors then determine the relative position of that job among other jobs.

4. Factor comparison method. This method consists of analysing, jobs on the basis of five factors, *viz.*, mental requirements, skill requirements, physical requirements, responsibility involved and working conditions. The jobs are ranked according to each one of these factors, one factor being taken at a time and each job is compared with the other with respect of its worth on this factor alone. The relative weightage of this factor on each job is done by applying money value (*i.e.*, rupees) to the ranking. After all the jobs are rated on each factor, a wage rate for each job is determined by the sum of money weightages determined for each of the five job factors. These wage rates become the basis for determining the wage scale.

MERIT RATING

Merit rating of an employee is the process of evaluating the employee's performance on the job in terms of the requirements of the job for the purposes of placement of workers on appropriate jobs, selection for promotion, providing financial reward and so on. In the words of Alford and Beatty, merit rating is the evaluation or appraisal of the relative worth of man's services on this job.

Objectives of Merit Rating

Merit rating serves the following purpose:

(*a*) It furnishes a periodic record of the relative value of each employee, as judged by his superior.

(*b*) It determines and justifies wage differentials existing for the same job.

(*c*) It provides more accurate information on which promotions, transfers and layoffs may be based.

(*d*) It provides a means of evaluating the selection and training techniques used.

(*e*) It provides information for counselling employees, so that the means of over-coming weakness can be pointed out and programmes for self-improvement developed.

(*f*) It provides a more effective tool for rating the personnel.

(*g*) It establishes better employer-employees relations through mutual confidence, which comes as a result of frank discussions between the leader and the follower regarding merit rating.

(*h*) It ensures better supervision as the supervisors must observe the employees closely if they are to rate them accurately.

Methods of Merit Rating

The method used for merit rating are as follows:

1. **Rank-order method.** Under this method, the rater is expected to keep a list of all the employees under his supervision. The various characteristics which are to be possessed by the employees are then determined. Ranks are assigned to these characteristics, depending upon the fulfilment of traits by the employees.
2. **Graphic rating scale.** Graphic rating scale provides a series of traits and their definition. The rater places a mark opposite to these traits on a line representing the full distance from the 'highest' to the 'lowest' rating. This approach is one of the most commonly used rating forms in industries today.
3. **Forced choice.** Under this method, the rater selects from a number of groupings of unrelated 'personal characteristics' statements, one that is most similar and another that is least similar to the rates. Numerical values are assigned on a statistical basis and thus scores are obtained.
4. **Critical incident.** The rater keeps a running record of activity incidents which are 'critical' for successful and unsuccessful performance. When this method is used over a period of time, it identifies those types of activity which are characteristic of suc-

cessful and unsuccessful employees in specific types of jobs. Thus, it furnishes the basis for continuing appraisals of subordinates and for day-to-day discussions with them for corrective and development purposes.

LABOUR PRODUCTIVITY

Labour productivity is an indicator of efficiency of employees in a factory. It refers to the quantity of output obtained for a given quantity of input. The quantity may be expressed in terms of quantity of output, sales value or cost and input in terms of weight of materials used, hours worked etc.

Measurement of Labour Productivity

The following are the important measurement of labour productivity:

1. **Output per man-hour.** Under this method the total output is divided by the total man-hours worked. This method can be applied where the output obtained is uniform in respect of quality, design, etc. The following formula is used:

$$\text{Labour productivity} = \frac{\text{Total output}}{\text{Total man - hours}}$$

2. **Labour hours per units of production.** Under this method the total labour hours are divided by the total output to get number of labour hour required for manufacturing certain units of products. This method can be used where different products are produced and where an overall productivity is to be measured covering all the production. The following formula is used:

$$\text{Labour productivity} = \frac{\text{Total labour hours}}{\text{Total output}}$$

It can be seen from the above formula that this method is reciprocal to the output per man-hour.

3. **Comparing actual time with standard time.** This method is adopted where production process is standardised and where standard costing is in operation. The following formula is used:

Labour productivity = Std. hours for actual output – Actual hours for actual output

4. **Extent of lost time.** Under this method the man-hours lost is divided by total man-hours and the quotient is expressed as a percentage. The following formula is used:

$$\text{Percentage of lost time} = \frac{\text{Man - hours lost}}{\text{Total man - hours}} \times 100$$

5. **Labour productivity based on money value.** The following are some of the measures used to know the labour productivity:

$$\text{Labour productivity} = \frac{\text{Sales value}}{\text{No. of workers}}$$

(*a*) ***Based on sales.*** Under this method the sales value is divided by the number of workers. The following formula is used:

$$\text{Labour productivity} = \frac{\text{Sales value}}{\text{No. of workers}}$$

(*b*) ***Based on value added.*** Under this method added value of the product is divided by total wages paid. Here added value represents the difference between sales value and material cost. The following formula is used:

$$\text{Labour productivity} = \frac{\text{Added value of the product}}{\text{Total wages}}$$

Where

Added value of product = Sales value – Material cost of product.

(*c*) ***Based on direct wages.*** Under this method the direct wages is divided by number of units produced. The following formula is used:

$$\text{Labour productivity} = \frac{\text{Direct wages}}{\text{Number of units}}$$

Measures to be Taken for Increasing Labour Productivity

Labour productivity can be improved by the joint efforts of the Government, employers and employees. The following steps may be taken to increase labour productivity:

(*a*) Recruitment and selection of right type and required number of employees.

(*b*) Training the employees.

(*c*) Provision of good working conditions to employees.

(*d*) Adopting production planning and control techniques.

(*e*) Standardisation and simplification of work.

(*f*) Fixation of reasonable rate of wages and incentives.

(*g*) Conducting of time, motion and work studies.

(*h*) Adopting job evaluation and merit rating techniques.

LABOUR TURNOVER

Whenever employees in a factory gets better terms and conditions of employment elsewhere, they leave the existing factory and join the new factory. This change in labour force is known as labour turnover. Thus labour turnover refers to mobility of employees from factory to factory for getting better opportunities in terms of earnings and position of authority. In concrete terms, labour turnover may be defined as the number of employees who leave the factory during a period in relation to the average number of workers employed during the year.

Although a minimum labour turnover is quite normal and can be allowed in factories, excessive rate of labour turnover is not desirable. This is because efficient and experienced workers leave the factory and new employees come and occupy their places. Naturally, the ability of such new workers is less as compared to that of the experienced workers. The desirable percentage of labour turnover is placed between 3 per cent and 5 per cent.

Causes of Labour Turnover

The causes of labour turnover may be listed under the following headings:

1. Causes arising from the point of view of employees

(*a*) Incompetence to perform a job satisfactorily.
(*b*) Insubordination to superiors.
(*c*) Accidents.
(*d*) Prolonged illness.
(*e*) Death.
(*f*) Marriage in case of women employees.
(*g*) Housing problem.
(*h*) Discharge on disciplinary ground.
(*i*) Retirement.
(*j*) Personal betterment.

2. Causes arising from the point of view of employer

(*a*) Payment of low wages.
(*b*) Bad working conditions.
(*c*) Failure to protect workers against accidents.
(*d*) Hostile attitude on the part of superior towards subordinates.
(*e*) Unfair promotion policies.
(*f*) Inefficient management.
(*g*) Lack of welfare facilities.
(*h*) Lack of job security, social security and training facilities.

Effects of Labour Turnover on Cost of Production

1. Increased wages due to less speed in production.
2. Additional expenses incurred on training the newly recruited employees.
3. Increased cost of labour arising out of rectifying the spoilt and defective products.
4. Increased idle time wages as new workers are always less efficient.
5. Overhead expenses will increase cost per unit owing to lower volume of production.
6. Cost of repairs and maintenance will increase.
7. Payment of higher compensation to employees involved in industrial accidents.

Remedial Measures to Prevent High Labour Turnover

The following measures are to be taken to control and reduce the high percentage of labour turnover:

1. Scientific recruitment, selection and training of workers.
2. Provision of better wages, allowances and other monetary benefits.
3. Provision of better working conditions.
4. Introduction of fair promotion policy.
5. Provision of social security measures such as pension, provident fund, gratuity and so on.
6. Better motivation and provision of welfare facilities to employees.
7. Cordial labour management relations.
8. Reducing fluctuations in the volume of work.

9. Ensuring job satisfaction and job security.
10. Measures should be taken to reduce labour disputes to the minimum.

Measurement of Labour Turnover

Labour turnover can be measured by any one of the following three methods. In this connection it is to be remembered that once a particular method is adopted, it should not be changed frequently as comparison of labour turnover becomes difficult.

1. Separation method. This is the most commonly used method of measuring labour turnover. Under this method, the total number of separations during a period is divided by the average number of workers on roll during that period and multiplying the quotient by 100 to determine the percentage of turnover. The average number of workers during a period is obtained by adding the number of workers in the beginning and at the end of the year and dividing the sum by 2. Expressed in the form of formula:

$$\text{Separation method} = \frac{\text{No. of separation during the period}}{\text{Average no. of employees during the period}} \times 100$$

2. Replacement method. This method takes into consideration only the actual replacement of labour *i.e.*, the number required to be replaced during the period, irrespective of total leavings. This is obtained by dividing the number of replacement during the period by the average number of employees during that period and then multiplying it by 100 to determine the percentage. Expressed in the form of a formula:

$$\text{Replacement method} = \frac{\text{No. of replacement during the period}}{\text{Average no. of employees during the period}} \times 100$$

3. Flux rate method. This method takes into account both the leavings and the new entrants. This is obtained by adding the leavings and replacements, dividing the total by the average number of employees during the period and multiplying the quotient by 100. Expressed in the form of a formula:

$$\text{Flux rate method} = \frac{\text{No. of separations} + \text{No. of replacements}}{\text{Average no. of employees during the period}} \times 100$$

Problem-1

From the following data given by the personnel department calculate the labour turnover rate by applying (*a*) separation method, (*b*) replacement method, (*c*) flux method.

Number of workers on the payroll:

At the beginning of the month	900
At the end of the month	1,100

During the month 10 workers left, 40 persons were discharged and 150 workers were recruited. Of these 25 workers are recruited in the vacancies of those leaving, while the rest were engaged for an expansion. *(ICWA, Inter, Dec. 1988)*

Solution:

Calculation of average no. of workers during the month

$$= \frac{\text{No. of workers at the beginning of the month} + \text{No. of workers at the end}}{2}$$

$$\frac{900 + 1{,}100}{2} = 1{,}000$$

(*a*) Separation method $= \dfrac{\text{No. of separations during the month}}{\text{Average no. of workers during the month}} \times 100$

$$= \frac{10 + 40}{1000} \times 100 = 5\%$$

(*b*) Replacement method $= \dfrac{\text{No. of workers replaced during the month}}{\text{Average no. of workers during the month}} \times 100$

$$= \frac{25}{1{,}000} \times 100 = 2.5\%$$

(*c*) Flux method $= \dfrac{\text{No. of separations + No. of replacement}}{\text{Average no. of workers during the month}} \times 100$

$$= \frac{50 + 25}{1{,}000} \times 100 = 7.5\%$$

Treatment of Labour Turnover Cost

Labour turnover cost can be classified into (*i*) preventive cost and (*ii*) replacement cost. Preventive cost includes all expenses incurred in preventing excess labour turnover. Such costs relate to providing welfare facilities. Replacement cost includes cost spent on new workers in place of workers who leave the factory, such as recruitment cost, training cost, cost of defectives and so on. Labour turnover cost is not treated as direct cost. Hence, they are accumulated over a period of time under the above two classification and are charged to various departments on the basis of number of workers in each department.

Problem-2

The cost accountant of Y Ltd has computed labour turnover rates for the quarter ended 31st March, 1997 as 10%, 5% and 3% respectively under 'flux method', 'replacement method' and 'separation method'. If the number of workers replaced during the quarter is 30, find out the number of (1) Workers recruited and joined and (2) Workers left and discharged.

(C.A., Inter., May 1997)

Solution:

Labour turnover rate (under replacement method)

$$= \frac{\text{No. of replacements}}{\text{Average number of workers on roll}} \times 100$$

$$\frac{5}{100} = \frac{30}{\text{Average no. of workers on roll}}$$

or Average no. of workers on roll $= \dfrac{30 \times 100}{5} = 600$

Labour turnover rate (separation method) $= \dfrac{\text{No. of separations}}{\text{Average no. of workers}} \times 100$

$$\frac{3}{100} = \frac{\text{No. of separations}}{600}$$

$$\text{No. of separations} = \frac{600 \times 3}{100} = 18$$

∴ No. of separations or No. left and discharged is 18

$$\text{Labour turnover rate (flux method)} = \frac{\text{No. of separations + No. of replacements}}{\text{Average no. of workers}}$$

$$= \frac{10}{100} = \frac{18 + \text{No. of replacements}}{600}$$

or $600 \times 10 = 100\ (18 + \text{No. of replacement})$

or $6{,}000 = 1{,}800 + 100\ \text{No. of replacement}$

or $6{,}000 - 1{,}800 = 100\ \text{No. of replacement}$

or $\text{No. of replacement} = \frac{4{,}200}{100} = 42$

∴No of replacement or No. of recruited and joined is 42.

Problem-3

The cost accountant of Adarsh Ltd., has computed labour turnover rates for the quarter ended 31st March, 2005 as 20%, 10% and 6% respectively under 'flux method', 'replacement method' and 'separation method'. If the number of workers replaced during the quarter is 80, find out the number of (*i*) Workers left and discharged and (*ii*) Workers recruited and joined including replacements. *(C.S., Inter., December 2005)*

Solution:

$$\text{Labour turnover (under replacement method)} = \frac{\text{No. of replacements}}{\text{Average no. of workers on roll}}$$

$$\frac{10}{100} = \frac{80}{\text{Average no. of workers on roll}}$$

or $10 \times \text{Average no. of workers} = 100 \times 80$

or $\text{Average no. of Workers} = \frac{8{,}000}{10} = 800$

(*i*) $\text{Labour turnover rate (separation method)} = \frac{\text{No. of separations}}{\text{Average no. of workers on roll}}$

$$\frac{6}{100} = \frac{S}{800}$$

or $100S = 6 \times 800$

$$S = \frac{4{,}800}{100} = 48$$

No. of separations or No. of workers left and discharged = 48 (*ii*) Labour turnover (flux method) rate $= \dfrac{\text{No. of separations + No. of replacements}}{\text{Average no. of workers on roll}}$

$$\frac{20}{100} = \frac{48 + R}{800}$$

or $20 \times 800 = 100(48 + R)$

or $16{,}000 = 4{,}800 + 100\,R$

or $16{,}000 - 4{,}800 = 100\,R$

or $11{,}200 = 100\,R$

$$R = \frac{11{,}200}{100} = 112$$

∴No. of workers recruited and joined including replacement is 112.

Problem-4

From the following information, calculate labour turnover rate and labour flux rate.

No. of workers as on 1-1-2000	7600
No. of workers as on 31-12-2000	8400

During the year, 80 workers left, while 320 workers were discharged, 1500 workers were recruited during the year. Of these 300 workers were recruited because of exits and the rest were recruited in accordance with expansion plans. *(C.S., Inter., May 2001)*

Solution:

(1) Separation method:

$$= \frac{\text{No. of workers left + No. of workers discharged}}{\text{Average no. of workers}} \times 100$$

$$= \frac{80 + 320}{8000} \times 100$$

$$= \frac{400}{8000} \times 100 = 5\ \%$$

(2) Replacement method:

$$= \frac{\text{No. of workers replaced}}{\text{Average no. of workers}} \times 100$$

$$= \frac{300}{8000} \times 100 = 3.75\ \%$$

(3) Flux rate method:

$$= \frac{\text{No. of separation + No. of replacement}}{\text{Average no. of workers}} \times 100$$

$$= \frac{400 + 300}{8000} \times 100 = 8.75$$

Problem-5

The following information relates to work force in a factory during the year 2001-02:

Number of workers on 1st April 2001	2350
Number of workers on 31st March 2002	2850
Number of workers who quit on their own	200
Number of workers who availed golden handshake opportunity	100

Number of workers employed during 2001-02 including those employed due to expansion

Calculate annual Labour turnover rate and equivalent monthly turnover rate under different methods. *(University of Delhi, B. Com., (Hons.) 2004 External)*

Solution:

Average no. of workers $= \dfrac{2350 + 2850}{2} = 2600$

(1) Separation method $= \dfrac{\text{No. of workers separated}}{\text{Average no. of workers}} \times 100$

$= \dfrac{200 + 100}{2600} \times 100 = 11.54\ \%$

Monthly rate $= \dfrac{11.54}{12 \text{ months}} = 1\ \%$ App

(2) Replacement method $= \dfrac{\text{No. of workers replaced}}{\text{Average no. of workers}} \times 100$

Note: It is assumed that those workers who had quit had been replaced:

$= \dfrac{200}{2600} \times 100 = 7.7\ \%$

Monthly rate $= \dfrac{7.7}{12 \text{ months}} = 0.64\ \%$

(3) Flux rate method $= \dfrac{\text{No. of workers separated + No. of workers replaced}}{\text{Average no. of workers}} \times 100$

$= \dfrac{300 + 200}{2600} = 19.23\ \%$

Monthly rate $= \dfrac{19.23}{12 \text{ months}} = 1.6\ \%$

CASUAL AND OUT WORKERS

A casual worker is a worker who is appointed on a temporary basis on a daily wage basis in order to meet the increased production schedule. Casual workers can also be appointed to replace workers who would have met with industrial accidents. As and when casual workers are appointed a separate accounting is to be maintained for such workers. They should be under the care of supervisor and their output must be certified by the supervisor.

The wages payable to the casual workers are to be treated as direct wages and as such it is charged directly to the job on which casual workers have been worked.

Out workers are engaged to work outside the premises of factory. Out workers may be classified under two categories *viz.*, (*i*) Those who work with their own tools in their own houses, (*ii*) Those who are sent to the premises of customers by the employers. No record need be maintained in respect of first category of employees. However, control is to be exercised over them with regard to issue of materials, prompt production of goods and quality of finished goods. For the second category of workers, it is necessary to maintain records for the purpose of recording attendance and time spent on the jobs.

Questions

I. A. Mark 'T' or F' in the space provided

1. The distinction between direct and indirect labour is not influenced by the use of a payroll summary account. *T/F*
2. The dial time recorder economises the clerical work involved in the preparation of the payroll. *T/F*
3. Muster roll is necessary for the preparation of payroll. *T/F*
4. Wages of a crane operator in a factory are direct wages. *T/F*
5. Metal disc method of time keeping can be profitably used in very large undertaking. *T/F*
6. Time keeping and time booking are one and the same thing. *T/F*
7. There is no need to record attendance of piece rate workers since attendance is not relevant for ascertaining the amount of wages to be paid. *T/F*
8. Time booking gives an analysis of the time spent by workers on various jobs. *T/F*
9. Time keeping record gives us the standard time of workers. *T/F*

[***Answers:*** *True*: 1, 3, 8, 9, *False*: Rest of the items]

(B) Fill in the blanks:

1. Wages sheet is prepared by .... department.
2. Recording of job time is known as ....
3. Wages which can be identified with and allocated to cost centre or cost unit is known as ....
4. .... department is concerned with proper selection and training employees.
5. An example of labour cost which is direct to a department and indirect of a product is ....

[***Answers:*** 1. payroll, 2. time booking, 3. direct wages, 4. Personnel, 5. formen's salary]

(C) Choose the correct answers:

1. Time and motion study is conducted by
   (*a*) Time keeping department (*b*) Payroll department
   (*c*) Personnel department (*d*) Engineering department

2. Time and motion study is essential for
(*a*) Rational promotion policy
(*b*) Completing a job on time
(*c*) Determining the standard time and the correct method of completing a task.
(*d*) Determining prices of products

3. The input-output ratio in case of labour means the ratio of
(*a*) The value of output to the wages paid.
(*b*) Standard time of the production to the actual time paid for.
(*c*) Abnormal idle time to normal idle time.
(*d*) Number of workers employed to the sanctioned strength.

4. Job specification is
(*a*) A list of operations to be performed for completing the job concerned.
(*b*) The requirement in terms of goods to be produced or work to be done.
(*c*) The list of qualities and qualifications which the employee concerned should have to do the job work.
(*d*) The name of the employee which will be assigned to a job.

5. Job evaluation aims at
(*a*) Comparing a job with others so as to ascertain the proper scale of remuneration for the job.
(*b*) Assessing the requirements in terms of personnel required.
(*c*) Assessing the profitability of the job.
(*d*) Establishing the hierarchical position of the holders of the job.

6. Direct labour means
(*a*) Labour which completes the work manually.
(*b*) Labour which is recruited directly and not through contractors.
(*c*) Permanent labour in the production department.
(*d*) Labour which can be conveniently associated with particular cost unit.

[***Answers:*** 1 (*d*), 2 (*c*), 3 (*b*), 4 (*c*), 5 (*a*), 6 (*d*)]

(D) Classify the following into direct and indirect labour

1.Repairman, 2. Shoemaker, 3. Baker, 4. Cabinet marker, 5. Time office clerk, 6. Foreman, 7. Bus driver in a transport company, 8. Carpenter, 9. Sweeper, 10. Watchman, 11. Lathe machine operator, 12. Factory clerical worker, 13. Workshop cleaner, 14. Internal transport men, 15. General Manager.

[***Answer:*** Direct labour 2, 3, 4, 7, 8, 11; Rest of the items is indirect labour]

II. Simple questions

1. Define direct labour.
2. State any four features of direct labour.
3. Define indirect labour.
4. State any four features of indirect labour.
5. Define direct labour cost.
6. Define indirect labour cost.

7. Distinguish between direct labour and indirect labour.
8. Mention the need for classifying the labour into direct and indirect labour.
9. Mention the five departments established to control labour.
10. What do you mean by time keeping ?
11. Mention two manual and two mechanical methods of time keeping.
12. What do you mean by time booking ?
13. Mention any four methods of time booking.
14. Distinguish between time keeping and time booking.
15. What do you mean by work study ?
16. What do you mean by method study ?
17. What do you mean by time study ?
18. What do you mean by motion study ?
19. What do you mean by merit rating ?
20. Distinguish between job evaluation and merit rating.
21. What do you mean by labour productivity ?
22. Define labour turnover.
23. What do you mean by separation method of labour turnover ?
24. What do you mean by replacement method of labour turnover ?
25. What do you mean by flux method of labour turnover ?
26. What do you mean by a casual worker ?
27. What do you mean by a outworker ?

III. Short and long answer questions

1. Explain the difference between direct labour and indirect labour highlighting the importance of such a distinction. *(ICWA, Inter., June 1992)*
2. Write a note on job evaluation. *(ICWA, Inter., June 1992)*
3. Explain the difference between work measurement and motion study. *(ICWA, Inter., December 1991)*
4. Write a note on labour turnover. *(ICWA, Inter., June 1991)*
5. Define productivity. Higher productivity does not always result in lower costs or increased efficiency. Give your comments on this statement. *(ICWA, Inter., June 1990)*
6. Define job evaluation and distinguish it from merit rating. Explain the methods and objectives of job evaluation. *(ICWA, Inter., December 1989)*
7. What is meant by the term labour turnover ? What is the effect of labour turnover on cost of production ? *(ICWA, Inter., December 1988)*
8. What is labour turnover ? How can it be improved ? Discuss the steps to be taken to increase labour efficiency and labour productivity. *(ICWA, Inter., June 1989)*
9. What is labour turnover ? Explain the important methods of measuring it? *(Nagarjuna University, B.Com., April 1992)*
10. Define 'Labour turnover'. What are the major causes for the same? *(Calicut University, M.Com., April 1992)*
11. Discuss the merits and demerits of disc method and dial time recorder. *(Mangalore University, B.Com., April 1991)*

12. Give the specimen rulings of the following documents and assess their importance (*i*) Pay roll (*ii*) Job card. *(Mangalore University, B.Com., October 1987)*
13. What is the meaning of 'labour turnover' ? How is it measured ? Write the avoidable causes (any three) and unavoidable causes (any three) of labour turnover. *(University of Chennai, B.Com., March 1991)*
14. What is labour turnover ? Describe the effects of high labour turnover. *(University of Delhi, B.Com. (Hons), 1990)*
15. Why is a job card 'maintained' ? How is it different from piece work card ? *(University of Delhi, B.Com. (Hons), 1988*
16. What is labour turnover ? What are its causes ? How is labour turnover measured. *(Sri Sathya Sai University, B.Com. March 1992)*
17. Distinguish between time keeping and time booking methods. Briefly explain the different method of time keeping. *(Sri Sathya Sai University, B. Com. October 1990)*

Exercise-1 (Labour Turnover)

From the following information, calculate the labour turnover rate under replacement method and labour flux rate:

Number of workers at the beginning of the year : 3,800
Number of workers at the end of the year : 4,200

During the year, 40 workers left while 160 workers are discharged. 600 workers are recruited during the year. Of these, 150 workers are recruited because of leavers and the rest are engaged in accordance with an expansion scheme. *(Bharathidasan University, B.Com., April 1988)*

[***Answer:*** Labour turnover rate under replacement method is 3.75 per cent and flux rate method is 20 per cent]

Exercise-2 (Labour Turnover)

The following information relates to the personnel department of a factory for the month of April, 1998

Number of workers on April 1, 1998	950
Number of workers on 30th April, 1998	1050
Number of workers who quit the factory in April	10
Number of workers discharged in April	30
Number of workers engaged in April	140

(including 120 workers on account of expansion scheme)

Calculate the labour turnover rate under:

(1) Separation method
(2) Replacement method
(3) Flux rate method

(Sri Sathya Sai University, B. Com., (Hons) March 2000)

Answer: (1) Separation method 4 %
(2) Replacement method 2 %
(3) Flux rate method 6 %

Exercise-3

From the following data provided to you, find out the labour turnover rate by applying:

(*a*) Flux method,
(*b*) Replacement method
(*c*) Separation method

Number of workers on the payroll:

At the beginning of the month	500
At the end of the month	600

During the month, 5 workers left, 20 persons were discharged and 75 workers were recruited. Of these 10 workers were recruited in the vacancies of those leaving, while the rest were engaged for an expansion scheme. *(University of Madras, B.Com., April 2003)*

[***Answer:*** Separation method = 4.55 %
Replacement method = 1.82 %
Flux method = 18.18 %]

Exercise-4

The labour turnover rates of a manufacturing organisation for the quarter ended 31st March, 2006 are 10%, 5% and 3% under "flux method", "replacement method" and "separation method" respectively. The number of workers replaced during the quarter is 120. Work out the number of workers

(*i*) Left and discharged and

(*ii*) Recruited and joined including replacements. *(C.S. Inter, December 2006)*

[***Answer:*** (1) No left and discharged 72
(2) No recurited and joined including replacements 168]

❑❑❑

CHAPTER 9

Labour Cost Accounting

INTRODUCTION

The remuneration payable to labour factor of production is known as wages. One of the major issues confronting the management of every factory is the determination of a satisfactory wage structure. This issue has been further complicated by the fact that many direct components of a wage structure have social and psychological implications. From the point of view of the employer, the selection of a particular system of wage payment determines the future earning capacity of the factory. From the point of view of employees, choosing the appropriate wage plan will play a prominent role in determining employees satisfaction, productivity, morale and turnover. Therefore, the management of every factory must determine how much of wages and salaries are to be paid to employees. The determination of wages payable to employees is based upon a thorough analysis of all factors affecting such remuneration.

CHARACTERISTICS OF A SOUND WAGE SYSTEM

The following are the essential characteristics of a sound system of wage payment:

1. The system must be agreed upon both by the employer and employees.
2. The wage system must be such that it must minimise labour turnover.
3. Wage system should include incentives for efficient and exceptional types of workers.
4. It should reduce absenteeism and late attendance.
5. The cost of operation of the system must be low.
6. The system of wage payment must take into account the working conditions of the employees.
7. It should guarantee a minimum amount of wages.
8. Wage system must be flexible and capable of being adjusted in case of need.
9. Wage system must be commensurate with the earnings of the factory.
10. It should be consistent with government policy.

METHODS OF WAGE PAYMENT

Originally two systems of wage payment were in practice viz., time rate and piece rate system of wage payment. In modern days a number of systems of wage payment have been devised based on the time and piece rate system. The following chart shows the various methods of wage payment:

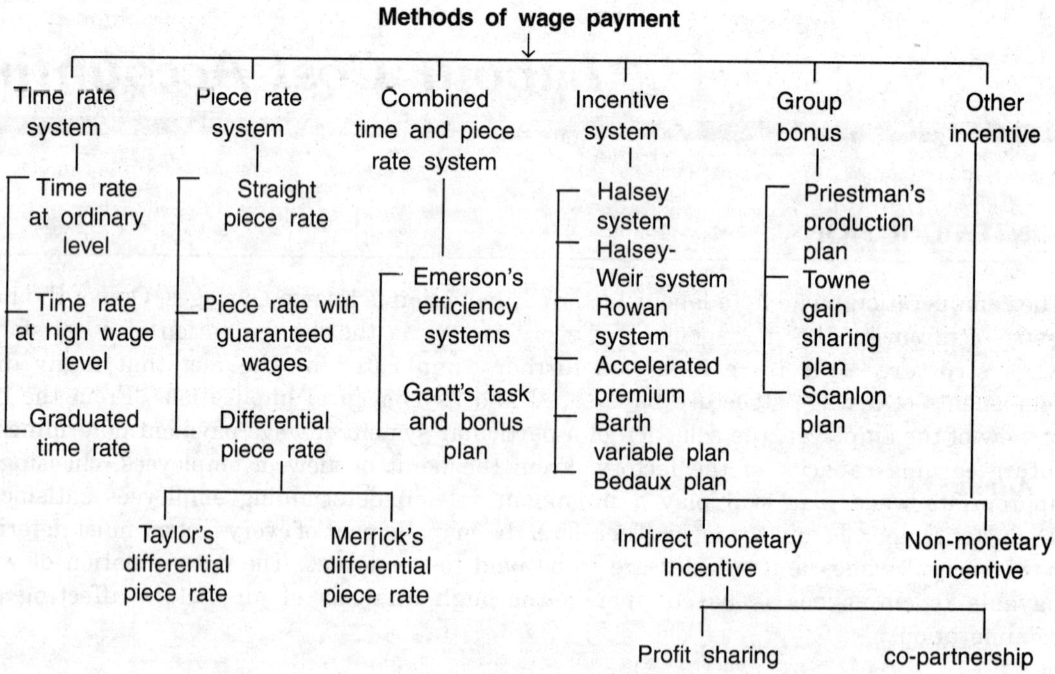

Fig. 9.1. *Chart showing various methods of wage payment.*

I. Time Rate System

Under this system wages are paid on the basis of time worked by the employees. Time rate system can take any of the following forms:

(A) Time rate at ordinary level: Under this system, the time rate is fixed beforehand and employees are remunerated at this rate. The time rate can be fixed in respect of hour, day or month. The following formula is used to calculate earnings under this method:

$$\text{Earnings} = \text{Time taken} \times \text{Time rate}$$

Suppose the time taken by an employee in a factory is 8 hours and the time rate fixed is Rs. 4 per hour, the employee will earn Rs. 32 under this method.

Time rate at ordinary level is suitable under the following circumstances:

(*i*) Where services rendered by employees cannot be tangibly measured, *e.g.*, watchman, office staff and other indirect workers such as repairer, inspector, etc.

(*ii*) Where quality is more important than quantity of output.

(*iii*) Where the speed of operation is governed entirely by the process time and the operator has little or no control over the rate of production.

(*iv*) Where a worker is learning a job.

(*v*) Where increase in production is not commensurate with the incentive paid, *e.g.*, wages payable to a night watchman.

(B) Time rate at high wage level: Time rate at a high wage level is used to attract and retain the highest quality labour for the purpose of obtaining and maintaining a high production level. The circumstances which favour this system are:

(*i*) Where the effort is strictly measurable in terms of units produced. In effect, the time rate is really a piece rate and high wage is an incentive to achieve a high task.

(*ii*) Where a uniform rate of high quality production is desirable, and

(*iii*) Where work can be graded according to skill and where a worker can be kept consistently at a job operation or machine demanding the same degree of skill.

(C) Graduated time rate: This is a form of time rate under which the time rate is fixed by adjusting to

(*i*) The cost of living index numbers,

(*ii*) Sale price of the product and

(*iii*) Merit rates.

Advantages of Time Rate System

(*i*) This system is very simple to understand and easy to operate. It does not involve any additional calculations excepting in the case of overtime work. The chances of committing mistakes under this system are very rare.

(*ii*) This system does not give scope for jealousy and hatred amongst the workers as all of them earn the same wages. So rival groups are not formed under this system.

(*iii*) Workers do not do the work in a hurry. So there is little loss due to breakage of tools and accessories.

Disadvantages of Time Rate System

(*i*) This system discourages efficient workers as no distinction is made between efficient and inefficient workers. All are paid the same rate of wage.

(*ii*) The workers tend to work slowly as they are certain about their wages. So in order to ensure that there is no waste of time, a supervisor is appointed which increases the total cost of labour.

II. Piece Rate System

Under this system wages are paid on the basis of the number of articles produced by the workers. This system offers a direct financial incentive to the workers who can earn more wages by producing more number of articles. Piece rate system can be of the following types:

(A) Straight piece rate: Under this system, each unit produced is taken as a piece. A piece rate is fixed for a unit of product produced. The number of pieces produced multiplied by piece rate will give piece wages under this method. The following formula is used:

$$\text{Earnings} = \text{No. of pieces produced} \times \text{Piece rate}$$

This system of wage payment is suitable under the following circumstances:

(*i*) Where there is an urgent necessity to increase production.

(*ii*) Where individual output can be easily and quickly determined and priced.

Advantages

(*i*) This system offers an incentive to the employees in as much as they can earn more wages by producing more number of units.

(*ii*) As the workers tend to work on their own initiative, the need for supervision does not arise.

(*iii*) Cost ascertainment is easy under this system.

Disadvantages

(*i*) Fixation of piece rate is not an easy task. A low piece rate may lead to discontentment among the employees.

(*ii*) The workers may sacrifice quality for the sake of quantity with a desire to earn more wages.

(*iii*) Excessive speeding up of work may lead to more spoilage and defective work. The cost of rectification may result in increased cost of production.

(*iv*) It is difficult to exercise control over the arrival and departure time of the employees.

(B) Piece rate with guaranteed wages: Piece rate with guaranteed wages is applicable for the new and inefficient employees. Those workers whose capacity is much below the required capacity will earn very meagre salary and hence instead of paying at the normal piece rate, they are given a minimum guaranteed wages. This encourages the workers to improve their efficiency gradually and there afterwards reach the standard of other workers.

PROBLEM ON TIME AND PIECE RATE SYSTEM

Problem-1

The employees in a plastic toy-making unit are paid wages at the rate of Rs. 7 per hour for an eight-hour shift. Each employee produces 5 units per hour. The overhead in this department is Rs. 10 per direct labour hour. Employees and the management are considering the following piece rate wage proposal:

Up to 45 units per day of 8 hours, Rs. 1.30 per unit
From 46 units to 50 units Rs. 1.30 per unit
From 51 units to 55 units Rs. 1.65 per unit
From 56 units to 60 units Rs. 1.70 per unit
Above 60 units Rs. 1.75 per unit.

The working hours are restricted to 8 hours per day. Overhead rate does not change with increased production.

Prepare a statement indicating advantages to the employees as well as the management at production levels of 40, 45, 55 and 60 units. *(ICWA, Inter, Stage 1, June 2000)*

Solution: **Present cost of making a toy**

Wages per hour	=	Rs. 7
Overhead per hour	=	Rs. 10
Conversion cost per hour	=	Rs. 17

Conversion cost per unit = $\frac{17}{5}$ = Rs. 3.40

Statement showing advantages to employees on piece rate wage proposal

Output (units)	*Time wages per day*	*Piece wage rate*	*Piece wages*	*Benefits to employees*
(a)	*(b)*	*(c)*	*(d)*	*(d) – (b)*
40	56	1.30	52	(–) 4
45	56	1.30	58.50	2.50
55	56	1.65	90.75	34.75
60	56	1.70	102.00	46.00

Statement showing advantages to the management

Output (units)	*Proposed piece rate*	*Piece wages*	*Over-head*	*Proposed total cost*	*Total cost as per existing scheme @ Rs. 3.40*	*Savings per day*
(a)	*(b)*	*(c)*	*(d)*	*(e)*	*(f)*	*(f) – (e)*
40	1.30	52	80	132	136	4.00
45	1.30	58.50	80	138	153	15.00
55	1.65	90.75	80	170.75	187	16.25
60	1.70	10.2	80	182	204	22.00

(C) Differential piece rate system: Under the differential piece rate system, the wages of workers, vary at different stages, within a certain range of output. This variation is sometimes more, sometimes less and sometimes in proportion to output. Workers often feel that beyond a certain stage, any further effort is not worthwhile. It is at this stage that an additional incentive is given to increase output. Differential piece rate system is useful under the following circumstances:

(i) Where production is undertaken on a continuous basis in order to maximise output.

(ii) Where learners are to be encouraged.

(iii) Where the time required to complete a job can be conveniently fixed.

(iv) Where the output can be identified with the individual workers.

(v) Where the production process is standardised.

The two systems which work under this principle are: (1) Taylor's differential piece rate system and (2) Merrick's differential piece rate system.

1. Taylor's differential piece rate system: This system was designed by F.W. Taylor in 1880. The features of this system of wage payment are as follows:

(a) Day wages are not guaranteed.

(b) A standard is established for each and every task by means of time and motion studies.

(c) Two differential piece rates are applicable for payment of wages to employees. The first rate is called 'low piece rate' and the second is known as 'high piece rate'. Low piece rate is used to remunerate those employees whose efficiency is below standard and high piece rate for those who are above the standard.

(d) Taylor's original system of wage payment includes a low rate which is 83 per cent of the normal piece rate. The high piece rate is 125 per cent of the normal piece rate plus 50 per cent incentive in the form of bonus (or 175 per cent of normal piece rate) of the given piece rate.

The main objects of Taylor's differential piece rate system are: (1) To discourage less than average workers denying guaranteed wages and fixing a low piece rate for low production and (2) For rewarding the efficient workers by offering a high piece rate for higher level of production.

Advantages

(i) This system attracts only the efficient workers.

(ii) With an efficient labour force, the output will increase considerably.

(iii) The incidence of overhead will be less with an increase in production.

Disadvantages

(i) This leads to discontent among employees, particularly among learners and sub-standard employees by setting a low piece rate.

(ii) This method is also not suitable for those employees whose efficiency level is just below the border line, *i.e.,* by a small margin.

(iii) It does not guarantee even the minimum day wages, which frustrates the employees.

(iv) Workers develop hatred and jealousy towards each other because of the differential wage rates.

PROBLEMS ON TAYLOR'S SYSTEM OF WAGE PAYMENT

Problem–2

From the following particulars calculate wages earned by workers A and B respectively under Taylor's system:

Standard time allowed : 10 units per hour

Normal wage rate : Re. 1 per hour

Differential rates to be applied:

90% of piece rate when below standard efficiency

125% of piece rate when at or above standard. Production on a day of 8 hours:

A–75 units, B–85 units. *(Sri Sathya Sai University, B.Com., March 1992)*

Solution:

	A	*B*
Standard output 10 units × 8 hrs	80	80
Actual output	75	85

Worker A's efficiency is below standard and therefor low piece rate is applicable. Low piece rate in this case is 90% of Re. 0.1 = 0.09

Worker B's efficiency is above standard and therefor high piece rate is applicable. High piece rate is 125% of Re. 0.1 = 0.125.

Earnings = Number of pieces × Rate per piece

A = 75 × 0.09 = Rs. 6.75

B = 85 × 0.125 = Rs. 10.63

Working Note:

$$\text{Calculation of piece rate} = \frac{\text{Rate per hour}}{\text{Pieces per hour}} = \frac{1}{10} = 0.1$$

Problem–3

The workwise production in a department is as follows:

Amar — 600 units, Akbar — 1,000 units, Anthony — 400 units

Calculate their earnings as per:

(*a*) Straight piece rate system at 10 paise per unit

(*b*) Differential piece rate system under which first 400 units are paid at 12 paise per unit, the rate increasing by 2 paise per unit for each subsequent 200 units produced. *(Osmania University, B.Com., April 1991)*

Solution:

(*a*) Straight piece rate system		=	No. of pieces produced × Rate per piece		
Amar		=	600 × 0.10	=	Rs. 60.00
Akbar		=	1,000 × 0.10	=	Rs. 100.00
Anthony		=	400 × 0.10	=	Rs. 40.00
(*b*) Differential piece rate system		=	No. of pieces produced × Rate per piece		
Amar	For Ist 400 units	=	400 × 0.12	=	48.00
	For next 200 units	=	200 × 0.14	=	28.00
					Rs. 76.00
Akbar	For Ist 400 units	=	400 × 0.12	=	48.00
	For next 200 units	=	200 × 0.14	=	28.00
	For next 200 units	=	200 × 0.16	=	32.00
	For next 200 units	=	200 × 0.18	=	36.00
					Rs. 144.00
Anthony	For 400 units	=	400 × 0.12	=	Rs. 48.00

STRAIGHT PIECE RATE AND TAYLOR'S DIFFERENTIAL PIECE RATE SYSTEM

Problem–4

Calculate the earnings of workers A and B under straight piece rate system and Taylor's differential piece rate system from the following particulars: Normal rate per hour Rs. 2.40, Standard time per unit 30 seconds. Differentials to be applied 80% of piece rate below standard, 120% of piece rate at or above standard. Worker 'A' produces 800 units per day and worker 'B' produces 1000 units per day. They work for 8 hours per day.

(Sri Sathya Sai University, B.Com. (Hons), March 2002)

Solution: ***Working Notes:***

(1) Calculation of normal piece rate

Standard production per 30 seconds = 1 unit

Standard production per minute

For 30 seconds ⟶ 1 unit

For 60 seconds ⟶ 2 units

Standard production per hour

2 units × 60 minutes = 120 units

Standard production per day of 8 hours

120 units × 8 hours = 960 units

$$\text{Normal piece rate} = \frac{\text{Piece rate per hour}}{\text{Output per hour}}$$

$$= \frac{\text{Rs. } 2.40}{120 \text{ units}} = 0.02 \text{ paise}$$

(2) Calculation of low piece rate

$$0.02 \times \frac{80}{100} = 0.016$$

(3) Calculation of high piece rate

$$0.02 \times \frac{120}{100} = 0.024$$

(4) Calculation of efficiency of workers

$$A = \frac{800}{960} \times 100 = 83.33\%$$

$$B = \frac{1000}{960} \times 100 = 104.16\%$$

Wages under straight piece rate system

No. of units × Rate per unit

A = 800 × 0.02 = Rs. 16

B = 1000 × 0.02 = Rs. 200

Wages under Taylor's differential piece rate system

No. of units × Differential piece rate

A = 800 × 0.016 = Rs. 12.80

B = 1000 × 0.024 = Rs. 24

Problem–5

From the following particulars calculate the total wages of an employee for a month.

(*i*)	Standard production	100 units
(*ii*)	Actual production of the employee	85 units
(*iii*)	Rate of wages	Rs. 50 per unit
(*iv*)	Dearness allowance	Rs. 500 per month

(*v*) Bonus for additional production: Rs. 5 for 1% additional production when actual production exceeds 80% of the standard production.

(*Calcutta University, B.Com. (Pass), 2002*)

Solution: ***Working Note:***

(1) Calculation of efficiency of worker

For a standard production of 100: Actual production is 85 units

$$\text{For } 100\% \longrightarrow \frac{85}{100} \times 100 = 85\%$$

Percentage of actual production beyond 80% of standard is 85%–80% = 5%. Production bonus is Rs. 5 for 1% increase in efficiency beyond 80% of standard *i.e.*, 5 × 5 = Rs. 25

Statement showing total wages for a month

Piece wages (85 units × Rs. 50)	Rs. 4250
Dearness allowance	500
Production bonus	25
Total wages	Rs. 4775

Problem–6

X Y Z Company employs its workers for single shift of 8 hours per day for 25 days in a month. The company has recently fixed the standard output of 40 units per day per worker for a mass production item and introduced an incentive scheme to boost output. Details of wages payable to the workers are as follows:

(*i*)	Basic wages	:	Rs. 3 per unit subject to a guaranteed minimum wages of Rs. 80 per day worked
(*ii*)	Dearness allowance	:	Rs. 40 per day worked
(*iii*)	Incentive bonus	:	
	Up to 80% efficiency	:	NIL
	For efficiency above 80%	:	Rs. 50 for every 1% increase above 80%

The details of performance of 2 workers for a particular month are as follows:

Workers	No. of days worked	Output (units)
A	25	820
B	18	500

Calculate the total earnings of both the workers for the month.

(University of Delhi, B.Com. (Hons), 2004)

Solution: ***Working Notes:***

(1) Calculation of dearness allowance

A = 25 days × Rs. 40 per day = Rs. 1000

B = 18 days × Rs. 40 per day = Rs. 720

(2) Calculation of standard output

A = 40 units per day × 25 days = 1000 units

B = 40 units per day × 18 days = 720 units

(3) Calculation of efficiency level

$$= \frac{\text{Actual output}}{\text{Standard output}} \times 100$$

$$A = \frac{820}{1000} \times 100 = 82\%$$

$$B = \frac{500}{720} \times 100 = 69.4\%$$

A's efficiency is more than 80%. So he is entitled to bonus. B will not get any bonus.

Statement of earnings

	A	B
Basic wages – A (820 × 3)	2,460	1,500
– B (500 × 3)		
Dearness allowance	1,000	720
Incentive bonus (50 × 2)	100	–
Total earnings	3,560	2,220

Problem–7

Based on the following data, calculate the total monthly remuneration of three workers P, Q and R, who are working in a factory.

(1) Standard production per month per worker – 2000 units.

(2) Piece work rate, Re. 0.50 per unit

(3) Production bonus to be given as follows:

Up to 85% efficiency	: NIL
Between 85% and 100% efficiency	: Incentive bonus at Rs. 40 for every 5% increase above 85%

Above 100% efficiency : Incentive bonus at Rs. 40 for every 5% increase above 85% plus 20% additional bonus on the incentive earned.

(4) P, Q and R had a production of 1600 units, 2000 units and 2200 units respectively during January 2001 *(ICWA, Inter, Stage I, June 2001)*

Solution: ***Working Notes:***

(1) Calculation of efficiency of workers

$$\frac{\text{Actual output}}{\text{Standard output}} \times 100$$

$$P = \frac{1600}{2000} \times 100 = 80\%$$

$$Q = \frac{2000}{2000} \times 100 = 100\%$$

$$R = \frac{2200}{2000} \times 100 = 110\%$$

(2) Calculation of incentive

P = Incentive is nil as his efficiency is below 85%

Q = 100% – 85% = 15%

For 5% increase in efficiency, incentive is Rs. 40

For 15%: $\frac{15}{5} \times 40 = 120$

R = 110% – 85% = 25%

For 5% increase in efficiency, incentive is Rs. 40

For 25%: $\left(\frac{25}{5} \times 40\right) = 200$

Add 20% additional bonus on the incentive earned = 40

$\left(\frac{20}{200} \times 200\right)$

Total incentive = 240

Earnings = No. of units × Piece rate + Incentive

P = 1600 × 0.5 + NIL

= Rs. 800

Q = 2000 × 0.5 + 120

= 1000 + 120 = Rs. 1120

R = 2200 × 0.5 + 240

= 1100 + 240 = Rs. 1340

2. Merrick's differential piece rate system. This system is also known as multiple pieces rate system. Under this system, three graded piece rates are used instead of two as in the case of Taylor's differential system. The features of this system are as follows:

(*a*) Minimum day wages are not guaranteed and thus remuneration paid is solely on the basis of output.

(*b*) The three rates of remuneration are as follows:

Up to 83 per cent standard output	— ordinary piece rate
83 per cent to 100 per cent standard output	— 110 per cent of ordinary piece rate
Above 100 per cent standard output	— 120 per cent of ordinary piece rate

Advantages

(*i*) When compared to Taylor's method, this system offers better terms for earning increased wages. Under Taylor's method, to earn a high piece rate wage, an employee has to improve his efficiency to 100 per cent, whereas to earn an incentive under Merrick's system, an employee has to reach only 83 per cent. Thus psychologically, the employee feels that Merrick's system is a better system of wage payment than Taylor's system, as it is felt that it is within their reach to attain 83 per cent efficiency.

(*ii*) Having thus reached 83 per cent efficiency, employees strive to achieve even 100 per cent efficiency to earn better wages.

Disadvantage

This system is mostly suitable at the intermediate range of efficiency, *i.e.*, it makes a good upgrading plan.

PROBLEMS ON MERRICK'S SYSTEM OF WAGE PAYMENT

Problem–8

Given the following data calculate wages payable under Merrick's differential price rate system.

Standard production		— 120 units
Actual production of workers	A	— 90 units
	B	— 100 units
	C	— 130 units

Rate per piece 0.10 per unit.

Solution:

Calculation of efficiency of each worker

$$A = \frac{90}{120} \times 100 = 75\%$$

$$B = \frac{100}{120} \times 100 = 83.33\%$$

$$C = \frac{130}{120} \times 100 = 108.33\%$$

Earnings = No. of pieces × Rate per piece

A = 90 × 0.10 = Rs. 9

B = 100 × 0.11 = Rs. 11

C = 130 × 0.12 = Rs. 15.60

Problem–9

Calculate the earnings of workers A, B and C under straight piece rate system and Merrick's multiple piece rate system from the following particulars:

Normal rate per hour : Rs. 5.40

Standard time per unit : 1 minute

Output per day is as follows:

Worker A — 390 units

Worker B — 450 units

Worker C — 600 units

Working hours per day are 8. *(C.A., Inter, May 1998)*

Solution:

Calculation of standard output per hour

For standard time of 1 minute the output is 1 unit

For standard time of 60 minutes or 1 hr. = 60 min × 1 unit

= 60 units

Calculation of normal wage per unit

$$\frac{\text{Normal rate per hour}}{\text{Pieces per hour}} = \frac{\text{Rs. } 5.40}{60 \text{ units}} = 0.09 \text{ paise}$$

Calculation of standard output per day

60 units × 8 hours = 480 units

Calculation of efficiency of employees

$$\frac{\text{Actual output}}{\text{Standard output}} \times 100$$

$$A = \frac{390}{480} \times 100 = 81.25\%$$

$$B = \frac{450}{480} \times 100 = 93.75\%$$

$$C = \frac{600}{480} \times 100 = 125\%$$

Earnings of workers under straight piece rate system

Earnings = No. of units × Rate per unit

A = 390 × 0.09 = Rs. 35.10

B = 450 × 0.09 = Rs. 40.50

C = 600 × 0.09 = Rs. 54.00

Earnings of workers under Merrick's multiple piece rate system

A = 390 × 0.09 = Rs. 35.10

B = 450 × 0.099 = Rs. 44.55

C = 600 × 0.108 = Rs. 64.80

Problem–10

The following piece rate system is followed in a small concern manufacturing a single product:

(*a*) Basic piece rate up to 85 per cent efficiency.

(*b*) 110 per cent of the piece rate between 85 per cent and 100 per cent efficiency.

(*c*) 120 per cent of the basis piece rate above 100 per cent efficiency. Guaranteed day rate is equal to 70% efficiency. Assuming that 100 per cent efficiency is 100 pieces per day of 8 hours and the piece rate is 50 paise per piece. Calculate labour cost per piece at 5 per cent intervals between 60 per cent and 120 per cent efficiency.

(University of Kerala, M.Com., May 1992)

Solution:

Statement showing calculation of wages

Output per hour	*Efficiency*	*Piece wages*	*Guaranteed time wages*	*100% Additional piece wages*	*20% Additional piece wages*	*Total wages*	*Wages per piece*
60	60	30.00	35	–	–	35	0.583
65	65	32.50	35	–	–	35	0.538
70	70	35.00	35	–	–	35	0.500
75	75	37.50	–	–	–	37.50	0.500
80	80	40.00	–	–	–	40.00	0.500
85	85	42.50	–	4.25	–	46.75	0.500
90	90	45.00	–	4.50	–	49.50	0.550
95	95	47.50	–	4.75	–	52.25	0.550
100	100	50.00	–	5.00	–	55.00	0.550
105	105	52.50	–	–	10.50	63.00	0.600
110	110	55.00	–	–	11.00	66.00	0.600
115	115	57.50	–	–	11.50	69.00	0.600
120	120	60.00	–	–	12.50	72.00	0.600

PROBLEM ON MERRICK'S MULTIPLE PIECE RATE SYSTEM

Problem–11

On the basis of the following information, calculate the earnings of Hari, Giri, Ravi and Suri under "Merrick's Multiple Piece Rate System"

Standard production per hour – 12 units

Normal rate per hour – Re. 0.60

In an 8 hour day, Ravi produced 64 units,

Hari 96 units, Giri 84 units and Suri 100 units.

(University of Madras, B.Com., May 2003)

Solution:

Working Notes:

Calculation of efficiency of workers:

Standard output:

For 1 Hr. — 12 units

For 8 Hrs — 12 × 8 = 96 units

$$\text{Ravi} = \frac{64}{96} \times 100 = 66.67\% \text{ (ordinary piece rate)}$$

$$\text{Hari} = \frac{96}{96} \times 100 = 100\% \text{ (110\% of piece rate)}$$

$$\text{Giri} = \frac{84}{96} \times 100 = 87.5\% \text{ (110\% of piece rate)}$$

$$\text{Suri} = \frac{100}{96} \times 100 = 104.17\% \text{ (120\% of piece rate)}$$

Calculation of standard piece rate:

$$= \frac{\text{Rate per hour}}{\text{No. of units per hour}}$$

$$= \frac{0.60 \text{ paise}}{12 \text{ units}} = 0.05 \text{ paise per unit}$$

Earnings = No. of units × Rate per unit

$$\text{Ravi} = 64 \times 0.05 = \text{Rs. } 3.20$$

$$\text{Hari} = 96 \times \left(0.05 \times \frac{110}{100}\right) = \text{Rs. } 5.28$$

$$\text{Giri} = 84 \times \left(0.05 \times \frac{110}{100}\right) = \text{Rs. } 4.62$$

$$\text{Suri} = 100 \times \left(0.05 \times \frac{120}{100}\right) = \text{Rs. } 6.00$$

PROBLEM ON STRAIGHT PIECE RATE AND MERRICK'S MULTIPLE PIECE RATE SYSTEM

Problem–12

Calculate the earnings of workers A, B and C under straight piece rate system and Merrick's multiple piece rate system from the following information:

Normal rate per hour = Rs. 1.80

Output per day is as follows:

Worker A	384 units
Worker B	450 units
Worker C	552 units

Working hours per day are 8 hours.

Standard time per unit 1 minute

(Sri Sathya Sai University, B.Com. (Hons.) March 2003)

Solution: ***Working Notes:***

(1) Calculation of normal piece rate:

Standard output per minute = 1 unit

Standard production per hour = 60 units

Standard production per day of 8 hours: *i.e.*, 60 × 8 = 480

$$\text{Normal piece rate} = \frac{\text{Rate per hour}}{\text{Normal output per hour}}$$

$$= \frac{1.80}{60} = \text{Re. } 0.03$$

(2) Calculation of efficiency of workers:

Worker A:

For a standard output of 480 units A's output is 384 units

For a standard output of 100 units A's output is ? units

$$\frac{384}{480} \times 100 = 80\%$$

Worker B: $\frac{450}{480} \times 100 = 93.75\%$

Worker C: $\frac{552}{480} \times 100 = 115\%$

(1) Wages under straight piece rate system:

No. of units × Rate per piece

A = 384 × 0.03 = Rs. 11.52

B = 450 × 0.03 = Rs. 13.50

C = 552 × 0.03 = Rs. 16.56

(2) Merrick's multiple piece rate system:

A = 384 × 0.03 = Rs. 11.52

$$B = 450 \times 0.033 = \text{Rs. } 14.85$$
$$C = 552 \times 0.036 = \text{Rs. } 19.87$$

III. Combined Time and Piece Rate System

This system of wage payment is based on the time rate and piece rate system of wages. The following method of wage payment fall under this classification.

A. Emerson's Efficiency System. This method of wage payment was introduced by Harrington Emerson who worked together with F.W. Taylor under scientific management movement. While Taylor introduced differential piece rate system of wages, Emerson devised an empirical system of wage payment which came to be called as Emerson's efficiency system. This system is suitable to (*a*) encourage slow workers to better their performance and (*b*) to facilitate an easy transfer from time wages to payment by result. The features of this system of wage payment can be enumerated as follows:

(*a*) Day wages are guaranteed.

(*b*) A standard is fixed in respect of output.

(*c*) Below $66\frac{2}{3}$ per cent efficiency, workers are paid at the normal time rate.

(*d*) Between $66\frac{2}{3}$ per cent and 100 per cent efficiency, payments are made on step bonus rates. Emerson himself has prepared a table which contains the efficiency level ranging from $66\frac{2}{3}$ to 100 per cent and the corresponding percentage of bonus on time wages earned by the worker. For 67 per cent efficiency, the bonus applicable is 0.01 per cent, for 68 per cent efficiency, it is 0.04 and for 100 per cent efficiency it is 20 per cent.

(*e*) Above 100 per cent efficiency, an additional bonus of 1 per cent of the time rate is paid for each 1 per cent increase in efficiency.

The following formula is used to calculate total earnings under this system:

$$\text{Earnings} = \text{Time taken} \times \text{Time rate} + \text{Emerson's bonus percentage} \times \text{Time taken} \times \text{Time rate}$$

PROBLEMS ON EMERSON'S EFFICIENCY SYSTEM

Problem–13

In a manufacturing concern the daily wages guaranteed for workers is Rs. 2. The standard output for the month is 1,000 units representing 100% efficiency. The rate of wages is paid without bonus to those workers who show up to $66\frac{2}{3}$ per cent efficiency. Beyond this, bonus is payable in a graded scale.

Efficiency	*Bonus*
90%	10%
100%	20%

Further increase of 1% of bonus for every 1% further rise in efficiency. Calculate the total earnings of Ramesh, Suresh, Umesh and Mahesh who worked for 26 days in a month and their output being 500, 900, 1,000 and 1,200 respectively.

Solution:

Calculation of efficiency of all four workers

$$\text{Ramesh} = \frac{500 \times 100}{1,000} = 50\%$$

$$\text{Suresh} = \frac{900 \times 100}{1,000} = 90\%$$

$$\text{Umesh} = \frac{1,000 \times 100}{1,000} = 100\%$$

$$\text{Mahesh} = \frac{1,200 \times 100}{1,000} = 120\%$$

Earnings = Time taken × Time rate + Emerson's bonus percentage × Time taken × Time rate

Ramesh = 26 × 2 + Nil = Rs. 52.00

$$\text{Suresh} = 26 \times 2 + \frac{10}{100} \times 26 \times 2$$

= 52 + 5.20 = Rs. 57.20

$$\text{Umesh} = 26 \times 2 + \frac{20}{100} \times 26 \times 2$$

= 52 + 10.40 = Rs. 62.40

$$\text{Mahesh} = 26 \times 2 + \frac{40}{100} \times 26 \times 2$$

= 52 + 20.80 = Rs. 72.80

Problem–14

An employee working under a bonus scheme saves 10 hours in a job for which the standard time is 60 hours. Calculate the rate per hour worked and wages payable to him if incentive bonus of 10% on the hourly rate is payable when standard time (namely, 100% efficiency) is achieved and a further incentive bonus of 1% on hourly rate for each 1% in excess of that 100% efficiency is payable. Assume that the normal rate of payment is Rs. 5 per hour.

(University of Madras, B.Com., September 1995)

Solution:

Hours worked = Standard time – Saved timed
= 60 hrs – 10 hrs
= 50 hrs

(*a*) Wages 50 hrs @ Rs. 5 per hr = Rs. 250
(*b*) Bonus 10% of Rs. 250 = Rs. 25

(c) Incentive 1% of excess of 100 efficiency $= \frac{60}{50} \times 100 = 120\%$

Incentive is 20% of 250	=	50
Total wages		Rs. 325

Effective rate per hour $= \frac{325}{50} = \text{Rs. } 6.50$

Alternatively:

Earnings = Time taken × Time rate + Emerson's bonus × Time taken × Time rate

$$= 50 \times 5 + \frac{30}{100} \times 50 \times 5$$

= Rs. 325

Problem–15

An employee working under a bonus scheme saves 12 hours on a job for which the standard time is 60 hours. Calculate wages payable to the employee if incentive bonus of 10% on the monthly rate is payable when 100% efficiency is achieved and a further incentive bonus of 10% on the hourly rate is payable when 100% efficiency is achieved and a further incentive bonus of 1% on hourly rate for 1% excess of that 100% efficiency is payable. Assume that the normal rate of wages is Rs. 10 per hour. *(Calcutta University, B.Com. (Hons), 2005)*

Solution: ***Working Note:***

(1) Calculation of percentage of efficiency:

$$= \frac{\text{Standard time}}{\text{Actual time}} \times 100$$

$$= \frac{60}{48} \times 100 = 125\%$$

For achieving 100% efficiency = bonus is 10% of hourly rate

Beyond 100% efficiency (125 – 100) = bonus is 25% of hourly rate. Therefore rate of bonus is 35% of hourly rate.

Earnings = Time taken × Time rate + Emerson's bonus% × Time taken × Time rate

$$= 48 \times 10 + \frac{35}{100} \times 48 \times 10$$

= 480 + 168 = Rs. 648.

Problem–16

The standard labour time required for the production of a certain component has been fixed as 4 hours. An incentive scheme was introduced recently to raise labour productivity. The relevant details of the scheme are as follows:

Efficiency	***Incentive as a percentage of basic wages***
Below 100%	No incentive
100% (*i.e.*, 4 hrs/unit)	10%

Above 100%	1% additional incentive for every 1% increase in efficiency above 100%, fractions excluded.

Four workers A, B, C and D produced 16, 12, 14 and 10 units respectively in a particular weak of 48 hours. The basic wages of all the workers is Rs. 15 per hour.

Calculate the efficiency, incentive bonus, total earnings and labour cost per unit in respect of each of the above four workers. *(ICWA, Inter, Stage I, December 2003)*

Solution: ***Working Notes:***

(1) Calculation of standard hours:

A = 16 × 4 hrs per unit = 64 hrs

or For 1 units → 4 hrs

For 16 units → ? (64 hrs)

B = 12 × 4 hrs per unit = 48 hrs

C = 14 × 4 = 56 hrs

D = 10 × 4 = 40 hrs

(2) Calculation of efficiency of workers:

$$= \frac{\text{Standard time}}{\text{Actual time}} \times 100$$

$$A = \frac{64}{48} \times 100 = 133\%$$

$$B = \frac{48}{48} \times 100 = 100\%$$

$$C = \frac{56}{48} \times 100 = 116\%$$

$$D = \frac{40}{48} \times 100 = 83\%$$

(3) Efficiency bonus:

A = At 100% efficiency 10% + 1% above 100% (133% – 100)

= 10% + 33% = 43%

B = 10% + NIL = 10%

C = 10% + 16% *i.e.,* (116 – 100) = 26%

D = NIL + NIL = NIL

Earnings = Time taken × Time rate + Emerson's efficiency bonus × Time taken × Time rate

$$A = 48 \times 15 + \frac{43}{100} \times 48 \times 15$$

= 720 + 309.60 = 1029.60

$$B = 48 \times 15 + \frac{10}{100} \times 48 \times 15$$

= 720 + 72 = 792

$$C = 48 \times 15 + \frac{26}{100} \times 48 \times 15$$
$$= 720 + 187.20 = 907.20$$
$$D = 48 \times 15 + \text{Nil}$$
$$= 720$$

(4) Labour cost per unit:

$$A = \frac{1029.60}{16} = 64.35$$
$$B = \frac{792}{12} = 66$$
$$C = \frac{907.20}{14} = 64.80$$
$$D = \frac{720}{10} = 72$$

Problem–17

XYZ Company employs its workers for a single shift of 8 hours per day for 25 days in a month. The company has recently fixed the standard output of 40 units per day per worker for a mass production item and introduced an incentive scheme to boost output. Details of wages payable to the workers are as follows:

(*i*) Basic wages : Rs. 3 per unit subject to guaranteed minimum wages of Rs. 80 per day worked

(*ii*) Dearness allowance : Rs. 40 per day worked

(*iii*) Incentive bonus :

Up to 8% efficiency : Nil

Above 80% efficiency : Rs 50 for every 1% increase above 80%

The details of performance of 2 workers for a particular month are as follows:

Workers	*No. of days worked*	*Output (units)*
A	25	820
B	18	500

Calculate the total earnings of both the workers for the month.

(University of Delhi, B.Com. (Hons.), 2004)

Solution: ***Working Notes:***

(1) Calculation of standard output

A = 40 units × 25 days = 1000 units

B = 40 units × 18 days = 720 units

(2) Calculation of efficiency of workers

A = For a standard output of 1000: Actual is 820

For 100 — ?

$$\frac{820 \times 100}{1000} = 82\%$$

B = For a standard output of 720 : Actual is 500

For 100 — ?

$$\frac{500 \times 100}{720} = 69.4\%$$

A's efficiency is more than 80%. So he is entitled to bonus. B will not get any bonus.

(3) Calculation of dearness allowance:

A = Rs. 40 × 25 days = Rs. 1000

B = Rs. 40 × 18 days = Rs. 720

Statement of earnings

	A	*B*
Basic wages:		
A – 820 × 3	2460	
B – 500 × 3	–	1500
Dearness allowance	1000	720
Incentive bonus 50 × 2	100	–
	3560	2220

B. Gantt's Task and Bonus Plan. This system was introduced by Henry L. Gantt. It is a combination of time rate system with a step bonus and differential piece rate system of wage payment. The purpose of this method is to reward those who reach a high level of production. The method also guarantees the minimum day wages and at the same time, encourages less skilled employees to improve their performance. Remuneration under this system is computed as under:

Output below standard — Time rate wages

Output at standard — Bonus of 20 per cent on time rate

Output above standard — High piece rate on whole output

Advantages:

(*i*) It provides security to less efficient workers.

(*ii*) It is beneficial to more efficient workers by offering a high incentive.

(*iii*) The increased output because of increased efficiency reduces the fixed cost per unit.

Disadvantage:

The trade union may not agree to the piece rate fixed. Instead, it may seek a high guaranteed time rate.

PROBLEM ON GANTT'S TASK AND BONUS PLAN

Problem–18

From the following particulars calculate the earnings of workers X, Y and Z under Gantt's task and bonus plan:

Time rate	—	Rs. 2 per hour
Standard output	—	10 units per hour
Number of hours	—	8 hours in a day
High piece rate	—	0.40 per unit
Output of X	—	70 units
Output of Y	—	80 units
Output of Z	—	90 units

Solution:

Calculation of efficiency of all the workers:

X's efficiency is below standard *i.e.,* his output is lesser than the standard output.

Y's efficiency is at standard.

Z's efficiency is at standard.

Earnings of X = Time taken × time rate
= 8 hrs × Rs. 2 = 16

Earnings of Y = 8 hrs × Rs. 2.40 = 19.20

Earnings of Z = No. of units produced × High piece rate
= 90 × 0.40 = 36

PROBLEM ON WAGES UNDER TAYLOR'S, MERRICK'S AND GANTT'S TASK AND BONUS PLAN

Problem–19

From the following particulars calculate wages under (1) Taylor's differential piece rate system, (2) Merrick's differential piece rate system and (3) Gantt's task and bonus plan.

Number of hours worked in a day	—	8 hours
Low piece rate	—	Re. 1 per unit
High piece rate	—	Rs. 1.50 per unit
Time rate	—	Rs. 2 per hour
Output of X	—	25 units
Output of Y	—	30 units
Output of Z	—	40 units

Solution:

(1) Taylor's differential piece rate system = No. of units × Rate per unit

X = 25 × Re. 1 = Rs. 25

Y = 30 × Rs. 1.50 = Rs. 45

Z = 40 × Rs. 1.50 = Rs. 60

(2) Merrick's differential piece rate system:

$$\text{Efficiency of X} = \frac{25}{30} \times 100 = 83.34\%$$

$$\text{Efficiency of Y} = \frac{30}{30} \times 100 = 100\%$$

$$\text{Efficiency of Z} = \frac{40}{30} \times 100 = 133.34\%$$

Earnings = No. of units produced × Rate per unit

X = 25 × Rs. 1.10 (Re. 1 + 10% of Re. 1) = Rs. 27.50

Y = 30 × Rs. 1.10 (Re. 1 + 10% of Re. 1) = Rs. 33.00

Z = 40 × Rs. 1.20 (Re. 1 + 20% of Re. 1) = Rs. 48.00

(3) Gantt's task and bonus plan

Earning of X at time rate	= 8 hrs × Rs. 2	= Rs. 16
Earnings of Y at time + 20% bonus	= 8 hrs × Rs. 2.40	= Rs. 19.20
Earning of Z at high piece rate	= 40 units × 1.50 per unit	= Rs. 60.00

IV. Incentive System of Wage Payment

The term, "incentive" has been defined as "the stimulation of effort and effectiveness by offering monetary inducement or enhanced facilities". It is clear from this definition that an incentive could be a monetary incentive, *i.e.,* cash bonus system or non-monetary incentive, like fringe benefits. Incentives can also be paid to an individual worker or collectively to a group of workers. In the former case, the worker directly gets his share of premium for his increased efficiency, while in the latter case, the incentive is shared by all the workers in an agreed proportion for their collective effort.

The incentive system is, in fact, a compromise between the time rate system and the piece rate system. Under the time rate system, the workers will not gain anything even if they complete production in less than the allowed time. On the other hand, under the piece rate system, employers get nothing if the time is saved. So under the incentive system, both the employer and employees benefit from the time saved.

The incentive systems have the following characteristics:

(*a*) In all incentive systems of wage payment, minimum wages are guaranteed.

(*b*) For every job, a standard time is fixed on the basis of time and motion studies.

(*c*) If a worker completes the job within the time allowed, he will be paid an incentive bonus on the time saved.

Essentials of a Good Incentive System of Wage Payment

David W. Belcher, in his "*Wage and Salary Administration*" enumerates the following essential requirements of a good incentive system of wage payment:

1. An incentive wage plan should be explained and discussed with all employees and supervisors before it is implemented. Employees' cooperation and participation is much more likely if they have a part in its inception.
2. The plan should allow for earnings to be in direct proportion to an employee's output above the work standard.
3. An incentive plan should be easily understood and easy to calculate by the employees. A complicated plan leads to doubts and distrust in the worker's mind.
4. The incentive should be paid in the same month during which the efforts are put. It should not be postponed to a future date.
5. The spread between the guaranteed and incentive pay rates should be large enough to encourage extra effort on the part of employees.
6. All incentive systems should guarantee a minimum day's wages. This infuses an element of security among employees.
7. The standard once set should not be changed unless (*i*) there is an error or (*ii*) a change in the working conditions has been affected.
8. The standard should be scientifically set and it must be within the reach of employees to attain it.
9. The entire production process should be standardised, such as standard control processes, etc.
10. Equitable adjustments should be provided for an employee who fails to meet the standard for reasons beyond his control.
11. Standards of output must be based on established and recognised quality requirements. Employees should not be paid for substandard work. In fact, some provision may be necessary to control waste if it is excessive.
12. Good working conditions are to be created to enable the workers to attain the established standard.
13. An incentive system should be extended so as to include even indirect workers.
14. No upper limit to be fixed for worker's earnings.
15. The incentive system should be conducive to setting up a standard cost and budgetary control.

The following are the most important types of incentive system of wage payment:

1. Halsey System

This system was introduced by F.A. Halsey, an engineer of America in 1891. The features of this incentive system are as follows:

(*a*) A standard time is allowed for each job. A worker who takes standard time or more than standard time to complete a piece of work receives his time rate.

(*b*) If the piece of work is completed in less than the standard time, the employee is paid an incentive of 50 per cent of the time saved. The remaining 50 per cent of the incentive is shared by the employer. The following formula is used to compute wages under this method:

$$\text{Earnings} = \text{Time taken} \times \text{Time rate} + 50\% \text{ of time saved} \times \text{Time rate}$$

Advantages:

(*i*) Time wages are guaranteed and thus it offers security to the employees.

(*ii*) As the incentive is also shared by the employer, he is interested in improving the working conditions in factories.

(*iii*) This method of wage payment is comparatively easy to operate and understand.

Disadvantages:

(*i*) The workers are dissatisfied because employer share half of the incentive earned by employees.

(*ii*) It is difficult to fix a standard time in actual practice.

PROBLEMS ON HALSEY SYSTEM OF WAGE PAYMENT

Problem–20

Calculate wages under Halsey system from the following particulars:

Time allowed — 16 hours

Time taken — 10 hours

Time rate — Re. 1 per hour

Solution:

$$\text{Halsey system} = \text{Time taken} \times \text{Time rate} + \frac{50}{100} \times \text{Time saved} \times \text{Time rate}$$

$$= 10 \times 1 + \frac{50}{100} \times 6 \times 1$$

$$= 10 + 3 = \text{Rs. } 13.00$$

Note: Time saved = Time allowed – Time taken

= 16 hours – 10 hours = 6 hours

Problem–21

A worker completes a job in a certain number of hours. The standard time allowed for the job is 10 hours and the hourly rate of wage is Re. 1. The workers earn at 50% rate bonus of Rs. 2 under Halsey plan. Calculate his wages under Halsey system.

Solution:

Here the time taken is not given. It is calculated as shown below:

Time allowed = 10 hrs

Time saved = 4 hrs

Time taken = 6 hrs

Time saved is calculated as shown below:

Bonus at 50% of time saved is Rs. 2

Bonus at 100% or total bonus = Rs. 4

Rate per hour is Re. 1. Hence time saved is 4 hours.

$$\text{Earnings} = \text{Time taken} \times \text{Time rate} + \frac{50}{100} \times \text{Time saved} \times \text{Time rate}$$

$$= 6 \times 1 + \frac{50}{100} \times 4 \times 1$$

$$= 6 + 2 = \text{Rs. } 8.$$

2. Halsey-Weir System

This system of wage payment was introduced by G.J. Weir in England. This is in fact modified form of Halsey system. All the features of Halsey system also apply to this system, excepting that the percentage of incentive payable to employees is $33\frac{1}{3}$ per cent of the time saved. The remaining $66\frac{2}{3}$ per cent is shared by the employer. The formula as was given under Halsey system holds good for this method also.

PROBLEM ON HALSEY-WEIR SYSTEM

Problem–22

Calculate the amount of wages and bonus earned by this worker:

Name	:	Surinder
Job commenced	:	Monday, 23rd Sept. 1982, 8 a.m.
Job finished	:	Saturday, 28th Sept. 1982, 1 p.m.
Quantity of pieces of work given out	:	638
Quantity of pieces of work passed	:	600
Worker's rate	:	50 paise per hour
Time allowed	:	10 pieces per hour
Bonus	:	40% of time saved

Assume that the employee worked for 9 hours a day and no overtime.

(Bharathidasan University, B.Com., October 1988)

Solution:

Calculation of standard time allowed = $\frac{600 \text{ pieces}}{10 \text{ pieces per hr}}$ = 60 hrs

Time taken: for 5 days @ 9 hrs per day (Monday to Friday)	= 45 hrs	
Saturday	= 5 hrs	= 50 hrs
Time saved		10 hrs

$$\text{Halsey-Weir system} = \text{Time taken} \times \text{Time rate} + \frac{40}{100} \times \text{Time saved} \times \text{Time rate}$$

$$= 50 \times 0.50 + \frac{40}{100} \times 10 \times 0.50 = \text{Rs. } 27$$

3. Rowan System

This incentive system was introduced by James Rowan of Scotland. Under this system also, the incentive is paid on the time saved as in the above-mentioned two methods. But a different method is used to calculate the bonus. Under this system, bonus hours are calculated as a proportion of the time taken which the time saved bears to the time allowed and they are paid on the basis of the time rate system. The following formula is applicable to compute wages under this system:

$$\text{Earnings} = \text{Time taken} \times \text{Time rate} + \frac{\text{Time saved}}{\text{Time allowed}} \times \text{Time taken} \times \text{Time rate}$$

Advantages:

(*i*) This system is more suitable to beginners and slow workers.

(*ii*) The employer benefits more from this system. So he provides good working conditions in the factories.

Disadvantages:

(*i*) This system of wage payment is not easily understood by employees.

(*ii*) This system is not beneficial to workers at high level efficiency.

PROBLEMS ON ROWAN SYSTEM

Problem–23

Mr. Avinash takes 9 hours to complete a job on daily wages and 6 hours on a scheme of payment by results. His day rate is Rs. 3 per hour. The material cost of the job is Rs. 20. Overhead are recovered at 150 per cent of the direct wages. Calculate the factory cost of the product under (*a*) Piece work plan and (*b*) Rowan plan.

(Mangalore University, B.Com., April 1992)

Solution:

Calculation of time saved

Time allowed	9 hours
Time taken	6 hours
Time saved	3 hours

(*a*) Earnings under piece work plan

Piece work wages are calculated on the time allowed at the rate Rs. 3 for 9 hours. It amounts to Rs. 27.

(b) Rowan plan

$$\text{Earnings} = \text{Time taken} \times \text{Time rate} + \frac{\text{Time saved}}{\text{Time allowed}} \times \text{Time taken} \times \text{Time rate}$$

$$= 6 \times 3 + \frac{3}{9} \times 6 \times 3$$

$$= 18 + 6 = \text{Rs. } 24$$

Statement of works cost

	Piece rate system	*Rowan system*
Materials	20.00	20.00
Wages	27.00	24.00
Prime cost	47.00	44.00
Works overhead	40.50	36.00
$\frac{150}{100} \times 27$		
$\frac{150}{100} \times 24$		
Works cost	87.50	80.00

Problem–24

A worker under the Halsey plan is paid Rs. 12 per week of 48 hours a week plus cost of living index bonus of 10 paise per hour. The time required to do a job is 8 hours which he completes in 6 hours. He is given bonus of 30% of time saved. Calculate the hourly rate of wage. Would it make any difference if he was paid under Rowan method?

(Gulbarga University, B.Com., November 1991)
(Nagarjuna University, B.Com., March 2003)

Solution:

Calculation of time saved

Time allowed	8 hours
Time taken	6 hours
Time saved	2 hours

$$\text{Calculation of hourly rate} = \frac{\text{Weekly wages}}{\text{No. of hrs in a week}}$$

$$= \frac{12}{48} = 0.25$$

$$\text{Halsey-Weir system} = \text{Time taken} \times \text{Time rate} + \frac{30}{100} \times \text{Time saved} \times \text{Time rate}$$

$$= 6 \times 0.25 + \frac{30}{100} \times 2 \times 0.25$$

$= 1.50 + 0.15 = 1.65$

Cost of living bonus 0.10 for 6 hours $= 0.60$

Total wages $= 2.25$

Calculation of wages under Rowan system

$$\text{Time taken} \times \text{Time rate} + \frac{\text{Time saved}}{\text{Time allowed}} \times \text{Time taken} \times \text{Time rate}$$

$$= \left[1.50 + \frac{2}{3} \times 1.5\right]$$

$$= 1.50 + 0.375 = 1.875$$

Cost of living bonus 0.600

2.475

Difference in wages

$2.475 - 2.250 = 0.225$

PROBLEMS ON COMBINATION OF DIFFERENT SYSTEMS OF INCENTIVES

Problem–25 (Time Rate, Guaranteed Piece Rate and Incentive System)

A workman's wages for a guaranteed 44 hour week is Rs. 10 per hour. The estimated time to produce one unit is 30 minutes and under incentive scheme, the time allowed is increased by 20%. During one week the workman manufactured 100 units. Calculate his gross wages under each of the following methods:

(*a*) Time rate

(*b*) Piece work with a guaranteed weekly wages

(*c*) Rowan system

(*d*) Halsey system *(Sri Sathya Sai University, B.Com. (Hons), August 2007)*

Solution: ***Working Notes:***

(1) Calculation of time saved:

Estimated time to produce one units $= \frac{30}{60}$ hrs

Estimated time to produce 100 units

in hrs $100 \times \frac{30}{60}$ $= 50$ hrs

Add 20% under incentives (20% of 50 hours) $= 10$ hrs

Time allowed 60 hrs

Time saved = Time allowed – Time taken

= 60 hrs – 44 hrs

= 16 hrs

(2) Calculation of guaranteed piece rate:

Time allowed for 1 unit = 30 mins

Add: 20% = 6 mins

36 mins

Piece rate:

For 60 mins Rs. 10

For 36 mins ?

$$\frac{10 \times 36}{60} = \text{Rs. } 6$$

(*a*) Time wages:

$$\text{Earnings} = \text{Time taken} \times \text{Time rate}$$
$$= 44 \text{ hrs} \times \text{Rs. } 10 = \text{Rs. } 440$$

(*b*) Guaranteed piece rate:

$$\text{Earnings} = \text{No. of units} \times \text{unit rate}$$
$$= 100 \times \text{Rs. } 6 = \text{Rs. } 600$$

(*c*) Rowan system:

$$\text{Time taken} \times \text{Time rate} + \frac{\text{Time saved}}{\text{Time allowed}} \times \text{Time taken} \times \text{Time rate}$$
$$= 44 \times 10 + \frac{16}{60} \times 44 \times 10$$
$$= 440 + 117.33 = \text{Rs. } 557.33$$

(*d*) Halsey system:

$$\text{Time taken} \times \text{Time rate} + \frac{50}{100} \times \text{Time saved} \times \text{Time rate}$$
$$= 44 \times 10 + \frac{50}{100} \times 16 \times 10$$
$$= 440 + 80 = \text{Rs. } 520$$

Problem–26 (Piece Rate and Incentive System)

Three workers Govind, Ram and Shyam produced 80, 100 and 120 pieces of a product 'X' on a particular day consisting of 8 hours a day in May 2005 in a factory. The time allowed for 10 pieces of product 'X' is one hour and the hourly rate is Rs. 10. Calculate the following for each of these workers.

(*i*) Earnings for the day and

(*ii*) Effective rate of earnings per hour under:

(*a*) Straight piece rate

(*b*) Halsey system

(c) Rowan system *(Sri Sathya Sai University, B.Com. (Hons), March 2006)*

Solution: ***Working Notes:***

(1) Calculation of time saved:

	Govind	Ram	Shyam
Production in units	80	100	120
Time allowed in hrs	80	100	120
@ 10 pieces per hrs	10	10	10
i.e., For 10 pieces = 1 hr			
For 80 pieces = $\frac{1 \times 80}{10}$ = 8 and so on	8	10	12
Time taken 1 day = 8 hrs	8	8	8
Time saved	0	2	4

(1) Piece rate

$$= \frac{\text{Rate per hour}}{\text{Units per hour}}$$

$$= \frac{\text{Rs. } 10}{10 \text{ hrs.}} = \text{Re. } 1$$

Earnings under piece rate system = No. of pieces × Rate per piece

Govind = 80 × 1 = Rs. 80

Ram = 100 × 1 = Rs. 100

Shyam = 120 × 1 = Rs. 120

(2) Halsey system:

$$\text{Time taken} \times \text{Time rate} + \frac{50}{100} \times \text{Time saved} \times \text{Time rate}$$

$$\text{Govind} = 8 \times 10 + \frac{50}{100} \times 0 \times 10$$
$$= 80 + 0 = \text{Rs. } 80$$

$$\text{Ram} = 8 \times 10 + \frac{50}{100} \times 2 \times 10$$
$$= 80 + 10 = \text{Rs. } 90$$

$$\text{Shyam} = 8 \times 10 + \frac{50}{100} \times 4 \times 10$$
$$= 80 + 20 = \text{Rs. } 100$$

(3) Rowan system:

$$\text{Time taken} \times \text{Time rate} + \frac{\text{Time saved}}{\text{Time allowed}} \times \text{Time taken} \times \text{Time rate}$$

$$\text{Govind} = 8 \times 10 + \frac{0}{8} \times 8 \times 10 = 80$$
$$= 80 + 0 = \text{Rs. } 80$$

$$\text{Ram} = 8 \times 10 + \frac{2}{10} \times 8 \times 10$$
$$= 80 + 16 = \text{Rs. } 96$$
$$\text{Shyam} = 8 \times 10 + \frac{4}{12} \times 8 \times 10$$
$$= 80 + 26.67 = \text{Rs. } 106.67$$

Calculation of effective rate:

	Govind	*Ram*	*Shyam*
(*a*) Straight piece rate	$\frac{80}{8} = 10$	$\frac{100}{8} = 12.5$	$\frac{120}{8} = 15$
(*b*) Halsey system	$\frac{80}{8} = 10$	$\frac{90}{8} = 11.25$	$\frac{100}{8} = 12.5$
(*c*) Rowan system	$\frac{80}{8} = 10$	$\frac{96}{8} = 12$	$\frac{106.67}{8} = 13.33$

Problem–27 (Halsey, Halsey-Weir, Rowan, Barth Premium System)

The following particulars apply to a factory where W, X, Y and Z work:

Normal rate per hour Rs. 5

Standard output per hour Rs. 5

In order to produce 200 units, time taken was as follows (in hours)

W	X	Y	Z
10	20	30	40

Required: Calculate the earnings per worker under:

(*a*) Halsey premium system.

(*b*) Halsey-Weir premium system.

(*c*) Rowan premium system.

(*d*) Barth premium system. *(Acharya Nagarjuna University, B.Com., June 2004)*

Solution:

$$\text{Standard time to produce 200 units} = \frac{200}{5} = 40 \text{ hours}$$

(*a*) Halsey premium system:

$$\text{Time taken} \times \text{Time rate} + \frac{50}{100} \times \text{Time saved} \times \text{Time rate}$$

$$W = 10 \times 5 + \frac{50}{100} \times 30 \times 5$$
$$= 50 + 75 = \text{Rs. } 125$$

$$X = 20 \times 5 + \frac{50}{100} \times 20 \times 5$$
$$= 100 + 50 = \text{Rs. } 150$$

$$Y = 30 \times 5 + \frac{50}{100} \times 10 \times 5$$
$$= 150 + 25 = \text{Rs. } 175$$
$$Z = 40 \times 5$$
$$= \text{Rs. } 200 \text{ (No bonus)}$$

(*b*) Halsey-Weir premium system:

$$\text{Time taken} \times \text{Time rate} + \frac{30}{100} \times \text{Time saved} \times \text{Time rate}$$

$$W = 10 \times 5 + \frac{30}{100} \times 30 \times 5$$
$$= 50 + 45 = \text{Rs. } 95$$
$$X = 20 \times 5 + \frac{30}{100} \times 20 \times 5$$
$$= 100 + 30 = \text{Rs. } 130$$
$$Y = 30 \times 5 + \frac{30}{100} \times 10 \times 5$$
$$= 150 + 15 = \text{Rs. } 165$$
$$Z = 40 \times 5 = \text{Rs. } 200 \text{ (No bonus)}$$

(*c*) Rowan premium system:

$$\text{Time taken} \times \text{Time rate} + \frac{\text{Time saved}}{\text{Time allowed}} \times \text{Time taken} \times \text{Time rate}$$
$$W = 10 \times 5 + \frac{30}{40} \times 10 \times 5$$
$$= 50 + 37.50 = \text{Rs. } 87.50$$
$$X = 20 \times 5 + \frac{20}{40} \times 20 \times 5$$
$$= 100 + 50 = \text{Rs. } 150$$
$$Y = 30 \times 5 + \frac{10}{40} \times 30 \times 5$$
$$= 150 + 37.50 = \text{Rs. } 187.50$$
$$Z = 40 \times 5 = \text{Rs. } 200$$

(*d*) Barth premium system:

$$= \text{Rate per hour} \times \sqrt{\text{Standard time} \times \text{Time taken}}$$
$$W = 5 \times \sqrt{40 \times 10} = \text{Rs. } 100$$
$$X = 5 \times \sqrt{40 \times 20} = \text{Rs. } 141.42$$

$$Y = 5 \times \sqrt{40 \times 30} = \text{Rs. } 173.21$$

$$Z = 5 \times \sqrt{40 \times 40} = \text{Rs. } 200$$

Problem–28 (Halsey and Rowan Incentive System)

A worker produced 200 units in a week time. The guaranteed weekly wage payment for 45 hours is Rs. 81. The expected time to produce one unit is 15 minutes which is raised further by 20% under incentive system. What will be the earning per hour of that worker under Halsey and Rowan system of wage system ?

(Sri Sathya Sai University, B.Com. (Hons), March 2007)

Solution: ***Working Notes:***

Calculation of time rate:

$$\frac{\text{Weekly wages}}{\text{Weekly hours}} = \frac{81}{45} = \text{Rs. } 1.80$$

Calculation of time saved:

Time allowed under piece rate system	=	15 mins
Add: 20% increase under incentive system	=	3 mins
		18 mins

For 1 unit	18 mins		
For 200 units	18 × 200	=	3600 mins
			or 60 hrs

Time allowed	=	60 hrs
Time taken	=	45 hrs
Time saved		15 hrs

(1) Halsey system:

$$\text{Time taken} \times \text{Time rate} + \frac{50}{100} \times \text{Time saved} \times \text{Time rate}$$

$$= 45 \times 1.80 + \frac{50}{100} \times 15 \times 1.80$$

$$= 81 + 13.50 = \text{Rs. } 94.50$$

$$\text{Earnings per hour} = \frac{94.50}{45} = \text{Rs. } 2.10$$

(2) Rowan system:

$$\text{Time taken} \times \text{Time rate} + \frac{\text{Time saved}}{\text{Time allowed}} \times \text{Time taken} \times \text{Time rate}$$

$$= 45 \times 1.80 + \frac{15}{60} \times 45 \times 1.80$$

$$= 81 + 20.25 = \text{Rs. } 101.25$$

$$\text{Earnings per hour} = \frac{101.25}{45} = \text{Rs. } 2.25$$

Problem–29 (Rowan System)

Sri Rajesh working under Rowan's plan earns Rs. 27.50 by completing the task for which the time allowed is 8 hours, at the rate of Rs. 4 per hour. Calculate the time taken to complete the task as well as bonus earned. *(Bangalore University, B.Com., April 2002)*

Solution:

Let time taken be denoted by 'T'

Earnings under Rowan system:

$$\text{Earnings} = \text{Time taken} \times \text{Time rate} + \frac{\text{Time allowed} - \text{Time taken}}{\text{Time allowed}} \times \text{Time taken} \times \text{Time rate}$$

$$27.50 = T \times 4 + \frac{8 - T}{8} \times T \times 4$$

$$27.50 = 4\,T + \frac{(8 - T)\,T}{2}$$

$$27.50 = \frac{8\,T + 8\,T - T^2}{2\,(\text{L.C.M.})}$$

$$27.50 \times 2 = 8\,T + 8\,T - T^2$$

$$55 = 8\,T + 8\,T - T^2$$

$$T^2 - 16\,T + 55 = 0$$

$$T^2 - 5\,T - 11\,T + 55 = 0$$

$$T\,(T - 5) - 11\,(T - 5) = 0$$

$$(T - 5)\,(T - 11) = 0$$

$$T = 5 \text{ or } 11$$

As time allowed is 8 hours T (Time taken cannot be 11)

$$\textbf{Bonus} = \left(\frac{\text{Time allowed} - \text{Time taken}}{\text{Time allowed}}\right) \times \text{Time taken} \times \text{Time rate}$$

$$= \frac{8 - 5}{8} \times 5 \times 4 = \text{Rs. } 7.5$$

Problem–30 (Halsey and Rowan)

Sri Chennabasappa finishes a work in 480 hours as against 600 hours allowed. His hourly rate is Rs. 5. He gets a dearness allowance of Rs. 16 per day of 8 hours worked in addition to his wages. Calculate his total income under Halsey (50 – 50) and Rowan incentive plans.

If the material cost be Rs. 5000 and factory oncost is recovered at 50% of wages, find out factory cost under both the methods. *(Bangalore University, B.Com., October 2001)*

Solution:

Time allowed	600 hours
Time taken	480 hours
Time saved	120 hours

(1) Halsey system:

$$\text{Time taken} \times \text{Time rate} + \frac{50}{100} \times \text{Time saved} \times \text{Time rate}$$

$$= 8 \times 5 + \frac{50}{100} \times 120 \times 5$$

$$= 40 + 300 = 340$$

wages under Halsey system =	340
Dearness allowance =	16
Total wages	356

(2) Rowan system:

$$\text{Time taken} \times \text{Time rate} + \frac{\text{Time saved}}{\text{Time allowed}} \times \text{Time taken} \times \text{Time rate}$$

$$= 8 \times 5 + \frac{120}{600} \times 8 \times 5$$

$$= 40 + 8 = 48$$

wages under Rowan system =	48
Add: Dearness allowance =	16
Total wages	64

Statement showing factory cost

	Halsey system	Rowan system
Materials	5000	5000
Wages	356	64
Prime cost	5356	5064
Factory overhead	178	32
Halsey — $\frac{50}{100} \times 356$		
Rowan — $\frac{50}{100} \times 64$		
Factory cost	5534	5096

Problem–31 (Piece Work with Guaranteed Wage–Halsey and Rowan Plan)

Wage negotiations are going on in a company with the Recognised Labour Union and the management requests you as the cost accountant of the company to formulate an incentive wage scheme with a view to increasing productivity.

The case of three representative X, Y and Z, who produce respectively 1500 units, 1200 units and 900 units in a normal week of 40 hours is taken up for study.

Assuming that day wages would be guaranteed at Rs. 5 per hour and the piece rate would be based on a standard hourly output of 25 units. Calculate the earnings and labour cost per 100 pieces of each of the above three workers under:

(1) Piece-work with a guaranteed weekly wage

(2) Halsey-premium plan

(3) Rowan premium plan *(Calcutta University, B.Com. (Hons), 1995)*

Solution:

Standard rate per hour = Rs. 5

Standard output per hour = 25 units

$$\text{Standard rate per unit} = \frac{\text{Rs. } 5}{25 \text{ units}} = 0.20 \text{ per unit}$$

(i) Day wages = Time taken × Rate per hour

= 40 hours × Rs. 5 = Rs. 200 for each worker

(ii) Piece wages = Units produced × Rate per unit

X = 1500 × 0.20 = Rs. 300

Y = 1200 × 0.20 = Rs. 240

Z = 900 × 0.20 = Rs. 180

Since Z's piece wages is less than time wages he will get the guaranteed piece wages of Rs. 200.

Calculation of time allowed

$$\frac{\text{Units produced}}{\text{Std units per hour}}$$

$$X = \frac{1500}{25} = 60$$

$$Y = \frac{1200}{25} = 48$$

$$Z = \frac{900}{25} = 36$$

Calculation of time saved

Time saved = Time allowed – Time taken

X = 60 – 40 = 20 hrs

Y = 48 – 40 = 8 hrs

Z = 36 – 40 = Nil

Halsey system

$$\text{Time taken} \times \text{Time rate} + \frac{50}{100} \times \text{Time saved} \times \text{Time rate}$$

$$X = 40 \times 5 + \frac{50}{100} \times 20 \times 5$$
$$= 200 + 50 = \text{Rs. } 250$$
$$Y = 40 \times 5 + \frac{50}{100} \times 8 \times 5$$
$$= 200 + 20 = \text{Rs. } 220$$
$$Z = 40 \times 5 + \frac{50}{100} \times 0 \times 5$$
$$= 200 + 0 = \text{Rs. } 200$$

Rowan system

$$\text{Time taken} \times \text{Time rate} + \frac{\text{Time saved}}{\text{Time allowed}} \times \text{Time taken} \times \text{Time rate}$$

$$X = 40 \times 5 + \frac{20}{60} \times 40 \times 5$$
$$= 200 + 66.66 = 266.66$$
$$Y = 40 \times 5 + \frac{8}{48} \times 40 \times 5$$
$$= 200 + 33.33 = 233.33$$
$$Z = 40 \times 5 + \frac{0}{60} \times 40 \times 5$$
$$= 200 + 0 = 200$$

Labour cost per 100 units under piece rate with guaranteed wages

$$= \frac{\text{Earning}}{\text{Units produced}}$$

$$X = \frac{300}{1500} = 0.20$$
$$Y = \frac{2400}{1200} = 2$$
$$Z = \frac{200}{900} = 0.22$$

Labour cost per 100 units under Halsey system

$$X = \frac{250}{1500} = 0.16$$
$$Y = \frac{220}{1200} = 0.18$$
$$Z = \frac{200}{900} = 0.22$$

Labour cost per 100 units under Rowan system

$$X = \frac{266.66}{1500} = 0.17$$

$$Y = \frac{233.33}{1200} = 0.19$$

$$Z = \frac{200}{900} = 0.22$$

Problem–32 (Rowan System)

A worker whose day-work wages is Rs. 2.50 an hour, received production bonus under the Rowan system. He carried out the following work in a 48 hour weak:

Job 1	1500 items at 4 hours per 1000
Job 2	1800 items at 3 hours per 1000
Job 3	9000 items at 6 hours per 1000
Job 4	1500 items for which no standard time was fixed and it was arranged that the worker would be paid a bonus of 25%. Actual time on the job was 4 hours.
Job 5	2000 items at 8 hours per 1000, each item was estimated to be half finished.

Job 2 was carried out on a machine running at 90% efficiency and extra allowance of $\frac{1}{9}$th actual time was given to compensate the worker.

4 hours were lost due to power cut. Calculate the earnings of the worker clearly stating your assumptions for the treatment given by you for the hours lost due to power cut.

(ICWA, Inter Stage I, December 2001)

Solution: *Working Notes:*

(1) Calculation of time allowed:

Job 1

For 1000 items = 4 hrs

For 1500 items $= \frac{1500 \times 4}{1000}$ = 6 Hrs

Job 2

For 1000 items = 3 hours

For 1800 items $= \frac{1800 \times 3}{1000} = 5.4$ Hrs

Add: Allowance $\frac{1}{9}$th = 0.6

= 6 Hrs.

Job 3

For 1000 items = 6 hrs

For 9000 items $= \frac{9000 \times 6}{1000}$ = 54 Hrs

Job 4

Actual time allowed on Job No. 4 = 4 hrs

Add: Bonus 25% thereof = 1 hrs = 1 hr

= 5 hrs

Job 5

For 1000 items = 8 hrs

$$\text{For 2000 items} = \frac{2000 \times 8}{1000} = 16 \text{ hrs}$$

But $\frac{1}{2}$ finished = 8 hrs

Total time allowed = 79 hrs

Time saved = Time allowed – Time taken

= 79 – 44 = 35

(2) Calculation of time taken:

= Gross time worked – Lost time due to power cut

= 48 – 4 = 44 hrs

(3) As 4 hours are lost due to power cut which is beyond the control, the wages payable *i.e.* 4 hrs × 2.5 = Rs. 10 should be treated as factory overhead.

(4) As 4 hours are not taken into account for arriving at time saved, the incentive is calculated on 44 hours and not 48 hours.

$$\text{Earnings} = \text{Time taken} \times \text{Time rate} + \frac{\text{Time saved}}{\text{Time allowed}} \times \text{Time taken} \times \text{Time rate}$$

$$= 48 \times 2.50 + \frac{35}{79} \times 44 \times 2.50$$

$$= 120 + 48.73 = 168.73$$

Problem–33 (Guaranteed Wages and Rowan System)

A company is undecided as to what kind of wage scheme should be introduced. The following particulars have been compiled in respect of three systems, which are under consideration of the management:

	Workers		
	A	*B*	*C*
Actual hours worked in a week	38	40	34
Hourly rate of wages	Rs. 6	Rs. 5	Rs. 7.20
Production in units:			
Product P	21	–	60
Product Q	36	–	135
Product R	46	25	–

Standard time allowed per unit of each product is:

	P	*Q*	*R*
Minutes	12	18	30

For the purpose of piece rate, each minute is valued at Re. 0.10.

You are required to calculate the wages of each worker under:

(*i*) Guaranteed hourly rates basis.

(*ii*) Piece work earning basis, but guaranteed at 75% of basic pay (guaranteed hourly rate) if his earnings are less than 50% of basic pay.

(*iii*) Premium bonus basis where the worker receives bonus based on Rowan scheme.

(C.A. Inter, P.E. II, November 2002)

Solution:

Wages under time rate system:

= Time taken × Time rate

A = 38 × 6 = 228

B = 40 × 5 = 200

C = 34 × 7.20 = 244.80

Working Note:

Calculation of piece rate

= Time per unit in minutes × Piece rate per minute

P = 12 × 0.10 = Rs. 1.20

Q = 18 × 0.10 = Rs. 1.80

R = 30 × 0.10 = Rs. 3.00

Wages under piece rate system: Worker A

= No. of pieces × Rate per piece

P = 21 × 1.20 = 25.20

Q = 36 × 1.80 = 64.80

R = 46 × 3.00 = 138.00

Total 228.00

Worker B

P = NIL = NIL

Q = NIL = NIL

R = 25 × 3 = 75

Total 75

Worker C

P = 60 × 1.20 = 72

Q = 135 × 1.80 = 243

R = NIL = NIL

Total 315

Since each worker has been guaranteed at 75% of basic pay, if his earnings are less than 50% of basic pay, therefore, workers A and C will be paid the wages as computed, viz.,

Rs. 228 and Rs. 315 respectively. The computed wage of worker B is Rs. 75 which is less than 50% of basic pay, viz., Rs. 100. Therefore he would be paid $\frac{75}{100} \times 200$ = Rs. 150.

Calculation of time allowed to each worker

Worker A = 21 units × 12 mins + 36 units × 18 mins + 46 units × 30 mins
= 2280 mins or 38 hrs

B = 25 units × 30 mins
= 750 mins or 12.5 hrs

C = 60 units × 12 mins + 135 units × 18 mins
= 720 mins + 2430 mins
= 3150 mins or 52.50 hrs

Calculation of time saved

Time saved = Time allowed – Time taken

A = 38 – 38 = NIL

B = 12.5 – 40 = NIL

C = 52.50 – 34 = 18.50

Rowan system

$$= \text{Time taken} \times \text{time rate} + \frac{\text{Time saved}}{\text{Time allowed}} \times \text{Time taken} \times \text{Time rate}$$

A = 38 × 6 + NIL
= Rs. 228

B = 40 × 5 + NIL
= Rs. 200

$$C = 34 \times 7.20 + \frac{18.50}{52.50} \times 34 \times 7.20$$
= 244.80 + 86.26
= Rs. 331.06

Problem–34 (Time Rate, Piece Rate, Halsey and Rowan System)

The existing incentive system of Alpha Limited is as under:

Normal working week	5 days of 8 hours each plans 3 late shifts of 3 hours each
Rate of payment	Day work Rs. 150 per hour
	Late shift Rs. 225 per hour

Average output per operator for 49-hours weak, *i.e.,* including 3 late shifts : 120 articles

In order to increase output and eliminate overtime, it was decided to switch on to a system of payment by results. The following information is obtained:

Time rate (as usual)	: Rs. 160 per hour
Basic time allowed for 15 Articles	: 5 hours
Piece-work rate	: Add 20% to basic piece rate
Premium bonus	: Add 50% to time

Required:

(*i*) Prepare a statement showing hours worked, weekly earnings, number of articles produced and labour cost per article for one operator under the following systems:

(*a*) Existing time rate

(*b*) Piece rate system

(*c*) Rowan system

(*d*) Halsey system

Assume that 135 articles are produced in a 40-hour week under straight piece work; Rowan premium system, and Halsey premium system.

(C.A., P.E. II, Group 11, November 2005)

Solution:

(*a*) Earnings under time rate:

Weekly wages:

	Rs.
Normal wages 40 hrs @ Rs. 160 per hr =	6400
O.T wages 9 hrs @ Rs. 225 per hr =	2025
	Rs. 8425

(*b*) Piece rate system:

Basic time: 5 hours for 15 articles.

Cost of 15 articles at hourly rate of Rs. 160 per hr

= Rs. 800

Add: 20% = Rs. 160

Rs. 960

$$\text{Rate of per article} = \frac{960}{15} = \text{Rs. } 64$$

Earning for the week = 135 articles × Rs. 64

= Rs. 8640

(*c*) Rowan system:

Basic time for 15 articles = 5 hrs

Add: 50% of time = $2\frac{1}{2}$ hrs

= $7\frac{1}{2}$ hrs

For 15 articles 7.5 hrs is time allowed

$$\text{For 135 articles } \frac{7.5 \times 135}{15} = 67.5 \text{ hrs}$$

Less: Time taken = 40 hrs

Time saved 27.5 hrs

$$\text{Earnings} = \text{T.T} \times \text{T.R} + \frac{\text{T.S}}{\text{T.A}} \times \text{T. T} \times \text{T. R}$$

$$= 40 \times 160 + \frac{27.5}{67.5} \times 40 \times 160$$

$$= \text{Rs. } 9007.\ 41$$

(d) Halsey system:

$$= \text{T.T} \times \text{T.R} + \frac{50}{100} \times \text{T.S} \times \text{T.R}$$

$$= 40 \times 160 + \frac{50}{100} \times 27.5 \times 160$$

$$= \text{Rs. } 8600$$

Problem–35 (Accelerated Premium System)

The standard hours of job 'X' is 100 hours. The job has been completed by Amar in 60 hours, Akbar in 70 hours and Anthony in 95 hours. The bonus system applicable to the job is as follows:

Percentage of time saved to time allowed	*Bonus*
Savings up to 10%	10% of time saved
From 11% to 20%	15% of time saved
From 21% to 40%	20% of time saved
From 41% to 100%	25% of time saved

The rate of pay is Re. 1 per hour.

Required:

Calculate the total earnings of each worker and also the rate of earnings per hour

(Acharya Nagarjuna University, B.Com., March 2004)

Solution:

Time saved = Standard time – Actual time taken

Amar = 100 – 60 = 40 hours

Akbar = 100 – 70 = 30 hours

Anthony = 100 – 95 = 5 hours

Percentage of time saved:

$$\text{Amar} = \frac{40}{100} \times 100 = 40\%$$

$$\text{Akbar} = \frac{30}{100} \times 100 = 30\%$$

$$\text{Anthony} = \frac{5}{100} \times 100 = 5\%$$

Earnings of Amar:

$$= 60 \times 1 + \frac{20}{100} (40 \times 1)$$

$$= 60 + 8 = \text{Rs. } 68$$

$$\text{Earnings per hour} = \frac{68}{60} = \text{Rs. } 1.13$$

Earnings of Akbar:

$$= 70 \times 1 + \frac{20}{100} (30 \times 1)$$

$$= 70 + 6 = \text{Rs. } 76$$

$$\text{Earnings per hour} = \frac{76}{70} = \text{Rs. } 1.09$$

Earnings of Anthony:

$$= 95 \times 1 + \frac{10}{100} (5 \times 1)$$

$$= 95 + 0.50 = \text{Rs. } 95.50$$

$$\text{Earnings per hour} = \frac{95.50}{95} = \text{Rs. } 1.005$$

PROBLEMS ON COMBINATION OF DIFFERENT SYSTEMS OF INCENTIVES

Problem–36

During the first week of April 1990, a workman Mr. Shyam manufactured 300 units. He receives wage for a 48 hours week at the rate of Rs. 4 per hour which is guaranteed. The estimated time to produce one article is 10 minutes, and under incentive scheme the time allowed is increased by 20%. Calculate his gross wages according to (*a*) piece work with a guaranteed weekly wages, (*b*) Halsey premium bonus, (*c*) Rowan system.

(University of Kerala, B.Com., April 1991; Andhra University, M.Com., April 1991)

Solution:

(*a*) Piece work with a guaranteed weekly wages:

Under this system Shyam is paid for 60 hrs at the rate of Rs. 4 per hour, *i.e.*, Rs. 240. This is in the absence of the availability of piece rate.

(*b*) Halsey premium bonus

Time allowed — Std. time for 1 article	= 10 mins
Add: 20% incentive under incentive system	= 2 mins
For 1 article	= 12 mins
For 300 articles 300 × 12 mins	= 3,600 mins

or in hours $= \dfrac{3{,}600 \text{ mins}}{60} = 60$ hrs

Time taken $= 48$ hrs

Time saved $= 12$ hrs

$$\text{Earnings} = \text{Time taken} \times \text{Time rate} + \frac{50}{100} \times \text{Time saved} \times \text{Time rate}$$

$$= 48 \times 4 + \frac{50}{100} \times 12 \times 4$$

$$= 192 + 24 = \text{Rs. } 216$$

(*c*) Rowan system:

$$\text{Time taken} \times \text{Time rate} + \frac{\text{Time saved}}{\text{Time allowed}} \times \text{Time taken} \times \text{Time rate}$$

$$= 48 \times 4 + \frac{12}{60} \times 48 \times 4$$

$$= 192 + 38.40 = \text{Rs. } 230.40$$

Problem–37

Out of the Halsey and Rowan plans of wage payment, which method will be more beneficial to a worker who saves less than 50% of the standard time? Illustrate your answer.

(C.S., Inter, June 2000)

Solution:

To a worker who saves less than 50% of the standard time, Rowan premium plan of wage payment is always beneficial as illustrated below:

Suppose the standard time to do a job is 10 hours

Actual time taken is only 6 hours

Wage rate is Re. 1 per hour

$$\text{Earnings under Halsey system} = \text{Time taken} \times \text{Time rate} + \frac{50}{100} \times \text{Time saved} \times \text{Time rate}$$

$$= 6 \times 1 + \frac{50}{100} \times 4 \times 1$$

$$= 6 + 2$$

$$= \text{Rs. } 8$$

$$\text{Rowan system} = \text{Time taken} \times \text{Time rate} + \frac{\text{Time saved}}{\text{Time allowed}} \times \text{Time taken} \times \text{Time rate}$$

$$= 6 \times 1 + \frac{4}{10} \times 6 \times 1$$

$$= 6 + 2.40 = \text{Rs. } 8.40$$

Problem–38

What is the difference between Halsey plan and Rowan plan of remunerating workers ? Which one is more beneficial to the workers ? *(C.S., Inter, June 1998)*

Solution:

Under Halsey plan, time rate is guaranteed. Standard time and work are predetermined. The bonus is 50% of the wages for standard time saved.

$$\text{Total wages} = \text{Time taken} \times \text{Hourly rate} + \frac{50}{100} \times \text{Time saved} \times \text{Hourly rate}$$

under the Rowan plan also, the time rate is guaranteed. But here the percentage of bonus to the wages earned is that which the time saved bears to the standard time.

$$\text{Total wages} = \text{Time taken} \times \text{Hourly rate} + \frac{\text{Time saved}}{\text{Time allowed}} \times \text{Time taken} \times \text{Time rate}$$

Comparison: If the worker finishes the work in half the time fixed for it, the wages earned under Halsey and Rowan plans will be the same. If the time saved is less than 50% of the standard time, the Rowan plan is better. If the time saved is more than 50% of the standard time, the Halsey plan is better.

Problem–39

A worker is allowed 10 hours to complete a job on daily wages. He takes 6 hours to complete the job under a scheme of payment by results. His day rate is Rs. 6 per hour and piece rate is Rs. 36. The material cost of the product is Rs. 40 and the overheads are charged at 150% of the total direct wages. Calculate the factory cost of the product under.

(*i*) Piece rate system

(*ii*) Rowan system

(*iii*) Halsey system *(C.S., Inter, December 1998)*

Solution:

(*i*) **Piece rate system**

Number of pieces are not given in this problem. Instead time allowed is given as 10 hrs to complete a job. Presuming that the worker completes one job and is paid Rs. 36 for that job, his piece wage for a day is Rs. 36.

(*ii*) **Rowan system**

$$\text{Time taken} \times \text{Time rate} + \frac{\text{Time saved}}{\text{Time allowed}} \times \text{Time taken} \times \text{Time rate}$$

$$= 6 \times 6 + \frac{4}{10} \times 6 \times 6$$

$$= 36 + 14.40$$

$$= 50.40$$

(*iii*) **Halsey system**

$$\text{Time taken} \times \text{Time rate} + \frac{50}{100} \times \text{Time saved} \times \text{Time rate}$$

$$= 6 \times 6 + \frac{50}{100} \times 4 \times 6$$
$$= 36 + 12$$
$$= 48$$

Factory cost under three system

	Piece rate	Rowan system	Halsey system
Materials	40	40	40
Wages	36	50.40	48
Factory overhead (150% of direct wages)	54	75.60	72
	130	166	160

Problem–40

A firm employs five workers at an hourly rate of Rs. 2.00 During the week, they worked for four days for a total period of 40 hours each and completed a job for which the standard time was 48 hours for each worker. Calculate the labour cost under the Halsey system and Rowan system of incentive plan payments. *(C.S., Inter, June 1996)*

Solution:

Calculation of time saved

Standard time allowed	48 hrs × 5 workers	= 240 hrs
Actual time allowed	40 hrs × 5 workers	= 200 hrs
	Time saved	40 hrs

1. Halsey system

$$\text{Time taken} \times \text{Time rate} + \frac{50}{100} \times \text{Time saved} \times \text{Time rate}$$
$$= 200 \times 2 + \frac{50}{100} \times 40 \times 2$$
$$= 400 + 40 = \text{Rs. } 440$$

2. Rowan system

$$\text{Time taken} \times \text{Time rate} + \frac{\text{Time saved}}{\text{Time allowed}} \times \text{Time taken} \times \text{Time rate}$$
$$= 200 \times 2 + \frac{40}{240} \times 200 \times 2$$
$$= 400 + 67 = \text{Rs. } 467$$

Problem–41

A skilled worker in XYZ Ltd. is paid a guaranteed wage rate of Rs. 30 per hour. The standard time per unit for a particular product is 4 hours. P, a machineman, has been paid wages under the Rowan incentive plan and he had earned an effective hourly rate of Rs. 37.50 on the manufacture of that particular product.

What could have been his total earnings and effective hourly rate, had he been put on Halsey incentive scheme (50%) ? *(C.A., Inter, November 1999)*

Solution:

Let 'T' hours be the total time worked in hours by machineman 'P'

Rate per hour = Rs. 30

Standard time = 4 hours per unit

Effective hourly earnings rate = Rs. 37.50

$$\text{Earnings} = \text{Time taken} \times \text{Time rate} + \frac{\text{Time saved}}{\text{Time allowed}} \times \text{Time taken} \times \text{Time rate}$$

$$37.5\ T = T \times 30 + \frac{(4 - T)}{4} \times T \times 30$$

$$37.5 = 30 + (4 - T) \times 7.5 \qquad \text{(T is common)}$$

$$37.5 = 30 + 30 - 7.5\ T \qquad \text{(By removing simple brackets)}$$

$$37.5 - 60 = -7.5\ T$$

$$-22.5 = -7.5\ T$$

$$T = \frac{22.5}{7.5} = 3 \text{ hours}$$

Halsey system

$$\text{Time taken} \times \text{Time rate} + \frac{50}{100} \times \text{Time saved} \times \text{Time rate}$$

$$= 3 \times 30 + \frac{50}{100} \times 1 \times 30$$

$$= 90 + 15 = \text{Rs. } 105$$

Problem–42

A job can be executed either through workman A or B. A takes 32 hours to complete the job while B finishes it in 30 hours. The standard time to finish the job is 40 hours.

The hourly wage rate is same for both the works. In addition the workman A is entitled to receive bonus according to Halsey plan (50% sharing) while B is paid bonus as per Rowan plan. The works overhead are absorbed on the job at Rs. 7.50 per labour hour worked. The factory cost of the job comes to Rs. 2,600 irrespective of the workman engaged.

Find out the hourly wage rate and cost of raw materials input. Also show cost against each element of cost included in factory cost. *(C.A., Inter, November 1997)*

Solution:

Calculation of time saved

	A	*B*
Standard time allowed	40	40
Actual time taken	32	30
Time saved	8	10

$$\text{Halsey system} = \text{Time taken} \times \text{Time rate} + \frac{50}{100} \times \text{Time saved} \times \text{Time rate}$$

$$= 32 \times x + \frac{50}{100} \times 8 \times x$$

$$= 32x + 4x$$

$$= 36x$$

$$\text{Rowan system} = \text{Time taken} \times \text{Time rate} + \frac{\text{Time saved}}{\text{Time allowed}} \times \text{Time taken} \times \text{Time rate}$$

$$= 30 \times x + \frac{10}{40} \times 30 \times x$$

$$= 30x + 7.5x = 37.5x$$

Statement of factory cost of the job

	A	*B*
Material cost (assumed to be)	y	y
Wages	$36x$	$37.5x$
Works overhead	240	225
Factory cost	2,600	2,600

The above particulars can be written as follows:

$$36x + y + 240 = 2,600 \quad \text{...(1)}$$

$$37.5x + y + 225 = 2,600 \quad \text{...(2)}$$

Substracting (1) from (2), we have

$$1.5x - 15 = 0$$

or $$1.5x = 15$$

or $$x = \frac{15}{1.5} = \text{Rs. 10 per hour}$$

On substituting the value of x in (1)

$$36x + y + 240 = 2,600$$

$$36 \times 10 + y + 240 = 2,600$$

$$360 + y + 240 = 2,600$$

$$y = 2,600 - 600$$

$$y = 2,000$$

Hence the wage rate per hour is Rs. 10 and the cost of raw material input is Rs. 2000 on the job.

Problem–43

Calculate the earnings of a worker under (*i*) Halsey plan and (*ii*) Rowan plan from the following particulars:

(*i*) Hourly rate of wages guaranteed 0.50 paise per hour

(*ii*) Standard time for producing one dozen articles—3 hours

(*iii*) Actual time taken by the worker to produce, 20 dozen articles—48 hours.

(C.A., Inter, November 1998)

Solution:

Calculation of time saved

Time allowed for producing one dozen articles	=	3 hrs
∴ Time allowed for producing 20 dozen articles	=	60 hrs
Time taken for producing 20 dozen articles	=	48 hrs
Time saved	=	12 hrs

Halsey system

$$\text{Time taken} \times \text{Time rate} + \frac{50}{100} \times \text{Time saved} \times \text{Time rate}$$

$$= 48 \times 0.50 + \frac{50}{100} \times 12 \times 0.50$$

$$= 24 + 3 = \text{Rs. } 27$$

Rowan system

$$\text{Time taken} \times \text{Time rate} + \frac{\text{Time saved}}{\text{Time allowed}} \times \text{Time taken} \times \text{Time rate}$$

$$= 48 \times 0.50 + \frac{12}{60} \times 48 \times 0.50$$

$$= 24 + 4.80 = \text{Rs. } 28.80$$

Problem–44

A worker produced 200 units in a week's time. The guaranteed weekly wage payment for 45 hours is Rs. 81. The expected time to produce one unit is 15 minutes which is raised further by 20% under incentive scheme. What will be the earnings per hour of that worker under Halsey (50% sharing) and Rowan bonus schemes ? *(C.A., Inter, May 1995)*

Solution:

Calculation of time saved

Time allowed under piece rate system	=	15 mins
Add: 20% increase under incentive system	=	3 mins
		18 mins.

For 1 unit	—	18 mins		
For 200 units	—	18 × 200	=	3,600 mins
Expressed in hours		$\frac{3,600}{60}$	=	60 hrs
Time taken			=	45 hrs
		Time saved		15 hrs

Halsey system

$$\text{Time taken} \times \text{Time rate} + \frac{50}{100} \times \text{Time saved} \times \text{Time rate}$$

$$= 45 \times 1.80 + \frac{50}{100} \times 15 \times 1.80$$

$$= 81 + 13.50 = \text{Rs. } 94.50$$

$$\text{Earnings per hour} = \text{Rs. } \frac{94.50}{45} = \text{Rs. } 2.10 \text{ per hour}$$

Rowan system

$$\text{Time taken} \times \text{Time rate} + \frac{\text{Time saved}}{\text{Time allowed}} \times \text{Time taken} \times \text{Time rate}$$

$$= 45 \times 1.80 + \frac{15}{60} \times 45 \times 1.80$$

$$= 81 + 20.25 = \text{Rs. } 101.25$$

$$\text{Earnings per hour} = \text{Rs. } \frac{101.25}{45} = \text{Rs. } 2.25 \text{ per hour}$$

Working Note:

$$\text{Calculation of time rate} = \text{Rs. } \frac{81}{45 \text{ hrs}} = \text{Rs. } 1.80$$

4. Accelerated premium system or sliding scale bonus system

Under this system as in the case of earlier methods a standard output or hour is specified. The actual performance or hours of time taken is compared with standard output or time. Bonus is paid at different rates for different level of efficiency. Under this method a direct relationship exists between the efficiency of workers and the wages earned by them.

Problem–45

What will be the earning of a worker at Re. 0.55 per hour when he takes 140 hours to do a volume of work for which the standard time allowed is 200 hours? The plan of payment of hours is on a sliding scale as under:

Within the first 10% saving in standard time, bonus is 40% of time saved.

Within the second 10% saving in time, bonus is 50% of time saved.

Within the third 10% saving in standard time, bonus is 60% of time saved.

Within the fourth 10% saving in standard time, bonus is 70% of time saved.

For the rest, bonus is 75% of time saved.

(University of Madras, B.Com., March 1992; Karnataka University, B.Com., April 1992)

Solution:

Standard time allowed	200 hours
Actual time taken	140 hours
Time saved	60 hours

Calculation of percentage of time saved to standard time

$$\frac{60}{200} \times 100 = 30\%$$

Calculation of the number of hours for which bonus will be allowed.

(*a*) For the first 10% of time saved, *i.e.*, bonus is allowed for 40% of time saved

$$200 \times \frac{10}{100} \times \frac{40}{100} = 8 \text{ hours}$$

(*b*) For the next 10% of time saved, bonus will be allowed for 50% of time saved, *i.e.*,

$$200 \times \frac{10}{100} \times \frac{50}{100} = 10 \text{ hours}$$

(*c*) For the next 10% of time saved, bonus will be allowed for 60% of time saved, *i.e.*,

$$200 \times \frac{10}{100} \times \frac{60}{100} = 12 \text{ hours}$$

$$30 \text{ hours}$$

Statement showing earnings of worker

Time wages — 140 hrs @ Re. 0.55 per hour	77.00
Bonus for 30 hours (30 × 0.55)	16.50
Total	Rs. 93.50

5. Barth variable plan

This incentive system is meant for new entrants, *i.e.*, beginners and for unskilled workers. The purpose is to encourage workers to learn the job and to improve their performance. The following formula is used to calculate earnings under this method.

$$\text{Earnings} = \text{Rate per hour} \times \sqrt{\text{Standard time} \times \text{Actual time}}$$

Problem–46

Calculate the earnings under Barth variable plan from the following data:

Time allowed	— 15 hours
Time taken	X — 12 hours, Y — 10 hours, Z — 8 hours
Time rate	— Rs. 4 per hour

Solution:

$$\text{Earnings} = \text{Rate per hour} \times \sqrt{\text{Standard time} \times \text{Actual time}}$$

$$X = 4 \times \sqrt{15 \times 12} = 4 \times \sqrt{180}$$

$$= 4 \times 13.4 = \text{Rs. } 53.60$$

$$Y = 4 \times \sqrt{15 \times 10} = 4 \times \sqrt{150}$$

$$= 4 \times 12.2 = \text{Rs. } 48.80$$

$$Z = 4 \times \sqrt{15 \times 8} = 4 \times \sqrt{120}$$

$$= 4 \times 10.1 = \text{Rs. } 40.40$$

6. Bedaux plan

This system was introduced by C.E. Bedaux. The following are the important features of this system:

(*a*) Day wages are guaranteed.

(*b*) Bonus is paid if the worker attains 100 per cent efficiency level. Under this method standard time and standard work is measured in terms of Bedaux points. These points are also known as B's, B refers to a standard work performed in a standard minute.

(*c*) Bonus of 75 per cent of B's saved is paid at the hourly rate.

The following formula is used to calculate earnings under this method:

$$\text{Earnings} = \text{Time taken} \times \text{Time rate} + \frac{75}{100} \times \frac{\text{Hourly rate}}{60} \times \text{B's saved}$$

Problem–47

From the following data calculate the earnings under Bedaux system:

B's got by the workman	90
Hourly rate	2.40
Time allowed in minutes	60

Solution:

$$\text{B's saved} = 90 - 60 = 30 \text{ B's}$$

$$\text{Earnings} = \text{Time taken} \times \text{Time rate} + \frac{75}{100} \times \frac{\text{Hourly rate}}{60} \times \text{B's saved}$$

$$= 1 \times 2.40 + \frac{75}{100} \times \frac{2.40}{60} \times 30$$

$$= 2.40 + 0.90 = 3.30$$

V. Group Bonus System

When bonus is paid collectively to a group of employees, it is known as group bonus system. In assembly-type of work such as radio, TV, typewriter, refrigerators, automobiles, etc. production depends upon the collective efforts of a group of workers as a whole. In such cases, the output of an individual worker cannot be measured and group effort is inevitable. The work of each worker is dependent upon the work done by one or more co-workers. So the workers constituting the group is considered for receiving incentives. This system is applicable under the following circumstances:

(*a*) Where individual output cannot be measured.

(*b*) Where output depends upon the combined efforts of group.

(*c*) Where management wants to encourage team spirit.

(*d*) Where workers constituting a group are almost of equal skill.

(*e*) Where indirect workers are also to be included under incentive system.

Advantages:

(*i*) This method of wage payment infuses cooperation and team spirit.

(*ii*) Absenteeism is reduced, as an absentee employee weakens the team which he does not like.

(*iii*) Accounting system is simplified as recording relates to the output of the group but not to individuals.

(*iv*) Supervision is reduced because efficient workers compensate for less efficient workers.

(*v*) Indirect workers can also be included in the team by taking them into the team.

Disadvantages:

(*i*) This system is unfair to efficient and hard working workers as efficient workers are penalised for their efficiency by the other members of the team.

(*ii*) Workers do not easily accept this plan.

(*iii*) It is difficult to fix group incentive and distribute it to employees.

The following are some of the important types of group bonus system:

1. Priestman's Production Bonus

Under this system, all employees are paid a guaranteed basic wage. In this system, a production standard is fixed every month. When the actual production exceeds the standard, worker's receive during the following month additional pay equal to the percentage on output over the standard.

2. Towne Gain Sharing Plan

Under this method, standard wages for a group of workers for a particular period is predetermined which is based on the output they are expected to produce. The actual wages of the group is ascertained and then compared with standard wages. When the actual wages is less than the standard wages, half of the gain resulting therefrom is paid to the workers as bonus apart from time wages.

3. Scanlon Plan

This plan was introduced by Scanlon in the USA prior to the Second World War. Under this system also day wages are guaranteed. The bonus payable is calculated from the effective reduction in labour cost which is expressed as a ratio of labour cost to total sales value. If the labour cost is reduced or sales value is increased, it results in increased pay for all the employees. This method enables more workers to participate and raise their productivity in factories.

Problem–48

In a factory group bonus system is in use which is calculated on the basis of earnings under time rate. The following particulars are available for a group of 4 workers P, Q, R and S:

(*i*) Output of the group	1,600 units
(*ii*) Piece rate per 100 units	Rs. 2.50
(*iii*) Number of hours worked by	P – 90, Q – 72, R – 80, S – 100
(*iv*) Time rate per hour for	P = Re. 0.80, Q = Re. 1.00, R = Re. 1.20, S = Re. 0.80

Calculate the total of bonus and wages earned by each worker.

(ICWA, Inter, June 1992)

Solution:

Time wages of the worker = Time taken × Time rate

P = 90 × 0.80 = Rs. 72

Q = 72 × 1.00 = Rs. 72

$$R = 80 \times 1.20 = \text{Rs. } 96$$
$$S = 100 \times 0.80 = \text{Rs. } 80$$
$$\text{Total} \quad \text{Rs. } 320$$

Total piece earning of the group $= \frac{1,600}{100} \times 2.50 = 400$

Total of bonus and wages earned by

$$P = \frac{400}{320} \times 72 = 90$$

$$Q = \frac{400}{320} \times 72 = 90$$

$$R = \frac{400}{320} \times 96 = 120$$

$$S = \frac{400}{320} \times 80 = 100$$

$$\text{Total} = \text{Rs. } 400$$

Problem–49

In a manufacturing concern 20 workmen work in a group. The concern follows a group incentive bonus system whereby each workman belonging to the group is paid a bonus on the excess output over the hourly production standard of 250 pieces, in addition to his normal wages at hourly rate. The excess of production over the standard is expressed as a percentage and two-thirds of this percentage is considered to be the share of the workmen and is applied on the notional hourly rate of Rs. 6 (considered only for the purpose of computation of bonus). The output data for a week are stated below:

Days	*Man-hours worked*	*Output (in pieces)*
Monday	160	48,000
Tuesday	172	53,000
Wednesday	164	40,000
Thursday	168	52,000
Friday	160	46,000
Saturday	160	42,000
	984	2,81,000

You are required to:

(*i*) Work out the amount of bonus for the week and the average rate at which each workman is to be paid the same.

(*ii*) Compute the total wages including bonus payable to Ram Jadav who worked for 48 hours at an hourly rate of Rs. 2.50 and to Francis Williams who worked for 52 hours at an hourly rate of Rs. 3. *(ICWA, Inter, December, 1990)*

Solution:

Day	*Man hrs worked*	*Std. output*	*Actual output*	*Excess output*	*% of excess output (see note 2)*	*% of bonus*	*Amount of incentive*
Monday	160	40,000	48,000	8,000	20%	13.40	128.64
Tuesday	172	43,000	53,000	10,000	23.26%	15.58	160.79
Wednesday	164	41,000	40,000	–			
Thursday	168	42,000	52,000	10,000	23.81%	15.95	160.78
Friday	160	40,000	46,000	6,000	15%	10.05	96.48
Saturday	160	40,000	42,000	2,000	5%	3.35	32.16
	984					Total bonus	578.85

Share of each individual workman

$$= \frac{578.85}{984} = 0.59 \text{ per hour worked}$$

Working Notes:

1. Standard output for Monday 160 × 250 = 40,000 and so on for other days.

2. Excess output for Monday = $\frac{8{,}000}{40{,}000} \times 100 = 20\%$ and so on for other days.

3. Bonus for Monday = $\frac{160 \times 13.40}{100} \times 6 = 128.64$ and so on.

Computation of wages to individual workers

	Ram Jadav	Francis William
Time wages		
48 × 2.50	120	
52 × 3		156
Share of Incentive		
48 × 0.59	28.32	
52 × 0.59		30.68
Total wages	148.32	186.68

Problem–51 (Group Bonus System)

In an assembly shop four workmen A, B, C, D work together as a team and are paid on a group piece rate. They also work individually on hourly rate jobs. In a 44 hour week, the following hours have been spent by them on group piece work: A – 40 hours, B – 40 hours, C – 30 hours and D – 20 hours. The balance of the time in the week has been booked by each worker on day work jobs. Their hourly rates are as follows:

A = Rs. 3.00, B = Rs. 4.50, C = Rs. 6.00, D = Rs. 6.00

The group piece rate is Rs. 6 per unit and the team has produced 150 units. Calculate the gross weekly earnings of each workman taking into consideration that each individual is entitled to dearness allowance of Rs. 50 per week.

(Calcutta University, B.Com. (Hons), 1993)

Solution:

Group production 150

Group earnings 150 × Rs. 6 = Rs. 900

Statement showing total time spent

Workman	*Time spent in group work*	*Time spent in day rate jobs*	*Total time spent*
A	40 hours	4 hours	44 hours
B	40 hours	4 hours	44 hours
C	30 hours	14 hours	44 hours
D	20 hours	24 hours	44 hours

Statement showing earnings by workers

Workman	*Wages on day rate jobs*	*Share of group earnings in the ratio of time spent for group work 40; 40; 30; 20*	*Dearness allowance*	*Total wages*
A	4 × 3 = Rs. 12	$\frac{40}{130}$ × 900 = 276.92	50	338.92
B	4 × 4.50 = Rs. 18	$\frac{40}{130}$ × 900 = 276.92	50	344.92
C	14 × 6 = Rs. 84	$\frac{30}{130}$ × 900 = 207.70	50	341.70
D	24 × 6 = Rs. 144	$\frac{20}{130}$ × 900 = 138.46	50	332.46
Total	Rs. 258	900	200	1358

VI. Other Incentive System

In addition to the above methods of incentive systems, some other incentive systems adopted by some industries can be classified under the following:

1. Indirect Monetary Incentives

Indirect monetary incentives are allowed on the understanding that employees contribute to profit earning capacity of the factory. This can take two forms.

(A) Profit-sharing scheme: Under this system, the employer agrees to pay a certain predetermined amount of profit in addition to the usual salary payable to employees. Profit-sharing scheme, differs from factory to factory in terms of coverage and method of distributing profit. In some factories, it is restricted only to executives, while in others, it is applicable to all employees. Again in some factories, it is paid for the year during which profit is earned while in others, the payment of profit is deferred. This is to enable the employees to get a sizeable fund at the time of retirement, disability or separation. The method of distributing profit also differs from factory to factory. In some factories, the length of service is taken as the basis for determining the percentage of profit. In others, a fixed percentage of the total wages or merit rating of the employees constitutes the basis.

Advantages:

(*i*) It reduces excess labour turnover.

(*ii*) It increases production on account of increased efforts of workers with a view to earn profit.

(*iii*) It eliminates conflicts between the employer and employees.

(*iv*) It leads to better cooperation, team spirit and increased efficiency of workers.

(*v*) It boosts up labour morale which is responsible for industrial peace.

(*vi*) Workers get a chance to participate in management. This creates a sense of belonging to the factory. Materials and machineries will be handled with care, thus minimising losses and wastages.

Disadvantages:

(*i*) Usually, the worker has no control over profit and it is not directly related to his effort.

(*ii*) Unless merit-rating is considered as the basis, both efficient and inefficient workers get profit at the same rate.

(*iii*) Payment of profit is at long intervals, usually once a year and the share received by employees is negligible.

(*iv*) Employees share only the profit but not the losses.

(*v*) When workers are habituated to the payment of profit on a regular basis, non-payment of profit in any particular year will discourage the employees.

(B) Co-partnership scheme: Co-partnership or co-ownership confers upon employees the opportunity to share in the capital of the factory and to receive a part of the profit that accrue to their share of ownership.

Co-partnership differs from profit sharing in two respects: (1) In co-partnership, employees invest capital in the factory, whereas in a profit sharing scheme, the employees do not contribute to capital. (2) In a co-partnership, the employees share profit and loss if there is any, whereas in profit-sharing scheme, the workers receive only a share in the profit but they are not called upon to bear the losses.

Incentives for indirect workers: In addition to paying incentives to direct employees, it is also paid to indirect workers for the following reasons:

(*a*) To reduce the cost of operating various departments by means of increasing their efficiency.

(*b*) To avoid discrimination between direct and indirect workers by extending incentives to both the categories.

(*c*) To infuse team spirit and cooperative attitude.

(*d*) To eliminate labour unrest and dissatisfaction among employees.

(*e*) To encourage efficient indirect workers by rewarding them.

(*f*) To enable them to improve their skill so that losses and wastages arising out of materials can be avoided.

(*g*) To provide better service by indirect employees to direct employees.

2. Non-monetary Incentives

Non-monetary incentives are offered with a view to attract better employees, to encourage loyalty, reduce labour turnover, promote better health and reduced absenteeism so as to build up a happy and contended staff. Non-monetary incentives are sometimes provided free of cost, while in some other cases, it may be subsidised. This usually takes the following forms:

(*a*) Canteens

(*b*) Educational facilities for training the employees or to educate children of employees.

(*c*) Financial assistance in respect of housing.

(*d*) Medical facilities.

(*e*) Transport facilities.

(*f*) Recreational facilities.

(*g*) Cooperative societies.

(*h*) Leave travel concession.

(*i*) Pension contribution to PF, gratuity.

(*j*) Free uniforms.

PREPARATION OF PAYROLL

The calculation of wages due to employees is entrusted to the payroll department of the factory. Wage sheets and wage slips are the two important documents used by the payroll department to calculate wages of employees. A payroll or wage sheet is a document which shows the details of gross wages earned by each employee for a particular period, the deductions made and the net wages payable. It is prepared generally once in a month, on the basis of department or shifts of work involved.

The preparations of payroll involve three steps, viz., (*a*) collection of basic data, (*b*) calculation of wages payable and (*c*) preparation of actual payroll.

Preparation of Payroll under Time Rate System

When time rate system of wage payment is adopted, the clock cards are used to ascertain the attendance time of workers. The cost accounting department then ascertains the normal working hours and overtime working hours. The normal working hours are paid at the normal time rate whereas, the overtime hours are paid at double the normal time. Having thus calculated the gross wages, the following deductions are made wherever applicable:

(*a*) Fines

(*b*) Employees state insurance contribution

(*c*) Income tax

(*d*) Toward house rent

(*e*) For recovering advances

(*f*) For life insurance premium

(*g*) Welfare facilities provided

Preparation of Payroll under Piece Wage System

When piece rate system of wage payment is adopted the number of pieces produced is obtained from piece work card or job cards. If there are any defectives, wages can be proportionately deducted out of the gross wages.

The cost accounting department checks the wages payable to the employees. Later on the payroll is prepared for each department separately. It is always better to prepare payroll departmentwise as it serves three purposes, viz., (*a*) the extent of work which is yet to be done can be distributed to various departments, (*b*) a departmental labour rate can be calculated for each department, and (c) control over departmental wages can be exercised by comparing actual wages with budgeted wages.

A payroll consists of the following particulars:

(*a*) Name of the department

(*b*) Duration for which wages are paid

(*c*) Workers name

(*d*) Normal hours worked and time rate

(*e*) Overtime hours worked

(*f*) No. of units produced and piece rate

(*g*) Total gross wages

(*h*) Dearness allowance

(*i*) Bonus payable

(*j*) Deductions

(*k*) Net wages payable.

A specimen of wages analysis sheet or payroll is given below:

Payroll of .... Department ....

Sl. No.	*Name of the worker*	*Hours worked*	*Rate*	*Basic wages*	*OT hours*	*OT wages*	*Leave pay etc.*	*Gross wages*	*Deductions*			*Net wages*
									Tax	*PF*	*ESI*	

Fig. 9.2. *Specimen showing wage analysis sheet.*

Having prepared a payroll for the entire department, the payroll department also prepares yet another document known as a pay slip. It contains all the particulars of a wage sheet. It is prepared for each individual worker and given to them before wages are distributed. This enables the workers to verify the amount of wages due to them.

Finally the exact amount of wages are drawn from the bank. The wages of each employee is put in an envelop and paid to all employees in the presence of departmental managers.

Measures to Prevent Fradulent Payment of Wages

Buyers and Holmes in their Cost Accountancy have summarised the following measures to prevent frauds while paying wages:

(*a*) The system of recording time of arrival and departure should be carefully controlled. Time clocks should be installed and the recording of time adequately supervised.

(*b*) Where piece work and bonus system are in operation, the quantitites produced should be certified by a competent Inspector and records should be signed by the foreman responsible. Extra allowances and payments for lost time should be recorded on forms provided for the purpose, which should be signed by a responsible official.

(*c*) Piece work rates should be clearly laid down and the terms of bonus schemes defined in writing so that no doubt can exist as to the method of payment.

(*d*) All overtime should be properly authorised and the form of authority should be passed to the wages department for verification of overtime bookings.

(*e*) Standard wage rates schedules should be prepared. All alterations in wage rates should be made out on proper forms and be approved by a responsible official.

(*f*) The clerks who prepare wage sheets should not take part in the make-up of the wages envelopes. Where this is unavoidable no clerk should know in advance which section of the payroll he will be required to make-up.

(*g*) All wages and bonus calculations should be worked out by one clerk and be checked by another and the totalling and cross-checking of the sheets should be done by accounting machine wherever possible.

(*h*) The wage sheets should occasionally be scrutinised by the Personnel Officer or Works Manager to guard against the inclusion of 'dummy' workers on the payroll.

(*i*) There should be a satisfactory system for ensuring that all workers are identified before they are handed their wage packets.

(*j*) Wages should not be handed to any person other than the worker concerned except on production of a signed request made out on an authorised form and this should only be permitted in exceptional cases, *e.g.*, disablement or sickness.

Problem–51 (Labour Cost)

Find the wage per hour from the following information:

Name of the worker	: Mr. Krishna
Wages per year	: Rs. 2400
Annual bonus	: 25% of wages
Employer's contribution to PF	: 10% of wages
Employee's contribution to PF	: 8% of wages
Employer's contribution to ESI	: 3% of wages

Total leave with pay permitted during the year – 60 days
Cost of labour welfare amenities – Rs. 8000
No. of workmen – 200
Normal idle time – 80 hours
Working days per annum – 320 days of 8 hours

(University of Madras, B.Com., October 2003)

Solution:

Statement showing wages per hour

	Rs.
Wages per year	2400
Annual Bonus – $2400 \times \frac{25}{100}$	600
Employer's contribution to P.F. – 10% of wages	240
Employer's contribution to ESI – 3% of wages	72
Cost of labour amenities for 200 workers Rs. 8000 Per one worker Rs $\frac{8000}{200 \text{ workers}}$	40
Total labour cost per year	3352

$$\text{Wage rate per hour} = \frac{3352}{2000 \text{ hrs}} = 1.676$$

Working Note:

Calculation of working hours per annum

	Hrs
Total working hours in a year 320 days × 8 hours per day	2560
Less: 60 days leave with pay @ 8 hours each	480
	2080
Less: Idle time hours	80
Effective hours per year	2000

Problem–52

From the following particulars, find the amount of cash required for payment of wages in a factory for the month of July 2005.

	Rs.
(*a*) Wages for normal hours worked	50000
(*b*) Overtime premium	4000

(*c*) Leave wages 2000

(*d*) Employees contribution to P.F. 8% of normal wages

(*e*) State insurance contribution (employees' share) 1000

(*f*) House rent is to be recovered from 20 employees at the rate of Rs. 15 per mensem.

(Acharya Nagarjuna University, B.Com., March 2006)

Solution:

Statement showing cash required for payment of wages

Wages for normal working hours		50,000
Add: overtime premium		4,000
Add: Leave Wages		2,000
		56,000
Less: Employees contribution to PF $50{,}000 \times \frac{8}{100}$	4,000	
Less: State insurance contribution	1,000	
Less: House rent recovered	300	
		5,300
Cash required for payment of wages		50,700

Problem–53

In a factory, 20 workers are employed in the production of a goods. From the following particulars compute the wage bill for the workers for the month of January 2002.

Basic wage – @ Rs. 1000 PM per worker

Dearness allowance – @ Rs. 900 PM per worker

Bonus for the month – @ Rs. 20% of Basic wages plus DA

Other allowances – @ Rs. 200 PM per worker

Own and Employer's contribution to PF – @ 10% of basic wages

Own and employer's contribution to ESI – @ 2% of basic wages

Professional tax deducted from salary – Rs. 20 PM

(Calcutta University, B.Com. (Hons), 2002)

Solution:

Statement showing wage bill for the month of January 2002

Basic wages 1000 × 20	20,000
Dearness allowance 900 × 20	18,000
Bonus @ 20% of basic wages plus DA	7,600
Other allowances 200 × 20	4,000
	49,600

Less:	Deduction from wages:		
	Own contribution to PF (10% of basic wages)	2,000	
	Own contribution to ESI		
	(2% of basic wages)	400	
	Professional tax (20 × 20)	400	2,800
Amount to be paid to the workers			46,800
Add:	Employer's contribution to PF	2,000	
	Employer's contribution to ESI	400	
	Deduction from wages	2,800	5,200
	Total wages for the month		52,000

Problem–54

Calculate the earnings of A and B from the following particulars for a month and allocate the labour cost to each job X, Y and Z:

	A	*B*
(*i*) Basic wages	Rs. 100	160
(*ii*) DA	50%	50%
(*iii*) Contribution to PF (on basic wages)	8%	8%
(*iv*) Contribution to ESI (on basic wages)	2%	2%
(*v*) OT	Hours 10	2%

The normal working hours for the month are 200. OT is paid at double the total of normal wages and DA. Employer's contribution to state insurance and PF are at equal with employees' contribution. The two workers were employed on jobs X, Y and Z in the following proportions:

	Jobs		
	X	*Y*	*Z*
Worked A	40%	30%	30%
Worked B	50%	20%	30%

Overtime was done on job Y. *(C.A., Inter, May 1992)*

Solution:

Statement showing earnings of workers A and B

	A	*B*
Basic wages	100	160
DA (50% of basic wages)	50	80
OT (Refer working not 1)	15	
Gross wages	165	240

Less: PF 8% of basic wages ESI 2% of basic wages	10	16
Net wages paid	155	224

Statement of labour cost

Gross wages (excluding OT)	150	240
Employer's contribution to PF & ESI	10	16
Ordinary wages	160	256
Labour rate per hour	160 / 200 = 0.80	256 / 200 = 1.24

Statement showing allocation of wages to jobs

	X	*Y*	*Z*	*Total*
Worker *A*:				
Ordinary wages (4:3:3)	64	48	48	160
Overtime	–	15	–	15
Worker *B*:				
Ordinary wages (5:2:3)	128	51.20	76.80	256
	192	114.20	124.80	431

Working Note:

$$\text{Overtime} = 2 \times \frac{(\text{Basic wages} + \text{DA})}{200} \times 10 \text{ hrs}$$

$$= 2\left(\frac{150}{200}\right) \times 10 = \text{Rs. } 15$$

Problem–55

Calculate labour cost per man day of 8 hours from the following particulars:

(*i*) Basic salary	—	Rs. 20 per day
(*ii*) Dearness allowance	—	50 paise per every point over 100 cost of living index for working class. Current cost of living index 500 points
(*iii*) Leave salary	—	10% of (*i*) and (*ii*)
(*iv*) Employer's contribution to PF	—	8% of (*i*), (*ii*) and (*iii*)
(*v*) Employer's contribution to ESI	—	2.5% of (*i*), (*ii*) and (*iii*)
(*vi*) Expenditure on amenities to labour	—	Rs. 20 per head per mensem
(*vii*) Number of working days in a month	—	25 days of 8 hours each.

(University of Kerala, B.Com., October 1989)

Solution:

Statement of labour cost for 25 days

(*a*) Basic salary — Rs. 20 for 25 days	500
(*b*) Dearness allowance — 400 points @ 0.50	200
(*c*) Leave salary — 10% of 700	70
(*d*) Employer's contribution to PF — 8% of 770	62
(*e*) Employer's contribution to ESI — 2.5% of 770	19
(*f*) Amenities to labour	20
Total for 25 days	871

$$\text{Per man – day} = \text{Rs. } \frac{871}{25} = \text{Rs. } 34.84$$

Problem–56

Calculate the labour hour rate of a worker P from the following data:

Basic pay	Rs. 200 PM
DA	Rs. 150 PM
Fringe	Rs. 100 PM

Number of working days in a year 300.30 days full pay and 20 days half pay leave in a year is availed and allowed. Assume 8 hours days.

What would be the effect on hourly rate if only 30 days full pay leave is allowed?

(C.S., Inter, June, 1990)

Solution:

Calculation of effective working hours for the year

Working days in a year	300
Less: Leave days (30 + 20)	50
Effective working days	250
Working hours in a day	8 hours

Total effective working hours = 250 × 8 = 2,000 hours

Statement showing total wages paid in a year

Basic wages	200 × 12	2,400
DA	150 × 12	1,800
Fringe benefits	100 × 12	1,200
	Total wages	5,400

$$\text{Rate per day} = \frac{5400}{300} = 18$$

Less: 20 days half pay.

For 1 day — 18

For 20 days — 360 and 1/2 pay is	180
Net amount paid	5,220

Hourly rate $\frac{5,220}{2,000} = 2.61$

If 30 days' full pay leave is allowed

Effective working days	270 days
Effective working hours 270 × 8	2,160 hours
Total wages payable	Rs. 5,400

Hourly rate $= \frac{5,400}{2,160} = 2.50$

Effect on hourly rate = Rs. 2.61 – 2.50 = Re. 0.11.

TREATMENT OF CERTAIN ITEMS IN COST ACCOUNTS

1. Idle Time

Idle time arises when time rate system of wage payment is implemented. It refers to the time during which workers will not attend to job although wages are paid for such time. In other words idle time is the time during which employees remain idle without producing any articles. In spite of this fact they are paid for such idle time. The existence of idle time can be known by referring to the attendance time and time booking which indicates the extent of idle time.

Idle time arises on account of the following causes:

(*a*) **Productive causes.** The productive causes are closely related to production function of the factory. Such causes are as follows:

- (*i*) Time involved in reaching the production department from factory gate
- (*ii*) Setting up time involved in adusting machines
- (*iii*) Time taken for attending to different jobs by the employees
- (*iv*) For want of instructions regarding the machine to be attended
- (*v*) Waiting for materials
- (*vi*) Waiting for tools and equipments
- (*vii*) Power failure
- (*viii*) Breakdown of machines

(*b*) **Administrative causes.** Administrative causes arises owing to decisions taken by management. Some such decision relates to operating the plant at a lower capacity, deliberate reduction in the production during depression, etc.

(*c*) **Economic causes.** Economic causes arise owing to general economic conditions prevailing in the country. Such causes are as follows:

- (*i*) Seasonality of products
- (*ii*) Non-availability of materials
- (*iii*) Lack of demand
- (*iv*) Period of depression

In addition to above causes, idle time may also arise for other causes like strikes, lockouts, natural calamities such as, occurrence of fire, floods, etc.

From the point of view of treatment of idle time, it is classified under two types, viz., (*a*) normal and (*b*) abnormal idle time. Normal idle time is regular in nature whereas abnormal idle time arise only under certain circumstances.

From the point of view of control idle time can be classified into (*a*) controllable and (*b*) uncontrollable idle time. It is very essential to control idle time as it has close relationship with cost of production and efficiency of workers. Controllable idle time is within the purview of management and it is possible to control it by an executive action. Whereas uncontrollable idle time is not within the purview of management to control it. Most of the productives causes resulting in idle time is controllable, whereas idle time arising out of economic and administrative causes are uncontrollable. An idle time card is used to book the idle time hours. This card helps in controlling the idle time. A specimen of it is shown below:

IDLE TIME CARD

Name of the worker .... Date ....

Clock no. ....

Department ....

Causes of idle time	*Time lost*		*Total hours lost*	*Rate*	*Amount*
	From	*To*			
Normal idle time (*a*) (*b*) (*c*) Abnormal idle time (*a*) (*b*)					

Signature of worker *Signature of foreman*

Fig. 9.3. *Specimen showing idle time card.*

Treatment of Idle Time in Cost Accounts

Treatment of normal and controllable idle time. Normal and controllable idle time is treated as overheads and charged to the department where such idle time is spent.

Treatment of abnormal and uncontrollable idle time. Abnormal idle time is charged to costing profit and loss account.

2. Overtime

Overtime work arises whenever normal production work is hampered by power failure, breakdown in machinery, non-availability of material, increase in demand for the products, rush orders from customers, etc. In all such situations overtime work is engaged and workers are paid at a higher rate than the normal rate. According to the Indian Factories Act 1948, any worker who works for more than 9 hours a day or 48 hours a week is said to have worked under overtime and is to be remunerated at double the normal rate. The treatment of overtime wages depends upon the circumstance under which it arises. As overtime wages results in excess payment of wages and thereby increases cost of production, it is necessary to control excess overtime work. The following steps are to be taken to control excess overtime work:

(*a*) It is to be resorted to only when it becomes inevitable.

(*b*) It should be authorised by competent authority.

(*c*) The efficiency of workers during overtime work should not be allowed to go down.

(*d*) Separate records must be maintained for overtime work and overtime wages.

(*e*) Overtime work must be properly supervised.

(*f*) More labourers are to be recruited if overtime work becomes a permanent feature.

(*g*) Arrangement for the prompt supply of materials and regular maintenance of machineries is to be ensured if materials and machine breakdown are responsible for overtime.

Treatment of Overtime Wages in Cost Accounts

(*i*) When overtime work is done at the specific instruction given by customer to complete production within a specific date:

Under this circumstance the overtime wages is charged directly to that job and treated as direct labour cost

(*ii*) When overtime work is done owing to power failure or breakdown in machinery:

Under this circumstance, overtime wages are charged to the number of jobs executed during the period as overheads.

(*iii*) When overtime work is done as a matter of policy due to shortage of labourers:

Under this circumstance, overtime wages is treated as direct labour cost and sperad over the various jobs completed.

PROBLEMS ON OVERTIME WAGES

Problem–57

Calculate the normal and overtime wages payable to a workman from the following data.

Days	*Hours worked*
Monday	8 hours
Tuesday	10 hours
Wednesday	9 hours
Thursday	11 hours
Friday	9 hours
Saturday	4 hours
	51 hours

Normal working hours : 8 hours per day

Normal rate : 0.50 per hour

Overtime rate : up to 9 hours in a day at single rate and over 9 hours in a day at double rate.

(University of Madras, B.Com., March 1991)

Solution:

Statement showing normal and overtime working hours

Days	*Total hours worked*	*Normal working hours*	*Overtime hours At single rate*	*At double rate*
Monday	8	8		
Tuesday	10	8	1	1
Wednesday	9	8	1	–
Thursday	11	8	1	2
Friday	9	8	1	–
Saturday	4	4		–
	51	44	4	3

Normal wages for 44 hours @ 0.50	=	22.00
OT wages— At single rate 4 × 0.50	=	2.00
At double rate 3 × 1	=	3.00
Total	Rs.	27.00

Problem–58

A firm's basic rate is Rs. 3 per hour and overtime rates are time and a half for earnings and double time for week ends. The following details have been recorded on three jobs:

	Job X Clock hrs	*Job Y Clock hrs*	*Job Z Clock hrs*
Normal time	480	220	150
Evening time	120	60	80
Week end	10	30	16

Calculate the labour cost chargeable to each of the jobs in the following situations:

(*i*) When the overtime is worked at the customer's request to advance the delivery time.

(*ii*) When overtime is worked occasionally under general pressure of work.

(Sri Sathya Sai University, B.Com., October 1989)

Solution:

(*a*) Under the first situation, the jobs are charged with the following amount of labour cost:

Job *X*	480 × Rs. 3	=	1,440
	102 × Rs. 4.50	=	459
	10 × Rs. 6	=	60
			1,959
Job *Y*	220 × Rs. 3	=	660
	60 × Rs. 4.50	=	270
	30 × Rs. 6	=	180
			1,110
Job *Z*	150 × Rs. 3	=	450
	80 × Rs. 4.50	=	360
	16 × Rs. 6	=	96
			906

(*b*) Under the second situation each job will be charged with labour cost for the number of hours worked at

Job *X*	480 + 102 + 10	=	592 @ Rs. 3	=	1,776
Job *Y*	220 + 60 + 30	=	310 @ Rs. 3	=	930
Job *Z*	150 + 80 + 16	=	246 × @ Rs. 3	=	738

The overtime wages chargeable to factory overheads will be

102 + 60 + 80	=	242 × 1.50	=	363
10 + 30 × 16	=	56 × 3	=	168
				531

Note 1: Rs. 1.50 is the difference between the evening overtime rate of Rs. 4.50 and basic wage rate of Rs. 3.

Note 2: Rs 3 is the difference between the double overtime rate of Rs. 6 and basic wage rate of Rs. 3.

Problem–59 (Overtime Wages)

From the following particulars you are required to calculate according to "Average wage rate" the labour cost chargeable to Job No. P-301 which was completed in 1998

Basic wage rate is Rs. 15 per hour and overtime rates are as follows:

Before or after working hours – 150% of basic wage rate

Sundays and other holidays – 200% of basic wage rate

During the year 1998 the following labour hours were worked:

Normal time	–	4,00,000 hours
OT before or after working hours	–	50,000 hours
OT on Sundays and holidays	–	40,000 hours
		4,90,000 hours

For Job No. P–301, 4000 hours were spent as follows:

Normal time	3,000 hours
OT Before or after working hours	700 hours
OT Sundays and holidays	300 hours

(Calcutta University, B.Com. (Hons), 1999)

Solution:

Statement showing average wage rate

Particulars	*Hours worked*	*Rate per hour*	*Wages paid*
Normal time	4,00,000	15	60,00,000
OT before or after working hours	50,000	22.50	11,25,000
OT on Sundays and holidays	40,000	30	12,00,000
Total	4,90,000		83,25,000

$$\text{Average wage rate} = \frac{83,25,000}{4,90,000} = \text{Rs. } 17$$

Wages chargeable to job no. P–301 under average wage rate:

4000 hours @ Rs. 17 = 68,000

Problem–60 (Treatment of OT and Idle Time Wages)

The normal working hours per week are fixed at 44 hours in a factory. An analysis of the time card of a worker shows that during a week he actually worked 43 hours (including 4 hours overtime) on production and remained idle for remaining 5 hours due to machine break down.

Normal rate per hour is Rs. 5. Overtime rate is 150% of the wages rate and the rate of wages for idle time is 80% of the normal wage rate.

Calculate total wages payable to the worker and show how the total amount shall be treated in cost accounts. *(Calcutta University, B.Com. (Hons), 1994)*

Solution:

Statement showing total earnings of the worker

		Rs.
(1) Normal wages (43 – 4) = 39 hrs @ Rs. 5	=	195
(2) Overtime wages 4 hrs × 5 × $\frac{150}{100}$	=	30

(3) Idle time wages 5 hrs × 5 × $\frac{80}{100}$ = 20

Total earnings for the week = 245

Treatment of Overtime Wages

Out of Rs. 245, Rs. 225 will be charged to the product (normal wages + overtime wages) assuming that overtime was necessary to finish the product in time.

Treatment of Idle Time Wages

Idle time wages of Rs. 20 will not be charged to the product. It will be charged to the costing profit and loss account, since the idle time was abnormal due to break down of machinery.

3. Holiday with Pay

Important festivals and days of national importance such as Independence Day, Republic Day, etc. are declared as holidays. On these days workers do not attend the factories and they are paid for these unproductive days. However, the wages payable for these holidays are charged to cost of production. There are two ways of treating holiday with pay in cost accounts, viz., (*a*) to treat it as factory overheads for the entire year and apportioned to the number of jobs executed during the year and (*b*) to charge as direct wages by inflating the wage rate chargeable to different jobs.

4. Leave with Pay

Workers are entitled to different types of leave in a factory such as casual leave, sick leave, special leave, etc. Leave days with pay again constitute unproductive working days. The wages payable for those days are again treated as factory overheads and apportioned to various jobs executed in that year.

5. Work on Holidays

Workers may be requested to work on holidays and other weekly off days owing to unavoidable circumstances. The rate of wage payment of those days are at higher rate than the normal rate. Such extra wages paid are treated as overheads and charged to jobs as indirect wages. However, the normal wages paid is treated as direct wages and charged directly to the jobs concerned.

6. Night Shift Allowance

The night shift allowance is treated as departmental overheads and charged to jobs executed as indirect wages.

7. Wages Payable to Defective Work

Defective units can be reworked in order to convert them into good units. The wages payable for converting defective units into good units may be treated in two ways, viz, (*a*) If the amount of wages is negligible it is treated as direct wages and charged to the work order, and (*b*) If the amount of wages is more it is treated as overheads and charged to the department concerned.

8. Wages Paid to Apprentices

A worker who learns a job cannot work efficiently when compared to other workers. He needs to be trained and the cost of training is treated as overheads. However, where a worker works on a job but takes more time, then his wages are partly charged to the job as direct wages and partly as overheads.

9. Fringe Benefits

Fringe benefits include all welfare facilities offered to workers by the factory such as medical, housing, recreational, educational and also other contributions such as PF, ESI, gratuity, pension, etc. The expenses incurred towards factory workers are treated as departmental overheads, whereas fringe benefit relating to office staff and selling department of the factory are treated as office and administration overheads and selling and distribution overheads respectively.

Questions

I. (A) Fill in the blanks

1. Coast of normal idle time is changed to ....

2. Time not spent on production is known as ....

3. In Taylor's differential piece rate system .... number of piece rates are set for each job.

4. Idle time arises only when workers are paid on .... basis of wage payment.

5. In Halsey-Weir system, a worker gets a bonus equal to .... percentage of time saved.

[***Answers:*** (1) overhead, (2) idle time, (3) two, (4) time rate, (5) 40%]

(B) Mark 'T' or 'F' in the space provided

1. When wages are paid on piece basis, the quality of work deteriorates. *T/F*

2. In Merrick's differential piece rate system, time wages are guaranteed to each worker. *T/F*

3. Holiday pay and leave pay are labour based cost. *T/F*

4. Rowan incentive system distributes the benefit of time saved equally between employee and employer. *T/F*

5. Cost of idle time due to labour strike should be treated as factory overhead. *T/F*

[***Answers:*** True (1); Rest are all false]

(C) Choose the correct answers

1. Incentive system of wage payment

(*a*) Pay bonus for the time saved besides guaranteeing wages for the time taken.

(*b*) Is a fruad on the employee compensation plan.

(*c*) Is intended to speed up work for the benefit of the employer.

(*d*) Pay increased bonus at an increasing rate as the efficiency increases.

2. Under Emerson's efficiency plan, the worker gets normal wages at

(*a*) $66\frac{2}{3}\%$ efficiency (*b*) $33\frac{1}{3}\%$ efficiency

(*c*) 80% efficiency (*d*) 100% efficiency

3. Under Bedaux system the point obtained as 'B' represents

(*a*) No. of units produced (*b*) No. of mintues taken for a job

(*c*) No. of hours taken for a job (*d*) No. of workers required for a job

4. Which one of the following is the basis on which bonus is calculated under Rowan system?

(*a*) $\frac{\text{Std. time}}{\text{Time saved}} \times \text{Std. time} \times \text{Std. rate}$ (*b*) $\frac{\text{Std. time}}{\text{Time taken}} \times \text{Time saved} \times \text{Time rate}$

(*c*) $\frac{\text{Std. time}}{\text{Time rate}} \times \text{Time taken} \times \text{Time saved}$ (*d*) $\frac{\text{Time saved}}{\text{Std. time}} \times \text{Time taken} \times \text{Time rest}$

5. Which one of the following is a system which combines both time and price rate system?

(*a*) Bedaux system (*b*) Merrick's differential system

(*c*) Halsey system (*d*) Emerson's system

6. Under Gantt's task and bonus plan no bonus is available to a worker if his efficiency is below:

(*a*) 50% (*b*) $66\frac{2}{3}\%$

(*c*) 75% (*d*) 100%

7. Under which of the following bonus system production budget of the department is taken as standard and the actual production, if exceeds the standard bonus is paid to all the workers?

(*a*) Rucker plan (*b*) Scanlon plan

(*c*) Bush plan (*d*) Priestman's plan

8. The formula to calculate wages under Barth system is

(*a*) $\sqrt{\text{Std.time} + \text{Actual time} \times \text{Time wage}}$ (*b*) $\sqrt{\text{Std.time} \times \text{Actual time} \times \text{Time wage}}$

(*c*) $\sqrt{\text{Std.time} \times \text{Actual time}}$ (*d*) Std. time × Time wage × Actual wage

9. Which one of the following factor is the most important for reducing the labour cost per unit?

(*a*) Low wage rates (*b*) Higher input-output rates

(*c*) Strict control and supervision (*d*) Longer hours of work

10. The benefit of time saved by a worker against the standard should

(*a*) go wholly to the employee

(*b*) be shared by the employer and the employee if the work is standardised

(*c*) be shared by the two if it is not standardised

(*d*) go wholly to the employer

[**Answers:** 1 (*a*), 2(*b*), 3(*b*), 4(*d*), 5(*d*) 6(*d*), 7(*d*), 8(*b*), 9(*b*), 10(*c*)]

(D) Match the following

A	*B*
(1) Halsey system	(*a*) Indirect monetary incentive
(2) Taylor system	(*b*) Group bonus system
(3) Emerson's system	(*c*) Combination of time and piece rate
(4) Co-partnership	(*d*) Premium bonus plan
(5) Production plan	(*e*) Piece rate system
(6) Barth system	(*f*) Time-rate system
	(*g*) Non-monetary incentive
	(*h*) 50% of time saved as bonus

[***Answers:*** 1. (*h*) 2. (*e*) 3. (*c*) 4. (*a*) 5. (*b*) 6. (*d*)]

II. Simple questions

1. State any two merits and two demerits of time rate system of wage payment.
2. State any two merits and two demerits of piece rate system.
3. State the feature of Taylor's differential piece rate system of wage payment.
4. State the features of Merrick's differential piece rate system.
5. State the features of Gantt task and bonus plan.
6. State the features of Emerson's efficiency system.
7. State the features of Halsey system of wage payment.
8. State the features of Rowan system of wage payment.
9. What do you mean by group bonus system ?
10. What do you mean by profit-sharing plan ?
11. What do you mean by co-partnership ?
12. Distinguish between profit sharing and co-partnership.
13. What do you mean by wage abstract ?
14. What is idle time ?
15. Distinguish between overtime and idle time.
16. What is a fringe benefit ?
17. How do you treat holiday with pay in cost accounts ?
18. How do you treat leave with pay in cost accounts ?
19. Mention any four types of group incentive system.
20. What do you mean by accelerated premium bonus ?

III. Short and long answer questions

1. Enumerate the causes of idle time indicating the treatment thereof in cost account. *(ICWA, Inter, June 1992)*

2. Write a note on plant register. *(ICWA, Inter, June 1992)*

3. Discuss the advantages and disadvantages of having piece rate system of payment of wages. *(ICWA, Inter, June 1990)*

4. Explain the differences between time rate wages and piece rate wages.
(ICWA, Inter, December 1988)

5. What are the various incentive plans of wage ? Explain.
(Andhra University, B. Com., May 1992)

6. Give a comparative study of Halsey and Rowan plan with imaginary data about actual time, standard time and rates of wages, etc.
(Kakatiya University, B. Com., November 1991)

7. Compare and contrast Halsey and Rowan premium plan.
(Kakatiya University, B. Com., October 1989)

8. Explain the different system of wage payment.
(Kakatiya University, B. Com., April 1990)

9. What is idle time ? From control point of view, how do you categorise different kinds of idle time? *(Nagarjuna University, B. Com., March 1992)*

10. What is idle time ? How is cost of idle time treated ?
(Osmania University, B. Com., April 1990)

11. Discuss the importance of the following (*a*) time booking, (*b*) time keeping, and (*c*) group incentive. *(Osmania University, B. Com., March 1992)*

12. Explain briefly the methods of treating overtime wages in cost accounts.
(Bangalore University, M. Com., May 1992)

13. Outline the general principles to be borne in mind in distinguishing a wage incentive scheme. *(University of Madras, B. Com., March 1992)*

14. What is idle time ? How is it treated in cost account ?
(Kakatiya University, M. Com., August 1991)

15. List the various causes for idle time of workers and machines and give the remedial measures you recommend. *(Mangalore University, B. Com., April 1988)*

16. Explain the following methods of wage payment: (1) Taylor's differential piece rate system, (2) Emerson's efficiency plan, (3) Gantt task and bonus plan, (4) Rowan scheme.
(Mangalore University, B. Com., October 1987)

17. What are the methods of group incentive payment ? What are its limitations ?
(University of Kerala, B. Com., May 1989)

18. How would you deal with the following expenses:

(*a*) Overtime wages,

(*b*) Expenses for welfare activities,

(*c*) Wages paid for re-operation of defectives,

(*d*) Research and development cost. *(University of Delhi, B. Com. (Hons.), 1991)*

19. What are the factors to be considered for the introduction of a wage incentive scheme ? Explain. *(University of Delhi, B. Com. (Hons.), 1991)*

20. What are the objectives of "Incentive plans of wage payment" ? Explain briefly the conditions necessary for their success. *(University of Delhi, B. Com. (Hons.), 1990)*

21. How will you deal with 'Idle time' in cost accounts ? How can you control such costs ?
(University of Delhi, B. Com. (Hons.), 1989)

22. How will you deal with "overtime premium cost in cost account" ?
(University of Delhi, B. Com. (Hons.), 1988)

23. What are the objectives of introducing an incentive scheme in a factory ? What factors would you take into consideration for the same ?
(Calcutta University, B. Com., 1991)

24. What do you understand by "Group bonus scheme" ? Briefly narrate its advantages and disadvantages. *(Calcutta University, B. Com., 1990)*

25. State the essentials of a good incentive wage plan. In the light of your answer discuss any two incentive wage plans you know of.
(Sri Sathya Sai University, B. Com., October 1991)

26. Draw a payroll sheet filling in imaginary details pertaining to the office staff of a small manufacturing concern. *(Sri Sathya Sai University, B. Com., October 1989)*

Exercise–1 (Taylor's Differential Piece Rate System)

Using the following data, you are required to ascertain the wages paid to workers Ram and Raj under the Taylor's system

Standard time allowed – 10 units per hour

Normal wage rate – Rs. 10 per hour

Differential piece rates to be applied:

(*a*) 75% of piece rate when below standard

(*b*) 125% of piece rate when at or above standard

The workers have produced in a day of 8 hours as follows:

Ram – 60 units: Raj – 100 units. *(Acharya Nagarjuna University, B. Com., June 2005)*

[***Answer:*** Ram's wages – Rs. 45
Raj's wages – Rs. 125]

Exercise–2 (Merrick's Multiple Piece Rate System)

On the basis of the following information calculate the earnings of A, B, C and D. Under Merrick multiple piece rate system:

Standard production per hour 6 units

Normal rate per hour Re. 1

In a day of 8 hours day:

A produced 32 units: B Produced 48 units

C produced 42 units: D produced 50 units *(University of Madras, B. Com., April 2002)*

[***Answer:*** A's Earnings Rs. 5.33
B's Earnings Rs. 8.80
C's Earnings Rs. 7.70
D's Earnings Rs. 10]

Exercise–3 (Gantt's Task and Bonus Plan)

Calculate the earnings of workers from the following details under Gantt's task and bonus plan:

Guranteed time rate is Re. 1 per hour

High piece rate Rs. 0.20 per unit

Standard output is 10 units per hour

In a day of 8 hours:

A produces 70 units, B–80 units and C–90 units (*University of Madras, B. Com., May 2002*)

[***Answer:*** A's Earnings Rs. 8
B's Earnings Rs. 9.60
C's Earnings Rs. 18]

Exercise–4 (Halsey and Rowan System)

In a factory guaranteed wages at rate of Rs. 1.80 per hour are paid in a 48 hour week. It is estimated that to manufacture one unit of a particular product 20 minutes are taken. The time allowed is increased by 25%. During one week Mr. 'A' produced 180 units of the product. Calculate his wages under: (1) Halsey system (2) Rowan system.

(*Sri Sathya Sai University, B. Com. (Hons), March 2001*)

[***Answer:*** Halsey system Rs. 110.70
Rowan system Rs. 117.10]

Exercise–5 (Rowan System)

Find out the total weekly earnings of Mr. Ramesh from the following information under Rowan plan:

Guaranteed time wages per week of 44 hours—Rs. 19 per hour

Time allowed to produce one article is 30 minutes

Under incentive scheme time allowed is increased by 20%.

Actual production for the week—100 articles. (*Mangalore University, B. Com., April 2006*)

[***Answer:*** Wages Rs. 1058.93]

Exercise–6 (Halsey and Rowan System)

Calculate the earnings of a worker under Halsey plan and Rowan plan from the following information:

Standard time	30 hours
Time taken	20 hours

Hourly rate of wage is Re. 1 per hour plus a dearness allowance at 50 paise per hour worked.

(*University of Madras, B. Com., May 2005*)

[***Answer:*** Total Earnings under (*i*) Halsey plan Rs. 35
(*ii*) Rowan plan Rs. 36.67]

Exercise–7 (Time Rate, Piece Rate, Halsey and Rowan System)

Standard time = 30 hours

Rate per hour = Re. 1 plans a DA of 30 Paise per hour worked

Actual time taken = 15 hours

Calculate the earnings under

(*a*) Time wage system (*b*) Piece rate system

(*c*) Halsey system (*d*) Rowan system

(*University of Madras, B. Com., May 2004*)

[***Answer:*** (1) Time rate system Rs. 19.50
(2) Piece rate system Rs. 24.50
(3) Halsey system Rs. 22.00
(4) Rowan system Rs. 23.25]

Exercise–8 (Halsey and Rowan System)

Standard time alllowed for a job is 100 hours. The hourly rate of wages is Rs. 4 per hour plus a dearness allowance of Rs. 5.50 per hour worked. The actual time taken by the worker was 80 hours. Calculate total wages on:

(*a*) Time rate basis (*b*) Halsey rate basis

(*c*) Rowan bonus plan

(University of Madras, B. Com., April 2001)

[***Answer:*** (1) Time rate basis Rs. 760

(2) Halsey rate basis Rs. 800

(3) Rowan bonus plan Rs. 824]

Exercise–9

From the following particulars, work out the earnings for the week of a worker under:

(*a*) Straight piece rate system (*b*) Differential piece rate system

(*c*) Halsey premium system (*d*) Rowan system

Number of working hours per week	–	48
Wages per hour	–	Rs. 3.75
Rate per piece	–	Rs. 1.50
Normal time per piece	–	20 mins
Normal output per week	–	120 pieces
Actual output for the week	–	150 pieces
Differential piece rate	–	80% of piece rate when output is below standard and 120% when above standard.

(University of Madras, B. Com., May 2003)

[***Answer:*** (1) Straight piece rate system Rs. 225

(2) Differential piece rate system Rs. 270

(3) Halsey system Rs. 183.75

(4) Rowan system Rs. 187.20]

Exercise–10 (Halsey and Rowan System)

Calculate the earnings of a worker from the following information under Halsey and Rowan plan

Standard time : 30 hrs

Time taken : 20 hrs

Wage rate is Rs. 2 per hour plus dearness allowance at the rate of Re. 1 per hour worked.

(Sri Krishnadevaraya University, B. Com., March 2006)

[***Answer:*** Halsey system – Rs. 70

Rowan system – Rs.73.33]

Exercise–11 (Time Rate, Halsey Plan and Rowan Plan)

Standard time allowed for job is 100 hours. The hourly rate of wage is Rs. 4 per hour plus a dearness allowance of Rs. 5.50 per hour worked. The actual time taken by the worker was 80 hours. Calculate total wages on:

(*a*) Time rate basis

(*b*) Halsey rate bonus

(*c*) Rowan bonus plan (*Sri Krishnadevaraya University, B. Com., October 2006*)

[***Answer:*** (*a*) Time wages Rs. 760
(*b*) Halsey rate basis Rs. 800
(*c*) Rowan bonus plan Rs. 824]

Exercise–12 (Halsey and Rowan System)

From the following particulars calculate the earnings of a worker under:

(*a*) Rowan premium bonus system and

(*b*) Halsey premium bonus system

Hourly rate of wages Re. 0.75

Standard time for producing 1 dozen articles is 3 hours

Actual time taken by the worker to produce 20 dozen articles is 48 hours.

(*Sri Krishnadevaraya University, B. Com., March 2005*)

[***Answer:*** (1) Rowan system Rs. 43.20
Halsey system Rs. 40.50

Exercise–13 (Halsey, Rowan and Halsey Weir)

From the following data calculate the earning of Ram, Gopal and Krishna who are working in a factory. The standard time allowed for a job is 48 hours. The job is completed by Ram in 45 hours Gopal in 40 hours and Krishna in 48 hours. Their wage rate is Rs. 4 per hour. They are allowed a dearness allowance of a 0.50 per hours calculate the earnings under: (1) Halsey plan (2) Rowan's plan (3) Halsey-Weir plan (40% bonus in time saved.) (*Nagarjuna University, B. Com., July 2007*)

[***Answer:*** (1) Halsey plan
Ram Rs. 208.50
Gopal Rs. 196
Krishna Rs. 216
(2) Rowan's plan
Ram Rs. 213.75
Gopal Rs. 206.67
Krishna Rs. 216.
(3) Halsey-Weir plan
Ram Rs. 207.30
Gopal Rs. 192.80
Krishna Rs. 216]

Exercise–14 (Piece Rate, Halsey Premium and Rowan System)

During the first week of January 2007. The workman Mr. Nagarjuna manufactured 300 articles. He receives wage for a guaranteed 48 hours week at the rate of Rs. 4 per hour. The estimated time to produce one article is 10 minutes and under the incentive scheme the time allowed is increased by 20%. Calculate his wages according to

(*a*) Piece rate system

(*b*) Halsey premium bonus plan and

(*c*) Rowan's plan (*Nagarjuna University, B. Com., March 2007*)

[***Answer:*** (*a*) Piece rate system – Rs. 240
(*b*) Halsey plan – Rs. 216
(*c*) Rowan's plan – Rs. 230.40]

Exercise–15 (Time Rate, Halsey and Rowan System)

From the following particulars, calculate the earnings of workers Abin and Biman for a day of under (1) Time rate system (2) Halsey system and (3) Rowan system

Standard production 8 units per hour

Normal time rate : Abin : Rs. 10 per hour

Biman : Rs. 12 per hour

Working hours of the day 8

Output: Abin : 60 units

Biman : 80 units

(Calcutta University, B. Com., 2004)

[***Answer:*** (1) Time rate system : Abin Rs. 80

Biman Rs. 96

(2) Halsey system : Abin Rs. 80

Biman Rs. 108

(3) Rowan system : Abin Rs. 80

Biman Rs. 115.20]

Exercise–16 (Halsey and Rowan System)

Time allowed for the production of 100 "Bolt" is 2 hours and hourly rate of wage payments is Rs. 12. M and N produced 600 and 500 pieces of "Bolt" respectively in a particular day of 8 hours. Calculate their earnings under Halsey premium bonus and Rowan premium bonus method.

(Calcutta University, B. Com. (Hons.) 2003)

[***Answer:*** Halsey system = M – Rs. 120

N – Rs. 108

Rowan system = M – Rs. 128

N – Rs. 112]

Exercise–17 (Calculation of Material Cost and Wage Rate)

In a factory a job can be executed either through workman Pradip or Arvindam. Pradip takes 32 hours to complete the job while Arvindam finishes it in 30 hours. The standard time to finish the job is 40 hours.

The raw material input cost and hourly wage rate are same for both the workers. Pradip is entitled to receive bonus according to Halsey plan while Arvindam is paid bonus as per Rowan plan. Works overheads are recovered on the job at Rs. 15 per labour hours worked. The factory cost of the job comes to Rs. 5200 irrespective of the workmen engaged.

Find out hourly wage rate and cost of raw materials input.

(Calcutta University, B. Com. (Hons.), 2001)

[***Answer:*** Material cost Rs. 4000

Wage rate per hour Rs. 20]

Exercise–18 (Halsey and Rowan)

A worker produced 180 units in a week. The guaranteed weekly wage payment for 44 hours is Rs. 77. The expected time to produce one unit is 16 minutes which is further raised by 25% under the incentive scheme. What will be the earnings per hour of the worker under the Halsey and Rowan schemes.

(Calcutta University, B. Com. (Hons.), 2000)

[**Answer:** Total wages under Halsey plan Rs. 91
Rate per hour 2.07
Total wages under Rowan plan Rs. 97.5
Rate per hour 2.22

Exercise–19 (Halsey and Rowan System)

From the following data, calculate works cost for jobs performed by Ajay and Saurav:

	Ajay	*Saurav*
Time allowed (per 100 units)	40 hrs	42 hrs
Rate per unit	Rs. 3	Rs. 4
Rate per hour	Rs. 8	Rs. 12
Actual time taken	48 hrs	70 hrs
Actual units produced	150 units	200 units
Material cost for jobs	Rs. 668	Rs. 1020
Bonus plan	Halsey	Rowan
Factory overhead	150% of wages	100% of wages

(Calcutta University, B. Com. (Hons.), 1998)

[**Answer:** Factory cost of Ajay Rs. 1748
Factory cost of Saurav Rs. 2980]

Exercise–20

Standard time allocated for a job is 20 hours and the rate per hour is Re. 1 plus a dearness allowance @ 0.30 paise per hour worked. Actual time taken by a worker is 15 hours. Calculate earnings under:

(*a*) Time wage system
(*b*) Piece wage system
(*c*) Halsey plan
(*d*) Rowan scheme

(University of Delhi, B. Com. (Pass) 2004)

[**Answer:** (1) Time wage system – Rs. 19.50
(2) Piece wage system – Rs. 24.50
(3) Halsey plan – Rs. 22
(4) Rowan scheme – Rs. 23.75]

Exercise–21 (Halsey and Rowan System)

A worker produced 200 units in a week's time. The guaranteed weekly wages payment for 45 hours is Rs. 1350. The expected time to produce one unit is 15 minutes which is raised further by 20% under the incentive scheme. What will be the earnings per hour of that worker under Halsey (50% sharing) and Rowan bonus scheme ?

(C.S. Inter, June 2005)

[**Answer:** Halsey system – Rs. 1575
Rowan system – Rs. 1687.50]

Exercise–22 (Labour Cost)

From the following particulars, find the amount of cash required for payment of wages in a factory for a particular month:

	Rs.
(1) Wages for normal hours worked	40,000
(2) Overtime wages	10,500
(3) Leave wages	5,000
(4) Contribution to provident fund:	
Employee's share	4,000
Employer's share	3,500
(5) House rent to be recovered from 10 employees @ Rs. 200 per month	

(University of Delhi, B. Com. (Hons.) 2005)

[***Answer:*** Cash requirement Rs. 49500]

Exercise–23 (Overtime Wages)

From the following particulars calculate normal wages and overtime wages of a worker.

Day	*Hours worked*
Monday	08
Tuesday	10
Wednesday	09
Thursday	11
Friday	09
Saturday	04
	51

Normal working hours per day is 8 hours. Normal rate per hour is Rs. 1.50. Overtime rate per hour is Rs. 3.00. *(Acharya Nagarjuna University, B. Com. March 2005)*

[***Answer:*** Rs. 87.00]

❑❑❑

CHAPTER 10

Direct Expenses

INTRODUCTION

Direct expenses, otherwise known as chargeable expenses, as the name itself indicates, are those expenses, other than direct material cost and direct labour cost, which are directly incurred on a specific cost unit. They form part of prime cost because they are incurred directly on a specific cost unit. The ICMA terminology defines direct expenses as "expenses which can be identified with and allocated to cost centre or cost units". However, in some cases, the direct expenses cannot be very easily identified with the cost unit but it can be identified with cost centre. In such cases these expenses are direct cost of the cost centre and it becomes indirect cost of all jobs manufactured in that department. A factory with large number of departments will have a greater proportion of direct expenses.

FEATURES OF DIRECT EXPENSES

1. Direct expenses are solely incurred on a particular cost unit or cost centre. The benefit of incurring direct expenses is available only for a particular cost unit or cost centre but not for others.
2. Direct expenses may sometimes include material, labour or indirect expense, *e.g.*, cost of a special mould.
3. Direct expenses vary in direct proportion with production volume.
4. The proportion of direct expenses to total cost of production is very less.
5. They can be controlled easily when compared to indirect expenses.
6. The direct expense can be identified with the total cost of production.

The following are some of the examples of direct expenses:

1. Carriage inward and import duty paid on materials purchased.
2. Excise duty and octroi paid on materials specifically purchased for specific job.
3. Primary packing materials.
4. Cost of patents and royalty paid.

5. Travelling expenses incurred in securing an order to supervise a work being carried out at the premises of customer.
6. Architect's or surveyor's fee.
7. Sub-contract cost.
8. Cost of spare parts.
9. Cost of special drawing, design, pattern or mould.
10. Cost of special tools or equipments hired.
11. Maintenance charges of such tools or equipments.

DIRECT EXPENSES VS. DIRECT MATERIALS

Though direct material cost and direct expenses form part of prime cost, yet there is a difference between the two. Direct materials can be conveniently identified with the finished product. Whereas direct expenses are incurred for providing services for the production and cannot be identified with the finished product. For example, when power is used substantially to produce goods, say to the extent of 75 per cent of the total cost of production it is to be treated as direct cost, because power is inevitable to production process.

DIRECT EXPENSES VS. INDIRECT EXPENSES

Direct expenses differ from indirect expenses in following respects:

(*a*) Direct expenses is part of prime cost whereas indirect expenses is part of overheads.
(*b*) Direct expenses vary in direct proportion of output, whereas indirect expenses do not.
(*c*) The benefit of incurring direct expenses ends with the completion of a job, whereas the benefit of incurring indirect expenses extends to other jobs also.
(*d*) The direct expenses can be identified with the total cost of production, whereas it is not possible in case of indirect expenses.
(*e*) Direct expenses can be allocated whereas indirect expenses are to be apportioned.
(*f*) Direct expenses can be easily controlled when compared to indirect expenses.

ACCOUNTING OF DIRECT EXPENSES IN COST ACCOUNTS

The following entry is passed when direct expenses are incurred.

Direct expenses a/c *Dr.*

To cost ledger control a/c

When charged to respective jobs, the following entry is passed

Individual job a/c *Dr.*

(In the work-in-progress ledger)

To direct expenses a/c

CONTROL OF DIRECT EXPENSES

Though direct expenses constitute only a small proportion to the total cost of production it should not be allowed to go unchecked. Care must be taken to see that these expenses do not exceed the predetermined amount. Standard cost can be fixed for direct expenses and the actuals can be compared with standard cost to know variances. In case of adverse variance, it should be analysed and reported for taking remedial measures.

Questions

Simple questions

1. Define direct expenses.
2. State any four features of direct expenses.
3. Give four examples of direct expenses.
4. Distinguish between direct material and direct expense.
5. Distinguish between direct expense and indirect expense.
6. How is direct expense accounted in cost account ?
7. How is direct expenses controlled ?

❑❑❑

CHAPTER 11

Factory Overheads

INTRODUCTION

Overheads constitute one of the important elements of the cost of production. The production of goods or services of every kind involves incurring of additional costs apart from the three prime cost elements. Such expenses which are incurred over and above the prime cost elements are known as overheads. Unlike prime cost elements the overheads cannot be easily identified with finished product. As such overheads cannot be allocated but can be apportioned to finished goods only on an equitable basis. Overheads are incurred both inside and outside the production department. The amount of overheads incurred depends upon the nature of industry and as such it cannot be precisely estimated as a percentage to total cost. However, it is inevitable to incur overheads in all factories.

The ICMA terminology defines overheads as the "aggregate of indirect material cost, indirect labour cost and indirect expenses".

There are two tests which can be applied to determine whether an item of cost is overhead or not. Firstly, identification of the item of cost with cost unit or cost centre. If it is not possible to identify the item of cost to a cost unit or cost centre then such item of cost is a overhead cost. For example, rent and rates, heating and lighting, power, etc., cannot be identified with finished products. Hence they are overheads. Secondly, the convenience with which an item of cost can be identified with finished product serves as a second test. Where it is not convenient to identify an item of cost with finished product, again it is a case of overheads. For example, nails used in furniture making and buttons used in readymade garments are overheads though they can be identified with finished goods.

The following are some of the distinctive features of overheads as an element of cost:

1. The proportion of overheads in the total cost of production is less.
2. Overheads are incurred both inside and outside the production departments.
3. They cannot be allocated but can be apportioned.
4. They cannot be controlled in the strict sense of the term.
5. Most of the overheads are charged on the predetermined basis.
6. Their benefit cannot be measured.
7. Most of them are period cost and not product cost.

Very often the term indirect expenses is interchangeably used to mean overheads. However, these two terms from accounting point of view differs. The term "indirect expense" is used to record the actual indirect expense incurred. Whereas the term "overheads" is used to record indirect expenses which are likely to be incurred.

Steps in Overhead Accounting

Unlike prime cost elements overheads cannot be charged directly to the cost of production. The following steps are involved in overhead accounting procedure:

I. Classification of Overheads

Overheads can be classified on the basis of number of characteristics. The following are the important basis of overhead classification:

1. Elementwise Classification. The method of classification is done on the basis of definition of overhead. Accordingly there are three elements of overheads. They are as follows:

(*a*) ***Indirect materials cost.*** The ICMA terminology defines indirect material cost as "materials cost other than direct material cost". It cannot be allocated but it can be apportioned to cost centres or cost units. The example of indirect material cost are: oil, grease, cotton waste, sand paper, nails, nuts, bolts, screws, carbon papers, etc.

(*b*) ***Indirect labour cost.*** The ICMA terminology defines indirect labour cost as "wage cost other than direct wages cost". Indirect labour cost cannot be allocated but apportioned to cost centres or cost units. The examples of indirect labour cost are wages payable to the staff of personnel department, purchase department, service and maintenance department. Idle time wages, overtime wages, leave with pay, holiday with pay, fringe benefits and so on.

(*c*) ***Indirect expenses.*** The ICMA terminology defines indirect expenses as "expenses, other than direct expenses". Indirect expenses cannot be allocated but apportioned to cost centres or cost units. The examples of indirect expenses are rent, rates, insurance, heating, lighting, power, depreciation, repairs and maintenance, etc.

2. Functionwise Classification. Under this method of classification, the various functions performed by the factory constitutes the basis. Accordingly overheads are classified as follows:

(*a*) ***Factory overheads.*** All overheads that are incurred in various production and service departments which are ancillary to production process is known as factory overheads. Factory overheads include indirect material cost, indirect labour cost and indirect expenses incurred in the various production and service departments. Some examples of indirect material cost used in the manufacturing process are consumable stores, tiny part of materials such as thread and button in readymade garment industry, nails and polish in furniture making industry and so on. Examples of indirect labour cost incurred in production process are wages and salaries of repair and maintenance staff, salary of foreman, supervisor, inspector, watchman's salary, works manager salary, etc. Example of indirect expenss incurred in production process are depreciation, repairs and maintenance, rent, rates, taxes of factory building, drawing office expenses and so on.

(*b*) ***Administration overheads.*** It is defined by the ICMA terminology as "the cost of formulating the policy, directing the organisation and controlling the operations of an undertaking, which is not reated directly to production, selling, and distribution function of an undertaking". Administration overheads include indirect material cost, indirect labour cost and indirect expenses. Some examples of indirect material cost are office stationery such as paper, pen, ink, carbon papers, stapler, etc. Some examples of indirect labour cost incurred in the administration department of a factory are salaries of managing director, accountant, secretary, clerks and attenders. Some examples of indirect expenses incurred in office are lighting and heating, rent and rates, repairs and maintenance, bank charges, legal charges, telephone charges.

(c) ***Selling overheads.*** The overheads which are incurred in promoting sales and retaining customers is known as selling overheads. Selling overheads include indirect material cost, indirect labour cost and indirect expenses. Some examples of indirect labour cost incurred in the sales department are salaries of sales manager, salaries and commission of salesmen. Some examples of indirect expenses incurred in the sales department are expenses incurred in training salesman, advertisement, market research expenses, rent, insurance, heating and lighting of sales showroom.

(d) ***Distribution overheads.*** These are expenses which are incurred from the time finished products are packed until they reach their destination. Distribution overheads include indirect material cost, indirect labour cost and indirect expenses. Some examples of indirect material cost incurred in the distribution department of a factory are packing materials, such as cardboard boxes, hammers, nails, etc. Some examples of indirect labour cost incurred in the distribution department are salaries of warehouse staff, salaries of drivers of delivery vans, etc. Some examples of indirect expenses are rent, heating, lighting, repairs of warehouse, freight, maintenance of delivery vehicles, etc.

3. Behaviourwise Classification. According to this basis overheads are classified by establishing a relationship with the output. There are certain overheads, which vary in sympathy with production while others remain static. With reference to such behaviour overheads are classified into the following:

(a) ***Variable overheads.*** The ICMA terminology defined variable overheads as "overhead cost related to production which, in the aggregate, tends to vary in direct proportion to changes in the volume of output. In other words variable overheads vary in direct proportion to output produced. Most of the indirect material costs are example of variable overheads.

(b) ***Fixed overheads.*** Fixed overheads tend to remain constant whatever may be the output obtained within the installed capacity of plant. All the indirect labour cost and indirect expenses are examples of fixed overheads.

(c) ***Semi-variable overheads.*** These overheads vary with production level but not in direct proportion. Indirect expenses such as depreciation of plant, repairs and maintenance, telephone charges, etc., are examples of semi-variable overheads.

4. On the Basis of Normality. According to this basis overheads are classified into the following two types:

(a) ***Normal overheads.*** Overheads which are not expected to be incurred in attaining a given output are known as normal overheads. Normal overheads form part of production cost.

(*b*) ***Abnormal overheads.*** Overheads which are not expected to be incurred in attaining a given level output are known as abnormal overheads. Cost of abnormal idle time is an example of abnormal overheads. It is taken into costing profit and loss account.

Advantages of Behaviourwise Classification of Overheads

(*a*) **Cost control.** Fixed overheads are not controllable at all points and levels of management. At the most fixed overheads can be controlled only by the top level management, whereas, variable costs are capable of controlling at all levels of management. Thus, a proper classification of overheads into fixed and variable helps in controlling overheads.

(*b*) **Flexible budgets.** A flexible budget is prepared for various levels of production capacity. In its preparation, classification of overheads into fixed and variable is very important. Fixed overheads remain constant for all levels of activity, whereas variable overheads vary with every change in the level of activity.

(*c*) **Marginal costing.** Under marginal costing technique only variable overheads are taken into cost of production, whereas fixed overheads are charged to costing profit and loss account. So, for the application of marginal costing technique it becomes inevitable to classify overheads into fixed and variable overheads.

(*d*) **Break-even analysis.** For preparation of break-even chart it is also very essential to classify overheads into fixed and variable. Only then it is possible to know the point of no-profit-no-loss in a business.

(*e*) **Managerial decision-making.** Management is very often confronted with number of problems and alternate proposals. To take decisions among various proposals it is necessary to classify overheads into fixed and variable. This is so because some decisions such as make or buy, fixation of price, etc., are affected by variable overheads but not by fixed overhead.

(*f*) **Cost analysis.** Analysis of overheads into fixed and variable is important because though fixed overheads remain fixed in respect of its amount, it decreases per unit when the volume of output is increased. Similarly, though variable overheads per unit remains same it increases when production volume is increased. When it is necessary to know the cost per unit, it is necessary to classify overheads into fixed and variable components.

(*g*) **Overhead absorption.** In order to charge overheads to various products or jobs it is essential to calculate two separate overheads rates, viz., fixed overhead rate and variable overhead rates. In order to calculate these rates overheads are to be classified into fixed and variable.

II. Codification of Overheads

Codification of overheads are useful in accumulating and control of overheads. After classification of overheads, the next step involved in overhead accounting is to codify them. This is so because there are number of overheads which are incurred in factories and unless proper attention is given, the chances of accounting of all overheads may not be possible. Thus all overheads falling under the category of depreciation relating to plant and machinery, factory building, factory furniture may be given a separate number. So that depreciation relating to all the assets can be properly accounted for. Codification of overheads refers to assignment of a number or symbol for each item of overheads with a view to accumulate them easily. To facilitate easy identification of different types of overheads different code numbers are given. The code numbers given for factory overheads is known as standing order number and that to administration, selling and distribution overheads is known as cost accounting number. These numbers are listed in a schedule for ready reference.

Objects to Codification of Overheads

(*a*) To accumulate overheads systematically.

(*b*) To facilitate control over them.

(*c*) To distinguish between different types of overheads.

(*d*) To account for all types of overheads.

(*e*) To facilitate convenience of identifying the overheads.

Methods of Codification of Overheads

The following are the important methods of codifying the overheads:

(*a*) **Numerical method.** Under this method numerical numbers are used to codify the overheads. In big factories, first of all the various expenses are first identified and a separate number (or main number) is given to each expense. Subsequently a sub-number is given for various overheads incurred under each category of expense. For example, depreciation is given a code number as 1. Then depreciation relating to factory building will be given a code number of 1.1 depreciation relating to plant and machinery 1.2 and that relating to furniture 1.3 and so on. Similarly repairs may be given a code number as 2. Then repairs relating to factory building is given a code number as 2.1 repairs relating to plant and machinery is 2.2 and repairs relating to furniture as 2.3 and so on.

(*b*) **Alphabetic method or mnemonic method.** Under this method alphabets are used to codify the overheads. Each item of overhead is given a code letter which happens to be the first letter of the overhead expenditure. However, items of overheads beginning with same letter will pose a problem. To avoid confusion the next letter of the overhead can be used along with the first letter.

(*c*) **Decimal method.** Under this method the various departments are first identified and a separate number is given to them. Then each and every overhead incurred in the respective departments are given a sub-number. For example, salary of clerk belonging to office department is given a code number as 1.1, the salary of clerk belonging to selling department is given a code number as 2.1 and so on.

(*d*) **Alpha-numerical method.** This method combines both the alphabetic and numerical methods. The alphabetic letter denotes the main expenditure while the numerical number denotes its sub-division. For example, depreciation of plant is coded as D_1, depreciation of plant and machinery as D_2, and depreciation of assets as D_3.

III. Collection of Overheads

The process of ascertaining the amount of overheads incurred for a period is called collection of overhead. The classified and coded overheads are collected and recorded under-standing order number and cost accounting number. To facilitate recording of overhead a separate ledger known as "overhead ledger" is maintained. Separate accounts are opened for standing order number and cost accounting number in this ledger. Generally, overheads are collected at the end of every month and after totalling them, they are recorded in the overhead ledger.

Sources from which Various Overheads are Collected

(*a*) **Material requisition slips.** Indirect materials such as oil, grease, cotton waste, tiny parts such as bolts, nuts, etc., are drawn by various departments on the basis of material requisition slips. At the time of issue the particulars of issue of indirect materials and the departments to which they are issued are recorded in the materials requisition slip. At the end of the month, the various material requisition slips are summarised in a sheet known as "materials abstract". From the material abstract the total of indirect material cost is posted to the debit of factory overhead control account and credited to stores ledger control account.

(*b*) **Invoices.** Those indirect materials which are directly requisitioned by departmental heads, such as stationery by the office superintendent does not pass through a material requisition note. Such type of indirect materials are collected from invoices. The various invoices supporting the purchase of indirect materials by various departmental heads are entered in purchase journal meant for the purpose of collection of overheads. At the end of the month, the totals from the purchase journal is posted to the debit of factory overhead account and credited to cost control account.

(*c*) **Wages abstract.** The indirect wages paid to various employees are recorded in the wage abstract on the basis of time cards or job cards. From wages abstract, the total indirect labour cost is posted to the debit of factory overhead account and credited to wages control account.

(*d*) **Cash book.** Sundry items of expenses or indirect expenses are recorded in an analytical petty cash book. The total of indirect expenses are collected from the petty cash book on the basis of standing order number and cost accounting number. They are then posted to the debit of factory overhead control account and credited to cost control ledger account.

(*e*) **Subsidiary records.** Certain items of overheads are recorded separately in some special or subsidiary records. For example, depreciation on machinery is recorded in a plant register. Similarly, scraps can be recorded in a "Scrap report" and postal expenses in a postage book. So overheads of these nature are collected from a subsidiary register or records meant for this purpose.

(*f*) **Journal.** All notional expenses and transactions requiring adjustments, such as accrued expense, prepaid expenses are posted into the journal. The total of these expenses are posted to the debit of factory overhead control account and credited to cost control ledger account.

IV. Departmentalisation of Overheads

In a large sized factories there exists number of departments. Some departments are concerned with production process, while other departments render useful services to production departments. The former type of department is known as production department and latter is known as service department. Whenever overheads are incurred in a factory, they have to be charged to these two types of departments. The process of allocation and apportionment of overheads to various departments is known as departmentalisation of overheads. Proper allocation and apportionment of overheads serve the following purposes:

(*a*) It helps in accurate ascertainment of cost.

(*b*) It helps in controlling of overheads by comparing actuals with budgeted overheads.

(*c*) An effective control can be exercised over service departments.

(*d*) Responsibility can be fixed over various executives for efficient functioning of the different departments of the factory.

(*e*) It facilitates correct ascertainment of work-in-progress.

(*f*) It helps in accurate forecasting and estimating.

Allocation of Overheads

The term "allocation of overheads" refers to identifying an item of overhead and the allotment of the whole amount to one department or cost centre. In other words it means charging the entire amount of overhead to a department or cost centre. Some examples of allocation are salary of a foreman, wages of a machine operator, power expenses if separate meter is installed for each production department.

Apportion of Overheads

Those overheads which cannot be allocated to a specific department or cost centre need to be apportioned to various departments or cost centres. The process of charging proportionate amount of overheads to various departments is known as apportionment of overheads. As overheads are to be charged proportionate to various departments it has to be done on some equitable basis. For example, salary of general manager is to be apportioned to various departments on the basis of time devoted by him on several departments.

Difference between Allocation and Apportionment of Overheads

Under allocation of overheads the entire amount is charged to a department. Under apportionment of overhead only a proportionate amount is charged to a department. Allocation is the first step in the departmentalisation of overheads, whereas apportionment comes next. Allocation is a simple process, whereas apportionment is a cumbersome process. In case of allocation overheads can be conveniently identified with a department, whereas it is not possible to identify overheads to a department under apportionment process.

Basis of Apportionment of Overheads

Items of overhead expenses which are incurred as a common expense is to be apportioned among all the departments. Though different basis are available for apportionment, it is essential to satisfy that the overhead is closely related to the basis selected. In other words the overheads should involve a direct impact on the basis selected. The basis should also ensure accuracy under the prevailing situations. Some of the basis used for approtionment are as follows:

(*a*) Direct wages. The following overheads are apportioned on this basis:

(*i*) Workmen's compensation. (*ii*) Contribution to provident fund.

(*iii*) Contribution to ESI.

(*b*) Number of labour hours. The following overheads are apportioned on this basis :

(*i*) Salaries of inspector. (*ii*) Salaries of supervisors.

(*iii*) Other administrative expenses.

(c) Number of employees. The following overheads are apportioned on this basis:
- (*i*) Canteen expenses,
- (*ii*) Welfare expenses.
- (*iii*) Salaries of time keeping staff.
- (*iv*) Medical expenses.
- (*v*) Fringe benefits.

(d) Floor area. The following overheads are apportioned on this basis:
- (*i*) Rent and rates.
- (*ii*) Taxes.
- (*iii*) Heating and lighting.
- (*iv*) Repairs and maintenance of building.
- (*v*) Accident prevention cost.

(e) Capital value of the asset. The following overheads are apportioned on this basis:
- (*i*) Depreciation.
- (*ii*) Repairs and maintenance.
- (*iii*) Insurance.

(f) Machine hours. The following overheads are apportioned on this basis:
- (*i*) Consumable stores.
- (*ii*) Supervision charges.
- (*iii*) Repairs and maintenance.

(g) Number of watts, kilowatt, hours or light points. The following overhead expenses are apportioned on this basis:
- (*i*) Electricity charges for lighting, heating, airconditioning.
- (*ii*) Electricity charges for productive purposes.

(h) Technical estimate. The following overheads are apportioned on this basis:
- (*i*) Sundry overheads which cannot be apportioned on any of the above mentioned basis.
- (*ii*) Internal transport cost.
- (*iii*) Director's salaries.

Principles on which Apportionment of Overhead is Based

Overheads which are incurred for various departments are to be apportioned by using a suitable criterion. The choice of a criterion for appropriate apportionment is referred to as principle on which overheads are to be apportioned. The following are the important principles adopted while selecting a basis for the apportionment of overheads.

1. **Service or use criterion.** This principle is based on the assumption that the service rendered to various departments are capable of easy measurement. Accordingly overheads are apportioned on the basis of service rendered to various departments. In other words that department which derives maximum service or benefit should share more amount of overheads, when compared to other departments.
2. **Analysis or survey criterion.** This criterion is adopted where it is not possible to measure the services rendered directly because of its variation from time to time. In such a situation a survey or analysis is made to know the impact of overheads on different departments and accordingly a fair share of overheads are apportioned to all the departments. The best examples are apportionment of salary of general manager to various departments based on the assessment of his time spent on different departments. Similarly, the salary of sales manager can be apportioned to different products based upon the time spent on promoting the sales of all products.

3. **Ability to pay criterion.** This principle is applied where overheads are to be apportioned to different departments or products of which one of them happens to be a new line. In such a situation it will not be proper to overburden a new department or new product by charging a higher share of overheads. According to this principle the overheads are charged on what is termed as "what the traffic can bear or ability to pay." This means those departments or products which earn more profit should bear a higher share of overheads as compared to a new department or products.

4. **Efficiency or incentive principle.** Under this principle production target is fixed for each department and overheads are apportioned according to the targets set. In order to encourage the departmental managers to attain the targets they are also given incentives. When the targets are attained, the unit cost of production decreases, which reveals the efficiency of the department. On the other hand, if the targets are not attained the unit cost of production will be high and thereby proves inefficiency of the department.

PROBLEMS ON APPORTIONMENT OF OVERHEADS

Problem–1 (Apportionment of Overheads)

The following information is taken from the cost records of a company. Prepare a departmental overheads distribution summary from them.

	Rs.
Rent	6,000
Maintenance	3,600
Depreciation	2,700
Electricity charges	600
Supervision	9,000
Insurance premium	3,000
Employer's contribution to provident fund	900
Power	5,400

	Dept. A	*Dept. B*	*Dept. C*	*Dept. D*
Area in sq. metres	150	110	90	50
No. of workers	48	32	24	16
Direct wages (Rs.)	8000	6000	4000	2000
Value of machinery (Rs.)	24000	18000	12000	6000
Stock in hand (Rs.)	15000	9000	6000	–

(University of Madras, B.Com., April 2005)

Solution:

Statement showing apportionment of overheads

Items of expenses	*Basis of apportionment*	*A*	*B*	*C*	*D*
Direct wages	Allocated	–	–	–	2000
Rent	Area	2250	1650	1350	750
Maintenance	Value of plant	1440	1080	720	360
Depreciation	Value of plant	1080	810	540	270
Electricity	Area	225	165	135	75
Supervision	No. of workers	3600	2400	1800	1200
Insurance on stock	Value of stock	1200	900	600	–
Employer's provident fund	No. of employees	360	240	180	120
Power	Value of plant	2160	1620	1080	540
		12315	8865	6405	5315

Problem–2

The Modern Co., is having four departments. *A, B* and *C* are the producing departments and *D* is a servicing department. The actual cost for a period are as follows:

	Rs.
Rent	2,000
Repair	1,200
Depreciation	900
Lighting	200
Supervision	3,000
Insurance — Stock	1,000
Employee's insurance — Employer's liability	300
Power	1,800

The following data are also available in respect of four departments:

	Dept. A	*Dept. B*	*Dept. C*	*Dept. D*
Area sq ft.	150	110	90	50
Number of workers	24	16	12	8
	Rs.	Rs	Rs.	Rs.
Total wages	8,000	6,000	4,000	2,000
Value of plant	24,000	18,000	12,000	6,000
Value of stock	15,000	9,000	6,000	–

Apportion the cost to the various departments on the most equitable method.

(University of Madras, B.Com., March 1991)

Solution:

Statement showing apportionment of overheads

Expenses	*Basis of apportionment*	*Total*	*Departments*			
			A	*B*	*C*	*D*
Direct wages	Allocated	2,000	–	–	–	2,000
Rent	Areas in sq ft	2,000	750	550	450	250
Repair	Value of plant	1,200	480	360	240	120
Depreciation	Value of plant	900	360	270	180	90
Lighting	Area in sq ft.	200	75	55	45	25
Supervision	No. of workers	3,000	1,200	800	600	400
Insurance	Value of stock	1,000	500	300	200	–
Employee's Insurance	Total wages	300	120	90	60	30
Power	Value of point	1,800	720	540	360	180
	Total	10,400	4,205	2,965	2,135	3,095

V. Reapportionment of Overheads

It refers to the process of apportioning service department's overheads to production departments. Reapportionment of overheads is necessary because service departments are established to render service to production departments and whatever expenses that are incurred in service departments must naturally be borne by production departments. The following guidelines are to be considered while reapportioning the services department overhead to production departments:

(*a*) The nature of service rendered by each service department.

(*b*) The extent of service rendered by each service department.

(*c*) Determining or identifying the production departments which derived services from service departments.

(*d*) Selecting the basis of apportionment.

PROBLEMS ON REAPPORTIONMENT OF OVERHEADS

Problem–3 (Reapportionment of Overheads)

A company has three production departments P_1, P_2 and P_3 and one service department *S*

	Rs.
Depreciation	7,000
Rent, Rates and Taxes	4,500
Electricity	6,000
Sundries	1,300
Canteen expenses	5,500
Insurance on assets	1,400
Power	1,200

Other informations are:

	Production dept.			Service dept.
	P_1	P_2	P_3	S
Value of assets (Rs.)	25,000	20,000	15,000	10,000
Floor space (sq.) metres)	300	250	200	150
Light points (Nos)	10	8	8	4
H. P. of machines	5	4	3	–
No. of employees	40	30	20	10
Direct wages (Rs.)	3,000	2,000	1,000	500

Cost of the service department is apportioned to production departments in the ratio of 3: 2: 1.

From the above particulars determine the total overhead cost of production departments.

(Calcutta University, B.Com., (Pass) 2000)

Solution:

Statement showing reapportionment of overheads

Particulars	*Basis*	*Total*	*Production dept.*			*Service dept.*
			P_1	P_2	P_3	S
Direct wages	Allocated	500	–	–	–	500
Depreciation	Value of assets	7,000	2,500	2,000	1,500	1,000
Rent, Rates and Taxes	Floor space	4,500	1,500	1,250	1,000	750
Electricity	Light points	6,000	2,000	1,600	1,600	800
Sundries	Direct wages	1,300	600	400	200	100
Canteen expenses	No. of employees	5,500	2,200	1,650	1,100	550
Insurance on assets	Value of assets	1,400	500	400	300	200
Power	H.P. of machines	1,200	500	400	300	–
		26,900	9,800	5,700	6,000	3,900
Overhead of Dept S apportioned 3: 2: 1		–	1,950	1,300	650	– 3,900
	Total		11,750	7,000	6,650	

Problem–4

From the following particulars, show distribution of overhead and calculate overhead rate per labour hour after redistribution of service department expenses.

Expenses	*Production departments*			*Service dept.*		
	Shop 1	*Shop 2*	*Shop 3*	*Tool room*	*Stores*	*Factory office*
Direct:						
Materials (Rs.)	1,80,000	1,20,000	1,00,000	–	–	–
Direct wages (Rs.)	1,00,000	80,000	60,000	40,000	–	–
Indirect labour (Rs.)	25,200	35,200	32,000	22,200	9,000	6,600
Indirect material (Rs.)	24,000	36,000	12,000	7,200	9,600	3,600
Value of machine (Rs.)	1,50,000	2,70,000	60,000	90,000	15,000	15,000
Area (sq. mt.)	2,000	1,500	3,000	1,000	1,500	1,000
H.P.	180	180	–	40	–	–
Labour hours	60,000	60,000	40,000	–	–	–
Machine hours	32,000	24,000	12,000			
No. of employees	600	600	400	100	100	200

Other information regarding the production: Insurance Rs. 12,000, Depreciation (10%) Rs. 60,000, Factory rent – Rs. 60,000, Light and Heat Rs. 24,000 and Power Rs. 54,000.

The expenses of service departments are to be apportioned to the shops as follows:

Tool room : based on value of machines.
Stores : based on direct labour hours.
Factory office : based on direct wages.

(Calcutta University B.Com., (Hons) 2003)

Solution:

Statement showing reapportionment of overheads

Items of expenses	*Basis of apportionment*	*Shop 1*	*Shop 2*	*Shop 3*	*Tool room*	*Stores*	*Factory office*
Insurance	Area	2,400	1,800	3,600	1,200	1,800	1,200
Depreciation	Value of machine	15,000	27,000	6,000	9,000	1,500	1,500
Factory rent	Area	12,000	9,000	18,000	6,000	9,000	6,000
Light and heat	Area	4,800	3,600	7,200	2,400	3,600	2,400
power	H.P.	24,300	24,300	–	5,400	–	–
Indirect labour	Direct Direct	25,200	35,200	32,000	22,200	9,000	6,600
Indirect material	Direct	24,000	36,000	12,000	7,200	9,600	3,600
Direct wages	Allocated	–	–	–	40,000	–	–
		1.07,700	1,36,900	78,800	93,400	34,500	21,300
Expenses of tool room 5 : 9 : 2		29,188	52,437	11,775			

Expenses of stores 3 : 3 : 2		12,937	12,938	8,625			
Expenses of factory office 5 : 4 : 3		8,875	7,100	5,325			
Total factory overhead		1,58,700	2,09,375	1,04,525			
Labour hours		60,000	60,000	40,000			
Labour hour rate		2.64	3.48	2.61			

Problem–5

In an engineering factory, the following particulars have been extracted for the quarter ended 31st December 2008. Compute the departmental overhead rate for each of the production departments, assuming that overheads are recovered as a percentage of direct wages.

	Production departments			*Service dept.*	
	A (Rs.)	*B (Rs.)*	*C (Rs.)*	*X (Rs.)*	*Y (Rs.)*
Direct wages	30,000	45,000	60,000	15,000	30,000
Direct material	15,000	30,000	30,000	22,000	22,500
Staff number	1,500	2,250	2,250	750	750
Electricity (kwh)	6,000	4,500	3,000	1,500	1,500
Asset value	60,000	40,000	30,000	10,000	10,000
Light points	10	16	4	6	4
Area sq. mts.	150	250	50	50	50

The expenses for the period were:

	Rs.
Power	1,100
Lighting	200
Stores	800
Welfare to staff	3,000
Depreciation	30,000
Repairs	6,000
General overheads	12,000
Rent and taxes	550

Apportion the expenses of service department *Y* according to direct wages and those of service department *X* in the ratio of 5: 3: 2 to the production departments.

Solution:

Statement showing overhead reapportionment

Expenses	*Basis of apportionment*	*Production dept.*			*Service dept.*	
		A	*B*	*C*	*X*	*Y*
Power	Kilo watt hrs.	400	300	200	100	100
Lighting	Light points	50	80	20	30	20
Stores overhead	Direct materials	10	201	201	147	151
Welfare to staff	No. of staff	600	900	900	300	300
Depreciation	Value of asset	12,000	8,000	6,000	2,000	2,000
Repairs	Value of asset	2,400	1,600	1,200	400	400
General overheads	Direct wages	2,000	3,000	4,000	1,000	2,000
Rent and taxes	Area	150	250	50	50	50
Direct materials	Allocated	–	–	–	22,000	22,500
Direct wages	Allocated	–	–	–	15,000	30,000
		17,700	14,331	12,571	41,027	57,521
Service Dept. *Y*'s overheads apportioned	Wages	12,782	19,174	25,566		(57,521)
Service Dept. *X*'s overheads apportioned	5 : 3 : 2	20,513	12,308	8,206	(–41,027)	
		50,995	45,813	46,343		
Overhead rate as percentage of direct wages		169.98%	101.80%	77.23%		

Inter-service Departmental Overheads

Under the reapportionment of service department's overheads to production departments, as discussed above, it was presumed that service departments render service only to production department. However in most of the industries, the service departments not only render service to production departments but also to other service departments. For example, canteen department provides service to both production and other. Service department, say, repairs department. The repairs department undertakes to serve not only the production department but also the canteen department. Thus, the overheads incurred in the canteen department is to be apportioned not only to production departments but also to the repairs department. Similarly, the overheads incurred in repairs department must be apportioned to canteen department apart from other production department. This process of reapportioning the service departments, overheads to other service departments is known as inter-service departmental overheads or secondary distribution of overheads.

There are two methods which are used for secondary distribution of overhead. They are as follows:

1. Repeated distribution method or step ladder method: Under this method the overheads are apportioned by adopting a repeated number of steps. As this method involves number of steps in apportioning overheads it is also known as step ladder method.

The following steps are involved under this method:

(*a*) By applying the given percentages, the primary distribution overheads of the first service department is reapportioned to all production and service departments. In this process the first service department's account is closed.

(*b*) The second service department now consists of primary distribution overhead and a share of overhead from the first department. The total of overheads of the second service department is now reapportioned according to the given percentages. This step closes the account of the second service department.

(*c*) The first service department now has only a share of overheads reapportioned from the second service department. Applying the given percentages this amount of overheads is again reapportioned to all the other departments.

(*d*) The above process is repeated until the amount of overheads become negligible for further reapportionment.

2. Simultaneous equation method: This method involves the following two steps:

(*a*) The amount of overhead for the two service departments is to be obtained by solving two simultaneous equations.

(*b*) By applying the given percentages the service departments overheads are reapportioned to production departments. This process involves only one step as compared to first method which involves number of repeated steps.

Problem–6 (Repeated Distribution Method)

A firm has three production departments. The following figures are extracted from the books of the firm:

	Rs.
Depreciation	4,000
Lighting	240
Rent	2,000
Indirect wages	600
Power	600
Others	4,000

Other particulars:

	A	B	C	D	E
Floor space (sq. ft.)	400	500	600	400	100
Direct wages (Rs.)	900	600	900	900	700
Light points	20	30	40	20	10
H.P. of the machines	75	30	35	10	–
Value of machinery (Rs.)	12,000	16,000	20,000	1,000	1,000
Working hours	3,113	2,014	2,033		

The expenses of service departments D and E to be allocated:

	A	B	C	D	E
D	20%	30%	40%	–	10%
E	40%	20%	20%	20%	–

You are required to distribute the service department expenses to the production departments (A, B and C) according to repeated distribution method and calculate hourly rate of each production department.

(Sri Sathya Sai University B.Com., (Hons) August 2007)

Solution:

Statement showing apportionment of overheads

Item of overheads	*Basis of apportionment*	*Production dept.*			*Service dept.*	
		A	*B*	*C*	*D*	*E*
Depreciation	Value of machinery	960	1,280	1,600	80	80
Lighting	Light points	40	60	80	40	20
Rent	Floor space	400	500	600	400	100
Indirect wages	Direct wages	135	90	135	135	105
Power	H.P. of machines	300	120	140	40	–
Others	Direct wages	900	600	900	900	700
Direct wages	Allocated	–	–	–	900	700
		2,735	2,650	3,455	2,495	1,705
Overhead of Dept. 'D' apportioned		499	749	998	– 2,495	249
Overhead of Dept. 'E' apportioned		782	390	391	391	– 1,954
Overhead of Dept. 'D' apportioned		78	117	156	– 391	39
Overhead of Dept. 'E' apportioned		15	8	8	8	– 39
		4,109	3,914	5,008		

$$\text{Hourly rate} = \frac{4,109}{3,113} \quad \frac{3,914}{2,014} \quad \frac{5,008}{2,033}$$

$$= 1.31 = 1.94 = 2.46$$

Problem–7

A company has 3 production departments A, B and C and two service departments X and Y. The following data are extracted from the records of the company for a particular given period:

	Rs.
Rent and rates	25,000
General lighting	3,000
Indirect wages	7,500
Power	7,500
Depreciation on machinery	50,000
Sundries	50,000

Additional data departmentwise:

	Total	*A*	*B*	*C*	*X*	*Y*
Direct wages (Rs.)	50,000	15,000	10,000	15,000	7,500	2,500
H.P. of machines used	150	60	30	50	10	–
Cost of machinery Rs.	12,50,000	3,00,000	4,00,000	5,00,000	25,000	25,000
Production hours worked	–	6,226	4,028	4,066	–	–
Floor space used (sq. mts)	10,000	2,000	2,500	3,000	2,000	500
Lighting points (Nos.)	60	10	15	20	10	5

Service department's expenses allocation:

	A	B	C	X	Y
X	20 %	30%	40%	–	10%
Y	40 %	20%	30%	10%	–

You are required to:

(*i*) Compute the overhead rates of production departments using the repeated distribution method if overheads are absorbed on the basis of production hours.

(*ii*) Determine the total cost of a product whose direct material cost and direct labour cost are respectively Rs. 250 and Rs. 150 and which would consume 4 hours, 5 hours and 3 hours in departments A, B and C respectively.

(Sri Sathya Sai University B.Com.(Hons), March 2005)

Solution:

Statement showing apportionment of overheads

Item of expenses	*Basis of apportionment*	*Total*	*A*	*B*	*C*	*X*	*Y*
Direct wages	Allocated	10,000	–	–	–	7,500	2,500
Rent and Rates	Floor space	25,000	5,000	6,250	7,500	5,000	1,250
General lighting	Light points	3,000	500	750	1,000	500	250
Indirect wages	Direct wages	7,500	2,250	1,500	2,250	1,125	375
Power	H.P. of machines	7,500	3,000	1,500	2,500	500	–
Depreciation on machinery	Cost of machinery	50,000	12,000	16,000	20,000	1,000	1,000
Sundries	Direct wages	50,000	15,000	10,000	15,000	7,500	2,500
Total		1,53,000	37,750	36,000	48,250	–23,125	7,875
Dept X's of apportioned			4,625	6,937	9,250	–23,125	2,313
Dept Y's of apportioned			4,075	2,038	3,056	1,019	–10,188
Dept X's of apportioned			204	306	407	–1,019	102
Dept Y's of apportioned			41	20	31	10	–102
Dept X's of apportioned			2	3	5	–10	
			46,697	45,304	60,999		

$$\text{Overhead Rate} = \frac{46{,}697}{6{,}226}\ \frac{45{,}304}{4{,}028}\ \frac{60{,}999}{4{,}066}$$

$$= 7.50 = 11.25 = 15$$

COST SHEET

Direct material cost				250
Direct labour cost				150
Prime cost				400
Overheads				
Dept. A	4 × Rs. 7.50	=	30	
Dept. B	5 × Rs. 11.25	=	56.25	
Dept. C	3 × Rs. 15	=	45.00	131.25
Total cost				531.25

Problem–8

M.N Ltd. has three production departments X, Y and Z and two service departments S and C. The following details extracted from the books of accounts in respect of indirect expenses incurred during April 2005.

Indirect cost	Amount (Rs.)
Indirect wages	9,000
Lighting and heating	1,200
Rent and rates	12,000
Electric power	6,000
Depreciation	24,000
Sundry expenses	7,800
	60,000

Following further details are collected for distribution of the above costs.

Particulars	*Departments*				
	X	*Y*	*Z*	*S*	*C*
Value of machinery (in Rs.)	60	50	80	10	–
Horse power of machines	40	45	60	5	–
Light points (Nos)	20	30	40	20	10
Floor space (sq metres)	150	200	250	100	50
Direct wages (in Rs. 000)	30	20	40	4	6
Machine hours worked	4250	3380	7120		

The costs of the service departments are apportioned percentagewise as follows:

Departments	X	Y	Z	S	C
S	20	30	40	–	10
C	40	20	30	10	–

Calculate:

(*i*) Overhead recovery rates showing the basis of apportionment.

(*ii*) Total cost of Job 321 (with elementwise and departmentwise cost break down). The job card of which contain the following details.

Particulars	Dept X	Dept Y	Dept Z
Direct materials used	Rs. 268	Rs. 131	Rs. 102
Direct wages	Rs. 300	Rs. 250	Rs. 300
Machines hours worked	10	12	12

(ICWA, Inter Stage, December 2005)

Solution:

Statement showing apportionment of overheads (Repeated Distribution Method)

Item of expenses	*Basis of apportionment*	*Total*	*Production dept.*			*Service dept.*	
			X	*Y*	*Z*	*S*	*C*
Indirect wages	Direct wages	9,000	2,700	1,800	3,600	360	540
Lighting and heating	No. of light points	1,200	200	300	400	200	100
Rent and rates	Floor space	12,000	2,400	3,200	4,000	1,600	800
Electric power	H.P. of machines	6,000	1,600	1,800	2,400	200	–
Depreciation	Value of machines	24,000	7,200	6,000	9,600	1,200	–
Sundry expenses	Direct wages	7,800	2,340	1,560	3,120	312	468
Direct wages	Allocated	10,000	–	–	–	4,000	6,000
Total		70,000	16,440	14,660	23,120	7,872	7908
Service Dept S			1,574	2,362	3,149	–7,872	787
Service Dept C			3,478	1,739	2,609	869	– 8695
Service Dept S			174	261	347	– 869	87
Service Dept C			35	17	26	9	– 87
Service Dept S			2	3	4	– 9	
Total			21,703	19,042	29,255		

$$\text{Overhead recovery rate} = \frac{\text{Total overheads}}{\text{Machine hours}} = \frac{21{,}703}{4{,}250} \quad \frac{19{,}042}{3{,}380} \quad \frac{29{,}255}{7{,}120}$$

(X, Y, Z respectively)

$$= 5.11 = 5.63 = 4.11$$

Statement of Cost of Job 321

	Dept X	**Dept Y**	**Dept Z**	**Total**
Direct material used	268	131	102	501
Direct wages	300	250	300	850
overheads X – 10 × 5.11 Y – 12 × 5.63 Z – 12 × 4.11	51	68	49	168
Total	619	449	451	1,519

Problem–9

Strongman Ltd. has three production departments *A*, *B* and *C* and two service departments *X* and *Y*. The following particulars are available for the month of March 1991 concerning the organisation:

	Rs.
Rent	15,000
Municipal taxes	5,000
Electricity	2,400
Indirect wages	6,000
Power	6,000
Depreciation on machinery	40,000
Canteen expenses	30,000
Other labour related costs	10,000

Following further details are also available:

	Total	*A*	*B*	*C*	*X*	*Y*
Floor space (sq. mts.)	5,000	1,000	1,250	1,500	1,000	250
Light points (No.)	240	40	60	80	40	20
Direct wages (Rs.)	40,000	12,000	8,000	12,000	6,000	2,000
Horse power of machines (Nos.)	150	60	30	50	10	–
Cost of machine (Rs.)	2,00,000	48,000	64,000	80,000	4,000	4,000
Working hours		2,335	1,510	1,525		

The expenses of service departments are to be allocated in the following manner:

	A	*B*	*C*	*X*	*Y*
X	20%	30%	40%	–	10%
Y	40%	20%	30%	10%	–

You are required to calculate the overhead absorption rate per hour in respect of the three production departments. *(ICWA, Inter, June 1991)*

Solution:

Statement showing apportionment of overheads

Expenses	*Basis of apportionment*	*Total*	*Production dept.*			*Service dept.*	
			A	*B*	*C*	*X*	*Y*
Rent	Floor area	15,000	3,000	3,270	4,500	3,000	750
Municipal taxes	Floor area	5,000	1,000	1,250	1,500	1,00	250
Electricity	Light point	2,400	400	600	800	400	200
Indirect wages	Direct wages	6,000	1,800	1,200	1,800	900	300
Power	H.P. of machine	6,000	2,400	1,200	2,000	400	–

Depreciation	Value of machine	40,000	9,600	12,800	16,000	800	800
Canteen expenses	Direct wages	30,000	9,000	6,000	9,000	4,500	1,500
Other costs	Direct wages	10,000	3,000	2,000	3,000	1,500	500
Direct wages	Allocated	–	–	–	–	6,000	2,000
Total primary distribution		1,14,400	30,200	28,800	38,600	18,500	6,300
Service dept. *X*			3,700	5,550	7,400	(– 18,500)	1,850
Service dept. *Y*			3,260	1,630	2,445	815	(– 8150)
Service dept. *X*			164	244	326	– 815	81
Service dept. *Y*			33	15	25	8	(– 81)
Service dept. *X*			3	1	4	(– 8)	
	Total overhead		37,360	36,240	48,800		
Rate per hour			$\frac{37,360}{2,335}$ = 16	$\frac{36,240}{1,510}$ = 24	$\frac{48,800}{1,525}$ = 32		

Problem–10

XYZ Ltd. have three production departments P_1, P_2 and P_3 and two service departments S_1 and S_2 the details pertaining to which are as under:

	P_1	P_2	P_3	S_1	S_2
Direct wages (Rs.)	3,000	2,000	3,000	1,500	195
Working hours	3,070	4,475	2,419	–	–
Value of machines (Rs.)	60,000	80,000	1,00,000	5,000	5,000
H.P. of machines	60	30	50	10	–
Light points	10	15	20	10	5
Floor space (sq ft)	2,000	2,500	3,000	2,000	500

The following figures extracted from the accounting records are relevant

	Rs.
Rent and rates	5,000
General lighting	600
Indirect wages	1,939
Power	1,500
Depreciation on machine	10,000
Sundries	9,695

The expenses of the service departments are distributed as under:

	P_1	P_2	P_3	S_1	S_2
S_1	20%	30%	40%	–	10%
S_2	40%	20%	30%	10%	

Find out the total cost of product LEO which is processed for manufacture in Dept. P_1, P_2, P_3 for 4, 5 and 3 hours respectively given that its direct material cost is Rs. 50 and direct labour cost is Rs. 30. *(Sri Sathya Sai University, B.Com., March 1999)*

Solution:

Statement showing apportionment of overheads

Expenses	*Basis of apportionment*	*Production dept.* P_1	P_2	P_3	*Service dept.* S_1	S_2
Direct wages	Allocated	–	–	–	1,500	195
Rent and rates	Floor space	1,000	1,250	1,500	1,000	250
Lighting	Light point	100	150	200	100	50
Indirect wages	Direct wages	600	400	600	300	39
Power	H.P. of machines	600	300	500	100	–
Depreciation of machines	Value of machines	2,400	3,200	4,00	200	200
Sundries	Direct wages	3,000	2,000	3,000	1,500	195
Total department overhead		7,700	7,300	9,800	4,700	929
Dept. S_1		940	1,410	1,880	(– 4,700)	470
Dept. S_2		560	280	420	140	1,399
Dept. S_1		28	42	56	(– 140)	14
Dept. S_2		6	2	4	2	
		9,234	9,034	12,160		
Hourly rate		$\frac{9,234}{3,070}$ = 3	$\frac{9,034}{4,475}$ = 2.101	$\frac{12,160}{2,419}$ = 5.02		

Statement showing total cost of product LEO

Materials cost		50
Labour cost		30
	Prime cost	80
Overheads		
Dept. P_1 — 4 × 3 = 12		
Dept. P_2 — 5 × 2.01 = 10.05		
Dept P_3 — 3 × 5.04 = 15.06		
		37.11
	Total	117.11

Problem–11 (Simultaneous Equation Method)

A factory near Peenya Industrial Estate has 3 production departments and 2 service departments. The following figures are taken from the books.

	Production depts. A	B	C	*Service depts.* X	Y
Factory overheads	31,240	50,172	18,188	16,000	10,400
X	30%	40%	10%	–	20%
Y	20%	20%	50%	10%	–

Estimated working hours of production departments are A–1000 hours, B–2500 hours and C–1400 hours. Prepare a statement showing the distribution of the expenses of two service departments using simultaneous equation method and also calculate hourly rate for each department. *(Bangalore University, B.Com., April 2003)*

Solution:

$$x = 16{,}000 + \frac{10}{100}\,y$$

$$y = 10{,}400 + \frac{20}{100}\,x$$

$$x = 16{,}000 + 0.1\,y$$

$$y = 10{,}400 + 0.2\,x$$

$$x - 0.1\,y = 16{,}000$$

$$-0.2\,x + 1\,y = 10{,}400 \times 5$$

$$x - 0.1\,y = 16{,}000$$

$$-x + 5\,y = 52{,}000$$

$$4.9\,y = 68{,}000$$

$$y = \frac{68{,}000}{4.9} = 13{,}877$$

Substituting the value of y in the first equation

$$x - 0.1\,y = 16{,}000$$

$$x = 0.1y + 16{,}000$$

$$x = 0.1 \times 13{,}877 + 16{,}000$$

$$x = 1{,}387 + 16{,}000$$

$$x = 17{,}387$$

Statement showing apportionment of overheads

	Production dept.			*Service dept.*	
	A	*B*	*C*	*X*	*Y*
Direct apportionment of overheads	31,240	50,172	18,188	16,000	10,400
Service dept. *x*	5,216	6,955	1,738	– 17,387	3,477
Service dept. *y*	2,775	2,775	6,938		
	39,231	59,902	26,864		

Problem–12 (Simultaneous Equation Method)

The New Enterprises Limited has three production departments *A B C* and two services departments *D* and *E*. The following figures are extracted from the records of the company

	Rs.
Rent and rates	5,000
General lighting	600
Indirect wages	1,500
Power	1,500

Depreciation on machinery	10,000
Sundries	10,000

The following further details are available:

	Total	*A*	*B*	*C*	*D*	*E*
Floor space (sq. ft.)	10,000	2,000	2,500	3,000	2,000	500
Light points	60	10	15	20	10	5
Direct wages (Rs.)	10,000	3,000	2,000	3,000	1,500	500
H.P. of machines	150	60	50	50	10	–
Value of machinery (Rs.)	2,50,000	60,000	80,000	1,00,000	5,000	5,000
Working hours		6,226	4,028	4,066	–	–

The expenses of D and E are allocated as follows:

	A	*B*	*C*	*D*	*E*
D	20%	30%	40%	–	10%
E	40%	20%	30%	10%	–

Calculate the absorption rates for departments A, B and C. Apply simultaneous equation method.

What is the total cost of an article if its material cost is Rs. 50, labour cost Rs. 30 and it passes through departments A, B and C for 4, 5 and 3 hours respectively?

(Sri Sathya Sai University, B.Com., (Hons) March 2007)

Solution:

Statement showing apportionment of overheads

Items of expenses	*Basis of apportionments*	*A*	*B*	*C*	*D*	*E*
Direct wages	Allocated	–	–	–	1,500	500
Rent and rates	Area	1,000	1,250	1,500	1,000	250
General lighting	Light points	100	150	200	100	50
Indirect wages	Direct wages	450	300	450	225	75
Power	H.P. of machines	600	300	500	100	–
Depreciation	Value of machines	2,400	3,200	4,000	200	200
Sundries	Direct wages	3,000	2,000	3,000	1,500	500
		7,550	7,200	9,650	4,625	1,575
Service dept. *D*		966	1,449	1,933	– 4,831	488
		8,516	8,649	11,583	– 206	2,058
Service dept. *E*		823	412	617	206	– 2,058
		9,339	9,061	12,200		
Rate per hour		$\frac{9,339}{6,226}$ = 1.50	$\frac{9,061}{4,028}$ = 2.25	$\frac{12,200}{4,066}$ = 3		

Let D Dept's Expenses = x

Let E Dept's Expenses = y

$$x = 4{,}625 + \frac{10}{100} y$$

$$y = 1{,}575 + \frac{10}{100} x$$

$$x - 0.1y = 4{,}625 \times 10$$

$$0.1x - y = -\ 1{,}575$$

$$10x - y = 46{,}250$$

$$+\ 1x - y = 1{,}575$$

On subtracting $9.9x = 47{,}825$

$$x = \frac{47{,}825}{9.9} = 4{,}831$$

Substituting the value of x in the first equation

$$10 \times 4{,}831 - y = 46{,}250$$

$$-\ y = -48{,}310 + 46{,}250$$

$$y = 2{,}060$$

COST SHEET

Material cost		50
Labour cost		30
Prime cost		80
Overheads		
A = 4 hrs × 1.50 =	6	
B = 5 hrs × 2.25 =	11.25	
C = 3 hrs × 3 =	9	26.25
Factory cost		106.25

Problem–13

You are supplied with the following information and required to work out the production hour rate of absorption for overheads in departments *A*, *B* and *C* under simultaneous equation method of distributing service departments costs to production departments:

Particulars	*Total*	*Production dept.*			*Service dept.*	
		A	*B*	*C*	*P*	*Q*
Total overheads	46,000	11,310	13,050	8,040	7,500	6,100
No. of hrs. worked		5,000	4,000	3,000		
Percentage of service rendered by dept. *P*		30%	40%	20%	–	10%
Percentage of service rendered by dept. *Q*		15%	25%	40%	20%	–

(Sri Sathya Sai University, B.Com., March 1993)

Solution:

Let x be the service dept. P

and y be the service dept. Q.

$$x = 7{,}500 + \frac{20}{100}y$$

$$y = 6{,}100 + \frac{10}{100}x$$

or $$x - 0.2y = 7{,}500 \quad ...(1)$$

$$-0.1x + 1y = 6{,}100 \quad ...(2)$$

or $$5x - 1y = 37{,}500 \text{ on multiplying (1) by 5}$$

$$-0.1x + 1y = 6{,}100$$

or $$4.9x = 43{,}600$$

$$x = \frac{43{,}600}{4.9} = 8{,}898$$

Substituting the value of x in 1st equation

$$5x - 1y = 37{,}500$$

$$5 \times 8{,}898 - 1y = 37{,}500$$

$$44{,}490 - 1y = 37{,}500$$

$$-1y = -44{,}490 + 37{,}500$$

$$y = 6{,}990$$

Summary of overhead distribution:

	A	*B*	*C*	*P*	*Q*
Primary distribution	11,310	13,050	8,040	7,500	6,100
Service dept. *P*	2,670	3,557	1,780	– 8,898	890
Service dept. *Q*	1,049	1,748	2,796	1,397	– 6,990
	15,029	18,355	12,616		
Production hour rate =	15,029 / 5,000 = 3	18,355 / 4,000 = 4.58	12,616 / 3,000 = 4.20		

Problem–14

Chandra Bhanu & Company has 3 production and 2 service departments. Distribution of overheads is done as follows:

Production departments		*Service departments*	
A	Rs. 3,000	*X*	Rs. 234
B	Rs. 2,000	*Y*	Rs. 300
C	Rs. 1,000		

Expenses of service departments are to be allocated on percentage basis as follows:

	A	B	C	X	Y
X	20%	40%	30%	–	10%
Y	40%	20%	20%	20%	–

Find out the amount to be distributed among production departments under simultaneous equation. *(Andhra University, B.Com., May 1992)*

Solution:

$$x = 234 + \frac{20}{100}y$$

$$y = 300 + \frac{10}{100}x$$

$$x = 234 + 0.2\,y$$

$$y = 300 + 0.1\,x$$

or $x - 0.2y = 234$ ...(1)

$-0.1x + 1y = 300$ ...(2)

or $5x + 1y = 1{,}170$ on multiply equation (1) by 5

$$-0.1x + 1y = 300$$

$$4.9x = 1{,}470$$

$$x = \frac{1{,}470}{4.9} = 300$$

Substituting the value of x in the first equation

$$x - 0.2y = 234$$

$$-0.2y = x + 234$$

$$-0.2y = -300 + 234$$

$$-y = \frac{66}{0.2} = 330$$

Statement showing secondary distribution of overheads

	A	B	C	X	Y
Primary distribution	3,000	2,000	1,000	234	300
Service dept. X	60	120	90	–300	30
Service dept. Y	132	66	66	66	–330
	3,192	2,186	1,156		

VI. Absorption of Overheads

This is the last step in the accounting procedure of overheads. After all the overheads are reapportioned from the service departments to production departments, it involves charging of production department overheads to the number of units produced in those departments. The process of charging the overheads from cost centre to cost units is known as absorption of overheads. In other words the recovery of overheads by the finished goods from various production departments is known as absorption of overheads. The finished products absorb the factory overhead through overhead absorption rates. The overhead absorption rates are obtained by dividing the overheads to be absorbed by a basis to be decided by the management.

Actual vs. Predetermined Overhead Rates

The absorption of overheads can be based either on actual basis or predetermined basis. Accordingly overhead rates are of two types: (1) Actual rate and (2) Predetermined rate.

1. **Actual rate.** An actual rate is obtained by dividing the actual overheads to be absorbed by the actual base selected. Actual overhead rate can be calculated only historically, *i.e.,* after the overheads are incurred and measured. This rate can be calculated either periodically or annually. Actual overhead rates are not popularly used because they suffer from the following limitations:
   (*a*) The cost ascertainment will be delayed as actual overheads are available only at the end of accounting period.
   (*b*) It is not possible to prepare tender statement for quotation. Thus prospective orders are lost if actual overhead rates are used.
   (*c*) Control cannot be exercised over actual overhead rates.
   (*d*) Cost comparison is not facilitated when actual overhead rates are used. This is so because certain overheads like overtime wages, leave and holiday pay, repairs and maintenance are not uniformly spread over the entire accounting year. So overheads rate fluctuates making difficult cost comparison.
2. **Predetermined overhead rate.** Because of the above limitations suffered by the actual overhead rate, in majority of the cases predetermined overhead rate is used. This rate is calculated in advance of incurrence of overheads. It is calculated by dividing predetermined overheads by a predetermined base. Budgeted overheads and budgeted base could be used to calculate this overhead rate.

Single or Blanket Rate vs. Multiple Rate

When a single overhead rate of absorption is set up for the entire factory it is known as blanket rate. This is calculated by adding up the overheads of all the production departments and dividing by the base which is the total of the quantity or amount. The use of a blanket rate may not give accurate result when the amount of overheads differ from department to department.

When a separate overhead rate is set up for each department for absorption of overheads it is known as multiple rates. This is calculated by dividing departmental overheads by the departmental base. Multiple absorption rates are popularly used because they give accurate results.

Methods of Absorption of Factory Overheads

The following are the various methods of absorption of overheads:

1. Percentage on direct material cost: Under this method the overhead to be absorbed is divided by direct material cost and the quotient is expressed as a percentage.

Expressed as a formula,

$$\text{Factory overhead rate} = \frac{\text{Amount of factory overhead}}{\text{Direct material cost}} \times 100$$

This method is suitable under the following situations:

(*a*) Where only one variety of product is manufactured

(*b*) Where the materials used are common for different jobs or process or products

(*c*) Where raw material prices remain stable

(*d*) Where material cost constitutes highest proportion to total cost.

Advantages:

(*a*) The method is simple and easy to operate.

(*b*) The method gives satisfactory results where prices are uniform, quantity and quality of materials used is uniform.

Disadvantages:

(*a*) Most of the factory overheads are not directly related to direct materials cost. So the method is not logically correct and hence gives misleading result.

(*b*) The method is again based on an illogical relationship, *viz.,* a job requiring costlier material requires more of overheads. This is wrong and instead the reverse is true because a job requiring cheap materials may require more of overheads.

(*c*) This method does not take time factor into account. Most of the overheads are related to time element. A job which requires a longer period to complete may need more of overheads than a job which is completed in a shorter period of time.

(*d*) This method also fails to take into account the jobs performed by skilled and unskilled worker. A job which is done to a large extent by unskilled workers requires more amount of overheads. Similarly this method also fails to distinguish the jobs done by manual labour and machines.

2. Percentage on direct labour cost: Under this method the overheads to be absorbed is divided by direct labour cost and the quotient is expressed in the form of percentage. This is the oldest method of overhead absorption and still it is more popularly used. Expressed in the form of a formula:

$$\text{Overhead absorption rate} = \frac{\text{Overhead to be absorbed}}{\text{Direct wages}} \times 100$$

This method is suitable under the following situations:

(*a*) Where labour cost forms a high proportion to total cost of production.

(*b*) Where the skill of labour, *i.e.,* grade and sex composition does not differ widely.

(*c*) Where the wage rate does not fluctuate widely.

Advantages:

(*a*) The method is simple to understand and easy to operate. All the details are available and there is no need to keep separate account for collecting particulars.

(*b*) Wages are directly related to time factor and so does overheads. Hence the method gives satisfactory results.

(*c*) Labour cost fluctuates less frequently compared to materials cost. Thus this method gives stable results.

Disadvantages:

(*a*) The method is not suitable where a large part of the work is done by machines.

(*b*) Where piece rate system of wage payment is adopted the method is again unsuitable as it ignores time factor.

(c) Where the work is done by both skilled and unskilled workers the method is again not suitable. As a matter of fact the overheads incurred will be more where work is done by unskilled workers. This fact is ignored by this method.

3. Percentage on prime cost: Under this method the factory overheads to be absorbed is divided by the prime cost and the quotient is expressed in terms of percentage. Expressed as a formula:

$$\text{Overhead absorption rate} = \frac{\text{Overhead to be absorbed}}{\text{Prime cost}} \times 100$$

This method is suitable where both direct material cost and direct labour cost are equally important and overheads are related to both.

Advantages:

(a) This method is simple to operate.

(b) Particulars about materials and wages are readily available and there is no need to keep separate account for them.

(c) The method takes into account both direct material cost and direct labour cost and hence gives satisfactory results.

Disadvantages:

(a) Equal importance is given for both materials and labour, though most of the overheads are closely related to labour cost.

(b) Where material cost is predominant element of cost, the method ignores time factor.

4. Labour hour rate method: Under this method overheads are absorbed on the basis of direct labour hours worked. The overhead rate is obtained by dividing the overheads to be absorbed by the number of direct labour hours. Expressed as a formula:

$$\text{Overhead absorption rate} = \frac{\text{Overhead to be absorbed}}{\text{Direct labour hours}}$$

This method is most suitable where manual labour is engaged in factories.

Advantages:

(a) This method recognises the time factor which is also closely related to overheads. Hence the method gives satisfactory result.

(b) This method is not affected by the method of wage payment.

Disadvantages:

(a) This method involves additional clerical work and separate records are necessary for recording direct labour hours.

(b) This method is not suitable where machines are used predominantly for production purposes.

5. Machine hour rate: It refers to the overheads incurred for running a machine for one hour. By far this is the most scientific method of overhead absorption when compared to all other methods. The ICMA terminology defines machine hour rate as "as actual or predetermined rate of cost of approtionment or overhead absorption, which is calculated by dividing the cost to be apportioned or absorbed by the number of hours for which a machine or machines are operated or to be operated". In simple words, machine hour rate is obtained by dividing the amount of overhead related to a machine by the number of machine hours. Expressed in the form of a formula:

$$\text{Machine hour rate} = \frac{\text{Overhead to be absorbed}}{\text{Machine hours}}$$

This method is most suited where machines are used predominantly for production purpose.

Types of machine hour rate: There are two types of machine hour rate, *viz.*, (*a*) simple or ordinary machine hour rate and (*b*) Composite or comprehensive machine hour rate. A ordinary machine hour rate takes into account only the fixed expenses incurred in operating a machine. The variable cost, mostly the direct wages is not included under operating expenses of the machine for calculating the machine hour rate. A comprehensive machine hour rate includes both fixed and variable cost per hour incurred for operating the machine.

Advantages:

(*a*) This is most scientific, accurate and logical method of overhead absorption.

(*b*) It is an ideal method for estimating the quotation price of a job.

(*c*) It helps in knowing the existence and extent of idle time of machines.

(*d*) This method takes into account time factor and hence gives accurate result.

(*e*) It helps in comparing the efficiency and cost of operating different machines.

(*f*) It helps management in choosing between manual labour and machines.

Disadvantages:

(*a*) This method is not suitable where most of the production work is done by manual labour.

(*b*) It involves maintenance of additional records for noting down the number of machine hours operated.

Computation of machine hour rate: The following steps are involved in calculating a machine hour rate:

(*a*) To allocate and apportion the factory overheads to all the production departments.

(*b*) To charge the departmental overheads to machine or a group of machines.

(*c*) Those overheads which can be allocated directly to the machine, such as depreciation, power, repairs and maintenance are charged, specifically to the machine.

(*d*) Where comprehensive machine hour rate is desired include direct wages along with other expenses incurred for operating the machine.

(*e*) Along with the above, include cost of standby equipment to calculate machine hour rate.

(*f*) Classify the overheads into fixed and variable overheads if possible.

(*g*) Make necessary adjustments for calculating the effective machine hours by deducting cleaning or warming up time.

(*h*) Divide the expenses incurred for operating the machine for a given period by the number of hours for which machines were operated for that period.

6. Rate per unit of output: Under this method the overheads are absorbed on the basis of number of units produced. The overhead absorption rate is obtained by dividing the overheads to be absorbed by the number of units produced. Expressed as a formula:

$$\text{Overhead absorption rate} = \frac{\text{Overhead to be absorbed}}{\text{No. of units produced}} \times 100$$

This method is suitable where the finished goods are identical in nature.

Advantage:

It is the simplest of all the methods.

Disadvantages:

(*a*) This method is not suitable where different varieties of finished products are manufactured.

(*b*) If historical overhead rate of recovery is adopted it involves considerable delay in computing the overhead rate as one has to wait for the completion of production for the given period.

7. Standard rate: This method is adopted by those industries which adopt standard costing technique. The standard overheads and a standard base is set on the basis of past experience and necessary adjustments are made based on the factors which affect it. The standard overhead divided by a standard base gives a standard rate of overhead absorption.

The following formula is applicable.

$$\text{Overhead rate} = \frac{\text{Standard overhead for a period}}{\text{Standard base for the period}}$$

Problem–15 (Absorption of Overheads)

The following information relates to the activities of a production department of a factory for a month:

Direct material consumed	Rs. 1,80,000
Direct wages	Rs. 1,50,000
Factory overhead chargeable to the department	Rs. 1,26,000
Labour hours worked	12,000 hrs
Machine hours worked	10,000 hrs

The relevant data relating to one order carried out in the department during the period are as follows:

Material consumed	Rs. 30,000
Direct wages	Rs. 24,750
Labour hours worked	Rs. 1,650 hrs
Machine hours worked	Rs. 1,200 hrs

Compute factory overhead rates of recovery and the amount of overhead chargeable to the order by the following methods:

(*i*) Direct material cost percentage

(*ii*) Direct labour cost percentage

(*iii*) Labour hour rate

(*iv*) Machine hour rate *(University of Delhi, B.Com., (Pass) 2000)*

Solution:

(1) Percentage on Direct Material Cost Method:

$$= \frac{\text{Factory overheads}}{\text{Direct material cost}} \times 100$$

$$= \frac{1,26,000}{1,80,000} \times 100 = 70\%$$

Amount of overheads chargeable to the order

= 70% of Rs. 30,000 = Rs. 21,000

(2) Percentage on Direct Labour Cost Method:

$$= \frac{\text{Factory overheads}}{\text{Direct labour cost}} \times 100$$

$$= \frac{1,26,000}{1,50,000} \times 100 = 84\%$$

Amount of overheads chargeable to the order

= 84% of Rs. 24,750 = Rs. 20,790

(3) Direct Labour Hour Rate Method:

$$= \frac{\text{Factory overheads}}{\text{Direct labour hours}}$$

$$= \frac{1,26,000}{12,000} = \text{Rs. } 10.50 \text{ per hour}$$

Amount of overheads chargeable to the order

= 1,650 × Rs. 10.50 = Rs. 17,325

(4) Machine Hour Rate Method:

$$= \frac{\text{Factory overheads}}{\text{Machine hours}}$$

$$= \frac{1,26,000}{10,000} = \text{Rs. } 12.60 \text{ per hour}$$

Amount of overheads chargeable to the order

= 1,200 × Rs. 12.60 = Rs. 15,120

Problem–16

The following information relates to the activities of a production department for the month of January

		Rs.
Material used		72,000
Direct wages		60,000
Machine hours	20,000	
Labour hours	24,000	
Overhead chargeable to the department		48,000

On one order to be carried out in the month of February, the relevant data were:

		Rs.
Materials		4,000
Direct wages		3,300
Machine hours	1,200	
Labour hours	1,650	

Prepare a comparative statement of cost of this order by using the following methods of absorption of overheads.

(*i*) Direct labour hour rate

(*ii*) Percentage of direct wages

(*iii*) Machine hour rate *(University of Delhi, B.Com., (Hons) 2003)*

Solution:

(1) Direct labour hour rate $= \dfrac{\text{Overhead}}{\text{Labour hours}}$

$$= \frac{48{,}000}{24{,}000} = \text{Rs. } 2$$

(2) Percentage of direct wages $= \dfrac{\text{Overhead}}{\text{Direct wages}} \times 100$

$$= \frac{48{,}000}{60{,}000} \times 100 = 80\ \%$$

(3) Machine hour rate $= \dfrac{\text{Overhead}}{\text{Machine hours}}$

$$= \frac{48{,}000}{20{,}000} = \text{Rs. } 2.40$$

Comparative statement of cost

	Direct labour hour rate	*Direct labour cost*	*Machine hour rate*
Materials	4,000	4,000	4,000
Direct wages	3,300	3,300	3,300
Prime cost	7,300	7,300	7,300
Factory overhead			
@ Rs. 2 per hour	3,300	–	–
@ 80 % of wages	–	2,640	–
@ Rs. 2.40 per hours	–	–	2,880
Factory cost	10,600	9,940	10,180

Problem–17

A manufacturing company has supplied the following particulars relating to the activity of its production department for the month of March 1988:

Materials used	Rs. 36,000
Direct labour cost	Rs. 30,000
Direct labour hours worked	24,000
Hours of machine operations	20,000
Factory overhead chargeable to the department	Rs. 25,000

On one production order wholly carried out within the department during this period, the relevant data were:

Material used	Rs. 2,000
Direct labour	Rs. 1,650
Direct labour hours	1,650
Machine hours	1,200

Prepare a comparative statement of cost of this order by using the following three methods of recovery of overheads:

1. Direct labour hour rate method.
2. Direct labour cost rate method.
3. Machine hour rate method. *(University of Delhi, B.Com., (Hons.) 1990)*

Solution:

1. Direct labour hour rate $= \frac{\text{Factory overheads}}{\text{Direct labour hours}}$

$$= \frac{25,000}{24,000} = \text{Rs. } 1.042 \text{ per hour}$$

2. Direct labour cost rate $= \frac{\text{Factory overheads}}{\text{Direct labour cost}} \times 100$

$$= \frac{25,000}{30,000} \times 100 = 83\% \text{ of direct labour cost}$$

3. Machine hour rate $= \frac{\text{Factory overheads}}{\text{Machine hour}}$

$$= \frac{25,000}{20,000} = \text{Rs. } 1.25 \text{ per hour}$$

Statement showing cost of the order

	(1) *LHR*	*(2)* *LCR*	*(3)* *MHR*
Materials	2,000	2,000	2,000
Direct labour	1,650	1,650	1,650
Overheads (See next page)	1,719	1,375	1,500
	5,369	5,025	5,150

Note: Overheads under each method is calculated as shown below:

1. 1,650 × Rs. 1.042 = 1,719
2. $\frac{5}{6}$ × Rs. 1,650 = 1,375
3. 1,260 × Rs. 1.25 = 1,500

Problem–18

Atlas Engineering Ltd. accepts a variety of Jobs which require both manual and machine operations. The budgeted profit and loss account for the period 1996–97 is as follows:

(Rupees in lakh)

Sales		75
Cost:		
Direct materials	10	
Direct labour	5	
Prime cost	15	
Production overhead	30	
Production cost	45	
Administrative, selling and distribution overhead	15	
		60
Profit		15

Other budgeted data:

Labour hours for the period	2,500
Machine hours for the period	1,500
No. of jobs for the period	300

An enquiry has been received recently from a customer and the production department has prepared the following estimate of the prime cost required for the job.

Direct materials	Rs. 2,500
Direct labour	2,000
	Rs. 4,500

Labour hours required = 80

Machine hours required = 50

You are required to:

(*a*) Calculate by different methods, six overhead absorption rates for absorption of production overhead and comment on the suitability of each.

(*b*) Calculate the production overhead cost of the order based on each of the above rates.

(*c*) Give your recommendation to the company. *(ICWA, Inter, December 1997)*

Solution:

1. Direct labour hour rate $= \dfrac{\text{Overheads to be absorbed}}{\text{Direct labour hours}}$

$= \dfrac{3,00,000}{2,500} = 120$

2. Machine hour rate $= \dfrac{\text{Overheads to be absorbed}}{\text{Machine hours}}$

$= \dfrac{3,00,000}{1,500} = 200$

3. Percentage on direct material cost $= \dfrac{\text{Overheads to be absorbed}}{\text{Direct materials cost}} \times 100$

$= \dfrac{3,00,000}{1,00,000} \times 100 = 300\%$

4. Percentage on direct wages cost $= \dfrac{\text{Overheads to be absorbed}}{\text{Direct wages}} \times 100$

$= \dfrac{3,00,000}{50,000} \times 100 = 600\%$

5. Percentage on prime cost $= \dfrac{\text{Overheads to be absorbed}}{\text{Prime cost}} \times 100$

$= \dfrac{3,00,000}{1,50,000} \times 100 = 200\%$

6. Production unit $= \dfrac{\text{Overheads to be absorbed}}{\text{No. of jobs for the period}}$

$= \dfrac{3,00,000}{300} = \text{Rs. } 10,000$

Statement showing overheads under the different methods

Methods		*Production overhead for the job*
1. Direct labour hour rate	80 hrs. × 120	9,600
2. Machine hour rate	50 hrs. × 200	10,000
3. Percentage of direct material cost	$\dfrac{300}{100} \times 2,500$	7,500
4. Percentage of direct labour cost	$\dfrac{600}{100} \times 2,000$	12,000
5. Percentage of prime cost	$\dfrac{200}{100} \times 4,500$	12,000
6. Production unit/job	1 × 10,000 = 10,000	9,000

Comments:

1. For labour hour rate and machine hour rate the rates are based on time and hence generally considered equitable as most overheads vary with time.
2. In case of percentage of direct material cost it may be suitable only if all the jobs use the same materials.
3. If wage rates vary, percentage of direct wages may cause distortion.
4. Percentage of prime cost is simple but has the disadvantages of percentage of direct material cost and percentage of Direct labour cost.
5. In case of production unit (Job) method, it is very simple and acceptable if all the jobs are same. If they are different, this method is not appropriate for charging overhead.

Recommendation:

Separate overhead rate based on labour hours and machine hours for absorption of labour related overhead and machine related overhead respectively is the ideal solution. However if the degree of mechanisation is very high in the factory and the management wants a single rate the machine hours rate may be used for absorption of production overheads.

PROBLEMS ON MACHINE HOUR RATE

Problem–19

From the following particulars, compute a machine hour rate:

	Rs.
Cost of machine	30,000
Estimated scrap value after the expiry of its life of 5 years.	3,000
Rent and rates of the department	2,000
General lighting of the department per month	200
Salary of supervisor per month	1,500

Power consumption 5 units per hour at the rate of 60 paise per unit.

Estimated working hours of the machine per year is 2000 hours. The machine occupies $\frac{1}{4}$ of the total area of the department.

The supervisor is expected to devote $\frac{1}{5}$ of his total time to this machine. General lighting charges are to be apportioned on the basis of floor area. The rent and rates charges are for 3 months. *(Sri Sathya Sai University, B.Com., (Hons.) August 2007)*

Solution:

Computation of Machine Hour Rate

Fixed charges: **P.A.**

Rent and Rates per quarter

$$2{,}000 \times \frac{1}{4} = 500$$

For 1 year 500 × 4 quarters = 2,000

General lighting for 1 month

$$200 \times \frac{1}{4} = 50$$

For 1 year 50 × 12 months	=	600
Salary of supervisor for 1 month $1500 \times \frac{1}{5} = 300$		
For 1 year 300 × 12 months	=	3,600
Total fixed charges per year		6,200
Fixed charges per hour $\frac{6,200}{2,000}$	=	3.10
Variable charges		
Depreciation $\frac{30,000 - 3,000}{5} \times \frac{1}{2,000}$	=	2.70
Power 5 units × 0.60	=	3.00
Machine hour rate		8.80

Problem–20

From the particulars finished below compute a machine hour rate.

Name of the equipment	:	Mobile crane
Date of purchase	:	1st April 2,000
Make	:	Lift 4 load corporation
Cost	:	Rs. 25,000
Power	:	Diesel 10 H.P. Engine
Estimated life	:	10 years
Depreciation	:	15% per annum on original cost
Insurance	:	Rs. 100 per annum
Repairs and maintenance	:	Rs. 600 per annum
Consumable stores	:	Rs. 300 per annum
Rent and rates	:	Rs. 750 per annum

Superintendence expenses for 5 similar machines estimated Rs. 1,300 per annum.

Assume that the crane can work for 200 hours per month but actually works for only 80% of the hours. Cost of diesel, oil per hour is estimated at Rs. 1.50.

(Sri Sathya Sai University, B.Com., (Hons.) March 2007)

Solution:

Computation of Machine Hour Rate

Standing charges:	**P.A.**
Consumable stores	300
Rent and rates	750
Superintendence expenses $\frac{1300}{5}$	260
Insurance	100
	1410

Hourly rate $\frac{1410}{1920}$ 0.734

Machine expenses:

Depreciation $\frac{15}{100} \times 25{,}000 = 3{,}750$

$\frac{3{,}750}{1{,}920} =$ 1.953

Repairs and maintenance $\frac{600}{1920} =$ 0.313

Power, diesel, oil per hour = 1.500

Machine hour rate 4.500

Problem–21

The following annual charges are incurred in respect of a machine shop where manual labour is almost nil and where work is done by means of five machines of exactly similar type and specifications:

(*a*) Rent and rates (all machines occupy floor space) for the shop: Rs. 4,800 p.a.

(*b*) Depreciation on each machine: Rs. 500

(*c*) Repairs and maintenance for the five machines: Rs. 1,000 p.a.

(*d*) Power consumed (as per meter) @ 5 paise per unit for the shop: Rs. 3,000

(*e*) Electric charges for lighting the entire shop: Rs. 540 p.a.

(*f*) Attendants: There are two attendants for the five machines and they are each paid Rs. 60 per month.

(*g*) Supervision: For the above machines in the shop, there is one supervisor whose emoluments are Rs. 250 per month.

(*h*) Sundry supplies such as lubricants for the shop Rs. 450 p.a.

(*i*) Hire purchase instalment payable for the machine (including Rs. 300 as interest) Rs. 1,200.

Each machine uses 10 units of power per hour. Calculate the machine hour rate for machine for the year. *(Sri Sathya Sai University, B.Com. (Hons.) March 2006, Kakatiya University, B.Com., March 2004)*

Solution: ***Working Note:***

Calculation of Machine Hours

Power consumed is the basis for calculating machine hours

Total amount of power consumed = Rs. 3,000

Rate of power (10 units @ 0.05 p) = 50 paise an hour

Total working hours of the machine = Rs. $\frac{3{,}000}{0.50}$ paise per hr

= 6,000 hrs.

Number of machines = 5

Machine hours per machine $= \frac{6,000}{5}$

$= 1,200$ hours

Computation of Machine Hour Rate

Standing charges:			**P.A.**
(1) Rent and rates	$4,800 \times \frac{1}{5}$	=	960
(2) Lighting charges	$540 \times \frac{1}{5}$	=	108
(3) Attender's salary for machine	$1,440 \times \frac{1}{5}$	=	288
(4) Supervision per machine	$3,000 \times \frac{1}{5}$	=	600
(5) Sundry supplies per machine	$450 \times \frac{1}{5}$	=	90
			2,046
	Standing charges per hr. $\frac{2,046}{1,200}$	=	1.70
Variable charges:			
(1) Depreciation	$\frac{500}{1,200}$	=	0.42
(2) Repairs and maintenance	$\frac{200}{1,200}$	=	0.17
(3) Power 10 units @ 0.05 paise per unit		=	0.50
	Machine hour rate		2.79

Problem–22

A machine costs Rs. 90,000 and is deemed to have a scrap value of 5% at the end of its effective life (19 years). Ordinarily the machine is expected to run for 2,400 hours per annum but it is estimated that 150 hours will be lost for normal repairs and maintenance and further 750 hours will be lost due to staggering. The other details in respect of the machine are:

(1) Wages (each operator is in charge of 2 machines)	6,000 per year
(2) Rent and rates of the shop	3,000 per year
(3) General lighting of the shop	250 per month
(4) Insurance premium for the machine	200 per quarter
(5) Cost of repair and maintenance for the machine	250 per month
(6) Shop supervisor's salary	500 per month
(7) Power consumption of the machine per hour	20 units
(8) Rate of power per 100 units	Rs. 10
(9) Other factory overheads attributable to the shop	4,000 per year

There are four identical machines in the shop. The supervisor is expected to devote $\frac{1}{5}$ of his time for supervising the machine. Compute a comprehensive machine hour rate from the above details. *(Sri Sathya Sai University, B.Com. (Hons), March 2005)*

Solution:

Computation of Machine Hour Rate

			P.A.		
Standing charges:					
Rent and rates	$3{,}000 \times \frac{1}{4}$	=	750		
General lighting	$250 \times \frac{1}{4} \times 12$	=	750		
Insurance	200×4	=	800		
Supervisor's salary	$500 \times 12 \times \frac{1}{5}$	=	1,200		
Overhead allocated	$4{,}000 \times \frac{1}{4}$	=	1,000		
			4500		
	Per hour = $\frac{4{,}500}{1{,}500}$			=	3.00
Machine expenses:					
Wages	$\frac{6{,}000}{1{,}500} = 4$				
For 2 machines = 4				=	2.00
For 1 machine = 2					
Power					
For 100 units	Rs. 10				
For 20 units	$\frac{10 \times 20}{100}$			=	2.00
Repairs and Maintenance				=	2.00
	$250 \times 12 = \frac{3{,}000}{15}$				
Depreciation:					
Book value			90,000		
Less: Scrap value	$\frac{5}{100} \times 90{,}000 =$		4,500		
			85,500		
For 19 years	$\frac{85{,}500}{19} = 4{,}500 = \frac{4{,}500}{1{,}500}$				3.00
For 1 year =					12.00

Problem–23

Following annual charges are incurred in respect of a machine in a shop where work is done by five machines of exactly similar specifications:

	Rs.
Rent of the shop	15,000
Depreciation on each machine	5,000
Repairs in total for all machines	10,000
Power consumed (as per meter) @ Rs. 1.50 per unit for the shop	12,000
Electricity charges for light in the shop	600
Sundry supplies for the shop	900
Hire purchase instalment payable for the machine (including Rs. 800 as interest)	2,500

Calculate the machine hour rate by considering the following additional information:

(1) The machine uses 5 units of power per hour.

(2) There are two attendants for the five machines each of whom is paid Rs. 200 per month.

(3) There is one Supervisor for the shop whose emoluments are Rs. 2,000 per month.

(Sri Sathya Sai University, B.Com. (Hons), March 2004)

Solution: ***Working Note***

Calculation of Working Hours

Total power bill = Rs. 12,000

Rate per unit = Rs. 1.50

Number of units = $\frac{12,000}{1.50}$ = 8,000 units for 5 machines

For 1 machine = $\frac{8,000}{5}$ = 1,600 units

Working hours = $\frac{\text{1,600 units}}{\text{5 units per hr}}$

= 320 hours per year

Computation of Machine Hour Rate

	P.A.
Rent $\frac{1}{5} \times 15,000$	3,000
Depreciation on each machine	5,000
Repairs $\frac{1}{5} \times 10,000$	2,000
Electricity charges $\frac{1}{5} \times 600$	120
Sundry supplies $\frac{1}{5} \times 900$	180

Attendants wages $200 \times 12 \times 2 = \frac{4,800}{5}$	960
Supervisor's salary $2,000 \times 12 = \frac{24,000}{5}$	4,800
	16,060

Per month = $\frac{16,060}{12}$ = 1,338.33

Per hour $\frac{1,338.33}{320}$ =	4.18
Power 5 units @ Rs. 1.50 per unit =	7.50
Machine Hour Rate	11.68

Problem–24

Calculate Machine hour rate of 'A' machine

	Rs.
Consumable stores	600 for 'A' machine
Consumable stores	1,000 for 'B' machine
Repairs	800 for 'A' machine
Repairs	1,200 for 'B' machine
Heat and light	360
Rent	1,200
Insurance of building	4,800
Insurance of machines	800
Depreciation of machines	700
Room service	60
General charges	90 (to be shared equally)

Additional information:

	Working Hours	Area (sq. meters)	Book value (Rs.)
'A' Machine	10,000	100	12,000
'B' Machine	25,000	500	20,000

(Sri Sathya Sai University, B.Com. (Hons), March 2002)

Solution:

Computation of Machine Hour Rate

	Machine A	Machine B
Consumable stores	600	1,000
Repairs	800	1,200
Heat and light (Area)		

$A = \frac{1}{6} \times 360$	60	300
$B = \frac{5}{6} \times 360$		
Rent (area)		
$A = \frac{1}{6} \times 1{,}200$	200	1,000
$B = \frac{5}{6} \times 1{,}200$		
Insurance of building (area)	800	4,000
$A = \frac{1}{6} \times 4{,}800$		
$B = \frac{5}{6} \times 4{,}800$		
Insurance of machine (value of machinery)	300	500
$A = \frac{3}{8} \times 800$		
$B = \frac{5}{8} \times 800$		
Room services (area)	10	50
$A = \frac{1}{6} \times 60$		
$B = \frac{5}{6} \times 60$		
General charges	45	45
	2,815	8,095
Machine hour rate =	$\frac{2{,}815}{10{,}000}$	$\frac{8{,}095}{25{,}000}$
	0.28	0.32

Problem–25

Calculate machine hour rate from the following:

	Rs.
Cost of machine	5,00,000
Cost of installation	50,000
Scrap value after 15 years	25,000
Rates and rent per month for the shop	1,000
General lighting per month	1,500
Shop supervisor's salary per month	3,000
Insurance premium for the machine p.a.	4,800

Estimated repairs per annum	5,000
Power 10 units per hour and the rate of power for 100 units	100
Estimated working hours per annum	2,200

This includes setting up time of 200 hours. The machine occupies $\frac{1}{4}$ of the total area of the shop. The supervisor is expected to devote $\frac{1}{5}$ of his time for supervising the machine.

(Bangalore University, B.Com., November 2003)

Solution:

Computation of Machine Hour Rate

			P.M.
Depreciation:			
Cost of machine	5,00,000		
Add: Cost of installation	50,000		
	5,50,000		
Depreciation per year $\frac{5,50,000}{15}$			
Per month = $\frac{36,666}{12}$		=	3,055
Rent and rates 1,000 × $\frac{1}{4}$		=	250
General lighting		=	1,500
Shop supervisor's salary 3,000 × $\frac{1}{5}$		=	600
Insurance premium $\frac{4,800}{12}$		=	400
Repairs $\frac{5,000}{12}$		=	416
			6,221
Per hour = $\frac{6,221}{2,000}$		=	3.11
Power $\frac{100}{100}$ × 10		=	10.00
	Machine hour rate		13.11

Problem–26

From the following data of textile factory machine room, compute an hourly machine rate assuming that the machine room will work on 90% capacity throughout the year and that a breakdown of 10% is reasonable.

There are 3 days holidays at Deepawali, 2 days at Holi and 2 days at Christmas, exclusive of Sundays. The factory works 8 hours a day and 4 hours on Saturday. Number of machines (each of same type) 40.

Expenses per annum:	*Rs.*
Power	3,120
Light	640
Salaries of foreman	1,200
Lubricating oil	66
Repairs to machines	1,446
Depreciation	785

(Acharya Nagarjuna University, B.Com., June 2004)

Solution: ***Working Note:***

Calculation of Effective Machine Hours

No. of holidays in a year:

Sundays	=	52
Deepawali	=	3
Holi	=	2
Christmas	=	2
		59 days

No. of working days = 365 – 59	=	306 days
No. of hours for 306 days = 306 × 8	=	2,448
Less: Half days (Saturdays) = 52 × 4	=	208
Working hours		2,240
Less: Machine breakdown 10%		224
Effective machine hours		2,016

Computation of Machine Hour Rate

		Cost per annum	*Cost per hour*
Standing charges:			
Light	$640 \times \frac{1}{40}$	16.00	
Salaries of foreman	$1{,}200 \times \frac{1}{40}$	30.00	
Lubricating oil	$66 \times \frac{1}{40}$	1.65	
		47.65	
Standing charges per hour:	$\frac{47.65}{2{,}016}$		0.024
Variable expenses per hour			
Power	$3{,}120 \times \frac{1}{40} \times \frac{1}{2{,}016} =$		0.039

Repairs to machines	$1{,}446 \times \frac{1}{40} \times \frac{1}{2{,}016} =$	0.018
Depreciation	$780.60 \times \frac{1}{40} \times \frac{1}{2{,}016} =$	0.010
	Machine Hour Rate	0.091

Problem–27

Following are the particulars relating to 3 machines for a particular period of 320 hours:

	Machine A	*Machine* B	*Machine* C
Cost of machine	Rs. 20,000	Rs. 30,000	Rs. 40,000
Power	Rs. 90	Rs. 160	Rs. 300
Direct wages	Rs. 600	1,600	2400
Area occupied	2,00 sq. mts	500 sq.mts	800 sq.mts
Number of workers	4	10	20
Light points	4	8	12

During the period following expenses were incurred:

	Rs.
Rent and rates	900
Depreciation	2,700
Power	550
Canteen expenses	102
Lighting expenses	96
Indirect wages	920
Repairs	3,600
Sundries	600

Compute comprehensive machine hour rate for each of the above machines.

(Calcutta University, B.Com. (Hons), 2004)

Solution:

Statement showing apportionment of overheads

Items of expenses	*Basis of apportionment*	*Total*	*Machines* A	B	C
Rent and rates	Area	900	120	300	480
Depreciation	Value of machine	2,700	600	900	1,200
Power	Direct	550	90	160	300
Canteen expenses	No. of workers	102	12	30	60
Lighting expenses	Light points	96	16	32	48
Indirect wages	Direct wages	920	120	320	480
Repairs	Value of machine	3,600	800	1,200	1,600
Sundries	Direct wages	600	78	209	313
Direct wages	Allocated	4,600	600	1,600	2,400
		14,068	2,436	4,751	6,881

Machine hour rate	$\frac{2,436}{320}$	$\frac{4,751}{320}$	$\frac{6,881}{320}$
	= 7.61	= 14.84	= 21.50

Problem–28

Three machines *P*, *Q* and *R* which are of different nature are used in a department of a factory. From the following information compute machine hour rate of machine *R*:

(*i*) Total cost of machine *P*, *Q* and *R* is — Rs. 50,000
out of which cost of machine *R* is — Rs. 10,000
Its estimated scrap value and working life are Rs. 1,000 and 18,000 hours respectively.

(*ii*) Rent (Total area 1,000 sq/ft and machine *R* occupies 250 sq/ft) — Rs. 780 p.a.

(*iii*) Lighting (Total light points 12, out of which 2 points used for machine *R*) — Rs. 288 p.a.

(*iv*) Insurance for all machines : Rs. 45 per quarter

(*v*) Consumable stores for machine *R* : Rs. 60 per month

(*vi*) Salary of supervisor (supervisor devotes $\frac{1}{4}$th of his time for machine *R*) : Rs. 6,000 p.a.

(*vii*) Repairs and maintenance for the entire life of machine *R* : Rs. 1,800

(*viii*) Machine *R* consumes 5 units of power per hour at a cost of Rs. 16 per 100 units.

(*ix*) Machine *R* will work 2,000 hours p.a., out of which normal idle time estimated at 8% of total working hours and time for routine maintenance estimated at 40 hours p.a. *(Calcutta University, B.Com. (Hons), 2001)*

Solution:

Computation of Machine Hour Rate of Machine R

Standing charges:		**P.A.**	**P.H.**
Rent	$780 \times \frac{250}{1,000}$	195	
Insurance	$45 \times \frac{10,000}{50,000} \times 4$	36	
Salary of Supervisor	$6,000 \times \frac{1}{4}$	1,500	
		1,731	1.517
Running charges:			
Depreciation	$\left(\frac{10,000 - 1,000}{18,000}\right)$		0.500
Repairs and maintenance	$\frac{1,800}{18,000}$		0.100
Lighting	$\left(288 \times \frac{2}{12} \times \frac{1}{1,800}\right)$		0.027

Consumable stores	$\dfrac{60 \times 12}{1,800}$	0.400
Power	$\dfrac{5 \times 16}{100}$	0.800
	Machine hour rate	3.344

Working Note:

Working hours	2,000
Less: Normal idle time 2000 × $\dfrac{8}{100}$	160
	1,840
Less: Maintenance	40
Effective working hours	1,800

Problem–29

A machine shop in a factory has five machines of exactly similar type and specification. One operator is employed on each machine at Rs. 20 per hour. The factory works a 40-hour week which includes four hours for set-up time for each machine. The operators are paid fully for 40 hours. Costs are reported for the machine shop on the basis of thirteen four-weekly periods.

The following details applicable to the cost centre/machine are available:

(1) Set-up time is unproductive and no power is consumed during the set-up time.
(2) Original cost of a machine is Rs. 1,30,000.
(3) Depreciation on machine is to be provided at 10% per annum on original cost.
(4) Maintenance and repairs per week per machine amounts to Rs. 25.
(5) Consumable stores per week per machine amounts to Rs. 27.
(6) Power consumed is 10 units per hour per machine at 80 paise per unit.
(7) Wages paid to the operators are considered as indirect.
(8) Overheads apportioned to the cost centre are:

Rent	Rs. 3,000 p.a.
Heat and light	Rs. 4,000 p.a.
Miscellaneous expenses	Rs. 6,000 p.a.

You are required to calculate:

(*i*) Cost of running one machine for a four-week period; and
(*ii*) The machine hour rate. *(University of Delhi, B.Com. (Hons), 2005)*

Solution: Working Note:

Calculation of machine hours

Number of machine hours	40
Less: set-up time	4
Effective hours per week	36

Effective hours per four-week = 36 × 4 = 144

Computation of Machine Hour Rate

For 4 weeks

(1) Rent	=	$\frac{3{,}000 \times 4 \text{ weeks}}{5 \text{ machines} \times 52 \text{ weeks}}$	46.15
(2) Heat and light	=	$\frac{4{,}000 \times 4 \text{ weeks}}{5 \text{ machines} \times 52 \text{ weeks}}$	61.54
(3) Miscellaneous overheads	=	$\frac{6{,}000 \times 4 \text{ weeks}}{5 \text{ machines} \times 52 \text{ weeks}}$	92.31
(4) Depreciation	=	$1{,}30{,}000 \times \frac{10}{100} \times \frac{4}{52}$	1,000.00
(5) Maintenance	=	25 × 4	100.00
(6) Consumable stores	=	Rs. 27 × 4	108.00
(7) Power	=	10 units × 36 hours × 4 × Rs. 0.80	1,152.00
(8) Wages of operator	=	200 × 40 hours × 4 weeks	3,200.00
			5,760.00

$$\text{Machine hour rate} = \frac{5{,}760}{144} = \text{Rs. } 40$$

Problem–30

The machine shop of a manufacturing concern has 6 identical machines manned by 6 operators. The total cost of the machine is Rs. 8,00,000. The following information relates to 6 monthly period ended 30th September 2002.

Normal available hours per month	208
Absenteeism (without pay) hours per month	18
Leave (with pay) hours per month	20
Normal idle time hours per month	10
Average rate of wages per hour per operator	Rs. 2.50
Production bonus	15% on wages
Power and fuel consumption	Rs. 9,000
Supervision and indirect labour	Rs. 3,300
Electricity, lighting	Rs. 1,200
Repairs and maintenance (per annum)	3% value of machine
Insurance (per annum)	Rs. 42,000
Depreciation (per annum)	10% of original cost
Allocated factory overheads (per annum)	Rs. 75,670

Calculate machine hour rate. *(University of Delhi, B.Com. (Hons), 2001)*

Solution: ***Working Note:***

(1) Calculation of machine hours:

Hours per month = 208 – 18 – 20 – 10 = 160

Hours for 6 months = 160 hours × 6 machines × 6 months

= 5,760 hours

(2) Calculation of wages:

Hours paid = 208 – 18 = Rs. 190

Wages = 190 hours × Rs. 2.50 × 6 machines × 6 months

= Rs. 17100

Computation of Machine Hour Rate

	6 months
	Rs.
Power and fuel	9,000
Supervision and indirect labour	3,300
Electricity lighting	1,200
Repairs and maintenance $8{,}00{,}000 \times \frac{3}{100} \times \frac{6}{12}$	12,000
Insurance (for 6 months)	21,000
Depreciation $8{,}00{,}000 \times \frac{10}{100} \times \frac{6}{12}$	40,000
Other overheads $75{,}670 \times \frac{6}{12}$	37,835
Wages	17,100
Bonus to workers $17{,}100 \times \frac{15}{100}$	2,565
	1,44,000

$$\text{Machine hour rate} = \frac{1{,}44{,}000}{5{,}760} = \text{Rs. } 25$$

UNDER-ABSORPTION AND OVER-ABSORPTION OF FACTORY OVERHEADS

As was mentioned earlier, the absorption of factory overheads could be based either on the actual rate or predetermined rate. When the actual rates are used the overheads are fully absorbed and no difference will arise between the overheads actually incurred and that absorbed. However, when predetermined rates are used, the overheads absorbed may not be equal to overheads incurred. This gives rise to under or over absorption of overheads.

When the overheads absorbed by the finished products are less than the actual overhead incurred, it is known as under absorption of overheads. For example, when overheads absorbed are Rs. 4,500 as against the actual overhead of Rs. 5,000, it is a case of under absorption of overheads. When the overheads absorbed by the finished products are more than the actual overheads it is known as over absorption of overheads. For example, if the overheads absorbed by the finished goods are Rs. 5,500 as against the actual overheads of Rs. 5,000 it is a case of over absorption of overheads.

The following are some of the causes which are responsible for the occurrence of over or under absorption of overheads:

(*a*) Wrong estimation of factory overheads.

(*b*) Change in the method of production which affects actual overheads.

(*c*) Change in the production capacity unexpectedly.

(*d*) Seasonal change in overheads.

(*e*) Change in production volume.

Treatment of Over-absorption and Under-absorption of Factory Overheads in Cost Accounts

The following methods are followed to treat the over and under absorption of overheads:

(*a*) **Use of supplimentary overhead rates:** This method is used when the over or under absorption of overheads are of considerable amount. The over or under absorbed overheads are adjusted to the cost of goods produced. Otherwise this will give rise to misleading picture. The cost of production is revised by making use of supplementary rates of overheads. The supplementary rates is obtained by dividing the amount of over absorption or under absorption of overheads by the actual base selected. There are two supplementary rates *viz.,* positive and negative supplementary rates. In case of under absorption the overhead is adjusted by adding it back through a positive supplementary rate. In case of over absorption, the over absorbed overhead is deducted through a negative supplementary rate. The effect of this treatment is overheads are absorbed at the actual rate.

(*b*) **Write off to costing profit and loss account:** This method is used when the over or under absorption of overheads are of small amount. According to this method the difference of under or over absorption of overheads is transferred to costing profit and loss at the end of accounting period. In case of under-absorption it is debited, and in case of over-absorption it is credited to costing profit and loss account.

(*c*) **Carry over to next year's overhead account:** Under this method the under absorption or over absorption of overheads of one year is carried forward to the next year in order to determine the overhead absorption rate of the next year. This method is criticised on the ground that the overheads of one year should be absorbed in the same year but not to carry over to the next year as it distorts the cost of production of next year.

Problem–31 (Under or Overabsorption of Overheads)

The factory overhead costs of three production departments of a company engaged in executing job orders for the accounting year 2003–04 are as follows:

A	Rs.	19,300
B	Rs.	4,200
C	Rs.	4,800

Overheads has been applied as under:

Dept A – Rs. 1.50 per machine for 14,000 hours

Dept B – Rs. 1.30 per direct labour hour for 3,000 hours

Dept C – 80% of direct labour cost of Rs. 6,000

Find out the amount of departmentwise under or over absorbed overhead.

(Calcutta University, B.Com. (Hons), 2004)

Solution:

Statement Showing Under/over Absorption of Overhead

	Dept A	*Dept B*	*Dept C*
Estimated overheads	21,000	3,900	4,800
Less: Actual overheads	19,300	4,200	4,800
	(+)1,700	(–)300	NIL
	(over absorption)	(under absorption)	

Problem–32

The budgeted activity and cost data for each half year of S.V. Ltd. were as follows:

	Rs.
Direct labour hours	68,000
Direct wages	42,500
Overheads: Fixed	37,400
Variable	64,600

During the 6 months January to June, the following actual results were achieved:

Direct labour hours incurred	65,000
Direct wages	45,500
Overheads: Fixed	38,700
Variable	65,800

The existing method of absorbing overheads is by a direct wages percentage rate. A proposal has been made to change the overhead absorption to a direct labour hour rate analysed into fixed and variable overheads.

You are required for the period January to June to calculate under the new proposal (*i.e.,* using direct labour hour rates of absorption):

(*i*) The budgeted direct labour hour rates of overhead absorption for fixed and variable overheads.

(*ii*) The absorbed overheads.

(*iii*) The over or under absorbed overheads.

(University of Delhi, B.Com., (Hons) 2002)

Solution:

$$\text{Rate for fixed overheads} = \frac{\text{Fixed overheads}}{\text{Direct labour hrs}}$$

$$= \frac{37{,}400}{68{,}000} = 0.55$$

$$\text{Rate for variable overheads} = \frac{\text{Variable overheads}}{\text{Direct labour hrs}}$$

$$= \frac{64,600}{68,000} = 0.95$$

$$\text{Total rate} = 0.55 + 0.95 = \text{Rs. } 1.50$$

$$\text{Absorbed overheads} = \text{Direct Labour} \times \text{Rate Hours}$$

$$= 65,000 \times 1.50 = \text{Rs. } 97,500$$

$$\text{Actual overheads} = 38,700 + 65,800 = \text{Rs. } 1,04,500$$

$$\text{Under absorption} = 1,04,500 - 97,500 = \text{Rs. } 7,000$$

Problem–33

Separate departmental overhead application rates based on direct labour hours are being used by a manufacturing company. At the end of the year, the following information is supplied to you:

	Dept. I	*Dept. II*	*Dept. III*
Overhead absorption rates used	Rs. 4	3	7
Actual overhead incurred	81,900	1,20,960	79,360
Overheads absorbed	72,800	1,00,800	86,800
Direct labour hours–recorded against:			
Work-in-progress	2,800	4,930	820
Finished goods stock	5,400	3,700	1,210

(*a*) Calculate the revised overhead application rate in rupees per direct labour hour in the light of actual figures for the year supplied to you.

(*b*) Calculate also the total amounts by which the work-in-progress and finished goods stock in each department will have to be increased or decreased in the light of the revision of the overhead application rate:

	Dept. I	*Dept. II*	*Dept. III*
(*a*) Actual overhead	Rs. 81,900	1,20,960	79,360
(*b*) Overhead absorbed	72,800	1,00,800	86,800
(*c*) Over (–) or under (+) absorption ($a - b$)	+ 9,100	+ 20,160	– 7,440
(*d*) Direct labour hours = $\frac{\text{Overhead absorbed}}{\text{Overhead rate}}$	18,200	33,600	12,400
(*e*) Supplementary rate $c \div d$	+ 0.50	+ 0.60	– 0.60
(*f*) Revised overhead rate	4.50	3.60	6.40
(g) Adjustment to work-in-progress:			
Labour hours × supplementary rate	+ 1,400	+ 2,958	– 492
(*h*) Adjustment to finished goods stock:			
Labour hours × supplementary rate	+ 2,800	+ 2,220	+ 726

Problem–34

The cost accountant of NOVO Chemicals Ltd., determined the overhead recovery rate for the year 1989 (based on direct labour hours) with the following estimates:

Indirect labour	Rs 1,15,000
Inspection	70,000
Factory supervision	50,000
Depreciation and maintenance	1,25,000
Total factory overhead	3,60,000
Direct labour hours	75,000
Hourly wage rate	Rs. 15

The actual results for the year are as follows:

Indirect labour	Rs. 99,000
Inspection	73,000
Factory supervision	51,000
Depreciation and maintenance	1,15,000
	3,38,000
Direct labour hours	67,600
Hourly wage rate	Rs. 16

Calculate the predetermined overhead recovery rate and find out the amount of over/under absorption if any. *(University of Delhi, B.Com. (Hons), 1991)*

Solution:

$$\text{Direct labour hour rate} = \frac{\text{Estimated total factory overheads}}{\text{Direct labour hour}} = \frac{3,60,000}{75,000}$$

$$= \text{Rs. } 4.80 \text{ per hour}$$

$$\text{Overhead recovered} = 67,600 \times 4.80 = \text{Rs. } 3,24,480$$

$$\text{Under absorption} = \text{actual total overhead} - \text{overheads recovered}$$

$$= 3,38,000 - 3,24,480$$

$$= \text{Rs. } 13,520$$

Problem–35

The actual total expenditure of a light engineering factory was Rs. 6,75,912. Overheads were recorded at the rate Rs. 2 per-hour at normal capacity of the factory. Out of 10,000 units produced, only 8,000 units were sold. 500 units were in work-in-progress. Actual hours worked were 2,84,756. Sixty per cent of the difference between the actual and applied overheads was due to fluctuations in material prices and labour rates. There was a fire in the factory during this accounting period and the company lost Rs. 50,000 of which the building accounted for Rs. 30,000 and the balance represented loss of materials stored in the godown. A sum of Rs. 10,000 was paid as wages to workmen during the strike period. The balance amount represented the difference between the actual and applied overheads due to operational efficiency or inefficiency.

Calculate the under/over absorption of production overheads for the period and state the appropriate treatment in cost accounts (Journal entries not required).

(University of Delhi, B.Com. (Hons), April 1999)

Solution:

Actual overhead	6,75,912
Less: Overhead recovered	
(2,84,756 × Rs. 2)	5,69,512
Under recovered overhead	1,06,400

Division according to reasons:

Due to price fluctuations	63,840
$1{,}06{,}400 \times \frac{60}{100}$	
Due to labour strike	10,000
Due to loss of materials	20,000
Due to inefficiency (balance)	12,500
Total	1,06,400

Under-absorption due to price fluctuations will be apportioned to total units produced at the supplementary rate calculated as follows:

Supplementary rate $= \frac{63{,}840}{10{,}000 \text{ units}}$ = Rs. 6.384

Charge to cost of sales = 8,000 units × 6.384 = Rs. 51,072

Charge to finished stock = 1,500 units × 6.384 = Rs. 9,576

Charge to work-in-progress = 500 units × 6.384 = Rs. 3,192

Balance of under-absorbed overhead will be transferred to costing P & L A/c.

Problem–36

ABC Ltd. manufactures a single product and absorbs the production overheads at a predetermined rate of Rs. 10 per machine hour.

At the end of financial year 1998–99, it has been found that actual production overheads incurred were Rs. 6,00,000. It included Rs. 45,000 on account of "written off" obsolete stores and Rs. 30,000 being the wages paid for the strike period under an award.

The production and sales data for the year 1998–99 is as under:

Finished goods	20,000 units
Work-in-progress	8,000 units
(50% complete in all respects)	
Sales:	
Finished goods	18,000 units

The actual machine hours worked during the period were 48,000. It has been found that $\frac{1}{3}$ of the under absorption of production overheads was due to lack of production planning and the rest was attributable to normal increase in costs.

You are required to:

1. Calculate the amount of under-absorption of production overhead during the year 1998–99.
2. Show the accounting treatment of under-absorption of production overheads.

(C.A. Inter, November 1999)

Solution:

(*i*) Calculation of under-absorption of production overhead during the year 1998–99

			Rs.
	Total production overhead actually incurred during the year 98–99		6,00,000
Less:	"Written off" obsolete stores	45,000	
	Wages paid for strike period	30,000	
			75,000
	Net production overhead actually incurred (A)		5,25,000
	Production overhead absorbed by 48,000 machine hours @ Rs. 10 per hour (B)		4,80,000
	Amount of under-absorption of production overhead (A – B)		45,000

(*ii*) Accounting treatment of under-absorption of production overheads

It is given in the statement of the question that 20,000 units were completely finished and 8,000 units were 50% complete, one-third of the under-absorbed overheads were due to lack of production planning and the rest were attributable to normal increase in costs.

(*a*) $33\frac{1}{3}\%$ of 45,000 = 15,000 of under-absorbed overheads were due to lack of production planning. This being abnormal, should be debited to the profit and loss A/c	15,000
(*b*) Balance $\left(66\frac{2}{3}\% \text{ of Rs. } 45{,}000\right)$ *i.e.,* 30,000 of under-absorbed overheads should be distributed over work-in-progress, finished goods and cost of sales by using supplementary rate	30,000
Total under-absorbed overheads	45,000

Calculation of supplementary absorption rate

$$\text{Rs. } \frac{30{,}000}{24{,}000 \text{ units}} = \text{Rs. } 1.25 \text{ per unit}$$

Apportionment of unabsorbed overheads of Rs. 30,000 over work-in-progress, finished goods and cost of sales.

Work-in-Progress

(equivalent completed)

Units $\frac{50}{100}$ × 8,000	= 4,000 × Rs. 1.25	=	5,000
Finished goods			
(20,000 – 18,000 = 2,000)	= 2,000 × Rs. 1.45	=	2,500
Cost of sales	= 18,000 × Rs. 1.25	=	22,500
(18,000 units)			
	24,000		30,000

Accounting Treatment:

Work-in-progress control A/c	Dr. 5,000	
Finished goods control A/c	Dr. 2,500	
Cost of sales A/c	Dr. 22,500	
Profit and loss A/c	Dr. 15,000	
To overhead control A/c		45,000

Problem–37

Sweet Dreams Ltd., uses a historical cost system and absorb overheads on the basis of predetermined rate. The following data are available for the year ended 31st March, 1997.

Manufacturing overheads:	
Amount actually spent	1,70,000
Amount absorbed	1,50,000
Cost of goods sold	3,36,000
Stock of finished goods	96,000
Work-in-progress`	48,000

Using two methods of disposal of under-absorbed overheads show the implication on the profits of the company under each method. *(C.A. Inter, November 1997)*

Solution:

According to first method, the total unabsorbed overhead amount of Rs. 20,000 will be written off to costing profit and loss A/c. The use of this method will reduce the profits of the concern by Rs. 20,000 for the period.

According to second method, a supplementary rate may be used to adjust the overhead cost of each unit. The under-absorbed amount in total money, at the end of accounting period, be apportioned on proportionate basis over cost of goods sold, stock of finished goods and work-in-progress. This is shown below:

Apportionment of Overhead under Absorbed

Cost of goods sold	3,36,000	14,000	3,50,000
Stock of finished goods	96,000	4,000	1,00,000
Work-in-progress	48,000	2,000	50,000
	4,80,000	20,000	5,00,000

Working Note:

Under-absorbed overhead to be absorbed by cost of goods sold $= \frac{3,36,000}{4,80,000} \times 20,000$

$= 14,000$

Under-absorbed overhead to be absorbed by stock of finished goods $= \frac{96,000}{4,80,000} \times 20,000$

$= 4,000$

Under-absorbed overhead to be absorbed by work-in-progress $= \frac{48,000}{4,80,000} \times 20,000$

$= 2,000$

Problem–38

A factory has three production departments. The policy of the factory is to recover the production overheads of the entire factory by adopting a single blanket rate based on the percentage of total factory overheads to total factory wages. The relevant data for a month are given below:

Department	*Direct materials Rs.*	*Direct wages Rs.*	*Factory overheads Rs.*	*Direct labour hours*	*Machine hours*
Budget:					
Machining	6,50,000	80,000	3,60,000	20,000	80,000
Assembly	1,70,000	3,50,000	1,40,000	1,00,000	10,000
Packing	1,00,000	70,000	1,25,000	50,000	—
Actuals:					
Machining	7,80,000	96,000	3,90,000	24,000	96,000
Assembly	1,36,000	2,70,000	84,000	90,000	11,000
Packing	1,20,000	90,000	1,35,000	60,000	—

The details of one of the representative jobs produced during the month are as under Job No. CW 7083.

Department	*Direct materials Rs.*	*Direct wages Rs.*	*Direct labour hours*	*Machine hours*
Machining	1,200	240	60	180
Assembly	600	360	120	30
Packing	300	60	40	—

The factory adds 30% on the factory cost to cover administration and selling overheads and profit required:

1. Calculate the overhead absorption rate as per the current policy of the company and determine the selling price of the Job No. CW 7,083.
2. Suggest any suitable alternative methods of absorption of the factory overheads and calculate the overhead recovery rates based on the methods so recommended by you.
3. Determine the selling price of Job CW 7,083 based on the overhead application rates calculated in (2) above.
4. Calculate the departmentwise and total under or over recovery of overheads based on the company's current policy and the methods recommended by you.

(C.A., Inter, November 1994)

Solution:

(i) Calculation of overhead absorption rate (as per the current policy of the company)

Department	*Budgeted Factory Overheads* *Rs.*	*Budgeted Direct Wages* *Rs.*
Machinery	3,60,000	80,000
Assembly	1,40,000	3,50,000
Packing	1,25,000	70,000
	6,25,000	5,00,000

$$\text{Overhead absorption rate} = \frac{\text{Budgeted factory overhead}}{\text{Budgeted direct wages}} \times 100$$

$$= \frac{6{,}25{,}000}{5{,}00{,}000} \times 100 = 125\% \text{ of direct wages}$$

Selling price of Job No. CW – 7083

Direct materials (1,200 + 600 + 300)		2,100
Direct wages (240 + 360 + 60)		660
Overheads $\frac{125}{100} \times 660$		825
	Factory cost	3,585
	Profit $\frac{30}{100} \times 3{,}585$	1,075.50
	Selling price	4,660.50

(*ii*) Methods available for absorbing factory overheads and their overhead recovery rates in different departments:

1. Machining department:

$$\text{Machine hour rate} = \frac{\text{Budgeted factory overheads}}{\text{Budgeted machine hours}}$$

$$= \frac{3,60,000}{80,000} = \text{Rs. } 4.50 \text{ per hour}$$

2. Assembly department:

$$\text{Direct labour hour rate} = \frac{\text{Budgeted factory overheads}}{\text{Budgeted direct labour hours}}$$

$$= \frac{1,40,000}{1,00,000} = \text{Rs. } 1.40 \text{ per hour}$$

3. Packing department:

$$\text{Direct labour hour rate} = \frac{\text{Budgeted factory overheads}}{\text{Direct labour hours}}$$

$$= \frac{1,25,000}{50,000} = \text{Rs. } 2.50 \text{ per hour}$$

Selling price of Job No. CW – 7083

(Based on overhead application rates calculated in (*ii*) above)

Direct materials	2,100
Direct wages	660
Overheads (see working note)	1,078
Factory cost	3,838
Profit $\frac{30}{100} \times 3,838$	1,151.40
Selling price	4,989.40

Working Note:

Calculation of overheads

Machining dept.	180 hrs. × 4.50	=	810
Assembly dept.	120 hrs. × 1.40	=	168
Packing	40 hrs. × 2.50	=	100
	Total		1,078

(iii) Departmentwise statement of total under or over recovery of overheads

(a) Under current policy:

	Machine deptt. Rs.	*Assembly deptt. Rs.*	*Packing deptt. Rs.*	*Total*
Actual direct wages	96,000	2,70,000	90,000	
Overheads recovered *i.e.*, 125% of Direct wages (A)	1,20,000	3,37,500	1,12,500	5,70,000
Actual overheads (B)	3,90,000	84,000	1,35,000	6,09,000
(under)/over recovery of overheads	(2,70,000)	2,53,500	(22,500)	(39,000)

(b) As per method suggested:

	Basis of overhead recovery			
	Machine hours	*Direct labour hours*	*Direct labour hours*	*Total*
Hours worked	96,000	90,000	60,000	
Rate per hr.	4.50	1.40	2.50	
Overhead recovered (A)	4,32,000	1,26,000	1,50,000	7,08,000
Actual overheads (B)	3,90,000	84,000	1,35,000	6,09,000
(under)/over recovery (A – B)	42,000	42,000	15,000	99,000

CAPACITY COST

The capacity of a factory is its ability to produce with the present resources and facilities which it commands. Plant capacity may be expressed in terms of physical unit of products, direct labour hour, machine hour, or value of production. The capacity of a plant is closely related to overheads. While discussing about the various methods of absorption of overheads, different bases such as direct labour hours, machine hours, number of units produced, etc., were used for the sake of absorption of overheads. Computation of overhead rates based on actual basis *i.e.,* capacity, is quite easy because the actual capacity is readily available. But a Problem–would arise while computing the predetermined rate, since the determination of the most suitable level of activity is somewhat difficult. The overhead recovery rates will vary if various levels of activities like maximum capacity, practical capacity, normal capacity, etc., are used as the basis. This has given rise to the study of various types of plant capacities adopted in factories.

Types of Capacities

1. **Maximum or theoretical capacity:** If the plant or department works without interruption and without any loss of operation it is known as maximum capacity. The maximum capacity cannot be achieved as the capacity is lost owing to normal operating interruptions such as time lost during repairs, breakdowns, set up time, labour absenteeism, etc., which are inevitable in factories and hence deducted from maximum

capacity. Because maximum capacity cannot be utilised in full, it is also known as theoretical capacity.

2. **Practical or operating capacity:** If the capacity is lost due to operating interruptions like time lost for repairs, supply of materials, etc., is deducted from the maximum capacity, the balance of capacity is known as practical capacity. Practical capacity will become the maximum capacity of the plant to manufacture the goods and services for all practical purposes, as in practice it is impossible to operate maximum capacity of the plant.
3. **Capacity to make and sell or capacity based on expected sales:** It is the capacity which is installed when there is lack of demand and it is not possible to sell the entire quantity produced in a factory. In other words it represents the capacity to meet the demand or sales.
4. **Actual capacity:** The capacity that is achieved during a given period of time is known as actual capacity.
5. **Idle capacity:** The excess of practical capacity over the actual capacity achieved is known as idle capacity. It represents the capacity which remains unutilised on account of lack of demand, scarcity of materials, or labour or other factors of production. The cost arising out of idle capacity is treated as factory overheads.
6. **Normal capacity:** It is somewhat difficult to define normal capacity, as what is 'normal' at one time may not be true at other time. Two views are expressed to indicate normal capacity. According to one view, the average of the sales level exepectancy for a period should be treated as normal capacity. The period so selected for this purpose should cover business cycle and seasonal fluctuations. According to a second view, the capacity which would be worked if there is no lack of orders should be treated as normal capacity. In other words, it refers to capacity available for utilising during a period.

Problem–39

A manufacturing unit produces electronic circuits at the rate of 6 pieces an hour. The unit works in a single shift of 8 hours during a six-day week and remains closed for 18 days in a year, on account of holidays. Average idle hours per month is 20 for cleaning and maintenance of equipments. Against an average annual output of 12,000 pieces during last 10 years, the actual output achieved during the year was 10,800 pieces. The fixed overheads for the year amounted to Rs. 5,40,000.

You are required to calculate the idle capacity on the assumption that overhead recovery rates are based on maximum capacity, practical, normal capacity and actual capacity utilisation respectively. *(ICWA, Inter, December 1993)*

Solution:

Ascertainment of Various Capacities in Terms of Hours

1. Maximum capacity = Total days during the year on single shift of 8 hours
   = 365 × 8 = 2,920 hours
2. Practical capacity = Maximum capacity – Idle time due to various reasons.
   Maximum capacity 2,920 hrs

Less: Idle capacity due to:

Sundays 52 × 8	=	416 hrs.	
Holidays 18 × 8	=	144 hrs.	
Maintenance 20 × 12	=	240 hrs.	
			800 hrs.
		Practical capacity	2120 hrs.

3. Normal capacity $= \dfrac{\text{Normal sales expected}}{\text{Rate of production}}$

$= \dfrac{12{,}000 \text{ pieces}}{6 \text{ pieces per hr.}} = 2{,}000$ hrs.

4. Actual capacity $= \dfrac{\text{Actual output}}{\text{Rate of production}}$

$= \dfrac{10{,}800 \text{ pieces}}{8 \text{ pieces per hr.}} = 1{,}800$ hrs.

Statement Showing Idle Capacity and Machine Hour Rate

Basis	*Base capacity (hrs.)*	*Capacity utilised (hrs.)*	*Idle capacity*	*Machine hour rate* $= \dfrac{\textit{Overheads}}{\textit{Base capacity (hrs.)}}$
Maximum capacity	2,920	1,800	1,120	184.93
Practical capacity	2,120	1,800	320	254.72
Normal capacity	2,000	1,800	200	270.00
Actual capacity	1,800	1,800	—	300.00

Statement Showing Idle Capacity Cost

Basis	*Overhead*	*Applied overheads*		*Idle capacity cost*	
Capacity	*Absorption rate*	*Hrs.*	*Amt. (Rs.)*	*Hrs.*	*Amt. (Rs.)*
Maximum	184.93	1,800	3,32,874	1,120	2,07,126
Practical	254.72	1,800	4,58,496	320	81,504
Normal	270.00	1,800	4,86,000	200	54,000
Actual	300.00	1,800	5,40,000	—	—

Questions

I. Classify the following costs into Prime Cost and Overheads. In case of overheads, classify by function.

1. Salary of the Accountant.
2. Temporary labour employed to increase production in order to meet unusual demand of product 'C'.
3. Uniforms of sanitary workers.
4. Gatekeeper's salary.
5. Dividends received on investments.
6. Freight on purchase of raw materials.
7. Remuneration for legal advise.
8. Consultation fee of advertisement designs.
9. Rent of godown for storing finished goods.
10. Rent of godown for storing raw materials.
11. Salary paid to the wife of the managing director. She is designated as whole time director but does not come to the factory at all.
12. Loss due to accidental falling of the roof of a section of the factory.
13. Primary packing material.
14. Secondary packing with the name of the company.
15. Packing of boxes of finished product in wooden cases for transportation.
16. Income for sale of bags in which raw materials were procured.
17. Depreciation of patterns and dyes.
18. Bad debts.
19. Cost of stolen materials.
20. Commission paid to salesman as a percentage of sales price.
21. Expenses incurred for repairs and maintenance of water supply lines, sewage pipes, etc.
22. Royalties paid on the basis of sales.
23. Amount paid to lawyer for appearing before a labour tribunal.
24. Allowance made to customers for late deliveries of goods.
25. Carriage inwards.

[***Answers:*** Prime cost—2, 6, 13, 16, 25; Factory overheads—3, 4, 10, 17, 21; Administrative overheads—1, 7, 23; Selling overheads—8, 16, 18, 20, 22; Distribution overheads—9, 15; Costing P & L A/c—5, 11, 12, 19, 24]

II. Classify the following costs into Fixed, Semi-variable and Variable

(*a*) Salary of M.D., (*b*) Salary of Foreman, (*c*) Raw materials, (*d*) Wages of permanent workers, (*e*) Commission to salesman as a percentage of sales, (*f*) Depreciation on plant, (*g*) Rent of factory, (*h*) Power consumption in the production process, (*i*) Canteen expenses, (*j*) Salary of storekeeper.

[***Answers:*** Fixed–(*a*), (*b*), (*d*), (*g*), (*i*), (*j*); Semi-variable—(*e*), (*f*), (*h*); Variable–(*c*)]

III. Mark 'T' or 'F' in the space provided

1. The actual overhead incurred in a month is the amount of overhead that is usually assigned to work-in-process and the production of the month. *T/F*
2. Manufacturing overhead consists of a rather homogeneous group of services that aid in the manufacture of a product. *T/F*
3. Factory overhead is said to be overabsorbed when actual costs are greater than the amount assigned to production. *T/F*
4. The amount of manufacturing overhead assigned to the production of a given month may be more or less than the amount to overhead costs incurred in that same month. *T/F*
5. Initially, overhead costs should be classified according to the function fulfilled by their incurrence. *T/F*
6. A cost accounting system may contain many sub-groups of accounts for overhead each of which contains an account with the same title. *T/F*
7. Generally, all indirect manufacturing overheads will be allocated to the production departments after being first accumulated in service departments. *T/F*
8. Any basis of allocating overhead costs to producing departments is arbitrary irrespective of its apparent logic. *T/F*
9. A factory may operate at a level greater than practical capacity. *T/F*
10. An idle capacity loss cannot be isolated if an overhead rate is set using expected activity. *T/F*
11. The overhead rate can be based on practical capacity even though the company fully expects to operate at a lower level. *T/F*
12. The machine hour rate is appropriate where direct labour costs are relatively low and machine costs are relatively high. *T/F*
13. The historical (actual) overhead rate is generally preferred over the predetermined overhead rate because it is precise and the predetermined overhead rate is only an estimate. *T/F*
14. If activity fluctuates widely during a year due to seasonal variations, the actual overhead rate will provide more constant unit costs from month to month than will a predetermined rate. *T/F*
15. Allocation of overhead costs to producing department is necessary to identify operating inefficiencies in service department. *T/F*
16. The actual overhead incurred in a month is the amount of overhead that is usually assigned to work-in-process and the production of the month. *T/F*
17. It is commonly accepted theory that a part of the overhead costs incurred in a period should be attached to every unit of product manufactured during that period. *T/F*
18. Factory overhead is said to be overabsorbed when actual costs are greater than the amount assigned or applied to production. *T/F*

[***Answers:*** 4, 6, 8, 9, 11, 12, 17; False and rest of the statements are True]

IV. Choose the correct answer

1. The allotment of whole items of cost to centre or cost unit is called
   (a) Cost apportionment (b) Cost reapportionment
   (c) Cost allocation (d) Cost absorption
2. Predetermined overhead is calculated as follows:
   (a) $\dfrac{\text{Budgeted overhead}}{\text{Budgeted base}}$ (b) $\dfrac{\text{Actual overhead}}{\text{Budgeted base}}$
   (c) $\dfrac{\text{Actual overhead}}{\text{Standard base}}$ (d) $\dfrac{\text{Standard overhead}}{\text{Standard base}}$
3. Information regarding depreciation is obtained from
   (a) Stores requisition (b) Cash book
   (c) Invoice (d) Plant register
4. Normal capacity of a plant is
   (a) The maximum productive capability
   (b) Maximum capacity less inevitable interruption
   (c) Actual volume of production overhead
   (d) Long-term average capacity based on sales expectancy
5. Idle capacity of plant refers to the service between
   (a) Maximum capacity and practical capacity
   (b) Practical capacity and normal capacity
   (c) Practical capacity and capacity based on sales expectancy
   (d) Maximum capacity and actual capacity.
6. Maximum possible productive capacity of a plant when no operating time is lost is its
   (a) Practical capacity (b) Normal capacity
   (c) Theoretical capacity (d) Capacity based on sales expectancy
7. Factory overheads include all of the following except
   (a) Taxes on factory building (b) Small tool expenses
   (c) Depreciation on delivery equipment (d) Salary of plant manager
8. The level of capacity or activity which when used in setting overhead rates would yield the lowest average unit product costs is most likely to be
   (a) Practical capacity (b) Normal capacity
   (c) Expected capacity (d) Actual capacity
9. Departmental overhead rates are used to
   (a) Allocate service department costs to production departments
   (b) Make sure that more overhead is applied to production
   (c) Assign overhead to production whenever a factory overhead applied account is used
   (d) Secure an assignment of overhead to production that reflects the benefits a product receives from a department better than does a single plant wide overhead rate

10. When fixed and variable overhead rates are used

(*a*) Both rates should be based on actual activity

(*b*) Both rates should be based upon expected activity

(*c*) The variable rate should be based upon expected activity, while several alternative bases may be used of the fixed rate

(*d*) Overhead will probably be rather fully absorbed when both rates are based upon practical capacity.

[***Answers:*** 1. (*c*), 2. (*a*), 3. (*d*), 4. (*d*), 5. (*c*), 6. (*c*), 7. (*c*), 8. (*a*), 9. (*d*), 10. (*c*)]

V. Match the following

A	B
1. Canteen expenses	(*a*) Sales
2. Depreciation of plants	(*b*) Hours used
3. Electric power	(*c*) Light points
4. Rent	(*d*) Weight
5. Electric light	(*e*) Asset value
	(*f*) Horse power
	(*g*) Floor area
	(*h*) Number of employees

[***Answers:*** 1. (*b*), 2. (*e*), 3. (*f*), 4. (*g*), 5. (*c*)]

VI. Simple questions

1. Define overheads.

2. Distinguish between indirect expenses and overheads.

3. Give two tests for identifying an item of expenditure as overheads.

4. Distinguish between standing order number and cost accounting number.

5. What do you mean by codification of overheads ?

6. What do you mean by collection of overheads ?

7. What do you mean by classification of overheads ?

8. Mention any four bases of classification of overheads.

9. Define allocation of overheads.

10. Define apportionment of overheads.

11. Distinguish between allocation and apportionment of overheads.

12. List out the important steps involved in the accounting procedure of overheads.

13. What do you mean by departmentalisation of overheads ?

14. What do you mean by reapportionment of overheads ?

15. Distinguish between primary and secondary distribution of overheads.

16. Define absorption of overheads.

17. Mention the different methods of overhead absorption.

18. What do you mean by percentage on direct material cost method of overhead absorption ?

19. What do you mean by percentage on direct labour cost method of overheads absorption ?

20. What do you mean by percentage on prime cost method of overheads absorption ?

21. What do you mean by direct labour hour rate method of overheads absorption ?

22. What do you mean by machine hour rate ?

23. Distinguish between direct labour hour rate and machine hour rate.

24. Distinguish between actual and predetermined rate of overhead recovery.

25. What do you mean by over-absorption of overheads ?

26. What do you mean by under-absorption of overheads ?

27. Distinguish between over- and under-absorption of overheads.

28. What do you mean by normal capacity ?

29. What do you mean by practical capacity ?

30. What do you mean by maximum capacity ?

VII. Short and long answer questions

1. State the need for pre-determined overhead rate in a factory.
(Calcutta University, B.Com. (Hons), 1991)

2. What is meant by absorption of overhead ? Explain briefly the different methods of absorption of overheads. *(University of Delhi, B.Com., 1989)*

3. Explain how will you deal with under or over-absorption of overheads in cost accounts.
(University of Delhi, B.Com., 1989)

4. Explain the different methods of apportionment of service departments costs over production department. *(University of Delhi, B.Com. (Hons), 1989)*

5. Briefly explain different methods of absorption of overheads.
(Andhra University, B.Com., May 1992)

6. Enumerate the different methods of absorption of overhead.
(Kakatiya University, B.Com., November 1991)

7. What is meant by machine hour rate ? Explain as to how it is ascertained using imaginary figures. *(Kakatiya University, B.Com., October 1990)*

8. Explain different methods of re-apportionment of service department costs.
(Nagarjuna University, B.Com., April 1992)

9. How do you treat the following in cost accounts (*i*) Bad debts, (*ii*) Expenses of costing department, (*iii*) Royalties, (*iv*) Packing materials, (*v*) Income tax.
(Osmania University, B.Com., April 1990)

10. How do you treat under-absorption and over-absorption of overhead in costing.
(Osmania University, B.Com., April 1990)

11. State the different methods of absorption of factory overhead.
(Osmania University, B.Com., April 1990)

12. Distinguish between "Allocation" and "Absorption".
(Calicut University, M.Com., April 1992)

13. Define overheads and state the problems connected with overhead accounting. Mention different methods of classification of overheads.
(Kakatiya University, M.Com., August 1991)

Exercise–1 (Apportionment of Overheads)

Ajit company has 5 departments P, N, R, S, are producing departments and T is a serivce department. The actual costs for a period are as follows:

	Rs.
Repairs	2,000
Rent	2,500
Depreciation	1,200
Supervision	4,000
Insurance	1,500
Employer's liability of employee's insurance	600
Light	1,800

The following data are also available in respect of the five departments:

	P	*N*	*R*	*S*	*T*
Area (sq. ft.)	140	120	110	90	40
No. of workers	25	20	10	10	5
Total wages (Rs.)	10,000	8,000	5,000	5,000	2,000
Value of plant (Rs.)	20,000	18,000	16,000	10,000	6,000
Value of stock (Rs.)	15,000	10,000	5,000	2,000	–

Apportion the costs to various departments on the equitable basis.

(University of Madras, B.Com., April 2004)

[***Answer:*** Total of apportioned overheads
P – Rs. 4,464 N – Rs. 3,638 R – Rs. 2,568
S – Rs. 6,982 T – Rs. 2,948]

Exercise–2

A manufacturing company has two production departments X and Y and three service departments: Time keeping, Stores and Maintenance. The departmental distribution summary showed the following expenses for January 1990.

Production Departments	
X	36,000
Y	24,000
Service Departments	
Stores	7,500
Time keeping	6,000
Maintenance	4,500

Other information relating to these departments were:

	Production departments		*Service departments*		
	X	*Y*	*Stores*	*Time-keeping*	*Maintenance*
No. of employees	20	15	10	8	5
No. of stores requisitions	24	20	–	–	6
Machine hours	18,000	12,000			

Apportion the costs of various service departments to the production departments.

(University of Madras, B.Com., October 2003)

[***Answer:*** Total overheads of Dept A Rs. 46,262; Dept B Rs. 31,738]

Exercise–3 (Apportionment)

The modern company has three production departments A, B and C and two service departments D and E. The following are extracted from the records of the company for the month of March 1993.

	Rs.
Rent and rates	20,000
Indirect wages	6,000
Depreciation of machinery	40,000
Power	6,000
General lighting	2,400
Sundries	40,000

The following further details are as follows:

	Total	*A*	*B*	*C*	*D*	*E*
Floor space (sq/ft)	20,000	4,000	5,000	6,000	4,000	1,000
H.P. of machines	300	120	60	100	20	–
Light points	120	20	30	40	20	10
Direct wages (Rs.)	20,000	6,000	4,000	6,000	3,000	1,000
Value of machinery	5,00,000	1,20,000	1,60,000	2,00,000	10,000	10,000

Prepare primary distribution summary. *(University of Madras, B.Com., October 2002)*

[***Answer:*** Total overheads of Dept A Rs. 30,200 Dept B Rs. 28,800, Dept C Rs. 38,600 Dept D Rs. 15,500 Dept E Rs. 5,300]

Exercise–4 (Repeated Distribution Method)

Superclass Company Limited has three production departments X, Y and Z and two service departments A and B. The following estimated figures for a certain period have been available.

	Rs.
Rent and rates	10,000
Lighting and electricity	1,200
Indirect wages	3,000
Power	3,000
Depreciation of machinery	20,000
Other expenses and sundries	20,000

Following are the further details which are also available:

	Total	*X*	*Y*	*Z*	*A*	*B*
Floor space (sq. ft)	10,000	2,000	2,500	3,000	2,000	500
Light points (Nos)	120	20	30	40	20	10
Direct wages (Rs.)	20,000	6,000	4,000	6,000	3,000	1,000
H.P. of machines	300	120	60	100	20	–
Cost of machinery (Rs.)	1,00,000	24,000	32,000	40,000	2,000	2,000
Working hrs.	–	4,670	3,020	3,050	–	–

The expenses of the service departments A and B are to be allocated as follows

	X	Y	Z	A	B
A	20%	30%	40%	–	10%
B	40%	20%	30%	10%	–

You are required to calculate the overhead absorption rate per hour in respect of three production departments.

What will be the total cost of an article with material cost of Rs. 80 and direct labour cost of Rs. 40 which passes through X, Y and Z for 2, 3 and 4 respectively ?

(Sri Sathya Sai University, B.Com., (Hons), March 2006)

[***Answer:*** Overhead absorption Rate X – 4, Y – 6, Z – 4 Total cost Rs. 178]

Exercise–5

Modern Machines Ltd. have three production departments A, B, C and two service departments D and E. From the following figures extracted from the records of the company calculate the overhead rate per labour hour.

Item of expenses	*Total*	*Departments*				
		A	*B*	*C*	*D*	*E*
Direct materials	60,000	20,000	10,000	19,000	6,000	5,000
Direct wages	40,000	15,000	15,000	4,000	2,000	4,000
Value of machinery	2,50,000	60,000	1,00,000	40,000	25,000	25,000
Floor area (sq ft)	50,000	15,000	10,000	10,000	5,000	10,000
H.P. of machines	150	50	60	30	5	5
No. of light points	50	15	10	10	5	10
Labour hours	15,000	5,000	5,000	2,000	1,000	2,000

Expenses:	*Rs.*
Indirect materials	15,000
Indirect wages	10,000
Depreciation on machinery	25,000
Depreciation on building	5,000
Rent, rates and taxes	10,000
Electric power for machines	15,000
Electric power for lighting	500
General expenses	15,000

The expenses of service departments D and E are to be apportioned as follows:

	A	B	C	D	E
D	40%	20%	30%	–	10%
E	30%	30%	40%	–	–

(Bangalore University, B.Com., October 2001)

[***Answer:*** Labour Hour Rate: Dept A – 7.31,
B – 6.68,
C – 12.47]

Exercise–6

Calculate the machine hour rate of recovery of overhead in departments A, B and C

Particulars	*Production depts*			*Service depts*	
	A *Rs.*	*B* *Rs.*	*C* *Rs.*	*P* *Rs.*	*Q* *Rs.*
Rent	4,800	5,000	3,000	2,000	800
Electricity	600	3,000	400	800	500
Indirect labour	2,000	3,000	1,000	800	1,000
Depreciation on machinery	3,000	3,200	400	500	200
Sundries	800	2,000	900	400	400
Estimated machine hours	1,000	2,000	3,000		

Expenses of service departments P and Q are apportioned as under:

	A	*B*	*C*	*P*	*Q*
P	30%	40%	20%	–	10%
Q	10%	20%	50%	20%	–

Use repeated distribution method for secondary distribution.

(Osmania University, B.Com., October 2003)

[***Answer:*** M.H.R. of Dept A – Rs. 13.097
B – Rs. 9.478
C – Rs. 2.815]

Exercise–7

A Ltd. has three production departments P_1, P_2 and P_3 and two service departments S_1 and S_2. The following data are extracted from the records of the company for a particular given period:

	Rs.
Rent and rates	25,000
General lighting	3,000
Indirect wages	7,500
Power	7,500
Depreciation on machinery	50,000
Sundries	50,000

Other information:

	P_1	P_2	P_3	S_1	S_2
Direct wages (Rs.)	15,000	10,000	15,000	7,500	2,500
H.P. of machines used	60	30	50	10	–
Cost of machinery (Rs.)	3,00,000	4,00,000	5,00,000	25,000	25,000
Floor space (sq ft)	2,000	2,500	3,000	2,000	500
No. of light points	10	15	20	10	5
Production hours worked	6,226	4,028	4,066	–	–

Expenses of the service departments S_1 and S_2 are apportioned as below

	P_1	P_2	P_3	S_1	S_2
S_1	20%	30%	40%	–	10%
S_2	40%	20%	30%	10%	–

You are required to:

(*a*) Compute overhead rate per production hour of each production department.

(*b*) Determine the total cost of product X which is processed for manufacture in department P_1, P_2 and P_3 for 4 hours, 5 hours and 3 hours respectively, given that its direct material cost is Rs. 250 and direct labour cost is Rs. 150.

(Calcutta University, B.Com. (Hons), 2000)

[***Answer:*** Total Cost Rs. 531.27]

Exercise–8

A manufacturing company has two production departments X and Y and three service departments time-keeping, stores and maintenance.

Time-keeping department is rendering services to two production departments and two other service departments, stores department is rendering services to maintenance department along with production departments and maintenance department is rendering services to production department only.

You are required to prepare a statement showing apportionment of overheads of service departments from the following information:

		Total
Production Departments:		
X	Rs. 16,000	
Y	Rs. 10,000	
		26,000
Service Departments:		
Time-keeping	4,000	
Stores	5,000	
Maintenance	3,000	12,000

The other information is:

	X	*Y*	*Time-keeping*	*Stores*	*Maintenance*
No. of employees	40	30	20	16	10
No. of stores requisitions	24	20	–	–	6
No. of machine hours	2,400	1,600	–	–	–

(University of Delhi, B.Com., (Hons.) 2004)

[***Answer:*** Total overheads of Dept. X – 22,845

Dept. Y – 15,155]

Exercise–9 (Simultaneous Equation Method)

A factory is having three production departments, A, B and C and two service departments namely, Boiler House (BH) and Pump Room (PR). The Boiler House is to depend upon the Pump Room for the supply of water and Pump Room inturn is dependent on the Boiler House for supply of power for driving the pump. The expenses incurred by the production departments during a period are:

A- Rs. 8,00,000, B- Rs. 7,00,000 and C- Rs. 5,00,000. The expenses for Boiler House are Rs. 2,34,000 and the Pump Room are Rs. 3,00,000.

The expenses of the Boiler House and Pump Room are apportioned to the production departments on the following basis.

	A	B	C	B.H.	P.R.
Expenses of Boiler House (%)	20	40	30	–	10
Expenses of Pump Room (%)	40	20	20	20	–

Show clearly as to how the expenses of the boiler house and pump room would be apportioned to A, B and C departments using simultaneous equation method.

(University of Madras, B.Com., April 2003)

[***Answer:*** Total overheads of Dept A on apportionment A–Rs. 9,92,000, Dept B–Rs. 8,86,000, C–Rs. 6,56,000]

Exercise–10

A company has three production departments and two service departments. For the month of March 2005 the departmental expenses were as follows:

Production Departments:

A – Rs. 10,000
B – Rs. 15,000
C – Rs. 12,000

Service Departments:

X – Rs. 2,500
Y – Rs. 1,100

The expenses of service departments are apportioned as follows:

	A	B	C	X	Y
X	40%	30%	20%	–	10%
Y	30%	40%	10%	20%	–

Prepare a statement showing the distribution of service departments expenses to production departments based on reciprocal services. *(Calcutta University, B.Com., (Hons.) 2005)*

[***Answer:*** Total overheads of Dept A- Rs. 11,612 Dept B- Rs. 16,209 Dept C- Rs. 12,679]

Exercise–11 (Machine Hour Rate)

The following expenses have been incurred in respect of a shop having four identical machines.

	Rs.
Rent and rates per annum	16,000
Power consumed by the shop at (1 Re per unit) per annum	48,000
Repairs per annum for each machine	12,000
Lighting for the shop per annum	8,000
Supervisor's salary per month	6,000
Lubricants per annum for all machines	4,800
Depreciation per machine per annum	30,000

Hire purchase instalment of Rs. 40,000 for the machine includes Rs. 10,000 for interest. Each machine consumes 10 units of power in an hour. From the above you are required to calculate machine hour rate. *(Sri Sathya Sai University B.Com. (Hons), March 2003)*

[***Answer:*** Machine Hour Rate Rs. 11.16]

Exercise–12

Calculate the machine hour rate from the following:

	Rs.
Cost of machine	8,000
Cost of installation	2,000
Scrap value after 10 years	2,000
Rent and rates for a quarter for the shop	300
General lighting	20 PM
Shop supervisor's salary	600 per quarter
Insurance premium for a machine	60 p.a.
Estimated repairs	100 p.a.
Power 2 units per hour. Each unit of power costs	Re 0.50
Estimated working hours per annum	2,000

The machine occupies $\frac{1}{4}$th of the total area of the shop. The supervisor is expected to devote $\frac{1}{6}$th of his time for supervising the machine. General lighting expenses are to be apportioned on the basis of floor area. *(Sri Sathya Sai University B.Com. (Hons), March 2001)*

[***Answer:*** Machine Hour Rate Rs. 1.86]

Exercise–13

From the following information compute machine hour rate for a machine for the month of April 1999

	P.A. (Rs.)
Rent and rates	12,000
$\left(\frac{1}{4}\text{th space is occupied by the machine}\right)$	
Machine operator's wages	3000
(10 operators are engaged in the department, out of them 4 are working on this machine)	
Supervisor's salary	6000
$\left(\frac{1}{3}\text{rd of time is devoted for this machine}\right)$	
Insurance	600
Lubricants and Cotton waste	60

The cost of the machine is Rs. 16,000 and its scrap value is estimated at Rs. 1,000. From the past experience it has been ascertained that

(*a*) The working life of the machine is 20,000 hours.

(*b*) The machine will work for 2,000 hours annually.

(*c*) The estimated cost of repairs and maintenance is Rs. 1,000 over the life of the machine.

(*d*) The machine consumes 4 units per hour, rate of power is 5 paise per unit.

(Sri Sathya Sai University, B.Com., (Hons), August 2000)

[***Answer:*** Machine Hour Rate Rs. 4.43]

Exercise–14

Calculate the machine hour rate for machine no. 45 from the following particulars:

		Rs.
Cost of machine		10,000
Estimated scrap value		250
Estimated working life		15,000 hrs.
Hours required for maintenance		200 hrs.
Productive working hours		2,000 hrs p.a.
Setting up time		5%
Power 20 units @ 7 paise per unit		
Cost of repairs	:	Rs. 1,500 p.a.
No of operators looking after 4 machines	:	2
Wages of operator	:	Rs. 150 per month each
Chemicals required	:	Rs. 100 per month
Overhead chargeable to this machine	:	Rs. 200 per month
Insurance premium		1% p.a.

(Bangalore University, B. Com., April 2002)

[***Answer:*** Machine Hour Rate Rs. 5.26]

Exercise–15

There are 5 identical machines in a workshop. The annual charges paid for them are as follows:

(*a*) Rent and rates proportion to floor space occupied – Rs. 4,800

(*b*) Depreciation on each machine – Rs. 500

(*c*) Repairs and maintenance for 5 machines – Rs. 1,000

(*d*) Power consumed as per meter @ 5 paise per unit for shop – Rs. 3,000

(*e*) Electric charges for light in the shop – Rs. 450

(*f*) Attendants:

There are two attendants for 5 machines and they are each paid Rs. 60 per month

(*g*) Supervision:

For the 5 machines in the shop there is one supervisor whose emoluments are Rs. 250 p.m.

(*h*) Sundry supplies such as lubricants, cotton waste, for the shop Rs. 450

The machine uses 10 units of power per hour. Calculate the machine hour rate for the year.

(University of Madras, B.Com., October 2002)

[***Answer:*** Machine Hour Rate Rs. 2.77]

Exercise–16

Calculate comprehensive machine hour rate from the following data:

Cost of machine	Rs. 1,50,000
Estimated scrap value	24,000
Estimated life	10 years
Number of working hours per annum (including 100 hours for repairs)	1,900
Diesel oil consumption per hour; 2 litres at	Rs. 3 per litre
Insurance	Rs. 1,500 p.a.
Repairs and maintenance	Rs. 5,400 p.a.
Wages of operator	Rs. 4 per hour of working
General overhead related to the machine	Rs. 3,900 p.a.

(Calcutta University, B.Com., 2005)

[***Answer:*** Machine Hour Rate Rs. 23]

Exercise–17

From the following information, calculate machine hour rate:

Cost of machine	Rs. 1,40,000
Installation charges	Rs. 10,000
Estimated scrap value	Rs. 24,000
Estimated life	10 years
Number of working hours per annum	1,800
Rate of power charges per 100 units	Rs. 20
The machine consumes 20 units of power per hour	
Insurance	Rs. 1,500 per annum
Rent	Rs. 7,200 per annum
Repairs and maintenance	Rs. 5,400 per annum
Supervisors Salary	Rs. 1,000 per month
General overhead allocated to machine:	Rs. 3,900 per annum

The machine occupies $\frac{1}{3}$rd of the total area of the shop. The supervisor is expected to devote $\frac{1}{4}$th of his time for supervision of the machine. *(Calcutta University, B.Com., (Pass) 2004)*

[***Answer:*** Machine Hour Rate Rs. 20]

Exercise–18

Calculate the machine hour rate from the information given below.

	Rs.
Cost of machine	1,00,000
Estimated scrap value after the expiry of its life (15 years)	5,000
Installation charges	10,000
Rent and rates for the shop per month	200
General lighting for the shop per month	300

Insurance premium for the machine per month	80
Repairs and maintenance expenses per annum	1,000
Power consumption–10 units per hour	
Rate of power (100 units)	20
Estimated working hours per annum	2,000
Shop supervisor's salary per month	600

The machine occupies $\frac{1}{4}$ th of the total area of the shop. The supervisor is expected to devote $\frac{1}{5}$ th of his time for supervising the machine. *(Calcutta University, B.Com., (Pass) 2002)*

[***Answer:*** Machine Hour Rate Rs. 7.95]

Exercise–19

A department has three machines. Calculate the machine hour rates in respect of three machines from the information given below.

	Machine I	*Machine II*	*Machine III*
Direct wages	Rs. 1,200	Rs. 2,400	Rs. 3,600
Power units	30,000	10,000	20,000
No. of workers	4	8	8
Light points	8	24	48
Space (sq. ft)	400	800	800
Cost of machine	Rs. 3,00,000	Rs. 1,20,000	Rs. 1,80,000
Hours worked	200	300	400

The figures indirect the departmental expenses:

	Rs.
Depreciation of machinery	12,000
Repairs to machinery	4,000
Insurance of machinery	600
Indirect wages	6,000
Power	6,000
Lighting	800
Other expenses	4,200

(Calcutta University, B.Com., (Pass) 2001)

[***Answer:*** Machine Hour Rate of Machine I Rs. 65.40
Machine II Rs. 22.53
Machine III Rs. 34.40]

❑❑❑

CHAPTER 12

Office, Administration, Selling and Distribution Overheads

DEFINITION AND FEATURES OF OFFICE AND ADMINISTRATION OVERHEADS

Office overheads are those overheads which are incurred in carrying out the day-to-day routine of office. Examples of office overheads are office rent, office insurance, printing and stationery, salaries payable to office clerks and office supervisors. Administration overheads are defined by the ICMA terminology as "the sum of those costs of general management and of secretarial, accounting and administrative services, which cannot be directly related to the production, marketing, research or development functions of the enterprise". In other words, the cost of formulating the policy, directing the organisation and controlling the operations of an undertaking may be termed as administration overheads.

Features of Office and Administration Overheads

(*a*) The amount of office and administration overhead constitutes lowest proportion to the total cost when compared to other types of overheads.

(*b*) Most of the office and administration overheads are fixed in nature.

(*c*) They are not amenable for control. This is so because the nature of these overheads are such that, it is not possible to set norms or standards against which actual overheads could be compared.

(*d*) These overheads cannot be charged accurately to cost of production. Hence cost ascertainment cannot be accurate.

CLASSIFICATION AND COLLECTION OF ADMINISTRATION OVERHEADS

Administration overheads are classified according to their type, nature, purpose or department. Each type of overhead is to be denoted by a specific cost accounting number. For the sake of exercising control it would be appropriate to classify administration overheads on the basis of various administration departments such as accounting department, secretarial department, general office and so on. The administration overheads are collected for each department by means of preparing a summary statement of administration overhead. A specimen of such a statement is shown below:

SUMMARY OF DEPARTMENTAL ADMINISTRATION OVERHEADS

Name of the Dept. .... General office ....
Month .... Year ....

Cost Account No.	*Expense*	*Actual*	*Budgeted*	*Variances*
A_1	Postage			
A_2	Telephone			
A_3	Printing and stationery			
A_4	Office lighting			
A_5	Office rent			
A_6	Salary of office staff			
Total				

Fig. 12.1. *Specimen of summary of departmental administration overheads.*

Where a common item of expense is incurred for all the administrative departments, it is to be apportioned to all the departments on some equitable basis. The following are some of the common expenses incurred in the administration department and the basis for their apportionment.

Items of expenses	*Basis of apportionment*
Filling expenses	No. of documents handled
Correspondence expenses	No. of documents handled
Typing expenses	No. of documents handled
Invoicing expenses	No. of documents handled
Personnel department expenses	Number of employees
Depreciation of office building	Floor area
Rent of office	Space occupied
Telephone expenses	Number of extensions

ACCOUNTING OF ADMINISTRATION OVERHEADS IN COST ACCOUNTING

There are three methods of accounting of office and administration overheads. They are as follows:

1. Apportionment to Production and Selling and Distribution Departments of the Factory

This method recognises the fact that a factory has two important functions to perform, *viz.*, production and distribution. As such office and administration overheads must be apportioned to these two departments. The effect of this treatment is administration overheads lose their identity and are absorbed by production and selling and distribution departments. The reasons advocated for adopting this method are as follows:

(*a*) Administration is only an auxiliary service which is rendered to the two important departments *viz.*, production and selling and distribution departments of the factory. So administration overhead should not have any separate entity and all such overheads should be borne by only these two departments.

(*b*) As administration overheads cannot be controlled easily, the merger of such overheads with factory and selling and distribution overheads facilitates easy control.

(c) Production and distribution costs can be correctly calculated only when administration overheads are charged to these two departments.

This method is subjected to the following criticisms:

(a) A suitable basis of apportionment may not to be available for apportioning administration overheads to production and selling and distribution departments. So the method will give absurd figure.

(b) Administration is also one of the important function performed in all factories. Administration department and the overheads incurred in this department is as important as overheads incurred in production and selling and distribution departments. Merger of such cost with other departments distorts the relationship between these functions.

(c) When administration overheads are not possible to control, its merger with other controllable overheads cannot make the former controllable.

The following entries are passed to record the office and administration overheads in the cost ledger:

(a) For recording administration overheads incurred:

Administration overhead control A/c *Dr.*
    To general ledger adjustment A/c

(b) When the overheads are apportioned between the production and selling and distribution overheads:

Works overhead control A/c *Dr.*
Selling and distribution overhead control A/c *Dr.*
    To administration overhead control A/c

The amount of administration overheads thus apportioned to production and selling and distribution departments are ultimately recovered in the total cost of sales.

2. Charging to Costing Profit and Loss Account

Under this method administration overheads are treated as period or fixed cost and hence written off to costing profit and loss account of the period in which it is incurred. This method is advocated on the following grounds:

(a) Administration overheads are related to cost of formulating the policies and are not directly related to production or selling function.

(b) The administration overheads are very small when compared to other overheads. So they must be charged to costing profit and loss account instead of apportioning to production and selling departments.

(c) These overheads have no direct bearing with production and sales. Hence it should not be taken into cost of production.

This method of accounting is criticised on the following grounds:

(a) It is as important as production and selling function and as such it should form an important component of total cost.

(b) If it is taken into profit and loss account, the cost of production of a job is understated.

(c) The static nature cannot be taken as a reason for excluding it from cost of production.

The following entries are passed under this method:

(*a*) When administration overheads are incurred

Administration overhead control A/c *Dr.*

To general ledger adjustment A/c

(*b*) When the overheads are charged to costing profit and loss account

Costing profit and loss A/c *Dr.*

To administration overhead control A/c

3. As a Separate Item of Cost

The method is based on the assumption that administration function is one of the distinct and important function in any organisation and as such its expenses should be borne by the finished products sold. So under this method, administration overheads are added as a separate item of cost to the number of units sold. According to this method, the stock of finished goods and work-in-progress should not bear the burden of administration cost.

For the sake of adding as a separate item of cost, the office and administration overheads are classified and collected under suitable cost accounting number. The various departments of the office such as cash, filing, secretarial accounting, etc., are identified as separate cost centres. Wherever it is possible to allocate the overheads to these cost centres, they are allocated. Other overheads are apportioned to these cost centres on some suitable basis. For the sake of calculating the rate the following basis can be used.

(*a*) Factory cost

(*b*) Factory overheads

(*c*) Sales value

(*d*) Units sold

(*e*) Units produced.

Control of Administration Overheads

It was already mentioned that administration overheads are fixed in nature and therefore not susceptible for exercising control over it. However, the top management can devise the following control techniques for the sake of controlling administration overheads.

1. Control through Classification and Analysis. The overheads incurred for various departments may be classified and compared with the budgeted figures. Similarly, overheads incurred for the previous year can be compared with current year to know whether more overheads are incurred. Alternatively, the absorption rates for different periods can also be calculated to know the increase or decrease in the overheads incurred.

2. Control through Budgets. Under this technique overheads are budgeted for different sections of the office. The actuals are compared with the budgeted overheads and variations are calculated and analysed. The person incharge of the concerned department has to report the variance to the top level management for taking remedial measures.

3. Control through Standards. Under this technique standard costs are set for each item of administration overhead. The actual overheads incurred in each section is compared with standards to know the efficiency or otherwise of the sections.

Definition and Classification of Selling and Distribution Overheads

The main aim of all business undertakings is to earn maximum amount of profit. This aim can be achieved by maximising the production and sales. Increased production results in decreased cost of production. But necessary efforts must also be taken to boost up sales of increased production. This is possible by incurring selling and distribution overheads for the sake of creating demand and promoting sales. Though technological development and automation to a large extent are responsible for lowering the cost of production still the total cost has not been able to be reduced owing to increased selling and distribution overheads. It is estimated that in most of the factories, selling and distribution overheads accounts for about 15 to 20 per cent and therefore requires proper accounting and control.

Definition of Marketing Cost

The ICMA terminology has used marketing cost as a broader concept to include three components, *viz.*, selling, publicity and distribution cost. Marketing cost has been defined by the terminology as the cost incurred in publishing and presenting to customers the products of the undertaking in suitably attractive forms of all relevant research work, securing of order, and usually, delivery of the goods to customers. In certain cases, after sales service and/or order processing may also be included.

Definition of Selling Cost

It is defined by the ICMA terminology as that portion of marketing cost which is incurred in securing orders.

Distribution Cost

It is defined by the ICMA terminology as that portion of marketing cost which is incurred in warehousing saleable products and in delivering products to customers.

Classification of Selling Overheads

Selling overheads may be classified into the following types:

1. Direct selling expense. The overheads which are directly related to securing orders, market research, retaining the customers etc., fall under this category. The common examples are salaries payable to sales manager, salesmen, showroom expenses, sales depot expenses, etc., expenses incurred in preparation and quotation of selling price, cost incurred in meeting enquiries and after sales service costs, such as repairs and maintenance.

2. Sales promotion cost. These are the overheads which are incurred in creating the demand for the products of the company. Examples of costs which fall under this cateogry are advertisement expenses, distribution of free gifts, cost of exhibition, expenses incurred for market analysis in order to expand the market and so on.

3. Financial cost. These overheads include actual or notional interest payable or working capital which is required to finance cost of stock of goods and for dealing on credit basis, credit collection expenses such as legal expenses, incurred for realising debts, and bad debts.

Classification of Distribution Overheads

Distribution overheads can be classified into the following types:

1. **Transportation cost.** These include expenses incurred for delivering goods sold and the cost incurred to receive back the goods when they are sold on sale or return basis. Examples are wages payable to the drivers of delivery van, depreciation of delivery van, insurance premium payable for goods in transit, etc.
2. **Warehousing cost.** All expenses incurred in storing the finished goods is known as warehousing cost. Examples are rent of godown, heating and lighting expenses, insurance of godown, wages of godown keepers, etc.

3. **Packing and cost of containers.** This include the cost of packing and employing the reconditioned containers for re-use. Examples are cost of secondary packing materials, cost of tools used in packing such as hammers, etc.

Though the term selling and distribution overheads are used together, they differ in the following respects:

(*a*) Selling overheads are incurred for promoting sales, whereas distribution overheads are incurred in moving the finished goods from the godown of the factory to customer's place.

(*b*) The object of selling overhead is to create demand and retain the customers, whereas the object of distribution overhead is to deliver the goods safely to the required place.

Accounting of Selling and Distribution Overhead

The accounting of selling and distribution overhead is necessary for the following purposes:

(*a*) To control selling and distribution overheads,

(*b*) To fix selling price,

(*c*) To determine optimum sales volume,

(*d*) To determine cost of sales of each product in order to know the profit.

The accounting of selling and distribution overheads involves the following steps.

1. Analysis of Overheads

Selling and distribution of overheads may be analysed under any of the following basis:

(*a*) According to nature and object. Under this basis the overheads are classified according to the purpose for which they are incurred. The examples of overheads which may be analysed on this basis are freight, warehousing expenses, packing material and so on. Some time these overheads can also be calssified on the basis of variability, such as variable, semi-variable and fixed. Best example is salary payable to salesman is fixed, travelling allowance is semi-variable and commission is variable.

(*b*) According to function. Overheads can be analysed based on the functional division of the factory. Examples are advertising and sales promotion, credit collection, storage, transportation, etc. The functional basis of analysis can also be made according to area covered by sales. The area may represent a territory, or sales office.

(*c*) Analysis by products. Overheads can also be analysed on the basis of products so that, those overheads which can be attributed to the products can be directly allocated.

2. Apportionment of Overheads

After collection and analysis, the second step involved is to apportion the overheads on suitable basis. The following are some of the basis used for apportionment:

Expenses	*Basis of apportionment*
Advertisement	Sales value
Warehousing	Sales value
Credit collection	Number of orders
Transport cost	Weight

3. Absorption of Overheads

Selling and distribution overheads may be absorbed under the following two methods:

(a) A percentage of sales value. Under this method selling and distribution overheads and sales value is predetermined. A percentage of this overhead is calculated over sales value. It is at this percentage that selling and distribution overheads are absorbed by the number of finished goods sold.

(b) An estimated rate per unit. Under this method the selling and distribution overheads and the number of units to be sold are predetermined. The predetermined selling and distribution overhead divided by the predetermined units to be sold gives a rate and it is at this rate the overheads are absorbed. This method can be conveniently used where only one variety of goods are produced and sold.

The following entries are passed in the cost books to record selling and distribution overheads:

(a) For recording the actual expenses incurred for selling and distributing the goods:
Selling and distribution overhead ledger control A/c *Dr.*
To cost ledger control A/c

(b) For issue of materials from store room for the purpose of selling and distribution function:
Selling and distribution overhead ledger control A/c *Dr.*
To stores ledger control A/c

(c) When wages or salaries are incurred towards this function selling and distribution:
overhead ledger control A/c *Dr.*
To wages ledger control A/c

(d) When selling and distribution overheads are recovered on goods sold:
Cost of sales ledger control A/c *Dr.*
To selling and distribution overhead ledger control A/c

Control of Selling and Distribution Overheads

There are three methods of controlling selling and distribution overheads. They are as follows:

1. By Analysis of Expenses and Comparison with Past Performance. This method is suitable only for a small organisation. Under this method selling and distribution overheads are analysed on the basis of nature, product, territory, etc. Each item of overheads is compared with the corresponding item of the previous year. Alternatively, the overheads can also be expressed as a percentage of sales and compared with similar percentages of previous year.

2. Budgetary Control. Under this method first of all a sales forecast is made and on this basis a sales budget is prepared. Then selling and distribution overheads are budget based on sales budget. The selling and distribution overheads are classified into fixed and variable overheads. These overheads are then compared with the budgeted overheads to know whether more expenses are incurred than the budgeted overheads. If so remedial measures are taken to minimise such overheads. Flexible budgets are used to control overheads in most of the cases.

3. Standard Costs. Fixation of standard cost for selling overheads in comparatively difficult than distribution overheads. Still, standard cost are set carefully for these overheads and actuals are compared with standards to know the variances. In case of adverse variances, the causes for the same are analysed and reported to the top level management for taking remedial measures to control such variance.

Problem–1

A company is making a study of the relative profitability of the two products – A and B. In addition to direct costs, indirect selling and distribution costs to be allocated between the two products are as under:

	Rs.
Insurance charges for inventory (finished)	78,000
Storage costs	1,40,000
Packing and forwarding charges	7,20,000
Salesmen salaries	8,50,000
Invoicing costs	4,50,000

		Product A	*Product B*
Selling price	(Rs.)	500	1,000
Cost per unit (exclusive of indirect selling and distribution costs)	(Rs.)	300	600
Annual sales in units		10,000	8,000
Average inventory	(units)	1,000	800
Number of invoices		2,500	2,000

One unit of product A requires a storage space twice as much as product B. The cost to pack and forward one unit is the same for both the products. Salesmen are paid salary plus commission @ 5% on sales and equal amount of efforts are put forth on the sales of each of the products.

Required:

(*i*) Set up a schedule showing the apportionment of the indirect selling and distribution costs between the two products.

(*ii*) Prepare a statement showing the relative profitability of the two products.

(C.A. Inter, May 1996)

Solution:

Statement showing apportionment of the indirect selling and distribution costs between the two products

Items	*Basis of apportionment*	*Total*	*A*	*B*
Insurance charges	Average inventory value (1,000 × 500: 800 × 100)	78,000	30,000	48,000
Storage cost	Average inventory storage space (1,000 × 2: 800 × 1)	1,40,000	1,00,000	40,000
Packing and forwarding charges	Annual sales in units (10,000: 8,000)	7,20,000	4,00,000	3,20,000
Salesmen salaries	Efforts of salesman (1: 1)	8,50,000	4,25,000	4,25,000
Salesmen commission	Annual sales value (5: 8)	6,50,000	2,50,000	4,00,000
Invoicing costs	No. of invoices (2,500: 2,000)	4,50,000	2,50,000	2,00,000
		28,88,000	14,55,000	14,33,000

Statement showing relative profitability of two products

		A	*B*
Annual sales:		50,00,000	80,00,000
	A 10,000 units × 500		
	B 8,000 units × 1,000		
Less:	Cost of sales	30,00,000	48,00,000
	A 10,000 × 300		
	B 8,00,000 × 600		
	Gross profit	20,00,000	32,00,000
Less:	Indirect selling and distribution	14,55,000	14,33,000
	profit	5,45,000	17,67,000

Profit percentage on sales $\frac{5,45,000}{50,00,000} \times 100 = 10.9\%$ $\qquad \frac{17,67,000}{80,00,000} \times 100 = 22.08\%$

Problem–2

Cosmos Ltd. produces three types of products A, B and C. The sales territory of the company is divided in three areas as North, South and Central. The estimated sales for the year as under

Product	*Territories*		
	North (Rs.)	*South (Rs.)*	*Central (Rs.)*
A	1,00,000	40,000	–
B	60,000	–	1,60,000
C	–	1,40,000	80,000

Budgeted advertising cost is as under:

	Rs.
North	6,400
South	9,000
Central	7,800
Common	11,600

You are required to work out the advertising cost per cent on sales for each product and each territory and prepare a suitable statement for presentation to the management.

(ICWA, Inter, June 1995)

Solution:

Apportionment of common advertising cost on the basis of sales value:

		Sales value		*Common advertising cost*	
Territory North –	A	1,00,000		2,000	
–	B	60,000	1,60,000	1,200	3,200
Territory South –	A	40,000		800	
	C	1,40,000	1,80,000	2,800	3,600
Territory Central –	B	1,60,000		3,200	
–	C	80,000	2,40,000	1,600	4,800
	Total		5,80,000		11,600

Apportionment of local costs on the basis of sales value

		Sales value		Common advertising cost	
Territory North	– A	1,00,000		4,000	
	– B	60,000	160,000	2,400	6,400
Territory South	– A	40,000		2,000	
	– C	1,40,000	1,80,000	7,000	9,000
Territory Central	– B	1,60,000		5,200	
	– C	80,000	2,40,000	2,600	7,800
	Total		5,80,000		23,200

Statement of advertisement cost

Product	*Territories*				*% on Sales*
	North	*South*	*Central*	*Total*	
A	6,000	2,800	–	8,800	6.29
B	3,600	–	8,400	12,000	5.45
C	–	9,800	4,200	14,000	6.36
Total	9,600	12,600	12,600	34,800	
Percentage on sales	6%	7%	5.25%		

Treatment of Certain Items in Cost Accounting

While treating certain items on cost accounting, the following guidelines are to be considered:

(*a*) To identify the item of expenditure with the units of production.

(*b*) Where it is not possible to identify the expenditure with the unit of production, or where the process of identifying is difficult or if the cost of identifying exceeds the cost of materials, then such an item of expenditure is to be treated as overheads.

(*c*) When an expenditure incurred results the benefit over a period of time, it is to be treated as deferred revenue expenditure and to be spread over the number of years during which benefit accrues. Only a part of the expenditure is charged to the production cost for that year.

(*d*) If the expenditure is of abnormal nature, it is to be included in the costing profit and loss account so that the cost of production is not distorted.

The following are some of the expenses which deserve special treatment in cost accounting.

1. Repairs and Maintenance Expenses of Machines. The repairs and maintenance department is a service department which is established in most of the factories. For the sake of treating this item of expenditure, repairs and maintenance can be classified into two types, *viz.*,(*a*) minor repairs and normal maintenance and (*b*) heavy repairs and major overhauls. The expenses of minor repairs and normal maintenance is to be treated as factory overheads. Heavy repairs and major overhauls can be undertaken for two purposes, viz., (*a*) to increase the earning capacity of the machinery and (*b*) to keep the machine in good running condition. In the latter case, it is treated as a deferred revenue expense and spread over to number of years' cost of production.

2. Audit Fees, Bank Charges, Legal Expenses and Postage and Stationery. These expenses are incurred in the day-to-day working of the office. Hence all these expenses are treated as office and administration overheads.

3. Advertising. This is one of the most commonly incurred expenses in most of the business enterprises. Advertising may relate to (*a*) common or general one to cover all the products to be sold, and (*b*) specifically spent on one existing line of product or for a new line of product. If the advertising expenses incurred is a general one to cover all products, it is treated as selling and distribution overheads and is recovered from the cost of goods sold on a suitable basis. If it is spent specifically to a particular line of existing product, it is treated as selling overhead and allocated directly to those products sold. If the advertising expenses are incurred specifically on a new line of product, then it is treated as deferred revenue expenditure to be recovered over a period of time.

4. Cost Accounting Department Expenses. This expenditure include salary of staff of cost accounting department and other expenses incurred to maintain it. Where the cost accounting department is established in small concern, then such expenses are treated as administration overhead. In big organisation, where the expenditure is large, it is charged to works, administration, selling and distribution overheads.

5. Bad Debts. When selling department bills the credit sales then bad debts is treated as selling overhead. If collection of accounting or administration department, then it is treated as administration overheads.

6. Transport Cost. The carriage inwards is treated as part of material cost. The cost of internal transport, *i.e*, cost of carrying materials from stores department to production departments and *vice versa* is treated as factory overheads. Carriage outwards is treated as distribution overheads.

7. Insurance of Building and Plant. The insurance policy in a factory may relate to fire insurance, burgalary insurance and so on. The premium paid on such policies is treated as overheads. Where a policy is taken in respect of a single department, the premium is allocated to that department. If the policy is taken for the entire factory, the premium is apportioned to all the departments on a suitable basis. Where a policy is taken to cover risk of administration and selling and distribution departments, the premium is apportioned to these departments.

8. Sales Commission. Commission on sales is paid to sales manager, salesmen or agents on a fixed basis for all products or as a percentage for each product sold. Where it is paid as a fixed rate it is charged to the cost of product sold. Where it is paid as a percentage for different products, then it is treated as selling overheads.

9. Discounts Received. Discounts on purchase of materials may be trade discount or cash discount. Such discounts are deducted from the invoice price of the materials bought.

10. Research and Development Cost. The ICMA terminology has defined research cost as "the cost of searching for new or improved products, new applications of materials, or new improved method." Whereas development cost as "the cost of the process which begins with the implementation of the decision to produce a new or improved product or to employ a new or improved method and ends with the commencement of formal production of that product or by that method."

The distinction between research and development costs thus lies in the fact that while research costs are incurred in the hope of getting a new or improved product or a new or improved method of production, etc., development costs are incurred on successful research projects only. The examples of research costs are salaries of research supervisor and of research assistants, *viz.*, chemists, technicians, etc., costs of materials used, cost of equipments etc.

Treatment of research cost. Research may normally be of two types, *viz.,* (*a*) fundamental research and (*b*) applied research. The aim of fundamental research is to increase the general fund of knowledge and no specific tangible results are aimed at. Nevertheless, they facilitate applied research work. If such research work is carried out on a continuous basis, the cost should be charged to the manufacturing overhead of the period in which the research work is carried out. However, if such research work is carried out at the intervals of certain periods, then the cost should be treated as deferred revenue expenditure to be spread over the manufacturing overhead of such periods.

Cost of applied research is treated in the following manner:

(*i*) ***For improvement of existing products or methods.*** Usually a lump-sum amount is earmarked every year for conducting research work on all existing products and methods. In such cases, the actual costs should be charged to manufacturing overhead of the period. If, any separate sums are allotted for any particular product, the actual expenses should also be collected accordingly and charged directly.

(*ii*) ***For new products and methods.*** Separate project number is allotted for each individual research project; cost collected accordingly, costs of incompleted projects are carried over. Costs of projects ending in failure are charged off to costing profit and loss account. Cost of successful research projects should be merged with development cost of the relevant project.

Treatment of development cost. For successful research projects, development costs should be merged with research cost and the total research and development cost for each such project temporarily capitalised and treated as deferred revenue expenditure to be spread over a number of future periods depending upon the size of the expenditure and period likely to be benefited. If the project is related to a product, the cost is charged directly and if it is related to method it is treated as factory overhead of the future periods.

11. Royalties, Patent Fees. The treatment of royalty depends upon the method of payment. If royalty is paid as a fixed amount or on the basis of a fixed percentage of output, it is treated as direct expenses. If it is paid on the units sold it is treated as selling expense.

The expenditure incurred in registering and renewal of patent as administration overheads.

12. Rent of Building. Depending upon the use of building for production, administration and selling, it is treated as overheads.

13. Heating, Lighting and Air-conditioning. Depending upon the location of installation, *i.e.,* production, administration, and selling, lighting charges are treated as overheads. However, where meters are installed lighting expenses are allocated directly to the departments. Where meters are not installed, it is apportioned on the basis of number or light points. Heating and air-conditioning expenses is, apportioned on the basis of cubic capacity of the department.

14. Head Office Expenses. Where a firm has number of plants, the expenses incurred in running the head office is apportioned to various plants on the basis of service rendered by the head office to each plant. In each plant such expenses is treated as its administration overheads.

15. Warranty Claims. A warranty clause is inserted in sales clause for replacing a defective part of a product. This clause will be in force for a specific period of time. Any expenses relating to replacement of defective parts within a stipulated period are treated as selling expenses.

16. Depreciation. Depreciation is the gradual and permanent decrease in the value of an asset from any cause. It has been defined as the dimunition in intrinsic value of an asset due to its use or lapse of time. The main causes for depreciation in an asset may be classified into physical and functional causes. The physical causes include wear and tear with constant use and the action of other element. The functional causes include obsolescence and supersession.

The depreciation of various assets are booked under various standing order number and the amount of depreciation is charged to the concerned departments as overheads. The following reasons are attributed for charging depreciation as overheads to cost of production:

(*a*) It will not be possible to calculate the correct cost of manufacturing goods without taking depreciation into account.

(*b*) It will not be possible to show the correct value of an asset in the balance sheet if depreciation is not provided for. In fact, the balance sheet will be overstated if depreciation is not provided for.

(*c*) It will become difficult to replace an asset if depreciation is not provided for.

(*d*) The profit and loss account also will not show the correct profit if depreciation is not taken into consideration.

(*e*) If depreciation is not provided for, it will show a higher profit. But the consequences of increased profit are (*i*) It leads to the entry of competitors, (*ii*) There will be no incentive to minimise the expenses, (*iii*) It involves payment of more tax, and (*iv*) Payment of more commission, if it is based on profit.

Methods of Calculating Depreciation

(*a*) Fixed instalment method. Under this method, the assets are depreciated at a fixed amount throughout its life span. The amount of depreciation is calculated by dividing the value of an asset by the number of years of the estimated life of the machine. At the end of its life, the value of the asset will become zero. This method of depreciation is followed where the services rendered by the asset is uniform as in the case of furniture. But the chief limitation of this method is that the amount of depreciation remains the same, although the value of the asset diminishes every year.

(*b*) Diminishing balance method or written down value method. Under this method, the depreciation is calculated every year on the diminishing value of the asset. For example, suppose, the original value of asset, is say Rs. 10,000 and the rate of depreciation is say, 10 per cent. Then according to this method, the asset will be depreciated by Rs. 1,000 in the first year. The diminished value of the asset in the second year will become Rs. 9,000. Then the depreciation for the third year will be charged on 9,000 which works out to Rs. 900 and this practice is continued till the end.

(*c*) Annuity method. Under this method, depreciation is calculated not only on the cost of the asset but also on the interest forgone which would have been earned had the amount been invested in some other form. The depreciation to be charged is obtained by referring to the annuity table.

(*d*) Depreciation fund method. Under this method, to facilitate ready replacement of asset without facing a financial problem, the depreciation amount is set aside from the divisible profit every year and a fund known as depreciation fund is created. The fund is invested in good securities. At the time of replacing the asset, the securities are sold out and the sale proceeds are utilised for the purchase of the new asset.

(*e*) Insurance policy method. This method resembles the above method but with a difference, *viz.*, the amount so set apart is invested in an insurance company in the form of premium. When the asset gets completely worn out, the policy money is realised from the insurance company and thus the asset is replaced.

***(f)* Annual valuation method.** According to this method, the asset is valued at the end of the year and if this valuation is less than the book value, the difference is treated as depreciation and charged to profit and loss account. However, if the valuation amount is higher, the excess amount is ignored as it is in the nature of a temporary charge and no depreciation is charged on this excess amount.

***(g)* Kilometer method.** This method of depreciation is used to depreciate motor vans, cars, and other delivery vehicles such as trucks. Under this method, depreciation is calculated by dividing the original cost of the asset by the estimated life of vehicle in kilometers.

***(h)* Machine hour rate method.** Under this method, derpreciation of machinery is calculated on the basis of hours for which it is used but not on a yearly basis.

***(i)* Replacement cost method.** Under this method, the replacement cost of the asset is estimated and depreciation is calculated on the replacement cost but not on the original cost.

17. Training Cost. It is compulsory under the Apprentices Act of 1961 to train apprentices by every factory. There are different schemes of training employees. Firstly, learners may be appointed and trained them before they are appointed as employees. Secondly, existing employees may be trained while they work in factory in order to make them more familiar with the work. Thirdly, before promotions, workers may be trained so that they can discharge their newly assigned jobs more satisfactorily.

The training cost comprises of cost of material and equipment used for training, pay and allowance of training staff, and the allowance payable to the trainees. There are two methods of treating training cost in cost accounting. Firstly, training expenses including the spoiled work is treated as factory overheads. Secondly, where the trainees are given some jobs to perform, part of the training cost is treated as factory overhead and the balance is charged to the job concerned as direct labour cost.

18. Erection and Installation Cost of New Plant and Machinery. The cost of installing the new plant and machinery is capitalised along with the acquisition value of the asset.

19. Re-erection Cost. The dismantling of an asset and its reinstallation may be on account of error or because of a policy decision of management. Where the cost of dismantling an asset and its refixation is due to an error it is treated as factory overhead. Where it is on account of management policy and the amount involved is more it is written off as a loss.

20. Interest on Capital. The inclusion of interest paid on capital in the total cost of production is a controversial issue. The following arguments are put forward for the inclusion of interest on capital in cost accounting:

(*a*) Just as wages are remuneration paid to labour factor, interest is the remuneration paid on capital. As wages forms part of production cost, interest must also form part of production cost.

(*b*) As interest paid on borrowed capital is included in cost accounting, under the same principle, the notional interest on capital should also be included in cost accounting.

(*c*) Cost comparison and profit evaluation is possible when interest is included in cost of production.

(*d*) The inclusion of interest in cost accounting also facilitates make or buy decision and to own or hire a machine.

(*e*) It enables in determining the cost of holding the inventory.

(*f*) If interest is not included in cost of production, the cost of goods sold is understated and profit is overstated.

The following arguments are put forward against the inclusion of interest on capital in cost accounts:

(*a*) The remuneration payable on capital is profit and as such interest should not be included in cost accounting.

(*b*) Actual interest paid can be included in cost accounting but not the notional interest.

(*c*) Interest is a matter of pure finance and hence it should be taken into costing profit and loss account but not to cost of production account.

(*d*) Interest need not be included in determining the comparative cost of installation of a new asset at it is governed by depreciation, repairs and maintenance cost, etc.

(*e*) It involves additional clerical work and creates unnecessary complications in cost accounting.

(*f*) Estimating the actual capital to be utilised and interest thereof is somewhat difficult. So interest is to be excluded in cost accounting.

(*g*) It increases the cost of closing stock-in-hand when there is not of much sales in an year. It results in increased value of closing stock which is not justified.

(*h*) Finally, it does not affect the profit figure. It increases cost of production on the one hand and simultaneously increases the profit on the other.

Where it is decided to include interest on capital in cost accounting, the interest amount for each department is to be recorded under standing order number. The following entries are passed in the cost ledger:

(*a*) For recording the notional interest:

Factory overhead control A/c *Dr*.
    To costing P and L A/c

(*b*) When interest is charged to cost of production:

Work-in-progress ledger control A/c *Dr*.
    To factory overhead control A/c

21. Rent. Rent paid on building is treated as overheads. It is apportioned on the basis of area occupied by production, administration, selling and distribution departments of the factory.

Questions

I. Choose the correct answer

1. Which one of the following is a cost of seeking to create and stimulate demand and of securing orders?

(*a*) Research cost (*b*) Administrative cost
(*c*) Selling cost (*d*) Distribution cost [ ]

2. Administration overheads are generally recovered as a percentage of

(*a*) Direct materials (*b*) Direct wages
(*c*) Prime cost (*d*) Factory cost [ ]

3. Warehouse expense in an example of

(*a*) Factory overhead (*b*) Selling overhead
(*c*) Administration overhead (*d*) Distribution overhead [ ]

4. Bad debts is shown under the head
   (*a*) Factory overhead
   (*b*) Administration overhead
   (*c*) Selling overhead
   (*d*) Distribution overhead [ ]

[***Answers:*** 1. (*c*), 2. (*d*), 3. (*d*), 4. (*c*)]

II. Simple questions

1. Define office overheads.
2. Mention the different methods of treating office and administration overheads in cost accounts.
3. Give four examples of indirect materials used as office overheads.
4. Define selling overheads.
5. Define distribution overheads.
6. Distinguish between selling and distribution overheads.
7. How is selling and distribution overheads accounted for in costs accounts ?
8. How are office and administration overheads and selling and distribution overheads controlled ?
9. How are the following expenses treated in cost accounts:
   (*a*) Royalty, (*b*) Research and development cost, (*c*) Inspection cost, (*d*) Drawing office expenses, (*e*) Transport cost, (*f*) Bad debts, (*g*) Advertising, (*h*) Tabulation expenses, (*i*) Repairs and maintenance cost, (*j*) Insurance on plant and building, (*k*) Office cost, (*l*) Erection of a new plant, (*m*) Dismantling and re-erection of old plant, (*n*) Subscriptions and donations, (*o*) Packing expenses.

Short answer questions

1. Explain the arguments for and against inclusion of interest in cost accounts.
2. Explain the arguments for and against inclusion of depreciation on cost accounts.
3. Explain the different methods of calculating depreciation on assets.

❑❑❑